LIKE UNTO MOSES

Indiana Studies in Biblical Literature
Herbert Marks and Robert Polzin,
general editors

LIKE UNTO MOSES

The Constituting of an
Interruption

JAMES NOHRNBERG

INDIANA UNIVERSITY PRESS
BLOOMINGTON & INDIANAPOLIS

" 'Must I not take heed to speak what the Lord puts in my mouth?' " (Num. 23:12, RSV). Photograph courtesy Peter C. L. Nohrnberg, of sculpture cast in bronze, owned by Stephanie L. Nohrnberg.

The paper used in this publication meets the minimum requirements of American
National Standard for Information Sciences—Permanence of Paper for Printed Library Materials, ANSI Z39.48-1984.

Manufactured in the United States of America

Library of Congress Cataloging-in-Publication Data

Nohrnberg, James, date
    Like unto Moses : the constituting of an interruption / James Nohrnberg.
        p.   cm. — (Indiana studies in biblical literature)
    Includes bibliographical references and index.
    ISBN 0-253-34090-X (alk. paper)
    1. Moses (Biblical leader). 2. Bible. O.T. Deuteronomy—Criticism, interpretation, etc. 3. Bible as literature.
    I. Title. II. Series.
    BS580.M6N64   1995
    222'.1092—dc20   94-18785

1 2 3 4 5 00 99 98 97 96 95

To my Father,
Carson Nohrnberg

Facesti come quei che va di notte,
che porta il lume dietro e sè non giova,
ma dopo sè fa le persone dotte . . .

[You did like one who goes by night
and bears the light behind him, who serves not himself,
but those after him makes learned . . .]
(Dante, *Purg.* 22.67–69)

CONTENTS

PREFACE

This book is a reflection—loosely speaking, "narratological"—on the canon of texts describing Moses *and* the exodus, especially as the story can be heard voicing the various latter-day concerns of Israelite identity, ideology, and history. I start from the principle that the Bible is a canon, which for my purposes here means a delimited and prescribed literature, and even a consolidated or completed or "collapsed" one.[1] A collapsed literature does not have the normal genetic relations of most literature, for it neither generates other examples of its kind, nor does it exhibit the same array of species. The Bible is often said to be a library, the work of an inspired school of bibliotechnicians. But if this is so, the Bible is not exactly a select library; rather, it is intent upon a kind of totalization, like an anthology without the cuts—a paradox that overcomes the usual objections to anthologies. And yet we must pay close attention to the very many shifts within the discourse, despite the Bible having somewhat lost a distinction between the intertextual and the intratextual. W. H. Auden warned the audience of his Phi Beta Kappa poem to avoid people who read the Bible for its prose;[2] but the truth is, that is exactly what we must do first, if we are to read the Bible satisfactorily at all. The prose one reads it for, however, is not the personal expression of the specialized sensibility of the individual stylist (which could be all that Auden really meant to disparage); rather, it is the cunning rhetoric of anonymous scribes who, like honest brokers, never wish to put themselves between their audience and its perceived need to know the world, the text, the tradition, and the design and dicta of the One God, of whom Moses was the greatest prophet—and sometime scribe.

Thus between the covers of the Bible we find not so much a member of the class *literature*, as a rival kind of organization. The contrast is between a number of authors each producing his own individual canon within the field of a technically canonless literature, and an ancient literature that has become, as it were, all canon. By definition, a canon is complete; its members form a literature of sufficiency, all members of the class *canon*, upon its formation, having been identified. In contrast, literature includes texts still waiting to be elicited from the order of words. It is the individual work that exhibits homogeneity in literature, while the field as a whole seeks to multiply diversity. The genres in literature signify, in part, this generativity. In the Bible, however, the homogenizing and heterogenizing tendencies actually coincide; thus while literature remains a molecular aggregate, the Bible has become an atomistic unity.

The Bible's own, interior assumption of an encyclopedic totality, starting from its account of the Creation on page one, is essential ground, at any rate, for the large number of comparisons offered by the present book. Nobody would care about the Bible as the Bible, that is, as a whole, if in fact nothing in it had prepared him or her to do so. The virtual absence of different narrators identifying themselves as different, for Genesis–2 Kings, is a studied effect, contributing to an impression of the Bible's design upon its own unity or homogeneity. The retailing of the revelation to Moses and Israel anonymously and omnisciently is apparently quite compatible with the Hebrew Bible's several annotative references to the survival of one institution or another "even unto this day," that is, to *our* day—but there is little trustworthy indication of what exactly that day might have been. The author comes forward only when he thinks his readers can temporarily stand in his place, observing the unity or continuity of his testimony about an Israel that is gone with their own knowledge of an Israel that has come to pass.

A traditional study of a traditional origin, the present essay makes no real contribution to composition history. Nonetheless, my arguments probably have some relevance to source-study, even as they may have to literary study. To those interested in the history of composition, this book may only be saying, initially, that the texts concerning Moses are largely a bafflement. Moses is treated by the texts as himself a source: the tracks back to where such a source came from must be pretty well covered, if he has been successfully put in their place. To literary study this book may only be saying, initially, that the texts concerning Moses are culturally self-apperceiving, in a way that compromises any attempt to treat the institution of narrative apart from the institutions of covenant, law, liturgy, and historiography. And to students of these institutions, in their Israelite forms, this book might only say that their existence in the Moses and exodus material is never wholly independent of a narrative; on the contrary, the narrative is to be numbered among these institutions itself. The biblical text re-understands the biblical institutions, where they are ancient, as including this specific "narrativization"—the thing that has helped make them "biblical" or "canonic" in the first place.

Although the theme of origins and originals is paramount in my essay, the urge of source-study to discern differ ent compositions making up the text cannot be; for, despite my numerous and somewhat presumptuous references to different textual voices, especially the so-called Priestly and deuteronomistic ones, I am not competent to study and pass judgment on the prevailing documentary hypotheses. If scholars ask, with Elijah in 1 Kings 18:21, "How long will you go limping with two different opinions?" (RSV), I can only answer that where source-study (the genetics of the text) discriminates strands, there is often an echo or a detail that *unites* the material that has been divided, whether divided by the scholars or by the texts themselves. At the same time, "Northern" and "Southern" biases, at least as I appeal to them, sometimes seem to *divide* material that has been united—again, whether the material has been joined by the scholars or conflated by the texts themselves. The result is both diacritical and harmonist, as if the Bible's "author" were both a documentarian and an incrementalist or unitarian. At times, I realize, it may seem as if I were talking out of both sides of my mouth, or as if my right hand did not know what my left was doing. In several places, at any rate, I have used "Northern" and "Southern" in ways that sometimes cut across the classical documentarian's favorite strands—"heteroglossically," if not ambidextrously.

To me it seems obvious that within the confines of the Bible we must define the story-text, like the myth in Lévi-Strauss, or like the law in the Talmud, as consisting in all its versions.[3] At the same time, I think we must orchestrate these versions hierarchically. In doing this, diachronic concepts such as "original," "early," and "latter-day" can hardly be ruled out as criteria, given the biblical rhetoric that refuses to be properly read without an appreciation for the exploiting of temporal shifts, which are not only diachronic (sequential), but also anachronic (or hysteron proteronic). It is in the nature of a tradition to grow outwardly, but also to recoup its development internally; in this sense, the Bible is a tradition.

I might add that the *fundamentalist* documentarian's picture of a blind redactor increasing the quotient of witness even while he is confusing it, merely because he has to get it all in, has only limited appeal for me. I think the text presents evidence of mastery, not incompetence, and where it is apparently the most cobbled I find it is often also at its most masterful; or, at least, at its most challenging—intent upon trying the powers of the reader while controlling multiple, collaborative levels of discourse. Such a thing is surely not unheard of in the arts proper, where the tour de force of complexity is not prima facie evidence of multiple authorship. Quite the contrary: the formal experiment in polyphony is often peculiar to the work of the singular mastermind who devises it.

I do not, however, suppose that only one person wrote the anonymous texts I will be discussing in this book; yet I do not doubt that they have been given their final form by virtue of a consensus concerning what is in them. In the retailing of the narrative, this consensus has created for some readers a virtual "master of the tale"—"the biblical narrator," Meir Sternberg writes, "is a plenipotentiary of the author . . . pursuing the same strategy, self-effacement included. . . . no ironic distance separates these figures of maker and teller."[4] In the well-made tale of Joseph and his brothers, attention is deliberately called to some of the embarrassments of this author's being, in his turn, the plenipotentiary of the Author of History; the story's all-powerful vizier reacts to the awe of his humiliated suppliants with, "Fear not: for am I in the place of God?" (Gen. 50:19).

The modesty of Joseph the plot-maker compels him to disown or retire from his Pharaonic status in relation to the more truly Pharaonic status of the Almighty. But both in Pharaoh's Egypt and in the matter of Joseph's manipulation of his Leahite brothers, the answer to this supposedly rhetorical question has been roughly yes—as the master of this particular section of the narrative must have known. Joseph claims the plot is God's (Gen. 44:16, 45:5–9, 50:20; cf. Gen. 42:28), but he partly says this to cheer up his kin. The masterful vizier and the closure-minded teller have, in fact, been very much in cahoots. This, however, is as near as the text of the pre-exilic history ever comes to a self-portrait of the author-narrator.

In the assembling of the canon we can postulate an analogous "master of the texts"—one like unto Moses, as the master of the Joseph tale is like unto Joseph. But this "master of the texts" is not Moses, except by imputation, because the author has neither denied himself Moses' human limitation of lack of access to the divine omniscience nor availed himself of the human freedom of an individuating authorial personality or the accent of self-assertion. In respect to omniscience, the author-narrator is like a prophet. In respect to personal choice, he is like a dutiful recorder of objective historical fact: his sole ostensible purpose is to inform the page with the signs and marks that tell what has transpired in the order of events. His ability to dramatize the facts is evident enough, with suspense, curiosity, and surprise arising merely from the order in which he chooses to tell things, and with the things which he chooses to tell more than once contriving to reveal the inner humanity and particular motives of individual actors in their characters. But the text does not say God wrote it, and that it is inspired; or that Moses did, and that it was hidden; or that some latter-day follower of

Moses did, and that he is Ezra. And, by its own rules, it cannot. For however many points of view and different sources the narrative has either assimilated or accommodated, it never breaks silence to name or otherwise designate them except for the odd poetic fragment. Authors must be inferred from the voices and offices assigned to the internal characters.

Given the choice between producing good literary criticism out of amateurish source-study, or good source-study out of amateurish literary criticism, the only recourse is to restudy the conventions, traditions, and comparisons embedded in the text. This means raising the question of how we are to know which texts and tradents are actually "different," rather than merely "variant," which ones embody the alleged "temporal shift." The conventions and traditions and schools and voices are surely sources of the texts, and, in the somewhat metaphorical sense developed in this book, they are at least as much like real sources as J, E, P, and D. A more supple theory of a D-Composition and a P-Composition—as recently proposed by Erhard Blum[5]—apparently shares at least my sense that anonymous synthesizings, exegeses, qualifications, accommodations of paradigms, and more scribal kinds of authorship deserve equal billing with sources; after all, in the case of "P" and "D," two of the four sources have developed more identifiable voices, idiom, vocabulary, ideology, and pursuits, while at the same time they have entered upon a manifesting of their own canons of narrations or of "history."

Conjectures upon what kind of author a putative "J" might have been have generally been less fruitful than the discussion of how or why an editor in the time of the scriptoria of the early or the later kings might have been inspired by received materials (or "tradents") to create or maintain a certain traceable line in Scripture—or how received and legendary materials might have been politicized, idealized, developed, reconstructed, and canonized by latter-day polities and their texts. But I do not pursue this discussion very far at all here—it is quite out of my competence—although I do occasionally identify—recognize—some of the primary evidence in the narrative for the activity in question, the activity of developing a tradition or "traceable line" through a chain of resemblance and allusion across different portions of the final text.

No comprehensive poetics of the Bible can neglect attempting a positive or constructive account of the various stereoscopic and anachronic structures within the canon. The texts pertaining to Moses and the exodus are an obvious example and starting point; for Moses, as the Bible's first lettered author, is already a double, beyond the story, of the Moses inside it. If our viewpoint sometimes puts us in the position of supposing that the Moses of the text is himself engaged in the search for the historical Moses, so be it. In this, we shall probably not have gone all that much beyond the authors who created the Moses of Deuteronomy.

In lieu of further explanations of my drift, discursive tabulation of the book's contents may be useful here. Seventeen essay-chapters are apportioned over four larger blocks. The first two of these blocks (chapters 1-5) treat Moses and his activity as in some sense or other an ideological and textual composite. Part I, "The Canonization of Moses," concerns this construct as Moses himself seems personally to constitute it. Part II presents a two-part study of Moses' legislating and "booking" activity (chapters 3 and 4); this is followed by a supplementary chapter (5) on the content of the Decalogue in relation to biblical narratives and discourses about sins and crimes within the covenanted society.

Part III, the longest part of the book, is called "Moralia in Exodum": it contains nine chapters of homiletic commentary on the major narrative of Exodus up to the deliverance at the Reed Sea. Here the reader will find the stories of Moses and the exodus treated in relation to each other (chapters 6-8), in relation to a proto-Mosaic society (chapters 9-11), and in relation to the theme of the creation of Israel (chapters 12-14). In this part of the book I reflect appreciatively on the career of Moses as it is entailed, first, in the revelation of Israel's right to existence and in the nation's own early history; second, in the will of God to be known aright, that is, to be known in *his* own right; and, third, in the national fable of identity. These chapters follow, more or less, the order of the narrative in Exodus 1–15. In chapters 13 and 14, however, I return to the Passover (Exodus 12–13), after having already expanded on the Reed Sea (Exodus 14–15). That is, the Passover narrative is only treated "narratologically" after explanations of what has been joined and divided by the Reed Sea narrative.

The remainder of the book is called "Allegories of Scripture," partly to indicate its overlap with another piece of that title, from which the present book has been separated. The bulk of this fourth part treats the story of Moses and the exodus in relation to the latter-day history of the Israelite state. As a kind of follow-up to Part II ("The Text of the Law"), it is mainly a study of the relation of the exodus to the politics of sovereign and priestly Israel, "The Text of History." (This discussion has already been initiated in chapter 10, where "Prophet unto Pharaoh" has been taken to mean also "prophet to the Israelite state.") The concluding chapter is retrospective: it is made up of three excursus on further allegories of (and analogies for) major narratives about Moses, also related to the kingship, the cult, and the landed Israel. A somewhat "deuteronomic" recapitulation offers to conclude this work, but long before this point the reader is likely to see that the Moses of the present book somewhat resembles the legendary ship Argo. The Argo made the maiden voyage of all voyages, but so many repairs to the vessel were required on the way to Colchis that by the time the Argonauts put into port their original ship had been entirely replaced. At the final destination it was the Argo in name only—yet it was no less the Argo for all that.

Regarding citations: the Bible, Jewish and Christian, is quoted in English translations, from the "AV," or Authorized Version (= King James Version) where not otherwise indicated. (The AV's transliteration of longish Hebrew names, however, is simplified according to the practice of some more modern English versions.) For several quotations— often where decidedly prosaic blocks or decidedly parallelistic verses are concerned—the Revised Standard Version, or "RSV," has been preferred. Only occasionally are other Bibles and translations employed: JB = Jerusalem Bible; NJB = New Jerusalem Bible; AR = author's revision of the AV; AT = author's translation, literal or synthetic of other translations; JPS = Jewish Publication Society. Septuagint, or LXX, refers to the Greek translation of the Hebrew Bible from the Hellenistic period. Hebr. = Hebrew biblical text or word; Gk. = Greek.

ACKNOWLEDGMENTS

Most of the ideas presented here derive from classes I have taught over many years, at Harvard in 1967, at Yale from 1969, and at Virginia from 1976. My readings—especially during 1970–1977—of Gerhard von Rad's *Old Testament Theology* and his commentary on Deuteronomy, Martin Buber's *Moses: The Revelation and the Covenant*, Brevard Childs's *The Book of Exodus*, and Freud's *Moses and Monotheism*—have been my main basis. More remote sources include graduate classes at Toronto from 1962, especially those under Northrop Frye and Marshall McLuhan. According to Blake, it was God who "in mysterious Sinai's awful cave / To Man the wondrous art of writing gave" (*Jerusalem*, prol.). Both of my Toronto mentors might have been present on the occasion in question: study in Canada proved an opportune remove from one's country of origin—and not less a call to one's true allegiance. I should add that without Yale's Morse Fellowship, a Guggenheim Fellowship, and paid sabbatical leave through the office of the late Dean Hugh Kelly of the University of Virginia, my ideas on Scripture would still lie house-bound in lecture notes, manuscripts, and wishful thinking. Besides my teachers in graduate school, support for fellowships and leave-time has come from persons in the literary-critical profession whose help it is an honor to acknowledge: I. A. Richards, Geoffrey Hartman, Robert Kellogg, Father Walter J. Ong, John Freccero, and Alastair Fowler. Many of my students, by way of inspired comments and papers, can also be reckoned as my colleagues and teachers: I am their considerable academic debtor. Grateful prompting has also come from old friends, including Michael Seidel and J. Daniel Kinney.

My title partly alludes to my own book's rather deuteronomic history. It is an expanded version of a long monograph, orginally written in 1978 at the University of Virginia's Center for Advanced Studies, thereafter radically abridged to produce the essay "Moses" for Burke O. Long's collection *God and Man in the Old Testament: The Old Testament Short Story in Literary Focus* (Almond Press, 1981). My ideas about Mosaic texts went back to graduate school pieces on *Piers Plowman*, begun under Derek Pearsall in 1963–64. In 1979 my manuscript was commented on by Richard Drake, Rachel Jakoff, and Stephen Barney (my longtime friend in the business, mented on by Richard Drake, Rachel Jakoff, and Stephen Barney (my longtime friend in the business, and again a Langland scholar). Deuteronomic, historicizing, and totalizing emphases had to be largely eliminated from my first published result. The next recasting of my material waited for the second of three Gauss Seminar lectures given at Princeton in 1987, thanks to Victor Brombert and David Quint. Parts were also read at Emory University, at the invitation of Walter Reed in 1989. Gary Anderson of the University of Virginia gave me valuable advice on my idea, at the point that it had indeed begun to be a book by having separated itself from an extended Bible project originally called *Allegories of Scripture*. The present study once formed nearly a third of that manuscript, from which a title essay has been published; I refer to it occasionally in my notes.

In what follows I cite the Hittite law code, which at paragraph 63 reads: "If anyone steals a plough-ox, formerly they used to give fifteen oxen, but now he gives ten." The numbers remind us of the gag in Mel Brooks's *History of the World, Part I*, where Moses appears before his people on Sinai with three tables, proclaiming to them, "I give you the fifteen—": but one table drops and breaks, and Moses hastily emends, "—*ten* commandments." This scene should be compared to my epigraph (for Part I) from Kafka, which is intended to illustrate the poesis of an origin. Brooks's routine explains, about as quickly as anything could, what is meant here by the narrativizing of textuality and the constituting of an interruption.[1] The analogous mechanism for Moses' exodus from my larger piece was a crashed and retrieved disk, the modern equivalent for the tables Moses broke at Sinai: the first full-length version of my study had to be rescued from its thousand shards by many volunteers, including my son, Peter, and his college roommates, Lester Ward and Michael Schoen, and two nameless and dedicated student employees at the University of Virginia Computing Center. My daughter, Gabrielle, also offered help during this unnerving time. Lester Ward, moreover, rescued the piece a second time, in 1992, at the Harvard Computer Science Center; Michael Schoen recovered this version again, through the kind offices of Microsoft Corporation's David Mckinnis. The magnetic script has been subject to much *recensio*.

In 1990 I had the happy opportunity of lecturing in Bloomington on my "Allegories" project before James Ackerman, Herbert Marks, and Meir Sternberg, at the invitation of Henry Remak of the Indiana Institute for Advanced Study. After a cautionary reader's report on the larger opus, I suggested "Moses" be published separately; the idea was heard graciously by both Marks and the Indiana University Press's literature editor Robert Sloan. Marks has been instrumental in overseeing and editing the form of the book represented here. His page-by-page queries, corrections, cuts, and suggestions for rejiggering the book's plan of organization have all been crucial: like unto Moses. This has also meant his being like unto Aaron—Aaron was appointed to translate for a stammerer and an outsider. Marks's co-editor, Robert Polzin, whose *Moses and the Deuteronomist*[2] should be read against much of the present text, has been equally gracious to let my book join his flock, and has provided me and the Press with a hopeful and valuable reading of my manuscript. Finally, Meir Sternberg has offered both corrections and, with terrifying penetration, a critique of my essential subject—and the invaluable encouragment of his counsels and his friendship over a growing number of years. He has particularly insisted I attempt to theorize both the poesis and the poetics of an origin.

Let me add my deepest thanks to my scholarly copy editor here: Nancy Miller's great pains have spared me many errors of style, form, emphasis, and, above all, citation.

My graduate students Ty Buckman and Stephen Fahringer have been critical help in the final stages of the preparation of copy and proof.

To record my greatest indebtedness, I go back to the fall of 1960. An ethnographer would see the occasion as a harvest-time festivity, with obvious tribal overtones and pronounced historicizing tendencies. Crowds of visitors—returning to a three-hundred-year-old seat of the New England ministry and renewing their membership in the symbolic *gens* of their youth—cross over a bridge in order to drink in tents and around booths and attend the annual restaging of an age-old conflict in which a group represented by an anxious American pilgrim seems meant to escape the hostile onset of another party whose partisans shout Eli and apparently identify themselves with the national dog of Great Britain! Gilgal perhaps it was not, but this was the occasion—at a party given by a college roommate—on which I met my wife, Stephanie. Since then she has kept many holidays—more oriented on children than Alma Mater, however. It is to her, even more than to my profession, that I owe the hours and years that it has taken to write for publication. From the first she has been finding what neither author nor feast can do without, the Aphikomon of the set-apart time, and the joy that makes us remember.

Charlottesville, Virginia

· I ·

THE CANONIZATION
OF MOSES

Leopards break into the temple and drink to the dregs what
is in the sacrificial pitchers; this is repeated over and over again;
finally it can be calculated in advance, and it becomes part of the
ceremony.

Franz Kafka, *Parables and Parodoxes*, III

· 1 ·

THE FACE OF MOSES

And when the Lord saw that he turned aside to see, God called unto him out of the midst of the bush, and said, Moses, Moses. And he said, Here am I.

And he said, Draw not nigh hither: put off thy shoes from off thy feet, for the place whereon thou standest is holy ground.

Moreover, he said, I am the God of thy father, the God of Abraham, the God of Isaac, and the God of Jacob. And Moses hid his face; . . .

(Exod. 3:4–6, AV)

Then Pharaoh said to him, "Get away from me; take heed to yourself; never see my face again; for in the day you see my face you shall die." Moses said, "As you say! I will not see your face again."

(Exod. 10:28–29, RSV)

i

In the Bible the heroic character is distinguished from the unheroic one by divine favor; God is the Bible's only real hero, and everyone else is at his disposal. The human protagonists of the Old Testament are merely human; their greatness is always contingent on God's will. The heroes are therefore God's servants. Moses was such a divinely favored servant, but so were many others. His uniqueness consists in his service being double, for he is also the servant of the equally contingent being Israel. Moses served Israel by bringing it into the service of God: his service is the brokerage of a relation. But Moses not only enlists Israel in the service of God, he also enlists God in the service of Israel. We owe the Bible's portrait of Moses to Israel's grateful memory or imagination of Moses' commensuration of incommensurables; God's greatest spokesman to his people is also depicted as their greatest spokesman to God.

Moses the spokesman, moreover, is Moses the lawgiver: because the difference between God-as-lord and man-as-subject determines that their relation be a legal one. Moses is thus in charge of Israel's papers, which are like a certificate of adoption or a bill of sale. For the texts have God

3

say, "I will take you to me for a people. . . . ye shall be a peculiar treasure unto me" (Exod. 6:7, 19:5). It is a Moses-like prophet in Isaiah who denies that exilic Israel possesses any Mosaic "bill of divorcement" (Deut. 24:1, 3, with Isa. 50:1). An earlier prophet shows us the content of such disadoption papers, where God tells Hosea's wife to name her last child after Israel's disinheritance: "Call his name Lō-ăm'-mī: for ye are not my people, and I will not be your *God*" (Hos. 1:9). But an Israel that had received a Mosaic torah could not be divinely divorced, even in exile.

Most of the heroes in the Old Testament are heroes of it, instruments of the promulgation of the biblical text itself, which is both their context and their object. Even a bookless character like Samson generates the riddles that make for the texture of his particular text. Such characters are heroes both "in Israel" and in the Bible, both within a revelation or an experience that is historical and within the context of the revelation to Israel in Israel's texts. Moses is this character par excellence, canonized in a canon, even as that canon is Mosaicized in him.

No doubt there is a type of "Mosaic hero," met in the more Yahwistic ideologues of the Bible itself—Elijah, for example—and also in works of Western literature attaching biblical typologies to themselves; but such an ideological type seems less exportable than the heroes of romance—an Odyssean hero in Aristophanes, a Byronic hero in a Brontë novel, the shell of the Byronic hero in Conrad.[1] Like the biblical patriarchs, Moses brings with him a specifically *Israelite* future. But he also brings a rendezvous with Israel's *ideological* destiny—and the sealing of the deed of a specific historical commitment. If the Bible is itself this deed or contract, its hero will always bring Moses with him.

Like territorial Israel after Moses, the Mosaic life is defined by the boundaries of the wilderness, but from the other side. Moses' life defines itself as the one shared with "*wilderness* Israel," set apart from both the Egypt of Pharaoh and the Israel of local jurisdictions and national rulers. This life is lived in the wilderness, but also in an "Israel of the text." For the wilderness defines a space within which the biblical authors have been free to construct Moses, apart from narrower historiographic constraints such as tribal memories and national chronicles, which are givens for the judges and the kings. Moses is not less a hero "in Israel" for his extraterritoriality, but he is more a projection of what Israel wished to see in itself: election, consecration, separateness. Moses is thus an ideological construct—a reinvented memory of the uniqueness of Israel's experience of itself before God—and before there was an Israel.[2]

Within Israel, Moses is a traditional hero, a received hero, a legendary hero, and a culture-hero. But Moses is also an ironic or handicapped hero, because of the preeminence of God over any other nescient being in the biblical narrative. Before he became a traditional founder-figure, Moses was an alien and an unknown. Before he came to Israel to be the official spokesman for the Hebrew God, he was an adoptive Egyptian. Before his words, delivered over a period of forty years, became sufficient to fill that large piece of the Bible that introduces itself into the history, as if in compensation for a missing record of four hundred years in Egypt, he was a stammerer. Moses is thus also "outside Israel," or at least outside the Israelite *state*. His negative identifications make him not a lawgiver, but an outlaw; not a leader of the people, but a murmurer before God; not a steadfast captain, but a fugitive slave; and not a chosen instrument, but a lost leader finally stricken by God himself. God can conjure, blight, blast, and make the darkness palpable (Exod. 10:21). If Moses is God's chosen agent, he is also his chosen victim.

Where did Moses' dual identity come from? From his relation to "the powers that be." All of his negative identifications find him outside the territorial Israel he is forbidden to enter, but also outside the territorial Egypt he is forced to leave. From Pharaoh's point of view, Moses and his deity share forbidden powers: the plagues are intrusions into the affairs of the royal house by the demonic and foreign "finger of God" (Exod. 8:19). Moses is a murmurer before Pharaoh, a faithless Egyptian overseer, and a state criminal. Moses is divided by the Egyptian state from his own magistracy in the state of Israel. In one state he might be heard and received as God's instrument, in the other be reviled and rejected as a demonic transgressor. So also Israel would itself divide, between Rehoboam ("freer of the people") and Jeroboam ("enlarger of the people").

As a traditional hero, Moses can only be partly described in the texts about him, for tradition is—putatively—always wider than any of its strands: it is always broadening toward the experience of the audience upon whose approval the perpetuation of tradition depends, beyond any given rendering or retailing of it. But while David, for example, is a strong character because the historical reminiscence about his strengths and weaknesses is strong, Moses is a strong character because of the tenacity of traditions that strengthened themselves—circularly—by invoking Mosaic authority. Moses would thus be a received hero because of the collateral reception of the law and the cult and the Yahwist oracles, or the judiciary and the priesthood and the prophets. He is not received as Abraham is, by an audience that uses traditional stories to establish its identity. Moses is necessarily received more as a prophet is, on the authority he obtains by invoking his *call* from Yahweh: "And Aaron spake all the words which the Lord had spoken unto Moses, and did the signs in the sight of the people. And the people believed; and when they heard that the Lord had visited the children of Israel and that he had looked upon their affliction, then they bowed their heads and worshiped" (Exod. 4:30–31). The shadow of this received Moses is the rejected one: the failure of the cultic order, of the Yahwist party, of the Yahwist leadership.

The reception of Moses requires a name around which the tradition consolidates, referring itself to a single life. Insofar as it is a historically limited life, the Mosaic vita also suggests some limits upon the Mosaic tradition. Nonetheless, the life is capable of legendary and exceptional features that make it exemplary or privileged, at least in the eyes of a Mosaic discipleship. Insofar as the life is generalized beyond the vocation of a select guild, becoming symbolic of a whole culture, the principal feature of the legend will be the hero's activity of finding, founding, instituting, transmitting, or sponsoring such institutions as the culture subscribes to. David is a harpist who dances before the ark, and who appoints the Levites to be temple singers in Jerusalem (1 Chron. 15:16–24)—a temple for which David has taken a city, purchased a site, and assembled the building material. David is thus the sponsor of the cult's localization in Jerusalem, and stands for the cult's patronage by the throne. The David who appoints the Levites to temple service anticipates the Nehemiah who restores the Levites' functions—and asks to be so remembered (Neh. 13:4–14). This mutual appropriation of the City of David and the Zadokite priesthood makes it impracticable to decide which adopted which. Moses seems to have a similar relation to the priesthood of Aaron. Moses is a culture-hero par excellence, since it is in and through him that Israel gets its cult. But Moses is also distinct from his priestly adjunct, and his own office is apparently set apart from the tenure track of priestly appointment. A significant part of the priesthood identified itself as "the sons of Aaron," yet Aaron's predeceasing of Moses suggests that Moses redeems the priesthood's original patron, vaguely in the way that a surviving brother raises up sons to a deceased brother by marrying the widow. The narrative shows God appointing Aaron to speak for Moses, but the logic of the relation shows Moses spoken for by the sons of Aaron: Moses is available. "Uncle Moses" appointed the landless Levitical priesthood in the wilderness sojourn, while "Uncle Aaron" stands for Israel in the way that "Uncle Sam" stands for the U.S. Post Office, Selective Service, or I.R.S. When, at his calling, Moses begs God to "send some other person" (Exod. 4:13), he in effect cedes his priestly-Levitical birthright to his brother, as Esau was understood to have ceded his Abrahamic birthright to Jacob. An implicit disjunction of Moses from Aaron is also found in the prophets. Amos (5:21–22, 25) disavows any divinely approved instituting of sacrifices in the wilderness; at the same time, he implicitly affirms wilderness auspices—hence Mosaic ones—for hallowing service to God. But the priesthood said that the cult of sacrifices, through which the priesthood fed itself, was founded by Moses, for his brother.

Although it is easy to see what Moses' life might be made to stand for, it is hard to see what it stands in place *of*. The texts about Moses do not seem to offer straight answers to the questions put by historical inquiry, but only to questions about the content of "the Mosaic." Moses as historical fact is buried under legends and interpretations that modify his personage for the use of Mosaic congregations and constituencies. The more complete the reception of the Mosaic persona, the more it interposes a veil of unknowability between us and any putative original. Moses wears a veil not when he is speaking to God, but when he is interpreting for God, when he is speaking to the people (Exod. 34:29–35). Without Moses we would not know what God was revealing to Israel, but without the veil we would know nothing of the actual Moses at all. Thus it is truly said, near the end of the biblical narration of Moses' career, that no man knows the place of Moses' burial to this day (Deut. 34:6). That is, insofar as Moses is merely the vehicle of God's will to speak, there is no burial place for Moses, since it is only the divinely commissioned words that abide; they make Moses present to us, in lieu of any other Mosaic remains. Insofar as Moses is spoken through by God, God speaks through the Mosaic veil.

The veil may result from the intensity of the Mosaic illumination by God, but it may equally result from the Mosaic imperfection. What Moses' face could not sustain, neither could Aaron and the people. Thus Moses' veil may cover the shininess of a skin that, in the Sinaitic encounter with the divine, has been terribly burned.[3] At the burning bush, Moses *hid his face* (Exod. 3:6). As with Moses' speech impediment, the emphasis may again be upon the obstacles Moses presents to the divine communication, rather than upon the priestly or prophetic medium for it. For if the shadow of the received Moses is the rejected one, then the veil of the glorified Moses is the "taboo" or stricken one. The priest whose body is marred cannot stand blameless before God's altar: "he shall not come near the veil" (Lev. 21:23, RSV). Moses' tongue-tiedness and his veiledness may imply that he, like Pharaoh's blemished courtiers, cannot stand blameless: i.e., "before *Moses*" (Exod. 9:11), or the ideal created by his own, self-disqualifying standards.[4]

What we know about Moses, his veiledness, is also what we do not know about him. We cannot be sure how he finally stood before God. We know his once being present, but we do not know what he looked like—he might as well as have been an Egyptian, the story tells us. Similarly, we know the time of his death, but not the site or the occasion. A cult of the dead Moses is symbolically ruled out by the obscurity of Moses' interment: no miracles can be worked at the miracle-worker's tomb where no tomb exists. But although such a cult is put out of the question, its being ruled out in this prevenient way is perhaps good evidence that Moses was a hero eliciting a worshipful response: a hero whose life became the object of a quasi-Sophoclean reverence for a human agent whose actions and commitments uniquely challenged human limits—his own as well as ours— challenged them on behalf of all of us.[5]

"The chair of Moses," as the Mosaic office is called in the New Testament (Matt. 23:2), seems impossible to fill, but also impossible to ignore. Specifying the office's contents may have been an obstacle from the start. The inauguration of Moses' mission looms large, precisely because its magnitude resists definition; Moses seems to be continually reinvested in his office or commission. His calling can be equated with a wide variety of pre- and post-Mosaic biblical vocations. These include *the call to military leadership*, such as the call of Gideon, who is also shown signs in the presence of God (Judg. 6:12–23), and of Saul, who is transformed into "another man" (1 Sam. 10:6; Moses is greeted by that "some other man" of Exod. 4:13 whom he asked to be sent in his place); *the call to priestly functions*, such as that of Samuel, who is addressed by a divine voice where a flame is burning (1 Sam. 3:3–4); *the call to a prophetic mission*, indicated by an inaugural vision and by participation in God's counsels (Amos, Isaiah, Jeremiah, Ezekiel); and finally the simple *call to a privileged relationship with God*, anticipated or repeated in the theophanic and conversational encounters between God and the patriarchs, or between the angel and Samson's parents (Judg. 13:15–24).

Moses is credited with such a range of functions from so many different historical periods that his is a name perpetually under suspicion of having been taken in vain: by a sacerdotal class, a warrior class, a scribal class (the law profession, roughly speaking), a ruling or administrating class. Inquiry into the historical Moses, buried under these various layers and superimpositions, must finally be addressed to a *datum absconditum*, if only because the signs of Moses' spiritual power have been sought in place of the evidence of his historical existence. We are catechized in the existence of a Moses like unto whom there have been no others (Deut. 34:10); and yet we overhear Moses himself devoutly wishing that all the Lord's people might become prophets (Num. 11:29). In such texts historicity is lost between the foreconceit of Moses' uniqueness and the back-reading of revivalistic congregations that would ideally be composed of many Moseses. The tradition is perplexed to the point that it principally represents itself and only secondarily any Ur-Moses behind it. The Moses of the text is thus his own "second Moses."

The search for the first Moses in such a tradition is perhaps only the building of a sepulcher for a prophet (Luke 11:47). The Moses of Deuteronomy seems in particular to be created out of longings for an original authoritative leader, one long since lost to the ravages of history and yet spiritually present in the very words of a latter-day "Mosaic" ministry.

Such a "second coming" of the original communal focal point dictates the text's report of the unknowability of the site of Moses' tomb (Deut. 34:6), at the terminus of the gospel of national salvation he has preached throughout the preceding text. "The word," this Moses has told Israel, "is very near you" (Deut. 30:14, RSV).

ii

> . . . when you had grown they brought you to the daughter of Pharaoh and you became her son. And Amram, your father, taught you writing. And after you completed three weeks (of years) they brought you into the royal court. (Jubilees 47:9)

> And Amram took him Jochebed his father's sister to wife; and she bare him Aaron and Moses; . . .
> These are that Aaron and Moses, to whom the Lord said, Bring out the children of Israel from the land of Egypt according to their armies. (Exod: 6:20, 26)

Each Mosaic figure—traditional, received, exemplary, and institutional—derives from the text. The traditionality of the figure is attested to by the plurality of the texts. His receivedness is attested to by the digesting of the plurality to form a canon. His exemplary character is attested to by the legendary vita attaching to him. And his character as an institution is attested to by the various institutions attributed to his sponsorship: cultic and ceremonial orders, jurisprudence, and national covenanting. The figure is heroic, not so much in his person as in the addition made to it by his many offices, through which he is textually magnified. Like a critical law case, he becomes a long-standing precedent.

The "chair of Moses" seems to be especially a legal one, one occupied by a law-speaker. While only God can be the hero of the Bible, Moses can be heroized through his agency in executing the dictates of God; but many of these dictates are, circularly, to deliver God's word to Israel, his statutes and judgments, what he commands, and to record the covenant he made between himself and the children of Israel, the things God said "by the hand of Moses" (Lev. 8:36, 26:46). So Solomon's dedicatory speech at 1 Kings 8:56b: "there hath not failed one word of all [God's] good promise, which he promised by the hand of Moses his servant." Indeed, the massing of the law corpus in the Pentateuch shows that Moses is one on whom much might depend because he is the one to whom much has been attached. But Moses does not initially speak the law. He is credited with *publishing* the Decalogue. The narrative of this publication insists upon a delay in the law's purchase upon authority and its obtaining of a hearing. Moses the stammerer brings a law he hesitates to deliver; he does not so much bring it, as bring it *back*, in the form of writing—inscriptions that others can thereafter speak.

The levitical law about the keeping of the law (Lev. 19:36b–37) implies conversion to the law as a way of life, or as subjection to a dispensation; but we could also refer it to the *study* of the law. The narrative of Exodus makes Moses function not only to promulgate the Divine Promulgation, but also to restore it. Over the course of the twentieth through the thirty-fourth chapters of Exodus, there are many more than a single repetition of the laws. These chapters, which make Moses the champion of Israel before God, make him at the same time the champion of a text that might be jeopardized by its singularity. Moses thus stands in place of any restorer of the law, anyone who safeguards the legal tradition by preserving or restoring its texts: for if it is God who writes on the tables the first time, it is Moses who writes on them the second. Moses thus prefigures the high priest Hilkiah, who recovered the Book of the Law from the repairs of the house of the Lord, the repairs suggesting that the priest had found a king apt to receive such a book. "When the king had heard the words of the book of the law . . . he rent his clothes" (2 Kings 22:11). The king was mortified, like St. Paul: "I had not known sin, but by the law . . . when the commandment came, sin revived, and I died" (Rom. 7:7, 9). What was death to Paul, however, was life to Josiah, who came to master all the law: "And like unto him was there no king before him, that turned to the Lord with all his heart, and with all his soul, and with all his might, according to all the law of Moses; neither after him arose there any like him" (2 Kings 23:25). The repetition of "none like him" doubles the king's uniqueness as "like unto Moses," and aligns it with key assertions about the uniqueness of the revelation to Moses as a prophet and confidant to whom God spoke "mouth to mouth" (Num. 12:6–8) and whom the Lord knew "face to face" (Deut. 34:10). Yet the Moses of Moab in Deuteronomy does not know God face to face so much as refer to his once having done so, when he was the former Moses of Sinai in Exodus (Deut. 4:5). By the time of Deuteronomy, he is not only keeping the legal corpora, but also the tradition of what had happened in his own prior existence, and in the prior existence of the wilderness Israel.[6]

Whether or not the levitical Yahwists were once priests in Egypt (since some of the Levites have Egyptian names, and since Eli's priesthood is dated from Egypt in 1 Samuel 2:27), Deuteronomy is surely a monument to the promulgation of Moses as the patron saint of a scribal-priestly corporation in Israel. Where Abraham's service to Israel stems from the keeping of the seed of his brother or grandfather Nahor, Moses' consists in the keeping of a text that is also kept by the priesthood of his brother Aaron. In spite of the absolute character of the pronouncements placed at the opening of Exodus 20, the effect of the subsequent ambiguities about what was written on the original tablets and the relation that they bear to any subsequent editions is to suggest that the law in Exodus is being characterized overall as a transcription, a transcription made from some lost or annihilated original, one we cannot consult. The story of a mediator's contact with an original document for which the mediator is himself the only source of information goes two ways: either toward identifying the mediator as inspired and present in the divine council, or toward identifying him as a pious fraud, one who claims an authority for his "transcription" which it would not otherwise have. The original plates for the Book of Mormon, for example, were allegedly destroyed, once Joseph Smith's translation from them had been made. Such an "author" thus denies his own originality for the sake of the more compelling one of the authority to which he defers. The authors who have constructed the story of what God told Moses have also created a story that shows us why we will never know what God told Moses in the first instance: because one or another Moses stands between us and his original, and has destroyed the primary transmission from God—though on behalf of its subsequent renewal. The activity of such a Moses can scarcely be distinguished from that of the authors who are depicting him, or from that of the Hilkiah in 2 Kings 22 who reenacts even as he transmits the story of the loss and recovery of a Mosaic revelation. Or from that of his brother Aaron, who is appointed as Moses' translator. This function of Aaron, from Exodus 4:14–16 and 7:1–2, does not appear in Deuteronomy. Eloquent in his own right, the deuteronomic Moses is adept in the tradition that had become styled as Mosaic, and he recapitulates the history of the exodus as if he himself were beginning—or rebeginning—at Moses.

Why does the "inaugural renewal" of the social contract include a story about a ruined and recovered text? Our answers throughout this book depend on bringing the convertible analogy between the history of the texts and the texts of the (hi)story to bear upon the comparisons suggested by the period of Josiah. In this period there is in fact a destroyed and reconstructed text recorded in Scripture itself, a parallel for the "lost and recovered" text of the Book of the Law of Moses, and containing some of the accents of Deuteronomy: Jeremiah, the prophet who enunciated the promise of a new covenant. Jeremiah's idea of a re-authoring of the covenant might well owe itself to the fortunes of his own texts—they were written "with ink in the book" by his secretary Baruch (Jer. 36:18), then burned by the king, and thereafter re-inscribed by Baruch.

> Then the word of the Lord came to Jeremiah, after that the king had burned the roll, and the words which Baruch wrote at the mouth of Jeremiah, saying,
>
> Take thee again another roll, and write in it all the former words that were in the first roll, which Jehoiakim the king of Judah hath burned. . . .
>
> Then took Jeremiah another roll, and gave it to Baruch the scribe, the son of Neriah; who wrote therein from the mouth of Jeremiah all the words of the book which Jehoiakim king of Judah had burned in the fire: and there were added besides unto them many like words. (Jer. 36:27–28, 32)

With these events we may compare the account in Exodus 34:

> And the Lord said unto Moses, Hew thee two tables of stone like unto the first: and I will write upon these tables the words that were in the first tables, which thou brakest. . . .
>
> And he hewed two tables of stone like unto the first; and Moses rose up early in the morning, and went up unto mount Sinai, as the Lord had commanded him, and took in his hand the two tables of stone. . . .
>
> And the Lord said unto Moses, Write thou these words: for after the tenor of these words I have made a covenant with thee and with Israel.
>
> And he was there with the Lord forty days and forty nights; he did neither eat bread, nor drink water. And he wrote upon the tables the words of the covenant, the ten commandments. (Exod. 34:1, 4, 27–28)

"And there were added unto them many like words": where Jeremiah had his secretary, Baruch, God may have had many secretaries called Moses.

The finding of the Book of the Law in Josiah's repair of the temple is the converse of the destroying of the scroll of the prophet in the court of the king who succeeded Josiah. Jeremiah might not have been closely involved in the Josianic revolution, and Josiah's high priest Hilkiah—whose scribe Shaphan brought the revolution's deuteronomistic program before the king (2 Kings 22:8–10)—might not be that Hilkiah who is named as Jeremiah's father (Jer. 1:1). But the restoration of the book of God's revelation to Israel functions like the restoration of the burned scroll or the broken tables.

Deuteronomy is an interpretation not only of Moses, but of such prophets as Hosea and Jeremiah *as* Moses. Both these prophets referred to Israel's systematic violation of the Mosaic torah (Hos. 4:2, Jer. 7:9), and both told Israel it had broken the covenant (Hos. 6:7, 8:1; Jer. 11:3, 10; 31:32, 33:21, 34:18). In Deuteronomy the "tables of the covenant" given on Sinai (Deut. 9:9) are preserved in "the ark of the covenant" (Deut. 10:2, 5, 8)—along with Deuteronomy itself. "Take this book of the law," Moses orders Israel, "and put it in the side of the ark of the covenant of the Lord your God, that it may be there for a witness against thee" (Deut. 31:26). The story of the broken and renewed tablets thus betokens the survival of written condemnations of Israel in the prophets—and their absorption in Deuteronomy. In Hosea and Jeremiah, along with Deuteronomy itself, Israel has kept the handwriting that was against it.

The hero who brings with him what is to be received—the offer of a new relation with God, or the divine legislation of a new national life—also brings with him the question of his own reception. There is no question regarding the acceptance of the patriarchal legacy; its acceptance is anticipated in the responsiveness of Rebekah, and it is something Moses himself can rely on. Like a family tradition, it encounters no resistance, because it offers itself as a prior condition—such a tradition no longer challenges belief in the present. To believe in Abraham is merely not to doubt that one has antecedents; for Abraham, to believe in God was required to believe that he, Abraham, would have descendants. Placed between those who call Abraham their father and those who will call themselves the sons of Jacob, Rebekah is required to believe both ways: to believe, that is, that she could be related to Abraham, both genetically, in the past, and legally, in the future, and that her son can lay claim to that relation, both genetically in the womb, and legally at the deathbed and in the marriage bed.

Beyond this belief that one is related to Abraham, there is the confidence in an Abrahamic legacy that includes significance as a people and inheritance of territorial possession (Gen. 12:1–2). The story commits Moses to the transmission and realization of the divine promises to the patriarchs of old, yet the reacceptance of these promises requires a further act of faith on the part of the sons of Israel. But the resources of faith are radically depleted. Thus the texts of Genesis and Exodus draw a contrast between an elect "father" who represents the steadfast orientation of an elder consciousness upon the far-off future, and the delegated intermediary of Yahweh who represents the immediate determination of a just conscience upon the desperate situation of the present. In Bunyan's *Pilgrim's Progress*, Hopeful is born out of the ashes of the martyred Faithful. But Moses comes to Israel with the faith of the patriarchs, and the people cannot hearken to him, "for anguish of spirit, and for cruel bondage" (Exod. 6:9). There has been no hope, and hence no survival of faith. The old faith cannot be reinspired by promises and prospects without a new hope quickened by signs and miracles.

Thus, while Moses is reconceived as a man of the old faith (by way of his immersion in Midianite equivalents of the patriarchal paradigms), he is also compelled to become the reluctant sponsor of a new hope or further investment in the faith. Moses therefore becomes what no patriarch is ever conceived as, namely, a man of the hour, the conveyor of the divine immediacy and givenness. This is as much as to say that he himself becomes a sign: not one to whom promises are made, but one who is caught up in the act of promising. Moses is conceived in terms of his reception, for a sign can either be accepted or rejected—either be compelling or be insignificant. His facial shine makes him such a sign, as if reflecting God's glory at the burning bush.

And what is such a sign "of"? What causes the bush to present itself to Moses in the way that it does, at the hour of his people's need? Essentially, it is a sign of the times—which is to say, of the time's at-handness, its historical pregnancy, its momentousness. The Pharaoh at the opening of Exodus forgot Joseph the provider, and then he was no longer alive to remember Moses the homicide. Then the time is at hand, when God remembers what Pharaoh, being dead, has necessarily forgotten. God remembers Israel down in the "iron furnace" of Egypt (Deut. 4:20, 1 Kings 8:51, Jer. 11:4), as he remembered Noah inside the ark (Gen. 8:1), and as indeed he remembered Abraham, when he remembered Abraham's nephew Lot inside of Sodom (Gen. 19:29)—for the smoke of Sodom "went up as the smoke of a furnace" (Gen. 19:28). In the exodus God "remembered his holy promise, and Abraham his servant" (Ps. 105:42). So one day he will remember the Israel of the exile, when he *chooses* it in the "furnace of affliction" (Isa. 48:10). But all the examples take their force from the example of the exodus, and not the other way round. This is even true when God, in Exodus 6:5, ostensibly referring to his relation to the patriarchs, says, "I remembered my covenant"; for the relation with the patriarchs is less a covenant proper than a promise, or proposal—implicitly a proposal to covenant with the patriarchs' unborn heirs. Thus while the Fathers are conceived almost wholly in terms of historical anticipation, Moses is conceived in terms of historical occasion. Though he is a legendary figure like the forebears to whom patriarchal legend attaches, he is also a vocational figure, whose legend specifically pertains to his hour. Thus his historicity is called into question, in a way that the historicity of the Fathers is not, because his legend, unlike theirs, is brought into proximity to an event of potential moment in world history: the exodus that creates the new legal entity Israel.

Moses' legend is actually more legendary than any of those stories attaching to the Fathers, because it stands in place of the critical question about the origins of an Israelite historicity: where did that historicity come from? Hence Moses' birth legend. But Moses' birth legend cannot, taken in itself, answer the question of where Israel got its sense of history. Even if Moses is somehow involved in the acquisition of a new sense of history, the birth legend only tells us that Moses' own origins are a mystery, and that the threats to the success of an Israelite leadership are to be read back into the chances against the leadership's emergence in the first place. And yet, even in the birth of Moses, there are anticipations of the Mosaic calling, and, with that calling, the calling-into-existence of a new sense of vocation, if not a new sense of history. For there is a sense in which Moses owes his existence to the midwives who defy and lie to Pharaoh in order to remain true to their profession. These protectors of infant life are given names by the text, and so are remembered by that text. God likewise remembers them, by giving them houses. Thus Shiphra and Puah are the patron saints not only of their particular calling but also of professionalism in general. And they anticipate—like the Hebrew etymology offered by the text for Moses' name—Moses' maieutic function, in drawing Israel out of the parent body of the land of the Nile.

Legends are vocational propaganda endorsing particular callings: the legends of Saint Francis tell us what ideally belongs to the vita of the Franciscan brother, the legends of Paul Bunyan tell us what ideally belongs to the life of the lumberjack (in terms meant to suggest the heroic proportions of the Northwestern timber industry), the legend of Saint George tells us what ideally belongs to Christian knighthood, the legend of Saint Anthony tells us what ideally belongs to desert monasticism, and the legend of Elisha tells us what ideally belongs to the ministry of "the sons of the prophets." Moses is so often addressed by God that it is almost his calling to be called, and hence to be renewed in some very broadly conceived Mosaic vocation. But what, besides being "Mosaic," is this vocation? Who is Mosaic after Moses, or in his place? Does his story, along with those of Samuel in the temple and Elijah in Horeb, tell us what belongs to being a Yahwist *prophet?*

"You shall be as my mouth," God tells Jeremiah (Jer. 15:19, RSV), and the words echo in the deuteronomic Moses' promise of the raising up of a prophet like the speaker: "the Lord said to me, ' . . . I will raise up for them a prophet like you . . . ; and I will put my words in his mouth' " (Deut. 18:17–18, RSV). Jeremiah seems to be recommissioned in Deuteronomy. For the deuteronomic Moses once delivered to the people the "fiery law" that came from the right hand of the God who came from Sinai (Deut. 33:2), and Jeremiah shares in the same affect: "I am making my words in your mouth a fire, and this people wood, and the fire shall devour them" (Jer. 5:14, RSV). This denunciatory power suggests that God will be "with" Moses' and Aaron's mouths when they go in to Pharaoh (Exod. 4:12, 15), because they have a prophet's power to speak *back:* to confound a hearer. Yet the partnership of Moses and Aaron also implies that their spokesmanship can be intercessory, like that of the "prophet" Abraham in Genesis 20:7. Moses can function, in other words, as Pharaoh's *priest,* as Abraham could intercede with God for Abimelech: "he is a prophet, and he will pray for you, and you shall live" (RSV).

The priest's office is hereditary and life-long. The burning bush might therefore stand for the divine sustaining of Moses' vocation through the length of the officeholder's life, beyond the fire's function as a sign (like the one given to Gideon in Judg. 6:12–21) of God's being "with" him and being able to make further signs for him. Thus Moses' ordainment to office seems to take place on an honorary priestly site, comparable to the temple in which a lamp of God burns on the night of the call of Samuel (1 Sam. 3:3). The divinely anticipated arrival of Aaron on the scene, in Exodus 4:14, coordinated with Moses' departure from the site, in Exodus 4:27, suggests that Aaron's calling to the priesthood enters into the same paradigmatic scenario that causes one to invoke the calling of Samuel for that of Moses. The alignment of the priestly and the prophetic callings is also found in historical times in the case of Jeremiah, who was from the priestly town of Anathoth (Jer. 1:1). At the time the young Samuel enters the temple service and is "girded with a linen ephod" (1 Sam. 2:18), a man of God visits Eli, and hearkens back to the call of the priesthood *in Egypt* (that is, before the appointment of Aaron in the wilderness, which took place after the exodus proper): "Thus saith the Lord, Did I plainly appear unto the house of thy father, when they were in Egypt in Pharaoh's house? And did I choose him out of all the tribes of Israel to be my priest, to offer upon my altar, to burn incense, to wear an ephod before me?" (1 Sam. 2:27–28). If this happened when Israel was in Egypt, then it took place at the call of Moses itself.

References to Moses and Aaron as co-present in Egypt have a way of deepening each brother's antecedents, while at the same time seeming to refer the leadership of Israel forward to the period of Samuel. For like Moses, Samuel is invested with memories of a guilty people's desertion of its divine leadership. According to a parallelism in Hosea 8:4, the people who have lost their faith in a Yahwist leadership either make a calf or a king (cf. Exod. 32:1 with 1 Sam. 8:2–5, 20). In applying for a kingship, God argues, the nation is not rejecting Samuel, but the God of the exodus (1 Sam. 8:7), which is to say, Moses and the Mosaic legacy for governing the nation. Thus the various official lives in Israel—those of priest, prophet, warrior, seer, scribe, jurist, and judge or governor—are all embodied in Samuel, and all receive Mosaic endorsement in the Pentateuch. Yet Moses himself is left free of their narrower or more bureaucratic claims. Moses' spokesmanship and his intercessory and ambassadorial functions draw him into the orbit of priestly and prophetic vocations; his magistracy draws him into the court and the assembly. But the result is an office that belongs uniquely to Moses.

In the story of the initial calling of Samuel in the temple, Samuel is called by name four times, and he will one day function as priest, prophet, warrior, and governor. It is thus his calling to be called, as the wordplay around his name (*ša'al*, ask, and *šam'a*, hear) and his being summoned up as a ghost also suggest. But what Mosaic function lies behind the multiplicity of the leader's role and the pluralizing of his summons to office? Roughly speaking, he is called to head up the critical development of the Israelite state. In the words of José Ortega y Gasset, "the State begins by being absolutely a work of imagination": "on the heterogenous basis of biology," it "imposes the abstract homogenous structure of jurisprudence," but the impulse to abandon a traditional structure of common life for a new one "is more substantial than mere legality." The state-enterprise, represented in Exodus by the tremendous energy expended upon the design and manufacture of the tabernacle, is not the kind of "project . . . possible to tiny groups related by blood. In the genesis of every State we see or guess at the figure of a great 'company-promoter.' "[7] The biblical question, of course, is whether this visionary is merely a Nimrod. For the Bible depicts such an enterprise in the story of the Tower of Babel in Genesis 11; Ortega y Gasset writes: "in its origins, the State consists of the mixture of races and tongues. . . . It is cross-bred and multilingual."[8] And so the architect of the Mosaic polity removes from one state—the imperial one—in order to create another: the theocratic one. This corporation, though equally marshaled by a "company-promoter," is as much a "congregation" as a state. Plagued by faction and cursed by confusion, the wilderness Israel nonetheless defines itself either by opposing or by rallying to the will and authority of the singular figure of Moses at the head of the congregation.

The Mosaic mission of eliciting the congregation-state embraces spokesmanship, stewardship, generalship, priestly functions in making covenants involving God, preaching, and the administration of a magistracy; and yet it also entails the assignment of all these functions to a Mosaic cadre that might serve in Moses' place and lay claim to Moses' appointment or endorsement. It is thus Moses' office or function to delegate office: to Aaron as speaker, aide-de-camp, and mediator and priest; to the seventy elders as arbitrators and councilors; to Joshua as "shepherd" and captain; to Joshua and Hur as military support; to Phinehas, whose armed intervention Moses confirms with a priesthood in Israel; to Joshua and Caleb as scouts and advance guard; and to the sons of Levi as devotees, priests, and educators (cf. the appointment of the Levites in Numbers 3 and 8, and the blessing of Levi in Deuteronomy 33:8–11). As a result, all of Moses' own offices seem provisional and pregeneric, unique to the Mosaic period and unique to Moses.[9]

Insofar as the functions he delegates fall to his successors and survivors, such as Joshua and "the sons of Aaron," Moses' own life might seem to be conceived as "pre-vocational." But we could also say "post-vocational," for Moses not only feels free to treat extensively with God without mediation, he is also freed from many of the demands of his various vocations. Thus in his set-apartness and dedication to God, he is like both the "pre-vocational" sojourner Abraham, called into a mountain to be given a sign, and the "vocational" Samuel, called to renew a seerlike experience of divine visitation among his people. But he is also something of a free floater, a "post-vocational" holy man, who has retired from the world to devote himself entirely to man's business with God. The mountain where he is called and the one that he ascends before he dies and in which God buries him apart from the sight of men bracket his public service with an exclusive communion with God that Exodus 33:17–23 also puts at its center: Moses asks to see God, and, *dia aenigmate,* he does so.

No one of the traditional offices in Israel is allowed wholly to conscript the life of Moses, which is not quite to say that they all do. The Israelite high command repeatedly approaches the scene of Moses' conferences with God on Sinai, yet is never fully included in them. Moses is not a judge in the narrower sense of a charismatic leader raised up solely by the singular emergency, as opposed to the demands of a whole dispensation. Moses gives his blessing to such a judge when he blesses Joshua down on the field of battle in the campaign against Amalek at Exodus 17:8–13. The story of Moses' arms being held up by Aaron and Hur during the battle suggests both the support of Moses by the priesthood and the priesthood's support of the holy war. But Moses is a military administrator, a long-term strategist, an officer in the resistance, and a commissar on a long march, rather than a warrior or army captain himself. Again, Moses is a magistrate, but not a sovereign. Rather, he is an elder ruling through a historical interregnum and exercising a dictatorship—properly God's—of the proletariat. And while he is of priestly stock, his priestly functions are divested to Aaron, leaving Moses a spiritual free agent. And though Moses is raised up as a prophet unto Pharaoh and called throughout his career to take continual dictation at God's mouth, his narrower prophetic function, within the daily life of Israel in the wilderness, is as a diviner, who takes an assay of God's will by means of lots and merely attempts to locate this will, as much as broadcast or promulgate or denounce it. Deuteronomy, on the other hand, treats Moses as an apologist for the divine will as specifically embodied in the divine word: yet it does not record the words of Mosaic oracles (such as the pronouncements of a seer like Balaam), but rather the words of Mosaic sermons and expositions of the law.

In Deuteronomy Moses has become both a kind of school of interpretation and a type for Levitical preaching activity. Since its Moses is relating the exodus tradition to the future, the discourse of Deuteronomy is something of an "art," both an art of preaching the Israelite kerygma and an art of interpreting the Israelite experience. Deuteronomy does not complete the story of the exodus by having Moses enter the promised land, for that might incorrectly imply a premature foreclosure of the postmortem career of Moses' word in Israel. And however late the composition of Deuteronomy, it is one with the wilderness Moses in keeping the name of Jerusalem off the record, even while the text's retiring spokesman frequently prophesies the place that God will choose for his worship at the royal capital. For Moses himself has "no lasting city," and he dies outside the promised land, and even outside the "camp" (cf. Heb. 13:13–14). The first campaign of the invasion under Joshua, the siege of Jericho, implies that the ancient Canaanite city-state, from the Israelite point of view, is a decadent institution. Joshua does not take over cities to rule them, he invades their territory to destroy them.

The text thus insists that the Israel that has shared its life with Moses' life is also an Israel that will be primarily understood as a congregation linked to its God, rather than as a place linked to its inhabitants. Just as God was understood as a "Kinsman" (Gen. 31:53, JB) attached to the persons of the sojourning Fathers, rather than to the shrines where the Fathers' god was worshipped, so the sojourning Israel is understood as an Israel of God, rather than as the land of Israel that Moses' people will subsequently come to occupy. In this connection, critics have aptly cited the evidence of the list of Near and Middle Eastern conquests recorded on the Merneptah stone, where the conquests other than Israel are all treated as territories—Israel is alone in being signified as a people.[10] Insofar as the Israelite people are represented as having had their Moses and their law before they had achieved any territorial sovereignty or jurisdiction at all, they are always back where they started, beyond Jordan, which is where Deuteronomy both starts and ends.

The birth of a historical kind of consciousness is discernible in precisely the charge that Israel forgot the mighty acts of the Lord in Egypt, before the people were delivered at the Reed Sea, even before the Reed Sea was divided: so Psalm 106:7 and Psalm 78:11–13. Or else the people forgot, subsequently, during the time in the wilderness: so Psalm 78:42–44. Both of these Psalms are histories of Israel's forgetfulness, and so it is not surprising that they find their subject virtually everywhere. Nonetheless, these texts suggest the function of a mediatorial and maieutic Moses in filling a void in Israel's historical explanation of itself. This would be a void between a legendary pre-Israel of the patriarchs and the covenanted Israel of the tribal league; a void between an international class of itinerant servants or hirelings called *habiru* and a people who had incorporated as the servant of God; and a void between an Israel in which each man was his own priest and an Israel in which the whole elect nation constituted itself as a nation of priests and holy men. Moses' portrait answers to Israel's sense that somehow it had traversed such a void, appropriating a history of a "time of troubles"—the plagues—as a time of consciousness-raising, and then departing from this history to enter upon the limbo of the wilderness. The wilderness is the space of preexistence, between nonentity in Egypt and identity in Israel; between vassalage in foreign lands and installment in the sovereign space of Israel's own country. Yet mediating the threshold over which Israel passes into historical existence, Moses finally becomes this threshold himself, at the borders of the promised land. The exodus of the Pentateuch begins with the charismatic kind of remembering that takes place at the burning bush. It ends with the bureaucratic kind of remembering that takes place in Deuteronomy.

·2·

"THE VOICE OF THE WORDS":
THE MOSES OF DEUTERONOMY

And the Lord spake unto you out of the midst of the fire: ye heard
the voice of the words, but saw no similitude, only ye heard a voice.
(Deut. 4:12)

When your eyes behold a king in his beauty,
When they contemplate the land round about,
Your throat shall murmur in awe,
"Where is the scribe? Where is the measurer?
Where is one that counts the towers?"
No more shall you see a savage nation,
The people of a speech too obscure to penetrate,
So stammering of tongue—not to be understood. (Isa. 33:17–19,
AT)

My heart is inditing a good matter . . . my tongue is the pen of a
ready writer. (Ps. 45:1)

Now go, write it before them in a table, and note it in a book, that it
may be for the time to come for ever and ever:
    That this is a rebellious people, lying children, children that will
not hear the law of the Lord. (Isa. 30:8–9)

Whoever writes is exiled from writing, which is the country—his
own—where he is not a prophet. (Maurice Blanchot, *The Writing of
the Disaster*)[1]

Deuteronomy posits itself as the late testament of Moses, a recapitulation
of the Mosaic experience given in the space between the generation that
died in the wilderness and the generation that possessed itself of the promised land. The text thus intervenes between Numbers and Joshua, as the
Joseph narrative at the end of Genesis intervenes between the patriarchal

21

and the Mosaic narratives. Like the Joseph story in Genesis, Deuteronomy's position in the Pentateuch dictates that it reify remembrance.
"Remember, and forget not, how thou provokedst the Lord thy God to
wrath in the wilderness," Moses says (Deut. 9:7); "And remember that
thou wast a servant in the land of Egypt," he asks in conjunction with the
commandment for sabbath-keeping and for providing time-off for workers
(Deut. 5:15). The maintenance of mindfulness is practically the whole
burden of Moses' teaching here, turning on a general injunction in his
song: "Remember the days of old, consider the years of many generations:
ask thy father, and he will shew thee; thy elders, and they will tell thee"
(Deut. 32:7). Deuteronomy assumes the existence of a "perverse and
crooked generation" (Deut. 32:5) that needs to be catechized—for there is
still hope that it may be converted. But despite God's having bought a generation's freedom, Israel's long-term conversion remains much in doubt.

Thus the Moses of this text convokes Israel as follows:

> . . . "Hear, O Israel, the statutes and the ordinances which I speak in
> your hearing this day, and you shall learn them and be careful to do
> them. The Lord our God made a covenant with us in Horeb. Not with
> our fathers did the Lord make this covenant, but with us, who are all of
> us here alive this day. . . ." (Deut. 5:1–3, RSV)

"The salvation . . . [God] will shew to you to day," as found at the Reed
Sea (Exod. 14:13) has been renewed in Moab, "That he may establish thee
to day for a people" (Deut. 29:13). Moses means that the new Moab generation, as opposed to the old Sinai one, is the object of God's address; but
the *deuteronomist* means that the latter-day statist Israel, as opposed to the
old Mosaic congregation, is also the object of Moses' address. The text
reaches out to catechize and constitute its proper audience within a current and vital Israel identical with a class of elected readers.[2] Deuteronomy
puts itself into the gap between the death of Moses outside Israel and the
edification of Israel inside Canaan, as its Moses puts his mediatorial offices
between the God whom Moses faced "at the mountain" and the Israel that
"did not go up" into that mountain. Hence the "temporizing" reversals
and deferrals in Deuteronomy 5:4:

> The Lord spoke with you face to face at the mountain, out of the midst
> of the fire, while I stood between the Lord and you at the time, to
> declare to you the word of the Lord; for you were afraid because of the
> fire, and you did not go up into the mountain. (RSV)

Yahweh spoke to the people face to face at the mount; yet Moses spoke for
him, and the congregation did not go up into the mount—Moses went in
its place. Yahweh spoke to the congregation out of the midst of fire, yet

Moses interposed himself between the congregation and the face of God, to face and withstand the fire—again, in the people's place. It is precisely this passage that buffers the space that "comes between" the original "covenant made with us in Horeb" and the deuteronomistic reiteration of its "statutes and ordinances," or between a latter-day covenant and the original Mosaic pronouncement at Sinai. "The word is very near you," Moses says (Deut. 30:14, RSV), near the end of his life, in his final exhortation to keep his book's law. In this text "the word" intervenes as a *concept:* it is *the* word, as in the prophets. The discursive protagonist is now the putative consolidator and promoter of the biblical word as a noetic entity mediating between man and God. The word administered by this Moses comes between God and Israel, like a prophet or a go-between. But by the same token, the word intervenes as an *interpretation* of the word; Moses is an expounder of dictates he has already spoken. The word is not near Moses' audience because the people are near the mountain but because they are near Deuteronomy.

Deuteronomy also signals the recognition of the law as such a noetic entity. And being given in Moab, this law revives a law it also revises, and so makes the law more conscious of itself. Acknowledgment of the law can also function as a pre-incriminatory recital of it: as Paul says, "I had not known sin, but by the law" (Rom. 7:7). "The word," the Moses of Deuteronomy tells his audience, is "in thy mouth, and in thy heart, that thou mayest do it" (Deut. 30:14), but he might almost have said, "is on the books so that you can know when you are not doing it." In Deuteronomy, this word and this law are understood in relation to the major narrative: having heard and understand the words of the law in Moab, Israel is in a position to "know sin" in Canaan.

Deuteronomy's reification of its own words puts it into a special class of biblical discourse. Beginning in Isaiah 40 an analogous reification of the prophetic word performs this reflexive function in relation to the archive of the writing prophets: "The grass withereth, the flower fadeth: but the word of our God shall stand for ever" (Isa. 40:8). The postulation of the preexistent *logos* in the prologue to the Gospel of John speaks similarly for the New Testament, and goes back to another example, Proverbs 8, which hypostatizes an analogous noetic entity for the wisdom literature. In these places where the text becomes notably conscious of itself as word, there also prophecy, law, gospel, and wisdom become subjects in their own right and stake their claim to be the Bible.

Although the deuteronomic word is in Israel's mouth and heart so Israel can do it, we could also say so Israel can *read* it. This does not necessarily mean read it privately, but it does mean aloud, on public occasions. The two obvious cases recorded by texts outside of Deuteronomy itself are the promulgations of Josiah and Ezra. Second Kings 22–23 reports Josiah's public reading of a book of the covenant in words that renew the speech-forms of this Mosaicizing text:

> And the king sent, and they gathered unto him all the elders of Judah and of Jerusalem.
> And the king went up into the house of the Lord, and all the men of Judah and all the inhabitants of Jerusalem with him, and the priests, and the prophets, and all the people, both small and great: and he read in their ears all the words of the book of the covenant which was found in the house of the Lord.
> And the king stood by a pillar, and made a covenant before the Lord, to walk after the Lord, and to keep his commandments and his testimonies and his statutes with all their heart and all their soul, to perform the words of this covenant that were written in this book.
> And all the people stood to the covenant. (2 Kings 23:1–3)

Josiah's rehearsal itself makes a start on fulfilling the book's newfound demand that it be read in all their ears (Deut. 31:11, 28).

Ezra's post-exilic publicizing of the text of "the book of the law of Moses" (Neh. 8:1) from a pulpit made for the occasion becomes an even more ceremonial performance: "And Ezra the priest brought the law before . . . all that could hear with understanding, upon the first day of the seventh month . . . And Ezra opened the book in the sight of all the people; (for he was above all the people;) and when he opened it, all the people stood up: And Ezra blessed the Lord, the great God. And all the people answered, Amen, Amen, with lifting up their hands" (Neh. 8:2–6). Where once the people rose at the approach of Moses to the tent of the meeting (Exod. 33:8–11), they now rise at the opening of the book of the Mosaic law: Exodus takes its cue from a practice that survived beyond the Exile.

Following the blessing by Ezra, in the scene just quoted, the Israelite saving history and the history of apostasy and the divine benefactions are publicly confessed by Ezra's audience, "And because of this we [the people] make a sure covenant, and write it; and our princes, Levites, and priests, seal unto it" (Neh. 9:38). Thus the people enter "into a curse, and into an oath, to walk in God's law, which was given by Moses the servant of God" (Neh. 10:29). This renewing of the law is also deeply embedded in the narrative of its original transmission, but Deuteronomy is uniquely positioned to expose the fact that extended biblical narratives concerning the law, the covenant, and the saving history always incorporate in themselves reincorporation, reinauguration, and recapitulation.

As a pertinent example of the principle just stated, we may take the "typological" rationale the post-exilic historians give for Ezra's celebration of the Feast of Booths. In Ezra 3:4, the people who had returned from Babylon "kept also the feast of tabernacles, *as it is written*, and offered the daily burnt offerings by number, according to the custom, as the duty of every day required," where "as it is written" may be glossed with Ezra 6:18, "as it is written *in the book of Moses*." So Nehemiah 8:14–16, upon the reading of the words of the law: "And they found written in the law which the Lord had commanded by Moses, that the children of Israel should dwell in booths in the feast of the seventh month," and that they should build these booths with branches "from the mount." The harvest feast is commanded in any book of the law of Moses we now have (Exod. 23:16, 34:22–23, Deut. 16:13–15); Ezra's purpose, however, is perhaps best stated by God in Leviticus 23:42–43: "all that are Israelites born shall dwell in booths: That your generations may know that I made the children of Israel to dwell in booths, when I brought them out of the land of Egypt." For "all the congregation of them that were come again out of the captivity made booths, and sat under the booths" (Neh. 8:17). Whether or not Ezra explicitly renewed the former levitical and deuteronomic interpretations of the festival, the leading scribe of the post-exilic period did cast himself in the role of a Mosaic interpreter, historicizer, and commemorator, merely by renewing a feast said to have been instituted by Moses. For Nehemiah's narrator has Ezra align the present, post-exilic observance of the feast with a former, immediately post-Mosaic occasion. The text says the Israelites had not made the booths from the days of Joshua son of Nun till that day (Neh. 8:17). Such a notice suffices to announce that the succession to Moses had rebegun in Ezra. In addition, Nehemiah's narrator has patently echoed a received description of the reform of Josiah, which was celebrated with an equally unique holiday: "Surely there was not holden such a passover from the days of the judges that judged Israel" (2 Kings 23:22). If Ezra as celebrant was a latter-day Josiah as well as a latter-day Joshua, this can only remind us that Josiah was himself an earlier second Moses.

Moses' success or failure with Pharaoh in Egypt, it follows from these examples, becomes itself the type of the success or failure of the levitical law-texts and festal calendars (those claiming Mosaic authority) in securing adoption by various Israelite leaderships. Royal sponsorship, of course, is just what Moses himself conspicuously failed to secure: Josiah heeded Hilkiah in Jerusalem, but Pharaoh chose to ignore Moses in Egypt. As if placed between these two alternatives, the Israelites may or may not hearken to God's spokesman in the plain of Moab in Deuteronomy.

Though Hilkiah was a priest, the exodus narrative casts the success or failure of the lawgiver in terms of an audience hearkening to—or ignoring—a prophet. Yet this prophet, as we meet him in Deuteronomy, is defined precisely by his being a deutero-Moses—and so a Levitical Moses as well. Ezra seems to have modeled himself on a "canonic" Moses, who has in turn been modeled on the Ezra canonizing the texts in Moses' name.

But what has the latter-day Moses of Deuteronomy himself been modeled on? A parallel for the "deuteronomicizing Ezra" may be found in the spokesmanship of Samuel, for example in 1 Samuel 12:6–15, where the prophet is recalling to the people "all the righteous acts of the Lord, which he did to [Israel] and to [its] fathers." Samuel's schema is the familiar deuteronomic one for the judges: the Israelites sinned by forsaking the Lord, they cried out for deliverance from their oppressors, the Lord sent them judges, and the judges delivered them into safe dwelling in their land. Thus, "When Jacob was come into Egypt, and your fathers cried unto the Lord, then the Lord sent Moses and Aaron, which brought forth your fathers out of Egypt, and made them dwell in this place" (1 Sam. 12:8). When Samuel recurs to this schema for the judges themselves, his history includes his own: "And the Lord sent Jerubbaal, and Bedan, and Jephthah, *and Samuel*, and delivered you out of the hand of your enemies on every side, and ye dwelled safe" (1 Sam. 12:11). The momentary lapse is indicative: the deuteronomic Samuel is a second one; the first has become history. The deuteronomic historian replaces the historical figure. So Moses the Yahwist became Moses the deuteronomist— and he thus becomes the deuteronomic redactor, or Ezra the scribe. Moses is less an individual person than the personification of an extended Mosaic succession.

Instead of saying that God led Israel out of Egypt by the hand of Moses, Hosea only says that the people were brought out "by a prophet" (Hos. 12:13). What Hosea puts in the past, Deuteronomy puts in the future:

> "The Lord your God will raise up for you a prophet like me from among you, from your brethren—him you shall heed—just as you desired of the Lord your God at Horeb on the day of assembly, when you said, 'Let me not hear again the voice of the Lord my God, or see this great fire any more, lest I die.' And the Lord said to me, 'They have rightly said all that they have spoken. I will raise up for them a prophet like you from among their brethren; and I will put my words in his mouth, and he shall speak to them all that I command him. And whoever will not give heed to my words which he shall speak in my name, I myself will require it of him. But the prophet who presumes to speak a word in my name which I have not commanded him to speak, or who speaks in the name of other gods, that same prophet shall die.' " (Deut. 18:15–20, RSV)

"Let me not hear again the voice of the Lord my God, or see this great fire any more, lest I die," the deuteronomic Moses says the people once said. " 'Did not our hearts burn within us while he talked to us on the road, while he opened to us the scriptures?' " Luke's apostles ask each other, after the disappearance of their risen teacher, whose exposition "in all the scriptures" of "the things concerning himself" began "with Moses and all the prophets" (Luke 24:32, 27, RSV). Hosea and the deuteronomic Moses answer to the latter-day need, much like the interpreter in the early church, whose office was a well recognized one (1 Cor. 12:10, 14:26). The relation between Hosea and the former "prophet," between the deuteron-omist and the former Mosaic Israel, and between Luke's latter-day prophet-interpreter and the Moses of Deuteronomy are successive phases in an ongoing relation.

Hosea appears to know a great deal of the legend of Israel's early expe-rience—the deliverance from Egypt, the wilderness, the sin of the calf, grapes, quails, the valley of Achor, Baal-Peor, and the divine ministry in general. But the prophet has spoken these things as similitudes: the grapes, for example, are not the promise of the promised land, as they are in the narratives; now they grow in the wilderness, and they are a simili-tude for the salad days of Israel's relation to God (Hos. 9:10). Nonetheless, we must go back to the text of Hosea, because it contains not only the first historically dateable reference to the exodus, but also the first dateable reference to Moses' part in it. But it is just this passage that attests that it was the writing prophets who invented the literary Moses. For Hosea refers to the Hebrew leader only by way of a reading of his own office as a prophet, for which Moses is a similitude; moreover, Hosea only refers to the exodus here in conjunction with its commemoration and renewal in the Feast of Booths:

> And I that am the Lord thy God from the land of Egypt will yet make thee to dwell in tabernacles, as in the days of the solemn feast.
> I have also spoken by the prophets, and I have multiplied visions, and used similitudes, by the ministry of the prophets. . . .
> And by a prophet the Lord brought Israel out of Egypt, and by a prophet was he [= Israel] preserved. (Hos. 12:9–10, 13)

Moses is chiefly adduced to provide supplementary authority for the saving ministry of prophet; and a historical repetition of the wilderness experience is only extended from its previous consecration in a liturgical calendar. Was the narrative invented to explain a rite like the one in Nehe-miah 8:4 renewed after the exile? If the legend of an exodus in the past is generated out of its repeating in the present and the future, then Moses' office seems to emerge as a similitude for that of his successors—whether a prophet like Hosea, or a liturgist like Ezra.

The existence of the Moses found in the dually "commemorative" and "revivalistic" text of Deuteronomy recognizes and advances the claim of the Moses of the Pentateuch to be one of Israel's canons of consciousness, a means of Israel's making itself *present* to itself. Such a canon functions in place of Moses himself: in his absence. The people in Exodus 33:8–11 rise when Moses approaches the tent, as a congregation might rise when its priest approaches the altar, because of a consciousness-raising function variously shared with the ark, the oracle, the public ceremony, and appeals to national norms (e.g., Gen. 34:7, Judg. 20:6). In the Pentateuch, most of the means to Israelite apperception fall under Mosaic auspices. When the people rise at the opening of Ezra's book, the Mosaic canon itself assumes the function. The Levites tell the people that God "camest down also upon mount Sinai, and spakest with them from heaven, and gavest them right judgments, and true laws, good statutes and commandments: And madest known unto them thy holy sabbath, and commandest them precepts, statutes, and laws, by the hand of Moses thy servant" (Neh. 9:13–14). Both leader and book are cast as "another Moses."

The same kind of claim is made for the Levites, in Deuteronomy itself, via Moses' blessing on Levi near the end of the text:

> And of Levi he said, Let thy Thummim and thy Urim be with thy holy one, whom thou didst prove at Massah, and with whom thou didst strive at the waters of Meribah;
> Who said unto his father and to his mother, I have not seen him; neither did he acknowledge his brethren, nor knew his own children: for they have observed thy word, and kept thy covenant.
> They shall teach Jacob thy judgments, and Israel thy law: they shall put incense before thee, and whole burnt sacrifice upon thine altar. (Deut. 33:8–10)

"*Give* to Levi thy Thummim" (RSV, vs. 8) is an addition of the Greek translation (LXX), which makes explicit what the original implies: the whole Levitical corporation is to be identified as "Moses." It comes to enjoy, through Deuteronomy, both the Mosaic imprimatur and the Mosaic bequeathal.

Owing to the deuteronomistic strand running throughout the major biblical narrative, there is a deep family resemblance between the Moses unto whose God no other is like (Exod. 8:10), the "prophet" of God like unto whom there has been no other since in Israel (Deut. 34:10), the Judaic king Hezekiah, whom there was no subsequent king like (2 Kings 18:5), and Josiah, like unto whom there had been no other king in Israel

(2 Kings 23:25)—and the prophet whom God promises to Moses in Deuteronomy that he will raise up "like unto" Moses (Deut. 18:18). The tendency toward an Israel-summarizing Moses—resulting from the coalescence of the traditional, received, and legendary Moses, and Moses as a cultural founder-figure—inevitably points us back toward the torah-teaching and torah-preaching Moses depicted in Deuteronomy itself. It is here that a Moses posterior to Moses emerges in his own right: as a legendary "prophet" and cultural sponsor of the received tradition, of which the earlier Moses of the exodus is now the content. Paradoxically, this "prophet" or deutero-Moses prophesies the place of the Mosaic tradition—or of the "past" Moses—in the future of Israel. For the critical prophecy that this deutero-Moses actually makes is somewhat circular: he prophesies the sending of a prophet to Israel—one like himself.

If the exhortative and admonitory deutero-Moses of the text is indeed identical with the anticipated prophet, then the reception of his "prophetic" message can only be synonymous with the revival or conservation of the Mosaic legacy or tradition. In thus dignifying Israel's hearkening to "Mosaic" tradition as a response to prophecy, Deuteronomy can hardly be defining prophecy as a particular address to the exigencies of the specific occasion or to a singular crisis. Rather, the relevance of deuteronomistic "prophecy" is analogous to that of the savingness of the exodus event, or to the promises, covenant, and law, or the Torah tradition as a whole. These things are the content, ready-to-hand, of the deuteronomic "word."

Insofar as a prophet's words themselves conduce to bring about what they anticipate, they are a speech with preternatural power, like that attributed to Jesus in Luke 4:32, 36 ("And they were astonished at his doctrine, for his word was with power. . . . And they were all amazed and spake among themselves, saying, What a word is this! for with authority and power he commandeth the unclean spirits, and they come out."). But just as the words of Moses in Deuteronomy do not aim at specific prediction, neither do they have the illocutionary force and efficacy of the thaumaturgic kind of conjuration. The law in Deuteronomy does not compel, it pleads. For if this kind of prophecy is a summons and a promulgation that are continuously in effect, it is also continuously open. An ongoing, steadily available relevance or applicability must also be a contingent and conditional one: these words may or may not be followed by what they threaten or promise or demand. Thus the preachment of Moses, in which Moses or God offers Israel again the decision of following the "ways" that God has shown to it, is anxiously situated in the borderline situation of Moab, where there is still a choice for salvation to be made, a "threshold of assent," in Dante's phrase (*Purg.* 18.63), yet to be crossed.

The covenant offered in Deuteronomy is conditional and revocable. The deuteronomic "exodus"—this time the leaving behind of the schooling in the wilderness—therefore implies not salvation from the subjection of the past, but rather a dangerous departure from obedience to the deliverer in the future: from the literal Moses that the text subtends, reconstitutes, and spiritualizes. The text knows of this defection, and gives Moses a grim foreknowledge of Israel's history in the land—the admonitory discourse visits it virtually retrospectively—and a further foreknowledge of exile, dispersal, and deracination abroad (Deut. 4:26–28). Here Moses calls Israel to the choice of life after its people have made the wrong choice many times, and offers them his perfected will and testament, even as he surrenders to his executors his own good offices as a Levitical mediator.

The blessing of Reuben in Deuteronomy 33 is characteristically dual: "Let Reuben live, and not die; and let *not* his men be few" (Deut. 33:6, AV, which has added "not"). But this could also mean, "Let Reuben survive and not die out—yet let his men be few." The blessings are paired with curses: their effectiveness resides less in the power of Moses' speech itself than in the receptivity of the audience. Moses predicts it will rebel against him, once he is gone, yet he or his author also is relying upon it to preserve the evidence of its apostasy. The words of such a text, dignifying choice and emphasizing persuasion and consent rather than compulsion and enforcement, must be very different from the effect of "words of power." There are singers whose voices can shatter glass, but there are others whose voices break hearts. According to Deuteronomy, the efficacy of Moses' speech lies less in the capacity of utterance to conjure and compel a rock than in the capacity of hearing to take in an unforgettable message—or to take that message to heart. But Moses may fail—that Deuteronomy's message may not convert its audience is acknowledged in every repetition of it, and God accuses Moses himself of omitting to hallow God in the midst of Israel at Meribah-Kadesh (Deut. 32:51). Moses did not heed God's word, or the letter of God's instructions: "Because ye believed me not" (Num. 20:12).

Since Deuteronomy defines the salvation tradition as continuously subject to a future vindication—or future belying—which more narrowly obtains when prophecy is predictive, it also defines the tradition as subject to a crisis of faith in its efficacy. The tradition itself may be a "false" or unreliable prophecy. Those who depart from it, in effect, succeed in disproving it. The long existence of the Israelite establishment seems to promise its continuation, yet in the time of Jeremiah it is precisely such an expectation that is falsifiable—the continuity of the history had become eminently breachable. The public falsification of prophecy is a notable feature of Jeremiah's prophetic career.

The potential contest, between the affirmation and refutation of the prophecies made by tradition and the falsifiable prophecy made by the survival of the Israelite establishment itself, defines so much of Jeremiah's life as a prophet that it is hard not to read his people's rejection of him into every summons and appeal made by the hero of Deuteronomy. With every objection that he raises to the future establishment of Israel, the "prophetic" and "belated" Moses of this text also threatens Israel with its discontinuance, as Jeremiah did. Nothing could be more significant, in this context, than Jeremiah's renouncing of a prophet's role as Mosaic and Samuelic (or "Shilonic"), in that rare, prophetic citation of Moses' name: "Then said the Lord unto me, Though Moses and Samuel stood before me, yet my mind could not be toward this people" (Jer. 15:1). "It's too late," Jeremiah in effect says, "for me to be Moses." But the Moses of Deuteronomy, excluded from the promised land, fears the same thing.

We may pause over the identification of Moses with Jeremiah. The line leading from Samuel's word concerning sacrifices in 1 Samuel 15:22–23, to Hosea 6:6 and Isaiah 1:11–17, and thence to circumcision of the heart as found in Deuteronomy (10:16, 30:6) and Jeremiah (4:4) is clear enough: the Lord does not require sacrifice per se, but repentance and sacrifice of the will; not the death of the firstborn, but the self-abnegation of the father—Jeremiah himself was commanded to remain a bachelor (Jer. 16:2; cf. also the ruined loincloth of Jer. 13:1–11). Jeremiah said that what the Lord wanted was a heartfelt knowledge of him, and he treated temple, cultus, king, and state as so many expendable shibboleths during a time when the existence of these things was about to cease. And he was emboldened to prophesy their replacement by the much-needed gift of a new heart. Moreover, in the latter day, God will restore Israel: "with my whole heart and with my whole soul," God himself promises through Jeremiah (32:41). God will do this because Israel will be searching for Yahweh in the same way: "with all your heart and all your soul," as the deuteronomic Moses invites Israel to do (Deut. 4:29, 10:12, 11:13, 26:16, 30:2, 6). In the end Israel may well return to Yahweh and listen to his voice, according to Deuteronomy 4:30. "I will give them a heart to know me," God tells Jeremiah (24:7), "for they shall return unto me with their whole heart." It is a "Mosaic" and deuteronomistic Jeremiah who says, "The sin of Judah is written with a pen of iron, and with the point of a diamond: it is graven upon the table of their heart, and upon the horns of your altars" (Jer. 17:1). Whatever else Judah's sin includes, it is still indicted in Jeremiah and Deuteronomy as if it involved an idolatry like that of the golden calf.[3]

Deuteronomy privileges the ministry of a preacher, or rather the consolidation of that ministry in a text, the product of an editorial process that creates the archive of a writing prophet. A somewhat similar development is found in the life of Jeremiah himself. As just noted, Jeremiah enjoyed the services of a secretary, Baruch, and Jeremiah's witness took the form of an epistle (Jer. 29)—a scroll that required a second edition after it was destroyed (Jer. 36)—and of a book of a new covenant: "The word that came to Jeremiah from the Lord, saying, Thus speaketh the Lord God of Israel, saying, Write thee all the words that I have spoken unto thee in a book" (Jer. 30:1). Baruch is even accused (by Jeremiah's opponents in the military party) of having put "all these words" in Jeremiah's mouth (Jer. 43:1–3). But there is necessarily a grain of truth in the accusation: Baruch's written descriptions of Jeremiah must indeed entail the scribe's putting words into his principal character's mouth.

There are two ways of looking at Deuteronomy, then. One way sees it as "packaged prophetism": [4] the attempt to reduce prophecy to the words of a unified canon of the law and a closed book. Prophecy is actually shut down by such an action, since Deuteronomy does not expect to be added to, and since the history it encompasses and alludes to possesses a kind of closure of its own. The only prophet God can raise up after Deuteronomy is another copy of Deuteronomy. But there is another way of looking at the matter: one can suggest that the explanation of Moses as a prophet in Deuteronomy intends to support a point made in Numbers 12:6–8, that there is a special kind of Yahwist prophet, for which the name Moses stands, and that this prophet has a Mosaic function, which is to say, the mediating of the covenant, thus reading that covenant as a "prophecy" of future covenants and turning the Mosaic prophet's office into that of covenant mediator. [5] For there is a kind of prophet, represented by Hosea, who is specifically the champion of the covenant. In Deuteronomy this prophet, like Jeremiah, has the power to sustain his word by making it over in the form of a new contract from God. A prophet like Hosea, who seems to be continually implying a marriage relation between Israel and God, speaks in a "similitude" for the covenant that Deuteronomy depicts Moses actually offering to Israel. As the Judaic prophets would provide the services of their word as an imprimatur for the election of the throne of David—God's gift—so the Northern prophets might provide the services of their word as a seal on the legal relation between God and Israel— God's offer. Both points of view see Deuteronomy as a "constitution" (or "package") claiming prophetic credentials. The question, then, is whether the package undermines those credentials and subverts the authenticity of Hosea and Jeremiah, by casting their prophecies in the form of terms for a covenant, or whether it extends the credentials and dignifies them as Mosaic, by recognizing these prophets as spokesmen for new founding events. Does the death of Moses in Deuteronomy betoken the silencing of the prophets, or does the survival of their words of promise and admonition in that text betoken the continued relevance of prophetism to Israel's situation? The answer depends on how you look at it, because a threshold faces both ways. In some of Hosea, Hosea faces the wilderness and sees hope and a new start. In some of Deuteronomy, Moses faces Canaan and sees the same old story—a very discouraging prospect indeed.

The deuteronomic Moses teaches that there is no God but Yahweh, and Deuteronomy teaches that Moses is his prophet. Such a Moses is not so much the individual prophet confronting the specific occasion, as a preacher on behalf of "the Mosaic"—because the speaker's audience is constituted as Moses' congregation. The text presents the coming of God's word as a saving event in its own right, and the congregation's response to this word as the completing of that event. Deuteronomy radically simplifies Israel's covenant obligations by submitting them all to the demand for sincere and loving response to them. God asks no more, and also no less. Hence his word as an utterance is virtually complete: what remains is only its promulgation through copying and repeating it. The reiterative, wooing style of the speech in Deuteronomy has not so much forgotten Moses' original slowness of tongue as transvalued it: Moses' uncircumcised lips are no longer doing the speaking. Or rather, his speeches come from the heart, that is, from the heartfelt desire that the words have ample opportunity to be heard, so that they might be heeded. It is Moses' devout prayer that his words not fall on deaf ears, poor hearing on the part of a latter-day audience being equivalent to the tied tongue on the part of its former spokesman. In preaching circumcision of the heart, the Deuteronomist has thrown all of his emphasis on the last of the first ten commandments, where intents have become subjects: his persona preaches the purification of motive in the answerable moral subject, as the authentic response to the one and only God. But "purification" and "authentication" are process terms that also might refer to the speech-act itself: to what the speaker ought to mean in speaking, and to what the hearer ought to understand in hearing.

Despite the idea of preaching in Deuteronomy, its word is preeminently a written one, and thus also a readable one. Paul once speaks of the "scripture" as having "concluded all things under sin" (Gal. 3:22); Deuteronomy has concluded all things under writing. If it is the unstated idea of Deuteronomy that Moses inevitably becomes "Mosaic" through the subsumption of his inheritors, it is also thanks to Deuteronomy that this idea is arguably something more than the mere notion of the mythifying back-projection into Moses of descendant vocational traditions. Of course Moses the character is depicted as sponsoring the Levitical and legalist traditions that originally sponsored him, but he also sponsors writing. Deuteronomy, for example, begins with Moses' creation of a judicial system. This might deserve no further notice, except that the invention of the judicial system is elsewhere attributed not to Moses but to his wife's father, who is concerned to relieve his son-in-law of a heavy caseload

(Exod. 18:13–27; cf. Num. 11:16–17). But Deuteronomy, which annexes to itself the subsequent historical narrative from Joshua through 2 Kings, puts Moses' establishment of the judiciary and his own magistracy at the head of the deuteronomic history, where the Priestly history puts the dominion of man over the earth. Moses' inaugural act in Deuteronomy is bureaucratic, and establishes a legal community for the hearing of causes. Moses is the hallowed patron of this community, and he comes to it—as if from Sinai—as the father of legal *writing*.

The divine commissioning of Moses to write is particularly strong in Deuteronomy, and much of the writing there is in fact simply *scriptural*. Despite a certain validation of the power of the word in Deuteronomy, the text hardly lets us forget—although its words were allegedly spoken—that Deuteronomy itself is cast in the deutero-speech of the writing in which its words are kept. A "writing Moses" is not peculiar to the conception of Deuteronomy, of course. He is found just previously in the activity of the Mosaic chronicler reported by Numbers 33:1–2: "These are the journeys [RSV 'stages'] of the children of Israel, which went forth out of the land of Egypt with their armies under the hand of Moses and Aaron. And *Moses wrote their goings out according to their journeys by the commandment of the Lord;* and these are their journeys according to their goings out." Such a record- or chronicle-keeping Moses was a kind of official historian of an expedition—the presumably more sedentary author of Numbers is his heir. The terminally placed Song of Moses—for a further example, from Deuteronomy itself—is said to be a piece that Moses was divinely commissioned to write down, at God's dictation, *before* its being delivered orally: "Now therefore write ye this song for you, and teach it the children of Israel: put it in their mouths, that this song may be a witness for me against the children of Israel . . ." (Deut. 31:19). Similar poems, when put into the mouths of other characters in the biblical narrative, are not identified as scripts in quite this explicit way—which makes Moses secretary, legal witness, and public catechizer.

Even at his most inspired, Moses is the hero of the text, and of the ghostwriters and editors who create and keep it. Those who have a desire to have the text written in the hearts of succeeding generations will also be moved to write it down in this one, especially if they foresee, with God, a hiatus (and its abridgment) in the succession of hearts: "When many evils and troubles are befallen them, . . . this song shall testify against them as a witness; for it shall not be forgotten out of the mouths of their seed" (Deut. 31:21). God urges Israel to " 'Remember what Amalek did unto thee by the way, when ye were come forth out of Egypt; . . . thou shalt blot out [*maḥah*] the remembrance of Amalek from under heaven; thou shalt not forget it" (Deut. 25:17, 19). God will "blot out" apostates from his book (Deut. 9:14, Exod. 32:33); yet the book has not forgotten to censure the roll call of the nations.

If writing is a kind of remembrance offered as an aid to a people otherwise possessing a short memory, the people whom Moses addresses in Deuteronomy are being characterized negatively: "Of the Rock that begat thee thou art unmindful," their accuser tells them, "and hast forgotten God that formed thee" (Deut. 32:18). This is also the accusation of the prophet Jeremiah, for the false prophets "think to cause my people to forget my name by their dreams which they tell every man to his neighbor, as their fathers have forgotten my name for Baal" (Jer. 23:27). Jeremiah is the prophet who wrote, and, when his writing was destroyed, wrote again.

Deuteronomy ends upon Moses' blessings on the tribes and the confirmation of Joshua's appointment. That is, the appointment of Joshua is in approximately the place where Genesis would put Joseph's blessing of Ephraim. Joshua will reveal even as he confirms the character of his succession when he first offers sacrifices on a proper altar: for Joshua did this "As Moses the servant of the Lord commanded the children of Israel, *as it is written in the book of the law of Moses*" (Josh. 8:31). These words contain the crucial ambiguity: was Joshua's authority the command of Moses, or his book? Did Joshua do what the book records Moses prescribing one do (i.e., follow those laws that the Lord established between himself and the people of Israel on Mount Sinai through Moses [Lev. 26:46]), or did Joshua do what the book reports Moses as having done? There is no real distinction to be made here, if Moses is himself portrayed, like Ezra in the post-exilic period, as regularly doing things "by the book" of which he himself is also the protagonist. It is especially in Deuteronomy that "the people of the book" are to be found in that book which they are the people of. The shift in emphasis, from saving event to saving word, or from those things that God did through Moses to those things he said through him, leads to the emergence of the Bible itself.

The deuteronomic Moses, failing a direct assault on Canaan, says the first thing he did was appoint administrators (Deut. 1:13–17). Similarly, the text's commission of Joshua is less the conquest itself than the publishing of "Moses" throughout the land: "thou shalt set thee up great stones, and plaister them with plaister: And thou shalt write upon them all the words of this law, when thou art passed over" (Deut. 27:2–3). Leaving "nothing undone of all that the Lord commanded Moses" (Josh. 11:15), Joshua executes his charge at Mt. Ebal: "he wrote there upon the stones a copy of the law . . . which [Moses] wrote in the presence of the children of Israel. . . . There was not a word of all that Moses commanded, which Joshua read not before all the congregation of Israel, with the women, and the little ones, and the strangers that were conversant among them"

(Josh. 8:32, 35). Joshua enjoys a Mosaic commission only insofar as he also possesses a Mosaic *canon.*

Though Moses treats almost exclusively with the divinity in the narrative about God and Israel in which he is involved, the text is quite innocent of any apotheosizing tendency. The Old Testament, at any rate, records no raising of Moses to the right hand of God, no prophetic translation of him to the court of heaven or paradise. His name in Egyptian is potentially theophoric, "Son of—," "—[his] child," but it names no god. Before God Moses is always the representative of the human, not the superhuman. Moreover, Moses is the man for Israel, not for Moses. When God makes offers to him personally, Moses refuses to divorce himself from Israel or to accept Israel's place as the deity's adopted or chosen one. The reverse side of his want of an apotheosis is his mediatorial self-abnegation. If the man Moses was indeed "very meek, above all the men which were upon the face of the earth" (Num. 12:3), this ambassadorial self-effacement stands at the opposite pole from the self-assertion of Jacob, who gets the blessing of a house. Jacob gets the house of Israel, in favor of which Moses disqualifies any house of his own (at Exod. 32:10–13).

God does not allow Moses to enter Canaan, but his life is not mocked by any cry of forsakenness, such as the one uttered by Jesus from the cross in Matthew and Mark. "Moses fails to enter Canaan not because his life is too short but because it is a human life."[6] Moses is humility incarnate, which is realistic, since life in general tends to be humbling. Deuteronomy thus shows Moses remaining outside the promised land that was the goal of the exodus—the goal endorsed by the Sinaitic revelation—while finishing his own life-work in the wilderness. Deuteronomy's teaching requires that its hero enjoy the length of life necessary to complete his work before he enters into death, for his purpose is to enable Israel to choose for a complete existence that is earthly. Length of years on the land is one of the essential promises of that existence.

Jacob and Moses both die outside of Canaan, and they likewise have in common the apotheosis-like emergence of their last wills and testaments in their place, upon the closing of their respective installments of the divine revelation as a narrative. Jacob's life ends with his blessing of his sons—his house—thus closing the canon of the patriarchal saga in Genesis, even while revisiting it after the intervention of the Joseph novella. Moses' life ends upon his blessing of the tribes of Israel, thus closing the exodus saga, while revisiting it after the intervention of the wilderness sojourn—during which virtually all of the original parties to the exodus have died. Moses is imagined as acting to close the Mosaic canon: his canonization takes the form of his completing his word and closing out further expressions of it.

As a consequence of his action in Deuteronomy, Moses uncovers within the law two further criteria that its completeness might imply: canonicity and traditionality. The canon of the law and the Mosaic canon are twin-born with the deuteronomic interpretation of law, and with its momentum toward the law's circumscription and universalizing. Neither disclosure is possible without some prior experience and acceptance of the summarizing power already present in previously revealed law codes, and without the tradition of such codes as embodying a Mosaically mediated communication from beyond Moses. As a latter-day Israel is commanded to add nothing to and subtract nothing from the deuteronomic law (Deut. 4:2, 12:32), so God originally spoke the Decalogue from the heart of the fire: "He added no more," Moses says, "And he wrote them in two tables of stone, and delivered them unto me" (Deut. 5:22). Yet Deuteronomy obviously adds much more through its own recitations, which include the criterion of completeness. Like the Sermon on the Mount, Deuteronomy is both a law and an interpretation of the law, poised forever on the margins of the deutero-canonical. Like the covers of a book, such a thing can only come into existence upon the interpretive decision that there exists a whole ready to be bound and circulated in a definitive form, for which Deuteronomy provides either the foreword or the afterword.

Deuteronomy, then, "packages" what a text like Exodus 20—the first instance of the Ten Commandments—merely records, and what Exodus as a whole finds a loose Sinaitic context for. Leviticus similarly takes Sinai for a colophon ("These are the commandments which the Lord commanded Moses for the children of Israel in mount Sinai" [27:34]), even though it begins with the Lord calling unto Moses and speaking to him "out of the tabernacle of the congregation" (Lev. 1:1). The editor's placement of Deuteronomy was a deutero-Mosaic activity in the same way that writing the last verse of Leviticus was. Paradoxically, because of the company it keeps—and at the same time subsumes—Deuteronomy could almost stand alone, in place of "the law and the prophets": for it renews the law of Moses, and canonizes a lawgiver who anticipates the prophets.

The first Moses, insofar as he is inside this second one's book, might seem to be a somewhat isolated figure. As self-contained works of art, books like Ruth and Job are easily isolated for literary-critical scrutiny, but they have a curious and symptomatic tendency to treat isolated personalities outside of Israel, and thus to locate these personalities in the buffer zone of a book. Perhaps similar "literary" forces are at work in the situating of the Moses of Deuteronomy in the buffer zone of Moab, where Moses' discourses fill the space between the activity of Numbers and Joshua. Such a Moses—placed by the canon as a whole upon the threshold between biblical installments, and prompted by the imminence of his own supercession to prophesy the future ascendancy of a Mosaic prophet synonymous with a sufficiently attentive Mosaic readership or audience—is a kind of belated Precursor, saying with John the Baptist, "One comes after me who is become before me: for he *was* before me" (John 1:30, AT).

It is a paradox that the totality of the Mosaic bequests is authenticated by a piece of genuine pseudepigrapha. Deuteronomy is not merely not a piece of prophecy *ex eventu*, nor a sentimentally attributed piece like a psalm "of David": apart from the epilogue, it presumes to be the words (or the spirit of the words) of Moses. The analogous New Testament case, the Gospel of John, advances a claim to be the witness or testimony of the beloved apostle. Both John and Deuteronomy are "inserts" into the narrative continuity framing them, Deuteronomy coming between Numbers and Joshua, which form a continuous narrative, and John coming between Luke and Acts, which possess the unity of the Lukan oeuvre. Yet the last chapter of Deuteronomy, with its "plains of Moab" returning from the end of Numbers, and the last chapter of Luke, with its brief post-resurrection Ascension reappearing in expanded form at the head of Acts, seem to belong to an "interim"—a gap that Deuteronomy fills retrospectively, and John prospectively. For it is here, in its last chapter, that Deuteronomy claims that there has never been a prophet in Israel like unto the Moses whom the narrative has seen to his quietus: yet the preceding text has promised the sending to Israel of just such a Moses (18:18), a promise provisionally fulfilled in the form of the text's own interpretation of Moses.

With its portrayal of Moses' self-effacing stance before God, Deuteronomy has qualities of a brave, renunciatory recessional:

> And the Lord said unto him, This is the land which I sware unto Abraham, unto Isaac, and unto Jacob, saying, I will give it unto thy seed: I have caused thee to see it with thine eyes, but thou shalt not go over thither.
> So Moses the servant of the Lord died there in the land of Moab, according to the word of the Lord.
> And he buried him in a valley in the land of Moab, over against Beth-peor: but no man knoweth of his sepulchre unto this day.
> And Moses was an hundred and twenty years old when he died: his eye was not dim, nor his natural force abated. . . .
> And there arose not a prophet since in Israel like unto Moses, whom the Lord knew face to face. (Deut. 34:4–7, 10)

Everything after this might well be a melancholy *bat qôl,* "the daughter of a voice," an echo heard at some latter-day remove from the immediacy of revelation itself. Yet Deuteronomy is itself this echo. Upon the threshold of the invasion of the land formerly promised to the Fathers, when Israel's need for confidence in God was greatest, the text's self-echoing style reconstitutes Moses in the very hour of his falling silent, and through writing makes the Mosaic word available for all of the history that follows. The congregation of Deuteronomy both was and was not at Horeb: memory can put the absent past at close remove, yet centuries separate Deuteronomy not only from Sinai but from Samuel. Deuteronomy's literary revisitation of the Mosaic voice subtly acknowledges the legendary and figurative status of much of the biblical Moses, but the existence of such a text also suggests the assertion of the Mosaic will and the continuity of the Mosaic courage as we have met them from the outset of Moses' ministry: they have now become the Mosaic longanimity. The hero of an older generation, Moses has outlived just such a generation, and yet he has hardly outlived his own relevance. Having survived so long, he can still speak to "all of us here alive this day" (Deut. 5:3).

To which one may add, "as for his generation, who considered that he was cut off out of the land of the living, stricken for the transgression of my people?" (Isa. 53:8b, RSV). Not taking direct possession of a goodly land and stigmatized with his doubting nation, Moses is indicted on narrower grounds at Numbers 20—yet would anyone in his own generation think that the man who resisted rebellion at the Meribah-Massah of Exodus 17:1–16 merited any such punishment for the latter-day version of this sin, at the Meribah of Numbers 20? Discriminating between instrumental rod and sanctifying word, the latter text disavows a materializing of prophetic speech as a magic wand. Deuteronomic authors, of course, have also looked critically at such identifications: man does not live by bread alone (even if divinely provided), but "by every word that proceedeth out of the mouth of the Lord" (Deut. 8:3). In practice, however, this has meant out of the pens of priestly scribes—like Ezra or the latter-day Zadok (Neh. 8:9, 12:26, 13:13, with 2 Sam. 20:25). Denied entry into Canaan for failing to hallow or adhere to a divine word (Num. 27:14, Deut. 32:51–52), Moses nonetheless enters on an estate that Deuteronomy itself deems essentially salvific: a Mosaic word calling Israel, whether forward or back, toward faith in an inscribed Mosaic canon. The Sinaitic Moses asked God to send some other man, and God provided Aaron as his prophet. The Moses of Moab conveys (or translates) to Israel a definitive version of the national experience which will go on speaking after his death: as his prophet. The Moses of the Pentateuch acquires the resources of the collective memory, through a comprehensive inscription which takes memory's place, and so he becomes Israel's "Homer." In the same motion, users of Deuteronomy are invited and enabled to assume to themselves enunciatory functions once belonging to a presumptive original, and so they become Israel's "Moses."

·II·

THE TEXT OF THE LAW

Then Joshua built an altar unto the Lord God of Israel in mount
Ebal.

As Moses the servant of the Lord commanded the children of
Israel, as it is written in the book of the law of Moses, an altar of
whole stones, over which no man hath lift up any iron: . . .

And he wrote there upon the stones a copy of the law of Moses,
which he wrote in the presence of the children of Israel. . . .

And afterward he read all the words of the law, the blessings and
cursings, according to all that is written in the book of the law.

There was not a word of all that Moses commanded, which
Joshua read not before all the congregation of Israel, with the
women, and the little ones, and the strangers that were conversant
among them.

(Joshua 8:30–32, 34–35)

But [Moses] took the tables of the Commandments and descended,
and was exceedingly glad. When he beheld the offense which they
committed in the making of the golden calf, he said to himself,
"How can I give them the tables of the Commandments? I shall be
obligating them to major commandments and condemning them to
death at the hands of Heaven; for thus it is written in the Commandments, 'Thou shalt have no other gods before me' (Exod. 20:3)."

(Judah Goldin, *The Fathers According to Rabbi Nathan*
[New Haven: Yale University Press, 1955], p. 20)

· 3 ·

THE BROKEN LAW-BOOK

The ascription to Moses of the texts that make up the Pentateuch is probably one reason why they are now all there: because of his name's authority, the Bible has apparently been edited so as not to exclude the testimony of any of the Mosaic texts, no matter how ideologically unlike their various versions of "Moses" may be. Despite the differences in provenance, the imposition of the Mosaic imprimatur must have ruled out an editorial committee's excluding anything bearing it.

The authors' continual use of the introductory phrase, "And the Lord spake unto Moses, saying . . . ," and its equivalent in Deuteronomy, "And the Lord spake unto me, saying . . . ," would come to mean, simply, "the Lord spake unto Moses." In the Gospel of John "Moses' disciples" say, "We know that God spake unto Moses" (9:28–29). They also wish to say that through Moses God spoke *to them*. Moses is put into similar relations with the sons of Aaron, with the sons of the prophets, with the Levites, with holy warriors, with the Calebites, with reformist parties at court, and with opposition to the monarchy; a wide distribution of Mosaic function results. All parties claim Mosaic patronage; each has its own idea of the patron.

The events narrated in Exodus provide many of the primary occasions for the giving of cultic, civic, and criminal ordinances. The book falls into three somewhat comparable divisions. We may tabulate them to show the motif of various orders as all fundamentally "Mosaic":

PART ONE

1) Proto-instituting of Mosaic *offices* through stories of Moses' nativity and early career (i.e., offices of Levite, "midwife," judge, intercessor, and "shepherd");

2a) Defective proto-*ministry* of Moses as public defender of the oppressed, *which leads to:*

2b) *Alienation* of Moses from Egypt and his dwelling with Midian's priest (= proto-instituting of the cities of refuge); Moses' circumcision (anticipation of Passover);

3) *Call* of Moses to office at Sinai by signs and wonders, and instituting of the Name;

PART TWO

1) Performance of signs and wonders *before Pharaoh* in Egypt; instituting of the Passover;
2a) Performance of signs and wonders *before Israel* in the nearer wilderness (pillars of cloud and fire, parting of the Reed Sea), *followed by:*
2b) *Alienation* of Israel from God at the wilderness of Sin and at Massah and Meribah, and performance of signs and wonders before Israel in the further wilderness, with instituting of the Sabbath; victory over Amalek (= proto-instituting of Holy War);
3) *Call* of Israel at Sinai; manifesting of God's holiness; instituting of covenant and law;

PART THREE

1) Instituting of priestly *office* and service (i.e., the tabernacle pattern indited at Sinai);
2a) Defective proto-*ministry* of Aaron (priestly service of the golden bull), *which leads to:*
2b) *Alienation* of sinful Levites from Moses, and Moses' subsequent glorification at Sinai, with instituting of Mosaic oracles (veil and the tent of meeting);
3) Fabrication and glorification of the tabernacle (comparable to the temple where the Name is to be kept in the future); priestly investiture of Aaron, holy unto the Lord.

Much of the narrative pertains to orders derived from a founding lawgiver; and much of the discourse articulates his actual, Sinaitic laws.

Despite some reservations about dividing observations on the text of the law from those on the text of the history, I propose to undertake discussion of the materials of the principal Sinai pericope under different heads. My treatment of the text of the law as it is also found in a narrative about an original Sinaitic covenanting occurs here, while discussion of the text of the *history*—as it might incorporate or echo political events and historic covenantings from the latter day—has been deferred to the fourth and final division of the present book. In the present chapter I wish to concentrate on that presentation which bulks so large in Exodus, the law's digestion to bills or codes or canons, as itself an event at the mountain.

When Moses comes to the scene of the golden calf, he implies that the noise of the orgy might equally be the noise of factions disputing with each other: "And he said, It is not the voice of them that shout for mastery, neither is it the voice of them that cry out for being overcome"

(Exod. 32:18a). "Geneticist" analysis suggests that the text may indeed be composed as the record of the voices of them that shouted for mastery, and the voices of those that cried out when they were overcome. I do not wish to add to the noise, but of course many readers can overhear and discern some of the different ideological voices that compete for a hearing in the narrative: these voices are heard more than once. For a start, there are really three decalogues in Exodus. And there are the three obviously different bodies of law in the Pentateuch—in Exodus, in Leviticus, and in Deuteronomy. And there are the differences between Moses and Aaron, Aaron and the Levites, and charismatics and officialdom. We may also guess that alternative versions and arrangements of material began to absorb more and more units until they also began either to absorb or to break with each other. The results of such a process are more obvious than the process itself can ever be; we shall nonetheless be arguing that the text of the law is, among other things, the type of its own production. Biblical law, wherever it is found, is wedded to narratives about its giving: its original cause.

The overall narrative of the Sinai story, from Exodus 19 to Exodus 35, is cluttered with legal formulations and lists of laws and obligations; in an analogous way, the text of the story of the tenth plague is interrupted by the ceremonial instructions for the Passover. To show that some of the seemingly artless displacements of consecutive narrative within the exodus complex are actually clues to the text's significance, I would argue, as *per* the quotation from Joshua 8 set at the head of the present section, that the inscribing of the law is indissociable from its reinscribing. The story of the preparation of a book of the law is embedded in narratives that are obliged to renarrate themselves in various mirror-forms. Joshua, for example, erects an altar of which the stones are sanctified by their being uncut, according to a Mosaic ordinance delivered at Sinai in Exodus 20:25; he cuts into the stones the words of a teacher who forbade the cutting of altar stones but who—at Deuteronomy 27:2–8—had prescribed the publication of the whole of Moses' dictates, "all the words of this law." This promulgation thus began from God's words to Moses in the mountain. But in the story of the people at Sinai we are also dealing with a compound narrative, one seemingly fatally botched by a perpetual grinding of narrative gears. Nothing meshes properly at all. The result is a texture that never allows us to forget that a text is always composed of other texts.

From Exodus 19 to Exodus 35:4, Moses is repeatedly summoned to Sinaitic conference with God, and commissioned to go to the people and keep them in a state of alert throughout the proceedings. Beginning with chapter 19—surely among the worst offenders in the Bible—the unfollowable sequence is roughly as follows. Moses goes up to the mount, and God tells him to offer the people his covenant; Moses goes and consults with the elders, and all the people answer that they will obey the Lord. (The elders are repeatedly dropped or ignored or upstaged or put in some kind of Sinaitic holding pattern, though they also enjoy at least one genuine and theatrical communion-encounter with God.) The Lord tells Moses he will let the people overhear Moses speaking with him, so they will believe. Moses reports to God their (having already) assent(-ed). The Lord tells Moses to go and sanctify and prepare the people for his appearance on Sinai, and to set boundaries they may not cross. Moses warns the people to be ready, and leads them out to a Sinai enveloped in smoke; Moses speaks and God answers. God now comes down on Sinai (perhaps in person, rather than in sound and smoke) and calls Moses up; Moses ascends. God orders him to go down and prevent the people from transgressing the limit set to their approach; Moses says he has already set the limits formerly commanded. God sends Moses down, telling him that he shall come up with Aaron; Moses goes down and speaks to the people. So chapter 19.

What are we to make of this huge harrumph? For the better part of a chapter God seems to be doing nothing more than anxiously clearing his throat, calling one press conference after another to announce that he will presently be calling a major press conference. God is making himself a nervous wreck. But whether or not Moses hears any laws (and whether or not what he hears are the Ten Commandments of Exod. 20:1–17), he has gone and told the people he has heard *something*. They in turn have heard *conditions*, assented to something, converted to obedience to God, been sanctified, and probably witnessed Moses' further trafficking with God.

At the end of chapter 19, Moses has gone down to the people to speak to them. Enter chapter 20, where the Ten Commandments, spoken by a self-announced God, lurch into place after the interminable narrative of preparations, but without any direct indication of where they came from: we do not know if Moses is quoting God, or if God is interrupting Moses, or if these laws are the terms for the impending covenant relation.

Stated in the negative and reduced to the minimum implied by their elsewhere being called "the ten words," the commandments are as follows:

I. Do not have (or serve or covenant with) other gods (do not treat any other gods as comparable to Yahweh the Jealous);

II. Do not have (or manufacture) any images of other gods;

III. Do not use God's name vainly (as part of a criminal purpose), or do not profane his name (cf. Lev. 18:21, 20:3);

IV. Do not neglect (or break) God's sabbath-rest (weekly day of rest);

V. Do not (—having a regard for your own future "in the land"—) dishonor your parents (i.e., by cursing them, possibly in the name of God, by physically violating them, by exposing them, by committing fornication with them);

VI. Do not kill;
VII. Do not commit adultery;
VIII. Do not steal (a man: cf. Exod. 21:16 and Deut. 24:7);
IX. Do not swear falsely (in court: cf. Lev. 19:12, "And ye shall not swear by my name falsely");
X. Do not covet your fellow's chattel (or do not engage in an evil plot to possess them).[1]

In the actual text, the fourth and fifth commandments are stated positively, a possibility for all five laws in the so-called "first table," which all suggest a general commandment to fear or reverence or magnify the Lord:

I. Fear and serve Yahweh, or have him in your midst exclusively;
II. Worship, honor, glorify, serve, or sanctify Yahweh, again exclusively, and thus give the lie to "other gods" and the cultic-magical use of their images (cf. Num. 20:12, ". . . to sanctify me in the eyes of the children of Israel," with Exod. 23:24, "break down . . . images" of the Canaanite gods);
III. Hallow Yahweh's name, exclusively; proclaim God's name; "swear by his name" (Deut. 6:13);
IV. "Keep the sabbath day to sanctify it" (Deut. 5:12)—to Yahweh; or, more generally, keep Yahwist holy days; (Lev. 19:30 adds, "and reverence my sanctuary");
V. Honor (or glorify or serve) your parents.

Positive forms of the first three laws, for example, are a basis for the injunctions of Deuteronomy 6:13: "Thou shalt fear the Lord thy God, and serve him, and shalt swear by his name" (slightly expanded at Deut. 10:20).

It is the first five commandments which particularly enable the association of the Mosaic law with the biblical covenant, since the Bible understands Israel as contracted to God through his service as redeemer. The narrative associates law and covenant immediately upon the departure from Egypt. After Israel's escape at the Reed Sea, God mentions instituting "a statute and an ordinance" for Israel at Marah, three days into the wilderness. He declares himself a patron-redeemer ("I am the Lord that healeth thee"), and offers Israel a deal: to spare it the plagues put upon the Egyptians, in return for keeping his statutes (Exod. 15:22, 25b–26).

One can appreciate the way in which Exodus 20 subsequently intervenes to lay down this law with no ifs, ands, or buts, but nonetheless there are obvious problems there for a conscientious reader. The covenanting narrative of chapter 19 has been totally displaced by a revolutionary manifesto, in which the power to command formerly belonging to the state is preemptively and rudely arrogated to the God who brought Israel out of

Egypt. None of the fussy preliminaries really prepares for this, nor does the succeeding narrative dispose of it. For having been temporarily suspended in favor of the anonymously and divinely voiced mandates of Exodus 20, the narration now reasserts itself to report that the people saw the violent commotion on Sinai, backed off from it, and put Moses in charge of speaking to God. We might think that the Sinaitic turbulence was an efflux of the giving of the law, but the text of Exodus 20 does not make this claim. Moses now reapproaches God, who tells him that he is to tell Israel that they have seen God talking to Moses! Next God gives four rules, all pertaining to worship, mainly in Canaan: no idols, a sacrificial altar, altars of undressed stone, and no steps to the altar—along with a promise that "in all places where I record my name I will come unto thee, and I will bless thee" (Exod. 20:24b). The Name is evidently a substitute for an idol. These are the first commandments actually given in the Sinai *story.*

The next three chapters (Exod. 21–23) then rebegin and list scores of statutes and judgments which God tells Moses to "publish," and into which the commandments of Exodus 20 now seem to be dissolved. Exodus 23:1–13 includes about five-tenths of a decalogue, with verses against perjury (1–2, 7a), murder (7b), sabbath-breaking (12), naming other gods (13), and perhaps taking the Name in vain (7c, "I will not justify the wicked")—i.e., commandments IX, VII, V, I, and III. These chapters conclude by setting out the conditions for the occupation of the promised land: the otherwise ahistorical material urges the people to obey the Angel of the Occupation (Exod. 23:21; cf. 23:20–23, 32:34, 33:2), even while it also presupposes the offensiveness of theft, murder, oppression, and like evils directed against the neighbor.

At the opening of chapter 24, Moses is summoned up, along with the Israelite high command; the others, however, are kept at a distance. Then Moses comes to the people and tells them all the statutes and judgments (we seem to be entitled to assume the whole of the preceding chapters 21–23). The people unanimously assent to keeping this law, and Moses puts it in a book, we again assume more or less identical with the three chapters we have just read. Further, he builds an altar and worships with sacrifice, and thus covenants with the people; he reads out the law (now called "the Book of the Covenant"), resecures the people's assent, and sprinkles them with blood to confirm that they are contracting to keep their word. In effect he pronounces that the blood is "the covenant which the Lord hath made with you concerning all these words" (Exod. 24:8). The book's final dictates also presumed covenanting: "Thou shalt make no covenant with them, nor with their gods" (Exod. 23:32). Not covenanting with "Them" is the prologue to—and the content of—covenanting with "Him."

Moses now returns to the mountain, dines there with God and the Israelite leaders, and is again summoned up; he hears for the first time that he will get a God-written law on stone (Exod. 24:9–12). Nothing says what this law will be, but the phrasing is significant for its distinguishing itself from what has so far transpired. For the three chapters of laws (21–23) are not at all specified at this new resumption of the narrative: "And the Lord said to Moses, Come up to me into the mount, and be there: and I will give thee tables of stone, and a law, and commandments which I have written; that thou mayest teach them" (Exod. 24:12). To judge by this sequel, the book does not seem to have been enough.

In spite of the fact that Moses has already communicated God's laws to Israel—presumably the laws of chapters 21 through 23—Moses now goes up with his minister Joshua; he puts Aaron and Hur in charge of the seventy-two elders (Exod. 24:13–14). Here, then, Moses explicitly delegates his office to Aaron. He now goes further into the mount alone, and God's glory abides on it; and on the seventh day God calls to him out of the cloud, and he again goes up and is there forty days and nights (Exod. 24:15–18). During this time God commissions Moses to tell the people all the prescriptions for the tabernacle and the priestly service; these take up the next six chapters (chaps. 25–30), ending with the announcement that God has called Bezal'el and Oholiab to build the tabernacle and its furniture (Exod. 31:1–6). This text then adds a lengthily enunciated commandment to keep the Sabbath as a sign of the covenant (Exod. 31:14–17). Finally we are told: "And he gave unto Moses, when he had made an end of communing with him upon mount Sinai, two tables of testimony, tables of stone, written with the finger of God" (Exod. 31:18). So far as a reader can tell, these miraculously inscribed tables could contain the ten laws of Exodus 20, or the Book of the Covenant again, or the prescriptions for the tabernacle (which will itself include "the ark of the testimony"), or the law of the sabbath obligation, or indeed any "testimony" or witness whatsoever. But one way or another, the writing on the tables was pertinent to—or made a sign concerning—the covenant God made with Israel in or around Sinai.

This covenant, if it is part of the deal made in the Book of the Covenant, contains the important commitment concerning the Canaanites: "Thou shalt not bow down to their gods, nor serve them, nor do after their works: but thou shalt utterly overthrow them, and quite break down their images" (Exod. 23:24). For in Exodus 32 the apparently abandoned people come to Aaron and commission him to make them gods and religious goods in Moses' absence, as if in despite of the advice regarding the Angel of the Occupation: "Behold, I send an Angel before thee, to keep thee in the way, and to bring thee into the place which I have prepared. Beware of him, and obey his voice, provoke him not; for he will not

pardon your transgressions; for my name is in him" (Exod. 23:20–21). At
the end of the forty days (the reader must assume) the Lord sends Moses
back to the camp to find the people disgraced by the sin of idolatry; and
he and Joshua do indeed find the people disgraced, as God has predicted.
But even before he returns, Moses pleads the people's case, and reconciles
a provoked deity. In place of the images the Israelites were commissioned
to break in Canaan, and before turning to the idols themselves, Moses
now breaks the tablets—it is something of a surprise to learn that Moses
has brought these tablets with him, and that an iconoclastic act is initially
visited on the text authorizing such an act (Exod. 32:19). Only after this
act does Moses drastically purge the people—or perhaps the Levites
among them—while God also plagues the people: because of their sin
(Exod. 32:35).

Moses now goes back to God, at Exodus 33, and hears God recommis-
sion the conquest of Canaan, and tell him that he, God, will not personally
be in Israel's midst henceforward. The people in turn hear this and
mourn, and do not wear ornaments as Moses has been ordered to tell
them not to do. They linger around the tabernacle (it cannot as yet really
be the tabernacle, but rather a more provisional tent of meeting), which
Moses has now pitched and where he consults with God. Here he asks to
see God's "glory." Apparently Moses is also back on the mountain—for he
is now positioned in a clift in the rock—and is, in part, satisfied; the revelation is to show that God intends to treat both Moses and the people graciously.

Though we might have guessed that Moses was in the mountain already,
because of the "clift of the rock" (Exod. 33:22) where he views God's
backparts, God in Exodus 34 summons Moses to the mount; he is to bring
newly hewn stones. These stones, "like unto the first" (Exod. 34:1, 4), are
for the purpose of receiving new tables with the same laws as were on the
original stones, "the words that were in the first tables," which Moses
broke (Exod. 34:1). God hereupon recommissions Moses with a further
declaration of God's abiding justice and mercy, and with a covenanting on
God's part to do marvels—and on Israel's part to drive out the Canaanite.

The subsequent orders, including the orders to desecrate Canaanite
idols and not to assimilate (Exod. 34:12–13), now modulate into ten commandments against (i) worshipping any other god than the Jealous one;
(ii) sacrificing to other gods or covenanting with Canaanites; (iii) intermarrying; (iv) making molten gods; (v) failing to keep the Passover; (vi)
sabbath-breaking (rest after sowing and harvest is also prescribed); (vii)
withholding the firstborn from God; (viii) appearing before God without
an offering; (ix) failing cultic observance at the three major agricultural
festival-times, including failing an (analogous) thrice-yearly presentation
of young men before God; and (x) seething a kid in its mother's milk

(Exod. 34:14–26). This last commandment has already appeared in a terminal position in one of the sub-tables—a code of ritual obligations—of the Book of the Covenant (at Exod. 23:10–19b). One can show that these are pretty much the same commandments as the first ones—if the first ones are to be found in Exodus 20—by reading for the equivalence of the moral and the ethnic law: but it takes some doing.

This time Moses himself is the scribe, in lieu of the "finger of God":

> And the Lord said unto Moses, Write thou these words: for after the tenor of these words I have made a covenant with thee and with Israel.
> And he was there with the Lord forty days and forty nights; he did neither eat bread, nor drink water. And he wrote upon the tables the words of the covenant, the ten commandments. (Exod. 34:27–28)

Here is the first time we hear that the commandments are ten in number (though they are much more clearly divisible into ten in Exodus 20); this is also the first time that these ten demands are also explicitly, themselves, *the words of the covenant.* Partly owing to the mention of Moses' own sacrificial regimen here, these two verses draw together the several expressions of the will of God so long in tension: divine word, ancient law, new contract, cultic orders, and memorial inscription. "The ten commandments" (Hebr. 'ten words') sounds like a gloss: the addition could be owed to a harmonist imperative common to editors. But the result is inspired: a coalescence revealing the narrative as a kind of chorale, poised upon a decisive resolution of competing elements.

This most recent set of commandments does not easily divide into two tables of obligations to God and neighbor, as the first set did; but this set does indeed prescribe covenanting with God simply by its giving of a law making it unlawful to covenant with anybody else (Exod. 34:15). The commandments at Exodus 20 did not specify covenanting at all, except by announcing (as if by fiat) that God (or "I") was the god of the "Thou"; this meant that God was the suzerain or patron, and that Israel was God's client. For the first commandment, at Exodus 20:3, "Thou shalt have no other gods before me," is revealed by the cognates at Exodus 19:4–6, 23:24–25, and 34:14–15 to have meant, in practice, "Thou shalt have no nationlike covenant partner, other than Yahweh." Or: "no covenant partner prior to Yahweh." In that Israel is not—allegedly—constituted until the beginnings made by the exodus and the Sinaitic conference, how could it have acknowledged any prior lord? Thus the first commandment is voiced into the text at the point that its actual form as an imperative is identical with its possible form as a proposition: when the truth for which the latter speaks would seem to be self-evident. The Israel of the exodus could have no other gods before it, because it scarcely existed in the presence of other gods—or patrons.

Moses has been apart from the people for forty more nights and has then returned, but any actual delivery of the tables (back to the people) is not mentioned here, though he does return with the two tables of testimony in his hand (Exod. 34:29), and with an unbearable shine emanating from his skin, to which attention is thereupon turned. In chapter 35, however, lawgiving briefly recommences: Moses assembles the people to announce the sabbath law (Exod. 35:1–3). Back in Exodus 31:12–18, the divine utterance of this particular ritual law immediately preceded the conferral on Moses of the first two tables of testimony; and Moses here adds the refinement that forbids the igniting of a fire in the house on the holy day (Exod. 35:3). He then invites the people to contribute to the material for the design of the tabernacle as the Lord has commanded it— the design is lengthily spelled out. Formerly Aaron invited a similar contribution to the smelting of the golden calf. Finally, Moses announces, as God earlier did, the inspiration of Bezal'el and also Oholiab in executing and teaching others the work (Exod. 35:30–35). Thus far to the end of chapter 35.

The law could never have been definitively issued, this perplexed narrative tells us, apart from the activity of the composers of the texts themselves, canonizing all the words comprising the laws, the next three books of the Bible included. They are the "Moses" through whom the law is being authored, and he is the common signature of their guild.

The number of ancient laws gotten onto ancient stelae is well represented by the story of the two tables in conjunction with the booking of the words of the Book of the Covenant, while the story itself speaks of the two tables as containing only ten words. We have encountered as many as ten issuings of prescriptions. We hear about, in order:

1: God's speaking to Moses the words on which covenanting is conditional (whatever the words are, they imply obeying God's voice and keeping his covenant), and Moses repeating them to the people, and the people hearkening and assenting, at Exod. 19:5–8;

2: The utterance of a specified decalogue, issued from God, but to no one in particular, in Exod. 20:1–17 (="Table 1," the "two tables" of obligations, to God and the neighbor; *idol-worship is forbidden,* and *the Sabbath is enjoined*);

3: God speaking to Moses *a specific commandment against making gold and silver gods,* and giving to Moses the *four prescriptions for altar worship,* in Exod. 20:22–26 (= "Table 2");

4: God then commanding the specific statutes and judgments of chapters 21–24 (= "Table 3"); these five chapters (20–24) include *sanctions against* homicide, kidnapping, brutality, theft, various irresponsibilities concerning others' life and limb and personal property, witchcraft, bestiality, *worship of foreign gods*, sexual seduction, exorbitant usury, abuse of parents, *sabbath-breaking*, involuntary indenture, etc.; several sub-tables can be discerned within this corpus (there are also found here various "thou shalt nots" without named penalties and sanctions—such as "thou shalt not revile the gods" [!], not delay to offer *firstfruits*, not oppress strangers, not take bribes);

5: Moses' speaking the laws to the people, apparently (but not unequivocally) the laws of "Table 3" above, at Exod. 24:3;

6: Moses putting the laws in a book—the Book of the Covenant—and reading it out (again apparently, but not unequivocally, the laws of "Table 3") at Exod. 24:4, 7, and pronouncing the covenant to pertain to all these words (Exod. 24:8);

7: God's speaking to Moses the specific laws pertaining to the *tabernacle decoration and ceremonial service*, for six-plus chapters, at Exod. 25–31:11 (= "Table 4-A"),

8: . . . and God speaking as well to Moses on this occasion, and giving *the laws of the Sabbath*, at Exod. 31:12–17,

9: . . . and God then issuing to Moses (the first) two stone tables of testimony (= "Table 4-B"), at Exod. 31:18, before the sin of the calf;

10: God's declaring to Moses the ten or so specific laws pertaining to the religious, political, and agricultural life in Canaan ("Table 5"—these are *laws proscribing both image-making and sabbath-breaking, and appointing feasts*), at Exod. 34:13–26 (the so-called Ritual Decalogue);

11. Moses or God (one cannot be sure which) inscribing the laws (apparently the cultural-cultic laws of "Table 5") on the second stone tables, at Exod. 34:28 (these are supposed to be the words that were on the first tables, or "Table 4-B"; they include *laws prohibiting sacrifice to other gods, and sabbath-breaking*);

12: Finally, Moses' issuing of *the sabbatical law* (its observance, with the specific added *prohibition of the kindling of fires*), at Exod. 35:2–3 (= "Table 6-A," or else a re-issue of "Table 4-B"),

13. . . . and Moses' issuing of the tabernacle prescriptions to the people, at Exod. 35:4–35 (= "Table 6-B," or a re-issue of "Table 4-A").

I have especially marked for attention, in all these texts, the devotion to the cultic order and cultic observance (sabbath-keeping, holy days, ceremonials, sacred artifacts, and iconoclasm). The chorale of the law does not slight religious obligation at any point: on the contrary. The quantity of law in all of the various Sinaitic "Tables" tremendously amplifies obligation—religious or otherwise—at just the place where the narrative has Israel contracting with God, at its critical rites of historical passage. And this amplification takes place in the Pentateuch as a whole: three books following Exodus add their versions of "Moses" to the pile, levitical, deuteronomic, and "Shechemite" tables of the ten words included.

In Exodus itself, the narrative of the giving of the law has been repeatedly interrupted by the enunciation of a minimum of six tables of laws and requirements (by our count), that is, by the actual giving of laws. But the more detailed these enunciations have been, the more indeterminate or sketchy have become the circumstances in which the laws were presented, and the more disembodied has become the voice delivering them. And the more specific the report of the writing down of something on the actual stone tables the likelier it is that the laws or conditions in question are bruited or understood but not actually specified. The disjunction is not particularly disturbing, but the account does not find it necessary to say that these and not some others are the specific laws that were inscribed on the tables or put in the book or read out to the people. The narrative fit—between law-speaking, on the one hand, and law-writing and law-reading, on the other—is loose. The exception is the "Ritual Decalogue" of Exodus 34:13–26: that is the table of laws that actually got inscribed, and in the Sinai narrative it is followed only by the single supplementation of the sabbath law. But if it is not the same decalogue as the earlier one, the one in Exodus 20, that the later tables reinscribe, then we can never be sure exactly which of the given laws did get inscribed. We can be confident, however, that some law or other was written down, if only for the somewhat deuteronomistic purpose of witnessing against those who might break it.

The disembodied character of the first decalogue, at Exodus 20, contributes immensely to the ambiguity, since it is introduced before all but one report of any giving of the law, and so hovers over any subsequent reference to a law being recorded; this decalogue is possibly such a record's content, but also possibly not. Nonetheless, the place where the text as a narrative breaks most dramatically, at Exodus 20:1, is the place where the authors have introduced the words that it is logical to think were destroyed when Moses broke the first tables. In a sense, then, the insertion of this decalogue into Exodus 20—like the harmonist's gloss, "ten of the words," in Exodus 34:28—restores what Moses broke, and thus reperforms the subsequent copy-work assigned by God to Moses himself.

The preceding description of the order of the text is sufficient to convince us that we are studying a case where the text of the narrative becomes its own story: that is, it becomes a case of elongation (or "dilation"), abbreviation, displacement, and interruption. Indeed, the digestion of a law of obligation to Yahweh to any ten principles or prohibitions will itself be an art of abbreviation, by virtue of its contrast with the text's own enlargement of the law to a fuller jurisprudence. The repeated giving of some laws, the exhortations, spellings out, and elaborations, along with the convocations and the descriptions of divine and human activities, offers a rather artless art of elongation; the causes for the repetition in apostasy and mediation suggest a parallel art of interruption; and the succeeding of one law table by another, and the alternation between cultic and civic law (or sin and crime), suggest an art of displacement. The narrative is prolix because the lawgiving activity of God upon the site of the people's dedication to Yahweh—Mount Sinai—has been accommodated to a wide and well-nigh archaeological confluence of interests. But the text also seems to be prolix because of an opposite impulse, repeatedly indulged, to digest jurisprudence to a definitive charter, to confine it to a specific, constitutional occasion, or to embody it in a single, unified composition, allegedly emerging from the conference at Sinai. Yet the law about the Sabbath, on just this account, has earned an occasion of its own at Marah, and has been definitively disclosed by Moses even before Israel arrives at the mountain. The narrative has kept the Sabbath, even before the tables have.

As one pores over the laws, one gradually hears the consistency of their preoccupations, the common denominators beneath the variety of enumerations. It might be hard to call this a studied effect, yet it is definitely an effect that causes study. God's jealousy, for example, is a motive clause in the *second* commandment against making *graven images* of other gods (in Exod. 20:5, and in the comparable motive clause in Deuteronomy 5:9); in the Ritual Decalogue's preface this motive is inserted into prescriptions urging iconoclasm *in Canaan*, in a statement also demanding the *worship* of no other gods (Exod. 34:13–14), as in the *first* commandment. In the Book of the Covenant the motive for the Sabbath is the refreshment of the workforce on the land, but it is directly followed by a rule of heedfulness that includes making "no mention of *the names of other gods*," nor letting "such be heard out of [one's] mouth" (Exod. 23:12–13, RSV), leading to the rules for Yahweh's three greater feasts. Is this ban on mentioning other gods commandment I in combination with commandment III, or commandment III with commandment IV?

However incumbent upon consciousness, the urge to perform this kind of collation is a more or less "editorial" motive—as opposed to an authorial one—whereby one comes to know the law comparatively, through possession of an anthology of the law, or a collection of its various editions. The whole text is a giving of the law pretty much inseparable from a pedagogical elicitation and reiteration of it. The more "authorial" motive—the motion toward digesting the law to a single, authoritative bill of obligations—runs counter to the reiterative and editorial motive. The counterpoint and the competition between the two motives creates the text's particular dialectic. A law code like that of the Hittites seems to be a recension compounded with various supplements: in the Pentateuch such a distinction is multiplied sevenfold, until it more or less complicates itself out of existence, somewhat like the historical fugue, when it comes into the hands of Bach. The end result is less a law, than an *art* of law.

The narrative is instrumental to this art. If we doubt, for example, the importance of God's Sabbath, we need not appeal to its embedment in the first creation narrative at Genesis 2:2–3, except where the exodus narrative itself does. We find the Sabbath, in advance of Sinai, in Exodus 16:4–5, where Yahweh not only provides the manna, but also a notable opportunity to break the law before we meet its Sinaitic enunciation as the fourth commandment in Exodus 20 (vss. 8–11):

> Then the Lord said to Moses, "Behold, I will rain bread from heaven for you; and the people shall go out and gather a day's portion every day, that I may prove them, whether they will walk in my law or not. On the sixth day, when they prepare what they bring in, it will be twice as much as they gather daily." (Exod. 16:4–5, RSV)

Moses, already in the position of having to expound what this "law" might be, even before it has been divinely stated in commandment form, goes on to explain the requirements of the Sabbath to the people, "a day of solemn rest, a holy sabbath to the Lord," which God has now commanded them (Exod. 16:23, RSV). "So the people," like God in Genesis 2:2, "rested on the seventh day" (Exod. 16:30, RSV). But they do not rest before they have broken God's law:

> On the seventh day some of the people went out to gather, and they found none. And the Lord said to Moses, "How long do you refuse to keep my commandments and my laws? See! The Lord has given you the sabbath, therefore on the sixth day he gives you bread for two days . . ." (Exod. 16:27–29a, RSV)

In this example, the law is articulated through a narrative of its being given *and* of its being broken. In effect, the redaction of Exodus 16 stammers, unsure as to when the people should be told what: it seems not to know whether it should inculcate sabbatical practice before or after the revelation of the sabbatical legislation, or whether it should enjoin Sabbath observance before or after its being ignored or being flouted. As in the case of virtually any of the biblical beginnings (e.g., those of the human creature, the Mosaic polity, the Israelite kingship, and the proto-Christian discipleship of the four Gospels), the law for the Sabbath is tempted to fail in the very event of its creation. Bidden to keep God's Sabbaths holy, Israel in Ezekiel 20 is also punished for having accepted laws that were "not good," or for having mistaken them (vss. 20, 25). Thus the law is tried at the outset, as if to help one decide whether it is *good*—viable, understandable, receivable, practicable, or even possible—or no.

The place of God in the narrative and on the tables may be similarly studied, in a sequence at Exodus 32–34:7. After the disclosure of Israel's idolatry, Moses urges the incensed deity to be more long-suffering and not forsake his people: God should maintain his newly established reputation among the Egyptians as Israel's champion (Exod. 32:12), and thus be jealous of his name for mercy. Moses could quote Isaiah 48:9–12, where God implies the I-am-ness of his name: "For my name's sake will I defer mine anger, and for my praise will I refrain for thee, that I cut thee not off . . . For mine own sake, even for mine own sake, will I do it: for how should my name be polluted? And I will not give my glory unto another . . . I am he." Thus Exodus credits zeal for the Name with having inspired God himself, "that [his] name may be declared throughout all the earth"—that is why he raised Moses up (Exod. 9:16). Pleading for mercy despite Israel's sin of going after other gods, Moses urges God to honor a form of the third commandment, to advertise the Name, if God indeed has a name for graciousness toward an elect nation. God will show Moses his glory by proclaiming to him "the name of the Lord . . . The Lord, The Lord God, merciful and gracious, longsuffering": "I will proclaim [*qāra'*] the name of the Lord before thee; and will be gracious to whom I will be gracious" (Exod. 34:5, 6; 33:19). About the same order appears in Exodus 20:4–7:

> Thou shalt not make unto thee any graven image, or any likeness of any thing that is . . . in the earth . . .
> . . . for I the Lord thy God am a jealous God, visiting the iniquity of the fathers upon the children . . . of them that hate me;
> And shewing mercy unto thousands of them that love me, and keep my commandments.
> Thou shalt not take the name of the Lord thy God in vain.

The narrative of apostasy through idol-making, followed by God's jealousy, mercy, and name-proclamation, in Exodus 32–34:7, preserves the order of these four declarations from the first decalogue. We may also compare Exodus 20:22–23, "Ye have seen that I have talked with you from heaven. Ye shall not make with me gods of silver," as a possible source for Deuteronomy's grounding of the image-ban in the fire-like formlessness of the Sinaitic theophany (Deut. 4:12, "ye heard the voice of the words, but saw no similitude"). God does not willingly give his glory to idols (cf. Ps. 106:19–20 with Isa. 48:11, Jer. 2:11, and Rom. 1:23), and "the Lord will not hold him guiltless that taketh his name in vain" (Exod. 20:7b). The Exodus 34 narrative moves from Moses' arrival on Sinai with new tablets to

God's name-proclamation and self-proclamation (vss. 5–6); it then segues into the formulations earlier found in Exodus 20:5–6—God is a god "keeping mercy for thousands, . . . and [one] that will by no means clear the guilty; visiting the iniquity of the fathers upon the children" (Exod. 34:7). Thus the narrative of Exodus 32–34:7 is an exploded view of the laws in Exodus 20:4–7. The laws digest this narrative, and then reappear on the new tables, circling back to an origin in Aaron's sin: "Thou shalt make thee no molten gods"; "For thou shalt worship no other god: for the Lord, whose name is Jealous, is a jealous God" (Exod. 34:17, 34:14). As the law keeps the Name, Jealous and Merciful, in place of the idol, so does the narrative.

ii

In much of what follows we will be considering the story of the Mosaic texts as they might narrativize covenanting, publishing, tradition-keeping, and reformation in the historical Israel. Such latter-day contexts tend to point toward the law text's future in Israel's history and in the Bible. But insofar as the legal corpora are archival, we may also ask after former-day contexts that would point toward the law's past in Israel's prehistory and in the Near East. This past again raises questions about both the law text's form and its content. One ancient content is suggested by the collection of statutes in the Book of the Covenant, in Exodus 21–23, while another ancient form is suggested by this collection's implied title (from Exod. 24:7)—the title, when taken with the concluding proscription of covenants with Canaanite peoples and their gods, points to the form now known as the suzerainty treaty. The content, however, is just a publishing or proclamation of the laws, such as a new regime might institute. The form is a royal "dispensation," minus any mention of a monarch, but with God understood in the monarch's place.

The laws of the Book of the Covenant stand in the text like a reminder of all such law corpora, with their rules about whose ox is being gored, whose dowry is still owing, and whose debt must be paid. But its title, as found in Exodus 24:7, is a quite significant misnomer. For the book itself does not contain a covenant, only a proscription of covenants with Canaanites: "Thou shalt make no covenant with them, nor with their gods" (Exod. 23:32). This is virtually the last law in the Book, and its final clause—"nor with their gods"—contains the whole secret of the Bible's sublimation of vassal-suzerain relations. For it is the covenant with the overlord's god, rightly redirected, that legalizes Israel's relation to Yahweh. The proscription of engagements to foreign gods implies a more kindred suzerain, who in fact will oblige himself to advance his protégé Israel over

Canaanite rivals. The Book of the Covenant does not, itself, set before a people the conditions of their vassalage or the suzerain's lordship, but only "judgments" (Exod. 21:1). It is not itself a formal contract, but a table of laws. The service of the law is thus put in place of conditions: therefore, the laws themselves might as well be the suzerain. Making the obligation to the law do duty for the obligation to the suzerain in effect breaks the mold of the Near Eastern suzerainty treaty. The observation of laws replaces the observation of covenant conditions.

And what are we to make of the first of these laws? What has it to do with the impositions of the overlord?

> If thou buy an Hebrew servant, six years he shall serve: and in the seventh he shall *go out* free for nothing.
> If he came in by himself, he shall *go out* by himself: if he were married, then his wife shall *go out* with him. (Exod. 21:2–3)

The first law states the condition for a release of a Hebrew from vassalage! Moreover, this particular formulation keeps repeating the verb for departure from the climax of the Passover narrative: "And it came to pass at the end of the four hundred and thirty years, even the selfsame day it came to pass, that all the hosts of the Lord *went out* from the land of Egypt" (Exod. 12:41). Putting a "law of release" (cf. Deut. 15) for the first condition of a covenant of obligation also breaks the Near Eastern mold, for every statement of biblical law that invokes Israel's obligation to the exodus-deliverer also implies an eternal law of release from any other lord.

The laws in Exodus are embedded in a story. Its primary episodes are the exodus out of Egypt and the meetings at Sinai, but its framing by the appeal to the God of the patriarchs and the discourse of Moses in the Moab of Deuteronomy shows that its overall content is the whole history of the covenanted and the history of their covenant. The law and the covenant are thus related by the narrative, insofar as both are depicted as coming into being, that is, as interchangeable divine *enactments*. Relations between law in the Pentateuch and in the exodus-Sinai narrative would therefore also include the analogy between law digested to principles and its diplomatic history abbreviated to an episode of forty-plus days; the analogy between law elaborated at length and narrative elongated to a history of forty years; the analogy between law broken and narrative interrupted, that is, a lawgiving interrupted and dilated by a breaking of the law, and a saving history deferred and delayed by an apostate generation that dies in the wilderness; and the analogy between law reinterpreted and narrative displaced—the narrative being displaced from the story about Moses at Sinai (in Exodus) to the recital by Moses in Moab (in Deuteronomy). When the people fail to take possession of the promised land,

God depicts himself as the narrator at Numbers 14:34: "After the number of the days in which ye searched the land, even forty days, each day for a year, shall ye bear your iniquities, even forty years, and ye shall know my breach of promise." God inevitably "constitutes" such an interruption.

Without saying much more than this, we can again see that Moses functions as the inspired author of both the law and the Pentateuch, that is, he stands for the keeping of the texts of the law and the keeping of the covenant history embodied in them. Moses is the only one who saw what the finger of God had written on the first set of tables before they were broken; the correspondence with the second set, which he wrote at God's dictation, presumes his faithfulness as an intermediary and scribe.

As Moses conveys the law to Israel and its sons, the transmitters of Genesis conveyed the patriarchal tradition. What the characters in Genesis kept genetically—the seed of Nahor—the Genesis texts likewise keep genealogically: thus character and text each stand, like the patriarchal grave and grave-register at Hebron, for the function of the other. The case is similar in the rest of the Pentateuch. Besides being the transmitter of the law to Israel, Moses is also presented as the transmitter of Israel's covenant history. Thus Moses publicly recites and recalls the history—the accumulating sequence of saving and obliging events—over the first third of Deuteronomy, much as Ezra is shown doing at the comparable covenant-making and lawgiving in Nehemiah (cf. Neh. 9:6–38 and following). Moses is in the position of doing this because he is the last surviving witness to the exodus; the new generation must depend upon him for its knowledge of—connection to—the world of its fathers. Moses is the keeper of the text of the covenant history, no less than of the law.

Moses is the sponsor and the restorer of the law because he is the one who would keep and safeguard the legal tradition by restoring its text, like Hilkiah in 2 Kings 22:8, who finds a king willing to restore the temple and so a sponsor apt to receive the law anew. For laws are like texts; to be kept they must needs be searched, codified, compared, redacted, reinterpreted, and emended. The golden calf is the sin of a people that has no patience with the prolonged absence of its leader while he is in the mount being exposed to a very lengthy version of the law. And yet Aaron, if he is the mouthpiece of his stammering brother, should have been the one to render the dictates of the law into articulate and communicable form. Not so paradoxically, however, Moses the stammerer has been compensated in the narrative by his also being cast as Moses the scribe. And where the Moses of Exodus 4:10 might almost be confessing to his difficulties in speaking Hebrew, the Moses of Deuteronomy is in no need of his brother as an interpreter: either the Mosaic tradition is able to do his speaking for him, or he is himself its interpreter, skillfully accommodating the tradition to the belated understanding of a secondary audience.

Those who receive the law are modeled on those who intervene, with Moses, to recover its text. But it is the genius of that text to have identified itself and its broken law with a broken *covenant*. By the time Moses has restored the text to Israel, "the words of the covenant, the ten command-ments . . . the two tables of testimony," in Exodus 34:28–29, Israel has already begun to establish the criminal record in question. It has *already* violated the laws against sabbath-breaking, image-making, serving other gods and honoring them with the glory owed to Yahweh, profaning his name, and dishonoring the god of its fathers.

This motif of incrimination might help explain Moses' climactic hesita-tion in publishing the ten words themselves, when he smashes the tablets: that is, if a guilty early Israel is also a naive and ignorant one. Doubled with (and breached by) the breaking of the tablets in Exodus 32, the lawgiving narrative tends to privilege Moses' awareness of Israel's sinfulness as prior to its denunciation. Thus one can postulate a tradition in which Israel had not yet received the laws of Exodus 19–24, before it went ahead and forged the calf in the sequel. Aaron's sin would be, in part, inadvertent—and his ignorance offer some excuse. Moses would then break the tables in order to delay or avoid Israel's condemnation by them: *Because the law worketh wrath; for where no law is, there is no transgression* (Rom. 4:15). In that case, Moses initiates his hasty purge of the Levites preemptively, before the people as a whole should fall under the divine wrath condemning their offense. Overall, the Pentateuch suggests that any imposition of the law revives it secondarily, whether Israel is found in sin forty days, forty years, or four hundred years after arriving at Sinai and separating from Moses. If, however, Moses himself turned away from lawgiving, then the story also offers a precedent for all returns to that vocation: in Moses' own, original faltering in and recovery of it.

·4·

THE BOOK OF THE COVENANT

And the Lord said unto Moses, Write thou these words: for after the tenor of these words I have made a covenant with thee and with Israel.

. . . And he wrote upon the tables the words of the covenant, the ten commandments. (Exod. 34:27, 28b)

And the king went up into the house of the Lord, and all the men of Judah and all the inhabitants of Jerusalem with him, and the priests, and the prophets, and all the people, both small and great: and he read in their ears all the words of the book of the covenant which was found in the house of the Lord.

And the king stood by a pillar, and made a covenant before the Lord, to walk after the Lord, and to keep his commandments and his testimonies and his statutes with all their heart and all their soul, to perform the words of this covenant that were written in this book. And all the people stood to the covenant. (2 Kings 23:2–3)

i

The length of the biblical law texts tells us that no idol can stand in for— or provide a shortcut for—the law's study and mastery, for yielding to its *copia* and persisting in its copying. It is no accident that Deuteronomy takes its title from the Greek for the following passage:

And it shall be, when [the king] sitteth upon the throne of his kingdom, that he shall write him a *copy* of this law in a book out of that which is before the priests the Levites:

And it shall be with him, and he shall read therein all the days of his life: that he may learn to fear the Lord his God, to keep all the words of this law and these statutes, to do them. (Deut. 17:18–19)

Within the framework of his commission to Joshua, "Be strong," at Deuteronomy 31:7 and 23, Moses writes and delivers the law to the Levites, commissioning them to read it at the Feast of Tabernacles, every seven years, on the site of the future Jerusalem: "When all Israel is come to appear before the Lord thy God in the place which he shall choose, thou shalt read this law before all Israel in their hearing" (Deut. 31:11). Given the interpolation of the Levites, Moses might as well have said, "Be strong *in the law*,"[1] which is virtually what God *does* say in his instructions at Joshua 1:7: "Be thou strong and very courageous, that thou mayest observe to do according to all the law, which Moses my servant commanded thee." The people in turn respond, telling Joshua that they will hearken to his commandment as they did to that of Moses, and put to death those who rebel against it; he should again "be strong" (Josh. 1:17–18): i.e., in the *execution* of the law.

In heeding Deuteronomy's behest to read its law over the ears of the people, the ruler is likening himself to the Moses of Exodus 24:4–7, who put the laws in a book and read it out to the people. This Moses, in turn, is like the Samuel of 1 Samuel 10:25, who "told the people the manner of the kingdom, and wrote it in a book, and laid it up before the Lord." But such a Samuel, in his turn, is like the high priest Hilkiah, who brought out a constitution to be read before King Josiah. Hilkiah, in his turn, is like Moses, in conveying the text of the words of the law to the leadership; and Josiah is again like Moses, in reading the text before the people. Josiah "read in their ears all the words of the book of the covenant" at a great assembly in Jerusalem (2 Kings 23:2; also 2 Chron. 34:30).

The Moses whom the narrative keeps having return to the people from Sinai is thus a second Moses, come back to abridge either the interruption of the revelation or the social contract, like the deuteronomic Moses who returns to the new generation that leaves the wilderness under Mosaic commission. For the story of the broken and renewed tables corresponds to the story of the lost and found generations, and indeed to the difference between those who left Egypt with Moses and those who grow up in the wilderness with legal traditions found in Leviticus and Deuteronomy. Thus the broken tables stand for the destruction and reconstruction of a text from God, since they also stand for the destruction and reconstruction of a covenant relation with him. In Exodus 16 the people prove to be the first sabbath-breakers. God means to test, he says, "whether they will walk in my law, or no" (vs. 4). This motive governs many of the narratives that follow.

Amidst religious preparations that sanctify their actions, the people in Exodus 19 subscribe to the essential agreement. God proposes to Israel, "If ye will obey my voice indeed, and keep my covenant, then ye shall be a peculiar treasure unto me above all people," and the people agree, "All that the Lord hath spoken we will do" (vss. 5, 8). Taken with the further negotiation of Exodus 20 ("Fear not: for God is come to prove you" [vs. 20]), following the divine declaration of the Decalogue, and the people's reaffirmation just before Moses' booking of the Book of the

Covenant—"All the words which the Lord hath said will we do" (Exod. 24:3)—we may assume that Israel and God have a legally binding contract. The people then violate this contract, especially if the keeping of the commandment against the worshiper's submission to graven images (the obeisance forbidden in Exod. 20:5) has become one of the contract's chief conditions. Likewise, if the keeping of ancient treaties in stone cairns or on inscribed stelae is what is meant by the preparation of the two tablets, then the contract-mediator's breaking of the tablets does double symbolic duty: as Israel through Moses' spokesman Aaron has been breaking the contract by molding and engraving the idols, so God through his spokesman Moses is annulling it by breaking the inscribed tables.

At the same time, Moses also engages in a standard covenant-making ceremony, the putting away of "other gods"—as in the great assembly in Shechem conducted by Joshua (Josh. 24:14, 23), and as per the first two commandments at Exodus 20 and the exclusion of foreign gods in Exodus 23:32. The story of the golden calf and its rejection therefore narrativizes the ceremonial scenario implied by a report like the one in 1 Samuel 7, where Samuel has the role of the Mosaic covenant-broker mediating the contract between a repentant Israel and an accepting deity—the God who will have no other gods "before him." The renewal of a relation to Yahweh again entails putting away other gods: "And Samuel spake unto all the house of Israel, saying, If ye do return unto the Lord with all your hearts, then put away the strange gods and Ashtaroth from among you, and prepare your hearts unto the Lord, and serve him only: and he will deliver you out of the hand of the Philistines. Then the children of Israel did put away Baalim and Ashtaroth, and served the Lord only" (1 Sam. 7:3–4). Moreover, the people gathered together at Mizpeh, Samuel prayed for them, they fasted, and they confessed they had sinned against the Lord (1 Sam. 7:5–6).

In this sequence the social order being reconsolidated under the judgeship of Samuel—after a twenty year hiatus (1 Sam. 7:2)—is divinely confirmed; for God protects the sacrifice he is offered from the interruption of the Philistines, who turn out to have gathered at Mizpeh as well. The covenant-making ceremony in this account is also considerably "narrativized": for "the Lord thundered with a great thunder on that day upon the Philistines, and discomfited them; and they were smitten before Israel" (1 Sam. 7:10b). This thunderous intervention is a Sinai-like sign of confirmation, but the protection God provides on this occasion is also an exodus-like miracle of power. For the thunder turns into a smiting of the adversary, and the smiting turns into a rout. We are told that the Philistines thereafter "came no more into the coast of Israel"; but the point remains "deuteronomistic," or "deutero-Mosaic," for the text adds that "the hand of the Lord was against the Philistines all the days of Samuel"

(1 Sam. 7:13). As with Moses at Sinai, covenant-making results in the extended ministry of the spokesman who brokered the exclusive relationship. "All the days of Samuel" treats the covenant as conferring lifelong benefits, and thus elongates the covenant-making to the experience of a whole generation: for "Samuel judged Israel all the days of his life" (1 Sam. 7:15). Yet the same report also treats the benefits as confined to a single generation; upon the death of this generation, the benefits lapsed and were exhausted, as in the succession of the Judges.

This example of covenant mediation is obviously relevant to Exodus, especially with Deuteronomy as its epilogue. But a closer example of the iconoclastic motif is found in the Josianic revolution—or revolutions. Josiah's reading out of the law in 2 Kings 23:2–3 is followed directly by his ordering Hilkiah "to bring forth out of the temple of the Lord all the vessels that were made for Baal, and for the grove, and for all the host of heaven: and he burned them without Jerusalem in the fields of Kidron, and carried the ashes of them unto Beth-el" (2 Kings 23:4). Moreover, the next thing Josiah does is to "put down the idolatrous priests, whom the kings of Judah had ordained to burn incense in the high places in the cities of Judah" (2 Kings 23:5). Such revolutions, it follows, have provided the basic scenario for Moses' legendary destruction of the calf and purging of the Levites, upon his delivery of the law.[2]

The story of the broken and restored tables also suggests that the legal as well as the social order is founded even while it is being refounded—or founded as a result of an immediately prior loss of it. Every crime precipitates the return of the law that incriminates the guilty for breaking it. Thus the relatively self-contained and well-reconciled account of the giving of the tables in Deuteronomy 9–10, with its insistence that Israel has been rebellious from the time that it came out of Egypt until the time that it came into "this place"—Moab—still centers on the destruction of the calf: "I took your sin, the calf which ye had made, and burnt it with fire, and stamped it, and ground it very small, even until it was as small as dust: and I cast the dust thereof into the brook that descended out of the mount" (Deut. 9:21). This action comports with the so-called Elohist conception of Moses as a prophet calling for a revival of the law and/or the covenant relation. And it agrees with the latter-day Moses we have found in Josiah: "And he brought out the grove from the house of the Lord, without Jerusalem, unto the brook Kidron, and burned it at the brook Kidron, and stamped it small to powder, and cast the powder thereof upon the graves of the children of the people," ". . . and the altars which Manasseh had made in the two courts of the house of the Lord, did the king beat down, and brake them down from thence, and cast the dust of them into the brook Kidron" (2 Kings 23:6, 12). The nameless brook that descended out of "the mount"—Sinai—in Deuteronomy is comparable to the brook

Kidron that runs below "the mount"—Zion—in 2 Kings. The renewal of the social contract, by means of the destruction of the symbols of a former contract, suggests the regular reenactment of the commandment that Israel shall have no other gods before Yahweh. Nations enjoying written constitutions are likely to be formed around an act of revolution. If Deuteronomy can be understood as the "covenant" (after Deut. 29:1, AV/ 28:69, JPS) or constitution of that latter-day Israel for which it was apparently written, or by which it was adopted, one may speak of the Josianic revolution. The act of breaking with other baals, or lords, in effect signs and seals Israel's new "suzerainty treaty" with God. But, because of "the allegory of Scripture," the original subscription to Yahweh is cast in the form of latter-day reaffirmations like Josiah's, which claimed to be a Mosaic *restauratio.*[3] As a result, the Mosaic dispensation has been equipped with a comparable *restauratio,* and the law appears to be twin-born with its own reformation.

The episodes of the biblical narration of the covenanting with God also belong to a convertible analogy with the history of the biblical text. The restructuring enterprise of (re-)establishing the Mosaic state provides us with an explanation for the manifest plurality and rehashing of the law texts as they have ended up in the terminal moraine of the Pentateuch— understood as an anthology not only of law texts but also of covenant stories. The breaking and renewing of the tables seem to acknowledge the process that has also given us the different codes in Exodus, Leviticus, and Deuteronomy. We may also read the Northern and Southern departures from Solomon as kinds of restructuring, with the condition of the temple taking the place of the tabernacle texts in Exodus. The very enterprise of establishing the Mosaic state, as we find it in the reforms of the priest Jehoiada and the kings Hezekiah and Josiah, may likewise be understood as such a retrospective, latter-day restructuring—that is, as a Mosaic reconceptualizing of the Davidic rulership as a whole. The story of the broken and renewed tables would have thus returned to Israel's consciousness as a symbol of the interruptions and renewals of the continuity of Israel's social contract, past and current. Hezekiah destroys the brazen serpent, as if Israel's wandering were again over, and Josiah discovers the Book of the Law in the repairing of the temple. Recovenanting, with a reading or rereading of the text, follows upon the decisive interruption of business as usual recognized in the stories of Jehoiada and Josiah; 2 Kings 23:25 reports that as a result of reading the rediscovered law-text Josiah "turned to the Lord with all his heart, and with all his soul, and with all his might, according to all the law of Moses." The Moses of Deuteronomy says to Israel that it "shalt love the Lord thy God with all thine heart, and with all thy soul, and with all thy might" (Deut. 6:5). Josiah was converted by reading "the words of the law which were written in the book that Hilkiah the priest found in the house of the Lord" (2 Kings 23:24). If this was a draft of Deuteronomy—as surely the specific echo of Deuteronomy's essential message means to declare—then Josiah may also have read the only fully coherent and digested account of the broken and restored tables that we now have (Deut. 4:13, 5:1–33, 9:8–10:5). Deuteronomy puts the story of the tables into the mouth of the chief witness—Moses—but insofar as this account was designed to be read out to his people by their king, it was being put into Josiah's mouth too.

Covenant renewal (as opposed to the various installments upon the original covenanting) takes place whenever the people who once covenanted with God and Moses in the wilderness rededicate themselves to Yahweh, whether under Joshua, Samuel, Josiah, or Ezra. Thus Josiah's priest Hilkiah unearths the Book of the Law in the repairs of the temple in a mimesis of Moses hewing the stones at the original salvaging of the Yahweh-Israel relation (i.e., at the reissuing of the tables). And Josiah does indeed "read over the people's ears" all the words of this newfound book, as Deuteronomy's own, parallel language prescribes (2 Kings 23:2, Deut. 31:11). Thus the renewing of the social order under a new regime involves a restoration of the legal order under God. And thus the frame for the kingship from Jeroboam to Josiah, in 1–2 Kings, is the disestablishment and reestablishment of Yahwist religion. The condition of the temple proves to be a framing motif for the history, as the double description of the tabernacle is a frame for the inscribing of the law.

The story of an interruption in the giving of the law suggests that there is nothing cyclic about the establishing of the social order. It is an arbitrary, even revolutionary act of God, and it is therefore characterized iconoclastically: it is not so much some sort of rhythmical coming around inherent in the nature of things, but rather a break with such a rhythm. Nonetheless, at the Reed Sea Israel was defined as the people which God *had redeemed* (Exod. 15:13), and this may imply a need to rebegin at an acceptable time. Deuteronomy 15, which prescribes the sabbatical reading of the law, also legislates the laws of release: the forgiveness of Hebrew debts and the liberation of Hebrew slaves (vss. 1–3, 12–15). The same formula as that for the reading is used to introduce the release legislation, "At the end of (every) seven years" (15:1 and 31:10). The release legislation remembers to remember the exodus: "And thou shalt remember that thou wast a bondman in the land of Egypt, and the Lord thy God redeemed thee" (Deut. 15:15). The "year of release" (Deut. 15:9) for the cancellation of debts and relief of the poor (15:1–2) is the same seventh year as the torah reading (31:10–11). Thus the reading and rereading of Deuteronomy, prescribed near the end of its text, intends to reinstate and renew the redemptive purposes of the exodus, which its laws otherwise remember near its middle.

Speaking from the point of view of the Israelite covenant, we have said that the meaning of the episodic sequence of the narrative is the covenant's unique representation of its own renewability, on the model of God's renewal of Israel's adoption, with the putting away of foreign gods. Deuteronomy prescribes a public reading of its text every seven years in Jerusalem at the Feast of Booths (Deut. 31:10–11). Although the laws do not elsewhere prescribe a fixed, annual, ceremonial observance of covenant-making, in the way that, say, the Bible attaches the celebration of the Passover to the springtime inception of the year, the narrative does assign the original covenanting and its confirmation to an initial seven and forty days. The breaking of the covenant and the renewing of the covenant are assigned to the following forty days: the second period reverses the pattern of the first, as in a mirror. Moses' account in Deuteronomy seems to agree with the schedule found in Exodus itself:

7 days: Moses covenants, the people accept (Exod. 19, Exod. 24);

40 days: Moses leaves, God confirms the covenant, and prescribes the tabernacle—Moses delays forty days (Exod. 24:18), and Aaron takes up the collection for the casting of the golden calf; the people idolize it, and Moses returns and breaks the tablets (Exod. 32);

40 days: Moses leaves and returns and leaves, God reconfirms—then Moses delays forty days, and returns with new tablets (Exod. 32:31, 34:2, 28–29), and takes up the collection for the tabernacle.

Despite the ways in which the periods might be mapped onto the Lent of the liturgical year and the Holy Week of Christians—the time when Christians join the Church—the nearer analogy is with the life of Jesus and his temptation. For the covenanting at Sinai equates with commitment and vocation. If this period schedules the call of Israel into partnership with God, then the temporal analogy governing the sequence of events is less an annual period of renewal than the legal sequence pertaining to nuptials: engagement (or precontracting), contracting, consummation, trial period (or honeymoon), confirmation, continuation, separation, annulment or cancellation, and disannulment or recontracting. Hence the metaphors in Isaiah 50:1—"Where is the bill of your mother's divorcement?"—and Jeremiah 3:8: "for all the causes whereby backsliding Israel committed adultery I [Yahweh] had put her away, and given her a bill of divorce." A marriage can be contracted, interrupted, broken, and renewed at any time (though only, in Israel's case, at the will of the divine party). Thus the Bible collapses the covenanting event to forty days while also expanding it to forty years. Something similar happened when Shakespeare reproduced the broken and mended nuptials of *Much Ado About Nothing* in *The Winter's Tale:* by the time of the writing of the later play, a new generation has intervened to renew the marriage of the earlier one.

ii

In delivering the law, both Josiah and Moses are also understood to be offering a contract *about* the law: to keep it. But we may understand this contract for obedience more narrowly. Exodus tells the story of a would-be nation—the Hebrews—that broke its labor contract with another nation—Egypt—in order to become itself—Israel. The Pharoah, who knew not Joseph, had basically violated the original conditions of the Hebrews' residency in Egypt, and God as judge intervened to annul the contract and impose damages. Annexed to the paralegal transaction of this story is a mirror-story, and it contains a morphologically similar transaction: the story of a people that became a nation at Sinai even as it violated its client contract with the overlord who had replaced Pharaoh, the Sinaitic God. But since God through Moses restores the tables, God renews the contract—a contract like the putative one that Israel broke in Egypt, where Pharaoh's quotas have the place of God's tithe.

The contract with God stated that Israel would be for God "a kingdom of priests, and an holy nation" (Exod. 19:6). The Hebrews in Egypt were heavy-laden; God's burden is light. "All the earth is mine," he states (Exod. 19:5); the ruler of the universe imposes himself on Israel as its lord and master only to volunteer to make it a ruling-class elite, a kingship, and a nationally independent, sacrosanct sovereignty. All this is in return for the enshrinement and enforcement of the contract's chief provision, that God's voice have legislative force in Israel: "if ye will obey my voice indeed, and keep my covenant" (Exod. 19:5). Israel broke a covenant with Pharoah, and it made one with God.

Everything that happens, happens somewhere, and Sinai provides the covenant with a place to happen—a place for God to remember his covenant, as he promises to do in Exodus 6:5. Because of the indications in Exodus 6, the script for the performance at Sinai is already in circulation by the time of Exodus 19. But the implication of Jeremiah 31:11, and the plain statement of Jeremiah 33:24, that God had chosen "two families," could well put the actual instituting of the covenants with Yahweh after the division of the monarchy between Israel and Judah, even if Exodus 6 and 19 put it at the head of the story of a landless Israel.

The narrative about covenanting at Sinai, however problematic as a *history*, establishes a critical juncture between covenant and *narrative*. That is, the covenant with God is not something that is merely one element among others in the story of the past, but rather covenanting is an action that has determined the form that the past has taken as a story. The brokerage of Israel's covenant with God, by landless priests, might have dictated its narrativization within the wilderness experience, but covenanting itself already suggested to the ancient Near Easterner a political instauration inseparable from a narrative-like agenda. This agenda is conformable to the bumps and hollows of the exodus narrative.

For the form of the text of the covenant in the ancient Near East was a somewhat standardized one: the script contained a rehearsal of deeds, it unfolded in a predictable order, and it announced a new relation, even while it commenced it. The form of this covenant as also found in the Bible generally features, in the famous analysis of George Mendenhall, two parties, suzerain and vassal, and hence it is a "suzerainty treaty."[4] The suzerain asserts his status and stature, what he has done for the vassal, his acts, and what the vassal is thereafter obliged to do for the suzerain, his liabilities or charge. The treaty typically obliges the vassal to covenant with the suzerain exclusively, to fight his battles and make the suzerain's enemies his enemies, to report conspiracies and to put down rebellions against the suzerain, and to pay him tribute. It cites the witnesses to the treaty, and names the place where or the form in which the treaty is to be preserved (for example, on silver tables). And it invokes the penalties or curses or execrations or plagues that are to fall upon the vassal should he prove a treaty-breaker. The exodus narrative is thus itself such a covenant: the suzerain Yahweh has delivered the vassal Israel from bondage in Egypt; the vassal is obliged to sacrifice to its deliverer, to keep his laws and holy days, and to have no other suzerains before him. In the Near Eastern treaties, there may be a kind of diplomatic prehistory attached to the preliminaries; this preamble, in one case, notes that the vassal's forefather rebelled against the suzerain's.[5] But it is the unique idea of the Bible to put the vassal nation's rebellion right into the middle of its contracting narrative, while narrativizing the contracting amidst various pieces of the contract. Both the Book of Exodus and the Pentateuch overall do this.

The act of witnessing the covenant is frequently invoked by the biblical text, the words of its inscriptions are themselves sometimes called upon as witnesses, and participants in the contracting event are instructed to report (again as witnesses) to subsequent generations. The words of the law are to be kept and repeated in specific places, much like the mountains Gerizim and Ebal in Deuteronomy 27:12–13, where curses on the treaty-breaker are also invoked. The reduction of the rebellious vassal to waste is a frequent threat in the treaties. The Bible reaches much further: the re-invocation of the dire predictions of Deuteronomy (28:36; 31:16–17, 29) in the oracle of Huldah the prophetess in 2 Kings 22 has both narratives recur to the bad end of the national history as a whole, with the destruction of Jerusalem by the Babylonians: "Thus says the Lord, Behold, I will bring evil upon this place and upon its inhabitants, all the words of the book which the king of Judah has read. Because they have forsaken me and have burned incense to other gods, that they might provoke me to anger with all the work of their hands, therefore my wrath will be kindled against this place, and it will not be quenched" (2 Kings 22:16–17, RSV).

A regular feature of the suzerainty treaties is the mutualization of the parties' allies or adversaries: "He who lives in peace with the King, shall live in peace with you; but he who is an enemy of the King, shall also be your enemy."[6] With such formulas for solidarity we may compare the promises of Deuteronomy 7:9–10, 15: "Know therefore that the Lord thy God, he is God, the faithful God, which keepeth covenant and mercy with them that love him and keep his commandments . . . And repayeth them that hate him to their face, to destroy them . . . the Lord will take away from thee all sickness, and will put none of the evil diseases of Egypt, which thou knowest, upon thee; but will lay them upon all them that hate thee."

A particular class of Near Eastern treaty, one with a purpose in common with the suzerain treaty's mutualization of foreign policy ("he who is an enemy of the King, shall also be your enemy"), deals with the exchange of fugitives between different jurisdictions; these extradition pacts prescribe penalties for retaining runaway slaves and receiving stolen property or booty from the suzerain-state.[7] The God of Exodus becomes, so to speak, a receiver of stolen property: not only of fugitive slaves, but also of Egyptian swag, since the jewelry the Israelites take from Egypt will one day be used to furnish his tabernacle. The spirit of the extradition laws pertaining to slaves is humbly transfigured in the Book of the Covenant, where the rule about the release of "Hebrew" slaves within Israel begins the book (Exod. 21:2ff.), and where the rule about returning a stray beast to its owner, *when the owner is one's enemy*, is directly followed with the rule about overcoming a selfish impulse not to help out with an ass that has fallen under its burden (Exod. 23:4–5).

Our knowledge of the extradition treaties helps us particularize the general characterization of the Egypt of the exodus as a suzerain-state, and God's reign as an uncooperative rival jurisdiction to which a suzerain's slaves have fled, and to which his property has been alienated: as per God's prediction that Israel shall not leave Egypt empty-handed (Exod. 3:21–22). Yet Egypt is also cast by the exodus narrative—and this is most curious—as itself a vassal-state: for Egypt is the state originally subjected to the world-ruler's impositions and plagues, which are otherwise the curse pronounced upon the rebellious treaty-breaker. "Thou shalt say to the house of Jacob," Moses is charged, "Ye have seen what I did unto the Egyptians" (Exod. 19:3–4), indicating what would happen to a future rebellious state at the hands of the vengeful suzerain.

By means of the story of the renewed tables, however, Moses is also charged with teaching Israel that the basis for the covenant relation of divine suzerain and mortal vassal is also renewable, from the covenant's very inception. The Book of Exodus presumes its own survival, beyond the murmuring of God's clients within it. As the text of Israel's adoption papers, in which a future Israel can see what God has done for it in the past ("how I bare you on eagles' wings" [Exod. 19:4]), the book is at the opposite pole from the "bill of divorcement" questioned by the prophets (Isa. 50:1, Jer. 3:8). Although the ancient treaties set down the dire consequences for treaty-breaking, they do not seem to prescribe for any renewal of a lapsed covenant relation. The biblical covenant, partly because of the transcendental nature of its suzerain, differs: God "keepeth covenant . . . to a thousand generations" (Deut. 7:9), because he can afford to—his regime knows no end. Unlike the case found in a prominent Assyrian example of such a treaty, God need not anxiously attempt to bind the client's allegiance to the royal succession.[8] Yet in Deuteronomy something like this happens: Deuteronomy seems to share the typical anxieties of a human suzerainty treaty. Similarly, God's own world-kingship cannot be destroyed by apostasy or rebellion or the temporary impositions of another regime, and so the covenant with him is eternally renewable. Yet, in a kind of inversion, God does transfer his gift of Canaan from one generation to another, remaining loyal to his client's children, when the client himself has not remained loyal to him. Although the Israel that left Egypt was replaced by the Israel that occupied the promised land, and the covenant was renewed in subsequent generations, God seems to have initially involved himself in the human politics of the suzerainty treaty, when he destroyed a generation in the wilderness.

Though numerous texts in the Pentateuch do indeed combine to suggest a suzerainty contract between a subject and his overlord, it could be one of the worst ever written. For suzerainty treaties do not try to impose their form on declarations of independence; neither do they try to impose it on codes of civil and religious law. Despite generic differences, however, the treaties and the codes share the common features of the prologues and epilogues. The prologues establish the authority of a royal speaker; the epilogues invoke the authority of the gods in curses on the desecraters of the text or the laws, or on rebels from the contract. The codes are longish, like textbooks, and unlike the Decalogue. The laws in the treaties may be long or short, but they only regulate civil existence insofar as it pertains to vassal-suzerain relations. And though the treaties are of various lengths, they are not books, in anything like the way Exodus is a book: which is to say, a canon of various texts. The prolix textuality of the particular treaty between God as suzerain and Israel as vassal, if we take it to be the Book of Exodus itself, is owed to the contract's being both multiplied and divided, by itself, and by law texts. The treaty-making is also lengthened by being narrativized: by the treaty's being annulled, reissued, amended, reinstated, prearranged for, and the like. The cobbledness and choppiness of a text are not, per se, good evidence of an "art" of interruption, but the breaking and restitution of the tables have proven to be suggestive manifestations of the text's own condition, its haltings and rebeginnings.

The oldest surviving example of the basic form of Exodus, as a law text, is the code of Lipit-Ishtar. Its prologue says the gods called the shepherd Lipit-Ishtar to the princeship of the land, to establish justice in Nippur. Then, verily, Lipit-Ishtar says, he procured "the freedom of the sons and daughters of Ur . . . upon whom slaveship had been imposed."[9] After the enunciation of the laws, the same speaker says, in his epilogue, "I caused Sumer and Akkad to hold to true justice," and "Verily, when I had established the wealth of Sumer and Akkad, I erected this stela":

> May he who will not commit any evil deed with regard to it, who will not damage my handiwork, who will [not] erase its inscription, who will not write his own name upon it—be presented with life and breath of long days; . . . may Enlil's bright forehead look down upon him. (On the other hand) he who will commit some evil deed with regard to it, who will damage my handiwork, who will enter the storeroom (and) change its pedestal, who will erase its inscription, who will write his own [name] upon it (or) who, because of this [curse], will [substi]tute someone else for himself—[that man, whe]ther he be a . . . , [whether he] be a . . . , may he take away from him . . . (and) bring to him . . . in his . . . whoever, may Ashnan and Sumugan, the lords of abundance, take away from him . . . his . . . may he abolish . . . May Utu, the judge of heaven and earth . . . take away . . . his . . . its foundation [. . .]

And so the mutilated text expires in a splutter of helpless, fragmented curses upon its future desecrater, which will ultimately be time itself.

This text suggests the original literary parent of the story of the desecration of the law text, as refigured and renarrativized in the story of the breaking and restoring of the Mosaic tablets. And perhaps the text discovered and read to King Josiah by the scribe Shaphan in 2 Kings 22:10 was found in the debris of a storeroom like the one invoked on the stela containing the Lipit-Ishtar law code. At any rate, the threefold structure of a saving sponsorship, a torso of legislation, and a coda of consecration is roughly that of Exodus itself, greatly expanded: Egyptian deliverance,

Sinaitic lawgiving, and priestly tabernacle. The tabernacle has the place of the list of sponsoring deities that concludes the Code of Hammurabi. But it is a longer step than at first it appears to be, from the epilogue of the Lipit-Ishtar law code to biblical curses on lawbreakers and covenant-breakers: in the Sumerian code, the voice of execration is not the voice of God.

The disembodied voice of God—the deity in Exodus whose glory-cloud will finally descend upon the tabernacle like a sign—contrasts radically with the voice of the ego of the state establishment, with its characteristic signature in self-memorializing public works. Lipit-Ishtar's royal monument hardly bothers to hide its inevitable mutability: the inscription in fact confesses the eventual silencing and disintegration of the state's voice. The biblical law is finally kept in the hearts of the people it creates and propagates, not in storerooms where thieves break in and rust corrupts; therefore the Bible transfers the anxiety of mutability to the responsiveness of the law-speaker's audience, and thus to Deuteronomy as a "kerygma," rather than as a tablet in the national archives.

iii

The great law codes derive, traditionally, from the great lawgivers, and these are kings. The law is an aspect of their magnanimity. But the lawgivers are sometimes disclosed by the laws as law-reformers, since within the codes are indications that their laws have been modified from earlier ones. Biblical law forms a library of comparative judgments, and the revisionary form is preserved in the rulings attributed to at least one lawgiver: "Ye have heard that it hath been said, An eye for an eye, and a tooth for a tooth. But I say unto you, That ye resist not evil: but whosoever shall smite thee on thy right cheek, turn to him the other also" (Matt. 5:38–39). Jesus radically adjusts the rate for damages. Thus the Hittite code reads: "If anyone steals a plough-ox, formerly they used to give fifteen oxen, but now he gives ten."[10] These examples make the point that laws generally have an economic basis in the regulation of scarcity—the Hittite law adjusts rates of compensation in terms of what looks like a cost-of-living index, and redistributes the wealth accordingly, damages included. Yet Jesus' ruling shows that such laws also have a basis in the regulation of justice, and indeed, of charity.

In theory the Mosaic Code might be something of an exception to this rule of internal revision of precedents, for the Mosaic rebellion from the former state—Egypt—ideally leaves no room for the authority of a pre-Mosaic tradition. And yet the story of the broken and restored tables seems to acknowledge, obliquely, the possibility of a law code basing itself upon earlier laws. The Bible certainly implies the issuing and reissuing of its own material, as in the supplementations Deuteronomy makes to the laws of release; and the Bible also implies, as we have shown, the negotiation and renegotiation of earlier covenants, as in the specific citation of two covenants at Deuteronomy 29:1 (28:69, JPS). Thus the Moses of Deuteronomy 15:12–15 can be imagined saying, "Ye have heard it said in the first Book of the Covenant that your Hebrew slaves are to be discharged as free in their seventh year, without payment of any release-price to you (Exod. 21:2); but I say unto you, in the book of this second covenant, let them be discharged at the end of their service gladly, with a handsome provision"—or compensatory gift: in lieu of back pay.

The law may change its mind, but it cannot change its principles. Thus the *moral* basis for the deuteronomic revision favoring the gift is already implicit in another law containing the original occurrence of the law of release: " 'If ever you take your neighbor's garment in pledge [as collateral for a loan], you shall restore it to him before the sun goes down; for that is his only covering' " (Exod. 22:26–27, RSV). We may compare Deuteronomy 15:1–2, where the "slave" has become the person bound by a debt, and the person whose money is tied up has become the slave-owner: " 'At the end of every seven years . . . every creditor shall release what he has lent to his neighbor' " (RSV). Forgiven and forgotten, the "debt" of work converts to the "gift" of rest. A *narrative* analogy for such gifts can be guessed in the original sabbath-giving in Exodus 16; the manna that God doubles and preserves on the sixth day makes a provision like the sabbatical year in a "week of years."

The Lipit-Ishtar law code has in common with the Bible the making of the lawgiver specifically a deliverer: one who delivers from "slaveship." Here is a broad hint of the Bible's narrativization of the legal code, a process that Exodus obviously takes a great deal further than Lipit-Ishtar did. Exodus similarly expands upon the narrativization of the traditional suzerainty treaty. If we ask what relation the narrativization of biblical covenanting has to ancient suzerainty treaties, the answer again points to the revolutionary character of the Israelite model. For the textbook examples of the treaties do not incorporate either the elaborate schedule of safeguards and procedures found in Exodus, nor the Bible's forelengthened "diplomatic history" of the treaty-making. Nor do they take occasion to promulgate the suzerain's legal system. But the narrative element has further reconstituted the form, because it presupposes what no other example comes close to contemplating or providing for: not only the instauration of the legal order, but also the restoration of a broken covenant. Moreover, Moses is shown acting to procure exactly the clause that allows for this development—we can be sure that if Assyria had been in

God's place, even Moses could not have succeeded. But Moses' success with God in obtaining the new tables can only remind us that the narrative also begins and ends by turning the vassal-suzerain relation of the treaties on its head: it begins with a subject who revolts from an Egyptian suzerain, Pharaoh, and it proceeds toward installing Yahweh's subject in his own sovereignty—the land of Israel.

There are further refinements to be made upon the broken analogy between the schema of the suzerainty treaty and the major narrative of Exodus. The (hi)story of the exodus is necessarily anachronistic to itself—for it presumes the existence of a legendary, revolutionary Israel, a state that preexisted the historical Israel (whether sovereign or colonial) that the exodus itself has yet to bring into existence; such an Israel would have to be in existence already in order to do the alleged revolting. We may suppose, then, that the vassal-suzerain relation governs not only the relation between Israel and God but also the relation between Israel (or "the house of Joseph") and Egypt: Israel is not only a slave that revolts from his master, but a vassal that revolts from his suzerain. But the vassal-state cannot revolt from the suzerain-state, unless the two have a prior covenant relation. And they cannot have this relation unless both are already states.

Potentially, Israel is an Egyptian "vassal," for it is an Egyptian slave; yet it is not a vassal, not being a state. Potentially, Egypt is the Israelite "suzerain," for it is a state with Israelite slaves; yet it is also not a suzerain, for it is not a suzerain Israel can recognize—namely God. When Israel breaks with Egypt, the "vassal" is not yet a state. When God contracts with Israel, the "suzerain" is not the state. Once again, the Bible has broken the mold of the ancient Near Eastern treaty texts. Yet the Bible has created its own text from the mold's two halves: an Egyptian suzerain, but without a vassal-state; and an Israelite vassal, but without a suzerain-state.

We may now take the vassal-suzerain model for the exodus a step beyond itself. If Pharaoh only knew better, he too would be the humble vassal of God, and not the overweening lord of Israel. God's show of power intends to impress Pharaoh with God's lordship, and so it may also be intended to compel Pharaoh's vassalage and submission to God. But that is not the form the story has taken by the time of the Reed Sea, where Pharaoh is defeated not only as an army but also as a kind of sea monster or Tiamat. Nonetheless, the model obtains, if we think of Tiamat's defeat as itself modeled upon the suppression of a rebellion. The stubborn Pharaoh, insofar as he is now cast as a rebel like Tiamat, would be rebelling from his vassalage to the divine suzerain who had already established authority over him. Egypt, in this sense, is a "rebellious nation" or "rebellious house" (Ezek. 2:3, 5). Yet the same language is more typically used of Israel itself. More particularly, it might apply to the "Israel" that "rebelled against the house of David unto this day" (1 Kings 12:19), and took its religious observance to the shrines of the North. In that case, the rebellion of Pharaoh from God reappears in Israelite history as the stubbornness of Rehoboam the son of Solomon; and the rebellion of Moses from Pharaoh likewise reappears, as the rebellion of Jeroboam the son of Nebat.[11]

The importance of a motif of rebellion in Exodus can scarcely be overstated for the purposes of our analysis. But rebellion has two different contexts: in the law codes, and in the suzerainty treaties. In law codes its place is small, because neither its offensiveness nor its punishability is in the least doubt. In suzerainty treaties its place is correspondingly large, and its offensiveness and punishability are almost the whole point of the contract. The Bible, one begins to see, has it both ways, or rather all four. Rebellion against God is surely proscribed throughout the first table of the law, and yet it is not called by name—because it has become apostasy. This same rebellion also bulks large in the narrative concerning the Mosaic covenant; but rebellion against an earthly suzerain, in Exodus, is practically a statement of the divine initiative, in which case it is no offense at all.

In the ancient world, "rebellion is as the sin of witchcraft," as Samuel says in 1 Samuel 15:23: an offense to the gods, in that it circumvents the power of the state and the authority of law. "The most serious offences were against the state and against the gods, which according to ancient views are really one and the same; in Mesopotamia the gods of a theocratic state were in fact the government, and amongst the Hittites, though the various local gods were not literally the city's rulers, yet an offence against the god involved the whole city or state in the god's displeasure."[12] The ancient view, indeed, is represented by a coupling found from ancient codes conserved in the biblical Book of the Covenant: "Thou shalt not revile the gods, nor curse the ruler of thy people" (Exod. 22:28). But the point about Samuel's invocation of the ancient principle is his Mosaic or prophetic reapplication of it: for Samuel applies his words to the state's departure from the demands of God—insofar as the state is the kingship, it cannot logically be charged with being in rebellion against its own offices, but only against the kingship of God. Moses, however, is in rebellion against the state, and therefore against the ancient principle itself, at least as embodied in Egypt.

The most serious charge against Moses, at the outset of his career, is his defiance of the state, presumably the most serious charge that could be brought against anyone: Moses interferes with the right of the master over the slave, and he defies the master's authority over his property; and so do the midwives. The Hittite law code prescribes capital punishment for defiance of the authority of the state (collectively, for rebellion) and for the slave's defiance of his master's authority; Hammurabi's Code prescribes it for connivance at a slave's escape or for sheltering a runaway slave.[13] Hammurabi's Code also introduces the death penalty for assaults on and offenses by the upper class of citizen, those essential to running the state enterprise[14]—an overseer such as Moses kills in Exodus 2:12 would seem to be a prime example. And yet, from Moses' point of view, it is not the subject who is in rebellion, but Pharaoh, or the state. Since the Bible does not contain particular sanctions for crimes against state functionaries or ruling-class persons, it too is in rebellion: against the Code of Hammurabi.

Laws concerning the relations between slaves and masters are found in the Bible and in other ancient law corpora, but the assertion of unequivocal differences between the just deserts of slaves and the just deserts of masters is far less pronounced in the Bible, because all men have one master—and he is not the king. The laws of the Bible differ from other ancient collections in just this respect: that the laws, though uttered through Moses, are God's laws. Both the stories and the rhetoric insist that God, not Moses, is their author. The laws do not come from a revered or semi-divine king, but from a revered mouthpiece of the otherwise disembodied divinity. The exodus story begins from an edict pronounced by an absolute monarch with the power to sentence babies to death. The midwives who defy this edict anticipate the claim made by the narrative and the major biblical codes alike, that the law binding Israel comes more or less directly from God, and not from the rulers of the state. In Deuteronomy 24:7, in fact, Moses prescribes the death penalty for stealing an Israelite man for sale into slavery, which is what Joseph's brothers did to Joseph, when they refused to know him as their brother. Pharaoh no longer knows Joseph, and so the Lord will take Pharaoh's son: "If a seignior has stolen the young son of another seignior, he shall be put to death." This rule from the Code of Hammurabi is right next to the one condemning Moses: "If a seignior has helped either a male slave of the state or a female slave of the state . . . to escape through the city-gate, he shall be put to death."[15]

iv

If the two most important laws represented in the various "tables" have turned out to be the ones against foreign gods and sabbath-breaking, then the charter or bill form of the law discloses an essential biblical variation on the model of a suzerainty treaty: the service or tribute required by the overlord or "boss"—Yahweh—is sabbath-keeping and worship. The Sabbath is a kind of levy paid to the suzerain. The fact that the levy is precisely a cessation from work—that is, work for other masters—merely shows that a transcendental suzerain can only be rendered a transcendental tribute. Work, or slave labor, is the kind of levy exacted by lesser suzerains; "rest," in contrast, is the service required by the God of the exodus. Deliverance from Egypt delivers from slavery or bondage or vassalage, while the holy day that serves God by giving his subjects a rest converts a debt to a gift.

Most of the ancient law codes maintain a double standard of justice for slave and free, and the Bible is no exception; the conscientious amelioration of the slave's lot, however, is peculiar to the law of Israel.[16] And this amelioration can obviously go very far. For example, the loss of a tooth owing to violence is basic to the ancient codes. In the Hittite law money is to be paid in compensation for this offense[17]; in the Code of Hammurabi, money can pay for the overlord's offense to a commoner, but "if a seignior has knocked out a tooth of a seignior of his own rank, they shall knock out his tooth."[18] But in Israel a servant who loses a tooth because of his master's violence *must be released from service* (Exod. 21:27); this is a remarkable conversion of the savage principle of retaliation, a tooth for a tooth, into a mandate for an altogether better treatment for human beings.

If the slave of Exodus 21:27 must be released not because he has been enslaved but because he has been abused, then the legal logic governing the narrative's inclusion of the episode of the abolition of the straw ration becomes clearer: the Israelite foremen are beaten, they say, but the fault— or *sin*—is in their Egyptian masters (Exod. 5:16). There are limits on the damage a master can do to a slave. The Egyptians made the Hebrews' lives bitter with *hard bondage;* and when Moses intervenes to secure a respite, Pharaoh tells his taskmasters, "Let there more work be laid upon the men" (Exod. 5:9); the men are forced to convert from using state-provided straw to foraging for stubble; and their officers suffer beatings. In the analogous development in 1 Kings 12, the house of Joseph pleads with Rehoboam, "Make thou the *grievous service . . .* lighter" (vs. 4); but Rehoboam tells his conscripts, "I will add to your yoke" (vs. 11), and promises to go from beating them with whips, to beating them with scorpions (whips with sharp or hard objects embedded in them). In both narratives the point is explained by the law, which distinguishes between servitude and slavery and contains sanctions against the degradation of the former into the latter.

According to the laws of release and redemption in Leviticus 25—which are combined with legislation pertaining to buying out longer contracts involving the Year of Jubilee—the bankrupt Israelite who has had to sell himself into servitude or *habiru* status under another Israelite is not to be treated like a compelled "bondservant" or slave during his service, nor is he to be used as Pharaoh used Israel, *with rigour* (Lev. 25:53, and vs. 46; Exod. 1:13–14). "For," God says in a parallel piece of legislation's concluding motive-clauses, invoking a distinction between servant and slave, "they are my *servants*, which I brought forth out of the land of Egypt: they shall not be sold as *bondmen* [= slaves]"; "unto me the children of Israel are servants; they are my servants, whom I brought forth out of the land of Egypt" (Lev. 25:42, 55). The levitical laws thus understand any indentured Israelite as an honorary Mosaic Hebrew, elevated out of slavery into service: the laws limit his term, and implicitly forbid his re-sale. The indentured person shall not be *re*-sold: i.e., as a slave.

It seems hard to overestimate the importance for the exodus narrative of the legislation that in the seventh year a slave's slavery ends (Exod. 21:2)—the existence of this year of release in Israel must have made the celebration of any Sabbath almost unimaginably more significant than it would have been otherwise, and also have made the Sabbath's connection with the exodus, in the fourth commandment at Deuteronomy 5:12–15, many times more apparent: "You shall remember that you were a servant in the land of Egypt, and the Lord your God brought you out thence with a mighty hand . . . ; therefore the Lord your God commanded you to keep the sabbath day" (Deut. 5:15, RSV). The Sabbath is thus a weekly memorial to the exodus; Deuteronomy tends to sponsor a recovery of the exodus tradition that it identifies with its prophet's teaching of it.

The same law in Deuteronomy also proposes the Sabbath as a weekly memorial to the laws governing the treatment of a whole class of menservants and maidservants, whose indentured or unrelieved condition, to judge by the laws in Leviticus 25, always threatened them with sliding into the condition of illegal aliens, men who had sold their land:

> "And if your brother becomes poor, and cannot maintain himself with you, you shall maintain him; as a stranger and a sojourner he shall live with you. Take no interest from him or increase, but fear your God; that your brother may live beside you. You shall not lend him your money at interest, nor give him your food for profit. I am the Lord your God, who brought you forth out of the land of Egypt to give you the land of Canaan. . . ." (Lev. 25:35–38, RSV)

Reading this, we may wonder what part the transition to a cash economy played in these matters. Marx warns us that money is a "jealous god" that "debases all the gods of man and turns them into commodities . . . it has therefore robbed the whole world, human as well as natural, of its own values"—"money," Marx adds, "is the alienated essence of man's work and being."[19] But in the Year of Jubilee, ancestral land that a man had sold, which he or his family could not thereafter afford to redeem, was released back to him: he could then return to his property (Lev. 25:25–28) and so recover the alienated essence of his work and being.

In Leviticus 25 the impoverishment of a brother is treated again, this time in a text that combines his treatment during service with the rehabilitation of his fortunes in the Year of Jubilee:

And if thy brother that dwelleth by thee be waxen poor, and be sold unto thee; thou shalt not compel him to serve as a bondservant:

But as an hired servant, and as a sojourner, he shall be with thee, and shall serve thee unto the year of jubilee:

And then shall he depart from thee, both he and his children with him, and shall return unto his own family, and unto the possession of his fathers shall he return.

For they are my servants, which I brought forth out of the land of Egypt: they shall not be sold as bondmen. (Lev. 25:39–42)

The combination here of the redemption of the man from servitude with the repatriation of him and his family to his land does more than appeal to the promises God anciently made and kept at the exodus: it epitomizes them. Is not God the patron of a race of enslaved workers in Egypt *because* in the law of Moses he is the patron of a class of dispossessed Israelites in Israel? The law has surely inspired the narrative as much as the founding events have inspired the law.

We may now want to look again at the biblical case overall, which is this: a national suzerainty treaty combines itself with a law relieving a vassal from slavery. For the story of the exodus goes both ways: it shows Israel covenanting with God at the same time that it has revolted against a suzerain. But we will also want to consider more closely the question of when a historical Israel might have been delivered from a historic vassalage, at the same time that its nation-state took leave from a slave-state. For this is a point at which covenant-breaking and lawbreaking might come together as cause and effect: the point when the suzerain breaks the law could be the point when the vassal breaks covenant, if it be thought the laws and the covenant could not be broken except together. This historic point, we will be arguing, is where "all Israel" broke with "David," leaving the established "house" of David for the more migratory "tents" of Israel, as at 1 Kings 12:16, after the people's confrontation with its new oppressor, Rehoboam, the son of Solomon:

> So when all Israel saw that the king hearkened not unto them, the people answered the king, saying, What portion have we in David? neither have we inheritance in the son of Jesse: to your tents, O Israel: now see to thine own house, David. So Israel departed unto their tents.

But what law had the house of David broken that might annul the labor contract? What law was Israel, in its break with David, bent on keeping? —A law applicable to the governance of the covenated relation. That law would seem to be the one in Exodus 21 governing the relation of master and slave, the very first law of the Book of the Covenant. The law accepts slavery, as we will see, only to legislate a particular case of it—*Hebrew* slavery—out of existence: "When you buy a Hebrew slave, he shall serve six years, and in the seventh he shall go out free, for nothing" (Exod. 21:2, RSV). If the term *Hebrew slave* once upon a time designated a member of the class *habiru*, and meant something like a non-Israelitish descendant of Abraham, then the application of the law to Israel would mean that "David" was guilty of treating Israel as Pharaoh did the ancient Hebrews, as *habiru*, or as servants that could be degraded into bondmen.[20]

The law of release, moreover, is not the only service law applicable to a secessionist Israel. A latter-day Moses could also have invoked the principles of asylum, as found within a law from Deuteronomy which might otherwise apply to Moses' own sojourn in Midian: "You shall not give up to his master a slave who has escaped from his master to you; he shall dwell with you, in your midst, in the place which he shall choose within one of your towns, where it pleases him best; you shall not oppress him" (Deut. 23:15–16, RSV). The retrieval of runaway slaves is understood in Israel as *per* the relevant stories in 1 Samuel 30:11–15 and 1 Kings 2:39–40; yet the question of the asylum owed the fugitive hovers around both cases, for David lets the slave of his Amalekite enemy buy his freedom from him while he is trying to recover his own chattel from captivity; and Shimei can only chase down his slaves by breaking a kind of parole—his asylum in Jerusalem is combined with house arrest there.

Of course there is no proof that the prophet Shemaiah, inspired by God, invoked a law against the servant's degradation to a slave, when, at 1 Kings 12:22–24, he prevented Rehoboam from attempting to recapture "Israel" for "David." Yet such a prophet might well have advised Rehoboam with something like the addition to the law of release found at Deuteronomy 15:18, "It shall not seem hard to you [Hebr., 'in your eyes'], when you let him go free from you; for at half the cost of a hired servant he has served you six years. So the Lord your God will bless you in all that you do' " (RSV). Pharaoh, at any rate, does send the people of Israel away with their flocks and herds, even while asking Moses for God's blessing (Exod. 12:32). And although we do not read that Rehoboam asked, in words like those attributed to Pharaoh, "What is this we have done, that we have let Israel go from serving us?" (Exod. 14:5, RSV), we do read that he assembled troops "to bring the kingdom again to Rehoboam" (1 Kings 12:21). As Shemaiah intervenes, so, centuries later, Jeremiah rebukes his king's reneging on a covenant made during the siege of Jerusalem, to release Hebrew bondpersons: Zedekiah had violated the covenant made "in the day that [the Lord] brought [Israel] forth out of . . . the house of bondmen, saying, At the end of seven years let ye go every man his brother an Hebrew, which hath been sold unto thee" (Jer. 34:13–14). And not unlike Nehemiah, who insisted that payments of corn, wine, and money be restored to Hebrew debtors (Neh. 5:6–11), Deuteronomy adds severance gifts to Exodus 21:2:

> "If your brother, a Hebrew man, or a Hebrew woman, is sold to you, he shall serve you six years, and in the seventh year you shall let him go free from you. And when you let him go free from you, you shall not let him go empty-handed [Hebr., 'empty']; you shall furnish him liberally out of your flock, out of your threshing floor, and out of your wine press." (Deut. 15:12–14, RSV)

In his original commission to Moses God specifically lays it down that Israel will not leave Egypt destitute: "when ye go, ye shall not go empty," he declares on his mountain (Exod. 3:21). True to this promise, "He brought them forth also with silver and gold" (Psalm 105:37a), re-endowed by their former masters with both favor and valuables (Exod. 11:2–3a, 12:35–36).

---

v

As a second consideration, I would like to return here to the relation between the specific words of Exodus 19 and the Mosaic covenant. How does this chapter—in concert with God and Moses within it—inaugurate the critical relation between God and Israel, and thus succeed as a discourse, in spite of the text's apparent failure as a coherently plotted narrative? For this text presents the major self-introduction of the overlord in the critical vassal-suzerain relation. It is the place where the nexus between covenant-making and narrative is formally established, because of the introduction and presentation—by the narrative, by God, and by Moses— of the two contracting parties to each other, through the good offices of a broker. Moses is a broker between master and servant in the way his law will eventually be; for the laws that deliver the slave also allow for the other possibility: that the servant will freely choose to remain in his master's service, and will accept the master-slave relation the rest of his life. That is, when and "if the slave plainly says, 'I love my master, . . . I will not go out free,' then his master shall bring him to God . . . and he shall serve him for life" (Exod. 21:5–6, RSV). There is likewise a class of slaves, purchased from among the strangers that sojourn in Israel, whom the owner may bequeath to his sons "to inherit as a possession for ever" (Lev. 25:46, RSV). It is a terrible phrase, but it seems to resonate with Israel's own relation to God.

On the prime occasion that Israel is "brought to God," God is driven to speak to Israel in a metaphor such as a prophet might resort to, when God uses the phrase "on eagles' wings." This eloquent expression can serve as a leitmotif. For the Sinai narratives as a whole would be very much poorer without the six opening verses in which the words occur. The question hanging over these lines is simple: How is Israel's now-to-be-covenanted relation with God proposed, brokered, explained, hedged, and qualified? Why has God borne Israel up toward his Sinai on eagles' wings, in a metaphor of aerial transport, rather than some other figure, such as, "I carried you as a mother carries a suckling child," or "I carried you up on my back," or "I drew you out of the depths of an abyss"? The existence of these other ideas is clear, when we compare the eagle here to the one with her nestlings in a parallel passage in Moses' final Song: "As an eagle stirreth up her nest, fluttereth over her young, spreadeth abroad her wings, taketh them, beareth them on her wings: So the Lord alone did lead him, and there was no strange god with him" (Deut. 32:11–12). God gives to a fledgling Israel some of his own cherub-like vehicular form, as it were: the capacity of wings. But without the passage from Deuteronomy, we are free to wonder whether the eagles' wings empower Israel, or abduct it.

In the Bible God the Father is always also God the Adopter. The I-Thou formula for God's and Israel's covenanting, "I shall be your God and you shall be my people," suggests the adoption formula, "I will be your sponsor, and you will be my progeny." The b-part of the parallelisms contains the b-member of the formulas:

> [I shall be your God, you shall be   my people]
>   I brought you to me
>   You shall be to me treasured possession
>   You shall be to me kingdom of priests
>   holy people (nation)
>   [I brought to me you]

Why has the text of Exodus 19 concealed the a-part of the formula, the readily available announcement, "I shall be your God"? We already know this form, from the Priestly version of Moses' authorization, in Exodus 6, which comes in the narrative as a reaffirmation of Moses' original Sinaitic call: "And I will take you to me for a people, and I will be to you a God" (vs.7). God's utterance, "I brought you to me," stands in place of more explicit declaration of God's status as a suzerain ("I will be to you a God"). It suppresses a declaration of sovereignty, but also any admission that the offer could be refused. It *obliges,* and its own, unspoken b-clause of "I brought you to me" would be: "and you are therefore mine." By saying that God brought Israel to him, rather than to Sinai, the clause ("I brought you to me") repeats the original "I bore you up," and develops the potential, possessive consequence: "therefore you have *no choice but* to be mine."

Is it really possible for God to bring any people to him, across a gap much larger than the one presented by the space between Egypt and Sinai—a gap which will be textually expanded to the distance between the Egypt of Exodus and the Moab of Deuteronomy? For surely a people is not properly brought to the God of the covenant by force. If God is only compelling from earthlings a yielding to him because the earth is already his, how is this different from pulling the strings of his puppets, from merely acting on Israel as an extension of himself? Does God mean, "I brought you to me, and therefore you have no choice"?

Everything in the story tells us that the gap between man and God is closeable, but how is it to be closed while also keeping it open so that both parties may remain free agents? The Targum of Onkelos says here that God brought Israel to *his worship*,[21] but the Sinai narrative overall makes it clear that God rather brought Israel to a *vision* of God, a chance to see God, or at least the divine affect, as represented by the tumult on Sinai. It is here we are told that the priest must never be seen mounting the steps of an altar that might expose his nakedness, while in Exodus 33:23 God specifically shows Moses his back-parts. Such texts cannot be made entirely consonant, unless we say that insofar as God did not and cannot bring Israel to himself without compromising and destroying Israel as an independent subject and deranging or scandalizing all its senses, he and the narrator bring Israel to God only through Moses. Israel is brought not directly to God, but rather to a Mosaic understanding of him.

Much depends here on the Sinaitic intervention of Moses. Only Moses can accomplish the bringing of the people home to God, or the bringing of God home to the people, or the bringing of God as Sinaitic to the people as pilgrims. The phrase "I brought you to me" repeats the idea that Israel was taken up by God, adopted from destitution or lack of sponsorship. How can an all-powerful deity do anything else than act compellingly? In making a people over "unto him," the question is, does God mainly make them holy, or does he mainly scare them silly, that is, terrorize and overwhelm them with the divine Sinaitic affect?

The hedging of God as God Almighty certainly appears in the text as the record of a theophany: God seizes upon a bush and makes it burn, yet without its burning up. God cordons off the mountain, and yet makes a show of himself upon it to all of Israel's representatives. God appears as both incomprehensible and unavoidable. Moses lays before the elders' faces all that God has spoken, and they see his thunders and trumpet-blast (Exod. 20:18), yet they are prevented from gazing on these things, lest they perish (Exod. 19:21). God orders them away from his exclusive precinct, and Moses has to point out that he has already done this on the basis of a prior order to the same effect (Exod. 19:23).

The giving of the contract (or the law or the Mosaic dispensation) is subject to some of the same dualities: the people are brought to Sinai and they capitulate to Moses' message without any hesitation ("All that the Lord hath spoken we will do" [Exod. 19:8]), yet they cannot be brought to approach God or deal with him themselves. God commands an unspecified object of address, a "thou," to have no other gods before him, yet he speaks about himself in the third person, as if he were Moses talking ("Thou shalt not take the name of the Lord thy God in vain . . . in six days the Lord made heaven and earth," etc., vs. "I the Lord thy God am a jealous god . . . shewing mercy unto thousands of them that love me"). Here God speaks about himself as if he were Moses speaking about Yahweh (Exod. 20:5–11; Deut. 5:9–10).

If "I brought you to me" doubles with "I brought you to Sinai," then the b-clause might be, "and you belong to Sinai." But Sinai is not quite a place on the map; it is only located apart from those places that were departed from to arrive at it, freed of human jurisdictions, and left in the jurisdiction of God. Israel is a "liminal community," undergoing rites of initiation;[22] Sinai is less its border than its horizon. An example of God's intention here is Ezekiel 37:26–27: "I will make a covenant of peace with them: . . . and I . . . will set my sanctuary in the midst of them for evermore. My tabernacle also shall be with them: yea, I will be their God, and they shall be my people." Israel's future as God's "treasured possession," object of care and keeping, advances the agenda beyond adoption to the results of it: treasuring and "possession" of the sponsored party by the sponsor. The treasured possession could again be a child, but a wife gives a better fit here, because of the "If-then" structure. If Israel accepts and observes the covenant faithfully, then Israel will be cherished and honored like a faithful mate. The contract, "If you will be my people, then I will be your God," is really restated as a proposal ("If you will have me to be your husband, then you shall be my wife"), and therefore an element of consent is at least rhetorically allowed for. Possession, of course, is already God's, the earth and everything in it being his. Yet God may suggest that Israel now has a power it might otherwise have lacked, to soar on God's own wings.

A greatly enriched version of the covenant formula is what Moses is commissioned to transmit to Israel, a series of promises: sponsorship by a party with the greatest claim to be the sponsor, preferred client, most favored nation trading status, partnership with a divine partner, honors and rights from the Disposer of All, livery and distinction as a class apart, and so forth. The offer is calculated not to be refused, as we have said. Its leading clause, "You have seen what I did to the Egyptians," takes the words right out of the Philistines' mouths at the battle of Aphek in 1 Samuel 4:8, rallying to the challenge of the ark ("these are the Gods that smote the Egyptians with all the plagues in the wilderness"), and again in

1 Samuel 6:6 ("when he had wrought wonderfully among them [the Egyptians], did they not let the people go . . . ?").

If "I brought you to me" is not entirely recognizable as "I will be your God," the reason may be its reservation for Exodus 20:2, where "I brought you up" is more or less immediately rendered as part of a law: "I am the Lord your God, who brought you out of the land of Egypt . . . You shall have no other gods before me." That is, "I will be your God and thou shalt have no other 'Thou.' " Exodus 20:2 thus transforms the covenant formula into the text of a commandment, out of the missing offer of an "I" for an I-Thou relationship. The effect is to turn covenant into law, while making law echo covenant. But by always keeping Moses in the foreground as the buffer and broker in this relationship, the text has represented something of its own purpose of delivering Israel from the bondage of a compulsion to the freedom of an allegiance.

A long homily from the scholar Perry Miller, writing about the purposes of the seventeenth-century Puritan "covenant theologians," might just as well have been about Raphael's explanation of the required but not necessitated "voluntary service" of God's angels in *Paradise Lost* (V.529):

> Through the maze of dialectic with which the covenant theologians rephrased conventional tenets runs one consistent purpose: they were endeavoring to mark off an area of human behavior from the general realm of nature, and within it to substitute for the rule of necessity a rule of freedom. They were striving to push as far into the background as possible the order of things that exists by inevitable equilibrium, that is fulfilled by unconscious and aimless motions, that is determined by inertia and inexorable law, and in its place to set up an order founded upon voluntary choice, upon the deliberate assumption of obligation, upon unconstrained pacts, upon the sovereign determinations of free wills. . . . They were inspired, even though but half conscious of their motive, with a desire to transform the concept of duty from something imposed brutally and irrationally by an ultimate datum into something to which man himself rationally and willingly consented. Obedience was no longer to be wrung from subjects by might, but accepted as a spontaneous token; . . . [23]

Even while God in Exodus 19–20 insists on his unilateral authority and his status as the sumptuary party of the suzerain, he also gives Israel its right to representation in Moses, and creates for it the legal status that recasts the relationship, changing it from a status relation to a contract relation.

As the Near Eastern suzerain, God makes that offer a vassal dare not refuse. But as a covenant-broker, Moses makes Israel an offer it has refused many times. Thus the relation that God must reinitiate at Exodus 19 is the essential bridge between the absolute deliverance given Israel by the

Moses of the exodus, and the contingent relation to a deliverer being offered to the people by the Moses of Deuteronomy. God hardens Pharaoh's heart, but he hopes to soften Israel's. That is, God subjects the Egyptian slave-owner to that bondage to another's will which is the slave's inevitable lot, while he delivers the Israelites into the voluntaristic sphere that ideally belongs to God's servants. Pharaoh's determination by the Other punishes his devaluation of the self-responsibility that the narrative anticipates for the people. Israel is freed from the very institution—slavery—to which Pharaoh proves captive. Thus the offer Israel cannot refuse is balanced by the command Pharaoh cannot obey. Yet there comes a day when Pharaoh is forced to let the people go, and Israel oftentimes proves unable to serve the Lord.

vi

God's remark to Moses, "I have remembered my covenant" (Exod. 6:5), is crucial, for it is positioned near the head of the story of Israel's covenant with the divine suzerain. The declaration that God has brought Israel out of Egypt, the prefatory history of relations, might theoretically include a diplomatic history of previous covenantings. So what covenant exactly did God remember? Is this a little like remembering the Sabbath in Genesis 2:2–3—it's never too early to get started? Or is there a genuine precedent in the covenant with Abraham?

God's address to Abraham, "I am the Lord [Yahweh] that brought thee out of Ur of the Chaldees" (Gen. 15:7a), certainly sounds like a covenant-maker's self-identifying preface and historicizing prologue, analogous to the preliminaries of the Mosaic covenant. But Yahweh does not go on to stipulate the conditions of vassalage (i.e., "you must have no suzerains other than the one making this contract"). Rather, the obligation falls on the covenant-donor: God's purpose in bringing forth Abraham, he tells him, is "to give thee this land to inherit it" (Gen. 15:7b). He is not taking Abraham as his vassal, but as his beneficiary. The obligation to the beneficiary lies with the donor. When the treaty donor is a benefactor, the covenant is redefined as his gift. Abraham's covenant is a gift certificate.

For here too an ancient form has been recognized: the certification or deed of a royal land grant to a faithful retainer, privileged to receive a fief donated to him from the royal bounty as a reward.[24] But the grant form, a kind of letter of patent, need not differ from the suzerainty treaty in regard to the need for provisions (protection of the recipient's interest, pledges on the part of the grantor's posterity), the need for registration (a keeping of documentation in some sort of depository), the need for witnesses or notarization (the gods, seals), and the need for sanctions (blessing and curses). To this may be added the need for a survey or map (specification of the property). If the gift is permanent and forfeiture is not contemplated, there is also a need to stipulate that the gift is conveyed to the recipient in perpetuity. So where the vassal had to swear loyalty to the suzerain's successor, the donor (with his posterity) contracts to honor the right of the recipient's heirs. The loyalty oath required of the vassal is replaced by the grantor's oath of his faithfulness to his commitments.

Could we arrive at this form from the Bible itself? Despite some remarkable variations, to be observed below, it is obvious that God makes such a donation to his faithful servant Abraham, and that it is just such a gift from God that Moses refuses. But how would we know? How would the Bible-reader be apprised of the model? Royal grants are certainly a familiar enough form of entitlement. Or the reader might rely on what he or she knows of, let us say, the weight of documentation accompanying a mailing from the Publishers Clearing House Sweepstakes, with its intention of convincing the addressees that they have already won, or the "Urgentgrams" giving the winning numbers for the free gifts that go with the acceptance of tours promoting investment in real estate for retirement. The bogus cases show the appanage of validation still exhibiting itself as a constant.

Gift certificates, at any rate, are a reasonable approximation of the donation procedure we are looking at: the certificate is a coupon telling the holder and the donor to whom the certificate belongs and what it is good for. Seals, for example: the reader knows that Noah has been granted the world as his farm, with the weather to go with it, and the same rights for his offspring. The rainbow is the "documentation," or the seal on it, and it corresponds to circumcision in Abraham. Its purpose, like that of certain ancient Near Eastern boundary markers, is to publicize the grant. The authenticating seal on a contract is to indicate the presence and consent of the party assuming an obligation. But the covenant with Noah is affected by other models. Treaties between the sun-god of Egypt and the storm-god of the Hittites, which are actually treaties between monarchs, are transcendentally literalized in the Noah story, and in God's covenants with the day and night, which Jeremiah in turn compares to the Lord's commitments to Israel and David (Jer. 33:25–26). Such treaties might be guessed in Israel's "covenant with Death," the Ugaritic Mot, where what is referred to is a nonaggression pact with Assyria (Isa. 28:15). It's only a myth, Isaiah seems to say, discounting any hope that Israel will be spared.

But there is a more specific case of the royal grant of privilege in the gift Pharaoh makes to Joseph of the land of Goshen, which seems to include a patronage offer to Joseph's dependents (Gen. 47:6, 11–12): Joseph is being paid for his services as vizier. The Pharaoh who knew not

Joseph is guilty of disregarding the crown's gift to Joseph's house. The phrases for the grant, whereby Pharaoh "gave them a possession in the land of Egypt, in the best of the land, in the land of Rameses, as Pharaoh had commanded" (Gen. 47:11, RSV), are legalistic and contractual, in the vein of the analogous boilerplate attaching to the grave site Abraham purchases in Hebron.

The Egyptian priests enjoyed a permanent land grant, parallel to the grant of Goshen Pharaoh made to the Hebrews. God's analogous grant to Abraham in Canaan reverted to Israel because it originally contemplated Abraham's heirs. But the Levites—Moses among them—are not included in the gift, in a reversal of the situation in Joseph's Egypt, where only the priests' land had not become Pharaoh's (Gen. 47:26). When God would like to renege on his gift, or rather transfer it to his faithful servant as Pharaoh had granted Egyptian land-ownership to the priests, he offers to make a "great nation" spring from Moses himself. But Moses recalls God to his legal and noble obligation to "Abraham, Isaac, and Israel, thy servants, to whom thou swarest by thine own self," and quotes the original deed of gift in which God obliged himself: "all this land that I have spoken of will I give unto your seed, and they shall inherit it for ever"—i.e., in perpetuity (Exod. 32:13). An eternally faithful God cannot annul the perpetuity clause of his deed of gift.

One example of the grant form is the deed-inscribed boundary markers that doubled as documents royally granting lands: "over eighty such monuments are extant," and "copies of these *kudurru's* on clay tablets were deposited in temples to insure their preservation."[25] Perhaps Jacob's pillow at Bethel (Gen. 28:11) is to be understood as such a "stake," since it is converted to a pillar (vss. 18, 22) to mark the land that God has just granted the third patriarch: "the land whereon thou liest, to thee will I give it, and to thy seed" (Gen. 28:13). Jacob gets part of Abraham's blessing on this same occasion (Gen. 28:14: "in thy seed shall all the families of the earth be blessed"); the corresponding curse is found in Deuteronomy 27:17, on the person moving a boundary marker. Where the marker bore the words of the grant, it could also have borne the words of the curse on the donor who failed to honor the terms of his gift. Jacob turns his particular grant deed into a covenant by vowing, in return for the land, to become God's subject, that is, to build him a temple as a payment for God's further sponsorship. The king's donation of a temple to a god develops a legal form similar to the land grant.[26] At the point where Jacob's pillar becomes part of a dedicated temple, the boundary marker will have been deposited in a shrine: the two forms will have converged.

What makes this more than a sterile exercise in either the obvious or the recondite is the way in which, once again, the biblical contract breaks the royal mold, by expanding beyond it. One reason the vehicle is less than obvious is precisely that Abraham does not get it in writing, that is, in legal writing, of which the echoes are much more apparent regarding the real estate he purchases from the Hittites (Gen. 23:9, 17–20; 25:9–10, 49:30, 50:13): the exactness of the specification of location and the publication of the terms of purchase both contrast with the invisibility of the actual cave and its contents. For it was very much against the spirit of ancient law to alienate land; the Hittites' resistance to selling their land is patent; in allowing the sale to a foreigner they may have violated their own laws against such a sale.

The legal devices for getting around ordinances forbidding the sale of land at Nuzi involved the would-be possessor's being *willed* the land, instead of his buying it.[27] Yahweh's deeding of the land to Abraham constitutes a form of the Nuzi evasion of the law. We can guess why the Bible is so insistent on calling the land of Israel an inheritance. The people, as slaves, may be a purchase, or something pawned that God redeems, but the land is conveyed to Israel as a bequeathal. The clearest example of God's use of the procedure of "fictitious adoption" comes from Jeremiah 3:19, where God explains how he will find a way to endow Israel with its inheritance in Canaan: "But I said, How shall I put thee among the children, and give thee a pleasant land, a goodly heritage of the host of nations? and I said, Thou shalt call me, My father; and shalt not turn away from me." In other words, God went to court and adopted Israel, so that he could legally assign it a parcel of heritable land.

That Israel is God's "inheritance" is especially the result of Moses' prayer for the people's reacceptance by God at Exod. 34:9: "I pray thee go among us . . . and take us for thine inheritance" ("I will take you to me for a people," God says at Exod. 6:7). In terms of the Nuzi forms, "take us for thine inheritance" could mean adopt us as your heirs, in order to convey your land to us as a bequeathal. The writing prophet supplies the text of the missing document. Without the critical words from Jeremiah, the biblical account would lack the writing or inscription that has ensured the survival of other royal contracts: for there is no mention in the narrative of a document being made or cut for Abraham, in order to be laid up in a temple or shrine or safe-deposit box. In Genesis itself there is no contract corresponding to the two copies that Jeremiah takes for his own protection in Jeremiah 32:8–14, "both that which was sealed according to the law and custom, and that which was open" (vs. 11), when, having the right of redemption and inheritance, he buys his cousin's field. There is no deed—and no promissory note—on which Abraham can collect. With the partial exception of Jacob's earthly mattress, there is no testamentary remainder, bill of bequeathal, or relicta of the transaction, suitable for posting or framing or entering in court. Nor is it missing because Abraham failed to ask for it: "And he said, Lord God, whereby shall I know that I shall inherit it?" (Gen. 15:8). In place of the contract itself, there is a covenant ceremony (the cutting of the sacrifice into pieces and the torchlight passing between the pieces) in which God obliges himself in the critical phrases, while Abraham is in the "deep sleep" Jacob might have needed to sleep on his rock; moreover, there is Moses' and God's exact repetition of these donative phrases (Gen. 13:15, 15:18, Exod. 32:13, 33:1), to show they were registered somewhere. Finally there is God's expression "Know of a surety," where "surety" has the force of the "evidence" of Jeremiah 32, though all the Hebrew itself says is "know to know" (Gen. 15:13; cf. English "Hear ye, hear ye").

The oracle given Abraham within his trance is a means to know. But the documentation is merely the oral pledge: the scribe or court recorder is successive generations to whom the pledge is repeated. God reissues the deed of grant to Isaac and Jacob (Gen. 26:3, "I will perform the oath which I sware unto Abraham thy father"; Gen. 28:13, "the land whereon thou liest, to thee will I give it, and to thy seed"): he grants the land to Jacob that Jacob himself claims by sleeping on it. Similarly, the terms of Abraham's purchase at Hebron are repeatedly spelled out in the text's description of his grave plot; but it is the actual occupation of the plot by the patriarchal remains, when the patriarch goes to sleep with his fathers, that takes the place of the deed originally proclaimed before the Hittites in the gate of their city (Gen. 23:18), like Jeremiah speaking to his scribe Baruch "in the presence of the witnesses that subscribed the book of purchase, before all the Jews that sat in the court of the prison": "Take these evidences, this evidence of the purchase, both which is sealed, and this evidence which is open; and put them in an earthen vessel, that they may continue many days. For thus saith the Lord of hosts . . . Houses and fields and vineyards shall be possessed again in this land" (Jer. 32:12, 14–15). Not only does the grave site in Hebron become a kind of registry—both a land registry, and a genealogical register—it is also the proof that the Israelite will be able to buy and sell land in Canaan after God has returned him to it.

It follows that the patriarchs are themselves the repository where the words for the transfer of Canaan were recorded and laid up:

> ask your father, and he will show you;
>   your elders, and they will tell you.
> When the Most High gave to the nations their inheritance,
>   when he separated the sons of men,
> he fixed the bounds of the peoples
>   according to the number of the sons of [Israel].
> For the Lord's portion is his people,
>   Jacob his allotted heritage. (Deut. 32:7–9, RSV [after Hebr.])

Moses attaches to this legal history because he "came and spake all the words of this song in the ears of the people, he, and Hoshea the son of Nun" (Deut. 32:44), so that later generations could ask their father and be shown the deed by their elders. "A land that I will show you," God said to Abram (Gen. 12:1, RSV); in Numbers 34 the map is finally shown—to Moses.

Besides the deed, what else is missing from the land grant to Abraham, yet also present in the Bible in some altered form or other? The donor's oath to be true to his pledge of the gift is apparent enough in Moses' version: "thy servants, *to whom thou swarest* by thine own self" (Exod. 32:13). This may be a bit of back-dating on the part of either God or Israel's lawyer: God may not swear in the original "document" in Genesis 15, but by the time of Genesis 26:3 he is telling Isaac he did. Ancient treaties have the treaty-maker swear by his gods. God is unlikely to say, "may the gods do thus to me and so, if I fail to do this other," but he also is unlikely to take his name in vain, perjure himself, or direct oaths against himself: we could not trust him to be faithful to his oath to pay back if he had not also been faithful to an oath to pay up. God's use of the first person itself constitutes an indirect oath not to forswear his commitments before God. For that is how Moses understands him in Exodus 32:13. Heaven, earth, and the stone of permanent inscriptions are not summoned as witnesses either, but if Abraham is as faithful to God as the narrator says, at Genesis 15:6, then he will need no other witness to God's oath-taking. God reckoned Abraham's faith to him as his righteousness, so Abraham would need no witness either.

God's gift to Abraham goes beyond the divinely patented royal land-grant in other ways too. First, the gift ordained in consideration of services seems to be offered from the outset, before very much of any actual service can have been performed. This may not matter, because the gift is not so much given in Genesis 12:1 as proffered: "a land that I *will* shew thee." Thus the gift is a kind of precontractual agreement on God's part. A mere commitment to contract is not so likely to issue in formal documentation. Second, the gift being contemplated is not only a land grant. It includes a continuing relation to the grantor as benefactor, and to the beneficiary as client and protégé. Where Abraham only gets a promissory note for the land, Israel seems to get a continued indebtedness: firstfruits paid to God are surely very like those paid by a tenant farmer to a landlord, as a condition of his tenancy upon a fief. Two places in the Hexateuch say the land belongs to God (Lev. 25:23, Josh. 22:19). Third, the gift includes a blessing, which does not function as a sanction but as part of the gift-deed stipulations: God obliges himself to give Abraham this blessing. But the grant of a blessing is rather less tangible than the blessing of a grant—even if the former serves as a recommendation for the latter. The blessing, of

course, provides for Abraham's prosperity; it is therefore a trust for
Abraham's posterity, in lieu of the king's actual gift; yet the blessing certi-
fies a gift—prosperity—will indeed be forthcoming.

Fourth, the power of the king to extend his gift to the recipient's heirs
is only part of what God's grant contemplates. God expects to give
Abraham a child of his body; moreover, God offers this gift again, when
the biology of Abraham's wife no longer allows it. If the typical gift rewards
loyal service, then it is likely to come late in life; hence the provision that
the land can be passed on to the recipient's posterity without interference,
giving his family a "house" or an estate. But though a king can give his
loyal subject an inheritance, he can hardly be expected to give him an
heir. In the Bible the provision for keeping the king's gift within a house's
possession has become the grant to provide that house. Such a gift is quite
beyond the powers of the king. The sheik Abimelech in Genesis 20 can
endow Abraham with his goods, and re-endow him with a half-sister wife.
But only God can grant a spouse fertility. The Hebrew women, at the
opening of Exodus, are blessed by this fertility; they are not like those
patriarchal wives who had difficulty bearing. God has made good on the
peoplehood clause in the grant he told Isaac he swore to Abraham. Finally,
one further dimension of God's gift to Abraham, the gift of a personal
relation to God, becomes specified and reconfigured in Exodus as the gift
of Israel's covenant relation to God. The biblical combining of the gift
treaty with the suzerainty treaty changes the relation between both the
sovereign and his vassal and the benefactor and his beneficiary. The noble
obligation of the grantor becomes the divine graciousness committing the
giver of all gifts to men. And the tribute exacted from the subject by his
overlord becomes the *obligation of the subject* toward law from God.

Nonetheless, at the time of the exodus the original basis for the divine
benefaction, the contract for a royal land grant, remained to be honored. It
is here that Moses figures: as God's agent, to execute God's long-standing
but unwritten commitment to provide Jacob's descendants a piece of land,
and as Israel's agent, to collect the unclaimed gift, held in abeyance, as
Genesis 15 provides, until the fourth generation (vs. 16). It becomes clear
why God's provision of the land, as found in the promises at Exodus 3:17,
6:8, 23:23, and 33:2–3, keeps being attached to the vassal-suzerain relation
of Exodus, yet also seems like foreign matter in it. What makes this provision of land like the vassal-suzerain material is the transcendence of the
suzerain, or rather the grantor. For the grantor does not give a fief, like
Pharaoh's plenipotentiary Joseph donating to his dependants the land in
Goshen; God is able to give nationhood itself—all the nations are within his
fief and power to give.

The land survey for the deed is necessarily less transcendental:

In the same day the Lord made a covenant with Abram, saying, Unto thy seed have I given this land, from the river of Egypt unto the great river, the river Euphrates,
The Kenites, and the Kenizzites, and the Kadmonites,
And the Hittites, and the Perizzites, and the Rephaims,
And the Amorites, and the Canaanites, and the Girgashites, and the Jebusites. (Gen. 15:18–21)

At Exodus 3:17, 23:23, 33:2, and Deuteronomy 7:1, the text repeats the list of native peoples who will lose the land owing to God's covenanting with Israel. Beginning as a "contract pending" notice, it is repeated with the passing on of the promise to Abraham's heirs, as the evidence of what God did or deeded. It is a basis for the domesday book of Joshua 12–21, and recurs in the account of the campaign of Abram in Genesis 14, Balaam's oracles in Numbers 24:15ff., and the list of intermarriages at Judges 3:5–6.

The land grant is the essence of the covenant being remembered in Exodus 6:5, since this is the covenant with God's servants the patriarchs that Moses will not let God forget in Exodus 32:13 ("to whom thou swarest by thine own self"), and which God rerecords at Exodus 33:1, "the land which I sware unto Abraham, to Isaac, and to Jacob, saying, Unto thy seed will I give it." Moses is the memory that the missing certificate would provide to the recipient: like God's, his words are as good as a text.

Moses' words, moreover, *are* this text. Hence God's mindfulness of the land grant, in Exodus 6:5, and Moses' own mindfulness thereafter, can be derived from (and compounded with) the concerns of the latter-day compilers of the Pentateuch, whom we can see as engaged in a kind of title search. Near the end of Leviticus God through Moses declares that in the future God will graciously "remember the land" of the Israelites exiled in Babylon: he will "remember the covenant of their ancestors" (Lev. 26:42, 45). In other words, the God of Exodus 6:5 obliges himself to honor his promise to give the forefathers the land in the same formula he uses to announce that he is going to give exilic Israel its land *back*.

· 5 ·

THE TWO TABLES, AND THE
MORALITY THAT LEGISLATES

He who dares to undertake the making of a people's institutions
ought to feel himself capable, so to speak, of changing human
nature, of transforming each individual, who is by himself a complete and solitary whole, into part of a greater whole from which he
in a manner receives his life and being; of altering man's constitution for the purpose of strengthening it; and of substituting a partial and moral existence for the physical and independent
existence nature has conferred on us all. He must, in a word, take
away from man his own resources and give him instead new ones
alien to him, and incapable of being made use of without the help
of other men. (Rousseau, *The Social Contract*, II.7, "The Legislator,"
trans. Cole)

In general the biblical narrative asks to be moralized legally. It can be read
as a double for either case law (the law based on the appeal to precedents
in judgment) or natural law (the law based on the appeal to necessary
consequences). At this point we may discern further analogies between
biblical narrative and jurisprudence, the text of each being found so much
in the proximity of the other. For the law in Israel is a "justified law." That
is, the Bible exposes how a law works, or why it might be compelling. Such
explanations contribute to the freedom and dignity of the legally bound
subject by acknowledging his power of choice and his capacity for understanding. But they also deepen the subject's answerability.

"An eye for an eye," in the Bible, is less a law than a "motive clause,"
an appeal to the principle of retaliatory equivalence. A crime's punishment is itself a kind of explanation—especially if we also understand the
penalty as an expiation for a sin, which purges it as *pollution*. Thus a
Mosaic legal background will throw the biblical narrative into special relief
from the outset. The commandment that the newly formed man shall not
eat from the tree of knowledge of good and evil, for example, is a dietary
law; the man is warned that transgressing will subject him to the death
penalty, a feature of Mosaic laws resembling those of "the ten words."

96

The knowledge of good and evil is a mixture; mixtures are levitically and epistemologically unclean, and therefore transgressive.[1] The motive clause about the bitter consequences of violating the taboo (Gen. 2:17b: "for in the day that thou eatest thereof thou shalt surely die") may not seem to be precisely this explanation of the taboo, yet everything in the story is vaguely explanatory of the kind of things that cause there to be taboos in the first place: restrictions pertaining to certain kinds of eating, certain kinds of undress, even certain kinds of speech ("Who *told* thee that thou wast naked?" [Gen. 3:11]). Before the man sins, the food of the story divides between the freely available fruit of immortality and the forbidden fruit of sophisticated perceptions (beauty, wisdom, and relish, according to the woman's appreciation at Genesis 3:6). After the man sins, it divides between the inedible thorns and thistles and the edible "herb of the field" (Gen. 3:18–19). Transgression is punished with the drudgery of farm life, the herb of the field got by the sweat of man's brow—perhaps we should recognize here the alienation of a pastoral people from farming the less arable lands where they have tended their cattle. After the man sins, there is also an explanatory cast in the difference between *unavailable, free* food—the "tree of life," which is the immortality reserved to the gods— and the thorns and thistles reserved as fodder for the beasts. Similarly, the *available, costly* food, the herb of the field, is reserved to farm laborers as bread, "the staff of life," while the tree of a forbidden knowledge is only available to transgressors, as if it were unclean. Whether he eats fruit from the orchard or fodder from the field (as it were, garbage), man is defined in both parts of the story as a discriminating eater: either he chooses wisely (does not get drunk with the gods or eat garbage or wild food—it would make him sick—with the animals), or he chooses unwisely (eats "foreign" or sophisticated food that does make him sick, i.e., mortal). The serpent is cursed for its crime: it is made to crawl on its belly (Gen. 3:14), and it thereby becomes inedible, which is to say, unclean. Thus the Mosaic law states that any small beast that crawls on the ground or moves on its belly is detestable to eat and makes one unclean (Lev. 11:41–47). The woman, who may get the uncleanness of childbirth (cf. Lev. 12) in the same motions that she gets its pains, suffers for having kept the wrong company.

The narrative is thus an appeal to interpretative understanding: an "explanation," rather subliminally inculcated, "justifying" dietary laws. The withdrawn food of immortality could as well be blood, the "life" in flesh that is reserved to God and wild or unclean animals (cf. Lev. 7:26–27, 17:10–16). The "justification" of the law might even include the obligations of penitence, since all dietary laws suggest the giving up of certain foods for the sake of undoing pollution. The humble food that Adam and the serpent eat is after all part of a penalty. A similar penalty is visited upon the humbled and excluded Nebuchadnezzar in the Book of Daniel as satisfaction for the king's presumption: a voice from heaven decrees "you shall be made to eat grass like an ox" (Dan. 4:32, RSV).

Other narratives of Genesis are no less haunted by the justificative concerns of the Mosaic law. The laws concerning the disinheriting of the firstborn at Deuteronomy 21:18–21, for example, might be used to justify Jacob's curse of Reuben at Genesis 49:3–4—*contra* the law upholding the firstborn's right to inherit a double portion, in spite of the firstborn's having a hated mother, in the immediately preceding law of Deuteronomy 21:15–17. For the conduct of the firstborn himself may be found culpable; hence the right of parents, in the second law, to discipline a rebellious and incorrigible son. The firstborn, Reuben, should not be disqualified because of his hated mother, Leah, but he may be disinherited if he defiled his father's bed with the maid of the beloved mother Rachel (Gen. 35:22). A narrative thronged with such cases doubles as a body of case law.[2]

The sequence of the two laws in Deuteronomy (the right of the firstborn to inherit, and the contrary right of the parent to disinherit the firstborn), almost suggests a plot in itself, a skeletal version of the A-B structure of biblical storytelling as found in the case of Esau and Jacob. In favoring Esau, Isaac might have been justified by the first law, for Esau is his firstborn; but if Esau's marriages are objectionable, Rebekah, in favoring the second-born, Jacob, is justified by the second law. Esau's embittered tears at Genesis 27:38 are justified not only by the terrible pain of his disinheritance by Isaac but also by the entitlement insisted on by the first of the two laws in Deuteronomy. Rebekah's estate-planning is equally justified, however, if the narrative and the second law share the idea that the firstborn might effectively disinherit himself, by marrying away his inheritance outside the tribe. Esau has threatened the Mosaic legal principle that "the inheritance of the children of Israel" shall not "remove from tribe to tribe" (Num. 36:7). The daughters of Zelophehad "were married unto their father's brothers' sons" (Num. 36:11). Moses brokers this marriage, and its kind, as Rebekah arranged that Jacob marry his mother's brother's daughters, and as Abraham's servant went "to take my master's brother's [son's] daughter unto his son" (Gen. 24:48).

When the narratives themselves lead to the establishment of a given social practice, they also constitute justifications—etiological in character—for the relevant laws. For example, the story of David's equal treatment of those who fight and those who stay with the baggage in 1 Samuel 30 concludes, "And it was so from that day forward, that he made it a statute and an ordinance for Israel unto this day" (1 Sam. 30:25). If the practice of David was compelling, how much more so the practice of Moses, whose statutes are from God himself. Moses' enunciation of the law as God's will is itself a motive clause, one in lieu of any other, but it too has explanatory force, equivalent to the appeal to binding precedent. On this point the narration of the Pentateuch is indeed monolithic; after Sinai, no part of its story derives the law from any other spokesman.

The statutes at the heart of the Mosaic law come with a singular sanction: the death penalty.[3] This "motive" also appears at both ends of the narrative overall. Adam was given, to go with the paradisal garden, the choice of life or death. If in the day he ate of the fruit he did not become liable to punishment, the gift of free will would be trivialized by the lack of consequences—man would have a limitless but inconsequential freedom. For if it did not matter what he chose, neither would it matter if he could choose at all. Like the law, freedom asks for justification. What choice would there be if there were no good and evil to choose between? "See, I have set before thee this day life and good, and death and evil; . . . I have set before you life and death, blessing and cursing," the deuteronomic Moses exhorts his nation: "therefore choose life" (Deut. 30:15, 19).

Israel's "penchant" for a justified law mirrors her need for a justified freedom.[4] A sinful mankind became subject to death and taxing labor; likewise, the serpent's bold kind became a dust-eater. But, conversely, Israel's *need* for a justified law mirrors its penchant for a justified history. Man and serpent are punished in their guilty clans, according to the rule "The fathers have eaten sour grapes, and the children's teeth are set on edge." (Ezek. 18:2, Jer. 31:29, RSV). When Moses says "therefore choose life," he adds, "that both thou *and thy seed* may live": he looks back at all the poor choices already made by the nation, and the generation that has died in the wilderness.

The Moses of Deuteronomy is not addressing himself to the choices of the individual, but of the collectivity, even though he knows the doctrine of individual responsibility (Deut. 24:16b, "every man shall be put to death for his own sin"). For the individual could only become the sole object of punishment for guilt when the nation had been destroyed, when he alone remained to be called by the later prophets to that repentance of his and his father's evil ways, which the prophets had urged to Israel as a house (cf. Jer. 31:29–34, Ezek. 18:2, 25–32). Having ignored the words of Moses, that house was punished by the captivity of the land. Thus the maimed Adoni-bezek in Jerusalem and the maimed Zedekiah in Babylon frame the whole of the narrative of the rulership in Judah (Judg. 1:1–7, 2 Kings 25:1–7): "As I have done, so God hath requited me," Adoni-bezek concludes.

The Mosaic legal sanction being the death penalty, Nehemiah and the deuteronomic historian agree that Israel was destroyed by Assyria and Babylon for having transgressed "the Law of Moses"—only Josiah had truly honored it (Neh. 1:7; 2 Kings 18:12, 23:25). The question was whether

Israel was to be doomed to the last man, or for whose sake might God spare the nation, as God had saved Judah out of Israel for the sake of David (1 Kings 11:34–36), or Caleb and Joshua out of Israel for the sake of the conquest (cf. Num. 14:15–38). "The Lord was angry with me for your sakes," Moses tells Israel in Deuteronomy 4:21, yet Exodus 32–34 suggests that it is also for Moses' sake that God has favored and adopted Israel, and so might someday save some portion of it as God's legacy, as promised in Deuteronomy 30:1–5 and Leviticus 26:41–45.

Societies utterly destroyed for their sin are portrayed in Lot's Sodom in Genesis 19, and in the Levite husband's Gibeah in Judges 19–20. Lot's connection with Abraham and the three men who visit him may have saved Lot out of Sodom, but it will not help Israel, according to the history of the land as projected by Ezekiel: "Though these *three men*, Noah, Daniel, and Job, were in it, they should deliver but their own souls by their righteousness . . . as I live, saith the Lord God, they shall deliver neither sons nor daughters; they only shall be delivered, but the land shall be desolate" (Ezek. 14:14, 16). The foreign witness whom Moses invokes in Deuteronomy 29:21–23 will compare the condition of post-Josianic Israel to that of Sodom and Gomorrah; he is anticipated not only by the prophets (e.g., Amos 4:11), but also by the Former Prophets: the narrators of Judges 19 have implicitly compared Gibeah to Sodom, by virtue of its impudent speeches and by its provocation to a systematic razing.

Considerations of group punishment apply more directly to the fate of the rebels' party in the Israelite camp in Numbers 16, or the leaders sacrificed for sin at Baal-Peor in Numbers 25:3–5. Abraham's questions at Genesis 18:23–33 concerning the justice of the judge of all the earth— Abraham argues for the exemption of the innocent from the general condemnation—are repeated in Moses' questions concerning the anger of the life-giving God over the Korahites: "Shall one man sin, and wilt thou be wroth with all the congregation?" (Num. 16:22). This intervention on Israel's behalf becomes a type of priestly mediation, owing to Moses' and Aaron's subsequent actions in the annexed incident of murmuring in Numbers 16:41–50 (17:6–15, JPS). Just as Moses' separation of Israel from Korah has prevented Israel as a whole from perishing in the general condemnation of a particular party, so now Aaron on Moses' instructions halts a plague with a rite of atonement that prevents the perishing of the whole group for its subsequent murmuring against Korah's fate: i.e., perishing in the wholesale condemnation for the sinfulness of only one of its particular actions. "shall we [all] be consumed with dying?" the Israelites ask at Numbers 17:13. For the offerings of the Levites have already been implicitly condemned in the prior case of Korah, and none of the rest of the community can placate Yahweh with priestly service—only the branch bearing Aaron's name has been favored in Moses' demonstration of his colleague's election (Num. 17:1–9 [17:16–24, JPS]).

Yahweh's further commissioning of Aaron in Numbers 18:1–7—in which Aaron's family, having been symbolically spared by the budding of their branch, is given the priesthood and responsibility to "bear the iniquity of [transgressions against] the sanctuary" (Num. 18:1)—provides Israel with a mechanism whereby God can charge one party with a whole community's transgressions against him, and, for the sake of one party, exempt a whole community from sin's consequences. Provided the Levites do not come near the sacred vessels or the altar, they are in no more danger of death than you, he tells Aaron, referring to the corps of ministering Levites, but also, by implication, to all of Israel's service to God (Num. 18:3).

We note the general and public "eventfulness" of all these institutions. Biblical law is like the biblical covenant in this respect: it presents itself by means of a historicized, Mosaic advent; it is crossed with an immense variety of advent narrative. From the point of view of the law, the "allegorical" meaning of the broken and restored tables is neither law reform nor covenant renewal, but the origination of the law in the sense that laws are revealed or forced into articulation as we are made conscious that a principle or a propriety or a person is being violated. At that point, "there oughta be a law." The Lord's intervention in the affairs of Israel in Egypt answers to this outcry, and the revelation at Sinai formalizes what the law should be.

But that there ought to be a law could mean, in practice, a revision or reapplication or renewal of a former law. The Bible is not interested in anything like readjustments or relaxations of the rate of compensation for damages, as found for example in the Hittite law, but it is interested in something like the opposite: a deepening and complicating of the extent of liability. The law against covetousness is certainly revisionary in this sense. The command to care for the neighbor as the self is perhaps no less revisionary—it tends to dissolve the very distinction between parties at law. Honoring the parent is also predicated upon self-interest: one honors the aged, "that thy [*own*] days may be long upon the land which the Lord thy God giveth thee" (Exod. 20:12).

At the same time, a law like the tenth commandment tends to make God the only being truly capable of righteousness. The Shechemite Duodecalogue reproves secret crimes, but its conclusion, "Cursed be he that confirmeth not all the words of this law to do them" (Deut. 27:26a), convicts this law of being virtually unenforceable except by God, or by the law-abider acting within himself. Through the dialectic of lawgiving, law-

breaking, and law reform within the narrative, one comes to understand
the tablets broken in Exodus 32:19 as saying that the law cannot long survive its being wantonly and repeatedly flouted. Lawbreakers cannot properly receive such a law: it cannot find sanctuary among them; not being its
keepers—law-abiders—they cannot expect to find protection within it, or
to escape a curse outside it. A case in point is the harsh treatment of
sabbath-breakers and blasphemers as persons who have excluded themselves from the law-community. It is a short step from the curses inherent
in the law, in the mind of Saint Paul, to the concept of the curse *of* the law,
which is the law's being unkeepable (Gal. 3:10–13). "For as many as are of
the works of the law are under the curse" (vs. 10). Liability could scarcely
be taken further, but the curses pronounced in Leviticus 26 and Deuteronomy 27 put the basis of liability in more than a broken law. Its source is
also historical, since the would-be law-community has accumulated a terrible record, deserving God's vengeance on "the quarrel of [his] covenant" (Lev. 26:25). But does the narrative containing this community's
record re-present the Sinaitic Decalogue?

The laws of the Decalogue are widely distributed through the Bible.
They appear in the Pentateuch several times (and as units in
Exod. 20:1–17; Exod. 21:12, 15–17; Exod. 34:10ff.; Lev. 19:3–4, 11–18;
Lev. 20:2–10; and Deut. 5:7–21, Deut. 27:15–26), in the prophets at least
twice (Hos. 4:2, Jer. 7:9), in Job's catalogue of wickedness in Job 24
(vss. 2–16), and in at least three places in the Psalms (81:9–10; 24:3–4,
50:16–20):[5] that is, in one or another listing or partially codifed form, or
in association with the covenant, or with climbing Sinai, Horeb, Ebal, or a
"mountain of Yahweh" (Ps. 24:3). The association of most of these
instances with a covenant, or a Sinaitic relation with God, speaks for the
biblical insistence that a Mosaic god-fearingness and human decency—
religious obligation and moral obligation—can neither one exist without
the other. The *lex* tying a person to God also ties him to other persons.

Turning to the content of the essential "ten words" themselves, we may
begin by noting that they divide into two parts, and that each part
advances the purposes of the other, since offenses against the neighbor
inevitably redound in offenses to God. Roughly speaking, the first table of
the Decalogue pertains to sins against God and authority, and the second
to crimes against one's fellow. Like a Roman with his *officiis*, the Pentateuch does not distinguish between law and religion, between civic and
cultic obligation. Duties are legislated, and in the Bible a law that forbids
and incriminates is one with a law that obliges and graces. The coexistence
of the demands on the two tables basically equates sins against the covenant with violations of the law. In the category of sins against the covenant—equivalent to covenanting with foreign gods (Exod. 23:32) and

so sinning against God and authority—also go conjuring the dead (Lev. 20:27), cursing one's parents (Exod. 21:17), abusing or profaning or failing to sanctify Yahweh's name (Lev. 24:16, 19:12, Exod. 23:13), casting an idol in secret or making molten gods (Deut. 27:15, Exod. 34:17), and engaging in witchcraft (Exod. 22:18; Lev. 20:6, 27; Deut. 18:10; 1 Sam. 15:23).

One almost feels the operation of an unspoken law against an anti-Mosaic secrecy or recusancy in some of these texts, though the secret is often an open one, as in this explanation of the fall of the Northern kingdom: "And the children of Israel did secretly those things that were not right against the Lord their God, and they built them high places in all their cities" (2 Kings 17:9). Through the witch of Endor Saul conjures the dead Samuel, while no one knows the place of Moses' burial. We may guess that Moses has no tomb in order to make the Mosaic legislation against necromantic practice and cults of the dead support the doctrine that Yahweh is specifically the god of the living. The system of levitical taboos attaching to a dead body can tell us the same thing.[6] The text never says in so many words that God delivers Israel from the mortuary obsessions of the Egyptians, but the creation of Adam and Eve in a combination of resuscitative and embalming procedures makes the point in inverted form.[7]

That neither table of transgressions and obligations could exist without the other appears both from the contexts in which the text embeds the various tables and from the criminality of sin and the sinfulness of criminality where the two tables overlap: as in the worship of Molech, which is both sinful and murderous (Lev. 20:2). The person who sinfully curses his parents might also criminally strike them (Exod. 21:15); the person who sinfully takes God's name in vain may criminally commit perjury in doing so (Lev. 19:12, Exod. 23:7). The obligation to honor one's parents is scarcely separable from honoring one's parents' god. The last law on the second table—against criminally coveting—is not altogether separable from avoiding sinful idolatry, for the Bible typically associates whoring after strange gods with a clutching, fetishistic possessiveness. Both idolatry and covetousness are possible to commit in secret (cf. Deut. 27:15), and both evince evil predispositions in a will that is hearkening to sin and crime by dividing itself from its proper objects in God and the neighbor. Murder is defined as a sin against God, because all life belongs to God: murder is bloodshed, and the life is in the blood. Theft is defined as a sin against God, inasmuch as the form of it criminalized by the death penalty is abduction, or man-stealing—again, a usurpation of God's prerogative in the taking of life. Adultery is likewise defined as a sin against God, because a theologically monogamous Israel is God's, and the overall testimony about sexual crime in the Pentateuch makes it miscegenous. That is, it

either involves practices (homosexual, incestuous, or bestial) that define
other peoples, as in the remarks on "the nation, which I cast out before
you" at Leviticus 20:22–23, or it involves actually going in to them, and
therefore creating them (as in the incestuous rape of Lot by his daughters
in Gen. 19:30–38, where an imitation of "the manners" of Sodom creates
Moab and Ammon). The sin of "whoring after" strange gods, such as the
Molech of Leviticus 20:5, is a natural accompaniment of the cognate social
practice of joining one's self with the foreign peoples who worship those
gods. The post-exilic Levites are cleansed of this evil in respect of Moab
and Ammon in Nehemiah 13, with a reference to the evil of Solomon's
wives (Neh. 13:26). Solomon built an altar for Molech (1 Kings 11:7) while
also breaking laws against intermarriage with the nations: for "the Lord
said unto the children of Israel," the author quotes, "Ye shall not go in to
them . . . for surely they will turn away your heart after their gods"
(1 Kings 11:2) One can also go awhoring after wizards, according to the
text in Leviticus 20:6 (cf. Isa. 8:19)—as they do in Egypt (Exod. 7:8–12,
Isa. 19:3), and in Babylon (Isa. 47:9, 12–13).

The codified commandments of Exodus chapters 20, 21–23, and 34, are
embedded in a narrative about covenanting and apostasy, worship and
idolatry, and service and rebellion, and so the first two commandments
are illustrated even while they are inscribed. The first commandment, **"No
other gods,"** which we could restate as "Be a faithful Yahwist," maintains
the exclusiveness of Israel's relation to God, which takes the positive-
negative form of forsaking and forswearing the other gods, especially in
Israel. As an action this first appears in the narrative sandwiched between
the two texts in Genesis where Jacob gets his name Israel (Gen. 32:28,
35:10), then again in the narrative of the last will and testament of Joshua
(Josh. 24:14, 20, 23), who has led the conquest. Jacob's orders to his
household in effect state the first commandment: "Put away the strange
gods that are among you, and be clean" (Gen. 35:2). Joshua's instructions
to Israel are three alternative versions of the same commandment: "*fear the
Lord*, and serve him in sincerity and in truth: and *put away* the *[foreign] gods*
which your fathers served on the other side of the flood, and in Egypt; and
serve ye the Lord" (Josh. 24:14).[8] The narrative of the mustering of Israel to
fight the Philistines has Samuel state it in a slightly more conditional form
that narrativizes the law by means of the process of conversion: "*If ye do
return unto the Lord* with all your hearts, *then put away* the *strange gods* and
Ashtaroth from among you, and prepare your hearts unto the Lord, and
serve him only" (1 Sam. 7:3). The placement of the apostasy and atonement
at Baal-Peor, in Numbers 25, also implies the putting away of strange gods
and strange wives on the threshold of the promised land (Shittim in Moab
is about ten miles east of the Jordan River). The daughters of Moab

"called the people unto the sacrifices of their gods: and the people did eat, and bowed down to their gods" (Num. 25:2). Phinehas's zealous intervention—on behalf of the jealousy of his God—earns his house a priesthood in his name (Num. 25:13).

"Ye shall not fear other gods, nor bow yourselves to them, nor serve them," God had admonished the sons of Jacob who became Israel (2 Kings 17:35). It is Yahweh who is "to be feared above all gods" (1 Chron. 16:25, Ps. 96:4), but God hearkens to God-fearers—according to the man born blind in John 9:28–31—whether they are Mosaic religionists or not. The converse of Israel's own dread of foreign deities, the fear of God is a more general motive; it explains, in Genesis, not only Abraham's conduct in acceding to the sacrifice of Isaac and Joseph's reprehension of Potiphar's lawless wife (22:12, 39:9), but also the host Abimelech's treatment of his potential brother-in-law Abraham (20:11). "The fear of God is not in this place," Abraham thinks in the Gerar of Genesis 20, but it is the Sodom of Genesis 19—where Lot preaches to his blinded hosts in vain—to which the thought properly applies. The fear of God governs the midwives' disobedience of Pharaoh, and presumably underlies the adherence of Rahab and the Gibeonites to the tribes invading Canaan (Exod. 1:17; Josh. 2:9–11, 9:9–10). Unlike the Pharaoh who did not fear God (Exod. 9:30), Rahab and the Gibeonites need no preaching to be converted—to the God of Joshua. The God-fearers to whom Paul speaks in Acts 13:16 may have been Gentile converts to the Synagogue; perhaps they were ripe to be converted once again. One of the thieves crucified with Jesus enlists himself among those saved when he questions his fellow, "Dost thou not fear God?" (Luke 23:40). The God-fearing centurions of Luke 23:47 and Acts 10:2 belong to the same history—which is to say, the same confession.

The rebellion of **idolatry** (Commandment II) is surely Aaron's immediate crime in Exodus 32, and its prominence near the head of the history of sin in Israel is important as an indication of what the editors of the overall history took to be the sin that caused the history to end in the Babylonian exile. Since all the world's "other gods" are represented by idols, it is scarcely possible to honor the first commandment, against divided worship, without honoring the second, against the use of cult images. Hezekiah "brake the images" and destroyed the brazen serpent as the receiver of idolatrous worship (2 Kings 18:4); Josiah as a deuteronomistic second Moses purges an idolatrous priesthood (2 Kings 23). The Bible associates the possession and use of the cult images with the resort not only to other gods but also to magic and magical apparatus. The Saul and Josiah who put the wizards out of the land (1 Sam. 28:3, 2 Kings 23:24) may thus be understood as effecting and obeying the second commandment in the spirit of the first, or vice versa. Saul ends as he began, by consulting Samuel as a diviner ("Behold, I have here at hand the fourth part of a shekel of silver: that will I give to the man of God, to tell us our way" [1 Sam. 9:8]). But the ghost of Samuel, whom the witch has been ordered to conjure, refers Saul to messages that Samuel had already delivered while he was alive; only now the ghost adds, "Tomorrow you and your sons shall be with me" (1 Sam. 28:19, RSV). On Gilboa Saul overtakes this Macbeth-like tomorrow. If those who consult the dead are soon numbered among them, then Samuel has spoken as a *Mosaic* prophet: "A man also or woman that hath a familiar spirit . . . shall surely be put to death" (Lev. 20:27).

The call of Moses conceals a statement of the first commandment in its positive form: "Ye shall *serve God* upon this mountain" (Exod. 3:12); so also Pharaoh's command, "Go ye, *serve the Lord*" (Exod. 10:24). Both services are informed by the more legalistic content of Exodus 23:24–25, "Thou shalt not bow down to [the Canaanites'] gods, nor serve them . . . ye shall serve the Lord your God," and Deuteronomy 6:13, 7:16, "Thou shalt fear the Lord thy God, and serve him . . . neither shalt thou serve their gods." Pharaoh asks who Yahweh is that he should obey him, and says he "knows not the Lord" (Exod. 5:2): for the wicked "say unto God, Depart from us; for we desire not the knowledge of thy ways. What is the Almighty, that we should serve him?" (Job 21:14–15). Exodus 23:33 and Deuteronomy 28:14 embed the formulae in warnings: "if thou serve [the Canaanites'] gods, it will surely be a snare unto thee," "thou shalt not go aside from any of the words which I command thee this day, . . . to go after other gods to serve them." But Deuteronomy 30:17 says Israel will indeed "worship other gods, and serve them." The final speeches of Joshua also predict this will come to pass—the people will "have gone and served other gods, and bowed [themselves] to them," and thus reverted to the pagan condition that antedated Moses' Israel, "on the other side of the flood, and in Egypt" (Josh. 23:16, 24:14). All expressions of faith in Yahweh honor the first commandment, whether they come from David facing Goliath (1 Sam. 17:45–47), or Job facing his own terrible condition (Job 19:25). "To him shalt thou cleave, and swear by his name," Moses instructs Israel at Deuteronomy 10:20. When Joab catches hold of the horns of the altar in 1 Kings 2:28, we understand the gesture as Jesus might: "Whoso . . . shall swear by the altar, sweareth by it, and by all things thereon" (Matt. 23:20).

The longer narrative of Israel's history illustrates Israel's criminal violation of the remaining commandments as well. **"Taking the Lord's name in vain"** (III) refers narrowly to the failure to perform promises after swearing oaths to God, or in his name. Such a failure seems to be proscribed throughout the Holiness Code in Leviticus, since its positive injunctions are all sealed by this same name: "he that blasphemeth [it] . . . shall surely be put to death" (Lev. 24:16). An example of the first and third commandments together in one formulation is found in Deuteronomy 6:13: "Thou shalt fear the Lord thy god, and serve him, and shalt swear by his name" (cf. Jer. 12:16, ". . . if they will diligently learn . . . to swear by my name"). Perhaps the prophet Balaam with his magical apparatus attempted to use God's name in some such way, though only with the purpose of giving God the lie. He finds out both for himself and for Balak that "God is not a man, that he should lie; neither the son of man, that he should repent" (Num. 23:19). The narrator thinks this important enough to put into the mouth of Samuel (1 Sam. 15:29), when the prophet rebukes Saul for a sinful duplicity comparable to that of the ban-violator Achan (Josh. 7). But it is really some sort of sin against the Name itself that seems implied by the commandment, and there are only two obvious cases of this sin: that of the Israelitish woman's son in Leviticus 24:10–16— he is a half-breed who curses an Israelite in a fight—and the false accusation brought against Naboth in 1 Kings 21. The sin is identified as blasphemy: a kind of verbal violence against God. Since Naboth is not guilty, and yet is killed as if he were, it appears to have been a sin easy to use for trumped-up charges.

Insofar as it implies ignoring the God whose name or chief epithet is Jealous (as per Exod. 34:14, "Yahweh, whose name [is] Jealous" [AT]), the sin against the Name might also imply mentioning or swearing by the names of other gods (as per Exod. 23:13, Jer. 12:16), or else misnaming God, or swearing by the Name unrighteously (e.g., Isa. 48:1). The sin therefore has a special association with Leviticus, if the Levites are the official keepers of the Name, and if Leviticus is the biblical text in which this name is most insistently kept within an enunciation of God's laws. God's commandments in Leviticus are routinely accompanied with God's self-identification by the name he disclosed to Moses on Sinai in Exodus 3. But zeal for the Name is equally a leading motive in the prophets, who prophesy in it, and suffer and intervene for its sake (cf. Jer. 11:21, 20:9); all false prophecy therefore sins against the third commandment by taking God's name in vain, and we should therefore not be surprised to hear Moses prescribing the death penalty for it in Deuteronomy 18:20 at the same place he is promising Israel that God will raise up a prophet like himself. Given the doubleness of the word of the prophet with the word of God, it is also not surprising that God himself is understood as acting zealously in the Name's behalf, as per Exodus 9:16, and through deutero-Isaiah. We have said that the narrative of Exodus 32–34:7 offers the keeping of God's name as Jealous and Merciful as remediation for the sin of the golden calf, and that the associated tables of the law are texts that keep God's name this way too.

Sabbath-breaking (IV) is implied by the mistrust of the would-be manna-gatherers of Exodus 16:27. The sin is comparable to that of Jonathan in eating during a fast that Saul has vowed to God in 1 Samuel 14:24, as if the words for sabbath and oath (*šebuʿah*) were related ("no man put his hand to his mouth: for the people feared the oath" [1 Sam. 14:26]). But it is the man who gathered sticks upon the seventh day in Numbers 15:32 who occasions Moses' inaugural imposition of the death penalty for this crime. Although it is not entirely clear, Naboth in 1 Kings 21 may have been technically guilty of breaking a fast, though he is certainly ignorant of any trespass into which he may have been lured. The biblical legislation does not require a fast for God in ordinary times, but rather a fast from work. Combining this legislation with the appeal to God's own fast from work (especially in Exod. 20:11) suggests that, on the Sabbath, work is to be replaced by a contemplation of God. The "crime" of sabbath-breaking, the failure to rest from "gathering," violates a *taboo* on the seventh day, which makes it "sin"; but the sin is otherwise inattention to the Creator, not observing his feasts, ignoring his behests. So God, speaking of the manna: "the people shall go out and gather a certain rate every day, that I may prove them, whether they will walk in my law, or no" (Exod. 16:4). As the text of Genesis 1–3 now stands, God creates man and woman in his image; therefore he vivifies the man with his breath. The Priestly author's God created the world for humans, and thus sanctifed it to their use: the world produces for man. But the Jahwist author's God created the man to serve a refraining law, and the man is profaned into a laborer by this law's abuse: man produces for the world. By dividing these accounts of the man-in-the-world with the institution of the Sabbath, the text divides on the question of which one was made for the other—or which was ordained to "keep" the other—the man or the Sabbath (Mark 2:27). Thus a particularly relevant narrativization of sabbath-keeping is found in those laws where the Sabbath is re-inscribed in various practices of release.

Dishonoring of the parent (V) is really the only commandment out of the ten that inculcates something like a duty to one's self. Thus its biblical violation includes a variety of mistreatment reflecting the abuse of one's neighbor—even if injuring the parent's glory also resembles the kind of insult that might otherwise be offered to God, in the form of profaning the glory of the Name, or "blasphemy." Injuring the parent's glory or authority seems especially apparent in the murder of Gideon's sons by their brother Abimelech (cf. Judg. 9:5, 18, 24, 56, "the wickedness . . . which he did unto his father"). This is the crime of Absalom against David, when he takes sexual possession of the king's harem on the king's rooftop (2 Sam. 16:20–23), and Reuben against Jacob, when he sleeps with Bilhah (Gen. 35:22). Reuben may receive his father's curse for this (Gen. 49:3–4, 7); if the fifth commandment is against *cursing* one's parents, as in Leviticus 20:9, then Jacob is fighting fire with fire (cf. the excommunication of Miriam in Num. 12:14: "And the Lord said unto

Moses, If her father had but spit in her face, should she not be ashamed seven days? Let her be shut out from the camp seven days"). The curse wished on those who "setteth light by their parents" in Deuteronomy 27:16 seems active in the incrimination of the Leahites for their mistreatment of their father's favorite, Joseph: "What is this that God hath done unto us?" they say to one another (Gen. 42:28). On the positive side—and the commandment is often stated positively—to "honour the face of the old" (Lev. 19:32) seems to be the whole psychological burden of Deuteronomy, if it calls on Israel to honor the memory of Moses, by honoring old Mosaic orders *today* (Deut. 5:1–3; cf. Ps. 95:7–11 with Heb. 3:7–19).

If cursing the God who made us is blasphemous—like the invitation of Job's wife to curse God, which was reproved by Job (Job 2:9–10), or like cursing or defying the king in other Near Eastern legislation—then cursing the parent can be reprehensible on similar grounds. But all crimes from the second table are especially heinous when committed against the parent: "Whoever robs his father and mother and says it is not wrong is the companion of one who is evil," Proverbs 28:24 (AT) reads, beginning its pronouncement as if it were citing an offender like Micah in Judges 17:2 and anticipating the penalty of a mother's curse. Since Micah had taken money that his mother "had wholly dedicated . . . to the Lord" (vs. 17:3), he was also robbing God.

Adultery is another example of a crime against a parent: "The nakedness of thy mother, shalt thou not uncover" (Lev. 18:7). Similarly, "Cursed be he that lieth with his father's wife; because he uncovereth his father's skirt" (Deut. 27:20)—Noah's cursing of his son Ham is relevant, because the reasoning is that sleeping with the father's wife is tantamount to sleeping with the father himself (Lev. 18:8, "the nakedness of thy father's wife shalt thou not uncover: it is thy father's nakedness"), and thus lying "with mankind as with womankind" (forbidden at Leviticus 18:22; cf. also 18:7, "The nakedness of thy father, . . . shalt thou not uncover"). The widowed Tamar, on the other hand, honors her father-in-law as a progenitor by seeking further husbands among his sons, and then, disguised as a prostitute, by seeking sons from her father-in-law himself (Gen. 38:6–26). The comparable honoring of a Judaic mother-in-law occurs in the story of Ruth. Ruth is as much a convert to Naomi as to Yahweh. Boaz (whose nakedness Ruth uncovers as her Lot-ite ancestress once uncovered that of her father Lot) honors Ruth's allegiance to Naomi over the pursuit of "the young men" (Ruth 3:10). Boaz sees in Ruth's loyalty the honor he may expect from her as her patron-husband.

One of Jesus' versions of the commandment recognizes the offense against the parent as slander (Mark 7:10, " 'For Moses said . . . "He who speaks evil of father or mother, let him surely die" ' " [RSV]). False witness against the parent is not directly represented in the Mosaic narrative, but we have the sense that Joseph's father finds himself in a court in which he cannot hope to hear the truth about a crime against his dearest son. The main point is, sins against the parent, at the end of the first table, can be translated into the crimes of the second table; conversely, the last commandment, against covetousness, refers the criminality of the second table back to the sinfulness of the first. Jesus maintains that the commandment to honor the parent can hardly mean the honoring of tradition at the expense of the parent's welfare, and puts the care of the parent in the place of service to God. Where the synagogue has coveted subsidies—Corban—otherwise belonging to the maintenance that a man owes his progenitor, it has made void the word of God through tradition (Mark 7:9–13). This point is "deuteronomic," because of the way in which it might figure in the book-by-book canon of transgressions listed below.

To turn to the second table proper: here our examples will naturally come from the life of Israel in the land, rather than in the wilderness. Covetousness (X) is indicated in David's desire for Uriah's wife (2 Sam. 11), and in Ahab's desire for Naboth's vineyard (1 Kings 21). The consequences are murder (VI), adultery (VII), and Nathan's pronouncing Yahweh's death penalty on the child conceived illegimately (2 Sam. 12:14). These two examples of **murder** (VI) seem comparable, given the treacherous orders of Jezebel's letter, at 1 Kings 21:9 (AT), "Proclaim a fast, and set Naboth at the head of the people," and those of David's letter at 2 Samuel 11:15 (AT): "you put Uriah in front of the faces of the fierce battle." Murder is a crime regularly associated with the power of the kingship, because the king is in the best position to usurp the right to life that belongs to God—as Pharaoh's genocidal edict in Exodus 1:16 shows. The god-fearing midwives defy the king of Egypt. The would-be king Abimelech (Judg. 9), who dies like Saul (vss. 52–55), becomes a king through murder (vs. 5); if he is assisted by his band, then the murderers were hired (vs. 4). Procured murder abuses power in a particularly heinous way. Saul's treacherous attempt on the life of David in 1 Samuel 19:11 is delegated to messengers by the king; David orders the death of Uriah through Joab; the death of Naboth is brought about through hire. The association of murder with conspiracy or treachery, or the abuse of proximity or intimacy, is also found in many of the political murders and murders that effect a coup: examples are Joab's murder of Abner during a truce (2 Sam. 3:27), the murder of Ishbosheth in his bed by his servants (2 Sam. 4:5–7), the killing of Ahab's son Joram by Jehu (cf. 2 Kings 9:23, "treachery"), and Hazael's murder of his bed-ridden master the Syrian king Ben-Hadad (2 Kings 8:14–15). Joab's killing of his rival Amasa, while they are both on a campaign-mission for the king, by means of a gesture of friendship and in an inquiry after Amasa's health (2 Sam. 20:9–11), is also murder. Joab's flight to the altar to save his life implies an appeal to the place of refuge that God will appoint for the manslaughterer, according to Exodus 21:12–13; but the same text also condemns Joab to "the judgment," for premeditated murder: "if a man come . . . upon his neighbor, to slay him with guile; thou shalt take him from mine altar, that he may die" (vs. 14).

Because of the principle whereby the legal confiscation of life belongs to God, the prophet who speaks against the murderous king may also pronounce and even execute the death sentence on God's enemies: examples are Samuel killing Agag before the Lord in 1 Samuel 15:33, and Elisha virtually commissioning Hazael to go ahead and kill his master at 2 Kings 8:11–14, as that act follows from God's commission to Elijah to anoint Hazael to be king over Syria at 1 Kings 19:15. The "message" given by the assassin Ehud to Eglon of Moab in Judges 3:20–22 combines a form of the treachery of the lawless Joab (a lethal weapon hidden under a cloak of dissimulated privacy-seeking at 2 Samuel 3:27—"to speak with him quietly") with a form of the prophet's word (a message that the king is subject to death for apostasy—e.g., Elijah to Ahaziah at 2 Kings 1:4). Killings identifiably murders certainly fall under the Noachic law in Genesis 9:5b: "At the hand of every man's brother will I require the life of a man." Murders offend both God and the parent, being directed against God's image in man as reproduced in human offspring. Cain is indicted on this account, since Abel's murder is compensated for by the begetting of Seth in Adam's likeness (Gen. 1:27, 4:25, 5:1–3, with 9:6). The sin of the brothers against Joseph causes them to invoke the Noachic law when they hear that they will have to take Benjamin from his father: "We are verily guilty concerning our brother . . . therefore is this distress come upon us . . . his blood is required" (Gen. 42:21–22). They are above all guilty before their father—in Genesis most violations of Mosaic law are conceived of as offenses to the parent, i.e., as offending traditional or patriarchal values.

The Noachic law puts murder quite out of the reach of monetary repayment, as the money in the brothers' sacks might have told them: God will repay (cf. Deut. 32:35 with Rom. 12:19), and blood-money is *not* what is meant. The requital in question is found in Isaiah 59:17–19: "he put on the garments of vengeance for clothing, and was clad with zeal as a cloak. According to their deeds, accordingly he will repay, fury to his adversaries, recompence to his enemies; to the islands he will repay recompence. So shall they fear the name of the Lord." An example of "life for life" is the rendering up of the seven Saulides in 2 Samuel 21, a collective compensation demanded and received from David by the Gibeonites—who refuse to be satisfied with a money offering, and also with the lives of just any Israelites (2 Sam. 21:4). The atoning Saulide lives allow for the repeal of a curse the Gibeonites have put on Israel in reaction to Saul's violation of the original oath of "the princes of the congregation" to preserve the Gibeonites in Israel (Josh. 9:15–21). Oaths are made on the oath-taker's life— that is their "surety" (Gen. 44:32). David probably has his own motives for surrendering lives that include the sons of a wife Saul denied him, but his appeal for a blessing (2 Sam. 21:3) may also justify him as refusing to take God's name in vain. The killing of Joab at the altar by Solomon (1 Kings 2:28–34) executes a general Davidic policy of life for life; but Joab also dies because he twice violated David's guarantees or oath, and perjured the state and its Lord.

The institution of *wergild,* which also appears in the Bible in Numbers 35, would seem incompatible with this formulation. Money for bloodshed is allowed not because the avenger is owed anything for the loss of a family member who is killed accidentally in the heat of a brawl, but because, again, all life (Heb. *nepeš,* "breath") belongs to God. Since only God can repay, the avenger must be prevailed upon not to take into his own hands what it is not his to take. What is bought by *wergild* is less life than time—time to settle the case, or purge the land of pollution. Otherwise it is forbidden: "Moreover ye shall take no satisfaction for the life of a murderer, which is guilty of death: but he shall be surely put to death" (Num. 35:31–34). The fugitive is *not* allowed to buy back his residency in the land he has polluted—and on which he would himself be a pollution—before the time prescribed by the rule for his exile in a city of refuge.

Adultery (VII), according to the commentary on the Decalogue that inaugurates Jesus' ministry, is committed with the heart (Matt. 5:27–28), which is why Job covenants with his eyes (Job 31:1, "I made a covenant with mine eyes; why then should I think upon a maid?"). But if it is an idol that ravishes the eye of a beholder (Isa. 44:9–20), and he commits spiritual fornication with it, then this kind of adultery is equally idolatry (Ezek. 23:30, 37: Israel and Judah have "gone a-whoring after the heathen" "and with their idols have they committed adultery"). In the words of the Geneva Bible, "the inventing of idols was the beginning of whoredom" (Wisdom 14:11). The prophet Hosea, who took a "wife of fornications," did so to allegorize Israel's idolatrous heart, its wayward "spirit of whoredoms" (Hos. 1:2, 4:12). Jeremiah 23:14 says Israel's prophets "commit adultery, and walk in lies." The prophets reserve their most heated sexual imagery for political promiscuity and the accompanying religious apostasy: Israel has enlarged its political bed to accommodate strange bedfellows (Isa. 57:8), and played the harlot to depart from God (Ps. 73:27). Adultery in this sense is a constant metaphor for religious and political impurity. Israel is a harlot when Hosea refers to the Name as "I am not her husband" (Hos. 2:2, RSV).

Insofar as adultery is impurity—in the way that bloodshed is pollution or defilement of the land (Num. 35:33)—it is a breaking down of any distinction given or made along sexual lines. God warns Israel against making itself unclean by homosexual relations or sexual relations with animals: "for in all these the nations are defiled which I cast out before you: And the land is defiled" (Lev. 18:24–25a). The same levitical code leaves adultery out of its version of the Decalogue at Leviticus 19 (vss. 3–4, 11–13, 30), but frames this chapter on both sides with elaborate prohibitions of sexual relations to various degrees of consanguinity (Lev. 18:6–23, 20:9–21). The text uses the metonymy of gazing on a given relation's nakedness for this kind of unchastity (Lev. 18:6–16); gazing on nakedness is the figure Joseph uses for the alleged crime of his brothers against Egypt (Gen. 42:9, 12), but this hostile gaze might seem to be interchangeable with their crime against him, in casting him naked into a pit. Ham's sin in viewing the nakedness of the drunken Noah (Gen. 9:22) also doubles as a crime, a man lying with a man (Lev. 20:13), if Ham "went in" to his father, and lay with him *incestuously*. The discretionary use of the metonymy, "to gaze upon another's nakedness," again points to the committing of adultery with the eyes, the sin being taken for the crime.

The sexual crime of Amnon against his half-sister Tamar is rape (2 Sam. 13:12, 14), an offense recognized in the Old Testament narrative in an almost programmatic way.[9] In 2 Samuel 13 it seems to be a variant on the occurrence of adultery in the House of David. Amnon's transgression reminds us that the Ammonites in Genesis are the issue of such an incestuous union, that of Lot and his daughters—the daughters took a rapist's advantage of Lot's drunkenness, if not his nakedness (Gen. 19:30–38). If the adulterous form of endogamy is incest, then the adulterous form of exogamy is miscegenation. Israelites are forbidden to marry Canaanites; Sodomites—being Hamitic—must be included. Intermarriage, or tribal adultery, leads to whoring after strange gods; at Exodus 34:16 the Ritual Decalogue mixes a ban on intermarriage with the one on idolatry; adultery is not otherwise specified. The Moabites descending from Lot's first daughter, however, are also "Lot-ites." So relations with them, while obviously promiscuous and idolatrous at the Baal-Peor of Numbers 25, might also subtly recoup a long-lost Nahorite solidarity; thus Ruth's approach to the bed of the drunken Boaz (Ruth 3:7–14) tends to confirm the Moabitess's descent from the daughter who caused Lot to beget Moab.

Coveting another man's wife is a crime analogous to coveting another tribe's daughters. Shechem's rape of Dinah (Gen. 34:1–2) is adulterous in this sense. Preaching spiritual purity, Paul is unwilling to see Christians make their bodies members of a harlot (1 Cor. 6:15); we can compare older concepts of the body of the congregation—the spiritual body of Christ, according to Paul—as *racially* pure. Anxieties about racial defilement can hardly have been far from the proselytizer's mind; Jacob becomes such a proselytizer in his attempt to accommodate Shechem's rape of Dinah, when she goes out to visit *the daughters of the land.* We might well replace the story's punchline, "Should he deal with our sister as with an harlot?" (Gen. 34:31), with the relevant injunction from the levitical decalogue: "Do not prostitute thy daughter, to cause her to be a whore; lest *the land* fall to whoredom, and *the land* become full of wickedness" (Lev. 19:29). Here the law contextualizes the seventh commandment in the threat of the land's defilement by the various sexual depravities of the Canaanite.

Dinah had also been kidnapped, and thus Jacob was hostage to Shechem's covetous demands. *Stealing a man,* the part of the crime that the commandment against **theft** (VIII) recognizes as capital (Exod. 21:16, Deut. 24:7), repeats the crime of the brothers against Joseph. To Jacob the money found in his sons' sacks must look very like the thievish earnings of slave-trading. The crime of which Joseph will finally accuse his brothers in court is in fact theft (Gen. 44:1–17), because the brothers have really tried to steal Joseph from Jacob, and thus to steal from them their paternal-filial *knowledge* of each other. Joseph aptly symbolizes this attempt on his brothers' part by alleging that his own alter-ego Benjamin has stolen his divining-cup. Such a narrative widens the crime of man-stealing to include stealth and fraud. Similarly, Moses in effect steals the body of the Egyptian he secretly kills, by hiding it in the sand (Exod. 2:12).

God calls Achan's furtive secreting of the enemy's goods from Jericho both theft and covenant-breaking (Josh. 7:11): here the crime of theft also includes bad faith and apostasy. Rachel steals Laban's images, a transgression that illustrates the common ground of idolatry and possessiveness; she seems to be punished by death (following from Gen. 31:32, "With whomsoever thou findest thy gods, let him not live"). Rachel's fraud illustrates that her desire has indeed been unto her husband, as per Genesis 3:16, as much as his had originally been unto her. But the theft may also be an attempt to take from God his right to bless whom he will bless, like the attempt of Balak in Numbers 22–23. The codes associate laws against witchcraft with repudiating the abominations of the nations (Exod. 22:18–20, Deut. 18:9–14), and thus Jacob's burying of foreign gods at Shechem (Gen. 35:2–4) has a closer association with the burial of Rachel in the way to Ephrath (Gen. 35:19) than at first appears. The gods are buried at Shechem under a local oak, as is Rebekah's nurse near Bethel (Gen. 35:4, 8). The oak and the nurse link the burials of the gods and the matriarch by way of Bethel's "oak of weeping." One kind of household god was called *teraphim,* "nourishers."

Assuming that they are a means to the inheritance of Laban's estate, Rachel's theft of the household gods from her father Laban is the parallel for her husband's theft of his blessing from his brother Esau—which is also a theft from his father Isaac. The scene of Laban's apprehension of Jacob, in Genesis 31, thus culminates in Laban's accusation, formerly leveled by Esau, that Jacob, in taking away both Laban's daughters and the offspring of his flocks, is twice a thief. The theft of Esau's blessing again widens the concept of theft toward the incrimination of covetousness, insofar as the blessing anticipates the whole patriarchal inheritance: for this is the kind of estate that can only be represented by the full listing of the objects of greed as otherwise found in enunciations of the tenth commandment. We may compare the narrative of Jacob's "oxen, and asses, flocks, and menservants, and womenservants" in Genesis 32:5, as they approach Jacob's rival Esau, with the manservant, maidservant, ox, and ass of the tenth commandment in Exodus 20:17. As for the "house" Jacob covets, he has mentioned it in his earlier question to his host Laban: "When shall I provide for mine own house?" (Gen. 30:30).

The theft-for-theft ethos of the Jacob narrative parodies the law of *talio*, but that does not seem to be the story's moral point. In the law, property thieves are not said to be punished by death, but neither are they rewarded—and Jacob is. His theft, like vengeance for bloodshed, must therefore in some sense be God's. Jacob's getting Israel is a theft so large that it can only be compensated for by donating its gains back to God. Jacob's offer of the tithe at Bethel (Gen. 28:22), the Lord's possessiveness in regard to the firstborn, the frequent description of Israel as God's inheritance, and the infrequent claim that the land belongs to God[10] all illustrate a principle of recompense in relation to Jacob's original design upon Esau's primogeniture. When God gives Jacob his other designation, Israel, at Penuel and Bethel (Gen. 32:28, 35:10–15), it is as if Jacob were relieved of the grasping selfishness betokened by his original name, or as if his theft were legitimatized, since he only contemplated the possession of—however covetously—the gift that Abraham's seed was originally promised.

Perhaps because of these implicit acknowledgments that the whole social order is founded on a theft—Israel's theft of the land from other occupants of Canaan—the extensive Near Eastern jurisprudence regarding more specific, individual thieveries is only feebly represented in the Pentateuch (a rare example is Exodus 22:7–15, on the abuse of safekeeping of goods). After Canaan, other thefts may look petty indeed; perhaps gratitude for the grant of the land sufficed to keep them that way, during the period of the formation of the Book of the Covenant. The most important thing about ordinary theft in the biblical legislation seems to be its simplification. In the Hittite laws there are so many rules about stealing and reparations that one suspects that in very materialistic ancient cultures theft constituted a kind of perpetual black market, and the laws were mainly the judiciary's attempt to regulate or rationalize this market according to rules of supply and demand. In such a code, theft seems to be an economic activity on a par with asking a price, setting a rent, paying a wage, fixing a rate, or making a trade. Every theft had its price: every recovery could therefore be treated as the calling in of an interest-bearing loan—the rules would be like those governing insurance claims. How much simpler, than tolerating this elaborate system of repayments and indemnifications, to simply ordain "Steal Not." (The turn away from such systems might also mean an end to *wergild* or blood money—as per Numbers 35:31, "take no satisfaction for the life"—though biblical allusions to the practice are found, for reasons earlier stated.) The thefts remaining in the biblical narrative, at any rate, are often thefts of persons or judgments, or theft from God. The young man who stole his mother's money, in Judges 17:1–6, is a case of theft from God: she was saving her silver for an idol (or at least for religious furniture). The mother gave her son the idol in return for his repentance, only to have both idol and priest stolen, in their turn, by those Danites who went on to found the shrine in Dan (Judg. 18:11–31)—this shrine is implicitly condemned as idolatrous by the link between the narrative of 1 Kings 12:28–30 and 13:1–6 with that of the golden calf of Exodus 32. If idolatry can also be theft from God, then covetousness can be a lust after false gods.

In the midst of the Chronicles version of Solomon's prayers dedicating the temple in Jerusalem, the king makes an entreaty to God on behalf of the social contract: "*If* a man sins against his neighbor and is made to take an oath, and comes and swears his oath before thy altar in his house, *then* hear thou from heaven, and act, and judge thy servants, requiting the guilty by bringing his conduct upon his own head, and vindicating the righteous by rewarding him according to his righteousness" (2 Chron. 6:22–23, RSV). This reprobation of perjury comes from the judge between the claims of the two mothers; he asks God to sanctify the temple by enforcing his ninth commandment there.

Solomon's appeal for divine sanctions against the bearing of **false witness** (IX) illustrates that this is a crime which is hard to witness: it is the very first offense treated in the Code of Hammurabi, because it subverts the royal justice system itself. In the biblical narrative the first important false witness in a royal state is Potiphar's wife (Gen. 39:7–20); the jail-sentence in which her perjury results is for the attempted ravishment of a master's wife by a master's slave, an offense that might appear in the class-conscious law codes of the ancient Near Eastern courts. The Old Testament narrative's last examples are the false witness of the elders against Susannah (she is a victim like Joseph), and Haman's testimony against the Jews. Haman accuses the Jews of disloyalty to the state, of flouting the king's laws, and accompanies his accusation with the promise of a large sum of money to the king for administering the Jews' persecution (Esther 3:8–9): "we are sold . . . to be destroyed," Esther declares (Esther 7:4). But in fact the Jews' leader Mordecai is on record as having betrayed a conspiracy to assassinate the king (Esther 6:1–2); he is an ideal *amicus curiae*.

Calumny, forbidden at Leviticus 19:16 ("Thou shalt not go up and down as a talebearer among thy people") and censured in Psalm 50:20 and Ecclesiastes 10:11, is linked to conspiracy to murder by Ezekiel 22:9 ("In thee are men that carry tales to shed blood"); it is punished with death in Psalm 101:5: "Him who slanders his neighbor secretly I will destroy" (RSV). The murmuring against Moses' (and Aaron's) presumptions to holiness in the wilderness is also calumnious, and its leaders are indeed cut off, in Numbers 16. The Korahites are also cut off, insofar as they are only Levites, from functions specifically Aaronid: their civil-political liability for rebellion is not really distinct from their religious-hygienic liability for a presumptuous proximity to the sacred vessels (Num. 18:3). Potiphar's wife is implicitly condemned by Proverbs 30:10, "Accuse [calumniate] not a servant unto his master, lest he curse thee, and thou be found guilty."

The jailing of prophets for speaking God's word offers a parallel for Joseph's jeopardy, if Joseph the dream-interpreter held in Pharaoh's prison is a parallel for Daniel the dream-interpreter thrown into King Darius's lions' den. The most important example of false witness is Jezebel, as the enemy of the Yahwist prophets; she uses her husband's seal to sign letters procuring the false accusation of Naboth (1 Kings 21:8–14). Pursuant to the plot in the letters, Naboth is accused of blasphemy by two scoundrels, a case which insists on the association of blasphemy with false witness: both transgressions abuse the name of God. The two witnesses violate the commandments of Exodus 23:1 and 7: "Thou shalt not raise a false report: put not thine hand with the wicked to be an unrighteous witness," and "Keep thee far from a false matter; and the innocent and righteous slay thou not: for I will not justify the wicked." Exodus 23:2 also convicts Jezebel of having inspired—and the people of having joined—a lynch mob: "Thou shalt not follow a multitude to do evil." As noted, the first law in Hammurabi's Code imposes capital punishment for the unproved murder charge. The life of a seignior, it appears, is owed for this kind of attempt on it. The blasphemy that Jezebel's witnesses allege appears to be what the Near East would in general have called rebellion, a crime against state-sponsored sacral orders, and thus offensive to both God and king. Moses' actions against the Korahites' calumny characterize it as rebellion against God. Something like bearing false witness is also implied in the wickedness that Balak attempts to purchase from Balaam, when he hires him to curse Israel, apparently in Yahweh's name

(Num. 22–24). Balak sins in trying to *hire* a witch to take Israel's life; Balaam sins in taking Balak's bribe: "And thou shalt take no gift: for the gift blindeth the wise, and perverteth the words of the righteous" (Exod. 23:8).

Job's comforters may not exactly be false witnesses, but his regular appeal for a courtroom hearing before God shows what he thinks of them: he has not done well in the slanderous court of men. One may compare the Psalmist pleading his good behavior toward those who have in return mocked and ruined him: "Plead my cause, O Lord, with them that strive with me. . . . False witnesses did rise up; they laid to my charge things that I knew not. They rewarded me evil for good to the spoiling of my soul" (Ps. 35:1, 11–12). Job charges God with about the same abuse. According to the prose, it is Satan who has made Job look so bad, like the confessed *satan* or opponent that opposes the advance of Balaam's ass in Numbers 22 (so vs. 32); but in Job this adversary has only been the agent of a test from the Father. God is thus implicitly accused of himself being the prosecutor of a false accusation: "he has shriveled me up," Job says, "which is a witness against me; and my leanness has risen up against me, it testifies to my face" (Job 16:8, RSV). The law in Leviticus 5:1, against keeping silent after witnessing a crime, also intentionalizes the sin of bearing false witness.

It is particularly the secret slander that Psalm 101:5 punishes, and it is chiefly the witness of the oath or curse that finds out the guilty accuser in Proverbs 30:10. This is even truer of the guilty in the Shechemite Duodecalogue: "Cursed be he that smiteth his neighbour secretly . . . Cursed be he that taketh reward to slay an innocent person" (Deut. 27:24–25). Almost all the crimes of the second table fall under a general offense of furtiveness: procured murder, adultery, theft, man-stealing, false witness, and covetousness—a curse is the only judicial means to a punishment. Job's catalogue of crime begins with fraudulently removing landmarks (Job 24:2a), the first crime against a neighbor cursed in the Duodecalogue (Deut. 27:17); the parallel member at Job 24:2b is cattle-rustling.

Covetousness (X) is listed with crimes, as if to promote this deduction, that no crime will bear inspection. Coveting another man's wife is hardly actionable, until the sin of coveting leads to the crime of adultery. The ordeal of jealousy in Numbers 5, for poisoning the guilty and exonerating the innocent through due process, confesses the unavailability of disinterested witnesses to such a crime; both the witnessing of the crime and the prosecution of the charge are left to God, as if the adulteress's offense were a sin punished by pollution, rather than a crime punishable by death. Curses in this area of the Shechemite Duodecalogue fall on sexual congress with family members (Deut. 27:20, 22–23); the pollution of mixing the category of wife with that of mother, sister, and mother-in-law is equivalent to that of mixing person with beast (Deut. 27:21).

The pairing of the coveting of another man's wife with the coveting of his house (Exod. 20:17) indicates that this sin tends to the violation of property rights. A man's house in the Bible may also be his posterity, which is to say, you cannot really take possession of his house unless you also take his life. Similarly, coveting another man's servant suggests a sin that tends toward the crime of stealing a man to sell him into slavery. The kidnapping of Joseph makes this motion exchangeable with murder. The sinful desire to take possession appears in Ahab's desire for Naboth's vineyard (1 Kings 21:18–19); murder is again the criminal consequence. Covetous intentions become criminal when they realize themselves in conspiracies: David's conspiracy to kill Uriah in order to be able to legitimatize his fathering of Bathsheba's child by taking her to wife parallels Ahab's conspiracy with a Baalist, Jezebel, to kill Naboth in order to legitimatize the state's confiscation of his land. Jezebel procures Naboth's murder, by stoning, by buying false witness to a capital crime; her two witnesses (as per Num. 35:30, Deut. 17:6) may have accused Naboth of cursing the king in ignoring a fast, as if he were a sabbath-breaker (cf. 1 Kings 21:9 and Jonathan's breaking of the king's fast at 1 Sam. 14:24–27).

The desire to take the wife, the life ("breath"), and the goods or house of the neighbor, and the willingness to commit perjury to avoid the legal consequences or to gain money, lead to crime in Israel. Thus covetousness is at the root of most of the evils of the second table, even if it is not punishable as a crime until it manifests itself in murder, adultery, theft, and false witness. Moses strongly denies any selfish reason for maintaining his authority over the people, in effect asking what evidence his accusers have of his covetousness and his abusiveness (Num. 16:15, "I have not taken one ass from them, neither have I hurt one of them"). In the possession of his evil spirit, Saul repeatedly seeks David's life (1 Sam. 22:23, etc.), as if the evil spirit was in fact some kind of covetousness. Saul's malady comes from God, and it is a kind of spirit of jealousy. It causes Saul to suspect David and try to kill him, even as he indicts Jonathan's love of David as undermining the son's right to his father's throne (1 Sam. 18:9–11, 20:30–31). Thus the jealous God of the first commandment and the first table is the counterpart of the evil spirit of covetousness of the last commandment and the second table. If all life belongs to God, then he is not only the paramount enemy of murder, but also, himself, the supreme taker of life. The obvious example occurs at the climax of the plague narrative, on the eve of the exodus itself. The life belonging to God does not belong to Pharaoh, or to the king.

This is also true of the life of the slave. The laws of release in Deuteronomy 15 might well have informed our understanding of Pharaoh's hin-
drance of Israel's departure, which the king does not suffer gladly. Since
Israel has gone out into the wilderness to serve God, Pharaoh is finally
guilty of a kind of covetousness toward another party's manservant. We
have noted that Israel departs from Egypt, in despite of Pharaoh, with the
severance-gift Deuteronomy prescribes. The same legislation warns against
regarding bondpersons covetously when the national year of release nears,
and therefore heartlessly stinting on charitable donations to the poor in
anticipation of the upcoming loss to one's estate (Deut. 15:7–10): " 'Take
heed lest there be a base thought in your heart, and you say, "The seventh
year, the year of release is near," and your eye be hostile to your poor
brother, and you give him nothing, and he cry to the Lord against you, and
it be sin in you' " (vs. 9, RSV). On this model Pharaoh has cursed himself—hardened his heart against the last commandment as well as the first.

If the Bible indeed describes virtually any sin one can imagine (as the
poet Blake says),[11] it nonetheless imagines them all in terms of infractions
of the relevant Mosaic commandments. We can tell that the various cited
episodes are all related to the Decalogue, because they typically become
causes célèbres: they are cases publicly aired, and are thus occasions for manifesting Mosaic, prophetic, or divine judgments, and for the taking of
public vengeance. In the New Testament, the account of Jesus in the Gospels breaks down any large distinction between teaching sign and healing
miracle; in the Old Testament, the record of judgments in Israel breaks
down any large distinction between the revelations made by statutory law
and case law. The Mosaic revelation recurs, whenever transgressions are
denounced by the narrative. We can tell that all these transgressions
involve covenant-breaking, like the one at Sinai, from pronouncements
like God's in the case of Achan in Joshua 7:15: "he that is taken with the
accursed thing shall be burnt with fire, he and all that he hath: because he
hath transgressed the covenant of the Lord, and because he hath wrought
folly in Israel."

Mosaic law assigns requital to God, and so equates sin, or guilt before
God, with crime, or guilt before men. Jesus, conversely, criminalized sinful
thoughts, equating sinful desires with illegal actions; the sinner should
abandon his sacrifice at the altar, if he has not surrendered his anger with
his brother before he gets there (Matt. 5:23–24). Similarly, Jesus treats
malicious speech as the thing that pollutes the mouth, from within rather
than from without (Matt. 15:11). Such prescriptions accord well—given a
context in various laws of holiness and purity—with Leviticus 19:17–18:
"You shall not hate your brother [neighbor] in your heart . . . you shall
not . . . bear any grudge against the sons of your own people" (RSV).

Samuel demonstrates that "the fat of rams" is useless to God if the sacrificer has not also yielded up his interior covetousness, and he tells a disobedient Saul that the real sin of idolatry is a failure of hearkening (1 Sam. 15:22–23). "None shall appear before me empty," the God of Moses commanded (Exod. 23:15, 34:20), and the barren Hannah felt her condemnation acutely from the outset: the humiliation of her barrenness left her with no heart to participate in the people's annual feast. But a broken and contrite heart is itself her sacrifice (Ps. 51:17), and so God hears her silent prayer that God give her a son to donate back to God. "Only her lips moved, but her voice was not heard" (1 Sam. 1:13), the text says, yet the prayer in question proves the opposite of lip service.

We may conclude that in the Bible sin and crime, ritual fault and moral fault, invisible and visible transgression are all opposed in order to be equated. We can recognize sin—crime against God—as crime, i.e., as sin against the neighbor, because of the metaphoric and metonymic qualities of the sins and crimes that translate into each other. The sin that Phinehas jealously reacts to at Baal-Peor is religious promiscuity and idolatry; but the episode, because of the sealing of pagan religious relations by temple prostitution, is cast in the form of an apprehension and punishment otherwise appropriate to an adulterer (Num. 25). The proscriptions connecting intermarriage with idolatry in the Ritual Decalogue speak to the same point: congress with the woman at Baal-Peor, Moabite or Midianite, is apostasy, because apostasy is promiscuous. Similarly, the destruction of the golden calf as "sin" seems to take the form of the "ordeal of jealousy," the trial by "bitter water" undergone by the woman accused of sexual crime (Num. 5:17–27). "I . . . am a jealous God" (Exod. 20:5)—or husband.

In all these cases, sinfulness is scarcely to be distinguished from criminality, the violation of a religious taboo from the violation of a civic law, incrimination from taint, and the malefactor's offense against a discerning God or his prophets from the certain cursing of a malefactor in Israel. The ordeal of jealousy is a special case of the general rule, that there is no great distinction in the pentateuchal law between purgative procedures for dealing with sin and judicial procedures for dealing with crime. The wife is practically put away like the golden calf. The ordeal also shows an attempt to get at the interior nature of sin. In the ancient laws a standard penalty for this sin was death by water, but insofar as the water procedure in the Bible and elsewhere tries to get God—or the water—to execute the sentence, it may also be trying to get the deity to render judgment upon guilt or innocence.[12] Hammurabi (no. 29), however, punishes the crime by first tying the accused parties together—there is little chance the water will prove them innocent. They will perish in their sins, having drowned each other in the immorality of their embrace.

Yahweh "is a jealous God; he will not forgive your transgressions nor your sins," Joshua tells the people; "God is jealous, and the Lord revengeth," the prophet deduces (Josh. 24:19, Nahum 1:2). To take the Lord's name in vain would be to ignore its weight, and so also to re-create it: for his name is Jealous (Exod. 34:14). The Lord who is jealous is also zealous, especially against the individual's attempt to usurp the divine prerogative in the taking of life. It is for crimes against the Decalogue that vengeance is primarily a jealous God's. These are therefore crimes for which vengeance is taken by the community, on God's behalf, because his community is the logical instrument for his reprisal for offenses to him. The purge of idolators, at Exodus 32:27–28, provides the first example. Thus what is originally meant by the sentence "Vengeance is mine, saith the Lord," is not that the community should ignore wrongdoers, but that God takes offense at those crimes and parties that undermine the constitution and well-being of his community, and to which the death penalty attaches. Phinehas clearly takes his vengeance on God's behalf, not his own. On the other hand, the community commissioned to take vengeance for crime is also obliged to provide refuge for the manslayer who has killed by accident (and so stained himself), to save the manslayer (within the place and period of sanctuary) from the private "avenger of blood"— whom the law recognizes as otherwise entitled to take life for life on behalf of the principle of *talio* (Num. 35:20–29). But generally God deprives kin of revenge for murdered kin: vengeance is mine, saith the king or the magistracy or the people. Only when the king does nothing about Amnon's rape of his half-sister (2 Sam. 13:21–22) does the obligation to take vengeance revert to her brother Absalom.

In many ways the Mosaic community is the keeper of its members' morality—as Jesus recognizes when he argues against removing the mote from the neighbor's eye when there is a log in one's own (Matt. 7:3–5, Luke 6:41–42). Jesus thus argues for a different priority, for the individual taking responsibility for his own morality. In the Gospel the individualization of the subject's answerability, as in the case of the woman taken in adultery, is the necessary precondition for the individual's conversion to the Kingdom of God, but in the sixth-century prophets the analogous individualization (especially in Ezekiel 18) is only the precondition for the survival of an Israelite morality in the face of the destruction of an Israelite polity. Threats against a failure to keep God's law cannot be visited upon the commonality, if these threats are already being made good in the impending demise of the state itself.

In the prophets, Israel was condemned for breaking the law. The most explicit text is Jeremiah 7:9, where Israel is asked, "Will ye steal, murder, and commit adultery, and swear falsely, and burn incense unto Baal, and walk after other gods whom ye know not?" Yahweh's house has become known as a den of robbers, and God will do to it what he has done to Shiloh. The first ten books of the Bible, as David Noel Freedman has suggested to me and others,[13] seem to agree with this prophet: Israel has become guilty for violating each of the Ten Commandments, and, at the end of a history of sin, the temple is destroyed. Using Jeremiah's reversed order for the sins of murder, adultery, and theft (i.e., reading VIII, VI, VII, theft, murder, adultery), Professor Freedman offers, makes the overall history a kind of roll call of offenses punishable by death:

1) Genesis: *contra* having other gods before the Lord (I): the revelation to Adam, Enosh (Gen. 4:26), Noah, Melchizedeck, and the patriarchs, and the putting away of foreign gods from beyond the river, as first promoted by Jacob after a communication from God to build him an altar at Bethel (Gen. 35:1–4); Rachel may die for retaining Laban's household gods; Israel's fathers served other gods before the revelation to Moses, according to Joshua 24:2, 14–15.

2) Exodus: *contra* making of graven images (II): idolatry of the golden calf (Exod. 32), for which the Levites slaughter the offenders, as demanded by Moses.

3) Leviticus: *contra* taking the name Yahweh in vain (III): the sin of the Israelitish woman's son, a "blasphemer" (Lev. 24:10–16), for which the blasphemer is stoned, as decreed by Moses—the Levites are the keepers of the holiness of God's name, and Leviticus invokes it the most often of any book in the Bible, notably in the formulae "I Yahweh your God [am] holy" and "I [am] Yahweh your God" (Lev. 19:2, 3, AR).

4) Numbers: observing of the Sabbath (IV): sabbath-breaking of a stick-gatherer who did not keep the day holy, for which the sabbath-breaker is stoned, as decreed by Moses (Num. 15:32–36).

5) Deuteronomy: honoring the parents (V): positively, the preservation of the Mosaic tradition itself as part of covenant-honoring (Lev. 19:32, "Thou shalt . . . honour the face of the old," with Deut. 34:10, "And there arose not a prophet since in Israel like unto Moses, whom the Lord knew face to face," and Deut. 32:7, " 'Remember the days of old, / consider the years of many generations; / ask your father, and he will show you; / your elders, and they will tell you' " [RSV]); *or*, negatively, the failure of the Israelites to honor the Lord's promise to give the land to their fathers Abraham, Isaac, and Jacob—after passing by the land God has given to the children of Esau, the children of Lot, and the children of Ammon (Deut. 1:8, 2:8–9, 19), God thus honoring his deal with their fathers—while the Israelites are sentenced to die in the wilderness with Moses for not promptly accepting the land-gift.

6) Joshua: *contra* theft (VIII): Achan's embezzlement from the Lord at

Jericho, for which he and his family are stoned, after the death sentence (by fire) decreed by Joshua (Josh. 7:18–26).

7) Judges: *contra* murder (VI): Abimelech's killing of his seventy brothers, for which Abimelech is killed under the wall (Judg. 9); and the Gibeahites' aggravated assault and murderous rape of the Levite's concubine, for which Gibeah is destroyed, as demanded by the Levite (Judg. 19:22–30), who may himself technically be the agent of her death.

8) 1–2 Samuel: *contra* adultery (VII): David's sin with Bathsheba, for which Nathan sentences their first child to die and David's harem to be used publicly by David's son Absalom as counseled by Ahithophel (2 Sam. 11; 16:20–22); and Amnon's rape of his virginal half-sister Tamar (2 Sam. 13), for which he dies at the hands of her brother Absalom.

9) 1–2 Kings: *contra* bearing false witness (IX): Jezebel's hiring of false witnesses against Naboth (1 Kings 21:9–13), for which Elijah pronounces on her a death sentence, which is carried out when she is thrown from a window at the behest of Jehu (2 Kings 9:30–37).

10) 1–2 Kings; *contra* covetousness (X): Ahab's coveting and possession of Naboth's vineyard (1 Kings 21)—for which the king is killed in battle, "according unto the word of the Lord which he spake" through Elijah (1 Kings 22:38).

The most important sin inveighed against in Deuteronomy is idolatry (Deut. 11:16; and 29:25–26: "they have forsaken the covenant of the Lord God of their fathers, which he made with them when he brought them forth out of the land of Egypt: For they went and served other gods . . . whom they knew not"). This is much the same sin—and in much the same words—which God warns Israel against in his covert prediction of the ruin of the temple, at its dedication (1 Kings 9:6–9, "they forsook the Lord their God, who brought forth their fathers out of the land of Egypt, and have taken hold upon other gods, and have worshipped them, and served them" [vs. 9]). The speeches point to about the same end, namely "the captivity of the land." If, as scholars generally suggest, we owe late forms of the second half of the overall narrative to the editing of a deuteronomic school, and if these books constitute or at least contain within them a canon of sins and crimes against the covenant, we are then likely to be impressed by the central place of Deuteronomy itself, at the place where the first table ends and the second begins, the break between Deuteronomy and Joshua corresponding to a formal division between the relation of the sinful Israelite to God in the wilderness and the relation of the criminal Israelite to his neighbor on the land.

If one is obliged to care for the neighbor as the self, this duty could well include preserving the neighbor from the baleful effects of his own potential immorality. But the force of the commandment against covetousness, taken with the cursed sins of the Shechemite Duodecalogue in Deuteronomy 27, is that morality cannot be legislated: the legislation cannot be enforced. The curse is the only sanction one can pronounce upon crimes doomed to remain secret and beyond the reach or perception of those offended by them. Secret crimes, like sinful intentions, are not subject to the collective enforcement of public morality, because they are beyond exposure to public agents. Covetousness is initially sin, not crime. Yet the idea of the Pentateuch is generally the other way. For while it may be impossible to legislate secular morality, the morality of the community gathered around one God will itself have virtually legislative force.

The first table implies the second, because God's adoption of Israel is a covenant relation, implying Israel's adoption of God: along with his oneness, truthfulness, sanctitude, purity, gravity, interior possession, jealousy, and righteousness. Knowledge of this God is indissoluble from moral awareness—and relations with him are conditional upon some degree of successful moral effort. God knows the sinner's sin, but only if the sinner can also be brought to know it is he in a position to know God, by beginning to know as God might. The pious man lives happily in the law, "For the Lord knoweth the way of the righteous" (Ps. 1:2, 6).

The knowledge of God includes the knowledge of the obligation to the neighbor. The levitical motive-clause for loving the neighbor as the self is: "I [Yahweh] am the Lord" (Lev. 19:18). The Lord is holy (Lev. 20:7–8). Devotion to the neighbor is prescribed as the relation is made sacred. To love the neighbor as the self is also to understand that the neighbor is the self sanctified in its communal aspect: "he" is "we." Crimes against him are alienations from the community's Yahwist self, insofar as it is constituted by both us and him. The community of man and God is divinely constituted: the community's alienation from itself cannot be other than man and God's alienation from each other: "For the Lord knoweth the way of the righteous"(Ps. 1:6) and cuts himself off from those who have only known the way of the wicked (Prov. 2:20–22, 4:18–19, 15:29, 21:12; Ps. 119:118–119, 146:9b): "The wicked are estranged from the womb" (Ps. 58:3).

The laws explicitly against begrudging charity to the neighbor (Deut. 15:10, Lev. 19:18) seem one with an unspoken law against begrudging obeisance to the law. But in Romans 7 Paul says the law convicts the sinner *provocatively:* it cannot remove the sins its declaration actually abets and takes advantage of, when it drives the tendencies it indicts underground, and so further ingrains them in one. Thus the Hebrews' release from slavery, if prescribed by a biblical law or edict of release, serves merely to aggravate Pharaoh's covetousness. Jeremiah says the tongue "is as an arrow shot out; it speaketh deceit: one speaketh peaceably to his neighbour with his mouth, but in heart he layeth his wait" (Jer. 9:8). Indicting the incorrigible evil of a human imagination—"The heart is deceitful above all things, and desperately corrupt; / who can understand it?" (Jer. 17:9, RSV)—his words recall the divine pronouncements framing the story of the Flood.[14] Hence Jeremiah must promise that men will receive a new heart, virtually at God's dictation (Jer. 24:7, 31:33, 32:39): in this way the law is to be graciously given anew, on clean slates, and defined again as a God-given gift. But even if forgiveness can give a transgressor back his former, lost acceptability, Moses also says, " 'to this day the Lord has not given you a mind to understand, or eyes to see, or ears to hear' " (Deut. 29:4, RSV): only in Moab could Moses' audience recover a heart to serve God. The Sinai events themselves incorporate indications of the law's latter-day recovery, if the text has to be re-issued at its first promulgation. Hence the narratives in which the text of the law is consolidated point not so much to an original revelation as to a latter-day moral rearmament.

The conversion of Israel to God's law is also one with its conversion to the holiness of the first-person voice speaking through Moses in the Holiness Code. For the law-speaker is dedicated to law-keeping through the law's very enunciation. Law-abidingness, after all, necessarily begins from keeping the law in plain view. "Ye shall be holy: for I the Lord your God am holy"; "Ye shall keep my sabbaths, and reverence my sanctuary: I am the Lord"; "Sanctify yourselves therefore, and be ye holy: for I am the Lord your God. And ye shall keep my statutes, and do them: I am the Lord which sanctify you"; "Ye shall therefore put difference between clean beasts and unclean: . . . and ye shall not make your souls abominable by [any] beast . . . which I have separated from you as unclean. And ye shall be holy unto me: for I the Lord am holy, and have severed you from other people, that ye should be mine" (Lev. 19:2, 30; 20:7–8, 25–26). These cannot be the words of one with unclean lips: repeating the prescribed terms to his people, Moses is remade in the image of divine righteousness, his speech having become—like his mouthpiece Aaron—"holy unto the Lord."

Leviticus 19 identifies law-keeping as keeping faith with God's sacrality. Other ancient law codes do not presume this feature, which belongs, rather, to the exclusivist royal legislation of ancient covenants. The narrative of Achan in Joshua 7 makes most of the pentateuchal points, because Achan steals from the community and its well-being, while at the same time stealing directly from God. In terms of the ancient treaties, Achan is a receiver of stolen goods—stolen from the king. Joshua's campaign against Ai goes badly, Achan having secretly withheld spoil from the victory over Jericho. The national will, as a result, is not correctly constituted: it is less than wholly consecrated. The things Achan takes sound like future temple goods—his sin is a kind of proto-sacrilege, against temple and tithe. Regarding Jericho's spoil, the narrative reports, "The silver, and the gold, and the vessels of brass and of iron, they put into the treasury of the house of the Lord" (Josh. 6:24)—before, indeed, there was any shrine to house this treasure. With a like exactitude, Achan reports how he sinned against Israel's God: "When I saw among the spoils a goodly Babylonish garment, and two hundred shekels of silver, and a wedge of gold of fifty shekels weight, then I coveted them, and took them; and, behold, they are hid in the earth in the midst of my tent, and the silver under it." And Joshua's agents indeed do find "it was hid in his tent, and the silver under it," "and they . . . laid them out before the Lord" (Josh. 7:21–23).

In his speech Achan totals up a take for which a tent-dweller seems unlikely to have much real personal use—in his actual circumstances, what could he do with such ill-gotten gains except go on hiding them under his rug? This hoarding in Achan's tent seems as anachronistic as the depositions in the Lord's "house." We cannot exactly understand why Achan has done what he did, except as he was driven to do it by its illegality—as Paul said, "I had not known lust [*epithumia*, ardor beside itself], except the law had said, Thou shalt not covet" (Rom. 7:7). But here is a man devoted to the Mammon of covetousness, even before the Mammon of money exists.

Indeed, the Mammon of covetousness does not exist either, except as a reclusive withholding of the clan-self from the nation-self: Achan had not known the anxiety for clan exclusiveness, except the collective effort had said, Thou shalt not covet it. He has thus made the swag more important than his communal membership, or the community's systematic enrichment of the treasury of the Lord. For Achan this membership was not "more precious than fine gold; . . . than the golden wedge of Ophir" (Isa. 13:12). It is thus significant that the prophetlike judgment that falls on him also falls on his hapless family: his maintenance of his private cache has blighted both a smaller and a larger community; he is punished both in himself, and in his part of the nation, those sharing his tent. They have harbored a thief—not altogether unwittingly, we might guess.

Jesus says, when a member of the corporate body offends that body, the body is obliged to cut it off and cast it away (Matt. 5:29–30). Joshua passes the same judgment on Achan, and the episode is a major one in his book. The dramatized representation of Moses' own concern with *ḥerem* (the ban on the private appropriation of the enemies' goods) is much smaller, but Moses' funding of the priesthood is much larger. Thus the Mosaic episode corresponding to the one concerning Joshua and Achan, namely the stoning of the man found gathering sticks on the Sabbath, in Numbers 15, makes a somewhat analogous point. The man's priorities were not Mosaically ordered. It is not enough, then, to explain that Moses' concern with constituting the priesthood—or indeed God's concern—reflects the interests of the Priestly authors, as if this ignored the larger interest. On the contrary, the priestly corporation is a representation of Israel as analogously constituted, "a kingdom of priests, and an holy nation" (Exod. 19:6), a nation that cannot serve itself without serving God. Observing his Sabbaths and furnishing his priests constitute the care of his nation.

Sins against the gods do not bulk large in the ancient Near Eastern law corpora. Rebellions against the whole establishment are little contemplated there. The sin of which Naboth is accused is a rare case of a crime that is at once against God and against the king: significantly, the accusation is false. And a crime like adultery is not ordinarily a crime against the king or the gods: it is merely offensive to a member of a given class. The story of Absalom's sin with David's harem is a notable biblical exception (2 Sam. 16:20–22), but it makes visible not only rebellion against the king, but also the king's own rebellion against God's law. Adultery in ancient Near Eastern law codes can earn vengeance or require compensation, and an offending woman is not treated mercifully.[15] Perhaps in doubtful cases arrangements can be made: some of the scenario necessarily turns on getting caught, and where the offense takes place.[16] But the gods do not, themselves, seem to be watching, even if they take cases at the river. The situation is quite different in the biblical narrative: a king himself is brought to the bar for committing adultery. The thing which David did he "didst . . . secretly," and it "displeased the Lord"; "And David said unto Nathan, I have sinned against the Lord" (2 Sam. 12:12, 11:27, 12:13). Yahweh is in the place of the jealous husband. Adultery is apostasy, and civil crime is no less sinful than religious pollution. The death of the first child of this union is surely as close to religious expiation as it is to payment of damages. "For all the firstborn of the children of Israel are mine," saith the Lord (Num. 8:17): he might have been speaking to Bathsheba. Or he might speak as the firstborn's parent. He is also in the place of the jealous property-owner, for it is his lots that discover the sacrilege of Achan.

If Achan was among the spies who gave Rahab the red thread to mark her window (Josh. 2:18–21)—being a Zerahite he might have worn on his wrist the red thread that was a Zerahite's birthright (after the birth of Zerah in Gen. 38:27–30)—then the spy has become the spied upon. The invader has become the invaded. Achan's furtiveness betokens a veritable fall into privacy and private wealth, a retreat into his own tent from the life of the community. Joshua provides him an opportunity to confess like the one that God offers the primal sinners: Joshua's "tell me now what thou hast done; hide it not from me" parallels God's question to Eve, "What is this that thou hast done?" (Josh. 7:19, Gen. 3:13). In a similar exposure of Adam's separation from God, God asked Adam who told him he was naked (Gen. 3:11). When the people are lamenting God's desertion of them, God orders them to put off their ornaments "that I may know what to do unto thee" (Exod. 33:5). God's omniscience is a projection from the collective surveillance of individual conduct. It is the presence of God and the community that tells the Israelite that he is naked. This surveillance is made possible, in some stories, by the lots. The lots discern Achan's "trespass in the accursed thing" (Josh. 7:1), as they discover that Jonathan is the violator of a wartime vow in 1 Samuel 14:36–46.

Of the many biblical retailings to the exodus, one of the most severe is found in Ezekiel 20, but this chapter's reduction of Israel's experience to that of a community under the constant threat of plague and pollution is not unfaithful to a strand of surveillance that runs throughout much of the Pentateuch, as if Israel's confinement in the wilderness were forty years of quarantine. The society that defines itself as constantly afflicted by plagues, and by such preventative practices as burning the edges of its encampments (cf. Num. 11:1–3), excluding the diseased from its midst (Lev. 13:45–46, Num. 5:1–4, 12:15, Deut. 23:10–11), performing rites of atonement (Lev. 16:3–10, 23:26–32; Num. 29:7–11), purging its cult (Exod. 32:27, Num. 9:13; 16, esp. vs. 26, "touch nothing of theirs"; Num. 25), and anticipating a "leprosy of houses" (Lev. 14:33–54)—this society is the same one upon which the law descends, having come from a similarly proscribed mountain (Exod. 19:12–13). A community afflicted by plagues is likely to be one regimented by laws for purification, and a society defining itself as a nation of priests is likely to cleanse itself on the model of a priesthood. The first woman shows this tendency when she adds to the commandment against eating the fruit, "neither shall ye touch it" (Gen. 3:3). She is already "making a fence around the law" (*Pirke Aboth* 1:1), as the biblical jurisprudence also tends to do for itself. She will have made herself "guilty" according to the language of Leviticus, "if a soul touch any unclean thing, . . . and if it be hidden from him; he also shall be unclean, and guilty" (Lev. 5:2; cf. 22:5–8)—contact with the fruit makes her not only guilty, but also unclean. Her offense is criminal and covetous, or sinful and sacrilegious.

As the nakedness of the original sinner indicates, this people is bent upon the project of a community-shared omniscience.[17] Rahab's marked window in Joshua 2 is significant, like the marked doors in Exodus 12:7 and 13. It is the point through which the Israelite informants pass to bring back their information about Jericho, but it is also the point where the confessing Yahwist Rahab can be recognized and thereby saved. And thus the story of Rahab in her house, in the wall of Jericho, is "Part A" of a narrative of which "Part B" has been the story of Achan, in his tent in Israel. In the story of Achan, the tent of the invader became the thing invaded, because a part of Jericho had surreptitiously found its way into his tent. Conversely, Rahab secured a house for her family in Israel, because she adopted the consciousness of the invaders: the house of the invaded became a house of the invaders. Both characters "confess": both have deserted the conscience of their original group. But where this conscience fails to remain in Achan, it returned with the invaders to turn his tent into his personal Jericho, and his private sin into his public crime.

The equivalence of "iniquities" (*'āwon*, perversity) and "sins" (*hattā't*, the kind of sin for which one makes an offering) is found in a parallelism in Isaiah 59:2: "your iniquities have separated between you and your God, and your sins have hid his face from you." The equivalence of sin and crime reappears as a synonymy in the formulation of 1 John 3:4: "Whosoever committeth sin transgresseth also the law; for sin is the transgression of the law." The God who will write the laws on his people's heart is also the God who must give them a heart that is one (Jer. 31:33, 32:39): one with both tables. According to the Achan episode, to keep the table of God is also to keep the table of Israel. Each table keeps the other.

·III·

MORALIA IN EXODUM

"Let the Lord, the God of the spirits of all flesh, appoint a man over the congregation, who shall go out before them and come in before them, who shall lead them out and bring them in; that the congregation of the Lord may not be as sheep which have no shepherd."

(Num. 27:16–17, RSV)

Hear ye, all people and the folk as many as they may be, I have done these things through the counsel of my heart. I have not slept forgetfully, (but) have restored that which had been ruined. I have raised up that which had gone to pieces formerly, since the Asiatics were in the midst of Avaris . . . and vagabonds were in the midst of them, overthrowing that which had been made. . . . I have made distant those whom the gods abominate, and earth has carried off [swallowed] their foot(prints). This is the counsel of the father of fathers [waters].

(Pharaonic temple inscription from Middle Egypt, *ca.* 1486–1469 B.C., after *ANET,* p. 231)

·6·

THE BIRTH OF THE
LIFE OF MOSES

Part A. The Birth of Moses, and the Divine Sponsorship

Moses is the human hero of the exodus, and the life of the human hero is determined by its singularity or individuation, and this is so even if the hero represents a collective: the collective itself is individuated in the hero's name, like the corporation of the Pharisees in John 9:28, who are the "disciples of Moses" (RSV). In the Bible this individuality manifests itself in four possible origins: (1) a beginning from conception, (2) from birth, (3) from conversion, and (4) from—so to speak—nowhere. The resulting narratives are, respectively, the annunciation story, the birth story, the call story, and the allusion (for no story can develop here) to the candidate's obscurity, oddity, or exceptional unlikelihood for distinction: he may be the least of his tribe, or depreciated by a question. The Gospel of John, for example, lacks Jesus' nativity story; in its place it has the question: "Can anything good come out of Nazareth?" (John 1:46, RSV).

Each origin can be colored by the others: a prophet who is "called from the womb" has a vestigial conception story, as well as a call story; his calling is, as it were, hereditary. Similarly, a conception or birth in adverse or humble circumstances counts as an obscurity allusion. A child born to a barren or virginal mother, to whom conception is announced and who bears in obscure circumstances and dedicates the child to a calling, or receives an announcement of what his calling will be, enjoys the blessings of all four origins. The more complete the cycle of these motifs, the more something larger than the advent of the individual hero is betokened.

An example of this larger advent is the introduction of Samuel at the opening of a subcanon in the Former Prophets. Samuel, called repeatedly, is called from the womb by an annunciation story that features his barren mother being asked the prophetic question, "How long?" (1 Sam. 1:14, "How long wilt thou be drunken?"). This call disestablishes the sons of Eli, who administer the temple where Samuel himself is subsequently called, as a boy, and whose credentials are said to go back to the time when Eli's forebears "were in Egypt in Pharaoh's house" (1 Sam. 2:27). The prophets as a whole ask "How long?" in the accents of Moses' God speaking to Moses about the sabbath-breaking Israelites in the wilderness, "How long refuse ye to keep my commandments and my laws?" or with Moses and Aaron pleading with Pharaoh, "How long wilt thou refuse to humble thyself before me?" (Exod. 16:28, 10:3). But vision and word are at low ebb in Eli's time, and prophets are not yet called prophets: thus the call of Samuel to go and renew the mission of Moses and Aaron is not only Samuel's, but that *of prophecy itself*: especially of the king-making and king-unmaking prophet twin-born with the monarchy.

The beginning from conception of course includes the subject's gene-alogy. There is no obscurity allusion in the case of Samuel himself, if the interruption of his genealogy by the barren Hannah is the very point of including seven generations of it, going back to the original Ephraim (1 Sam. 1:1). But such an allusion is thrown back on Samuel's profession, in the question asked about the ecstatics among whom Saul is found in 1 Samuel 10:12, "But who is their father?" The question is asked both about the prophets and, covertly, about Saul as king; it makes doubtful descent a figure for doubtful authority. The Priestly genealogy of Moses attempts to claim Moses for the priesthood, since many of the Levite clans are also priestly orders, and the orders are thus at least genetically prior to Moses himself. But while the text gives the obscure Levites who sired Moses in Exodus 2 their specific names and lineage, it also confesses to the breach in the tradition it constructs: not only by anxiously insisting three times that "these are that Moses and Aaron" who sponsored the exodus (Exod. 6:26–27), but also by confining the descent from Levi to Moses to just three generations. It accomplishes its aims by making the Levites out-live the divinely imposed age-limit of one hundred and twenty years (Moses' own), and by making the wife of Moses' father that father's aunt. Such a genealogy is insisting that it can be remembered, since any given generation can witness to the two generations before it, or the two after it, or the one before it and the one after it. At the same time this text recurs to Moses' obscurity, by changing his being "slow of tongue" (Exod. 4:10) to his having "uncircumcised lips" (Exod. 6:12): Moses' speech, meta-phorically speaking, is outside the covenant of circumcision.

Extrapentateuchal examples of the biblical rhetoric for the obscurity of origins, and for the doubtfulness of authority, make the Mosaic case even more visible to us. Pharaoh will finally treat Moses and his Israel as a run-away slave, the way the heedless Nabal reacts to David: "And who is the son of Jesse? There be many servants nowadays that break away every man from his master" (1 Sam. 25:10). The rebellious Hebrew of Exodus 2:14 questions Moses as if he were an illegitimate successor to the presump-tuous Joseph: "Who made thee a prince and a judge over us?" Some time thereafter, in Midian, Moses asks the same kind of question about himself:

"Who am I, that I should go unto Pharaoh, and that I should bring forth the children of Israel out of Egypt?" (Exod. 3:11), just as David will ask God who he is, or what his house is, that he should be made heir to the kingship (2 Sam. 7:18). "Is not this the carpenter's son?" the Galileans find themselves asking after Jesus' performances in his own country: "Whence then hath this man all these things?" (Matt. 13:55, 56). The temple leadership's remarks about Jesus in the Gospel of John—"We know that God spake unto Moses: as for this fellow, we know not from whence he is" (John 9:29)—are designed to characterize the speakers as themselves Pharaoh-like: these "disciples of Moses" cannot hearken to the new Moses. But the exodus narrative had originally redirected the standard aspersion on status from God's servant to the servant's god: "Who is the Lord," Pharaoh asks, "that I should obey his voice?" (Exod. 5:2).

Pharaoh's preemptive denial of Yahwistic authority, *a fortiori*, echoes those who-questions that are the touchstones for human authority. Yahweh himself is now the dubious character. The questioning of divine and human credentials is also heard in Moses' original anticipation of rejection: "They shall say to me, What is his name?" (Exod. 3:13). Taken with all the pentateuchal texts in which Yahweh has indeed "spoken unto Moses," the question lets an audience hear a future law-speaker as if he were also a prophet who had come in God's name.

The only obvious "annunciatory" motif in Moses' birth story is the giving of his name; this nomination has been displaced from a natural prophetic position, prior to the birth of an announced savior, and it has not been assigned to the child's parents. It could, of course, have been placed directly after the birth, and still been explicitly annunciatory: as in Lamech's naming of Noah at Genesis 5:29, "he called his name Noah, saying, This same shall comfort us concerning our work and toil of our hands." The place of such an announcement is taken by the report of the lying midwives, who inform (or misinform) Pharaoh of the preternatural fertility of Israelite women. Their lie is the environment's malevolent projection, back toward the king, of Pharaoh's fear of the future, and of a future savior. But Moses' name and its etiology do not obviously identify him as a savior, unlike the titles, say, for the wonderchild Emmanuel (Isa. 9:6). Moses is, rather, a saved one, who has himself been "drawn out" of Egypt's waters.

The birth story is otherwise largely determined by its mediation of the Hebrew/Egyptian polarity found in the child's dual extraction: Moses is alternatively and alternately Moshe. In Hebrew, he is *drawn out*—of Egypt. In Egyptian, he is *born of*—the Hebrews. Moses' singularity is his duality, a Hebrew Egyptian and an Egyptian Hebrew. The interface points to the almost constitutive role the royal house will have in Moses' vocation. But what is combined in Moses is what is separated in the exodus. The birth story also points to this eventuality. Fated to be thrown into the Nile by Pharaoh's edict in Exodus 1:22, Moses is paradoxically saved by his mother's exposing him on the river. On the one hand, the bondwoman's son is adopted by Pharaoh's maternally-inclined daughter, while his fellow Hebrews have been conscripted for Pharaoh's work; on the other hand, the bondwoman is able to hire herself out as the foundling's nurse, and thus get herself reinstated as the child's mother. The servants are doing their masters' living for them, and the royal house is paying for what ordinarily a child secures for free. For the mother takes wages for nursing her own son. The despoiling of the Egyptians, a motif that turns up three times in the exodus narrative proper (Exod. 3:21–22, 11:2, 12:35–36), has already begun.[1]

The marked trace of an adoption formula in the princess's commission is likewise proleptic.[2] Her pronouncement, "*Take* this child," suggests she only adopts the child to put it up for further adoption; similarly, the mother only abandoned the child to preserve its life—and restore it to its mother. The princess's further action reconfirms Moses' status as "foundling," while the mother's reconfirms the child's status as "son": the two mothers change places twice. The law from Hammurabi's Code helps explain the logic: "If a seignior, upon adopting a boy, seeks out his father and mother when he [the seignior] had *taken* him [the boy], the foster child may return to his [biological] father's house."[3] This ruling provides for Moses' repeated repatriation to Israel, since the Princess, in seeking out a nurse for her adopted child, has sought out its biological mother, however inadvertently. In the double motion of both orphaning and parenting the child, the mother and the princess cooperate to identify the human sponsorship of the infant Moses with the religio-political sponsorship of an unborn Israel. For the text shortly has God say, "I will *take* you for my people" (Exod. 6:7, RSV): the birth story shows that the house of Pharaoh will be made instrumental in putting Israel up for divine adoption.

Further examples of Israel's divine adoption—beyond God's declaration of fatherhood in Exodus 4:22 and Hosea 11:1 and 1:10—are: "Is not he thy father that hath bought thee?" (Deut. 32:6); and "They shall come with weeping, and with supplications will I lead them: I will cause them to walk by the rivers of waters in a straight way, wherein they shall not stumble: for I am a father to Israel, and Ephraim is my firstborn" (Jer. 31:9). But cases of literal adoption procedure in the Bible are largely confined to the narrative of national origins; strikingly, in view of other codes, they do not figure in the laws of Israel. There are, however, no less than three biblical examples of adoption connected with either a foreign party or a foreign place: besides Moses the Levitical child in Egypt, adopted by the Egyptian royal house, there are Esther, the orphaned Jew in Babylon, adopted by her ethnic compatriot Mordecai, and Ruth's half-Moabite son in Israel, adopted by his Judaic grandparent Naomi. The other major instances are out-of-house adoptions by Abraham and in-house adoptions by Jacob and Joseph:

House of Abraham:
  Abraham designates Eliezer of Damascus as his heir, before the patriarch has any biological sons (Gen. 15:2);
  Abraham asks God to make Ishmael, born of the Egyptian Hagar, his heir, after Sarah has "obtained [a child] by her" (Gen. 17:18, 16:2).
House of Jacob-Joseph:
  Rachel names Bilhah's two (half-Nahorite) sons, after bearing them on her knees (Gen. 30:3–8); Leah names Zilpah's two (half-Nahorite) sons (Gen. 30:9–13);
  Jacob blesses his two (half-Egyptian) grandsons Ephraim and Manasseh from between Joseph's knees (Gen. 48:5–14);
  Manasseh's (one-eighth Egyptian) grandchildren, the sons of Machir, are borne on Joseph's knees (Gen. 50:23).

These familiar instances can seem poor preparation for appreciating God's momentous declaration of his resolve in Exodus 6:6–7: "I will redeem you . . . with great judgments: And I will take you to me for a people, and I will be to you a God," where God in the legal originals would have merely been "father," and where the great judgments would have been the decree of a court legalizing or notarizing the adoption. Nonetheless, spiritual adoption is a step away from legal adoption, as adoptive parentage is a step away from biological parentage. And it is the predominance of the latter-day political-legal *figuration* over the former ethnic-tribal *ground*, in which our point about the theologized sonship of Exodus 4:22 and Hosea 11:1 consists, if indeed the Bible reconfigures the Near Eastern practice of "fictitious adoption" for its expression of divine sponsorship.

If some of the examples cited are post-exilic, then the adoption they promise to Israel is a form of the abridging of a critical *interruption* in the nation's sponsorship. The same interruption is expressed by the narrational "blank" between the period of Genesis and that of Exodus. The Hebrews of the exodus could have said to God, with the exiles in Babylon: "Doubtless thou art our father, though Abraham be ignorant of us, and Israel [i.e., *Jacob*] acknowledge us not: thou, O Lord, art our father, our redeemer" (Isa. 63:16). The flurry of blessings and adoptions at the end of Genesis designs to abridge an analogous "blank." For the number of generations between Jacob's son Joseph and Machir's sons is the same as that between Jacob's son Levi and Moses: four. God twice declares he will be gracious even to the third and fourth generation (Exod. 20:5–6, 34:7). Jacob's curse on Levi, however, disjoins him from his brothers and scatters him in Israel (Gen. 49:5–7). This curse is transformed by the adoption of the Levites into the landless priesthood, but one also wonders if it might not figure in keeping Moses out of the promised land.

Is there a further reason, besides the metaphor of God's post-Abrahamic adoption of Israel, why Moses should appear as a foundling in Egypt, and as a stranger in Midian? Why might Moses, in particular, be shown dependent on foreign care? This way of asking the question suggests that Moses' birth itself illustrates the appeal to mercy in the motive clauses of the Mosaic legislation, especially in the deuteronomic rendition of its demands. For the Israelite is to treat people considerately and well, because he is to consider that he was once himself a stranger in Egypt. He is to succor the orphan and the widow, and, in a significant injunction in Deuteronomy (12:18–19, etc.), he is to care for the Levite. Moses is a Levite, and there are reasons to believe that the situation of the Levite could become precarious—he had no land, and in the time of the dispossession of the Northern sanctuaries he may even have become something of a charity case, like the priesthood of Shiloh, according to the prediction of the "man of God" to Eli in 1 Samuel 2:36: God is to raise up a faithful priest—and a more exclusive priesthood—"And it shall come to pass, that every one that is left in thine house shall come and crouch to him for a piece of silver and a morsel of bread, and shall say, Put me, I pray thee, into one of the priests' offices, that I may eat a piece of bread." Moses' blessing of Levi in Deuteronomy 33:8–11 insists that the sons of Levi are virtually Moses, and that the priestly services of God's word and covenant have required the Levite to forgo the normal benefits of the tribal network. In order to be adopted of God, Levi "said of his father and mother, 'I regard them not'; he disowned his brothers, and ignored his children" (vs. 9, RSV).

The narrower question is the treatment of foundlings, as opposed to the dispossessed. There seems to be, in all the very considerable legislation of the Old Testament, no provision for the foundling. Yet such a phenomenon is well known in ancient societies. The story of Moses, after all, itself begins from an edict commanding infanticide. There is a feeling, in the story of Moses' infancy, as in the story of the Egyptian bondwoman Hagar, that the exposing of children is indeed something that happens in the world, but that the God of the oppressed is a guarantee against its happening in Israel. Those who call Abraham their father do not sacrifice their children. Those who have adopted Moses' God do not expose those children. Both the young Isaac and the unborn and outcast Ishmael were saved by the God who provides (Gen. 22:8, 13–14; 16:11–13, 21:19). So Israel had its life preserved by the God who found it in the wilderness

(Hos. 9:10, Ezek. 16:4–6 with 20:10–11), and so Moses was saved by the providential interventions of his mother. Yet a suspicion crosses the birth narrative. The mother hid the newborn, "when she saw that he was a *goodly* child" (Exod. 2:2): what might she have done with him had he *not* been?

We have commented on the traditional legislation represented by the Babylonian law that gives a father the power to legalize natural children for the purpose of giving them a part in the father's estate, where the father's declaration "You are my children" suffices.[4] In the Bible such a procedure is replaced by the divine action making Israel God's inheritance, heir, as it were, to God's relation to the patriarchs (like the landless Aaronites at Num. 18:20), and to that part of his creation which is Canaan (cf. Deut. 4:20–21). The God who calls his son out of Egypt also calls a subject into sonship: "I will declare the decree: the Lord hath said unto me, Thou art my son; this day have I begotten thee" (Ps. 2:7).

Whether or not we consider the "obscurity" of Moses' origin to be unobscured or reobscured by the story is less important, perhaps, than its indications of an epochal break with the past. The bitumined ark in which Moses is set upon the Nile cannot help but allude to the ark in which Noah crossed the gap between the Sethite and Semite genealogies in Genesis 5 and 11. The comparison of Flood stories to accounts of origins—those of founder figures included—is suggested by the frequent occurrence of either one as a motif in the other. Thus Sir James Frazer, writing on the story of Moses as foundling, also remarks on the story of Moses as founder:

> Such marvellous tales appear to have been told particularly of the founders of dynasties or of kingdoms, whose parentage or upbringing were forgotten, the blank thus left by memory being supplied by the fancy of the story-teller. Oriental history furnishes an instance of a similar glamour thrown over the beginning of a powerful empire. The first Semitic king to reign over Babylonia was Sargon the Elder. . . . [5]

Sargon was found by the court gardener, or a superintendent of irrigation, in the requisite floating basket.[6] Frazer's reasoning here is compatible with that of George E. Mendenhall on "the function of Flood stories in many cultures" as "a way to explain a gap resulting from failure of historical memory or due to a period of accelerated social change."[7] Northrop Frye prescribes a similar "motif of amnesia" as inaugural for a romance:

> Whether romance begins with a hero whose birth is, as Wordsworth says, a sleep and a forgetting, or whether it begins with a sinking from a waking world into a dream world, it is logical for it to begin its series of

adventures with some kind of break in consciousness, one which often involves actual forgetfulness of the previous state. We may call this the motif of amnesia. Such a catastrophe, which is what it normally is, may be internalized as a break in memory, or externalized as a change in fortunes or social context.[8]

But such a "break in memory," itself, is not unique to romance; it may be implicit at the outset in any comprehensive history whatsoever. Thus Thucydides, proposing to describe the polarization that led to "the greatest movement yet known in history," the Peloponnesian War, has assured himself, "by means of an inquiry carried back as far as was practicable," that no comparable events had ever occurred before in "Hellas": "on the contrary, before the time of Hellen, son of Deucalion, the appellation itself did not exist."[9] Hellen resembles Shem, whose Flood-hero father marks a limit beyond which inquiry into a given *gens*—or development—cannot go.

Livy, similarly, begins his history of the rise of "the mightiest empire the world has ever known" from the founding legend of Romulus and Remus. The Roman author suggests that the story of the conception of the twins, through the rape of a Vestal Virgin by Mars, may have only been offered to explain an illegitimate pregnancy—similar things, of course, have also been said about the origins of the story of the Egyptian princess who found Moses. The Italic king, at any rate, was not having it: he ordered the scandalous twins to be exposed on the Tiber. Because a flood prevented the men assigned the task from reaching the shore of the river itself, "the basket in which the infants had been exposed was left high and dry by the receding water."[10] (The she-wolf then found and nursed the twins, followed by the king's herdsman and his wife—but, Livy says, this woman may have been a common whore.) Illegitimacy is logically doubled with exposure in such stories (twice, in Livy), because the emergence of the hero challenges the legitimacy of the powers that be—and that would put him to death. Thus the Cyrus of Herodotus is exposed after the announcement of his future greatness to King Astyages, whose daughter had been destined to give Cyrus birth: for the king dreamt that he saw "so much water passing from her, as to fill an entire city and innundate all Asia."[11] Otto Rank, in his famous study of such legends, also cites Ctesias's lost account from Nicolas of Damascus (Frag. 66), where it is Cyrus's mother who reports the dream, to Cyrus himself: she had dreamt it while giving him birth.[12] Psychoanalytic interpretation of the aqueous imagery here points to the infant's passage through the birth canal, as the "latent content"; but the "manifest content" is the onset of a floodlike revolution in the world order being entered by the protagonist of an epoch.

In Ctesias's account, the mother's dream of Cyrus's future greatness was hushed up, but the king heard of it all the same; then he sent his horsemen after the emergent rival, to whom he had previously been a patron. When Cyrus prevails over the attackers, the king goes into hiding in his palace; his hiding place is found out, and Cyrus kills Astyages' chief protector. Thereafter he marries this man's wife. Finally he turns to honor Astyages as a father. Also in this account, Cyrus was born of poor parents; but he had distinguished himself at court as a cup-bearer, and the chief cup-bearer (a eunuch) offered to adopt him. Subsequently, Cyrus's fortunes were advanced by the king himself. Cyrus summoned his parents to court to join him in his success—then it was that his mother recurred to her prophetic dream. The sequence shows us that not only does Moses' birth story occupy the head of a new history, but so also might the tale of Joseph. For Cyrus's stories contain a replete account of a hero's exposure and being "found," his social promotion and dynastic destiny, and his repatriation. We can constitute an equivalent account for the exodus, by taking the Joseph and Moses materials to be no less complementary. The emergence of Moses, moreover, asks to be grounded in even broader "saving histories," with which it shares these dialectical relations as well.

Part B. The Career of Moses, and the History of Israel from Joseph to Joshua

The Mosaic birth sequence illustrates a much vaster narrative pattern than its own, stretching from Joseph to Joshua, a story of which it is first recapitulatory, and then prefigurative. The stages of this story are as follows: (1) the subject's birth in the house of Israel; (2) the subject's "immersion" in Egypt; (3) the subject's appeal to the Egyptian ruling house (Moses as an infant "appeals" to the daughter from the river; as an adult he appeals to Pharaoh by the river [Exod. 7:15]); (4) the subject's negotiation with the ruling house (Moses' sister arranges for Moses' mother to be hired as his nurse; the Israelites are permitted to depart with gifts—even the most nuclear version of the story has Egypt endowing the Hebrews); (5) the restoration of the subject to "Israel" (as an infant Moses is returned to the care of his mother; as an adult he goes out to see the condition of his countrymen, and returns with his people to the borders of Canaan).

The story of Moses' birth belongs to a widely distributed story-type, even though it seems to challenge that type at every point.[13] This is the "rags to riches" story which is constituted as the sequel to a "riches to rags" story. A rejected but potentially royal child—or a technically royal but disinherited or rejected or endangered child—is cast out or exposed, thereby becoming a foundling. He is typically found in package form: swaddled, bundled, boxed, cribbed, encapsulated, or otherwise bound. The child is rescued from exposure and succored, or guarded, kept, preserved, suckled, or adopted: by rustics, servants, animal-tenders, animals, nature-spirits, or some socially marginal being—or by a god. He is reared "abroad," that is, during the period of rustication. He grows capable and "goodly," and then returns to his home, either succeeding to honors, recognition, or his original high status in the ascendant social class, or earning promotion, vindication, and removal of his original stigma while regaining his natural identity. The story of Oedipus is a deeply ironic rendition of this romance of vindication which turns the recognitions and family reunions into a tragedy of indictment.[14] In Neoplatonic allegorizations of it, the romance stands for the descent and return of the soul, orphaned in the material world and initiated into immortality in the spiritual one.[15] Indeed, both descent and foundling themes are not far from the biblical story in its enlarged form, which encompasses both the descent of Jacob-Israel into the "Sheol" or shadow-world of Egypt, and the finding and nurturing of the foundling Israel in the desert: the wilderness is the liminal state occupied by the candidates in an initiation rite.[16]

As the paradigm of the "family romance" applies to Moses, however, we can only note, with Freud quoting Otto Rank's study, that the paradigm is turned inside out: because of "national motives."[17] Moses is not a royal/rejected child; he is a low-born/sponsored child. He is not abandoned by his parent, or stolen from it, but preserved by it. That is, he is abandoned under very careful supervision: he is exposed not so much to the elements as to the literary motif of exposure. Nor is he the child of the royal house, or the princess, even if he might have been. He is reared (nursed) first by his mother, and thereafter in unspecified circumstances that make him appear to be "Egyptian." He is then adopted a second time, as an adult, by his wife's family and his father-in-law in Midian. Only then is he found sojourning among shepherds or peasants—when he is able to succor others (the sheep of the daughters of Midian), and when he has become a parent himself (the father of Gershom). It is his son who is named according to the rustication motif ("he called his name Gershom; for he said, 'I have been a sojourner [*ger*] in a foreign land'" [Exod. 2:22, RSV]). The paradigmatic story, as the example of Oedipus shows, makes the child alternately the child of Fate and Fortune; the Hebrew story, on the contrary, gives the Hebrews themselves a hand in shaping the activity of Providence. Moses returns from rustication not to reclaim princely status in Egypt, but to repudiate Egyptian status there altogether. And he seeks to reclaim status not for himself, but for Israel. He is born in "exile," and so his "home" is revealed as being "abroad"—his people's homeland in Canaan, toward which he turns his people, without ever actually returning himself.

Thus Moses' story keeps disturbing the paradigm, yet the paradigm keeps echoing through the story. Why? Not, I would argue, as Freud thought, because Moses is an Egyptian. Freud implies that, in some other story, Moses, son of—say—Ra, would have been saved from exposure by a peasant—say a Hebrew—in order to be restored subsequently to the royal house of Egypt; it is the princess who would be the original mother, and she is the one who would have cast him out in the first place. But why bring this paradigm into the reading of the Bible? The reason is, I would suggest, because we have heard another, biblical version of it before. This would be the almost equally nonconforming story of Joseph.

Joseph is highborn, but only by tribal standards, as the first son of his father's more honored wife. He is given a token recognizing his status, his coat, and much more livery follows. He is rejected, not as a child by his parent, but as a young man by his wicked half brothers. He is exiled from the tribe at just the age he should be joining it. It is the tribe that exposes him to die, and brings back the evidence that the missing "child" is dead. Here Judah or Reuben or the satyr-like Ishmaelites have the role in preserving Joseph that in Moses' story falls to Moses' anonymous sibling, a sister, who is subsequently identified as Miriam, sister of Aaron. In the Hebrew story the maternal instincts of the original family are not being successfully denied. Preserved abroad and rising to honors, Joseph does not eventually return to his home, but he does return his family to him and is recognized and vindicated. Had Jacob had his way, Joseph would have been born first, but Laban succeeded in putting Leah ahead of Joseph's mother Rachel. When Joseph seats his brothers in the order of their birth he may well be insisting upon the fact that he is missing from the sequence and that Rachel's remaining son, Benjamin, should be treated doubly well as a consequence and compensation; at the same time, he seems to be restoring his brothers to honor, by putting them in festal gowns. Joseph knows there is no rehabilitation for himself if the community to which he returns has not been rehabilitated as well.

These initiatives in the Joseph story anticipate those of the Mosaic ministry. Moses, when he was grown, "went out unto his brethren" (Exod. 2:11) and tried to call them to their responsibility to each other; so Joseph, son of Jacob, at age seventeen went out *seeking his brothers* (Gen. 37:16). The "Oedipal" theme of the "family romance" (the gratifying fantasy of a more aristocratic parentage) is hardly to be found in a story in which the hero satisfies both his adoptive father in Egypt and his natural father in Israel, and redeems all his rivals rather than destroy or replace any of them. Pharaoh does behave like the father in the Oedipus story, when he orders the death of the male children, but Pharaoh is not responding to an oracle, a prophecy, or a dream, unlike Laius in relation to Oedipus, Herod in the story in Matthew 2, and Pharaoh in the Moses story in Josephus.[18] Joseph's half brothers, however, *are* responding to a prophetic dream: Joseph's own, egotistical, self-proclaiming dream in Genesis 37:5–11. And Pharaoh *is* responding to his fear of the Hebrews: his own self-fulfilling prophecy of the danger they pose to the state.

It seems, then, that the biblical stories of Joseph and Moses each exhibit about half of the paradigm, complementarily distributed, and also critically qualified. The Egyptian/Hebrew dialectic is likewise present, not only in each character, but between the two of them. Joseph is a Hebrew who assimilates with Egypt, acquires an Egyptian name from the court, and becomes "father to Pharaoh" (Gen. 41:45, 45:8). He calls the Hebrews into Egypt, and, in a series of repeating scenes, confronts and judges over the brothers who formerly disputed his dreams of ascendancy; now he stands in the place of Pharaoh and God. Moses is an Egyptianized Hebrew who becomes the reverse, a Hebraicized Egyptian. He is the adopted son of Pharaoh's daughter, from whom he has his name, who alienates himself from the land of his birth, calls the Hebrews out of Egypt, and, in a series of repeating scenes, confronts and judges over Pharaoh on behalf of God and the kinsmen who formerly questioned his authority over them.

Joseph sponsors his own family reunion in Egypt, bringing his family toward a reconciliatory self-recognition that depends on each brother making himself his brother's keeper, that is, his redeemer or bondsman. At the same time he is credited with creating the monopolistic unity of Pharaonic Egypt, the tax of the fifth, and the corps of Egyptian slaves (Gen. 47:13–26). Moses rejects—in the phrase of George Mendenhall— "the monopoly of force"[19] enjoyed by an imperial state, even while he brings his people to form a polity recognizing the world sovereignty of God and its debt to him for redemption from state bondage.

The Hebrews of Exodus 1:11 "built for Pharaoh treasure cities, Pithom and Raameses." The store cities being built with forced labor at the time Moses is born must extend the kinds of plans instituted by Joseph the provider. But the projects also pervert those plans, for Joseph "placed his father and his brethren, and gave them a possession in the land of Egypt, the best of the land, in the land of Rameses, as Pharaoh had commanded" (Gen. 47:11). The settlement Joseph gave his family to possess, "the best of the land, in the land of Rameses," is the site of the oppression Moses leads the Israelites out from under. "The children of Israel journeyed from Rameses to Succoth" (Exod. 12:37): from the slavery of Son-of-Ra's public works to the service of Yahweh's tabernacle.

The patriarchal narrative is a kind of saga, the "ongoing" story of God's covenanting through three generations with the line descending from Abraham. The Joseph story is a small novel, and what is novel in it, and an innovation beyond the patriarchal serial, is the sense of lateral, mutual obligations (rather than vertical, paternal-filial ones, or avuncular-nepotistic ones) binding the individual member of the family or kinship group to securing the welfare of the fellow members of his generation.

This study in communal sentiment provides a literary introduction to the mutuality of the Mosaic covenant and a sympathetic foundation for the Mosaic legislating of social concern. Joseph does not promote anything like welfare laws; yet the experience of Joseph as victim—of parental favoritism, kidnapping, slave-trading, immigrant status, estrangement in Egypt, and criminal conviction on the (false) accusation of one witness—constitutes a prefatory argument for all kinds of civil legislation subsequently found in the Pentateuch. This argument is repeated by three stories of Mosaic intervention at scenes of abuse, after the foundling story.

For purposes of eliciting the scope of the life of Moses, Moses' refuge in Midian also will carry us beyond the family paradigm deriving from Joseph, to theological and legal paradigms deriving from Pharaoh. The Egyptians, the text alleges (Gen. 46:34), cannot abide shepherds, and so the Israelites are separated into Goshen. The priest of Midian is also a flock-keeper, but this episode takes us quite off the reserve in Egypt. As other writers have suggested, Moses' exile in Midian stands not only before Moses' repatriation to "Israel," but also in place of it.[20] That is, Moses' sojourning in the pastoral world points to Israel's future with its shepherds in the wilderness. Yet this prefiguration draws on story elements from the past—the *patriarchal* past. The betrothal encounter at the well and the call at the burning bush are recognizably patriarchal—the latter explicitly so. Unlike the patriarch, however, Moses at the well does not meet a wife to whom the future husband is precontracted by kinship ties. Nor is Moses invited home by the family because that is how betrothal arrangements are properly managed. Moses helps at the well, unlike Rebekah and Jacob her son, not because he is making a case for his eligibility for patriarchal marriage, but because he is a stranger reacting to the daughters' own exclusion from their right. Owing to the hospitality motif, however, there is a trustworthy feeling here that we are back among the pieties of the patriarchal world and that Moses has recovered a home in Midian despite his having lost Pharaonic patronage back in Egypt.

Joseph—to extend his story in a similar way—will also return home temporarily, prior to returning home finally. All the Hebrews in Egypt carry the corpse of Jacob to the promised land of Canaan, in a proto-exodus carefully placed near the end of Genesis (Gen. 50:7–9). Comparably, in the actual exodus, the Israelites leaving Egypt come under the direct leadership of the pillars of cloud and fire at the point in the text (Exod. 13:19–22) where they are taking the embalmed or Egyptianized corpse of Joseph with them: the embalming of Joseph is the last event in Genesis (50:26). These actions, taken together, symbolically and textually assert the continuity of the story of Mosaic Israel, as found in the rest of the Pentateuch, with the patriarchal saga and its innovative Josephic sequel, as found in Genesis. Similar conveyances across the periodizing thresholds of the narrative link up the whole sequence from Genesis through 2 Kings.

Insofar as Joseph's remains are literary, the story of Joseph's being carried down into Egypt and surviving there is "wrapped around" the eventuality of the Northern exodus traditions being carried down into Judah and surviving in the South. The bones of Joseph, the ark of the covenant, and the goods of the tabernacle all seem like so many importations, into the future, of the memory represented by the texts themselves—in which these remains and their translation into subsequent dispensations are anticipated. Lesser examples of such "carry-overs," like the crown of Saul and the mantle of Elijah, are found at places where the texts of Samuel and Kings have been editorially divided to be reinitiated.

So far we have viewed the Mosaic life story mainly in terms of the antecedent story of Joseph. But Moses' office, unlike Joseph's, could not exist without the existence of Israel. The reader will note that where the paradigmatic story has the infant founder-figure exposed on the water or in some other way, the story in Exodus 1 begins with the newborn Hebrew males *as a whole* cast into the water (Exod. 1:22, LXX). It is argued that Pharaoh's attack on the people originally was only directed at the infant Moses, as a would-be rival, and not at the exploding numbers of his fellows. Such a motive may be the original source of Pharaoh's motions, yet the main point of the tale, as it now stands, is not merely Pharaoh's "motiveless malignity," but the imposition of adversity on all Hebrew nativity in a way that recognizes the people as a whole to be the threatened personage that is seeking its place in the sun. The midwives then appear as the underlings or peasants who act to preserve the infant life of a *collective,* or congregation.

The parallels between the story of Moses and the story of Israel suggest that we are dealing with a comparison whereby two things that are "like" each other—namely, the leader of a nation and the proto-history of that nation—have also become assimilated to each other; viz.:

Moses is born in Egypt, where he seeks to intervene on behalf of his countrymen there.	Israel finds itself in Egypt, where it is ministered to by Moses, who intervenes with Pharaoh.
Moses departs from Egypt as a fugitive.	Israel departs from Egypt in haste, being expelled.
Moses sojourns with the priest of the Midian.	Israel wanders with Moses and priest Aaron.

Moses is called by God at the mountain of God, his hand is touched by God, and he is met by Aaron.	Israel is encamped at the mountain of God, and Aaron and Hur support Moses' hands in the battle with Amalek.
Moses parts from his father-in-law in Midian, and is symbolically circumcised by his wife by being touched with blood.	Israel parts from Moses' father-in-law, after covenanting with God at Sinai and being sprinkled with blood.
Moses returns to rejoin the people of "Israel," and to intervene with Pharaoh on their behalf.	Israel sets out from Sinai to return to the land of "Israel" after Moses has intervened with God on its behalf.
Moses works signs before Pharaoh, then sends plagues that leave the Israelites unharmed and culminate in the death of the Egyptians' firstborn.	Israel is plagued by God for bad faith and is destroyed in the form of the elder, Egyptian-born generation's dying in the wilderness.
Moses and Israel enter the wilderness west of the Reed Sea, and then pass through the waters unharmed, while Pharaoh and his captains and his army all die there.	Israel leaves the wilderness, passes through enemy territories undefeated, and enters the Transjordan, where Moses confirms Joshua and then dies there.
Moses and Israel enter the wilderness beyond the Reed Sea, where God feeds his people with manna.	Israel crosses the Jordan out of the Transjordan with the Transjordan tribes in the vanguard and enters a land flowing with milk and honey.

Moses' earlier life establishes a paradigm for the exodus as a whole.

It was in the mountain that it was revealed to Moses that he was to return to Israel in Egypt, and that this Israel would return to the mountain and to the territorial Israel. This pattern is one more of the blueprints that God shows Moses in the mountain. Moses shares the life *of* his people, and so shares his life *with* them. His life is thus converted to Israel's, while its life is converted to his. He preparticipates in the life of his people in Egypt and Midian, then repossesses that life through the stories in Exodus.

Confessional texts show that both later generations and individual Israelites believed not only in the redeeming power of the exodus but also in the redeeming power of the wilderness experience. In a sense this accounts for the seconding of Moses by Joshua. The conqueror of the land is imagined as repeating several features of the Mosaic ministry in the wilderness. Viz.:

Moses sends spies to Hebron, Joshua being one of them (Num. 13:16–26).	Joshua sends spies to Jericho (Josh. 2).
Moses crosses the Reed Sea without being swallowed up (Exod. 14:22, 15:19).	Joshua crosses the Jordan dry-shod (Josh. 3:12–17).
Moses is circumcised symbolically, when Zipporah circumcises their son (Exod. 4:25–26).	Joshua circumcises Israel "again" (Josh. 5:2–9).
Moses is told to celebrate the Passover, and how to do this (Exod. 12–13, Num. 9:2–14).	Joshua celebrates Passover (Josh. 5:10–11).
Moses is told to put off his shoes at the mountain of God, where he is promised the Angel of the Occupation (Exod. 3:5).	Joshua is told to put off his shoes by the Angel of the later Occupation (Josh. 5:15).
Moses is told to extend his hand in a gesture that betokens conquest (Exod. 10:12, etc.).	Joshua is told to extend his hand in the gesture of conquest at Ai (Josh. 8:18–19, 26).
Moses gives the law at Mt. Sinai, and God writes it on tables that are like earlier ones (Exod. 24:12, 34:28).	Joshua puts a stone copy of law at Mount Ebal (Josh. 8:30–32).
Moses announces the levitical cities of refuge (Num. 35:1–28).	Joshua appoints the cities of refuge by name (Josh. 20–21).
Moses sentences the apprehended sabbath-breaker to death (Num. 15:32–36).	Joshua sentences the apprehended *herem*-violater to death (Josh. 7:24–25).
Moses prescribes the inheritance rights of the daughters of Zelophehad (Num. 36).	Joshua gives the five daughters of Zelophehad an inheritance as the Lord through Moses prescribed (Josh. 17:3–4).
God and Moses summon Israel to covenant with God at Sinai (Exod. 19).	Joshua summons Israel to covenant with God at Shechem (Josh. 24).

This schedule does not present us with the assimilative analogy of the lives of Moses and Israel; rather, it suggests a secondary imitation of certain features of the Mosaic offices by the first successor.[21] Joshua's imitations are loyal "observances" of hallowed Mosaic precedents and practices. The crossing of the Reed Sea is a miracle; the crossing of the Jordan is more like a holiday for celebrating or observing a miracle— even if the miracle is scheduled and expected to take place again: at a comparable place.

Such an imitation recommends to future leaders of Israel that they be like Joshua in being like Moses: the most significant of these leaders will celebrate the Passover as a kind of New Year's resolution, rededicating the nation to a Mosaic ideal: Joshua (Josh. 5:10), Josiah (2 Kings 23:21–22), and Ezra (Ezra 6:19). The New Year's feast celebrated by Solomon (at the dedication of the temple at 1 Kings 8:2, 65, with 9:25) is rather the feast that symbolizes the total possession of the land, "from the entrance of Hamath unto the Brook of Egypt" (1 Kings 8:65, JPS). Such an agricultural feast of "ingathering" might have been as much Canaanite as Israelite, but the king's invocation ends on the setting apart of Israel to be God's inheritance, "as thou spakest by the hand of Moses thy servant" (1 Kings 8:53).

The imitation of Moses by successors shows a desire to import into Canaan the Moses of the wilderness, as well as the Moses of the exodus victory. So does a text like the one in Exodus advocating vengeance on the Amalekites, where a book-sponsoring Moses and a Joshua-inspiring one are equated parallelistically: "And the Lord said unto Moses, Write this for a memorial in a book, and rehearse it in the ears of Joshua" (Exod. 17:14a). In its wilderness sojourn Israel is imagined as possessing an enhanced consciousness of itself—even if its mission was cast much in doubt—both as a lost and found generation and as an isolated and initiated "self." For the wilderness experience amounts to a prolonged "rite of passage," or life-crisis ritual, that alienates the younger community from the older one, in order to rejoin the community as a whole to its future in the succeeding generation. Like Moses in Midian, the Hebrews in the wilderness constitute what the anthropologist Victor Turner calls a "liminal community," that is, a group of neophytes temporarily deprived of the status and support of the more established society they are on the threshold of joining.[22] They exist peripherally, and in a critical polarity to that society, in a "limbo" of the virtually pre- and post-existent: with the ancestors and unborn. Shrouded from public view, vulnerable and afraid, thrown upon the mercy of their guides and the voice of one beyond them, they live in fear of their lives (for it is their lives that are indeed in doubt), exceptionally dependent and in need of exceptional care and succor and graciousness. The conditions of this precovenanted state are well described in Ezekiel 16:4–7, where the prophet employs the figure of a postnatal and postpartum isolation:

> And as for your birth, on the day you were born your navel string was
> not cut, nor were you washed with water to cleanse you, nor rubbed with
> salt, nor swathed with bands. No eye pitied you, to do any of these things
> to you out of compassion for you; but you were cast out on the open
> field, for you were abhorred, on the day that you were born. And when I
> passed by you, and saw you weltering in your blood, I said to you in your
> blood, "Live," and I made you a myriad like a plant of the field. And you
> grew up and became tall and arrived at full maidenhood; your breasts
> were formed, and your hair had grown; yet you were naked and bare.
> (RSV)

The comparison of the Israelites in the wilderness to Moses in Midian suggests that the wilderness texts describe the introversion, sequestration, and
quarantine of a corporate personality betaking itself to the uncultivated
wastes to discover the patterns that will govern its subsequent nationally
bound existence. Israel is on a prophetlike retreat, prior to joining the
clan or organization—the "congregation"—procreated out of its future
constituents' and present candidates' accession to group membership. But
like some of the prophets, the people are made faint and "bitter" by their
isolation and extremity (Exod. 15:23, 16:3; 1 Kings 19:4; Ezek. 3:14).

The wilderness period itself is an expanded threshold between two
spaces, a threshold that has widened to become itself a space, with two
thresholds of its own. These are the thresholds marked by one generation's going out (out to the wilderness), and another generation's going in
(out of the wilderness into the promised land). The movement across
such a threshold space might constitute a single momentum, as the parallelism of Psalm 106:9 allows: "He rebuked the Red Sea also, and it was
dried up: so he led them through the depths, as through the wilderness."
This condenses the buffer space into an abridgment of chaos. Instead, the
narrative offers various objections to such an advance, whether these are
generated by considerations of military strategy, or by hesitations upon the
threshold which are punished by wandering or abiding there. In some way
Israel was qualified for the promised land by the wilderness, either penally,
or through probation and trial, or by preliminary service to God.

Into the threshold space the authors of the Pentateuch have interpolated the whole of the Mosaic legislation, thus confirming the space's
enlargement both theologically and textually. The narrative anticipates
this development at the outset, for it shows us a miniature expansion of
the wilderness tradition upon its very threshold—and therefore a doubling of the threshold—through Moses' doubling back and camping along
the Egyptian side of the Reed Sea, in its "wilderness" (Exod. 13:18).
Moses' delay upon this threshold is divinely inspired, and seems to anticipate a future dilation of the wilderness texts and narratives. Apparently, by
keeping Israel within the range of Egypt, Israel's encampments by the Sea

provoke Pharaoh's pursuit. But this very jeopardizing of Israel's escape, while it appears to cooperate with an enemy that seeks to capture Israel back to Egypt, is actually instrumental in securing Israel's final emancipation from Egypt, by bringing Pharaoh and his troops into range—God's— where it was alleged Israel itself would be swallowed up: "For Pharaoh will say of the children of Israel, They are entangled in the land, the wilderness hath shut them in" (Exod. 14:3). Because of the distich form, God seems to predict here that Pharaoh will employ the parallelistic accents that otherwise might have come from poems like the Song at the Sea (Exod. 15:1–21), or the Song of Deborah (Judg. 5).[23] The Israelites themselves promptly (and repeatedly) fall into this way of thinking: "And they said unto Moses, Because there were no graves in Egypt, hast thou taken us away to die in the wilderness?" (Exod. 14:11a) These phrases seem intromitted into this present account from their recurrence beyond the Reed Sea: "ye have brought us forth into this wilderness, to kill this whole assembly with hunger"; "Wherefore is this that thou hast brought us up out of Egypt, to kill us and our children and our cattle with thirst?" (Exod. 16:3, 17:3b). The litany is expanded and recycled in the people's criticism of Moses, Aaron, and God in Numbers: "and the whole congregation said unto them, Would God that we had died in the land of Egypt! or would God we had died in this wilderness! And wherefore hath the Lord brought us unto this land, to fall by the sword, that our wives and our children should be a prey? were it not better for us to return into Egypt?" (Num. 14:2b–3). God had predicted that the Israelites would give up in the land of the Philistines: that is, "when they see war" (Exod. 13:17; cf. also Num. 14:42).

As "the earth swallowed" the Egyptians (Exod. 15:12), so it swallows Korah and Abiram (Num. 16:31–35); this follows the condemning of the evil generation in the wilderness at Numbers 14, where Israel is ordered to "get you into the wilderness by way of the Red Sea" (vs. 25). A clue to these echoes of the threshold-crossing is given by Dathan and Abiram being Reubenites, for it is the Reubenites who settle down before the Jordan River yet volunteer to be the first to cross it, and so undertake the risk of being swallowed up by the waters, as well as by the wilderness (Josh. 1:12–15). (The death of the Korahites is mingled in with that of Dathan and Abiram, but the text seems to finally dispose of the rebellious priests holocaustically [Num. 16:35], rather than cataclysmically.) God's decree that the people tarry in the wilderness partly concedes to their motion to appoint themselves a captain back to Egypt, yet also takes a positive step toward crossing into Canaan, by allowing for the development of a bolder generation on its threshold (Num. 14:4, 20–23).

The term *captain* is important here; it occurs just after Joshua's being ordained (by being renamed, at Num. 13:8, 16) to conduct the abortive reconnaissance mission of Numbers 13–14. For the wilderness sojourn links itself to the migratory patterns and seasonal nomadism of pastoralists, who enter pastureland annually, only to return at the season's end to the borderlands from which they came—where some fodder survives through the winter.[24] The seasonal circling of the shepherd is thus opposed to the kind of campaign leadership provided by the captain, who takes for his own the land a shepherd shares with an agriculturalist, rather than merely visiting it as a seasonal guest. The anxiety surrounding the exodus, if we combine the hazard in which the lives of the young stand with the impending hostility of Amalek, is that of a shepherd eating his last safe meal (the Passover) before invading the rich farmland belonging to agriculturalists—who may or may not be friendly to a sojourner come to graze his flocks among them. The "myth" of Moses' jeopardized birth is thus controlled by the overall pattern of his mission. Like other heroes, he travels in a loop, escaping from a danger that brings him toward his destiny, which is only to confront the original danger anew. But Moses' life story is scripted this way twice. The threatened hero flies from Egypt to meet dangers abroad, then returns to meet his original antagonist at home. Making his escape a second time, he revisits his danger in the Sinaitic desert. He oscillates between dual jeopardies—Pharaoh and God.

The exodus story of Israel's call into sonship constitutes its subjects vocationally, and many are called: the midwives, to be given houses of their own; the mother, to nurse her son; Pharaoh's daughter, to adopt him; the sojourner, to keep shepherdess and sheep; Gershom, to a priesthood descending from Moses in Judges 18:30; and Israel, to be "a kingdom of priests" (Exod. 19:6) like Aaron. But, like Moses, Israel is "drawn out" of another nation, a rival jurisdiction. After Herod's death, Matthew 2:15 quotes from Hosea 11:1, "When Israel was a child, then I loved him, and called my son out of Egypt." So, after Pharaoh's death, Moses' family was brought out of Midian. Each call has characterized the other. Deuteronomy 1:31 announces God's paternity with Moses' own Hosea-like similitude: "the Lord thy God bare thee, as a man doth bear his son, in all the way that ye went." Moses disavows a paternal role for himself: "Have I conceived all this people? have I begotten them, that thou shouldest say unto me, Carry them in thy bosom, as a nursing father beareth the sucking child . . . ?" (Num. 11:12). Nor was he called to be God's son. Yet Pharaoh must free God's son so that he may become God's servant. Moses departs from Pharaoh's adoption, Israel enters into God's protection: the story oscillates between rival patronages. Therefore both Pharaoh and God also try to kill Moses—as if to say, Moses cannot serve two masters.

·7·

SOJOURNER IN MIDIAN

The purposes of the story of Moses' pre-Sinaitic career seem both recapitulatory and proleptic. Trying to act as his brother's keeper, Moses
murders an Egyptian furtively, and consequently becomes a fugitive: we
compare the condition of Cain. Trying to raise his brothers' consciousness
of their obligations to each other, Moses is rebuffed by a question that
casts him as a foreign bureaucrat: we compare Joseph rejected by his
brothers for his pretense to lordship. Moses then reimmerses himself in
the intervening patriarchal past as a sojourner with the local priest of
Midian, with whom he secures an alliance through an encounter with his
future wife, or one of her sisters, at a local well—contact is initiated when
he assists his future wife in watering her flock, and she and her sisters are
sent back to the stranger by their father to bring the outlander home as a
guest: we compare Jacob assisting Rachel and marrying Leah. With the
new father-in-law in Midian Moses finds safety from Pharaoh: we compare
Jacob finding safety from the murderous Esau in the house of Laban. Both
Moses and Jacob tend their father-in-law's flock. Moses names his child
Gershom (by his Midianite wife), after his adjustment to abroadness: we
compare Joseph naming his child Manasseh (by his Egyptian wife, likewise
the daughter of a priest) after his success abroad. As if to extend the equivalence between Moses and Joseph, a chapter featuring Moses' father-in-
law, Jethro, gives Moses a second and otherwise unmentioned son, Eliezar,
cited in tandem with the Gershom named in Exodus 2:22. During the
exodus Jethro has kept Moses' wife in Midian,

> And her two sons: of which the name of the one was Gershom; for he
> said, I have been an alien in a strange land:
> And the name of the other was Eliezer; for the God of my father, said
> he, was mine help, and delivered me from the sword of Pharaoh.
> (Exod. 18:2–4)

With these verses we compare a similar pair in Genesis:

> And Joseph called the name of the firstborn Manasseh: For God, said
> he, hath made me forget all my toil, and all my father's house.

> And the name of the second called he Ephraim: For God hath caused
> me to be fruitful in the land of my affliction. (Gen. 41:51–52)

Moses is reunited with his children in the wilderness as once Jacob was
reunited with Joseph and these children in Egypt. With this renewal of the
repatriation motif from the end of Genesis we are come full cycle, back to
the genesis of Exodus; for where Jethro greets Moses in Exodus 18, there
Aaron greeted Moses in Exodus 4: on his return to his erstwhile people.

Once we have recognized the recapitulatory elements in Moses'
sojourning, we may review them for their difference from these Genesis
originals. First, Moses only turns into a Cainlike fugitive after he has tried
to protect his brethren from a kinsman's violence. He himself is protected
not by God but by an alliance with a priest. Again, Moses is identified as
being a would-be prince of Joseph's kind only after he has separated from
Pharaoh and gone out from the house to which Joseph the future prince
had yet to come. In Midian Moses is not a kinsman abroad at a well at
which the migrant is welcomed, but an alien at a well that is disputed. Not
only is the woman at the well not kin, but she is a member of a foreign
clan, or house: for she is one of seven, a plausible number for a completed
tribal unit (like an Irish "sept"). Thus Moses' impending marriage is not
intratribal, it is "political," between persons each of whom is foreign to
the other: no one objects when the woman describes Moses as an Egyptian—in Midian he might as well be. The father of the woman at the well is
not defined relationally, as an Abrahamic kinsman, but vocationally, as a
priest: the marriage is therefore between persons with a possible religious
difference and implies a new ideological commitment on the part of a
previously "unchurched" or uncircumcised party. This could have also
been the case with the Nahorite Rebekah marrying Yahwist Isaac; the religious innocents are Rebekah and Moses, in the respective cases. But the
ambassador catechizing Rebekah's family in relation to Abraham is not a
priest, the official of a cult, even if he is an eager proselytizer for the family
guardian and numen. Finally, the bargaining initiated by the encounter at
the well is not for family service or sanctuary from revenge for wrong to a
brother, but rather for community membership and sanctuary from the
death penalty for a crime against an overlord. Jacob puts himself out of
Esau's reach, in another country or homeland; Moses takes himself out of
the state, in another jurisdiction—it is significant that Midian is the province of a priest. In Egypt, priests were the only landholders apart from
Pharaoh himself (Gen. 47:22, 26).

Curiously, the pedigree of the Midianite priest derives from Abraham,
through the Keturah who bore Midian as her fourth son (Gen. 25:2). We
scarcely remember this, until we ask in what sense Moses might be
rejoining the family of Abraham: not genetically, but ideologically. For

Moses is less like Ruth, the Moabitess, recovering the genetic share in Abraham that got lost through Lot, than like Rebekah, called to become the bridge between past and future deals with Yahweh: in the case of Rebekah, the former deal with Abraham and the latter one with Jacob; in the case of Moses, the former deal with the patriarchs and the latter one at Sinai.

Jacob was increasing his own holdings while herding his father-in-law's flock: he was enriching the future house of Israel in the exercise of his vocation. While Moses is keeping the analogous flock, he is being called toward Sinai: that is, toward the care of the future people of Israel. However, Moses is not, occupationally speaking, a shepherd like Jacob, who is a shepherd from his youth. Rather, Moses begins his career as a kind of public defender and a mediator, almost a would-be Good Samaritan, one who fights other people's battles for them. His first contact with shepherding, in fact, takes the form of disciplining other shepherds, who are apparently accustomed to abusing the priest's daughters at the well. The person who is occupationally a shepherd in the story is actually Moses' father-in-law; but again Jethro is at the same time also an officeholder: a priest, with a flock of daughters in his care. In other words, Moses' stewardship of Jethro's flock is mainly metaphorical, and anticipates the Mosaic office of leading his congregation out of Egypt and into the wilderness, and out of the wilderness and into the Transjordan. Moses is exposed to shepherding in the way he is exposed on the river: under something like laboratory conditions. As an infant Moses was less exposed to the elements than to the motif of being exposed; as an adult he is less of a flock-keeper than the keeper of flock-keepers. He is a shepherd in the way that the entertainer Roy Rogers was a Western cowboy or the poet Robert Frost was a New England farmer: as part of a consciously chosen role.

To the reader coming to Exodus from Genesis, the name Midian in the Keturah story merely advises us that any rivals to Isaac were "pensioned off" (Gen. 25:6): it does not suggest a place where the patriarchal identity might be symbolically renewed, or the patriarchal career symbolically reenacted. In the patriarchal story the names exist to become part of any proper recital of the patriarchal pedigree. The expansion of Abram's name to Abraham, at Genesis 17:5, makes him over from the actual father of Ishmael to the potential father of many. Isaac's name laughingly takes issue with the promise to Abram and Sara—the promise of issue (cf. Gen. 17:17, 18:12–15). Jacob's name makes him the supplanter of his twin. When this supplantation is about to be realized his name is doubled with Israel, as God adopts him into the promises to Abraham (Gen. 25:26, 27:36, 32:24–28, 35:9–12). The names in the Moses story lack this genetic-ethnic future, but their political, civic and historical significance also emerges from etymologizing and supplementation.

The name of Moses is Egyptian, if it is an Egyptian suffix, like the "son" in the name Wil*son*; but "Moses" is explained by the story itself as the Hebrew name of one who *was drawn out* from the waters (in Hebrew he should perhaps have been one who *draws out* from the waters). The founder of Babylon, the foundling Sargon, was found and adopted by a water-drawer called Akki, according to the legend.[1] The Egyptian princess in Exodus 2 is in the sponsoring position of this water-drawer. Sargon's actual mother, however, was not a resident alien like Jochebed, but a priestess or vestal; and his sponsor was not a princess like the daughter of Pharaoh; Akki could have been a peasant. The story of Moses' infancy, however, is less about restoring princely status to a dynast than about restoring ethnic identity to the deracinated. Thus the story is also less about changing or maintaining class than about changing or maintaining allegiances. Moses might not know of whom he was the son—the culture of Egypt or the seed of Israel—but he is taken from the Nile so the children of Israel can be delivered from the Reed Sea of Egypt.

There are hints of the Egyptian root in Moses' Egyptian name in the name [Ra-]mose. The enslaved Hebrews "built for Pharaoh treasure cities, Pithom and Raamses," and they leave Egypt through "Rameses" (Exod. 1:11, 12:37), named for the "Son of Ra." Moses' own father is named Amram (Exod. 6:20). Thus the name "Son-of" is removed from the pedigree of one gens to be put up for adoption by another. The princess's command "Take this child" might have been, in Egyptian, "Take this *mose.*" Somewhat unwittingly, she also etymologizes a Hebrew meaning for Moses' name, for she is unaware that this etymology will attach to the future deliverance at the Reed Sea, when her idea is realized in the drawing out of Israel, not of Moses. God or Moses becomes the drawer-out, taking the Hebrew subject up from his imperiled Egyptian beginnings.

Another valorized name in the story is that of Moses' son Gershom. Looking backward to the patriarchal sojourner even while looking forward to sequestration in the wilderness, Moses in Midian names his son after his father's being a stranger in a strange land (Exod. 2:22, 18:3). But Gershom's name points more specifically at Moses' criminality and deportation, since the same *grš* root is used when God promises that the Hebrews in Egypt will be delivered by their being *driven* or *thrust out* (Exod. 6:1, 11:1). His estrangement is tantamount to their banishment.

The doubling of names in the case of Moses' father-in-law, the priest of Midian, may also point to the legal and Mosaic character of banishment. The priest is first named Reuel, at the point (Exod. 2:18) when Moses arrives in Midian as a fugitive from Pharaoh and is thrown upon this locale for sanctuary: apparently Midian is beyond the reaches of Egyptian jurisdiction. But when the need for sanctuary has passed, at the death of that Pharaoh in whose reign Moses killed the Egyptian, God remembers his people Israel and calls Moses away from the priest to go back to his brethren in Egypt. It is at this juncture that the priest's name mysteriously changes from Reuel (at Exod. 2:18) to Jethro (at 3:1, and again at 4:18 and ch. 18; the "harmonist" LXX 2:16 puts Jethro in early).

How are we to explain the Hebrew text's change, from Reuel the host to Jethro the employer? Is the textual anomaly in some way significant? Why is the name of Moses' father-in-law so plural? It includes the name Hobab as well, and, in Numbers 10:29, Hobab is said to be the son of Raguel the Midianite, Moses' father-in-law: this presumably does not mean that Hobab is Moses' brother-in-law, Hobab being an otherwise unmentioned male sibling of Zipporah. Nonetheless, the clue to the priest's identity might be found in this most exceptional case: for the implications here are, (1) the priest of Midian is an "office," (2) this office is heritable, and (3) Moses' connection with the official in question is bigenerational.[2] Nothing says that the priest Reuel/Raguel died and was succeeded in the local priesthood by Jethro or by Hobab, or that Reuel was the girls' grandfather rather than their father, but these would be ways of harmonizing the text. More importantly, the two names in Numbers suggest that what matters is not the name itself but rather the mechanism for changing it. For the mechanism is potentially dynastic.

On the level of the story, the death of the Pharaoh marks the end of Moses' danger, but on the level of the story's implications, the lifetime of Pharaoh also figures in a statute of limitations; his death is the means of determining the expiration of sanctuary and the time of Moses' return to Egyptian jurisdiction. Thus the narrative's giving of a new name to the priest, at the point of the expiration of a Pharaoh's reign, means something more specific than the mere ending of a novitiate with the beginning of a proper ministry. For the narrative of the encounter at the burning bush is framed, on both sides, with a separation of Moses from Jethro and the remarking of the old Pharaoh's being dead—the narrator himself tells us this at Exodus 2:23; then God tells Moses something similar at 4:19, after Moses asks Jethro's permission to go and see if his brethren are still alive.

Why does the priest's name change when the Pharaoh or ruler changes? For this is indeed one way of asking the question. In some sense, the Reuel who offered Moses protection at the outset is not the same man as the Jethro under whose auspices Moses departs into Sinai and Egypt: it's "Hello, Reuel," but "Good-bye, Jethro." The implied change in the holder of priestly office would constitute a peculiarly Mosaic allusion to officeholding, because, at the other end of his ministry, Moses will himself appoint the Levitical or priestly cities of refuge in Canaan. These cities, assigned to the priesthood as their lot in Canaan, are the places where the manslayer may find sanctuary: but only for a circumscribed period, during which the danger of hasty family vengeance, without negotiation, may have time to pass. The time specified is that of the remaining lifetime of the city's high priest (Num. 35:25, 28). Thus a given high priest is in effect the patron of the manslayer's cause, as Reuel has been of Moses' life. This indirect discovery that the priest can be defined as a patron, rather than as a strictly literal father-in-law, also comports well with our feeling that Moses owes more to the priest than his mere physical survival. For he might also owe him the concept of a political priesthood itself.

There is a second way of arriving at somewhat similar conclusions. Jethro, in Exodus 18, is credited with conceiving Israel's judicial system of seventy elders, in order to distribute "Moses" among the people. The Israelites, before they get there in Exodus 19, are already "encamped at the mount of God" (Exod. 18:5), where they will be told "Thou shalt not kill" (Exod. 20:13). Yet in Exodus 17:8–16 they must fight the war with the Amalekites, on the way to Sinai; and this war seems to be perpetually instituted as a result, "from generation to generation" (Exod. 17:16). Joshua is therefore mentioned here for the first time, as the agent of such an institution, the holy war (Exod. 17:9–10a, 13–14). Indeed, this is the first time God commissions Moses to put something in a book: for Joshua (Exod. 17:14). The holy war is thus instituted before the covenant itself. It is upon hearing the news of the success of the new polity that Moses' father-in-law, Jethro, comes out to greet Moses and—a bit like the Gibeonites in Joshua 9—to acknowledge his conversion to Yahweh's cause.

If Jethro is "Hobab, the son of Raguel [Reuel] the Midianite," as per Numbers 10:29, and yet Hobab is "Hobab the Kenite father-in-law of Moses," as per Judges 4:11, then Jethro, a.k.a. Hobab, is *Kenite.* What could this mean? The Amalekite and Kenite aspects of Israel's wilderness sojourn are distinguished in Exodus 17 and 18 as the war with Amalek and the peace—since their relation is sealed by a meal—with Jethro; this distinction reappears in 1 Samuel 15, where Saul divides between these same opposed treatments that Israel received in the exodus, and enjoins the old Kenite ally to withdraw from the old Amalekite enemy before he makes war on it. The presumption of Kenite sanctuary is also a feature of the prose version of the story of the killing of the general of the Canaanite king Jabin at Judges 4:17: "Howbeit Sisera fled away on his feet to the tent of Jael the wife of Heber the Kenite: for there was peace between Jabin the king of Hazor and the House of Heber the Kenite." Yet Heber's wife betrays the fugitive—that is, takes his life—on behalf of the Israel of Deborah and Barak. It is thus Israel, rather than Canaan, who actually enjoys the protection of the Kenite female in the story.

The Kenite will one day be offered sanctuary and protection by Saul's Israel, in a continuation of these intramural relations (see 1 Sam. 15:6). But why did the Moses who had become an outlaw acquire a Kenite father-in-law in the first place? Why does being touched with the blood of his wife's son's circumcision save his life? What is the connection between being adoptively Kenite and finding sanctuary? The Kenite's eponymous ancestor was Cain. His archetypal killing of Abel involved Cain in genocide, fratricide, murder, homicide, and manslaughter. Yet Cain was offered sanctuary and protection, by a Kinsman in lieu of a kinsman. He had killed his clansman Abel, yet his clan had its mark from God.

The patriarchal "type scene" governing Moses' meeting with the daughters at the well is the "hospitable" encounter at the watering place abroad that leads to the betrothals of Isaac and Jacob with one of the daughters of the land of Nahor (Gen. 24:10–58, 29:1–19).[3] The scene is repeatable in the same momentum that it is predictable, and it contains an element of prearrangement: Abraham's servant is sent to the old country only after Rebekah is born (Gen. 22:20–23), Jacob's engagement to Laban is a month old before he engages to serve for Rachel—even if he has kissed her first (Gen. 29:11–18). The site "abroad" (if one is from Canaan) is still the homeland of a living kinsman; the scenes in Genesis advance a social contract previously implicit in the kinships of the parties to it.[4]

In contrast, Moses has no hereditary link to the clan from which he takes his spouse, no family tie across the patrilineages that the patriarchal betrothals lateralized and maintained. The Midianite girls he helps at the well might be merely "daughters of the land," in the sense of the nameless Shechemite progeny Dinah goes out to visit in Genesis 34:1. But an alliance with such daughters—even to the point of one party's adoption of the scarification practice of the other party's god (circumcision)—has ideological and ethical consequences in the Midian of Exodus 2:15b–4:24 altogether different from those found in Genesis 34. At Genesis 34:7, the rapist Shechem "had wrought folly in Israel." Reuel, in contrast, has his daughters call the helpful Egyptian, "that he may eat bread" (Exod. 2:20): "And Moses was content to dwell with the man, and he gave Moses his daughter Zipporah. She bore a son, and he called his name Gershom; for he said, 'I have been a sojourner [*ger*] in a foreign land' " (Exod. 2:21–22, RSV). Provocatively camping *in the face of* Shechem (Gen. 33:18, after Hebr.), and about to expose his daughter to being raped, Jacob was on the verge of vitiating the thing that Moses, apart from Egyptian jurisdiction in Midian, is in the process of conceiving: namely, the right of Israel. In a land named "Contention," this right is to be deduced from that of the *ger*.

Its name confesses that Midian is not, itself, securely in the territory of an ideal Mosaic Israel. Nonetheless, Midian gives Moses the idea of a renewable homeland. For when he waters the daughters' flock, he commences that circle between guest and host whereby a host invites his guest

to make himself at home, and where the guest's response to this invitation
is to undertake some of the host's work. The helpful stranger is soon *owed*
the privileges of the guest—his host, after all, should be helping him. Even
without this impetus toward the hospitality Moses is shown by the priest in
Midian, the story polarizes the difference between a society like Gibeah's,
where aliens who are merely out-of-towners are treated as fugitives without
rights, and a society like Abraham's, where strangers—almost foreign
agents, in the case of Abraham's visitors in Genesis 18—are treated as
guests and honorary kinsmen. These opposed societies collide in the story
of Lot in Sodom. All of Sodom tries to behave like the brutish men of
Gibeah, while a part of Lot tries to behave like the gracious host Abraham.
The "inhospitable" Sodomites are checked by Lot's divine guests, but the
house of Lot is compromised by his "hospitable" offer of his daughters to
the vicious Sodomite "hosts" outside his door.

The hospitality of Abraham and Lot, insofar as it is extended to angels,
is clearly of a different order than the hospitality found at the patriarchal
wells of betrothal: for it is not extended to a directly eligible member of
the other moiety of the tribe, but rather to a "sacred stranger." The patriarchal hospitality is equally productive, however, since the divine guests in
each case prove the host's genetic salvation. The visiting angels cause the
aging Abraham and Sarah to conceive, and they save Lot and his daughters from perishing—they survive as Ammonites and Moabites.

Moses also comes to his hosts as a deliverer, but not a genetic one. The
annunciation scene leading to Isaac, and the betrothal scenes leading to
Jacob and the sons of Jacob, might have a more Mosaic counterpart in a
homeless or homeland-less person at a well. Such is the case of the outcast
Hagar. Moses' well is in Midian, and the tribesmen the Bible associates
most closely with the Midianites are the Ishmaelites. The Ishmaelites are a
tribe deriving from the fugitive bondwoman Hagar, whose son Ishmael is
cast out with her both when she is pregnant, and thereafter, when she is a
mother. In both stories (Gen. 16:1–7; 21:9–21) the ancestors of the future
Hagarenes are found at a well: found, that is, by God—a God who *hears*
and *sees* their plight.[5] While the annunciation and betrothal scenes for
Isaac belong to the matrimonial saga of patriarchal election, the scenes of
the abused women at the well belong to the complex of vindication pertaining to excluded, intermarrying parties—that is, those parties who
recruit seed or childbearers outside their gens. Zipporah marries an
"Egyptian," namely, Moses. This Egyptian Moses marries a half-Semitic
outlander, a Midianite, Zipporah. And later, as an Israelite, Moses marries
a "Cushite," a violation of the taboo on intermarriage; Moses' *family*,
Aaron and Miriam, protest this liaison (Num. 12:1). Hagar, who is Hamitic, is concubine to a Semite, Abraham. She marries her half-Hamitic and
half-Semitic son Ishmael to a woman she takes from Egypt (Gen. 21:21).

Yet the identities of these intermarrying characters all include a genetic or protogenetic stake in the elect identity of the first patriarch: Hagar is a surrogate for Sarah, Ishmael's father is as much Abraham as is Isaac's, Zipporah is a descendant of Abraham (through the fourth son of Abraham's wife Keturah), and Moses' god declares himself the god of Moses' fathers Abraham, Isaac, and Jacob.

But is the patriarchal connection sufficient to assert that the abused Hagar and the abused Midianite daughters have their Abrahamic rights violated at the well? Shouldn't they too, no less than Isaac, be able to bless Abraham for their existence? Despite what we know about the racial identities of the parties at the three biblical wells of a woman's abuse—the two in Genesis 16 and 21, and the one in Exodus 2—both the racist overtones of the wrong, and the correction God makes in the case of Hagar, are absent from the well of the daughters in Midian. Transactions here are only superficially interracial. As with Jesus and the Samaritan woman at the well in John 4, an ideological component somewhat latent in the earlier encounters now prevails over the ethnic component. The God of Abraham vindicated Hagar's genetic right to a collective future; he did not seem to address the question of a civil right to redress for grievances. In the Book of the Covenant, the God of Moses will.

Hagar's annunciation scene and well scene are the result of a separation—an informal divorce, if a surrogate mother can be divorced, rather than being fired, like a maid. The story has the fugitive bondwoman rest from her flight by a spring, where the sacred stranger appears in order to console her with the announcement of the alternative election of Ishmael. Two things here already suggest Mosaic criteria for the tale. First, since Hagar is a bondwoman, the annunciation at the well constitutes a restoration of rights and an extending of divine protection to the uncovenanted. Second, since Ishmael's election is announced when Hagar's rights (or her claims upon existence) are in abeyance, Ishmael is created—or marked as being—outside of any social contract other than the one constituted by the natural bond between mother and child. The son who is promised to the pregnant and abused bondwoman "shall be a wild ass of a man, his hand against every man and every man's hand against him; and he shall dwell over against all his kinsmen" (Gen. 16:12, RSV). The Ishmaelite has run wild. A domesticated beast of burden that has revolted and become feral is the logical consequence of the runaway maidservant's troubled pregnancy. It is therefore the abuse of a pregnant woman (during the violence of a male brawl) that issues, with sudden and arresting ferocity, in the first and most complete Mosaic version of the Near Eastern *lex talionis*: "If men strive, and hurt a woman with child, so that her fruit depart from her, and yet no mischief follow: he shall be surely punished, according as the woman's husband will lay upon him;

and he shall pay as the judges determine. And if any mischief follow, then thou shalt give life for life, Eye for eye, tooth for tooth, hand for hand, foot for foot, Burning for burning, wound for wound, stripe for stripe" (Exod. 21:22–25).

The law of "life for life" or "skin for skin" (Job 2:4) is originally stated in the Bible as *a brother for a brother*, in the Noachic code (Gen. 9:5), and that is the law's basis, when enforced among phratries. The Ishmaelites are such a brotherhood, even if they are defined by being at odds with all other tribes. Ishmael, according to the prediction, will treat himself like a fugitive, the kind Cain dreaded becoming, dwelling over against all his kinsmen, where kinsmen can be read "tribes to which his clan is related by blood." His marginal status denies him the protection of other Abrahamites. Only God protects him, as he formerly protected Cain. Yet the Kenites also aspired to protect themselves, killing as many as "seventy and sevenfold" in reprisal for the loss of a life (Gen. 4:24). From such potentially sociopathic conditions Moses might hope to save Israel.

The hospitable Reuel invites Moses into a quasi-patriarchal community that betokens his progress back toward the rights enjoyed—or the obligations undertaken—by a covenanted member of a just society. Nonetheless, the shadows of the earlier annunciation scenes involving Ishmael and his Egyptian mother fall across the story. For the encounter of the Midianite daughters and their "Egyptian" deliverer at the well leads to betrothal and pregnancy, and Moses names Zipporah's son after his own alienation from a homeland. Furthermore, Zipporah will include Moses in the community of *her* blood, by touching him with the blood of his son's circumcision. Gershom and Moses are being included in a covenant of circumcision, like Ishmael and Abraham at the announcement of Isaac in Genesis 17: father and son were circumcised together in a show of ethnic solidarity at Ishmael's rites of social puberty, or political coming of age.[6]

But despite Abrahamic auspices, the inclusion of Moses in the covenant of circumcision only takes ethnic election as its "vehicle," and not its "tenor." For Moses is saved from being murdered by God, at Exodus 4:24–26, in the way that Israel is saved from the plague on the firstborn, in Exodus 12. Celebrating the Passover meal with the Jews does not necessarily make one a Jew; yet it numbers one, as a guest, among those who might be spared: among the Abrahamites. For if all persons may *come* to this meal, only the circumcised are finally *invited* (Exod. 12:48). Reuel's call to Moses, to eat bread and thus share a shepherd's meal (Exod. 2:20), thus anticipates Moses' subsequent inclusion in the community of the circumcised and the converted. For Zipporah knew about a saving rite of circumcision, where Moses evidently did not. She knew how a bridegroom was made part of the wife's family's blood, how a genetically unrelated person could be included in a community defining itself genetically, yet constituting itself ideologically. One is not born circumcised, but, once circumcised, or symbolically scarified for life, one dies this way.

Circumcision is a means to inclusion in a community that one can join, whether or not one is born into it, through participation in rituals of initiation. Still, we may wonder why a practice that was known in the ancient world as part of the Egyptian system of purifications[7] should have to be extended to an adopted subject who is Egyptian by an outlander priest who is Midianite in order to save the adopted subject from the patriarchal God of an enslaved people who are Hebrews. The Moses whom God meets in Exodus 4:24–26 will have already celebrated his first Passover: before rejoining his brethren in Egypt. His vicarious circumcision is not a fragment, but a fraction: not a stray trace, but a carefully placed sign.

To explain Moses' present salvation in Midian by means of Israel's future rescue at the institution of the Passover, however, is to jump ahead to a story that has not yet been told, in Egypt, while ignoring a story that is being retold, in Midian. When Moses marries into the family whose part he has taken, he is not so much joining this family, as rejoining the family itself—for it is a large one: seven daughters. Moses is joining a family deriving from a patriarchal lineage, a family that knows about Abrahamic circumcision. Yet this family is also associated, by way of the Joseph story, with kidnapping and the sale of human chattel into Egyptian servitude. The Midianites were party to this sale, and so were the Ishmaelites (Gen. 37:25–28, 36). Thus the family in Midian is Abrahamic (Gen. 25:1–2, 4), yet only half-Nahorite; at least half-Semitic, yet perhaps not more than half-Sethite (if Keturah was Hamitic). Its dual identity is thus a match for Moses' own, especially if joining with a Midianite clan should result in a new identity: one based on doubling the family's dynastic components. For Moses and Reuel can both claim descent from the patriarch Abraham. But this ethnic identity is again a vehicle for a nongenetic, latent, ideological tenor. Moses is a son of Levi, even though there are not yet any Levites; similarly, Reuel is a priest, even though it is never clear what he is a priest of, apart from Midian itself. God has not yet declared to Reuel, perhaps, "Thou shalt have no other gods before me." But a priest should still stand for a spiritual idea. What could this idea be?

Moses' encounter with the daughters at the well does not lead to the genetic conservation of his ancestors or any "keeping of Nahor," but rather to the concept of sanctuary. Without this notion, the Mosaic version of the national homeland could not exist. Moses has earned the daughter at the well by service, like Jacob paying the bride-price of Rachel, and like Jacob engaging for sanctuary (Gen. 27:42–45; 29:15–20, 27–28). In patriar-

chal society, sanctuary is an augmentation of the basic protections otherwise offered by kinship; but in nonpatriarchal society, sanctuary proves to
be the original of these protections—it is their symbolical *sine qua non.*

And while sanctuary is a type of shelter—shelter being a kind of prevenient sanctuary—it is also a type of the supervenience of Franklin Roose-
velt's "Four Freedoms." The first of these are freedom from fear and
want, but latterly freedom of thought and religion. Yahwism hardly contemplates what we mean by freedom of religion, but in the ancient world
what it would mean is freedom from the worship of the state. Moses finds
safe harbor with a priest, not because this priest needs must be the source
of Moses' religion but because he is the source of sanctuary, without the
conception of which the Mosaic ideology could not have developed at all.
As we have noted, the priest, as Hobab, not only is Midianite
(Num. 10:29), but also is said to have a descendant who is Kenite
(Judg. 4:11). If such a priest knew about the Kenite law of retaliation,
perhaps he also knew about God's protection of Cain.

Again, the priest in Midian may or may not have known the levitical
motive-clause in the name of Yahweh, but he clearly could guess the
requirements of the Holiness Code appertaining to the naturalization of
the stranger in Israel: "the stranger that dwelleth with you shall be unto
you as one born among you, and thou shalt love him as thyself, for ye were
strangers in the land of Egypt" (Lev. 19:34)—the name of Moses' Midian-
born son Gershom (*ger* = 'stranger') echoes in the diction. As traditional
stories about the hospitality owed to strangers attest, the provision of sanctuary rests on divine imperatives, for the stranger may turn out to be a
god.[8] Even the outcast may become a source of good luck, as Laban
learned Jacob the flock-keeper was: "I have learned by divination that the
Lord has blessed me because of you" (Gen. 30:27, RSV). So Abimelech
and his friends found Isaac the dowser to be: "We saw certainly that the
Lord was with thee" (Gen. 26:28). A little like Laban and Abimelech, the
Moses of Midian might at least enjoy these references to the blessing of
Abraham vicariously.

· 8 ·

DELIVERING JUSTICE:
THE PREHISTORY OF MOSAIC
INTERVENTION

God calls the patriarchs to a knowledge of his promises to them or to their
posterity. But Moses is called to know the divine will in a much more vol-
untarist sense. He is called to know God's will to justice. Though he is not
called from the womb, there being no announcement to his parents—i.e.,
no evidence of his *precocity*—yet there *is* a cryptic annunciation to Pharaoh, through the midwives. Moses' own call, however, is preceded by his
maturation. Yet this in itself constitutes a kind of call, since as a man he
responds to the plight of his people before God himself hearkens to it: by
his re-calling Moses. Moses' preliminary, precall ministry is thus quite as
vital to the birth of his life as the birth itself. It may have inspired God.

The preministry contains three cases of Moses' intervention on behalf
of some weaker party. These episodes belong to what is really a four-part
story; the remaining part is the story of Moses' stay in Midian. He earns
sanctuary there by his action in the third of the four episodes; sanctuary is
required by his action in the first episode, and the reaction in the second.
The first incident, Moses' murder of an Egyptian abusing a Hebrew,
incriminates him as an interfering bystander. But he interferes again, this
time in the quarrel of two Hebrews, one of whom is beating the other; he
now reveals himself to Israel as a spokesman. But this second episode also
reveals him to himself as a transgressor, potentially a fugitive from justice.
For the rebuked Hebrew throws Moses' own, earlier violence in his face:
he may be a wanted man, faced with a likely informer.

Outside of any formal judicial structure or vocation, Moses begins his
ministry by acting to police a world polarized into aggressors and victims;
but his private intervention on behalf of abused parties only shows that
the protection he offers is as much the protection he needs. Where there
is no justice, none can be done; there can be no law made or kept without
the prior securing of respect for persons under the law. But there is no
law, and little respect, in evidence. Indeed, without an executive order to
point to, the executive Moses is an outlaw. And without authorization or

appointment, the deliberative Moses is presumptuous, virtually a pre-tender: his authority is disputable, under suspicion of being usurped, no less an encroachment of force than the one he thinks to take issue with.

The third incident shows the same formal elements, but deductions from it—about the kind of law it inculcates—cannot be the same. In the first episode Moses could only defend the traduced Hebrew by killing the traducing Egyptian. Like Othello killing the malignant Turk, the violence of the Egyptian provokes the reciprocal violence of Moses; but as with Othello at the end of his play, it is also a violence against something in himself. For to violence Moses has added stealth. He looks both ways, murders in secret, and hides the body, in effect "man-steals" it. Moses seems to break the sixth commandment, but also eight, nine, or ten, if we think of them as forbidding the furtive or dishonest action. Moses is similarly compromised by the second episode, where he tries to stand back from abuses, rather than fall into repeating them. But Moses cannot get away with murder, without also flying from its scene—yet even after his getaway to Midian, the scene of violence comes back to him.

In the first episode Moses kills the Egyptian because the Hebrew in Egypt had lost his civic status, the rights or obligations to which one might appeal on the slave's or Hebrew's behalf. But in protecting his own, he is like the unforgiving Kenite Lamech, who promises to be avenged "seventy and sevenfold" (Gen. 4:24): as things stand, Moses might have to kill all the Egyptians to save a single Hebrew. In the second episode Moses merely appeals to the Hebrew's lost rights—the "right" that one Hebrew might have to kind treatment or favorable judgment by another Hebrew—yet it is hard to avoid sin even here: "Thou shalt not hate thy brother in thine heart: thou shalt in any wise rebuke they neighbour, and not suffer sin upon him" [RSV: "you shall reason with your neighbor, lest you bear sin because of him"] ". . . nor bear any grudge against the children of thy people" (Lev. 19:17–18). The Hebrews are perhaps breaking the fifth commandment, by not honoring their father—they are all sons of Jacob. There would be no wronging of the Hebrew by his fellow if the honoring of their fathers had not fallen into disuse or disregard. There is hardly any difference between appealing to a tribal covenant long since lost and a civic status not yet found: in the first case, Pharaoh knew not Joseph; in the second, Joseph knows not Abraham.

The story does not yet tell us how rights are got, or from whence rules of conduct derive their authority; but when we consider the dictates of biblical law, the presence of justification in the form of the "motive clause" comes to seem as important as the law itself: "You shall not stand forth against the life of your neighbor: I am the Lord . . . You shall love your neighbor as yourself: I am the Lord" (Lev. 19:16, 18, RSV). But the dissent of the murmuring Hebrew—"Intendest thou to kill me as thou killedst the Egyptian?" (Exod. 2:14)—could make it painfully clear to one that Moses had put the fear of Moses into the offender, but not the fear of God.

The first two episodes show degenerative progressions within themselves, and within their sequence. In the first case, the repression or disadvantaging of a class begets reprisals in kind; but it also begets fraud, by driving the forms of open coercion underground, into secret forms. A society characterized by this devolution is finally cursed, in the sense that only a curse can reach its criminality. "Cursed be he who slays his neighbor in secret," the Shechemite Duodecalogue charges the people (Deut. 27:24, RSV), "And all the people shall say, 'Amen.' " But what "Amen" effects the curse? The one cursing the crime's perpetrator must be a transcendental subject: who else could see the criminal's secret act?

In the second episode, dispute begets violence; the attempt to intervene begets rebellion. The only authority the schismatic Hebrew acknowledges is found in his reference to Moses' previous intervention; Moses' might is his right, he *may* kill if he *can*, having the power to get away with it. The Hebrew's resistance to Moses' authority organizes itself on the same principle as Moses' resistance to the Egyptian. Driving his and the Hebrew's violence into furtive forms, Moses has only created a criminal subclass. For the Hebrew indicates that Moses failed to kill in secret and is in a position to be blackmailed. But the Hebrew's taunting murmur— must Moses now do to him as he did to the Egyptian?—also constitutes an epiphany: Moses could kill the Egyptian because no one was looking, for he looked both ways first (Exod. 2:12). Yet someone was looking. This is the revelation to Cain, and it makes a murderer into a fugitive.

Moses' status will change again, when the fugitive becomes a "landed immigrant." This causes one to ask how the episodes in Egypt differ from the sequel, in which Moses successfully secures the rights of the Midianite daughters, that is, their claim upon the Midian well. For rights really do seem to be an issue here, despite their almost complete absence, conceptually and terminologically speaking, from the law codes of the Pentateuch, apart from property rights. Yet in one of the curses in the Shechemite Duodecalogue, rights of a civil kind are notably recognized: "Cursed be he that perverteth the judgment of the stranger, fatherless, and widow" (Deut. 27:19). Significantly for our theme, these rights (i.e., favorable judgments in behalf of a party at law) are those of the relatively defenseless, or the disadvantaged. Such rights are fiercely defended in the Book of the Covenant itself, where God personally volunteers to take the part of the offended kinsman of abused widows and orphans and inflict a kind of *talio*: "If thou afflict them in any wise, and they cry at all unto me, I will surely hear their cry; And my wrath shall wax hot, and I will kill you with the sword; and your wives shall be widows, and your children father-less" (Exod. 22:23–24). The logic is, one way or another the cry of the bereaved will not go unheard—God will take revenge in battle, using the chance to add to the numbers of those classes blighted by Israel's neglect: he will make more widows and orphans. The argument leads into the circle that the disaffected Hebrew so resisted entering: the community's obligation to others is also its obligation to itself as a community.

The first two episodes might show that doing justice is a matter of securing—or pre-securing—dominion or lordship over the future violator, whose violence violates not only persons but their rights and security, should they have any. The traduced Hebrew had no civil rights, and the weaker Hebrew had no claim on the stronger Hebrew. In Egypt there was no sovereignty, tribunal, or compact to which the aggrieved could appeal. And in Egypt Moses had no claim upon either Egyptian or Hebrew. He was either a helpless bystander, or an endangered fugitive.

Where no rights are prescribed, there are none to secure; where no claims are honored, none need be made. And yet we feel with Moses that the weaker party might have a right or a claim, if only because existence itself seems to constitute such a claim, once its minimal condition has been granted. The person with existence has a claim to it, and thence to welfare, protection, and—circularly—the right to recover the rights they might have enjoyed except for being disadvantaged. The disadvantaged need an advocate, one to exercise a preliminary right to claim rights. But the claim cannot be heard unless someone is found strong enough, and willing, to act out of compassion or graciousness on the weaker party's behalf, in their place—but also to act on behalf of principle, and its articu-lation. Society itself will want to take this advocate's part, once he has made himself known, if the generalization of intervention makes it avail-able to all: everybody will want their new right—to have their rights—pro-tected.

Justice may be more than a defensive mutualizing of security, but that must be better than the polarization of coercion that has led us from bat-tery to murder in the first episode and from assault to blackmail in the second. The stronger Hebrew discounts his interest in his right to protec-tion by a weaker one. The Pharaoh "knew not Joseph," but neither did the Hebrew: he need not be his brother's keeper. Just as surely, he knew not Moses, for the story has him ask who made Moses "a prince and a judge over" him and his fellow (Exod. 2:14). Joseph's alienated brothers—who did not know their brother reigning in Egypt—put him such a ques-tion back in Canaan: "Shalt thou indeed reign over us? or . . . have dominion over us?" (Gen. 37:8). The aggressor rebels against Moses' future leadership proleptically, but also retroactively, if he reacts in terms of the prior figure of Joseph. He resembles the Miriam and Aaron who take, as their occasion for exception to Moses, his "outlandish" marriage to a Cushite wife—for Moses' Egyptian side has its precedent in Joseph's Egyptian wife. All three questions could come from the Southern kingdom, objecting to a Northern spokesmanship so Josephic-Mosaic as to be anti-Aaronid: "Hath the Lord indeed spoken only by Moses?" Miriam and Aaron ask (Num. 12:2).

The Hebrew's original question also echoes the rebellious words of Dathan and Abiram, the priests who argue in the wilderness against the arrogation to Moses of a holiness that they maintain belongs to the whole congregation. When summoned by Moses to face the charges of insubordination, the two priests refuse, saying that it is bad enough that Moses has led Israel into the wilderness, without his also being compelled to lord it over them (Num. 16:13: "Is it a small thing that thou hast brought us up . . . to kill us in the wilderness, except thou make thyself altogether a prince over us?"). Moses had no sign to make before the rebellious Hebrew, but in his call he is touched by leprosy; his hand becomes as white as snow (Exod. 4:6). God punishes Miriam and Aaron with the same sign, and Miriam becomes white as snow (Num. 12:10). The rebellious priests, however, are consumed by fire, and swallowed by the earth. These are Mosaic signs too, for the bush burning on Sinai was not consumed, and the people crossing the Reed Sea were not drowned.

The question of the political identity of those searching Moses' title will occupy us elsewhere, but it can only confirm that having a consistent ideology is a prerequisite for the exercise of sway. The murmur of the disaffected Hebrew informs Moses that his bid for power conspicuously lacks authority. His dialogue with God in Exodus 3 acknowledges this. Until God says, "Thus shalt thou say unto the children of Israel, The Lord God of your fathers, the God of Abraham, the God of Isaac, and the God of Jacob, hath sent me unto you: this is my name forever" (Exod. 3:15), Moses' cause lacks ideological support.

The Hebrew's question might also show Moses that the grounds of any authority he might hope to have are not "in Egypt," even while the would-be magistrate will have to secure a virtually Egyptian dominion over his people. Oppression and demoralization in Egypt have robbed the Hebrew people of their claims to protection, subscription to leadership, and concern over each other. In Egypt they are all outside the protection of the law, and Moses himself, the self-appointed protector and adjudicator, is the most outside of all. For once Moses the protector was revealed to himself as an outlaw, he became Moses the fugitive.

A fugitive from the scene of a murder seems to be a figure for a man without rights, at least if we see him from the back. His claims upon society drop away from him as he is precipitated into flight. For him it is the land of Nod (that is, Wandering), and no one will care for him. Whoever finds him is free to take away his life. But if we see this fugitive coming toward us, a different perspective may obtain. He is in flight *toward* us; he appears to be in danger and in need. He may have claims on our help. He may have fled a place where decent people are not surviving, where violence and the *modus vivendi* have tragically become inseparable.

The third episode in Exodus 2:11–22, at the well in Midian, shows Moses again standing up for the rights of the downtrodden. The fugitive still feels called upon to undertake the role of public defender. But here his action is more successful: he secures the use of the well for the daughters, and he also secures their rights. But what are the various parties' rights? What claims do the various parties have upon the various things claimed? Why might their rights be honored here and not in Egypt?

First, Moses abides in the land, and second, he sits beside its well. Wells are themselves landmarks, and digging them makes a claim upon the land and its use, as in the stories of Isaac finding water at Gerar and Beersheba. The well stories in Genesis 26 exhibit the same four-part structure that controls the stories of Moses' preministry, because the stories anticipate the same dénouement. Isaac digs four wells. The first three are in a valley in Gerar. And the first two are taken away from him. "The water is ours," the locals say; the wells are the site of conflict, not negotiation: "and he called the name of the well Esek; because they strove with him" (vs. 20). But at the third well things go better for Isaac, and he calls the site Rehoboth, "For now the Lord hath made room for us, and we shall be fruitful in the land" (vs. 22). Thanks to Isaac, the locals have their water, and now are willing to share. The site name ("enlargement") tells us Isaac has become recognizably Abrahamic, for he now migrates to Beersheba, where God reasserts his promises to him. Here his servants begin to dig his fourth well. And now Abimelech, who originally sent Isaac and his "mightier" numbers away from him, reappears to claim a peaceable relation with Isaac, now that Isaac, like Abraham, is "blessed of the Lord" (26:29; '*āsûm*, 'mighty,' is God's word for Abraham's future at Gen. 18:18). A covenant is offered, accepted, and sealed, and the servants then report that the fourth well has also produced water (Gen. 26:31–32). Isaac names the site Beersheba after the oath of this new social contract. We may compare Moses' inclusion in Midianite society by his marriage into its priestly family.

Where Isaac was seeking water rights, Moses is seeking justice: twice unsuccessfully, when resources and justice are scarce, and twice successfully, when living room and sanctuary are also found. His abiding by the well tends to define Moses as a sojourner *in* a land (rather than as a fugitive *from* one): he will need to use the land's water, however little, whether or not he has any acknowledged right to it. But the story does not have him try to use the well to water a flock or caravan, for he has none. It is the daughters who try to use the well and have their claim violated: "the shepherds came and drove them away" (Exod. 2:17). Are these shepherds suffered to do this regularly? If they are, do they do it whenever they meet a weaker party, or just in repeated tellings of this story? Do they happen to be in the neighborhood only this once, ready and able to take water by force, or have they a known priority or prerogative?

We suspect that the shepherds are habitual offenders, because Reuel questions the early return of his daughters. He implies that it ordinarily takes his daughters a longer time to water the flock—because, we assume, others regularly are permitted to take their turn before them. We also note here that the water for the flock has already been raised and poured into troughs when the shepherds commandeer the well; they not only appropriate the young women's turn, but also rob them of the results of their work. Where Rebekah eagerly watered the camels that accompanied Abraham's ring-bearing ambassador, Reuel's defrauded daughters will have watered the flock of the shepherds without any return. They are thus put into the expropriated position of Moses' enslaved kinsmen in Egypt, and Moses is therefore moved to intervene on their behalf.

We cannot decide the answer to the question of whether the shepherds' "right" is purely *de facto*, or also somewhat *de jure*, but in neither case are we likely to assume that they are the only party here with any rights. Moses is only a sojourner, but the daughters are tied to the well by locality; they are not divorced from the land, unlike the Hebrews in Egypt. A well and a priesthood might both be central to Midian existence, if theirs is a traditional society. For the father is a *local* priest: it is not implied he is visiting from somewhere else. The less the shepherds are equally Midianite, the more their right is only a sojourner's claim on privileges, or a stranger's claim on the consideration of locals. But in defending a right belonging to all parties, the right of those on the land to the use of its resources, Moses defends the claim of the shepherds as much as that of the daughters: visiting shepherds cannot have a stronger claim than locals, even though they are better equipped to defend a weaker claim.

If Moses is defending the right of "daughters" over that of outsiders, then he is already defending the right of the future female progeny of Zelophehad: the right, in the absence of sons, of a man's daughters to inherit his land. But Moses will also establish the right of the daughters' tribe to keep their inheritance within that tribe (Num. 26:33, 36:1–12): by marriage. If we omit the insertions of Deuteronomy, the clarification of these inalienable land-rights is the very last of "the commandments and the judgments, which the Lord commanded by the hand of Moses unto the children of Israel in the plains of Moab by Jordan near Jericho" (Num. 36:13), before the report of Moses' death and the march on the promised land at the opening of Joshua: "Every place that the sole of your foot shall tread upon," God declares, "that have I given unto you, as I said unto Moses" (Josh. 1:3).

Like the freedom of speech and motion that define a "free country," or the safe water that defines a livable environment, the right to the land's available resources seems to be one everyone might aspire to have, if they have existence on the earth at all. But at the same time that Moses defends an elementary aspiration to exist, he defends those things his own presence at the sources of life could particularly symbolize: the orphan's right to succor, and the fugitive's right to sanctuary. Moreover, he asserts the worker's right to the fruits of his labor—or to the means of production: for the daughters produce, out of the ground, the water others benefit from. But these are rights no longer tied to one's own locality; they are rights to regain locality itself, when they are sought for those whose locality and shelter or means to subsistence have been lost or displaced.

Thus Moses in Midian has essentially been brought to a Pisgah-sight of the idea that a country is a sanctuary for rights that otherwise do not exist: that is, the rights of his countrymen in Egypt, whose rights are lost insofar as Egypt is not their country. Midian is only a stopgap for another country, and Moses will not ever enter the actual sovereign territory of Israel; but that is just why he is able to project its legislation, that is, from an ideal standpoint outside it. "An *Egyptian* delivered us," the daughters report (Exod. 3:19). They almost could have said, a Samaritan.

All four parts of the preministry of Moses touch upon the means to social security: reciprocal violence and a counterbalance of coercive force in the first case, and the imposition of a judge's restraining order in the second; mutual protection pacts and a dwelling place or permanent guest status in the remaining two cases of the well scene and the marriage into Midian. Yet the stories also touch on "pre-securities." For no one has appealed to any laws in these stories, yet there can be no justice without a prior elaboration upon violence as the violation of the law—when someone cries foul. Yet the only right that provides a right to other rights has turned out to be the seemingly exceptional right to sanctuary, the right within society to a free zone of unmolested security from society.

For where can the law come from, how can the check on violence and violations assert itself independently, if the law is only a check upon offenses because it occasions and sanctions reprisals that in turn become further offenses?

> To take the life of an enemy is to help him,
> a little, towards destroying your own. Indeed, that is why
> we hate our enemies: because they force us to kill them.

A murderer hides the dead man in the ground:
but his crime rears up and topples on to the living,
for it is they who now must hunt the murderer,
murder him, and hide him in the ground: it is they
who now feel the touch of death cold in their bones.[1]

This origin for the law makes all who enforce it potential fugitives from further just reprisals: so the first encounter extends itself into the second.

But where can the law come from, if it is the creation of precedent, that is, of cases already brought before the law, before an authority that must have been pre-acknowledged to be effective? So the second encounter extends into the third: for the quarreling Hebrew never agreed to submit to arbitration, nor to observe the rights of a fellow whom Egypt had deprived of these rights. When Moses the Israelite suggests to the Hebrew that he should be his brother's keeper, the Hebrew replies that Moses the Egyptian has not been *his* brother's keeper. Why should the Hebrew submit the judgment of a violent quarrel to a fugitive slave stained with the blood of his master? Why should he be answerable to one of two violent "Egyptians" now taking issue with his own, Egyptian treatment of another Hebrew?

And how or why—in Moses' third encounter itself—does the class of the weak qualify for the assistance of the strong? Does the well merely belong to whomever is strong enough to possess it? And how—in the fourth encounter—has the priest come by his knowledge of the obligations of sanctuary, apart from living in a "circumcised" community that might already honor them? The circle of questions raised by Exodus 2:11–22 paradoxically points toward the monopoly or priority of means that an unquestioned righteousness or rightness enjoys over decideable rights; that preemptive power enjoys over the remedial correction of violations; that divinely ordained sanctuary enjoys over the application of secular sanctions; in short, to the priority of divine intervention over human interference. In that case, the social contract is hardly social at all. Far from being a bilateral settlement made between consenting parties—parties to a social consensus—it is a divine fiat and a unilaterally donated gift, like the light in Genesis 1:3. Thus the questions raised by Moses' first encounters do not initially point him back toward his lost homeland in Egypt, but neither do they allow him to remain anchored in his new homeland in Midian. Rather, they point him away from society altogether, toward the mountain of God.

·9·
"THUS I AM TO BE REMEMBERED":
SINAI AND THE NAME

BUT THIS FURTHER SHOULD BE SAID BECAUSE OF THE BOWMAN. Lo, the
wretched Asiatic—it goes ill with the place where he is, afflicted
with water, difficult from many trees, the ways thereof painful
because of the mountains. He does not dwell in a single place, but
his legs are made to go astray. He has been fighting ever since the
time of Horus, but he does not conquer, nor yet can he be conquered. He does not announce a day in fighting, like a thief who
[scouts and works] for a gang.
BUT AS I LIVE! I AM WHILE I AM!
("The Instruction for King Meri-Ka-Re," after *ANET*, p. 416)

Sinai is in the wilderness (Exod. 19:1, Num. 1:1, 33:15), and the wilderness
is less a place than a space. It is not Egypt, the place where there is no
justice for Hebrews. Neither is it an alternate homeland, such as Midian,
where there is a family, clan justice, traces of peoplehood, and a priesthood. Sinai is permanently out in the territories, with the feral creature,
the bedouin, and the storm. Set apart, well-nigh empty, this extraterritorial space is almost perforce holy. If it cannot be inhabited, it cannot be
profaned—it can be visited, but its only "native" is one whose presence is
wholly and starkly Other.

The mountain of God is in the desert (Exod. 19:2, Num. 33:16, "the
desert of Sinai"); the desert can be startling testimony to the presence of
God, because it effectively reduces all other possible presences to their
status anterior to the Creation. One might truly say here, "Behold, the
Lord maketh the earth empty, and maketh it waste, and turneth it upside
down, and scattereth abroad the inhabitants thereof" (Isa. 24:1). "Now
Moses . . . led [Reuel's] flock to the backside (*'aḥar*) of the desert, and
came to the mountain of God" (Exod. 3:1). Moses' charges are led here
indeed, and here their leader sees the back parts (*'aḥôr*) of God (Exod.
33:23).

---

i

The story of Moses in Midian begins with the sojourner watering a local flock; it culminates in God's call to return from a literal pastoral care in Midian to a metaphorical pastoral care in Egypt. Moses is ordained to represent the greater shepherd who will lead the congregation to water to heal its thirst—for in the wilderness Moses heals the bitter water (Exod. 15:25) and cures the thirst-causing bites of the fiery serpents (Num. 21:6–9). The miracles of the new exodus, in so-called Deutero-Isaiah and Trito-Isaiah, are largely the water miracles of the old one (Isa. 41:17–20; 43:2, 16–21; 48:21; 58:11a; 63:11–14), along with the pillars of cloud and fire that conduct Israel at the outset (cf. Isa. 58:8: "Then shall thy light break forth as the morning, and thine health shall spring forth speedily: and thy righteousness shall go before thee; the glory of the Lord shall be thy rereward"). In part because it occurs in the narrative twice, Paul at 1 Corinthians 10:4 understands the water-bearing rock of Exodus 17 and/or Numbers 20 to have also been part of Israel's escort. On the first occasion, God orders Moses, "Go on before the people . . . I will stand before thee there upon the rock in Horeb; and thou shalt smite the rock, and there shall come water out of it, that the people may drink" (Exod. 17:5–6). On the evidence of the "token" in Exodus 3:12, where God predicts that Moses will bring the people out of Egypt and "shall serve God upon this mountain," God will also have waited for Moses' return to "the mountain of God, even to Horeb" (Exod. 3:1). It is such a faithful rock that Yahweh is appointing for the foundations of the Israelite congregation, by directing the attention of Moses in Midian to this same headland in the wilderness. "Is there a God besides me?" the all-encompassing Yahweh of Isaiah 44:8b will ask exilic Israel: "There is no Rock; I know not any" (RSV).

Moses *remembers* this rock, that is, the God of several Psalms, who is above all "the Mighty One of Jacob . . . the Stone of Israel" (Gen. 49:24, JPS).[1] That Jacob's God is a rock helps explain the narrative's insistence on Jacob's dealings with pillar, cairn, and stone. One of these is the great rock he single-handedly rolls from a well, as he otherwise takes on God (Gen. 29:2–10, 32:24); other stones he takes and puts to be his pillow, whereupon he dreams about God (Gen. 28:11–15). When Moses sets up twelve pillars at Sinai he is "re-membering" the twelve sons of the Jacob associated with rocks (Exod. 24:4). He indicts forgetfulness in his Song at the Jordan: "Of the Rock that begat thee thou art unmindful, and hast forgotten God that formed thee. . . . their rock is not as our Rock" (Deut. 32:18, 31).

The Bible puts an analogous prayer in Moses' mouth at the Reed Sea:

"plant them in the mountain of thine [= God's] inheritance" (Exod. 15:17). But as yet there is no Zion—"the mountain of his holiness" in Psalm 48:1—to apply the phrase to, nor any Psalm 48 to help an Israelite apply it. The wind, fear, and flight of Moses' Song at the Reed Sea (Exod. 15:10, 14–16) approximate the same divine affect in the Psalm (48:5–7), but with the Zion of David so much in the province of another era, what can Moses' prayer foresee in Sinai, beyond a rendezvous? A volcano in a desert is quite outside the pale of arable land—it cannot be a plantation for anyone. Yet Sinaitic *experience* is heritable, and God does indeed wait for every subsequent Israel to come to this appointed and devoted rock.

The deity established by the patriarchal narrative is attached to persons before places: he is attached to places only incidentally. He is not called a *particular* rock. The biblical ambiguity about the mountain of God, where Moses meets the god of the fathers, and where this god first "visits" his people Israel (so Exod. 4:31, and Moses' report, at Exod. 5:3)—whether the place is Sinai or Horeb—shows that the Sinaitic god is really no exception to the rule of God's omnipresence, despite the place's being sanctified by his visit, or even by his coming *from* there (Deut. 33:2, Judg. 5:5). The rock, in the passage quoted from Exodus 17:5–6, is not understood as a sacred place per se, but as a place consecrated by a particular *assignation.* God's present or former address is nothing like his permanent residence. It is less a rock in space than an event in time.

In the loneliness of Sinai, Moses is unlikely to have any other gods before him, or before *Him.* He is on "holy ground" not because a mountain on the margins of Midian is sacred to God or because God is devoted to difficult terrain generally: *contra* the mistaken assertion of Ben Hadad's servants that the Israelites' God is only powerful in the mountains (1 Kings 20:23). Sinai is the kind of place where God can be heard, because it is isolated from human and national jurisdictions. The meeting at such a set-apart site is a sacred event, if it issues in commandments pertaining to holiness, offerings, and the exclusiveness of God's jurisdiction; sacrifice is offered, and a meal with him is taken there (Exod. 24:5, 9–11). Yet no holy day is instituted on the occasion, and no altar consecrated to God's name on the site. The meeting place of God and Moses betokens a jurisdiction not of men, and an inheritance not of land.

ii

Like Moses' life in Midian, his Sinaitic conversation with God asks to be understood by means of patriarchal criteria. Both Abraham and Jacob seem to have bartered with the deity: Abraham over the number of righteous persons needed to redeem Sodom from destruction (Gen. 18:16–33), and Jacob over the return he is owed for the angel's release from their mutual embrace (Gen. 32:24–29). The righteous Abraham invoked God's moral obligation to the innocent; the strong wrestler Jacob attempted to extract his attacker's name from him, and to gain the advantage of a blessing. God recognized Jacob with his name Israel; he "remembered Abraham, and sent Lot out of the midst of the overthrow" (Gen. 19:29)—despite Lot's unpatriarchal treatment of his daughters. Perhaps God reckoned Lot righteous more on account of Abraham than of Lot; he later makes his promises to Isaac because of his father's heedfulness (Gen. 26:5). Abraham's negotiations had in view Lot's deliverance from the overthrow of the cities of the plain, the smoke of which "went up as the smoke of a furnace" (Gen. 19:28), when God decided to act upon the human outcry against the wickedness there. The Bible also says God delivered Israel from Egypt as from a "furnace of iron" (Deut. 4:20, 1 Kings 8:51), after the people's cry came up to God. Moses also intercedes with God when his own are come under the wrath: "Shall one man sin, and wilt thou be wroth with all the congregation?" (Num. 16:22).

What emerges from these conversations—to paraphrase Hans-Georg Gadamer[2]—is each party's right to a hearing, and the right of the addressed human party to an interrogation of the divine intentions. The conversationalists have a common purpose of doing their subject justice. Abraham secures the right of the human party to a plentitude of assurances and the right of rebuttal. For God will speak to Moses, as one place says, "mouth to mouth" (Num. 12:8), which is to say, with Moses speaking *back*.

The conversation between God and Moses takes the form of question and answer, because it is a mutual inquiry, undertaken by the two parties, as to the possibility of their dialogue, of conversation *between* them. So long as it lasts, a conversation (again paraphrasing Gadamer) is governed by an agreement between the partners to seek further grounds of agreement. To ask God his name, as Moses does, might well be to ask a conversation partner how, for purposes of further and more familiar conversation, he is to be addressed. God himself declares he has known Moses "by name," a usage that means showing Moses favor (Exod. 33:12).

The question of God's name, in Exodus 3, proves a means for eliciting considerable further conversation, a further demonstration, beyond the Name itself, of God's actuality and its verbal mode. The long exchange shows God is *with* his human addressee. Such a conversation, however, also shows its partners doing more than merely conducting a talk that establishes parity and cooperation: it also shows each of them allowing himself to be governed in the presence of the other by conversational norms. Being on speaking terms, the speakers can conduct themselves from different standpoints toward a common object of mutual understanding. This is true even between unequal parties; even conversations that begin merely because one party has a bone to pick may seek to "draw out" the other party. "God's controversy with Israel," for example, seeks to bring Israel to the point of participating in its own indictment, along with its human prosecutors the prophets.

Abraham's posture of intercession and negotiation in Genesis 18, like Moses' protests inviting God's rebuttals in Exodus 3–4, illustrates that conversations of some length are exercises in testing the commonness or compatibility of the parties' object. As Job shows, such conversations also test or challenge the limits of each party's knowledge. Both Moses and God have seen the suffering of Israel, just as Abraham and God both knew something of what there was in Sodom. If, in the course of mutual testing, the conversation degenerates into a mere challenging of the prerogatives and presumption and status of the other conversationalist, it reduces itself to a sterile contest. Such a deadlock appears in the story of Jacob and the angel in Genesis 32; verbal temptations, like that of Jesus by Satan in the nativity gospels (Matt. 4:1–11, Luke 4:1–13), tend in the same direction. This kind of dialogue only superficially respects the differences and the respective dignities of the conversationalists, each speaker attempting to kidnap the common object of conversation for his own, or to prevent its being kidnapped by his rival. Jacob devises his strategy for getting himself blessed, it seems, so that he may at least come out even in a contest that otherwise will lame him. Jacob's object is himself and his house, and his questions are levied as demands. Behind them lie the twin's demand for recognition as an individual son, and the son-in-law's demand for recognition as the father of a family. At the time of this story, Jacob is near to being reconciled with the brother he has formerly cheated out of his father's blessing, and so the adversary relation governing the conversation is nearly exhausted. Yet without this adversary relation, Jacob might have had little to talk about. When he meets his brother, he comes loaded with gifts and comparisons of Esau to God (Gen. 33:10). In modern parlance, he comes on strong. So must anyone who would deal with him, *in that he hath been strong against God* (Gen. 32:28, AT).

The attacking angel, the symbolic addresser in Jacob's conversation, begrudges Jacob any but an elliptical disclosure of his name, and Jacob in Genesis 32 wins his blessing and his new theophoric cognomen, Israel, only in return for letting his fellow wrestler escape from their temporarily common ground. Indeed, the escaping motion is as much Jacob's own: in the sequel Esau will go to Edom, but Jacob escapes to Succoth, as he once escaped from Esau to go to Padan-Aram, and as he thereafter escapes from Laban to return to the land of his birth. Jacob's controversial stance polarizes conversation to the exclusion of any common object: each party is dominated by the address of the other, bringing them each, through their will to overpower the other, to a fixed likeness as rivals and contestants, but to an ambiguous discrepancy as respondents or communicators. Jacob names the site of the match Face-of-God, or Peniel, but since Jacob leaves at the break of day, God retreats unseen. Yet he has been partly forced to acknowledge his divinity, even if he bears a suspicious resemblance to the Esau whose countenance Jacob subsequently says is like the face of God.

We are not surprised that Jacob's powerful protector-god, watching over Jacob and his interests, tests his subject's fitness, rather than his loyalty or obedience. God regularly tests or approves whatever he has created, here Jacob's ability to turn the tables on an alienated Other and make his demands himself. Jacob leaves lame, yet not wholly bested by this other. Thus Esau is compelled to accept Jacob's gift (Gen. 33:11), and to allow his brother's existence generally; Jacob quickly puts as much space between them as is otherwise indicated by the fact that they only meet again at Isaac's funeral. Some conversations end on a new plateau of mutualized understanding, and some in an impasse: a kind of frustrated duelists' draw.

The testing in the conversation of Moses and God does not obliterate the parties' differences: God and man are in no way equals. But where Abraham in Genesis 18 maintains his claim to consideration, and where Jacob in Genesis 32 does not lose his nerve, Moses in Exodus 3–4 is both intimidated and out-maneuvered. But even if he does not come off so well as the others, Moses is probably brought much further. Abraham successfully asserts that the righteous should not be permitted to suffer with the wicked, but God and Abraham never actually acknowledge to each other that it is Lot they are talking about, because, as subsequent events suggest, Abraham could not have faithfully asserted that Lot was the real Simon Pure. Between the speakers there may remain a barrier, an unspoken distrust. In contrast to its physical intimacy, Jacob's parley is even more of a standoff: controversy is prolonged, communication abbreviated.

Jacob comes away from his contest with the earnings of his self-assertion, his nameability and his lameness: he wins a somewhat self-defeating identification with his genius for controversy and self-assertion, which otherwise appears in his shadowy, attacking other. He gets himself a name—"Striver with" or "Strong against" El—that derives an awareness of God from affirmations of Israel's own unity of consciousness, or from an underdog twin's strong instinct for surviving his other: from the womb.

Moses, in contrast, is born to be put up for adoption; his cradle's *here am I* puts him at the conversational dispose of another from the outset.

iii

There are sacrifices at Sinai, but the mount has no site-in-life as a cult center; Moses' encounter there after the exodus involves an elaborate calendar of forty-day intervals, but no festival names Sinai as its inception. The chief memorial motif in the call story is the disclosure of the name by which God is to be remembered. No less than other biblical inaugural occasions, reiteration is built into it. And like the exchanges between the parties in the birth story, the conversation is eductive: it draws out the two parties concerned. For it draws out, from God himself, the etiological etymon of the name Yahweh, just as the birth story ended up by drawing the name Moses from Pharaoh's daughter. Pharaoh's daughter stumbles on Moses' future name in the way she happens upon Moses and his nurse—by the predesign of someone hidden from her. The storyteller and Moses' sponsors are of one mind in this matter, putting Moses in a postnatal situation that will allow the princess to invent Moses' name out of circumstances of a mysterious origin, even as these circumstances have cast her in the role of the midwives whom Pharaoh has formerly attempted to compromise: *all* children, after all, are "drawn out." The princess (or else the storyteller through her) reinvents the name Moses on etymological principles for an audience that knows the vocable and the name. At the same time, the princess as narrator departs slightly from the name that she would have chosen as an Egyptian: for the name's original meaning, roughly "Junior," serves as the suffix for a name derived from the bearer's parent or sponsor. Again, *all* children are "born of." But "born of" cannot stand by itself—one must be the offspring of *someone*, and Moses' parentage is precisely what the princess's discovery of the foundling calls into question: "Born of *whom?*" Moses is not Born-of-Ra, the Rameses whose name-city the enslaved Hebrews build, but of Am-ram ("people exalted"), whose name appears in a genealogy the princess may never hear.

The situation is not altogether similar with the name of God. To begin with, God is necessarily more knowing than the princess, and so in eliciting a name perhaps he is also a good deal wittier. Unlike the princess, God begins from a foregrounding in the present conversation, rather than in the facts of nativity. The Hebrew god is not in any sense "born," so the Name is sought in the Hebrew language God has been using about being the god of Moses' father. As Moses was formerly "Son of whom?", God is now "God of whom?", for Moses' father has not been named: he was dropped as soon as he was introduced, as "a man of the house of Levi," upon his having *taken* Moses' mother (Exod. 2:1). From our point of view, it is as if God had said to Moses, "I am the god of a man of the house of Levi," or "I am the god of a man who was your father." No wonder scholars have wanted to make him the god of the priest of Midian.

The text itself does not shy away from having God discover his name—and hence his identity—in the way one might discover a hat size, by trying on different possibilities. God arrives at his name out of a quasi-Cartesian deduction from his givenness, "I am that I am." But the relative pronoun seems to lack a proper antecedent—"I am *that* that I am," which can be understood as "I am *the one* that I am." Or else the antecedent is understood to be the whole preceding clause: " 'I am,' that exists"; or else, perhaps, "I that am, am." But there is something incomplete, defective, or contracted about the sentence "I am, that am," since the sentiment lacks any predication or suggestion of what the "I" denotes, apart from the self-avouching, first-person voice of a possible existent.[3] The Name, in this form, does not seem to be used elsewhere, in the way that "I am Yahweh" and "I am he" are used. The sentence is unlike "I am gracious to whom I am gracious," or else the *idem per idem* structure, used in a context of divine self-disclosure at Exodus 33:19, is only superficially like.[4] Merciful is a kind of prosopopoeia through an attribute, like The Kindly Ones for the Furies. Biblical personal names are regularly formed this way—e.g., Jehohanan, God-is-gracious (1 Chron. 26:3, Neh. 12:13), and Jerahmeel, God-is-merciful (1 Chron. 2:9, 24:29, Jer. 36:26)—but "I am [——] that I am," or " 'I am,' that am [——]," does not answer, *What* am I? As well have said, Anything But.

God nonetheless seems to declare his name to be a "word" in the sense of a message: "I am that I am." But God does not ever actually say "My *name* is I-am-that-I-am," in the way Odysseus says "My name is No One."[5] Possibly God is not answering Moses' question, but refusing to answer it, censuring any Hebrew mistrustful enough to attempt to uncover what God has reserved to himself.[6] The thought of God as any *thing* one might think him to be is likely to be specious,[7] and thinking of him in terms of what he has *done*—that is, as the savior revealed by the exodus—is not yet possible. Whoever he is, that "whoever" is sufficient, and a proper trust in his existence or givenness as the kind of being entitled to use the personal pronoun, or "I," will abort any further, potentially idolatrous inquiry.

If the long name is naggingly incomplete as a grammatical construction, as if the sentence had fallen in on itself, its dehydration may suggest a kind of introversion in God, a movement toward self-enclosure that necessarily accompanies any authentic gesture of self-revelation to another on the part of the divine. God withdraws from the questioner, expressing reluctance to answer a poor question. If his name implies that he is something other than what he is, namely "the god," he is best referred to pronominally. Long lists of names for several principal gods in ancient Near

Eastern texts lead to the same conclusion: God is really unnameable: he cannot be known in the way Rumpelstiltskin can.

God does not leave it at that, however. He is made to anticipate a good deal of evidence in the Bible for a tradition of variations on Yahweh's "I-am-ness."[8] For however unnameable, the whole point about God is that he can be called upon. The story has him keep refining upon his initial declaration, accommodating and tailoring it to a growing sense of Moses' most pressing need. Yet like the law tables, God gives Moses the Name in a form in which it might repel and/or be repelled. Despite the potential for rejection, however, God graciously reverses his self-withholding or reservation across the three critical verses in Exodus 3:13–15, and offers the shortened form "I am" as a practical way for Moses (or covenant-makers) to refer to him; he seems to have settled on this form himself when—almost an afterthought—he varies the "I am" to the invariable form Yahweh. Thereafter he suffixes the three titles of the god of the fathers; and only then does he ratify this final form as that name which he is henceforth determined to be remembered by. The net result—of whatever redaction-history has led to the present text of Exodus 3:13–15—is a remarkably high quotient of names and/or periphrases for God.

The quantity of speculation and the versatility of interpretations found in this text imply both freedom and reverence: freedom to question the Name, and reverence for a particularly tautologous understanding of it. The Name seems almost negotiable, God himself being willing to play with ways of arriving at it, or deriving it from what he has already committed himself to. The audience knows the final name, as it knew the name the princess would arrive at for Moses. Yet by means of this kind of story an audience can be taught—or can acquire—a new value for the Name, even while refamiliarizing itself with it, by hearing a story character arriving at a state of awareness like Israel's own. Unlike the princess, however, God does not look to external circumstances for his inspiration; he looks to the more elemental circumstance of his being present—and being self-aware. At Genesis 16:13 Hagar witnesses to a God of Seeing, while she is pregnant with the Ishmael whose name means God Hears. All self-consciousness implies a division of consciousness on the model of the subject-object relation: "I am" will also mean "I am *hereabouts*," consciousness alone being able to be present to itself. If names indicate natures, God's unnameability also clues us in to the ban on dumb images: amorphous images like the burning bush encourage one to imagine God as residing in a living vocable: "ye . . . saw no similitude; only . . . a voice" (Deut. 4:12). But in speaking, God makes himself present to anyone within hearing, in order to make him know God in his *word*. He begins the name-verses assuring Moses he will be *with* him, hence *with his mouth* (Exod. 3:12, 4:12). In Exodus 33:14 he promises Moses, "My presence shall go with thee, and I will give thee rest." The I-am etymology is thus suited to Moses' need for assurance in his ministry. It insists on God's being as his bond: he will be, as he has said, "with." With God, God is; what *is*, must needs be trusted.

The etymology of God's name is a reminder, a reiteration. Being given reiteratively, the Name shows us the Sinaitic God as the one who will say to Moses "I cause my name to be remembered": it is a memorable name story that God uses for the purpose, while at the same time prescribing how he is to be remembered by it (Exod. 20:24, 3:15). It is startling to hear God offering Moses an etymological substrate for his name, as if he were a rabbi exploring the choice of a peculiar word in a text. Far from its being taboo, God may even make light of the Name, its future unmentionability included. He not only fixes on the right vocable, he also offers an embarrassment of riches for its meaning; it is his kind of joke, the most solemn things hardly ever being the most exempt from jest.

God is the only character in the Bible who must needs be naming himself, but he is not the only one with two names, one of them being taken on at the character's accession to his or her spiritual majority. God's self-naming stands in for both his birthday and his saint's day. "Call me Jacob's god," the Jahwist's deity might say at Bethel (Gen. 28:13, "I am Yahweh God of Abraham," with vs. 21, "then shall Yahweh be *my* God" [AT]); then the Elohist and Priestly God would say, "Call Israel's god Yahweh" (Exod. 3:13ff., 6:3). Hosea 1:9 and Isaiah 52:6 particularly refer to the name's Sinaitic etymology, but these parallels, being in the prophets, tend to prove that the Name pericope is not wholly inspired by the need of the cult to attach itself to its namesake, as opposed to a nation needing to attach itself to the Name cult. In Genesis 32 this is ambiguous, but not in Exodus 3. For the prophets, God's name means he can be no other than he who has proven to be the sole god of a *nation*: God is there for an Israel of God. Their monotheistical program is political: i.e., *under God, one nation.*

Moses is a prophet who, like Hosea, can know this reading of the Name, and be charged with keeping it. But if indeed "the Lord God will do nothing, but he revealeth his secret unto his servants the prophets" (Amos 3:7), the revelation of the Name to his prophet Moses contains this secret as well, that the God who is for Israel can also *not* be for it. For in Hosea it is above all the covenant-making and covenant-breaking god who is the real content of God's I-am-ness: "And he said, call its name Not-My-People, for you are not people to me and I am not I-Am to you" (Hos. 1:9, AT).

The practice of self-naming is otherwise the prerogative of kings, who may take for themselves a new name, often divine or theophoric, upon their installation on the throne. So the newly elected Pope takes on names typically apostolic or titularly sanctifying, "Innocent," "Pious," "Blessed." Analogously, the name story ends upon its point of departure, when

Yahweh invokes the apostolic succession of the patriarchs, where he accedes in an inheritance of traditional titles and roles. But even as these names are drawn into the official train trailing after God's new name, there is a disinheriting of the patriarchal titles. For while God circles back to the God of the fathers with the new name, he puts the latter first. Now the patriarchal titles become merely titular, retaining only honorific and commemorative force—like the English monarch's "Defender of the Faith." The Sinaitic God says "Thou shalt have no other gods *before me*"; he could add, "Before the God of Abraham was, *I am.*"

Despite any consideration of revised precedence, we may deem the so-called Elohist text essentially correct: the use of the name Yahweh constitutes a Mosaic innovation. Exodus 3:13–15 recognizes a history for the coming-into-being of the Name, even in the space of the three verses themselves. There is also the Priestly summary at Exodus 6:2–3: "And God spoke to Moses, and said to him, I am Yahweh; and I appeared to Abraham, to Isaac, and to Jacob, as God Almighty, but I was not known to them by my name Yahweh" (AT). Zeal for the Name is peculiarly Mosaic. Whatever God's name is, only with the advent of the Mosaic dispensation does it become a prime object of the divine solicitude. So the theophany at Sinai in Exodus 34:5–6: "Yahweh came down in the cloud, and stood with Moses there, and proclaimed in the name of Yahweh. And Yahweh passed by before him, and proclaimed, Yahweh, Yahweh God" (AT).

God can hardly make himself famous with Pharaoh if he has no name with which to do this, nor can Moses come and speak to Pharaoh and Israel in Yahweh's name if he has no knowledge of it. Even if the Name itself were not the discovery of the exodus period, the discovery and promotion of its range, use, serviceability, and sanctity all must be the discovery of *some* period, with which all subsequent Yahwists might identify, even if they themselves lived, paradoxically, in a period in which Yahweh's name or reputation seemed in danger of being forgotten.

As we have said, the call pericope is colored by motifs belonging to the cult legend of a religious site, and yet no possession is taken of it; the legend attaches to a place, yet no dramatizing cultic observance is prescribed by it, or synchronized with it. In place of the original hallowing of the site the story hallows the Name. In place of cultic observance the story prescribes the sign of a return to the mountain, to the momentous beginning made by the publishing of the Name. But in stressing the Name's obliquity, the story implies that there are theological dangers in the new serviceability ascribed to the Name. The third commandment (Exod. 20:7) forbids its use "in vain." The second commandment forbids the making of idols, and idols are accused of speaking vanity (Zech. 10:2). Thus God hesitates to provide Moses with a disposable idol, which is not as it is, but as the worshipper's anxieties and magical usages compel it to be.

The story of God's potential suppression of the Name acknowledges that he is the one whom it is presumptuous to name, yet also the one to whom it is presumptuous not to defer. We have argued that the third commandment implies a courtroom context: the guilty who swear their innocence by Yahweh will not thereby make themselves less guilty. But the commandment cuts two ways: against the profanation of the Name by vain and perjurious usage, and against the vanity of using some *other* name! In the Meribah incident in Numbers 20 Moses is charged with not having sanctified Yahweh in the midst of Israel, and we may wonder if in some way Moses failed to hallow the Name, to do as Moses himself commands in Deuteronomy 6:13: to fear the lord, serve him and swear by his name. Israel rallies to the Name, and only with the Name can Israel articulate its proper confession. For whether or not the Name was first revealed on the mount, at least its sacrality—its weightiness or "glory"—was.

Only a name taken seriously can be threatened by its being taken in vain: the names of the idols are always taken in vain, and they can never be taken in any other way. Concealed in this reflection is the hint that the only and exclusive name of God is esoteric *necessarily*, since it names the one and only god. In that case, the author of Exodus 3 is not only essentially right, but also essentially wrong. Or he has gotten his history backwards. The use of the name Yahweh over Elohim is not the innovation, but the intellectually and historically prior datum, the discipline that made for monotheism. Hence the commandment of discretion in Exodus 23:13: "And in all things that I have said unto you be circumspect: and make no mention of the names of other gods, neither let it be heard out of thy mouth." Do not give the other gods even a linguistic purchase on existence, because, however nominal, that existence would be specious.

By the use of the Name, men were trained to use the word *God*: meaning not my god, but *our* god; and meaning not a god, but *the* god. For the typical English, Greek, and New Testament translation of God's name as the Lord (*kyrios*) contains an understanding it would be impossible to arrive at without someone's first having possessed the Name that the euphemistic usage will suppress. God's solity is first established by using the Name exclusively, a preliminary conditioning that distinguishes him from the other gods potentially "beside" him as rival lords, baals, and idols.

The Name implies God's own lordship, when it is linked with words like "hosts" and "almighty" (Isa. 1:9, Joel 1:15). But the question "Who is on the Lord's side?" cannot be asked in this way without some prior understanding of another side, on whose behalf the question is *not* being put. Subscription to any other principle is "beside" him, but if there were no other gods, who would *not* be on the Lord's side? The distinctiveness of the Name provides a basis for that summons by means of which the faithful are marshalled against the rival principle, which begins as the local Canaanite baal, but ends as the baal-idol of imperial polytheism.

"Thou shalt have no other gods before me": only God's personal disclosure is sufficient to make the gods beside him into the irrelevance and impossibility they are. Moses foresees the first commandment when he asks the Name, if he sees that his mission is to secure allegiance to one who will become *the* one, besides whom there can be no other. "Before *whom?*" the uninitiated might ask; "Who besides?" Isaiah 44:8 might ask back.

The name the princess gives Moses had an end in view, to make Moses an Egyptian Hebrew or a Hebrew Egyptian, one immersed in a body of Egyptian water in order to be drawn out of it: the name provided a terminal augmentative distillation of Moses' birth story, a joke-like bonus in return for an audience's attention. The name of God is more central to the story of Moses' call, since Moses is raised up as a spokesman of this god: for the promulgation of his name is itself a purpose of his service. Moses is called to help God get for himself a name. God is explicit: "for this cause have I raised thee up, for to shew in thee my power; and that my name may be declared throughout all the earth" (Exod. 9:16).

The Name is supposed to be serviceable in this calling, to secure a belief in God's visit. Moses might as well have come to Pharaoh in the name of the Unknown God, yet the name-gift declares that God is determined upon new status as a legal entity, a "person" as it were, entitled to treat with other legal entities, such as the state. But "Who is Yahweh [*mi Yahweh*], that I should heed [*'ašer 'ešma*] his voice?" Pharaoh will ask (Exod. 5:2, AT), sounding not only a little like Yahweh, who will be as he will be, but also like French President Charles de Gaulle, who, on being told of the accession of Nuygen Cao Ky to the last of the increasingly short-lived premierships of the Republic of South Vietnam, inquired "Qui est Ky?" Ky was only a question mark—what authority had a Whosis?

We cannot perhaps get much further on the question of *what* the word *God* names in the narrative in Exodus 3–4, except to note the El who is the specific god of the fathers. The assertion that El is Yahweh does not occur here, in the form found in the name Elijah, and in the chant of his claque at Carmel in 1 Kings 18:39, confessing and proclaiming the Lord's divinity. The Exodus narrative *is* meant to assure us that the *El* that matters has the personality or ethnicity of Yahweh, the personlike quality implicit in his having a personal name. But this *El* resists further attempts to impose on the meaning of his name, by assigning to it the sole and only etymology that prevents its meaning from being delimited by an assertion of *what* he is. Pagan thought arrives at an analogous point when it has a goddess, through an inscription on a temple, say, "I am all that was and that is and that shall be, and no mortal hath lifted my veil."[9] But the Sinaitic context in which the Name is introduced shows that it does not mean primarily "I exist"; nor does it primarily mean that God possesses an essential core of human peculiarity or originality, like a character in Shakespeare.[10] The personal name means that "God is the one who is proclaimed, invoked, questioned, supplicated, and thanked"[11]—consulted, heeded, propitiated, glorified, and served—in matters of greatest moment.

The effect of the conversation in Exodus 3 on the biblical narrative is momentous, if it is to have God pronounce on his name so as to change it, rather than having his human addressee change his. But why would God change his name? In many respects the Yahweh of Moses and the El of the fathers are not that different: *except in the scope of the history they make.* There had come a Pharaoh in Egypt who knew not Joseph; and Moses guesses that his present people are unlikely to put their faith in the God of the Abraham who was. Moses has guessed right: reference to the god of one's father will not be adequate to treat with the state, or to authorize the sudden creation of the national purpose, or to invoke God's peculiar cause, which is that of justice. Doubtless the fathers' names are the recognizable and authoritative ones, and doubtless the fathers' migrations anticipate the motions toward a march upon territorial sovereignty. Abraham is told his descendants will leave Egypt to possess Canaan, and moreover Yahweh rather than Terah brought Abraham out of Ur (Gen. 11:31, 15:7, 13–14). But despite an endorsement of Abraham's campaigns by the high god's priest Melchizedek (Gen. 14:18–20), the patriarchs are not shown as undertaking a mission that would require their coming in God's name: a campaign to seek new religious auspices apart from their present place, or to plunder Egypt by carrying off its portable property, slaves and chattels—the Israelites themselves.

The visitations from God experienced by the patriarchs were personal, even idiosyncratic ones, barely mediated at all, except through their bequeathal from father to son, and inasmuch as these visits were the content of the "blessing of Abraham." The name of the God of the fathers is formed on the name of the one whom the god has adopted, and is then re-formed through the process of reissuing it in the successively augmented editions of the son and grandson. The process exhausts itself in the fourth generation, which divides the Abrahamic-Nahorite genetic inheritance among the sons of Jacob, and unites their political-tribal inheritance as the sons of Israel. Joseph refers to the God of the fathers as the one who has put money in his brothers' grain sacks (Gen. 43:23), perhaps to hint at his brothers' alienation from such a deity in their present straits. Jacob asked for the god's name, upon returning to the promised land, the demand suggesting the emergence of the need to know the name of the personal numen, at the very time that Jacob's own identity seemed most jeopardized—by his impending meeting with his twin. But

Jacob does not, himself, acknowledge the future, collective need for the Name.

The numen's visit vouched for the god's existence; he had been *experienced* as Shield, Awe, Rock, and Mighty One.[12] The visitation of one's father guaranteed virtually the same presence, the father's reporting to the son the god's visit being scarcely less direct than the visit itself. Thus the revelations to Jacob at Genesis 46:3 and 28:13 ("I am El, God of your father," and "I, Yahweh, am the God of Abraham your father, and the God of Isaac" [AT]) differ significantly from the revelation to Moses at the burning bush, despite a superficial similarity in the form. For the identity of the patriarchal recipient's father (or fathers) was no small part of the recipient's own identity. Hence God read himself back into the migration of Terah from Ur—he inspired the father as well as the son (Gen. 15:7 *versus* 11:31). Such a family god needed no name to be experienced as a force moving, guiding, and illuminating the family's counsels. But the purposes of the Mosaic God require a name with which his agent can sign the communications addressed to a circle beyond that of the family's immediate members. The coming of the Name implies the publishing of God's will for a wider audience, the securing of a wider response. It gives Moses' whole people someone to cry out to (Exod. 2:23), to call upon, as individual men in the time of Enosh had done (Gen. 4:26). And it gives God something with which to secure credit and treat with other sovereignties in the earth.

·10·

PROPHET UNTO PHARAOH

---

i

"By a prophet the Lord brought Israel out of Egypt" (Hos. 12:13). From the moment Moses answers God's summons with his own "Here am I," we can guess he will accede to a prophet's call to manifest God's will to a people. During his stay in Midian, Moses cannot have been unmindful of his fellows—how else could he understand his call? Yet his pre-acceptance is contradicted by the shirking "Who am I?" that follows—an "obscurity allusion." Moses' last speech is the self-pitying, "Oh, my Lord, send, I pray, some other person" (Exod. 4:13, RSV). This appeal is angrily brushed aside, while it is also immediately and ironically granted. God assigns Moses the help of his fluent brother Aaron; in a sense Moses had not meant, Aaron provides the other "hand." The alter ego of the tongue-tied appointee will be the high priest; the priesthood can speak in the authoritative voice of its brother Moses. Is Aaron too among the prophets?

The first sign Moses is shown after his interview with God is the coming of his brother, confirming God's prediction that Moses will shortly meet with him. A similar fulfillment confirms the appointment of Saul. After Samuel has anointed him king, he meets a band of the prophets; Samuel has forecast in this company he will be "turned into another man," and it is so: "God gave him another heart" (1 Sam. 10:6, 9). God has singled out Saul upon hearing the outcry of an afflicted people; like Moses also, Saul is given prophetic confirmation and the support of prophetic company. Both stories show a pressure on the savior-designate to share his role with that of a prophet, yet both divide his functions with a priest. Like Samuel, the high priest is an adoptive prophet: Moses' own spokesman, in the Priestly interpretation of Aaron's role as his brother's mouthpiece (Exod. 7:1). Moses is among the priests. But despite officiating with Aaron, he does not really seem to be a priest himself, even if he is an ordainer of other men to the priesthood. As if to say Moses cannot be a priest, he is divinely touched with leprosy at his very call (Exod. 4:6); after meeting with God on Sinai, he wears a veil (Exod. 34:29–35). If this is to cover a damaged countenance, Moses is not alone: his opposites in Pharaoh's court are afflicted with unsightly boils. They "could not stand before Moses because of the boils"

189

(Exod. 9:11)—rather like Miriam, the leprous prophetess shut out from the camp for seven days (Num. 12:14–15). Aaron is spared these stigmata: priests must be unblemished to stand before God—"no one who has a blemish shall draw near, . . . or one who has a mutilated face . . . *he shall not come near the veil* or approach the altar" (Lev. 21:18, 23, RSV). But a burned and tongue-tied Moses might well find himself among the prophets; the cauterized lips of Isaiah (6:5–7) and the seizures of Ezekiel (3:25–26) make the prophet's calling a hazardous one.

"Who hath made man's mouth? or who maketh the dumb, or deaf, or the seeing, or the blind? have not I the Lord?" (Exod. 4:11). Here God says Moses' calling is *prophetic;* he invokes not only the creator of all flesh but also the phenomenology of Yahwist prophecy. Less rhetorical than he makes them out to be, the questions may be translated into others, to which the answer is prophecy itself. Who gives speech to prophets like Amos or Balaam? "The Lord God hath spoken, who can but prophesy?" (Amos 3:8); "have I now any power at all to say anything? the word that God putteth in my mouth, that shall I speak" (Num. 22:38). Who touches Jeremiah's mouth and puts words in it when he does not know how to speak (Jer. 1:6, 9)? Who made Ezekiel mute, and then opened his mouth again (Ezek. 3:26, 24:27, 33:22)? Who makes the prophet see visions with the company in Numbers 12:6 and Balaam in Numbers 24:4, 16? Who makes the true prophet see a lie with the prophets rebuked in 1 Kings 22:21–23 and Ezekiel 13:1–10? Who makes the prophet's audience blind and deaf in Isaiah 6:10? And who could cause a prophet to be heard, even if he were sent not to the house of Israel but to a "people of a strange speech and of an hard language," whose words he could not understand (Ezek. 3:4–6)? If prophecy itself is the cause of these things, then in making Moses' mouth God is making an Adam for the prophets.

That God's creative power is involved emerges from a passage in the *Enuma Elish.* "Having placed in their midst the Images," the gods who appoint Marduk their firstborn also look to him for a sign:

"Lord, truly thy decree is first among gods.
Say but to wreck or create; it shall be.
Open thy mouth, the Images will vanish!
Speak again, and the Images shall be whole!"
At the word of his mouth the Images vanished.
He spoke again, and the Images were restored.
When the gods, his fathers, saw the [outcome of his mouth]
Joyfully they did homage: "Marduk is king!"[1]

Here is a demonstration of divine power close to the sign Aaron will make with his metamorphic rod; but "the magicians of Egypt . . . did in like manner with their enchantments" (Exod. 7:11). "Marduk is king!" the

Babylonian pantheon exclaims; but the Egyptian king does not concede that Yahweh is God. For if Marduk can impress the gods, then Moses cannot succeed with idolators.

So why does Exodus have God doing signs to impress Moses, and Aaron doing signs to impress Pharaoh, in the way the *Enuma Elish* had Marduk doing signs to impress older colleagues? The answer would seem to be, so *Moses* will say "Yahweh is God," or else so his people will, when they come to the Reed Sea: "Who is like unto thee, O Lord, among the gods? who is like thee, glorious in holiness, fearful in praises, doing wonders?" (Exod. 15:11). Recognizably Psalmic, this utterance relates the sign to the miracle. Like Marduk raised to the supremacy, the Psalmist's deity is "exalted far above all gods" (Ps. 97:9); "God standeth in the congregation of the mighty; he judgeth among the gods" (Ps. 82:1). "Worship him, all ye gods," the Psalmist says (Ps. 97:7), reminding us of the gods who grant Marduk kingship over their entire universe and promise that no one among them will transgress his bounds. "The Lord is a great God, and a great King above all gods" (Ps. 95:3). "He is to be feared above all gods. For all the gods of the nations are idols: but the Lord made the heavens" (96:4b–5). There is ultimately a difference, perhaps, between a Marduk who makes the images disappear in the presence of the gods and a God who reduces all the other gods to the appearance of images. For the gods of the images are not indestructible: "I have said, Ye are gods; and all of you are children of the most High. But ye shall die like men, and fall like one of the princes" (Ps. 82:6–7). Pharaoh is such a perishable god— though neither willing or able to hear it. God begins by performing for Moses alone; perhaps the performance remains esoteric, even when presented at court.

In hardening Pharaoh's heart God is turning Egypt into the national obstacle met by the prophets, a people "which have eyes to see, and see not, . . . ears to hear, and hear not: for they are a rebellious house" (Ezek. 12:2; and cf. 2:7–8); for Egypt also has its eyes and ears from God. At Exodus 4:8, God promises Moses, "it shall come to pass, if they will not believe thee, neither hearken to the voice of the first sign, that they will believe the voice of the latter sign." Like a prophet, God is making a sign in Egypt, and even if Moses were to prove a poor speaker, he is empowered with the prophetic voice of the sign, which becomes human mortality itself.

In its immediate context, the "latter sign" in Exodus 4:8 is God's striking Moses' hand with leprosy, and restoring him from it. Egypt, God implies, will listen to the voice of a sign in the flesh. But Moses does not, in fact, strike Pharaoh's house with leprosy, or wither the king's hand to restore it; nor does he do this to himself. But a man of God in 1 Kings 13, who announces "the sign which the Lord hath spoken" (vs. 3), does something very like it. King Jeroboam, putting his hand forth from the altar the man has condemned, says, "Lay hold on him":

> . . . And his hand, which he put forth against him, dried up, so that he could not pull it in again to him.
> The altar also was rent, and the ashes poured out from the altar, according to the sign which the man of God had given by the word of the Lord.
> And the king answered and said unto the man of God, Entreat now the face of the Lord thy God, and pray for me, that my hand may be restored me again. And the man of God besought the Lord, and the king's hand was restored him again, and became as it was before. (1 Kings 13:4–6)

So Moses' leprous hand: at God's bidding, "it was turned again as his other flesh" (Exod. 4:7). Thus God does to Moses what Moses might do to the sign-despising Pharaoh, but what the man of God in 1 Kings actually does do to the sign-despising Northern king. And God does this to Miriam's flesh in the same chapter of Numbers in which he declares to Israel what kind of prophet Moses has become. Jeroboam and Miriam are struck as Moses was, and as the threatened Aaron might have been (Num. 12:11). Moses is empowered to treat Pharaoh as God treats those who resist the word of a prophet—and to intercede as a prophet intercedes for a king.

<hr>

ii

<hr>

To answer further the question of what kind of prophet Moses became, we turn now toward explaining how his prophetic identity might help advance the "cultural" mission which we have previously attributed to the received and traditional Moses of the text. For as Moses became "prophet unto Pharaoh," so the Yahwist in Israel came as a light to lighten Israel's own darkened understanding of itself. At one point in the Samuel narration we are told that prophets in Israel were formerly called seers (1 Sam. 9:9), and the suggestion is that the historical change in status for prophets passed through Samuel himself, with non-Yahwist seers who employed familiar spirits being hunted out of the country or put to death (1 Sam. 28:3, as per the law of Lev. 20:27). Both Samuel and his ghost speak to Saul with the voice of Yahwist prophecy, but Moses functions rather like a seer, insofar as his absorption in Sinai is in the foreground of our understanding of him, with any Yahwist message in the background. Members of Moses' rather synthetic family can seem like ecstatics and miracle-workers too, as if they all constituted a professional class of

Balaam-like diviners. The links of Moses, Aaron, and Miriam with Kadesh suggest something similar. The Bible's first name for Kadesh is "Fountain of Judgment" (Gen. 14:7), as if the family pronounced oracles for the people at this site. If Balaam is any evidence, pagan magicians did "in like manner with their enchantments" (Exod. 7:11; cf. Num. 23:23, 24:1).

The revelations of the patriarch and seer are confined to a circle of immediacy, and are made present to the audience through the presence of the recipient himself. The mantic's rictus, or rigidified facial expression, speaks for the somewhat transitory character of what he speaks. Such communications will not themselves travel far or well, though the vision lets the prophet himself go about in the spirit (2 Kings 5:26: "Went not mine heart with thee?"). Balaam is a borderline case, since his seven oracles are cast very wide indeed. Prophecy also implies a greater power than the seer's ecstatic translation out of himself. The prophet has the power to overtake a further-off future, to broadcast and "denounce" it, and to pass far-reaching judgments on God's will in the event. Similarly, the priesthood: while Deuteronomy 33:8–10 says God's "holy one," deriving from Levi, has been given the Thummim and Urim, it also says he observes God's word, keeps his covenant, and teaches his dictate and torah.

It would be hard to miss the visual effects belonging to the divine vision in the fire and smoke that envelop Mount Sinai. But even as Moses is drawn into the intensities of the Sinaitic interior, he leaves behind him other appointed leaders who have followed him to its periphery, as if they represented a way back from the dangers of a seerlike absorption in mere visionary affect. Moses is credited with laying down the whole of the law, and such a function implies the power of codifying results of divine consultations of an altogether different magnitude from those mediated by a seer. The results, if they are the Decalogue, are not for the use of the immediate situation at all, but for establishing sacral orders (e.g., sabbath-keeping) and rendering civic judgments. The seer does not produce bills.

Moses, in particular, has been given the abiding significance of the Name—a significance which prophets will subsequently attach to their own communications from God. The Mosaic-Yahwistic imprimatur, "Thus says Yahweh," serves to publish God's message to all receiving the divine name, even while detaching the reception of God's message from the acceptability of the immediate speaker. At the first the Name could be used to give particular messages authority and distinction; in time it could also be used to distinguish authentic from inauthentic messengers (Deut. 18:19–22 and 13:1–3, with Jer. 2:8 and 23:13). The text, by entrusting Moses with the name of Yahweh, presecures an audience for later prophets coming in the name of the One in whose name Moses came. Yahweh's name, attached to many different messages, also argues for their possible unity, just as Moses' name, attached to many different laws, has argued for the unity of the

Pentateuch. And if the various messages spoken on various occasions are all the word of God, their putative coherence may unify our conception of the will of God. Thus the "Elohist" attribution of the divine name to the Mosaic revelation implies a claim of Mosaic authority for the unification of Israel's religious experience as a canon of "the law"—meaning the Mosaic law. At the same time, the attribution of a prophetic office to a canon-minded Moses reendorses the Bible's assembling of the various oracles from Yahweh into a canon of "the prophets"—meaning the Mosaic prophets. But this is the Bible's doing, not that of the prophets themselves. Though the Torah (or the Mosaic and Levitical instruction found in the Pentateuch) supports the prophets' teaching, and though the prophets' teaching supports the Torah, there is little enough direct reference to the Sinaitic Moses himself in the texts of Amos, Hosea, Micah, and Isaiah. For the prophets to have made the law strictly "of Moses" would have been to bring it down to the level of the Code of Hammurabi—to make it a law of men and not of God. It was the prophets' gradual assimilation of the law to the covenant, and the eventual characterization of Moses' career in terms of the biographies of these prophets themselves, that produced the replete Moses of the Bible, versus the very much sketchier Moses of the prophets.

For the "law of *Moses*" is simply not appealed to, by this name, apart from the Pentateuch, Joshua, and the historical books referring to the kings and leaders influenced by what the Pentateuch itself embodies (Josh. 1:7–8, 8:32–34, 23:3, 6, 16, 24:26; 1 Kings 2:3, 2 Kings 14:6, 23:25; cf. Ezra 3:2, 6:18, 7:6; Mal. 4:4, "Remember ye the law of Moses my servant," is a rare, late, canon-concluding exception). But the text of Jeremiah uses the heartfelt language of Deuteronomy, implying its renewal of a Mosaic covenant or law, and preaching its circumcision of the heart (Jer. 4:4, Deut. 10:16). Accusing Israel of breaching its contract with Yahweh, Ezekiel likewise uses the language of the Priestly author in Leviticus.[2] But even if these prophets have turned to texts crucial to any bid for Mosaic authority, neither one uses Moses' *name* to authorize his teaching.

Even before Jeremiah, Hosea's God complained, "they have not cried unto me with their heart" (Hos. 7:14). This prophet couples widespread ceremonial insincerity with a failure to hearken to Yahweh's law. God speaks about the way in which a pluralizing worship has turned idolatrous:

> Because Ephraim has multiplied altars for sinning,
>   they have become to him altars for sinning.
> Were I to write for him my laws by ten thousands,
>   they would be regarded as a strange thing.
> (Hos. 8:11–12, RSV)

This text implies that a proliferation of sanctuaries in the North has its counterpart in a proliferation of law codes. This widespread legal promulgation, if it dates from Hosea's time, comes a quarter century in advance of the Assyrian capture of Samaria, near the advent of written prophecy itself. Apparently the chirographic dissemination of the law did not lessen the North's actual disregard of God's behests, it only made it more visible. As a consequence, Hosea predicts, his people "shall return to Egypt" (Hos. 8:13)—the law and its publishers are powerless to deliver them from their fate. If literacy had widened the promulgation of the law, it had not prevented its foundering. Was the hearkening that followed a law-book's publication unique to Josiah's reign? Might not the picture of Moses' Egypt as an illegal society derive from the prophets' denunciation of policies pursued by Josiah's more recent predecessors?

"Be ye therefore very courageous to keep and to do all that is written in the book of the law of Moses, that ye turn not aside therefrom": despite the patronage of the book of the law of Moses by an ideal Joshua (as in Joshua 23:6), the codifications in question are much more likely to have become the law of Moses as the result of a comparatively late royal sponsorship. When that sponsorship faltered, the texts would owe their subsequent survival to the continuing persistence of their priestly keepers. Such historical reversals include the failure of the post-Solomonic succession (the reign of Rehoboam) to obtain in Northern Israel, the failure of the Northern kingdom to survive deportation to Assyria, and the failure of the Judaic kingship to survive the Babylonian exile. To these royal sponsorships and failures roughly correspond, it has been argued, the creation and/or survival of the Levitically sponsored law texts which appear in the pentateuchal strands known as "E," "P," and "D."[3] Whether or not we allow the documentary hypothesis, and such modifications as Hezekiah's possible endorsement of the Priestly legislation,[4] we can readily grant that the law of Moses became authoritative not only as it secured royal sponsorship but as the kingship faltered, and more and more monolithic versions of "Moses" came to stand in the kingship's place: in the constitution according to Ezra.

---

iii

The Bible depicts Moses as the agent of a saving ministry. The first of the servant songs in Isaiah 40–55 tells us that this ministry has obtained an honorable place among the creations of God—God is pleased to issue Moses in a new edition, and to speak through his exalted servant again:

> Behold my servant, whom I uphold,
>   my chosen, in whom my soul delights;

I have put my spirit upon him, . . .
He will not fail [or: *burn dimly*] or be discouraged
    till he has established justice in the earth;
    and the coastlands wait for his law. . . .
I am the Lord, I have called you in righteousness, . . .
I have given you as a covenant to the people . . .
to bring out the prisoners from the dungeon, . . .
I am the Lord, that is my name! (Isa. 42:1, 4, 6–8, RSV)

Testifying to the force of this exilic version of the Mosaic commission, all
the Gospels inaugurate Jesus' ministry from its opening verse, this being
the scriptural basis for the Baptism. Those receiving the good news joined
a new Israel, as if "baptized into Moses" (1 Cor. 10:2) in the latter day.

Such a passage depends upon the widening of the prophetic mission by
the Mosaic office—which is that of covenant-mediation—and the widening of the Mosaic mission by the prophetic office—which is that of humbling the human pretense to worldly power by means of God's word.
Again, the point is the coalescence of different functions in the tradition.
Thus the sermonizing Deutero-Moses of Deuteronomy can begin his
sermon in Moab by citing his own former career up until that point, as it
might have been found in "JE," and he can quote God's words (apparently in the Priestly author) about reserving the invasion of Canaan to the
young (Num. 14:31), thus recalling the accuracy of the divine predictions
through Moses at the time of the invasion forty years later (Deut. 1:39). It
is illogical that Moses' ministry should benefit from Mosaic endorsement,
but so be it.

Though the prophets do not say they came from Moses, and Moses
does not say he came from the prophets, an imitation of Moses by Elijah,
or an imitation of Elijah by Moses, is surely implied by the story of Elijah's
forty days of fasting and his visit to Horeb to communicate with God in
1 Kings 19:4–18 during the baalist apostasy of the Northern regime. Nonetheless, Moses differs from a prophet like Samuel: for the story necessarily
presents Moses—himself, the founder—as unable to appeal to a prior
cultic order. His plan to carry out sacrifices three days into the wilderness
is a made-up excuse for the occasion. Moses originally has no cult, just as
he has no homeland. And while a prophet is not honored in his own
country (Matt. 13:57, Exod. 4:1), that differs from not having a country.

Even if Moses' audience in Israel had been able to derive the name of
God from the verb for being, Moses' first audience in Egypt would nonetheless have had no earlier prophets by means of which to identify the
spokesman's activity. Rather, Moses must secure his authority over his audience—always on God's behalf—by the working of signs. Moses is thus magnified by the story as having secured that authority among men upon

which Israelite prophets had subsequently relied. The prophets delivered God's word, but Moses is portrayed as having delivered God's power. The prophet's words would not be important unless they had come from a source of power. The "signs and wonders" manifest that power.

Moses' signs are direct expressions of force, as we can see in the accounts of those plagues where Moses does not "denounce" the word of God to Pharaoh at all, that is, with a conditional threat and its fulfillment upon Pharaoh's noncompliance. For in the case of the third, sixth, and ninth plagues (gnats, boils, and darkness), Moses simply acts to produce a wonder-*cum*-disaster. Thus Moses comes not as a prophet, but as a thaumaturgically equipped proselytizer for the prophets: which is to say, a proselytizer for God's power, rather than his word. Yet the power in question is almost that of Yahweh's own name, which is, after all, a word too. *God's* power is also verbal: "By the word of the Lord were the heavens made; and all the host of them by the breath of his mouth . . . For he spake, and it was done; he commanded, and it stood fast" (Ps. 33:6, 9).

Moses' campaign is thus for a wider fame for God—or God's name, as being a "word with power" or "authority" (cf. Luke 4:32, 36). For once the Name has been revealed as a kind of fact, God is shown determined upon its widest promulgation, a worldwide confession equivalent to that of the foreign general—Naaman—making his grateful presentation to his healer Elijah: "Behold, now I know that there is no God in all the earth but in Israel" (2 Kings 5:15). Thus Exodus 9:14, 16: "I will at this time send all my plagues upon thine heart, and upon thy servants, and upon thy people; that thou mayest know that there is none like me in all the earth. . . . for this cause have I raised thee up, for to shew in thee my power; and that my name may be declared throughout all the earth." Kings like the Ahaziah of 2 Kings 1 had to be brought to acknowledge that there was a God in Israel, whose word was truth and law ("Is it because there is no God in Israel that you are going to inquire of Baalzebub, the god of Ekron?" the king is asked [vs. 3, RSV]). But Pharaoh is made an example, "that *all the earth* may know that there is a God in Israel," as David will say to Goliath (1 Sam. 17:46). For why should the earth care, except this god were the great God, doing things for Israel in the world at large?

At the same time, the world at large can merely be *Israel* at large, an Israel that is not wholly Yahwist, or that has half-forgotten its own deity. Though their prophecies oftentimes reach beyond Israel, the Yahwist prophets are not themselves shown in foreign courts until the Babylonian exile. Prophets in the time of the divided kingship are sometimes found, however, in courts away from their homes, in courts somewhat foreign or alien to them by being in the other part of the divided kingdom (i.e., 1 Kings 13:1, RSV: "And behold, a man of God came out of Judah by the word of the Lord to Bethel"). Thus the mission to Pharaoh can be seen as securing the widest possible reception for Yahweh's messengers, within a more and more worldly Israelite sphere; the Name constitutes their ambassadorial credentials, even if it is only the word itself, and not the prophet, that undertakes the actual embassy abroad.

Pharaoh, however, proves unreceptive to the Name, the ambassadors, and the message. Indeed, the words of the message are mainly delivered *pro forma,* like mail destined not to be opened. Pharaoh's unheedingness is prescribed and found in all but the plague of locusts, where his softening and hardening of heart has been interpolated into the middle of the announcement-enactment sequence, being taken out of its usual late position in order to illustrate the breakdown of negotiations—Pharaoh's bad faith—definitively, before the final disasters (darkness, watch night, and Reed Sea) that rescue Israel for good and all. (In the case of the locusts, Exod. 10:3–20, the usual concession by Pharaoh, made after a given plague itself, is placed before it, and then reneged on, thus bringing on the locusts, along with Pharaoh's prayer for forgiveness of his sin, minus any further indication of a concession.) After the plague of darkness that follows upon his hardening toward the disaster of the locusts, Pharaoh makes his fullest concession to the Israelites, but then he rehardens and expels Moses from court altogether; Moses concludes that, indeed, Pharaoh will not see him again (Exod. 10:21–29). Pharaoh has precipitated the "one plague more" (Exod. 11:1) by means of which God can make himself definitively known. God now announces—and Moses reannounces—Egypt's final disaster, the death of its firstborn; but the narration does not say Pharaoh himself ever hears this sentence in advance of its execution.

All along, the narrative supposes that Yahweh can only be made known if Pharaoh puts Moses off long enough for God to be known in some very terrible and decisive way. The king's uncooperation cooperates in the necessary accumulation of unrecompensed injustice. His hard-heartedness provides the occasion to bring on the plagues, which includes the sending of all God's plagues *upon Pharaoh's heart* (Exod. 9:14): the signs cannot be effective in softening this heart, if they are also causative in hardening it. Indeed, one of God's motives is to take advantage of the opportunity hard-heartedness presents, in order to multiply his signs (Exod. 7:3, 11:9–10): hard-heartedness causes the signs-as-plagues, but, conversely, the making of the plagues into signs has a cause in hard-heartedness. Every time Pharaoh fails to respond to a plague as a sign, the sequence makes that much more of a sign out of the plague Pharaoh has himself become.

Pharaoh's confessions of sin and error are only so many palliations of the deeper ignorance and unresponsiveness to which they unwittingly attest. For although Pharaoh can hearken unto Moses as a troublemaker and a nuisance-bringer, he cannot hear him as a compelling bringer of God's word: a prophet of the admonitory kind of word Ahab hears when he humbles himself after Elijah's prediction of the fall of the royal house as punishment for the king's apostasy (1 Kings 21:17–29). Like Naaman, Pharaoh is a foreigner or non-Yahwist whom the story compels to seek prophetic intercession with God; but the story in 2 Kings 5 shows Elisha dealing with an Israelite king's lack of faith, as much as a foreigner's lack of knowledge. And unlike Elisha's cure of Naaman, the cures Moses works do not succeed as signs to break through the foreigner's inexperience in the greatness of God or the powers of his prophet. Only once, before the plague of locusts and after the alleviation of the plague of hail (Exod. 10:7), does Pharaoh's court respond to the prophet's announcements with any awareness of what the word of God has in store for it. Even here, the king continues to trifle over terms, as if you could sign a contract with God without believing or trusting in him, or in the voice of the latter signs.

It is Pharaoh's servants, rather than Pharaoh himself, who see the disaster looming over them; but the narrative lacks an equivalent Israelite for the captive servant-girl who is Elisha's disciple, and who is an index of the popular faith the prophet inspires: "And she said unto her mistress, Would God my lord were with the prophet that is in Samaria! for he would recover him of his leprosy" (2 Kings 5:3). Moses has not quickened such faith in Israel. "Our fathers understood not thy wonders in Egypt," Psalm 106 confesses, "they remembered not the multitude of thy mercies; but provoked him at the sea, even at the Red sea"; only after the miracle "believed they his words"—not before (vss. 7, 12).

---

iv

Two conceptions emerge from these observations on Moses' mission to Pharaoh. There is the "prophet of power," who works miracles and disasters, and the "prophet of threats," who brings God's word into court and oversees the fulfilling or suspending of it.[5] But the latter function is not well illustrated by the fulfilling of Moses' announcements, even though the message formula itself ("Thus says Yahweh") is repeatedly found in Moses' mouth. For God's original declaration of the death of Pharaoh's firstborn (Exod. 4:22–23), the message that might be fulfilled "according to the word of the Lord, which he spake by the hand of his servant . . . the prophet" (1 Kings 14:18), is never explicitly delivered to Pharaoh, and is only announced in Egypt (at Exod. 11:4–9) when the approach of the event is virtually concurrent with the event itself.

The announcements of the plagues are not really conditional threats, namely, that if Pharaoh does not let the people go God will bring such and such a disaster on Egypt. The announcements are more in the nature of performative utterances, for the speaking of the threat is virtually one with the executing of its sentence. Where prophecy and fulfillment are not merely conformable but also consubstantial, the effectiveness of the prophet does not derive from the prophet's having God's word in his keeping, but from his having God's creative power at his immediate dispose. We may compare the Exodus plague narrative with the story in 2 Kings 1, where Elijah intercepts a king with a word from God, but where, in the space between the report of the threat and its finally being made good on—that is, in the interval created by the prophet's message having polarized the king's intransigence—he calls down disaster on the king's servants.

Thus there are two rather different words of God entrusted to Moses by the plague narrative. One is God's intention of delivering Israel. The other is God's intention of hardening Pharaoh. For the hardening of Pharaoh is the conclusion deriving from each of Moses' addresses to the ruler. Instead of a prediction being fulfilled according to the word of the prophet, the concluding formula always ought to be, as it once is, "And the Lord hardened the heart of Pharaoh, and he hearkened not unto [Moses and Aaron]; as the Lord had spoken unto Moses" (Exod. 9:12). The hardening is the fulfilled word, but it is to Moses this word is spoken, by God as Moses' prophet, and not to Pharaoh, by Moses as Pharaoh's prophet. All the time Moses is bringing God's word to Pharaoh, God is bringing another word to Moses: that Pharaoh will not hear either one of them. "The wicked . . . are like the deaf adder that stoppeth her ear; Which will not hearken to the voice of charmers, charming never so wisely" (Ps. 58:3–5). God says he has raised Pharaoh up in order to "send all my plagues upon [his] heart" (Exod. 9:16, 14): the plague God really sends on his heart is indifference—a heartless indifference to the effect of the plagues.

We now come upon a third conception of the prophet. This is the prophet who, being called upon to deafen his hearers, is called *not* to be heard.[6] This "call unto rejection" implies a somewhat subtle apperception of the prophet's mission, one that perhaps informs Moses' fears of Israelite rejection in Deuteronomy, and his exclusion from the promised land in Numbers (Num. 20:12, with Deut. 1:37, 3:26, 32:51–52). "The Lord hath not given you an heart to perceive, and eyes to see, and ears to hear, unto this day" (Deut. 29:4): *until now*, says Moses, with the deuteronomist sounding his own trumpet in the background. Moses is commissioned as Isaiah was, to satirize or mock the callousness of his audience by declaiming the very word that would prompt it to avert disaster if it were not too obtuse to hear it, or rather were not deafened by hearing it

(Isa. 6:9–13). God promises Aaron as a mouthpiece, and that he will be with Moses' mouth, but there is a wonderful congruity between a God who knows Moses cannot speak well and one who knows Pharaoh will prove so hard of hearing.

At the outset God's means seem economical: why waste a good speaker on a poor listener? Similarly, God has his uses for both Moses' disappointment in his pre-Midian ministry and Moses' subsequent resistance to God's call. Through the action of this spokesman, the destruction God has foreseen and planned for Pharaoh will not be averted, but confirmed. Isaiah's call, placed six chapters after the opening of his collection, seems to be a reconstructed one, since it implies Yahweh's knowledge of a record of fruitless preaching to Israel. So the frustration of Moses' ministry among Pharaoh's Hebrew subjects may have served as a vocational failure preparing Moses for a vocation that can only succeed *by* failing and for the task of persisting in the face of Pharaoh's sinful persistence.

Before drawing further conclusions about his performance before Pharaoh, we may recur to Moses' call, which suggests so many prophetic norms for his mission. He seems to be selected, to judge by the length of his prophetic career as a whole, for longanimity. If he is gifted at his call with a power to work wonders, he is not charismatically transformed. At the ordainment of Isaiah (6:5–7) the prophet's unclean lips are purified, but at Sinai Moses' slowness of tongue is unalleviated. God next visits Moses to circumcise not his lips but his manhood: the event betokens collective as much as individual initiation (Exod. 4:10, 24–26). Such visits are not depicted as conversions: unlike the circumcised Abram/Abraham in Genesis 17, or the lamed Jacob/Israel in Genesis 32, there is no name-change. At Exodus 6:12 Moses is still only himself: "Behold, the children of Israel have not hearkened unto me; how then shall Pharaoh hear me, who am of uncircumcised lips?" God "maketh . . . his ministers a flaming fire" (Ps. 104:4), and at the burning bush Moses is touched—but not consumed. He must needs be fortified, his being a lifetime's calling; the appointment cannot be *narrowly* charismatic. Saul's possession after his anointing recurred, yet he was sustained only spasmodically (1 Sam. 10:5–13, 11:6, 16:14, 18:10, 19:20).

All offices are from God, and the call of Moses doubtless plays on the difference between the demands of divine office and the limitations of human officeholders. Moses protests his handicap or inaptness not to show that God hires the handicapped, nor even that the articulation of God's will requires less fluency than persistence, though both are true. In this case, the objection to the calling is created by the unreadiness of *any* candidate for high office, especially an office directly from God. Without divine support, any man might be a stammerer in the presence of the

Sinaitic commission. Moses' portrayal as defective merely expresses this gap in human preparation. Though he will endorse the activity of a group of ecstatics outside the camp in Numbers 11, Moses himself lacks the gift of tongues. But all power is from God, and he glosses this over.

We may now ask why the account of Moses' call dwells so insistently on his resistance. As suggested, the shadow of the latter-day rejection of God's prophets has been allowed to fall over the constituting of the Mosaic office. But the story also anticipates the resistance Moses is preordained to meet from Pharaoh. Jonah carries a prophet's resistance a step further: he recoils from the likely success of a commission to condemn Nineveh that will prove him a false prophet when the city repents. Pharaoh, however, seems not to have been in much danger of repenting willingly, or too soon. At the opposite pole from Jonah, Moses resists being asked to do a thing that will not be done. Yet it will be done, if he is commissioned to create Pharaoh's resistance, in contrast to the threat of the Ninevehites to repent. Thus Moses acts out in advance the role of Pharaoh himself, as a preconditioning necessary for his success. God also gets in on the act: he practices on the resistance of Moses, for ultimately breaking that of Pharaoh. Thus God's call turns the strength to resist into the strength to persevere, where Moses' mission turns Pharaoh's ignorance of God into a will to deny him. As Moses' fear of rejection turns into a rejection of fear, Pharaoh's lack of concern turns into a ruinous defiance. The text thus arrives at a reconstruction of its human parties: a rejected yet increasingly emboldened prophet, and a heedless yet increasingly provocative kingship.

v

From what history can the narrative of the exodus have taken this scenario, if not from the subsequent history of Israel itself? According to the narratives of the kingship, apostasy is denounced before the king by the prophet; the king either persists or repents, and the threat to him is either fulfilled or alleviated (to be fulfilled thereafter, at some further remove). The king's securing of respite introduces a second rhythm into such a narrative, much more recognizable in the stories of the Judges, who secure deliverance for the people, and who are raised up as a result of the people's repentance for the apostasy that has brought oppression upon them. Traces of this rhythm in the plague narrative appear in the hearkening of the Egyptian people to Moses. Just as characteristic, however, is the charge that the people *did not hearken to their judges* (Judg. 2:17), where we can substitute *prophets*. Moses complains to God that the people of Israel have not listened to him; the passage from Exodus 6:9–12 implies the recurrent rebuff that makes any call to greatness a lonely one.

"Thus saith the Lord," saith the prophet. Moses is the first biblical character to use this tag in its presumptive site-in-dialogue, God's spokesman addressing a royal audience (Exod. 5:1, 9:13). Pharaoh, according to the norms provided by the stories in the Kings narratives, stands in place of a kingship only intermittently responsive to the ministry of the prophets. In Pharaoh's magicians, this interpretation recognizes rival prophets, a state-supported corps of professional sign-doers, such as we meet in the Jezebel-supported prophets of Baal who contest with Elijah, and the guild of prophetic yea-sayers who support Ahab when the true prophet Micaiah opposes him (1 Kings 22).[7] Since God's commission to Moses has him threatening the life of Pharaoh's firstborn, the prophet sent to condemn a dynast deserves special mention here: Nathan prophesying the death of David's first son by Bathsheba and bringing David to confess—and earn remission of—his sin (2 Sam. 12:1–14); and Ahijah of Shiloh prophesying the death of Jeroboam's son Abijah and the elimination of their house because of the king's sponsoring idolatry (1 Kings 14:1–18). Ahijah's prophecy is fulfilled with Abijah's death and Baasha's subsequent murder of Jeroboam's successor Nadab and the rest of Jeroboam's house. In Leviticus Moses himself will pronounce sentence on a Nadab and an Abihu, the condemned sons of Aaron who die for offering strange fire before Yahweh and Moses (Lev. 10:1–3). The stories from Leviticus and 1 Kings seem to be aligned not only by the similar names of the victims, but also by the attention that the disposal of the corpses and the funeral arrangements command from the Yahwist spokesman in each story (Lev. 10:4–6, 1 Kings 14:11–13).

In Moses' part in the plagues we recognize the role of earlier prophets in procuring drought, rain, and fire from heaven, and also in meteorological prediction.[8] Insofar as the people were agriculturalists, their prophets were weather-seers; it is hard to separate this kind of prediction from a more shamanistic activity of intervention; those who talked about the weather with Yahweh were also in a good position to do something about it. Nonetheless, the meteorological phenomena we meet in several prophet stories suggest that the prophet's power over the weather can be a power over its interpretation: the weather carries a message, it is the preeminent sign of the times. For example, in 1 Samuel 12, an antimonarchial Samuel convokes the people and chronicles their apostasies, and warns them that the kingship for which they are asking is likely to be another of these. He then calls down unseasonable thunder and rain on them, that they might know their wickedness is great in the sight of Yahweh. The intimidated people ask the prophet to pray for them—his servants—that they may not perish for having added the kingship to their sins. Samuel encourages them to follow the Lord, for God will not cast them off, "for his great name's sake" (vs. 22), nor will Samuel cease praying for them. Here the prophet-mediator menaces the people as much as the kingship with his parting shot, that if the people persist in wickedness both they and their king shall be consumed (vs. 25).

A second story from the history of the kingship is no less illustrative of the rhythm of the plague narrative. In 2 Kings 1 we hear that King Ahaziah suffered a near-fatal accident, whereupon he sent to the Baal of Ekron concerning his life. At God's instance the prophet Elijah intercepts the king's messengers with the threat that the king shall indeed die. This follows upon the motive-question "Is it because there is no God in Israel that you are going to inquire of Baalzebub, the god of Ekron?" (2 Kings 1:3, RSV). The messengers return to the king and deliver Elijah's message from Yahweh. Recognizing the message's more immediate source, the king seeks to lay hands on the prophet. He repeatedly sends "a captain of fifty men with his fifty" to bring Elijah into custody. Elijah retaliates by calling down fire from heaven that consumes the first and second expeditions sent against him. The third captain, amply warned by these demonstrations of the forces at Elijah's disposal, falls on his knees before him and prays for his and his men's lives. God now tells Elijah that he may come down from his perch, and the prophet returns with the captain. He then delivers his death-dealing message to the king in person, and the king dies, "according to the word of the Lord which Elijah had spoken" (2 Kings 1:17a). We conclude that a prophet has the power to bring down disaster so long as hearts remain hardened against true submission to the will of God, and that God will humiliate the kingship that is not faithful to him or humble before him. The agency that converts word into event also converts event back into word.

A similar account is found in the story in 1 Samuel 19:19–24. This story contains a peculiar twist that converts word and event dynamistically:

> And it was told Saul, "Behold, David is at Naioth in Ramah." Then Saul sent messengers to take David; and when they saw the company of the prophets prophesying, and Samuel standing as head over them, the Spirit of God came upon the messengers of Saul, and they also prophesied. When it was told Saul, he sent other messengers, and they also prophesied. And Saul sent messengers again the third time, and they also prophesied. Then he himself went to Ramah, and came to the great well that is in Secu; and he asked, "Where are Samuel and David?" And one said, "Behold, they are at Naioth in Ramah." And he went from there to Naioth in Ramah; and the spirit of God came upon him also, and as he went he prophesied, until he came to Naioth in Ramah. And he too stripped off his clothes, and he too prophesied before Samuel, and lay naked all that day and all that night. Hence it is said, "Is Saul also among the prophets?" (RSV)

The narrator of this story wanted to make it a good one, so he did not write paraphrasingly, to the effect that "Saul sent three successive sets of messengers to arrest David at Naioth in Ramah, and each of them fell into a prophetic trance—and then so did Saul, when in turn he attempted the mission himself." Rather, the story pictures Saul's obtuseness as it compounds itself through perseveration. Thus the story is partly told for the sake of the refrains, "at Naioth in Ramah" and "and they also prophesied." The repetition is not merely narrative boilerplate, designed to satisfy a childish and quizzical and musical appetite to hear it again; the whole point is the reemergence of the formulas at the point of their visitation upon Saul himself: "he prophesied . . . and he also prophesied." The "messengers" became the message: those officers sent to arrest David at Naioth in Ramah were themselves arrested by the Spirit at Naioth in Ramah. And the king who would not hear this message became, in turn, a final instance of an arrested sender, and of the byword, "Is Saul also among the prophets?" After Saul's call (1 Sam. 10:12), this is *already* a byword.

The story is the mirror-opposite of the successful unsuccess of Moses' mission to Pharaoh. The obtuse Pharaoh, through the repeated process of his rejecting Moses, is also being made into a byword. But is Pharaoh ever in any sense among the prophets, in the way that the dreaming Pharaoh of Genesis is, or in the way that Abraham is, as the prophet to the dreaming Abimelech? In the seventh plague, the plague of hail, a new kind of exchange takes place. Moses not only predicts the plague, but also prescribes precautions to be taken against it: man and beast should be put under shelters. And certain of Pharaoh's servants, namely those "that feared the word of the Lord" (Exod. 9:20), do put their cattle and slaves in sheds. Joseph is momentarily in the court, and the court is momentarily among the prophets. For the clause describing the reaction of the heedful Pharaonic servants refers us to two semitechnical Mosaic concepts: God's word, and fearing God. Pharaoh's servants have departed from a heedless kingship that has "rejected the word of the Lord" (1 Sam. 15:23), because it is bent on becoming a deuteronomistic laughingstock (Deut. 28:36–37, with 1 Kings 9:7, 2 Chron. 7:20, and Ps. 44:14).

Pharaoh himself is not afflicted with any real repentance, unlike Saul, or Manasseh (in 2 Chron. 33), or Nebuchadnezzar (in Dan. 4). In Daniel we can see traces of the interpreter Joseph who ministered to the dreaming Pharaoh of Genesis, and the outspoken Moses who urges Pharaoh to mend his ways—but the Egyptian king is not accessible to troubling dreams or madness or instruction or genuine humiliation. Nor is he to be found among the prophets on the impending Passover, in the way that Pilate will be found, entitling Jesus "the king of the Jews" (John

19:19–22). Pharaoh does not think to have spoken prophetically at the critical juncture, before the plague on the firstborn. Yet when he orders Moses never to see his face again, on penalty of death, Moses' reply seizes on the inadvertent prediction, and throws its fatality back in Pharaoh's face. "And Pharaoh said to him, 'Get away from me; take heed to yourself; never see my face again; for in the day you see my face you shall die' " (Exod. 10:28, RSV). Pharaoh speaks like the retreating God of Deuteronomy, who hides his face (Deut. 31:17–18), or the harsh Egyptian vizier reported to Jacob, who threatens to deprive Jacob's sons of interviews (Gen. 43:3, 5: "Ye shall not see my face"). Moses replies in kind: "Thou hast spoken well, I will see thy face again no more." (Exod. 10:28–29). Pronouncing a sentence of mutual banishment, he turns away from the terrible face of the god-king, toward the face of the living God.

The finality in Moses' self-dismissal from the royal presence could remind one of the separation of Samuel from the Saul who had "rejected the word of the Lord": "And Samuel came no more to see Saul until the day of his death" (1 Sam. 15:26, 35). Even if the motif of "royal apostasy from Yahweh" is only allegorically present in the plague narrative, bad faith surely stands in its place—along with the king's failure to make a lasting confession of God's sovereignty or deity. On the night of the passing-over, God promises to execute judgment "against all the gods of Egypt" (Exod. 12:12). David is also made to speak of God's redeeming Israel from Egypt, "from the nations and their gods" (2 Sam. 7:23). Later tradition, such as Wisdom 11:15, saw the plagues as virtually the scourge of idolatry. But the plagues in Exodus do not so much allude to the gods of Egypt as to those of Canaan: Baalzebub, lord of flies, and Dagon, lord of mice with a departmental interest in tumors. Both these gods are associated with Ekron—it was at Ekron that the ark of God caused the Philistines a plague of tumors and a plague of mice (1 Sam. 5–6). Egypt is punished in the shape in which kingships in Canaan sinned.

The "Canaanite" typology for the plaguing of Pharaoh is reflected in a comparable "Egyptian" typology for the ark's peregrinations between the Israelites and the Canaanite Philistines in 1 Samuel 4–7. The ark's Philistine hosts at Gath and Ekron return it to Israel with interest, to avert the fate that befell the Egyptians (1 Sam. 5:9–6:8). Similarly, when Abraham's alleged sister Sarah caused plagues among his Egyptian hosts, Pharaoh (having divined that Sarah was Abraham's wife) released her from the royal harem and sent his guest on his way with all he had (Gen. 12:17–20).

Unlike the stories about the prophet-threatened kings, the plague narrative conflates the cyclical rhythm of forecast and fulfillment preemptively: Moses delivers the message even as it is being fulfilled, and Pharaoh is hardened against hearing it until disaster has overtaken him. The reprieves Pharaoh is granted differ fundamentally from the one Ahab earns at 1 Kings 21:27–29: Moses' reprieves only arrest disaster after it is fully upon a willful malefactor. And the narrative does not show God and the course of events *eventually* keeping faith with the prophet's words: the vindication is without pause. It does not so much justify the prophet's word as avenge his cause in the very announcing of it. Yet all this effectiveness has no lasting effect on Pharaoh.

Like certain powerful foreigners (Ben-hadad in 1 Kings 20:31, Naaman in 2 Kings 5:13) Pharaoh is advised by his own servants to make a submissive response; and like certain kings in Israel Pharaoh must entreat the prophet's intercession with God after being punished for his offense to him: Jeroboam's hand is withered after he has offered violence to the prophet (1 Kings 13:3–6). But where the stories in 1–2 Kings portray the intermediate effectiveness of the prophet figure with the ruler figure, and the temporary staving off of the bankruptcy the ruler's policies threaten, the exodus narrative shows neither sign nor threat-word, miracle, disaster, better advice, intervention, clemency, or remediation prevailing with Pharaoh.[9] The narrative marshals just as many reasons for the ruler's intransigence as for its breaching: hardness of heart, God's design, Pharaoh's skill in double-dealing, the temporary success of his magicians in duplicating the signs, his aloofness from disasters not directly affecting him, Moses' indulgence of his insincerity. Where so many reasons for failure are given, none seems altogether trustworthy. The multiplication of unpersuasive signs and wonders is subject to the still greater wonder that they all failed to work: the wonder, in short, of Pharaoh's bureaucratization of charisma.

·11·

THE BURDEN OF EGYPT

And it shall come to pass, if they will not believe thee, neither
hearken to the voice of the first sign, that they will believe the voice
of the latter sign. (Exod. 4:8)

Isaiah 19 bears the title "The Burden of Egypt": 'burden' or *massā'* means
the refrainlike argument of a chant or preachment. Isaiah predicts that God
will smite the Egyptians with economic, political, and ecological disasters.
The oppressed will in turn cry out, and God will send a savior to deliver
them; as a result, "in that day there shall be an altar to the Lord in the midst
of the land of Egypt, and a pillar at the border thereof to the Lord"
(Isa. 19:19). Isaiah's burden is like the cyclic one in Judges and the plague
narrative. But Exodus 7–13 also establishes its own internal models, and its
markedly "chronic" or dilated character probably had become a standard
feature of any burden of Egypt long before the Bible became the Bible, and
however later than the Song at the Sea (Exod. 15) now found in the sequel.

In the present section it will be our task to analyze this narrative as a
prophetic *massā'*, starting from the anticipatory signs that Moses is shown
as a prophet and extending to the self-prescribing sequence of the plagues
as they renew the divine signifying.

i

The exodus primarily demonstrates God's *power*, as with the "waters
above" in Psalm 148:4–5: "He commanded and they were created." The
fulfillment of God's *word* is necessarily secondary to this demonstration,
though of course every time God's word is fulfilled it is, perforce, a demonstration of God's power to fulfill it. Thus, when God's spokesman
doubts God's prediction that he will feed Israel in the wilderness with the
quails, "the Lord said unto Moses, Is the Lord's hand waxed short? thou
shalt see now whether my word shall come to pass unto thee or not"
(Num. 11:23). The sign compels belief in God's power, but also in his
word. Nonetheless, Moses' main role in Egypt is as an instrument of the

208

approaching event; he is the bringer of God's word only as it conduces to disaster. Moses' signs in Egypt witness to the absoluteness of divine power before they witness to the compellingness of the divine word. But the signs in the call story were promises of further signs and stand as installments upon an unfolding meaning, as well as an unfolding demonstration; they take their place in the sequence of sign-making out of which a connected meaning or sentence or judgment emerges. If indeed significance is "determined by delays in understanding and registration, the dilation of comprehension, and the belatedness of the word's coming, not into event, but into meaningfulness," Pharaoh's being a very slow learner has a purpose. His retardation serves to open—in the "meantime"—that "hiatus between what is said, and what is *being* said, between the positing of the sign and the depositing of its significance."[1]

Pharaoh's counselors invoke the temporality of significance when they say, "This is the finger of God" (Exod. 8:19): for the magic of the third plague, in which dust is turned into lice, is not only an *act* of God but also a *sign* of his unfolding will or design. It bears the unmistakable signature of both the realization of a divine intent and its future. Egypt is the home of embalming, but the magi confess that only God can give life to dust—as if they knew Genesis 2:7. They are being pushed toward confessing the creator, but also the God who told Jacob his seed should be as the dust of the earth for the breadth of its distribution (Gen. 28:14).

The ten laws written with the finger of God (Exod. 31:18, Deut. 9:10) are also a sign. The hand of El is so insistently invoked for God's acts in the exodus that one comes to agree with the midrash explaining the ten plagues as God's fingers.[2] The Sinaitic call story has at least five of them:

(1) the mysterious sign (or nonsign) of Exod. 3:12, signifying the fulfilling of the promises of deliverance and return to the mountain;

(1a) the burning bush: this may be the unnamed sign of Exod. 3:12, or the sign of a sacred service to be conducted on the mount in the future;

(2) the transformation of Moses' rod into a serpent, and the serpent into the rod again;

(3) the plaguing of Moses' hand with leprosy, and its restoration to health (the hand is an agent like the rod, and so this sign repeats the preceding one, but in the flesh);

(4) the promise of the power to turn the Nile water to blood on dry ground (the leprous hand was unclean; the blood also points to pollution);

(5) the promise of the sign—directly fulfilled by God—of Aaron's coming to meet Moses.

The sequence predicts the plague narrative, as a sign of the signs to follow. It exemplifies the narrative's transformation of announcement into event, and the convertibility of its events into signs. The encounter with Aaron in the wilderness provides the mysterious sign that Moses is initially promised, that the Israelites will be called out of Egypt to return to a homeland apart from the land of their servitude. The family re-union in the wilderness makes an early start on fulfilling this promise.

The promise contained in the first sign, at Exodus 3:12, is all the "event" there is, apart from the post-exodus and therefore *post eventu* sign of return to the mountain. Conversely, the last sign, the rendezvous with Aaron, is only a promise: but its almost immediate fulfillment becomes the first "event" of the following narrative. This event supplies the quizzical substance of the report to Pharaoh that "The God of the Hebrews hath met with *us*," Yahweh in fact having met with no one other than Moses himself—yet the people *believe* in the visit (Exod. 5:3, 4:31). They are already turning toward the mountain of God's return.

Between word-of-promise and fulfillment-in-event comes, first, the sign of the rod, which Moses will show Pharaoh initially; then the coming and going of leprosy from Moses; and finally the promise of the metamorphosis of the Nile water. This last "word" is closely related to the second sign Moses subsequently shows Pharaoh, the bloodying of the Nile. But the second sign to Pharaoh is also the first plague, a plague of thirst and a pollution of Egypt. For the water of the Sinaitic sign was poured on the ground and became blood. In the levitical legislation, blood poured on the ground signifies either sacrifice or—oppositely—the pollution of bloodshed (Num. 35:33–34): the blood ought not to be on the ground, unless it is sacrificially offered in exchange for flesh-eating (Lev. 17:13). This sign reaches as far forward as the life-taking of the last plague in Egypt, and even to the "dry ground" in which Pharaoh is mired at the Reed Sea.

The central sign of leprosy must stand for the plagues between the pollution of the Nile and the drowning of Pharaoh's troops, since the sign after it, the Nile sign, suggests the Reed Sea. Leprosy is a form of plague, as is easily recognized from events in the wilderness. Analogously, the central plague between the bloodying of the Nile and the closing of the Reed Sea is the sixth one, boils. But this is not the "latter sign" that God predicts Pharaoh will "hear" (Exod. 4:8), though Pharaoh's counselors certainly do ("And the magicians could not stand before Moses because of the boils" [Exod. 9:11]). Boils are a sign in their flesh, and just as the flesh of a prophet may be made into a sign, so Moses' own flesh is affected in the central sign of the call narrative: his vocation is potentially a plague-like affliction. Yet his hand is healed, numbering him with those able to walk whole or present themselves before God.[3] Despite his speech impediment, he is freed from his uncleanness, a lack of soundness and uprightness thereafter visited on Egypt. Only later does God's touch cause Moses to take the veil.

God's questions about who makes man what he is suggest that at his call Moses receives from God a panoply of spiritual gifts: revelation (the promise to return to Sinai), power and wisdom (the power over the rod, and the wisdom of one who has power over serpents), integrity (the healing of the afflicted hand), life (the power to turn water to blood—for the life is in the blood), and the spirit (for Aaron is moved by God to go into the wilderness to meet Moses). Spirit is not itself mentioned, but the meeting with Aaron leads directly to the announcements that God has visited or met with his people (Exod. 4:31, 5:3).

ii

Comparison of the sequence of signs in the call narrative and the sequence of events in the plague narrative might suggest that rehearsal as recapitulation is one of the most insistent features of the Exodus narration overall, whether it is studied as a composition or as a story. But despite an analogous agenda, the sign-doing promised by the call story only hints at the complex exfoliation of the plague narrative itself. The story is heavily invested in its own retelling or restaging. This feature of redoing makes for the text's appropriation for liturgical purposes, as a litany retailing the exodus, or a script for a commemorative reenactment, a reproduction as an anniversary oratorio.

The call story has a critical codicil in the commandment that Moses do before Pharaoh the miracles that God has put in his power, and that he threaten the life of Pharaoh's firstborn in the event of Egypt's noncompliance. The corresponding "Priestly" call narrative, placed in Exodus 6:1–7:7, beyond Moses' first announcement to Israel and the initial unsuccess of his mission, more explicitly recognizes that God will *multiply* his signs and wonders in Egypt, and that Pharaoh will not heed—with the result that God will lay a heavy hand on Egypt. But neither the storm produced by Samuel nor the fire summoned by Elijah suggests the incessance and numerosity of the plagues announced in Moses. Scripture does not really credit the prophets—however adversarial their posture—with such an unrelenting campaign or sustained schedule, and we will want to look elsewhere for clues to the meaning of the multiplication in question.

There are two kinds of number represented by the plagues: their number overall, and the numerosity of frogs, lice (gnats, RSV), flies, and locusts. The vermin especially reflect God's creative activity, if we think of him as either "he who causes the hosts of heaven to be," or as he who causes the hosts of the enemy to disintegrate—to panic and stampede as if driven by a horde of wasps (cf. Exod. 23:28). Egypt's troops will be drowned in the Reed Sea, like the locusts that are driven there by the wind—the same divine wind that returns the sea's waters on these troops (Exod. 15:10, "Thou didst blow with thy wind, the sea covered them").

God created and ordered all things in the world by measure, number, and weight (Wisd. 11:20, Job 28:25, Isa. 40:12, Prov. 8:27–30), especially the waters, and he said all that he created was good; both his methods and his evaluation show that he is "a master workman," whose "work" is that "of a master hand" (Prov. 8:30, RSV; Song of Songs 7:1, RSV). Plagues present a somewhat different kind of number and mastery, but once again the acts of the creator cannot be far from mind, since these too exhibit a kind of method; they constitute a calendar-like schedule of disasters, and insist on God's control over the weather, the elements, the deep, increase, "the issues of life," and "the issues from death" (Prov. 4:23, Ps. 68:20). The two narratives present the protagonist—God the creator and Moses the spokesman—in the priestly role of ministering to the world through a divinely ordaining word. Each presides over a liturgy-like recitation that acknowledges the acts of God even as it presents them as a doxology.

The mastery of the plague narrative, like the deliberative unrolling of the week in the creation narrative, can also be seen as characteristic of a work of art. Its steady and purposive elaboration provides a long bridge from the call of Moses to the removal of Israel from Egypt. In this it again resembles the creation narrative, because it presents itself as a work of art in which the narrator's own accomplishment depends on that of God, even while coinciding with it. God dilates his activity like a performer. "By now I could have put forth my hand and struck you and your people with pestilence," Moses is instructed to say that God says to Pharaoh after the sixth plague (boils), "and you would have been cut off from the earth" (Exod. 9:15, RSV): Pharaoh is mortal, a mortal can be no match for the God of nature. But, God tells Moses, he has not come down on Pharaoh in one fell swoop: "I have hardened his heart and the heart of his servants, that I may show these signs of mine among them, and that you may tell in the hearing of your son and of your son's son *how I have made sport* of the Egyptians and what signs I have done among them" (Exod. 10:1–2, RSV). Pharaoh is unable to read the signs of the times, and he can be no match for the God whose métier *is* the times—the God whose art is the narrative kind, of which time is the medium. It takes time to make sport of the Egyptians. Moses is also a beneficiary of the delay: he has begun to read God's intention more fully, and Pharaoh's just accusation that Moses keeps changing his terms (Exod. 10:10–11)—now he wants to take *everyone* for the sacrifice, their flocks included—shows that Moses believes it more and more likely that God can deliver on his promises to remove the people from Egypt.

---

iii

In trying to explain further the rationale for the forelengthening of God's sign-making activity in Egypt, we need to establish what kind of work of art this narrative suggests. A purely chronological retailing of events might be historiographic but inartistic, because it might not construct itself according to the creation, puzzling, decoying, ambushing, and fulfilling of expectation: in the artistic narrative the sequence of disclosure and the sequence of events are not necessarily synchronous. But while considerations of "the plot thickens" kind are found in abundance in the Joseph novella, they have little to do with the art of the plague narrative, where the chronological order of events and the artistic order of disclosure are kept strictly in step, and where the order contains no real gaps to be filled in a final unsorting, dénouement, or disambiguation.

Darkness comes into the narrative of Genesis 1 only after vs. 1 declares that God created the heavens and the earth: the order is serial, but also artistic. The subsequent *geneses* are subject to the divine will, they do *not* generate it: *"These* are the generations of the heavens and of the earth[:] when they were *created"* (Gen. 2:4), the narrator of the story pointedly says, eliminating the genealogical kind of beginning from precisely the place where it would turn the narrative into a pagan theogony.[4] In dealing out the "unnatural" plagues to Egypt, God asserts for himself a similar priority. Instead of inverting the received metaphysic, in which abstract principles generate the gods, God now inverts the received historiography, in which dynasts and regimes set the agenda. When Pharaoh's magicians proclaim that Moses has done his sign by virtue of "the finger of God" (Exod. 8:19), they introduce a new idea into court. The hand of God is critical in Exodus, because it invokes God's own historical agency. But God's freedom from sequences he has not caused also tells us that the chronicle of the plagues, like that of the Creation, is not history-telling itself, only a second narrative obeying a rhythm of regularity, a "burden" of temporality.

"The history of time" or "the history of the weather" are not History. In the case of the creation narrative the "foreign content" is mainly an inventory of the earth, with the categories periodized as the "days" making up the pseudo-chronological sequence of God's acts. This activity mimes the kind of program that establishes a new dynasty or dispensation: the new king proclaims an amnesty, rebegins the calendar, names new ministers, creates new offices, proclaims new boundaries, and sets a new agenda. But at the outset the new dispensation has no history of its own— even the weather is deferred to the "second creations" of Adam (when a pre-rain mist rises from the earth, at Gen. 2:6) and the Flood.

The last thing Deuteronomy says about Moses is that he was unequaled as a prophet because of "the great terror" he showed in the sight of Israel (Deut. 34:12). In the case of the plague narrative, the content of such a demonstration is an almanac-like inventory of dismal ecological anomalies (cf. *dies mali*, 'bad days'). The divine acts are "pseudo-historical," yet they mime a program of political terrorism, one intending to destabilize the control over life exercised by a state establishment. Such a program hardly disguises the fact that the Mosaic polity has no history of its own. God seems very conscious of its difference from Egypt in this respect: he says he "will cause very heavy hail to fall, such as never has been in Egypt from the day it was founded until now" (Exod. 9:18, RSV). The implication is that Egypt has kept very good records; which only reminds us that Israel, 430 years in Egypt, has kept no such annals for itself; it has every reason for an anxiety of belatedness.

How can "the history of getting a history" be written at all? In practice, of course, the historian will establish his or her ground in geographical and demographic surveys. And the beginnings made by both the history of the world in Genesis and the history of Israel in the Pentateuch are vaguely understandable in this way. For God's passing over the Israelites in the tenth plague must constitute a kind of census of survivors analogous to the census found in Numbers 1 and 26. More particularly, we may com-pare the census God institutes in Numbers 3:14–15, which he reinstitutes in Numbers 3:40: "And the Lord spake unto Moses . . . saying, Number the children of Levi after the house of their fathers, by their families: every male from a month old and upward shalt thou number them"; "And the Lord said unto Moses, Number all the firstborn of the males of the chil-dren of Israel from a month old and upward, and take the number of their names." In this context, the rod in the hand of Moses is the baton with which the shepherd counts his flock.

---

iv

The creation and plague narratives resemble each other as sequences that put the action of God at the head of the history. Like works of art, God's actions exhibit mastery. The creator of Genesis 1 sees that what he has made is good, like a successful artisan; the history-maker of Exodus 7–12 contrives to extend the plagues in order to make them as memorable as possible, like a good story (Exod. 10:1–2, 1 Sam. 6:6). To further reveal the artistic métier of the plague narrative, we may start from the evidence of form in an instance of the naive, unrevised, cyclical, and verbatim kind of repetition, which belongs to the "tell-it-again" or Goldilocks and the Three Bears type of folk and fairy tale. The Sternbergian "members of forecast"[5] that introduce the central nine plagues in Exodus 7–10 regularly begin in three different ways: "Go to Pharaoh in the morning" (7:15, cf. 8:20, 9:13), "Go in to Pharaoh and say to him" (8:1, 9:1, 10:1), and "Then the Lord said to Moses, 'Say to Aaron . . . ,' " or do such and such (8:16, 9:8, 9:22; cf. 8:5). This kind of repetition is combined with a steady increase in results in both the creation narrative in Genesis 1 and the plague narrative in Exodus 7–12, according to a design and schedule, because God does not repeat a miracle without going beyond its given disclosure to some further advance upon it. God's dual activity dictates the text's recourse to both verbatim refrain and revisionary restatement. The dilation also follows from the resumptive techniques of the telling, which can be analyzed into members of "forecast," "enactment," and "report":

"And God said, 'Let there be light' " (= forecast →);

"and there was light" (= → enactment ←);

"and God saw that the light was good" (= ← report);

"and God separated the light from the darkness" (= second enactment).

"God called the light Day, and the darkness he called Night" (= third enactment: but also perhaps a second report, insofar as God is reporting the previous act of separating the light from darkness);

"And there was evening and there was morning, one day" (= third report, insofar as there being evening and morning is equivalent to there being a light separate from darkness).

The different kinds of members keep blurring into each other, however, where "enactments" are the results of speech-acts (performative utterances with illocutionary force), "speech-acts" are those of preordaining, summoning, pronouncing, or judging, and "reports" imply further acts of recognition or mental speech. This consonance between the members makes them virtually coinherent. All the variation is merely for the sake of insisting upon the execution of what God has ordained, or its wider promulgation. The purpose is not—*contra* that of Sternberg's examples of local repetition—to show the miscarrying of human enactment, or the inaccuracy of human forecast, or the imperfection or deviance of human report and acknowledgment. God, after all, does not mess up. "He commanded, and they were created" (Ps. 148:5).[6]

God's telling Moses what to do before the narrator's recording Moses' doing it, and Moses' announcing events to Pharaoh before they take place, function in the plague narrative like the repetitions in the creation narrative: forecasts are repeatedly and inevitably followed by wholly congruent enactments. The discourse rapidly shuttles through various cycles of the three modes without hitch. Thus Exodus 8:16–19 (RSV):

Then the Lord said to Moses, "Say to Aaron, 'Stretch out your rod and strike the dust of the earth, that it may become gnats throughout all the land of Egypt.' " [*dual forecast*]
And they did so; [*narrator's report of enactment of the main event*]
Aaron stretched out his hand with his rod, and struck the dust of the earth, [*first enactment of the main event and narrator's second report of it*]
and there came gnats on man and beast; [*second enactment of the main event and narrator's first report of its second half*]
all the dust of the earth became gnats throughout all the land of Egypt. [*narrator's second report of second half of the enactment*]
The magicians tried by their secret arts to bring forth gnats, [*a new enactment, but also an attempted re-enactment*]
but they could not. [*narrator's report of this new enactment*]
So there were gnats on man and beast. [*narrator's second (or reiterated) report of second half of the enactment of the main event*]
And the magicians said to Pharaoh, "This is the finger of God." [*a character's report of second enactment, itself a further event*]
But Pharaoh's heart was hardened, and he would not listen to them; [*last, new enactment (concluding event, but also a reaction)*]
as the Lord had said. [*narrator's report of last enactment, and of a prior, original forecast*]

Here the final, confirmatory report records the fulfillment of the prophecy found in the inaugural forecast that governs the whole series of plagues: God's predictions that he or Pharaoh will harden Pharaoh's heart. When there is no intervention on the part of Pharaoh and Moses, then a given plague—whether announced by God to Moses alone or also by Moses to a heedless Pharaoh—runs the course of forecast, enactment, and report or acknowledgment. Pharaoh's heart being regularly hardened, all the plagues forecast to him commence on schedule. Eight of these have been announced by the narrative, and six to Pharaoh, before he attempts to intervene in advance of a plague's arrival. The formulas "Pharaoh's heart was hardened," "Pharaoh shall not hearken unto you," "And the Lord hardened Pharaoh's heart," are all offered to explain the "so" in "So that he would not let the children go." God is enabled to increase and multiply his wonders in the same motion that the narrator is enabled to increase and multiply his formulas.

Despite such regularities, seemingly parallel expressions are differenti-ated by temporal modes. The end of Exodus 11, for example, concludes God's forecast of the death of the firstborn with what have become almost purely reflexive formulas, tedious predictions of what has by and large already happened, which sound like a broken record:

> And the Lord said unto Moses, Pharaoh shall not hearken unto you; that my wonders may be multiplied the land of Egypt.
> And Moses and Aaron did all these wonders before Pharaoh: and the Lord hardened Pharaoh's heart, so that he would not let the children of Israel go out of his land. (Exod. 11:9–10)

These sentences exhibit a recapitulative feature of biblical narrative that has been called "resumptive repetition," or *epanalepsis*.[7]

Biblical narrative uses such sentences, virtually editorially, for linking up an episodic and self-paralleling cycle of pericopes; they allege a kind of status report on the narrative's progress. The following sequence, extracted from 1 Samuel 2–3, is integrated into the account of the dises-tablishing of Eli's sons, while evincing a design of its own:

1. And the child did minister unto the Lord before Eli the priest.
2. But Samuel ministered before the Lord, being a child, . . .
3. And the child Samuel grew before the Lord . . .
4. And the child Samuel grew on, and was in favour . . . with the Lord . . .
5. And the child Samuel ministered unto the Lord. . . . And the word of the Lord was precious in those days;
[Now Samuel did not yet know the Lord, neither was the word of the Lord yet revealed unto him.]
6. And Samuel grew, and the Lord was with him, and did let none of his words fall to the ground . . .
7. . . . the Lord revealed himself to Samuel . . . by the word of the Lord. (1 Sam. 2:11, 18, 21, 26; 3:1, 7, 19, 21)

Thus Samuel ministered unto or before the Lord three times (1, 2, . . . 5); he grew three times (3, 4, . . . 6); and the Lord responded to him in some way three times, favoring him, being with him, and revealing himself to him (4, . . . 6, 7). The refrain assumes and resumes its burden in different combinations and at various intervals; "the word of the Lord," for example, is introduced at Samuel's last ministering (5), but only after "child" has disappeared does it actually come to him, at the third asser-tions of growth and of the Lord's special relation to him (6, 7).

Such a cyclic burden has also been used to describe a younger person's development elsewhere in the Bible. Samuel's progress as Eli's protégé compares with Joseph's development under his patrons in Egypt, David's emergence as a rival in the service of Saul, and the favoring of Jesus as the son of man and God in Luke. Pharaoh is as resumptively *dis*favored: the recurring burden about his hardness of heart characterizes him as a case of arrested development. Indeed, the arresting-resumptive feature of this narrative has migrated from the frame into the center of the picture: the subject, after all, is Pharaoh's and God's *perseveration*. Each episode is set apart and ministered to by God's and Moses' words, as if a formal petition were being made through the conduct of an extended rite—we note the ashes Moses as priest sprinkles "toward the heaven in the sight of Pharaoh" (Exod. 9:8) and their transformation. The final result is the instantiation of another rite: the Passover.

---

v

We might not be inclined to recognize the widely and haphazardly used pentateuchal formula "And the Lord said unto Moses" as a genuine instance of resumptive repetition; yet we note its specific introduction into the much more controlled and deductive narrative of the plagues. The phrase that authorizes and authenticates the mandates of virtually all the pentateuchal legislation is happily introduced, with God's self-naming or self-declaration at Exodus 3:14, as "*God* said unto Moses" (cf. also 6:1–2, 29); God has become "the Lord" (Yahweh) by the time of Moses' commission as his prophetic spokesman (at Exod. 4:19, 21, 6:1, 10, 13, 7:1). He also is the Lord at God's disclosure of Pharaoh's hard-heartedness (Exod. 7:14). Thus the introductory phrase has been standardized before its occurrence in the plague cycle itself.

It is used in the three cases where the Lord resumes a conversation with Moses that is not conveyed further, to Pharaoh, i.e., at the third, sixth, and ninth plagues. It is from this repetition that we learn that the cycle of plague-instructions is itself threefold: "Go to Pharaoh in the morning" is used for plagues 1, 4, and 7 (blood, flies, hail); "Go in to Pharaoh and say" for 2, 5, and 8 (frogs, cattle murrain, locusts); and "The Lord said to Moses" for the plagues precipitated without warning, 3, 6, and 9 (gnats [RSV], boils, darkness). If to the instructions for the ten plagues we add the instructions for the sign of the rod ("And the Lord spake unto Moses and unto Aaron, saying" [Exod. 7:8]), a cyclical pattern of four three-part rounds reveals itself, where the Reed Sea event completes the last round:

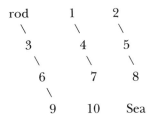

The narrative uses the general formula, "And the Lord spake unto Moses," for those three plagues that are not thereafter published by Moses to Pharaoh. Thus three of the divine utterances to Moses using the general formula belong to a commissioning and a revelation that is exclusive to the Mosaic leadership. Ordinarily, when the Pentateuch says "the Lord spake unto Moses," it means he did so in order to be heard by the people, and overheard by the reader: Yahweh is typically publishing for all to hear. But in the special case of the phrase's use at the onset of the third, sixth, and ninth plagues, Egypt is defined as "not spoken to."

Being the confidant to whom God has spoken exclusively—in the case of the three unannounced plagues—Moses is cast as a witness powerless to intervene before it is too late; he does not report the onset of gnats, boils, and darkness, nor does Pharaoh, in these cases, call on him to procure the sparing of an alienated people. Thus the set of unannounced plagues emphasizes exclusive or esoteric revelations to Moses, even while the overall narrative systematically embeds this set within those cases where Moses has been told to seek Pharaoh out like a king ("Go to Pharaoh in the morning"), or where he is supposed to make a public announcement in court ("Go in to Pharaoh and say"). In place of Moses the messenger to Pharaoh, *God* is the prophet; and, in place of the Egyptian adversary, *Moses* is the catechized subject. Moses, rather than Pharaoh, is being shown what God can do—through Moses. He is also being shown what Aaron can do, in cooperation with him, since, in the first two of the three unannounced cases—gnats (lice) and boils—he is told to act in concert with his brother. Aaron is thus preordained as a priest, for lice and boils are the two afflictions that would have made an Egyptian priest unpresentably *unclean*.

vi

God is a teacher who uses the plagues as both carrot and stick, inducing hard-heartedness while preaching repentance. The first fully roundlike course of events, or "full-cycle plague," is the multiplication of the frogs (Exod. 8:1–15), the second plague:

the announcement of the frogs through instructions to Moses,
the precipitance of the frogs,
the summons of Moses by a repenting Pharaoh,
the entreaty before God by Moses,
the remission of the frogs,
and the rehardening—and, in this case, reneging—of Pharaoh.

The result is to lure Pharaoh into a game of cat and mouse.

The first and last of the three unannounced plagues, the gnats and darkness (3, 9), follow on Pharaoh's reneging on promises made during what are his first and last repentances, after the frogs and locusts (2, 8), as if these two unannounced plagues were brought directly on by the king's preceding bad faith, and were themselves punishments, each following on the unheeded warning of the preceding plague. But the intervening unannounced plague of boils (6) does not follow upon such a further tempting of God by Pharaoh, and the two other examples of Pharaoh's bad faith, the false repentances after the onsets of the plagues of flies and hail (4, 7), are not followed by another plague without there also being a further remonstrance; it is Pharaoh's ignoring of such remonstrance, or second chance, that brings on the succeeding, announced afflictions of the cattle-murrain and locusts (5, 8).

Pharaoh is not called upon to repent after the onset of the three unannounced plagues (3, 6, 9), no communication with him having been initiated; and these plagues cease without any repentance. Yet they are not the only plagues that are exhausted without Moses' and Pharaoh's intervention—so also the plague of blood (1), and the cattle-murrain (5). Since presumably the death of the firstborn (10) only stops when all the firstborn are dead, and no entreaty otherwise is made, it is the last example of six self-exhausting plagues: 1, 3, 5, 6, 9, and 10. Moses intervenes to arrest the other plagues of frogs, flies, hail, and locusts: 2, 4, 7, and 8. The result is an alternating rhythm that compounds or doubles midway through the sequence, viz.:

$$
\begin{array}{lcccc}
\text{unarrested:} & 1, & 3, & 5,6, & 9,10... \\
 & \searrow\nearrow & \searrow\!/\!/ & \searrow\!\searrow & /\!/ \\
\text{arrested:} & & 2\text{-;} & 4\text{-;} & 7\text{-;}8\text{-;}
\end{array}
$$

The lower register ("arrested") shows Pharaoh readier to reverse himself late in the sequence (at hail, 7, and locusts, 8). In the previous cases of frogs and flies (2, 4), Pharaoh may have reconsidered only after he had been reached personally by the nuisance in question. "Entreat the lord," Pharaoh says to Moses during the second plague, "that he may take away the frogs from *me*" (Exod. 8:8); "and there came a grievous swarm of flies," the narrator reports of the fourth plague, "into the *house* of Pharaoh" (Exod. 8:24). The word *house* is a sinister anticipation of the plague that *will* finally reach Pharaoh: in Hebrew it can mean family, while in Egyptian the name *Pharaoh* derives from the word meaning "great house." Pharaoh's *son* is his house.

As Moses accumulates the advantage of his threats being fulfilled, in plagues 2, 4, 5, and 7, he raises the ante—and Pharaoh always lags behind. If he ever wanted to soften his heart, he is prevented from doing so fast enough. First he says the Israelites can sacrifice in Egypt, but Moses demands they be allowed to leave, and Pharaoh insists they not go very far, after the onset of the flies (4). Then he is ready to let the men go, but Moses has asked that those allowed to leave include all Israel, before the locusts (8). After the locusts Pharaoh will let the men and children go, but tries to detain the flocks. Finally, after the death of the firstborn (10), he indeed lets all the people and their cattle go: but then he sends his troops to bring them back. Thus Pharaoh is shown neither fully acknowledging the trouble of his own people, nor fully conceding the "right" of Israel. "Knowest thou not yet that Egypt is destroyed?" his counselors ask him in vain (Exod. 10:7), before the impending plague of locusts. "Not yet" is the right answer, since the locusts, in reply, are finally scotched at the Reed Sea. For beyond ruining Egypt, Pharaoh is determined to create Israel— without ever quite knowing what he has done.

Pharaoh contrasts with Moses, who early on begs God to clarify his purpose in wishing Moses upon God's suffering flock (Exod. 5:22–23). Moses rejects Pharaoh's penultimate confession of being in the wrong, as merely the stratagem of an oppressive regime desperately attempting to buy itself extra time. It is here that God says that his purpose is to *make sport of* the Egyptians (RSV, but otherwise "deal harshly with") and to create a series of episodes worth the retelling (Exod. 10:1–2; cf. Ps. 44:1, 78:4–6). After the alleviation of the eighth plague (locusts), Pharaoh becomes more obdurate than ever; and his final permission allowing the Hebrews to depart *en masse* (after the plague on the firstborn) is not accompanied by any admission of sinfulness. Rather, he is presumptuous enough to request a blessing in the midst of the disaster that condemns his policy as that of a fool. And he reneges, yet once more, upon his permission—after the Hebrews have left. His folly will not let him go. The extending of the narrative has thus made its initial point both actually and conjecturally: a temporizing Pharaoh has been no less obstinate and resistant than an unmitigatedly adamant one would have been.

The Reed Sea event is annexed to the plague narrative by the repetition of the features of Pharaoh's preliminary hardening, God's large announcement, Moses' performance with his rod, Egypt's benighting (from the ninth plague), and the visitation of destruction on the sinful party. But as an event it also belongs among victories recorded in the Book of the Wars of Yahweh: "Wherefore it is said in the book of the wars of the Lord, What he did in the Red sea, and in the brooks of Arnon" (Num. 21:14), a possible paralleling of Moses and Joshua. For it belongs with the judges' miracles in the field—one of these was poeticized in a poem found in a similar "Book of Jasher" (Josh. 10:13). Moses and Miriam, as prophets and celebrants of God's victory on its site, are like the Deborah and Barak who sing Deborah's Song in Judges 5.

Defining features of this war-song genre are thrown into relief by the copresence in the Bible of prose versions of the various occasions. The first feature is simply this poetical detachment of the epos—which exhibits its own parallelistic, self-rallying rhetoric, and embodies its cause in the figure of the singer as prophet or judge—from the event the song originally commemorated. But a second feature of the poems finds its way back into the prose versions: the (epideictic) dramatization of a favorable turn of events as the sign of a mysterious or extraordinary intervention—epiphanic, prophetic, supernatural, or providential. The sea opens, the sun stands still, the tent-keeping woman prevails over the general off the battlefield. However miraculous, the feat-legend is surely inspired by actual turning points in military history: it is difficult to believe that these biblical border ballads celebrate events that did not occur at all.

A verse-like prediction of the Israelites' plight announces the arrival of the rhythms peculiar to the genre: Moses' lines, "The depths have covered them; they sank into the bottom as a stone," compare readily with Pharaoh's: "They are entangled in the land, the wilderness hath shut them in" (Exod. 15:5, 14:3). But it is God who forecasts that the hardened heart of Pharaoh will be led to say this. "We had the enemy up against a wall," Pharaoh would say, "they were completely trapped"—with God as his poet. The predicted distich, in other words, belongs to a *putative* Egyptian verse-epic on the defeat of Israel at the Reed Sea. The maids of Sisera's mother, in the Song of Deborah, are similarly made to speak lines from a putative ballad on the projected victory of Sisera over Israel (Judg. 5:30). Pharaoh and Moses—like the maids and Deborah—are presented as composing rival distiches on the same event, as if each speaker were commissioned to work up a panegyric on behalf of his or her side's victory. Both texts internalize the other side's ideal verse-version of what happened.

Yet we should also see the poetical episode as *having* happened, apart from having been poeticized. Such a turning point is marked by the generic gear-change itself, from the tell-it-again story of the plagues to the war-song of a victorious underdog: rallied to a national cause, and oriented on an engagement at a specific location where opposing forces were mustered and decided between. Joshua's God stayed the sun and conjured the moon (Josh. 10:12–13), but he also delivered up the Amorites to the Israelites. The plagues end where this verse-epos begins, because history-keeping itself rebegins here—at a point where Moses-functions convert to those of Joshua.

---

viii

The plague of frogs is the first "full-cycle" plague. The preceding seven-day plague on the Nile (back into which the conjured frogs will crawl) is as much a sign as a plague; the Egyptians can circumvent it by digging for water, and it ends without Mosaic intervention—and perhaps partly with Egyptian intervention. In advance of this sign-making plague had come the sign of the rod, which was no plague at all, and which the Egyptians are definitely able to duplicate, as they are also able to do with the plague of frogs (Exod. 8:7). Thus the first round of Moses' performances begins from a sign (rod), adds a second sign (blood), which is also a threat and a temporary disaster (pollution of the Nile's water for seven days by the blood, the first plague), followed by a second disaster (frogs, the second plague), and culminating in Pharaoh's repentance and Egypt's deliverance by Moses. Signs alone are not effective (rod), threats need to be maintained (blood), and feckless negotiation can bargain away the gains of God's demonstrations of power (frogs).

We can argue that the sequence of these first three demonstrations constitutes a group—a narrative "round"—and that the remainder of the twelve-demonstration total falls into three more rounds. We have identified these further rounds by the simple observation that the narrator has placed one of the three unannounced plagues (3, 6, 9) at the head of a cycle, in place of the inaugural sign of the rod. In the resulting four rounds, each round's demonstrations or wonders recapitulate some feature newly introduced by the preceding round, as the initial sign of the rod renews the signs Moses was shown on the mountain.

The overall pattern of the twelve signs-wonders-plagues-disasters is:

I. rod	blood (1)	frogs (2)		
II.	gnats (3)	flies (4)	murrain (5)	
III.		boils (6)	hail (7)	locusts (8)
IV.			darkness (9)	firstborn (10)	Reed Sea

The first round begins from a self-contained sign (rod-serpent-rod), while the second (plagues 3 through 5) begins from an unannounced and self-contained plague (gnats: 3): as the first wonder (rod) leads to the first self-contained plague (blood: 1), so the first round leads to the second self-contained plague—the first unannounced plague, gnats (3). This plague improves on the attempt of the Egyptians to work a demonstration of their own, because it introduces "the finger of God." Pharaoh does not intervene for the plague's cessation, yet Israel's presence *may* be sparing Egypt. This self-containing plague is followed by a full-cycle plague, that of flies (4). The gnats seem duplicated by the flies, but this time deliverance is secured *only* through Pharaoh's intervention with Moses, and Moses' express intervention with God. The gnats *may* be a plague on flesh, but the concluding demonstration of this round is the first plague *definitely* on flesh: the cattle murrain (5). But Israel's cattle are spared, a specific deliverance unprocured by Mosaic intervention and therefore *restricted* to the elect nation, whom God himself is now intervening for.

The sparing of Israelite flesh now becomes a constant, for the third round of demonstrations, like the second, begins from an unannounced and self-contained plague—boils (6)—this time a visitation exclusively on *Egyptian* flesh, but flesh more narrowly considered, since the Pharaoh's own court is the most affected party. This plague is followed by a full-cycle economic and meteorological plague and disaster, hail (7), in which Israel *and also the heedful among the Egyptians*—and therefore even some part of the Egyptian crop—are spared. Moses and God are looking out not only for Israel now, but also for Israel's partisans and converts. This affliction may also be considered a plague on flesh, like the cattle-murrain, since its victims are physically smitten. The concluding plague in this round, locusts (8), is also a full-cycle one, like the concluding plagues of the two preceding rounds: the locusts destroy the remainder of the Egyptian crop, but thereafter Moses again procures deliverance for all. In this case, however, the new feature of the full-cycle, follow-up plague in the third position of the round is not Moses' intervention from the plague of frogs (2), or the victimizing of specifically Egyptian flesh from the plague of cattle murrain (5), but rather an expansion of the event's significance both semiotically and prophetically. Perhaps because the deliverance from this plague is, for the first time, negotiated between Pharaoh and Moses *before* as well as after the plague's onset, the results of the second, follow-up negotiation also take proleptic form; that is, they reach over and beyond the deliverance itself—to the Reed Sea, in which the locusts are drowned by a divine wind. Locusts, in biblical parlance, can stand for armies, and it is just such a divine wind that blows the Reed Sea waters back on Egypt's troops, according to Moses' Song at the Sea (Exod. 15:10). By the end of round three, the locusts have overtaken the final result of round four. They are a late plague, but an early sign.

Like the second and third rounds, the fourth and last round of demonstrations begins with an unannounced, self-contained plague: darkness (9). As with the earlier example of the boils (6), the elect nation is set apart: but now in a way suggesting the Israelites are *already absent* from Egypt, since presumably the benighted Egyptians can no longer actually see them. Darkness is followed by the watch-night, with the sign of the blood ensuring both the passing over of God's adoptive son Israel, and the death of Pharaoh's natural son in Egypt's firstborn (the tenth plague). The deaths throughout Egypt are yet another plague on Egyptian flesh, but also now on Egypt's *elect*: that is, on the primary class of heirs.

The plague of darkness sets Israel apart from Egypt for *three days*, this being the original amount of time that Moses proposed to journey into the wilderness to offer sacrifice to God. Apparently it is on the third day into the wilderness, moving at night, under cover of darkness, that Israel is overtaken by Pharaoh's pursuing army. There follows the final member of the final round: God's destruction of the remaining sons of Egypt in the Reed Sea. This devotion of Egypt to destruction completes a schedule of demonstrations in accordance with Moses' original provisions for setting Israel three days apart from Egypt, in order to make a *sacrifice*.

The canon of the twelve signs and wonders forms a kind of thematic *terza-rima*, a-b-c, b-c-d, c-d-e, d-e-f. The system of advance, retardation, and recapitulation is built on the following base:

a	b	c	d	e	f
sign,	plague,	deliverance;			
	plague,	deliverance,	Israel spared;		
		deliverance,	Israel spared,	salvation sign;	
			Israel spared,	salvation sign,	sign realized.

We may fill in this pattern with some of the variables and constants:

I)	ROD	BLOOD	FROGS	
	sign	threat and plague	—deliverance for all	
II)		GNATS	FLIES	MURRAIN
		unannounced	—deliverance for all	—deliverance of cattle, but Israel's spared

III)	BOILS	HAIL	LOCUSTS	
	unannounced; human flesh (Egyptian) temporarily afflicted	—sparing of Israel & the heedful Egyptians	—deliverance, but with a sign/threat	

IV)	DARKNESS	FIRSTBORN	REED SEA
	unannounced; Israel set apart in Egypt	sign, plus sanctification of Israel	—Israel set apart from Egypt

The center of narrative gravity is shifted across the first round from sign to announcement, from threat to plague, and from remission to brokered deliverance. It is shifted across the second from disaster to deliverance for all, and then to a sparing of animal flesh. It is shifted across the third from a sparing of Israelite flesh, to sparing of the heedful, to deliverance in the ironic, admonitory form of a sign of the final setting apart of Israel from Egypt. It is shifted across the fourth from oblivion in Egypt, to the sanctification and deliverance of Israel by a second sign, to Israel's putting Egypt behind it with the destruction of its pursuers. Indeed, the crossing of the Reed Sea after a sojourn apart from Egypt not only enters Israel on the wilderness, but anticipates deliverance from it forty years later, if crossing the Sea is a sign of eventually crossing the Jordan.

Thus the plague narrative provides a long bridge over which the sign-making activity of the prophet or deity is gradually transformed into the very revelation of history. Across this bridge the narrative moves inexorably from sign to event; from striking announcements to unannounced strikes; from ineffective warning to performative utterance; from the temporizing of occasion to the precipitance of disaster; from Israel's intercession with God for the heedful to God's repudiation of the intransigent for wickedness; from the wicked's indifference to God to the wicked's foolish persistence in defying him; from the prolongation of the night of a people's adversity to the dawn of its vindication; and from the deliverance of the creation to the creation of deliverance.

·12·

THE GENESIS OF THE EXODUS

> Praise him, ye heavens of heavens, and ye waters that be above the heavens.
> Let them praise the name of the Lord: for he commanded, and they were created.
> He hath also stablished them for ever and ever: he hath made a decree which shall not pass.
> Praise the Lord from the earth, ye dragons, and all deeps:
> Fire, and hail; snow, and vapour; stormy wind fulfilling his word.
> (Psalm 148:4–8)

According to Isaiah 40–66, Yahweh has *created* salvation (45:8). God has called his servant "for a covenant of the people . . . to bring out the prisoners from the prison, and them that sit in darkness out of the prison house" (42:6–7). A fifth-century formula recorded for the manumission of a slave is "You are released . . . from the shade for the sun, and no other man is master of you . . . You are released for God."[1] According to Psalm 105:43, the Lord "brought forth his people" not only with "gladness," but also with a loud cry of rejoicing, a song or proclamation, or *rinnâ*. According to Wisdom, it was wisdom "who delivered a holy people . . . and withstood fearsome kings with wonders and signs," and "drowned their enemies, then spate them out from the depths of the abyss": "For the whole creation, submissive to [wisdom's] commands, had its very nature re-created" (Wisd. 10:15–16, 19; and 19:6, NJB).

These texts do not make Moses the leader of Israel's emigration out of Egypt: it is God who has this office. The Mosaicization of the exodus is the project of a particular kind of prophecy found in the eighth-century Hosea, who says, "by a prophet the Lord brought Israel out of Egypt, and by a prophet was he preserved" (12:13). This prophet was Moses. For Psalm 103:7 says of Yahweh: "He made known his ways unto Moses, his acts unto the children of Israel," which confirms Moses' prayer in Exodus 33:13, "Now therefore, I pray thee, if I have found grace in thy sight, shew me now thy way, that I may know thee . . . and consider that this nation is thy people." Moses is thus understood as an informed initiate, one who prayed in order to be able to instruct Israel not only in the law, but also in the exodus itself. Moses is only credited with effecting the exodus-deed, insofar as he also *revealed* it—as *God's* deed, and God's way. The exodus is thus acknowledged as "torah." It is something to be taught. Can we say what?

Israel is always guilty of apostasy. The cause of the national disaster is much the same in the mouth of Ahijah, speaking against Solomon, as in the mouth of Huldah, speaking against the last Judaic kings: "because that they have forsaken me" (1 Kings 11:33, 2 Kings 22:17; cf. 2 Chron. 7:22, 34:25, etc.). With this refrainlike motif goes the indictment of the nation's shortness of memory: after Joshua's generation "there arose another generation . . . which knew not the Lord, nor yet the works which he had done for Israel. And the children of Israel . . . forsook the Lord God of their fathers, which brought them out of the land of Egypt" (Judg. 2:10–12). Indeed, according to Psalms 78 (vss. 11, 32, 42) and 106 (vss. 7, 21, 24), the nation had forgotten the Lord's mighty acts in Egypt almost before it was delivered from there—even before the Reed Sea event. As rebukes of ingratitude, disbelief, and forgetfulness, these psalms find their subject everywhere, while also recalling those same mighty acts.

If the newly delivered people did forget God's mighty acts, it was not for want of their being cast in memorable form: three days of darkness, but with light for the children of Israel, before the institution and sacrifice of the Passover night; three days' journey into the wilderness with the pillars of cloud and fire, before the "sacrifice" at the sea in which the locusts had perished; and three days further to Marah, before the divine healing of the waters there and the institution of the Sabbath. Like Moses at the Reed Sea (and perhaps Jacob at the Jabbok in Gen. 32), the narrative *doubles back*, hemming in (or reincorporating) recapitulative features.

The need to catechize Israel in the record of God's recurring effectiveness accounts for this "structure of recall" being built into the saving events from the outset. God *will be* remembered (Ps. 45:17, Exod. 3:15). Moreover, Moses is commissioned to reveal a particular *interpretation* of the exodus, if we consider what he is told at Exodus 4:22: God would have him say, "Thus saith the Lord, Israel is my son, even my firstborn: And I say unto thee, Let my son go." The fact that Moses does *not* go on to say this shows that God's getting it said to his spokesperson—or in the text—is more important than his getting it said to Pharaoh, or in Pharaoh's court. The revelation of Israel's adoption into God at the exodus is implicitly identified as the essential kerygma of the Old Testament, near the opening of the New: "Out of Egypt have I called my son" (Matt. 2:15). In Hosea itself, however, the adoption message mediated by the prophet falls on deaf ears. It is a call to which Israel refuses to be recalled:

When Israel was a child, I loved him,
  and out of Egypt I called my son.
The more they [Gk.'I'] called them,
  the more they went from me;
They kept sacrificing to the Baals,
  and burning incense to idols. (Hos. 11:1–2, RSV)

—As if to say, the more the Mosaicizing prophets—the "they" of the Hebrew version—called Israel into adoption by God by means of an appeal to the saving fact of the exodus, the more Israel addicted itself to idols and captained itself back to Egypt. Moses spoke his exodus message "unto the children of Israel: but they hearkened not unto Moses" (Exod. 6:9). But even if Moses failed to reveal to Israel the kerygma of its deliverance and adoption from Egypt, Yahwist prophets or a Yahwist priesthood must have kept it. *Pace* Moses' song regarding Israel's forgetfulness at Deuteronomy 32:15–18, Israel could never really disown the deity who had made it.

The effect of all the repetition in the plague story is to tell one episode over and over, as if Israel had only this single story to tell—or only one story really worth the retelling. The story culminates in the Passover, which tends to turn the built-in retelling in the narrative into the Passover liturgy. It may be significant that there are seven plagues that Moses announces to Pharaoh. For like the creation itself, Passover is scheduled for seven days (Exod. 12:15–16); and like the drying up of the Flood—which takes place during two weeks—its date is set for the beginning of the New Year (Gen. 8:11–13, Exod. 12:2), on the fourteenth day of the first month (Exod. 12:17–18). In the ancient Near East, New Year's festivals celebrating the establishment of the world order were used to renew the kingship, with a creation story featuring the combat myth as their liturgy.

If Passover occupies the place of such a springtime feast, then its purpose is to re-inaugurate the biblical "kingship of God," in conjunction with the defeat of the divine king's would-be rival, the king of Egypt. Essential evidence for the nature of God's action in the exodus occurs in Isaiah 51, where vss. 14–16 reveal God's role as sponsor, consoler, reliever, proclaimer, suzerain or covenant partner, but also creator and founder:

  The captive exile hasteneth that he may be loosed, and that he should not die in the pit, nor that his bread should fail.
  But I am the Lord thy God, that divided the sea, whose waves roared: The Lord of Hosts is his name.
  And I have put my words in thy mouth, and I have covered thee in the shadow of mine hand, that I may plant the heavens, and lay the foundations of the earth, and say unto Zion, Thou art my people.

Like Babylon, Israel traced its antecedents from the foundation of the world, but what is the poetic logic that connects the Lord's saving of his people from oppression with the Lord's stirring up of the sea? Is this also an interpretation of the exodus?[2]

In the story of how Israel was finally and definitively set apart from her Egyptian pursuers, the parting of the Reed Sea opens upon the aboriginal abyss, even while revealing the original dry land and the foundation of the firmament. So Exodus 15:8 and 14:21b–22:

> And with the blast of thy nostrils the waters were gathered together, the floods stood upright as an heap, and the depths were congealed in the heart of the sea.
>
> . . . the Lord caused the sea to go back by a strong east wind all that night, and made the sea dry land, and the waters were divided.
> And the children of Israel went into the midst of the sea upon the dry ground: and the waters were a wall unto them on their right hand, and on their left.

At Isaiah 51:10 the same divine deliverer has brought the ocean to heel: "Art thou not it which hath dried the sea, the waters of the great deep; that hath made the depths of the sea a way for the ransomed to pass over?"

With these verses we may compare Genesis: "the Spirit of God moved upon the face of the waters . . . And God said, Let there be a firmament in the midst of the waters, and let it divide the waters from the waters. And God made the firmament, and divided the waters . . . And God said, Let the waters under the heaven be gathered together unto one place, and let the dry land appear: and it was so" (Gen. 1:2, 6–7, 9). For the gathering of the waters into two walls at the Reed Sea must also "divide the waters from the waters." The doxology of Psalm 33:6–9 shows the same divisive gesture:

> By the word of the Lord were the heavens made; and all the host of them by the breath of his mouth.
> He gathereth the waters of the sea together as an heap: he layeth up the depth in storehouses.
> Let all the earth fear the Lord: let all the inhabitants of the world stand in awe of him.
> For he spake, and it was done; he commanded, and it stood fast.

Moses' invocation of the Lord's punishment of Dathan and Abiram also couches itself in cosmogonic terms, as both a sign from God *and* a new creation: "But if the Lord make a new thing, and the earth open her mouth, and swallow them up, with all that appertain unto them, and they go down quick into the pit; then ye shall understand that these men have provoked the Lord. And . . . the ground clave asunder that was under them: And the earth opened her mouth, and swallowed them up" (Num. 16:30–32). God makes this "new thing" when he defeats Pharaoh, in the Song at the Sea: "Thou stretchedst out thy right hand, the earth swallowed them. Thou . . . hast led forth the people which thou hast redeemed" (Exod. 15:12–13).

It follows that it is Pharaoh, not Moses, who is finally the one the narrative exposes on the waters. God destroys Pharaoh's army as the god-hero Marduk destroyed the belligerent water-monster Tiamat:

> Sheol is naked before God,
> and Abaddon has no covering.
> He stretches out the north over the void,
> and hangs the earth upon nothing.
> He binds up the waters in his thick clouds,
> and the cloud is not rent under them. . . .
> By his power he stilled [Hebr. *rāga‘*, AV 'divideth'] the sea;
> by his understanding he smote Rahab.
> By his wind the heavens were made fair;
> his hand pierced the fleeing serpent. (Job 26:6–8, 12–13, RSV)

God *divides* the sea in the same way in Isaiah 51:15 and Jeremiah 31:35. In Isaiah 30:7b Egypt's value as an Israelite ally is mocked: "I have called her 'Rahab who sits still' " (RSV). Here we may reread the texts from Isaiah:

> Was it not thou that didst cut Rahab in pieces,
> that didst pierce the dragon?
> Was it not thou that didst dry up the sea,
> the waters of the great deep;
> that didst make the depths of the sea a way
> for the redeemed to pass over? (Isa. 51:9b–10, RSV)

The exodus account in Psalm 105 names a variety of plagues, including caterpillars (vss. 34–35), but it is silent about the Reed Sea event; nonetheless, it does not fail to say that God "opened the rock, and the waters gushed out; they ran in the dry places like a river" (vs. 41). Water is an issue here too:

> Is my hand shortened, that it cannot redeem?
> Or have I no power to deliver?
> Behold, by my rebuke I dry up the sea,
> I make the rivers a desert;
> their fish stink for lack of water,
> and die of thirst. (Isa. 50:2b–c, RSV)

The first plague that Moses causes is a plague of thirst: it forces the Egyptians to dig wells beside the Nile (Exod. 7:18, 21, 24). One thinks of the Egyptian Hymn to the Aton: "Thou makest a Nile in the underworld, / Thou bringest forth as thou desirest / To maintain the people (of Egypt) / According as thou madest them for thyself."[3] It is thus the Near Eastern Sovereign God who is the source of Moses' power to still or imprison water, and his converse power to release water from captivity. In the Babylonian creation epic Tiamat in her primal union with Apsu engrosses all the world's water, and Marduk thereafter will enlarge her with an evil wind, and bring her waters under the control of the bars of the cosmos.[4] As God smote Rahab and pierced the *fleeing* serpent, so Moses struck the Nile and the rock (Exod. 7:20, 17:5–6, Num. 20:11, Ps. 78:20) and confounded the fleeing Pharaoh (Exod. 14:25–27). And as the heavens were made by the word of the Lord and the breath of his mouth when, in Psalm 33:6–7, he gathered the waters together in a heap, so, in Psalm 78:13 and in Exodus 14–15, the waters of the Reed Sea are stood up in a heap. Moreover, in Psalm 106:9, these waters are stayed at the Lord's *rebuke.*

At God's rebuke would mean at his word, as in the case of the summoning God of Isaiah 50:2: ". . . when I called, was there none to answer? . . . at my rebuke I dry up the sea." Such a word of rebuke is implied by the primeval stilling of the seas described in Psalm 89:9–11, which links this stilling with the dividing of Rahab, the scattering of enemies, and the founding of the world. Similarly, in Psalm 104:3, 5–7, the primeval waters stood above the mountains and fled at the creator's rebuke, at the laying of the beams of his creation in the waters and the covering of the foundations of the earth with the deep; and these waters are bound that they may not again cover the earth (vs. 9).

By a strikingly ironic chance of intertextuality, the Hebrew Psalm in which God the creator definitively rebukes the primeval waters takes much of its depiction of God's universal activity from the Egyptian Hymn to the Aton. The Psalm says that God "makest darkness, and it is night: wherein all the beasts of the forest do creep forth," and that when the sun rises "Man goeth forth unto his work and to his labour until the evening" (Psalm 104:20, 23); but it does not say that God who covers himself "with light as with a garment" (vs. 2) is the sun, and that these things happen when he sets and rises, or that God has made "the distant sky in order to rise therein, / in order to see all that (he) dost make." Nonetheless the Egyptian hymn contains a rough sketch for the acts of the creator in Genesis 1:

> Though didst create the world according to thy desire,
> Whilst thou wert alone:
> All men, cattle, and wild beasts,

Whatever is on earth, going upon (its) feet,
And what is on high, flying with its wings.[5]

This "sole god, like whom there is no other," makes a Nile in the underworld and a Nile in Heaven, as God "divided the waters which were under the firmament from the waters which were above the firmament" (Gen. 1:7). Like God creating in Genesis 1, the Aton acts without strife; darkness is delimited, not conquered—there is no turbulence. The God of Genesis 1 had no occasion to defeat great sea-monsters, if he created them in the first place (Gen. 1:20–21: "God said, Let the waters bring forth abundantly, . . . And God created great whales"). Psalm 148 shows such creatures called forth as part of a universal doxology: "Praise the Lord from the earth, ye dragons, and all deeps: Fire, and hail; snow, and vapour; stormy wind fulfilling his word: . . . Beasts, and all cattle; . . . Kings of the earth, . . . princes, and all judges" (vss. 7–8, 10, 11).

And here questions arise. Why would the narrative of Genesis and Exodus defer a divine victory over chaos from its initial account of the activity of the creator to the story of the events at the Reed Sea? Why is the Reed Sea account a demythologized and historicized theomachia of the kind found in the Near Eastern creation epic with its "combat myth"?[6] In some of the cosmogonic, proto-diluvian, and theomachic materials adduced to explain God's intervention in the natural order, a Bible-reader may feel a scruple: that even a scholarly initiate cannot be fairly counted on to read these materials as constituting a genuine *allusion* to them on the Israelite storyteller's own part.[7] Yet the parallels, however much displaced, dissociated, condensed, or omitted, give us a sense of what the storyteller may have held in reserve, to be invoked sparingly, in his story's frame.

The God of the Sea-miracle is surely the Creator from the poetry: "Thy way is in the sea, and thy path in the great waters, and thy footsteps are not known" (Ps. 77:19); he "alone spreadeth out the heavens, and treadeth upon the waves of the sea" (Job 9:8). Jeremiah 51:15–16 links the sound of God's creative voice with the turbulence of his creative power:

"It is he who made the earth by his power,
    who established the world by his wisdom
and by his understanding
    stretched out the heavens.
When he utters his voice there is a tumult of waters in the heavens,
    and he makes the mist rise from the ends of the earth.
He makes lightnings for the rain,
    and he brings forth the wind from his storehouses." (RSV)

The wonder-working God of the Psalmist deploys all the power originally released in a cataclysmic victory over the aboriginal *tehôm* of Genesis 1:2:

> When the waters saw thee, O God,
>   when the waters saw thee, they were afraid,
>   yea, the deep [*tehôm*] trembled.
> The clouds poured out water;
>   the skies gave forth thunder;
>   thy arrows flashed on every side.
> The crash of thy thunder was in the whirlwind;
>   thy lightnings lighted up the world;
>   the earth trembled and shook.
> Thy way was through the sea,
>   thy path through the great waters;
>   yet thy footprints were unseen.
> Thou didst lead thy people like a flock
>   by the hand of Moses and Aaron. (Ps. 77:16–20, RSV)

God raises and then quiets the storm at sea, his voice is greater than that of all the waters, he established their bounds, and set the unruly sea its bars and doors, the deep and its monsters obey his decree (Ps. 93:3–4, 107:25–30, 148:6, Job 38:8–11, Ps. 148:7–8), he tamed the original abyss and all things cohere through his word (Ecclus. 43:23, 26). His commands dispatch the snow and the ice, and "He sendeth out his word, and melteth them: he causeth his wind to blow, and the waters flow" (Ps. 147:15–19).

"Command is his lips," one might say, which is indeed what an Egyptian hymn to Amon does say: "When he enters the two caverns which are under his feet, the Nile comes forth from the grotto under his sandals."[8] But the peaceful creation event and the warlike exodus event, which the utterances of psalmist and prophet alike have clearly united, and which are back to back in Psalms 104 and 105 even when they are separated, are just as clearly the events that the Pentateuch has divided between Genesis 1 and Exodus 14–15. Why is this so?

The answer seems twofold. First, the combat myth is really a victory myth. But the victory of the one and only god over all other gods—the victory of monotheism—eliminates the combat myth itself, which could only be a weapon in the hands of the antagonist: "the enemy, although and precisely because he is fearful, always receives cult."[9] The propitiation of Tiamat, even in the form of including her in the literature about her defeat, is not wanted on the opening page of the total history: God is not a second- or third-generation deity triumphing over a predecessor, or indeed even a deity who was "the first to come into being in the earliest times . . . at the beginning," like the post-Amarna Amon.[10]

The second part of the answer looks to the social context for the literary cultivation of the combat myth. The prebiblical creation epic was attached to regimes that celebrated and dramatized their own ascendancy: as the re-creation of the victory of god-heroes, like Marduk, over the opposing forces of inertia and disorder. Marduk was the Babylonian "man of the hour" who defeated the insurgent forces of chaos, or Nature, when Culture proved incapable of defending itself, without resorting to the impositions of Civilization.[11] While the first creation-narrative is a litany without a drama or a ritual, the plague narrative is a litany with both: in this *agon*, the Prince of the Nile-lands, pretending to the supremacy, is humbled by the God of nature—and the God over it. God-as-Marduk defeats Pharaoh-as-Tiamat: his defeat provides a founding event for Israel, as Tiamat's did for Babylon. Tiamat is supposed to have said "Let us make monsters,"[12] in order to overthrow the gods' regime by visiting chaos on it. So while Pharaoh-as-Marduk is rallying his forces to defend the social order on the land, God-as-Tiamat is conjuring up and unleashing the hosts of an unruly nature on the established order. Pharaoh is a Near Eastern sovereign hoisted with his own mythological and dramatic petard.

In the following passage from Ezekiel, for example, the prophet presents himself as a Moses commissioned to announce the defeat of Pharaoh's pretensions in terms that suggest the plaguing of the Nile as the divine defeat of the water-monster who is the river's god:

> Son of man, set your face against Pharaoh king of Egypt, and prophesy against him and against all Egypt; speak, and say, Thus says the Lord God:
> "Behold, I am against you,
>   Pharaoh king of Egypt,
> the great dragon that lies
>   in the midst of his streams,
> that says, 'My Nile is my own;
>   I made it.'
> I will put hooks in your jaws,
>   and make the fish of your streams stick to your scales;
> and I will *draw you up* [*'ālāh*] out of the midst of your streams,
>   with all the fish of your streams
>   which stick to your scales.
> And I will cast you forth into the wilderness,
>   you and all the fish of your streams; . . .
> Then all the inhabitants of Egypt shall know that I am the Lord."
> (Ezek. 29:2–5a, 6a, RSV)

God, as in Job 41:1, can "draw out leviathan with an hook," since he *will*. Ezekiel works a specific reversal on the Reed Sea event. Pharaoh's troops perish in the wilderness, like a fish out of water, or a water-monster out of his element; conversely, in Isaiah 63:11, God *drew up* the shepherd of his flock—it was the pursuers who drowned. But such reversals are also implicit in the original narrative: Pharaoh predicted that the wilderness would shut in the Israelites. But it is a "wilderness of the sea" (Isa. 21:1, RSV) that shuts in Pharaoh. So Psalm 106:9, "[God] led them through the depths, as through a wilderness," because, as he says, "I dry up the sea, I make the rivers a wilderness"; "[His] way is in the sea," yet "He turned the sea into dry land" (Isa. 50:2; Ps. 77:19, 66:6). Ezekiel certainly understands an application of the combat myth to Near Eastern history—the text (Syriac) employed above for rendering 29:3 has Pharaoh offer himself as a rival for the creator (Pharaoh *made* the Nile). The following verse has God destroy this rival as a fish out of water, but also out of his theological element. Such a ruler cannot defeat "nature": nature is subject to acts of God—and in this case human rulers are subject too.

In the Babylonian creation epic mortal men are created by Marduk and Ea out of what looks like remains and refuse: the blood vessels of a defeated and scapegoated rebel-god, Tiamat's firstborn and prime minister, Kingu, Tiamat herself being something like mud. The job of these mortals is to be the servitors of the victors, in the gods' new temples in Babylon.[13] The job stands for the fate of subject peoples under their Babylonian masters. This dénouement reminds us of Pharaoh's action "in the beginning": Pharaoh-as-Marduk enslaves the Hebrews-as-humankind—to build his cities with the mud and straw that in another myth might have been humankind's flesh and bone.

Yet Marduk could also be Moses, for at his accession to office the deity proves himself to be endowed with extraordinary verbal powers, a kind of demonstrable "word of power" equivalent to Moses' command over serpents and God's power in Moses' hand. We may quote the appointment of Marduk from the *Enuma Elish*:

> "Say but to wreck or create; it shall be.
> Open thy mouth, the Images will vanish!
> Speak again, and the Images shall be whole!"
> At the word of his mouth the Images vanished.
> He spoke again, and the Images were restored.[14]

Similar signs are worked into the miracle at the Reed Sea. Thus, by means of the pillar of cloud, God gave light to the Israelites, but benighted the Egyptians (Exod. 14:19–20): ". . . And it came between the camp of the Egyptians and the camp of Israel; and it was a cloud and darkness to them": "Thou makest darkness, and it is night" (Ps. 104:20). In the event, God tells Moses to divide the waters, and Moses does as he is told: "For

[God] spake, and it was done; he commanded, and it stood fast" (Ps. 33:9). Moses' Marduk-like achievements depend on his following *God's* word of command. The instrumentality of the divine *word* in accomplishing such signs and wonders is an important part of them, to judge by the punishment Moses receives for *not* using the word in the obtaining of water from the rock (Num. 20:12, 27:14; Deut. 32:51–52). Yahweh's prophet should be at least as resourceful as Marduk.[15]

Exodus 15:16 speaks of the stilling of the peoples who are Israel's enemies, by means of their wonder at the deliverance God works there. Israel's own murmuring is subject to an analogous silencing: "The Lord said to Moses, 'Why do you cry to me?' "; "Moses said to the people, '. . . you have only to be still' " (Exod. 14:15, 13–14, RSV). As these rebukes and stillings show, the Reed Sea event, in common with the Creation, came to be understood as the work of God's word, a deutero-word of creation addressed to the waters. Psalm 114 implicitly gives Joshua these powers too: "The sea looked and fled, / Jordan turned back . . . What ails you, O sea, that you flee? / O Jordan, that you turn back?" (vss. 3, 5, RSV).

Perhaps the most telling text of this kind is the cataclysmic theophany in Psalm 18, a piece put into a Davidic archive at the end of 2 Samuel, where it is associated with David's rescues from Saul (e.g., "He brought me forth into a broad place; he delivered me" [22:20, RSV]). The Psalm reads:

> Then the channels of waters were seen,
>   and the foundations of the world were discovered
> at thy rebuke, O Lord,
>   at the blast of the breath of thy nostrils.
> He sent [RSV 'reached'] from above, he took me,
>   he drew me out [*māšāh*] of many waters.
> (Ps. 18:15–16, lineation added; approx. = 2 Sam. 22:16–17)

The drawing of the delivered party from the waters gave us the princess's etymology of Moses' name ("Because I drew [*māšāh*] him out of the water" [Exod. 2:10]). A parallel recollection occurs in Isaiah 63:11–13a:[16]

> Then he remembered the days of old,
>   of Moses his servant.
> Where is he who brought up ['*ālāh*] out of the sea
>   the shepherds of his flock?
> Where is he who put in the midst of them
>   his holy Spirit [Hebr. 'wind'],
> Who caused his glorious arm
>   to go at the right hand of Moses,

> Who divided the waters before them
> to make for himself an everlasting name,
> Who led them through the depths? (RSV)

Perhaps the Reed Sea event also colors the deliverance alluded to in Jeremiah 31:3: "The Lord hath appeared of old unto me, saying, Yea, I have loved thee with an everlasting love: therefore with lovingkindness have I drawn [*māšak*] thee." Israel was drawn as much from the wilderness as from the Sea, but the language of deliverance is an abiding one.

In Isaiah 63 it is the human shepherds—Moses and Aaron—who are brought out of the waters, as Israel was brought out of Egypt. More typically, as in Psalm 77:16–20, the shepherds are themselves the saviors. An invisible Savior walks ahead of them, the waters fear the worker of wonders, earth trembles at his voice of thunder, his way is in the sea, yet his own footprints are unseen: "Thou leddest thy people like a flock by the hand of Moses and Aaron" (vs. 20).

The text of Micah speaks of the days when Israel came out of the land of Egypt, and promises that God will again show his people marvelous things: moreover, he will *cast all their sins into the depths of the sea* (7:15, 19b). Such a deliverance, if it applies to the Reed Sea event itself, may go considerably beyond a remission of the people's sin of doubt. Micah also says that Israel was led by Moses, Aaron, and Miriam (6:4). We may wonder what these two versions of the exodus have in common. For there is a curious doubling of the text at the Song at the Sea. First we are told that Moses and the people of Israel sang this song, "saying, 'I will sing to the Lord, for he has triumphed gloriously,' " and it is explained in prose why the song says "the horse and his rider he has thrown into the sea." Then the text adds: "Then Miriam, the prophetess, the sister of Aaron, took a timbrel in her hand; and all the women went out after her with timbrels and dancing. And Miriam sang to them: 'Sing to the Lord, for he has triumphed gloriously, the horse and his rider he has thrown into the sea' " (Exod. 15:1, 20–21, RSV). Miriam is thus introduced by name, for the first time: as the teacher of the Song at the Sea, at the very point that Israel is acquiring its hymnody and God's people is being brought forth with the glad cry of Psalm 105:43. On the analogy of Deborah, and as a member of the Mosaic corporation who is like Moses and Aaron in performing oracular functions, Miriam may well have invented the song. But at this point the sister of Moses has appeared only once before, at the time the midwives were acquiring their houses and her infant brother was being saved out of the water and getting his name. As for her name, it is only drawn out at the Reed Sea: at the Sea she reoccupies her place in a story of deliverance, which she formerly shared with the midwives, the Princess, and Moses' mother. Moses' postnatal birth legend, after all, was practically Miriam's creation: we should therefore not be surprised to find her on the scene again, at the literary creation of Mosaic Israel.

Thus Moses' function in regard to the a-borning Israel is vocationally maieutic (Greek *maieutikos*, obstetric, "bringing ideas to birth," from *maieusthai*, to act as midwife). Moses-as-Miriam is commissioned to draw Israel out, and to interpret its emergence to itself—a little like Otto Rank, who not only studied the myth of the birth of the hero but also postulated the existence of birth trauma.[17] As Psalm 114:3 equates the exodus from Egypt through the Reed Sea with the entry into Canaan through the Jordan river, so the Song at the Sea more or less immediately telescopes the defeat of Pharaoh into the conquest of Canaan: "The peoples have heard, they tremble; pangs have seized on the inhabitants of Philistia. . . . Terror and dread fall upon them . . . they are still as a stone, . . . till the people pass by whom thou hast purchased" (Exod. 15:14, 16, RSV). These pangs may be interpreted as "pangs as of a woman in travail," as in Jeremiah 50:43, where the news of the impending ruin of the king of Babylon causes anguish to seize the king (cf. also Ps. 48:6). The cry in the Song echoes both the crying out of the people under oppression, and the great cry throughout Egypt on the night its firstborn die (Exod. 11:6, 12:30). Such a cry recurs in the prose narrative of Israel at the shore of the Reed Sea (Exod. 14:10). The summary at Nehemiah 9:9 collapses the parallel events on the basis of the common element: "[thou] didst see the affliction of our fathers in Egypt, and heardest their cry by the Red Sea."

The parallel crying out of Israel and Egypt argues for the obstetrical interpretation of deliverance we also find in Paul's letter to the Romans:

> I consider that the sufferings of this present time are not worth comparing with the glory that is to be revealed to us. For the creation waits with eager longing for the revealing of the sons of God; for the creation was subjected to futility, not of its own will but by the will of him who subjected it in hope; because the creation itself will be set free from its bondage to decay and obtain the glorious liberty of the children of God. We know that the whole creation has been groaning in travail together until now; and not only the creation, but we ourselves, who have the first fruits of the Spirit, groan inwardly as we wait for adoption as sons, the redemption of our bodies. For in this hope we were saved. (Rom. 8:18–24a, RSV)

If this homily is inspired by the exodus, then we must read its hope as the one originally generated by God's visiting of Moses. According to a related text, it was the divine Wisdom who brought a holy people across the Red Sea, "whereas she drowned their enemies, then spate them out from the depth of the abyss"; it was then that "the whole creation, submissive to

[Wisdom's] commands, had its very nature re-created, so that [her] children should be preserved from harm" (Wisd. of Solomon, 10:18–19, 19:6, NJB). As Isaiah 45:8 says: "Heavens above, rain down, and let the clouds shower righteousness; let earth open, and let salvation and righteousness spring up; let it grow together—I Yahweh have *created* it" (AT). The heavens create deliverance, and all the earth is set free.

· 1 3 ·

THE CREATION OF ISRAEL (I):
THE EXODUS AND THE
NUMBERING OF ISRAEL

. . . and there shall be a time of trouble, such as never was since there was a nation even to that same time: and at that time thy people shall be delivered, every one that shall be found written in the book. (Dan. 12:1b)

According to the commandment of the Lord they were numbered by the hand of Moses, every one according to his service, and according to his burden: thus were they numbered of him, as the Lord commanded Moses. (Num. 4:49)

The Lord doth build up Jerusalem: he gathereth together the outcasts of Israel . . . .
He telleth the number of the stars; he calleth them all by their names. (Psalm 147:2, 4)

The Book of Exodus begins with "the names of the children of Israel, which came into Egypt; every man and his household came with Jacob" (1:1). Household implies family and retainers, which the text numbers at seventy souls; but the list of names at Genesis 46:8–27 reports itself as retailing the same number (vs. 27), and they are all family, "Jacob, and all his seed with him" (Gen. 46:6). The word family, however, first occurs in the Bible in Genesis 7:14, where it is often translated "kind": all the animals—"both man, and beast, and the creeping thing, and the fowls of the air" (Gen. 6:7)—went into the ark *after his family.* Following the Flood story the "generations of the sons of Noah" are discriminated and enumerated in Genesis 10:1–5, "every one . . . after their families."

The Israelite nation is born even as its people are delivered from a malign census and world inventory. Thus to the metaphors of calling forth and recalling, and creation and procreation, we may add a third way of understanding the origination of exodus: in terms of the motifs of proliferation, numbering, and "visiting," from which biblical story typically begins. God himself begins by creating humankind male and female, and blessing this creation with the injunction to increase and multiply (Gen. 1:27–28a), yet thereafter multiplying the woman's pain in childbirth and cursing the man with a return to dust and preventing him from acquiring immortality (Gen. 3:16, 19, 22–24). Similarly, the Flood story begins from the multiplication of men, and shortly finds God resolving to limit the human life-span. The evil Noachic generation of Genesis 6 was destroyed for its violence and evil (vs. 5), but the interpolated story of the generation of the giants (vss. 2 and 4), combined with the proliferation of humankind already observed (vs. 1), and God's giving notice of a human life-span (vs. 3), suggests that God's enmity is also directed against a population explosion and/or against longevity. Longevity and overcrowding qualify as honorary forms of evil gigantism.

In the Babylonian creation epic, Apsu is not happy with the noise made by the second generation of gods that he and Tiamat have spawned; he proposes to destroy the lot, mother Tiamat's objections notwithstanding. A god's reaction to overcrowding is a motif that is also found in one of the Near Eastern versions of the story of the Flood.[1] Flood motifs abound in a story in which a host is overwhelmed between walls of water, and the hero is preserved in a bitumen-sealed basket on a river. The sealing of the ark with bitumen is common to all four forms of the Near Eastern flood myth: the Sumerian Ziusudra, the Mesopotamian Atrahasis, the Babylonian Utnapishtim (Gilgamesh, Tablet XI), and the biblical Noah are all moved to prepare their boats in this way. The killing of the male race in Exodus 1 and of the Egyptians in Exodus 14 have analogous precedents: a divine party's resolve to destroy a human race because of its ubiquity is an inaugural motif in Atrahasis and in Genesis 6:1ff; somewhat like the causal wrath found in the mythopoesis of epic.[2] The drowning of human numbers, in the Atrahasis epic, because they have been able to *survive* a series of divinely sent plagues offers a second cause—the catastrophe now threatens the race as a result of the *failure* of the initial plague-program to destroy it. In the Flood story of the Gilgamesh epic, the god who wants to plague the lone flood-survivor, Utnapishtim, with wolf, famine, and disease seems to be reinvoking the afflictions humankind has *already* survived, *before* the main catastrophe, in the Atrahasis story. Thus the genocidal program of Pharaoh prefaces the exodus as the presiding deity's jealous program of population control prefaces the biblical Flood story.

In the Atrahasis epic, the proliferating human population has become so noisy that the god Enlil is losing his sleep; he attempts to quiet the race by sending plague after plague on it. This is Part A of a story of which Part B is the Flood: as a last resort, Enlil sends the Flood to eliminate the noise-makers, and only Atrahasis in his boat survives the destruction of his kind.

The Bible divides this Enlil's destructive schemes (in Part A), between Yahweh the plaguer of Egypt and Pharaoh the plaguer of the Hebrews. And it divides the story of destruction and survival (in Part B) between the Egyptian host that Yahweh-as-Enlil drowns in the Reed Sea and the flock that Moses-as-Atrahasis leads to safety between the walls of water. In Moses' infancy story, the same survival and destruction motifs are divided between the survival of the infant in the bitumined ark (Exod. 2:3) and the destruction of all male children when it is commanded that "every son that is born" be thrown into the Nile (Exod. 1:22). The text's neglect to specify *Hebrew* sons at this point tends to characterize Pharaoh's frustrated demand as a reaction to half the human race—his half, since he also is male. Genocide necessarily has some form of self-destruction as its underlying intent.

The motive that logically disguises this intent is that of playing god. There is of course such a god to play. By the seventh plague, God could have put forth his hand to depopulate Egypt totally, cutting its people off from the earth (Exod. 9:15). But the cosmic and holocaustic devastation of which the Creator is quite capable is not really contemplated on the apocalyptic Richter scale announced in Joel 1–2. Egypt will not be impressed with the weight of God's glory if there is no Egypt left to impress it on.

Pharaoh's attempt to destroy the very generation of Hebrews that he has enslaved makes very little *economic* sense and must be attributed to politics: the politics of terror. Or to pure animosity. Or else to a metaphor: the cheapening of Hebrew life through slavery amounts to eliminating it.[3] But in practice, slaves should be cheaper the more there are of them, while the state as the slave-owner should be wealthier when its property breeds than when it is being purged. And if Pharaoh were interested in breeding selectively, he presumably ought to be killing the females, not the males. But while we cannot explain the link of infanticide and enslavement logically, we could make sense of either one alone, as attempts to rationalize or check an unbridled or otherwise ungovernable numerosity. The imperial ruler is a creator *manqué*, attempting to impose a kind of state order on the potential chaos of unused or useless subjects.

If there is a parallel with the kingship, Pharaoh's inspiration can be considered demonic: "Satan stood up against Israel, and provoked David to number Israel. And David said to Joab and to the rulers of the people, Go, number Israel . . . ; and bring the number of them to me, that I may know it" (1 Chron. 21:1–2). The same story in 2 Samuel 24 ends with David given a choice of punishment by a prophet (vss. 12–13). David chooses to subject Israel directly to the punishment of God, three days of plague (vs. 14). Plague is one of the forms in which God "visits" his people, or "numbers" them (so *pāqad* in Num. 16:29, when taken with the plagues in the same text at vss. 35, 46–50).

Thus numerosity and its assessment tend to come into a biblical narrative together: large numbers result in attempts to terminate their growth, and assessment of large numbers brings a plague on the people of the assessor. The generous plenitude celebrated in the table of nations in Genesis 10 is followed by the monopolistic unity plagued with confusion at the Tower of Babel in Genesis 11. Numbers have a positive, sanctified, prolific form, and a negative, unclean, swarming, and epidemic form. Numbering is thus both positive and negative in its efficacy. Moses is told to number Israel for war at the opening of Numbers, the initial sense being positive. And yet the census must be taken again, for the death of a whole generation in the wilderness has intervened (the first to die die by plague), and not a man numbered originally remains (Num. 26:64–65). The language of Numbers 1:2–3 is also found in God's prescriptions for the temple tax, in Exodus 30:11–16, with the added idea of ransoming or redeeming a debt owed to God. The census ordered by Caesar Augustus in the Gospel of Luke is positive, for it is *ecumenical*, like the analogous congress at Pentecost in the Book of Acts (Luke 2:1, Acts 2:1–6). But it is also negative, for it is part of the levying of a tax: the equivalent levy in the Gospel of Matthew is Herod's slaughter of the innocents (Matt. 2:16–18). Indeed, Matthew has got his version of the genocidal motif from the legend of the Pharaoh of the exodus, for the legendary Pharaoh—a dreamer of dreams like the Pharaoh in the Joseph novella—has had a warning dream about the coming of Moses.[4] Matthew mirrors this legendary dream with the three dreams warning the wise men not to return to the hypocritical Herod, warning Joseph of Nazareth about the king's murderousness, and advising him about his child's safety upon the king's death (Matt. 2:12, 2:13, 19–20).

The assessment of numbers provides a kind of Ur-historical ground in lieu of some more historical beginning. If there is a numberer or census-taker inspiring the Pharaoh from the past, it is of course the forgotten Joseph, the legendary tax-gatherer who not only bought up Egypt for its ruling house but also reorganized the population: "And as for the people, he removed them to cities from one end of the borders of Egypt even to the other end thereof" (Gen. 47:21). Moses is a similar assessor, particularly in taking the sum of the sons of sons of Levi, whom he is conscripting for a service involving the burdens of the sanctuary, in Numbers 4. The kerygma of the exodus always treats it as a deliverance, with Yahweh as the savior. But its *text*, as a collection of records, also treats it as a conscription, an assessment, an exaction, or a recruitment.

The record might well begin from a census-like survey, insofar as the recordkeeping and bookkeeping institutions of society themselves begin the record this way. Lists of the king's possessions are among the earliest known uses of writing in the ancient Near East: whole regimes seem founded on the inventories inscribed in the clay memorializing them. In the Bible the place of these lists is taken by accounts of goods and specifications belonging to the tabernacle. Yet all the hardware catalogued for Solomon's temple pales in comparison to its possession of God's name, to which the Pentateuch attaches the inscription and collection of his law. Numerosity and its containment otherwise furnish material for accounts of the impositions of an ascendant bureaucracy: to taxation and military conscription we may here add forced labor. In the historical period, we can point to an allusion to the North's decisive break—under Jeroboam—with Jerusalem's policy of forced labor under Solomon, as found in the account of 1 Kings 12. For the Solomon who multiplied horses, wives, treasures, and public works, whose tribute flowed in from all the earth, and who made collections and inventories of proverbs, hymns, and the vegetable and animal kingdoms (Deut. 17:16–18, 1 Kings 10:14–11:8, 10:24–25, 4:32–33) is also the Solomon who "raised a levy of forced labor out of all Israel; and the levy numbered thirty thousand men"—to get him timber from Lebanon (1 Kings 5:13, RSV).

"Of the children of Israel did Solomon make no bondmen," 1 Kings 9:22 asserts; 2 Chronicles 2:17–18 varies the Kings account of Solomon's workforce, yet adds significant details for our theme: "Then Solomon took a census of [AV: *numbered*] all the aliens [Hebr. *gērim*] who were in the land of Israel, after the census of them which David his father had taken . . . seventy thousand of them he assigned to bear burdens, eighty thousand to quarry in the hill country, and three thousand six hundred as overseers to make the people work" (RSV). The workers are not all "aliens" in this version of this story, yet that is what they are to become: in Judah they will one day be Samaritans, as in Egypt they had been Hebrews.

In the Bible the genesis of recounting mirrors the recounting of "geneses." In the positive Genesis narrative, man is ceded a Pharaonic world-sovereignty and blessed with reproduction; in the negative one he falls into hard labor and is cursed with death and the labor of childbirth. The positive pattern is repeated in the story of Noah, but so is the negative one: men in Noah's time hope that Noah will give them relief from their labor (Gen. 5:28–29), but their population is radically purged. The Creation narratives suggest the beginnings of the exodus: the population explosion and world-mastery, or the population purge and universal toil. On these models, God's purposes and Pharaoh's were once the same: while God multiplies the Israelites, Pharaoh enslaves them and afflicts their birthing. Pharaoh's programs express resistance to God the creator, but also a usurpation of his prerogatives.

The plagues mirror the creator's original motions in dividing night from day on the fourth day, and populating the earth on the third and fifth. For God created "every living creature that moves, with which the waters *swarm*," and "blessed them, saying, 'Be fruitful and multiply and fill the waters in the seas' "—and he blessed the multiplication of "winged" things "on the earth" (Gen. 1:21–22, RSV). Pharaoh, like a god, would control the evil of this blessing. For basically he considers the Hebrews to be a plague: they were many in the land, and the plagues are on, over, and throughout the land (Exod. 1:7, 5:5, 8:2, 10:14–15, 21–22, etc.).

Thus Pharaoh's house is punished by a nightmare in the very shape of its founder's anxieties: by epidemics of uncontrollable numbers and by a vast uncleanness that has everything spilling and swarming out of its proper category and ratio and number. Besides this punishment of the first Pharaoh's attempt to limit nature at the mouth of the womb, we must also consider God's action as the divine creator's punishment of the empire-building of a rival. The plagues offer a divine critique of the wasteful afflu-ence of the universal slave-state, with its atomization of the human commu-nity, its production schedules and quotas and shortages of raw materials, and its systematizing of its labor force into uniform building-blocks even while its human raw materials are treated like stubble and vermin. With the remission of the second plague, the Egyptians piled the dead frogs up in heaps and the land reeked of them (Exod. 8:14). This poisonous landfill is the revenge taken by a gross national product.

Thus the schemes of the two Pharaohs are a parody of state planning: the "store-cities" presumably anticipate shortages, but the court's original reaction to the burgeoning Hebrew population alleges a threat to state security that the first Pharaoh's edict itself sets about bringing into exis-tence. He anticipates a danger posed to his state by a dispossessed class, but his delusion is that the way to avoid trouble is to stir it up (Exod. 1:9–14). The second Pharaoh may know, but only dimly, that his shrewdness is actually re-creating the very problem the first Pharaoh thought to avoid.

What neither Pharaoh knows is that they are both fulfilling the terms of a larger plan to reconstitute the Hebrews as Israel, a plan variously announced in Genesis to Jacob (46:3) and through Joseph (50:20). One way to advance this plan would be to create the nation's future unity by making it a class, though a class of slaves is hardly the obvious choice for a nation of priests and holy men or for a nation to whom kings and queens will be nursing fathers and mothers (as per Isa. 49:23). Pharaoh's house is initially conscripted by the same plan, for its daughter is inveigled into temporarily offering her protection and patronage to the future leader-ship for the Israelites as a class. Even the midwives take advantage of this Pharaoh, for the lie they tell him—that the Hebrew women bear virtually spontaneously (Exod. 1:19)—is just the lie his edict shows him readiest to believe: that the Hebrews are somehow very different from the Egyptians. However ironically, this lie serves as the annunciation to Pharaoh.

Although one may speak of the first Pharaoh's initiative as genocidal, such a motif is really only the shadow cast backwards over the Israelites by the second Pharaoh's enmity to Moses. The hereditary leader who disregards his own people's trouble is thus opposed to an unborn leader who "sees" and heeds his people's cry for deliverance. The first Pharaoh's murderousness toward (Hebrew) males only arrives at a proper *human* motive if the threat of extinction applies specifically to the infant Moses.

The first Pharaoh's motive is *not* entirely genocidal, if by this we mean the systematic liquidation of a truly distinctive group which has become the object of such attention by its being (in Hegelian-Marxist terms) the alienated essence of established society.[5] Only Moses finally furnishes Egypt and/or Israel with such an object or object lesson, for only Moses is both an Egyptianized Hebrew and a Hebraicized Egyptian. Esther will tell her king that she could have held her tongue at the *sale* of her Jewish people, but not at their liquidation (Esther 7:4). But that may be just the point being made by her speaking up, or not speaking up: a slave population loses the voice of a people's leadership, while any given people is likely to have its outspoken survivors. Paradoxically, peoplehood is enhanced, however negatively, by the threat of genocide, while it is vitiated by the effects of enslavement. Servitude, unlike genocide, denies and degrades the *nationality* of the slave, for the slave is portable property and is thus separable from his original homeland. But the slave may also be *reduced* to his racial identity, if he is of a notably different race than his owners: the race of Ham is identified as slavish in Noah's curse on his son's descendants in Genesis 9:25–27, where, ironically, Ham is called Canaan as if he were a people; but he is condemned to be the servant of the Israelites ("Shem") and the Philistines ("Javan") who have pitched their tents in Canaan's *land* and turned the dispossessed locals into their slaves.

Slave or Israelite, however, the question asked by the exile in Psalm 137, "How shall we sing the Lord's song in a strange land?" (vs. 4), cannot be wholly asked, until the "we" has acquired land to be estranged from. Neither can this song be sung until the singer has the psalms, some of which celebrate the exodus, or celebrate Zion as if it were a realization of a Sinai which Israel could actually possess.[6] Moses, exiled from Egypt in Midian, "a stranger in a strange land" (Exod. 2:22), actually suffers the estrangement from the land of his birth presupposed by the psalmist's question; but only when he returns to the holy mountain has he begun to consolidate the Israelite cult—by then he has the Passover as well as the divine name. Only when he has brought the people to the other side of the Reed Sea, and they are set on the shore of land that is not Egypt's, do they actually acquire the exodus: "Then sang Moses and the children of Israel this song unto the Lord, . . . saying, I will sing unto the Lord" (Exod. 15:1). In the Lord's victory at the Reed Sea they have possessed the historical basis for the saving narrative that is so often a subject of the hymnody itself.

King Saul's persecution of his son's sworn friend at court seems to lead to the throne's establishment in Judah; and Paul's persecution of the Christians in the synagogue creates the martyred body of the church. The Hebrews in Egypt, however, are no such scapegoat as the Christians in the synagogue, or even David at Saul's court. Moses tells us as much when he says that the Hebrews might become the object of Egyptian retaliation if they carried out their sacrifices in Egypt: " 'If we sacrifice offerings abominable to the Egyptians before their eyes, will they not stone us?' " Exod. 8:26, RSV). What do the Egyptians so abominate? Moses' doubt hardly disguises the fact that to date the Hebrews have no sacrifices, and no cult—they are going out into the wilderness to get one. Moses tells Pharaoh the Israelites attending the feast must take all their livestock with them: they do not know what rites God will institute in respect of this feast (Exod. 10:9).

The object of genocide is identified racially—genocide depends on establishing the identity of its victims by means of their parentage and characteristics conveyed genetically. But the practice of "cleansing" a culture of a people, or separating an offending gens for its religion, implies finding that gens offensive *culturally*; the purge does not obliterate nationality, but instead creates its opposite and its double—in the other gens' unassimilable cultural difference. Thus the kind of antisemitism that battens on repugnance to the allegedly sinister content of Jewish rites cannot yet exist in Pharaoh's Egypt if no one can say what those rites are. The Hebrews are an enslaved *race*, but the condition of their servitude is not promising for their future as a sovereign *people*. The infant Moses only survives through subsequent assimilation to the dominant race. Yet he initially survives genocide, thanks to a kind of conspiracy. His own culture has begun to organize itself to exist, and so he will survive assimilation too.

We may again compare and contrast the situation of the Jews in Babylon in the Book of Esther. Like the exodus, Esther's story events become the pre-text for a religious holiday. But here the Jews are already religiously differentiated from the Babylonians, by virtue of their refusal to worship the Babylonian king (Esther 3:2–6). In Exodus 9:4 Moses is instructed to tell Pharaoh that the Lord "shall sever between the cattle of Israel and the cattle of Egypt." In the book of Esther it is Mordecai who is dividing between Judah and Babylon—unlike the Hebrew in Pharaoh's Egypt, Mordecai does not need God to do it for him. The Babylonian Jews have a well-placed leadership already, for Mordecai is the "father" of the new queen (as Joseph was "father to Pharaoh"), and Esther is herself Jewish. Moses, as the "son" of the princess, is well-placed too; but as the narrative's beginning from his infancy tells us, the Hebrews do not yet have enough of a political identity to have a fully developed leadership.

Thus Pharaoh's attempt on the life of the unborn Moses falls into place as an attempt to prevent the Hebrews from begetting that historical identity represented in Esther by Mordecai. Yet Pharaoh's precautions prove to be self-fulfilling prophecies (a characteristic effect of the paranoid point of view), and thus the instrument of God's overall design of producing a national leadership. Pharaoh's midwives might well say, with Joseph or with the wise men in Matthew, "God sent me before you to preserve you for a remnant on earth," indeed "to save your lives by a great deliverance" (Gen. 45:7a [RSV], 7b [AV]): "God meant it unto good, to bring to pass . . . to save much people alive" (Gen. 50:20). The midwives are members of a union: the increased pressure on the Hebrews in Egypt also unionizes them and readies them for a new, divinely inspired leadership—out of Egypt.

·14·

THE CREATION OF ISRAEL (II):
THE EXODUS AND THE
"VISITING" OF ISRAEL

The Lord said to Moses, "When you take the census of the people of Israel, then each shall give a ransom for himself to the Lord when you number them, that there be no plague among them when you number them. Each who is numbered in the census shall give this: half a shekel according to the shekel of the sanctuary (the shekel is twenty gerahs), half a shekel as an offering to the Lord. Every one who is numbered in the census, from twenty years old and upward, shall give the Lord's offering. . . . And you shall take the atonement money from the people of Israel, and shall appoint it for the service of the tent of meeting; that it may bring the people of Israel to remembrance before the Lord, so as to make atonement for yourselves." (Exod. 30:11–14, 16, RSV)

But the Lord said to Moses, "Whoever has sinned against me, him will I blot out of my book. But now go, lead the people to the place of which I have spoken to you; behold, my angel shall go before you. Nevertheless, in the day when I visit, I will visit their sin upon them." (Exod. 32:33–34, RSV)

Israel and Moses will be found written in God's book—Exodus itself, as it seems to be invoked from within the narrative. There is a kind of slippage, however, from the list of the Israel that went into Egypt in Genesis 46, to the recapitulation of the list in Exodus 1. Judah's sons Er and Onan are listed in Genesis 46, yet the text also annotates itself contradictorily: they were left behind in Canaan (vs. 12). The Dinah who is violated and avenged in the Canaan of Genesis 34 is also listed at Genesis 46:15, yet she is omitted from the list of Jacob's children in Exodus 1:1 and is not mentioned again. "Blot me, I pray thee, out of thy book," Moses asks; "Whosoever hath sinned against me, *him* will I blot out of my book," God answers (Exod. 32:32, 33). But Shechem's sin against Dinah seems to have been visited on *her*: it has blotted her out of the rest of God's book.

We must now find out how the text signals that the broken-spirited Hebrews, whom we meet at the outset of the narrative (Exod. 6:9), can be redefined as the elect group recorded in the divine book. How does one become "family" at the same time that one becomes God's "inheritance"? How can the Hebrews as a group acquire the essential national prerequisites for covenanting with God at Sinai? Circularly, as the opening of Exodus shows in various ways, the prerequisite is being numbered among the Israelites. Yet membership in Israel cannot be sealed until the occurrence of the events of the Passover. How is membership thus defined?

i

The giving of the Passover is obviously essential to the instauration of membership in Israel. The national feast of set-apartness is given through Moses—the role of instituter falls to an outsider. Yet Moses has been included in a priestly community in the land of Midian, a proto-Israel apart from the pre-Israel that is lost in Egypt. Just as we find in Midian traces of the patriarchal experience, before the exodus, so we find a rite of incorporation there before the Passover. The peculiar account of Moses' circumcision at Exodus 4:24–26, makes more sense when it is read in the light of the Passover than it does alone; for God met Moses, "and sought to kill him," as if Moses had failed to sacrifice. Moses and Aaron will ask to make their three days' journey into the wilderness to sacrifice to the Lord their God, "lest," they say, "he fall upon us with pestilence, or with the sword" (Exod. 5:3). The Lord, they say, has met with them (Exod. 5:3; cf. 3:18); the encounter can take the form of a violent visitation.

The symbolic touching of Moses with the blood of circumcision—in Midian, after his first visit to Sinai, and between the earlier and later biblical versions of his appointment to office—suggests the late inclusion of Moses in the covenants with the patriarchs. The flint or rock of the Mosaic circumcision narrative combines the food knife and the fire of the sacrifice of Isaac (Gen. 22:6), the occasion when the martial form of the blessing of Abraham (to possess the gates of his enemies) was conferred on Isaac (Gen. 22:17b). Similarly, the mutual initiation of father and son recalls the solidarity of Ishmael and Abraham at their circumcision, when the blessing of Abraham as forefather was shared with the Ishmaelites, who have a destiny like that of Israel: like Jacob, they are to have twelve princes (Gen. 17:20). Finally, the community includes the Midianite Zipporah. Thus Moses is symbolically repatriated in relation to all of Abraham's wives: Sarah by descent from Isaac, Hagar by Gershom's "Egyptian" circumcision, Keturah by marrying a Midianite.

The demonic nocturnal attack resulting in permanent bodily harm also recalls the blessing of Jacob, when the attacker recognized Jacob as a prince and as "Israel" (Gen. 32:28). But the attack on Moses is distinctly sinister, because it not only re-presents the initiations into "Abraham" and "Israel" from the past, but also pre-presents the impending membership rite of the future: namely, the Passover itself.

This may be the place to answer the objection that circumcision is not originally a Semitic but an Egyptian institution, to judge, for example, by its occurrence in Herodotus (2.37), where it is mentioned as part of Egyptian hygiene and purification regimen. At first we may believe that the Bible does not know of an Egyptian origin for this practice. Yet circumcision is something that first appears when Abraham *adopts* it. Circumcision is first instituted when Ishmael is included in God's promises to the patriarch, and in God's contracts with him. At this time Ishmael has reached "social puberty";[1] at thirteen years of age, Abraham's son is old enough to join his father's tribe. But Ishmael's mother, Hagar, is Egyptian, and takes her son a wife from Egypt (Gen. 16:1, 21:21). And Abraham himself is ninety-nine years old when he converts all his people to the practice, including servants bought with money (Gen. 17:12, 23, 27). Thus Abraham, through circumcision, declares ethnic solidarity with the son of a Hamitic mistress, even as God institutes a covenant with a Semite, with circumcision as its sign. The sign makes Abraham's election the less genetic the more it is cultural: his people are all converts, like the men of Shechem in Genesis 34, to a practice that is cultural, if it is also Hamitic.

While this history cannot fully explain where the Midianite Zipporah got the practice, it does show circumcision's place in assimilating two ethnically different parties (Hagar and Abraham, or Ishmael and Isaac) to a common cultural order, under the guise of an appeal to a common genetic ancestor (Abraham). If Zipporah were continuing to think of Moses as an Egyptian, and if circumcision were also Egyptian, then Zipporah's circumcision of Gershom would only be uniting Moses and their son to Moses' own Egyptian identity and heritage. But circumcision has already been adopted by Abraham as a sign of membership in Abraham: and Abraham is an ancestor Moses and Zipporah have in common, despite their ethnic differences (Keturahite vs. Nahorite). In other words, the Bible, through the story of Ishmael's circumcision in Genesis 17, redefines the "Egyptian" practice of circumcision as (adoptively) Abrahamic, and then renews the adopted practice, in the story of Exodus 4:24–26, to redefine the Egyptian Moses as (adoptively) Midianite—thus converting him to be *culturally* Abrahamic while reminding us that his genetic identity is also Abrahamic. Egypt, through Hagar and Genesis 17, was included in the loop, before the exodus; but by the time Moses is introduced to the practice, Egypt has dropped out: the institution now characterizes the patriarchal tribe, not the Pharaonic establishment.[2] For at the other end of this story the acculturative purpose reappears, where it is served by circumcising the new generation in the wilderness. "All the people that came out were circumcised; but all the people that were born in the wilderness *by the way* as they came forth out of Egypt, them they had not circumcised" (Josh. 5:5). Moses is thus initiated vicariously in anticipation of his solidarity with an Israel reunited to itself beyond Egypt; so Moses was joined to God *"by the way* in the inn" (Exod. 4:24).

It was then that Moses was adopted into the fathers. The flint of Zipporah's circumcision goes back to both Abraham's offering of Isaac to God on Mt. Moriah (with "fire" and knife) and his giving up of Ishmael for Isaac in Genesis 17; it brings with it circumcision's peculiar biblical character as a substitute for, or symbolic version of, the sacrifice of a firstborn. But this interpretation means here that circumcision is *a symbolic sparing of the subject thanks to the circumcision of the son.* Moses is spared, during a nocturnal attack from God, because he is marked with the blood of a sacrifice made in place of the life of his own firstborn son. But if God's *passing over* Moses is this story's special feature, then the blood shed by Zipporah and her son is that of the Passover lamb. Moses' circumcision (as a linked sequence at Josh. 5:5–10 shows) is the first Passover.

In the rite as portrayed in Exodus, a part is given up to save the whole— the whole being the remainder of the individual or family unit; in that case, it can again be compared to the taking of the life of the Israelite paschal lamb or of the Egyptian firstborn, indifferently, in place of the life of Israel. In the Ritual Decalogue, God dictates the Passover with a critical motive-clause: "The feast of unleavened bread shalt thou keep. . . . All that openeth the matrix is mine" (Exod. 34:18, 19). Exodus narrativizes circumcision's "Egyptian" provenance uniquely; it is not denied, but recreated, as a mark or sign of participation in Israel's Egyptian experience. This experience culminated in the passing over of Israel in Egypt.

ii

The symbolic economy of sanctification and violations in the Passover event itself proceeds by a series of substitutions—Pharaoh's firstborn son, Moses and Moses' firstborn son, the sign of the son's blood, the Israelite's firstborn in Egypt, the animal firstling, the lamb firstling, the Passover lamb and the sign made with lamb's blood, the Egyptian firstborn, and the Egyptian cavalry. The narrative involves a similar chain of substitutions, in that it is intent on saving Israel, God's firstborn son by adoption, for service as a priestly nation. Yet the service is sacrifice, and Moses and Aaron tell Pharaoh that their God has demanded of them a three-day journey into the wilderness for this purpose: "lest he fall upon us with pestilence, or with the sword" (Exod. 5:3).

In the golden calf episode, sword and pestilence will indeed fall upon the Israelites (Exod. 32:27–28, 35): not in Egypt, but in the wilderness. The pairing of Gershom's circumcision with Moses' divinely endangered return from Midian, following Moses' call in the Sinai theophany, suggests that the rite's equivalent, in the analogy between Moses and Israel, is a purgative "circumcision of the tribe" in the wilderness, following Israel's own call, which is by another Sinai theophany. The threatening of the people at Sinai culminates in the slaughter of a part of the idolatrous priesthood with the destruction of the golden calf. The plaguing and purging of the priesthood at the time of the apostasy, in turn, recall the events of Leviticus 10, where the death of two of Aaron's sons coincides with the investiture of the Aaronid priesthood in its office of sacrificer. Sacrifice, like the Levites, appeases the divine demand that a plague or purge satisfies otherwise, the demand the exodus-God makes of the first-born in return for Israel's deliverance: Numbers 8:13–19 more or less implies that the Levites were given to Aaron to sacrifice in the firstborn's place.

We may take the rulings about the Levites, both at Numbers 3:40–45 and at 8:9–19, to be as serious as their narrative equivalents in the transaction effected by the exodus itself. It is hardly surprising to find that the Bible refers the final singling out of Israel in Egypt to the obliging that makes the Israelite so religiously distinct—his perpetual indebtedness to the one and only living God. As long as Israel lives, it will be like the child Hannah promises to the Lord if he will redeem her barrenness: *on loan to the Lord* (1 Sam. 1:28). —Or like Isaac after his sparing on Mount Moriah, on loan *from* the Lord. The Israelite insists he is obliged to God for his life: being always under a threat of forfeiture, it is always in need of ransom.

Numbers justifies the sparing of the firstborn by choosing the Levites:

> And thou shalt set the Levites before Aaron, and before his sons, and offer them for an offering unto the Lord.
> Thus shalt thou separate the Levites from among the children of Israel: and the Levites shall be mine. . . .
> . . . and thou shalt cleanse them, and offer them for an offering.
> For they are wholly given unto me from among the children of Israel; instead of such as open every womb, even instead of the firstborn of all the children of Israel, have I taken them unto me.
> For all the firstborn of the children of Israel are mine, both man and beast: on the day that I smote every firstborn in the land of Egypt I sanctified them for myself. (Num. 8:13–17)

"The Levites shall be mine" (also at Num. 3:45) parallels "all the firstborn of the children of Israel are mine, both man and beast," which gets itself partly quoted in the Passover prescription itself: "Sanctify unto me *all the firstborn*, whatsoever openeth the womb among the children of Israel, both of man and of beast: it *is mine*" (Exod. 13:2). The rationale for Israel's celebrating the exodus, at Exodus 34:18ff. ("The feast of unleavened bread you shall keep") is also substitutive, and leads to an analogous law:

> The firstling of an ass you shall redeem with a lamb, or if you will not redeem it you shall break its neck. All the first-born of your sons you shall redeem. And none shall appear before me empty. (Exod. 34:20, RSV)

As the lamb might save the ass, so the Levite might save the firstborn. The ass is almost, by definition, a beast of burden—in the legislation of Exodus 23:5, he and his owner are offered a kind of Good Samaritan's relief.

The sacrificers are pre-elected in Egypt by the narrative's introjection of the Passover rite on the watch-night, and in the wilderness the passover is reenacted by the election of the Levites. They are recruited in place of those firstborn whose lives are levied from Egypt, but whose counterparts in Israel are deferred from service. The Egyptians are the victims of a levy that God will inevitably "seize as forfeit," in its turn, from Israel: "None shall appear before me empty." As the birth of the firstborn might redeem the barrenness of the wife in 1 Samuel 1, so the lifelong loan of her firstborn to service in God's house might redeem God's gift of life to the Hebrew. The firstborn are the price exacted for God's delivering Israel from the like exactions of Pharaoh. God's place in the story-pattern is like that of the confiscatory demon in *Rumpelstiltskin;* the impossible task of turning the king's straw into gold has taken the place of the impossible task of turning Pharaoh's mud into brick without straw. Such a story puts into memorable form the idea that God's demands and exactions are no less a divine visitation than are his mercies and deliverances.

iii

The first regular sacrifice commanded of the Hebrews is that of the Passover. Sword and plague, or draft and census, it is administered by an angel that strikes the Egyptian class likeliest to form an army. The Passover occupies the place in the narrative originally projected for the sacrifice in the wilderness, in that it is preceded by a three-day interval: namely, the plague of darkness. This darkness anticipates the absenting of Israel from Egypt before the sacrifice, for during this interval of eclipse the Hebrews enjoy a divinely provided light (Exod. 10:23), while they are guided nocturnally in the wilderness by the pillar of fire. The three days of darkness constitute a "little wilderness"; so also do the three days that seem to be spent in the wilderness on the Reed Sea's nearer side. Two nights intervene before the day on which God again distinguishes between Israel and Egypt, giving Pharaoh a military defeat of the kind that Israel elsewhere dignifies by the name of sacrifice.

An example of this sacrificing of Egypt is found in Jeremiah 46, an oracle on Nebuchadnezzar's defeat of the army of Pharaoh Neco at Carchemish. Jeremiah suggests that God has destroyed Egypt at the Euphrates in a debacle analogous to the one in which Moses destroyed the army that encountered the Hebrews at the Reed Sea:

> "Who is this, rising like the Nile,
>   like rivers whose waters surge?
> Egypt rises like the Nile,
>   like rivers whose waters surge.
> He said, I will rise, I will cover the earth, . . .
> Advance, O horses,
>   and rage, O chariots!
> Let the warriors go forth:
>   men of Ethiopia and Put who handle the shield,
>   men of Lud, skilled in handling the bow.
> That day is the day of the Lord God of hosts,
>   a day of vengeance,
>   to avenge himself on his foes. . . .
> For the Lord God of hosts holds a sacrifice
>   in the north country by the river Euphrates. . . .
> for warrior has stumbled against warrior;
>   they have both fallen together." (Jer. 46:7–10, 12b, RSV)

"Terror and dread fall upon them," says the Song at the Sea, referring to the enemy; "They are dismayed and have turned backward . . . terror on every side," Jeremiah repeats, referring to the dissolution of Pharaoh's forces (Exod. 15:16, Jer. 46:5, RSV).

The Egyptians' loss of life makes manifest what the Egyptians' subsequent attempt to recover their slaves in effect denies—that all life belongs to God. To God, therefore, there also belongs the "visiting" of life. In the words of a "passing over" described in Isaiah:

> O Lord our God, other lords beside thee have had dominion over us: but by thee only will we make mention of thy name.
> They are dead, they shall not live; they are deceased, they shall not rise: therefore hast thou visited and destroyed them, and made all their memory to perish.

Thou hast increased the nation, O Lord, thou hast increased the nation: thou art glorified: thou hadst removed it far unto all the ends of the earth.

Lord, in trouble have they visited thee, they poured out a prayer when thy chastening was upon them.

Like as a woman with child, that draweth near the time of her delivery, is in pain, and crieth out in her pangs; so have we been in thy sight, O Lord. (Isa. 26:13–17)

This passage tells us that Israel was created in its being visited, and that it is God's visitation—rather than Pharaoh's—which really "counts."

Pharaoh's visitation of the Hebrews in Egypt can be no more—and no less—than the instrument of God's visitation of Pharaoh. Pharaoh has hardened his heart, but it has also been hardened for him: by God. The Bible does not mean that God has coerced Pharaoh's army into the Reed Sea against Pharaoh's will, but that Pharaoh's will-to-omnipotence has necessarily polarized the will of God. In asserting his would-be mastery over history, Pharaoh discounts—and therefore badly underestimates—his divine rival; the very defiance through which he thinks to retain control must perforce overreach itself. God's hardening of Pharaoh's heart only presents the paradox that the more refractory the human will, the more it undermines its self-dispose, and the more it puts itself into the power of Another. Hence Pharaoh's will was actually *self*-determined—in the words of Dante's drowned Ulysses—"as it pleased *Another*" (*Inf.* 26.141).

---

iv

God levies his demand for historical recognition by taking the life of Pharaoh's firstborn, and the Hebrews mark themselves as different as they take the life of a sacrificial animal, even while they also single out their own firstborn (Exod. 13:1–2). The death of Egypt's firstborn culminates the *sign-making activity* of the narrative, as the Hebrews make a sign for themselves, that of the blood on their doors: as they become the Israelites, they also become cosponsors in the sign-making of the exodus. But what sign does God make in the death of *Egypt's* firstborn? How would this sign help historicize the departure meal of the people whom Pharaoh once admitted into Egypt as shepherds (Gen. 46:31–34)? Why is the narrative's "latter sign" directed against Egypt's heirs, or its rights of primogeniture?

In saying "out of Egypt have I called my son" (Matt. 2:15; cf. Hos. 11:1, Exod. 4:22), God is also saying "whatsoever openeth the womb among the children of Israel, . . . it is mine" (Exod. 13:2), conferring on Israel a spiritual firstbornness that, historically speaking, can only belong to it in the latter day, anachronistically, by virtue of God's *choice* of this son. Thus the narrative postulates an unprecedented suspension or interruption of Egyptian history: never has there been hail like that of the seventh plague *since Egypt became a nation* (Exod. 9:24). God's visiting of Israel comes into a critical alignment with that of the land of the Nile—where it scarcely ever rains and where "the main source of taxes was the harvest, which was calculated on the height of the inundation recorded annually at least since the First Dynasty" (*incip.* 3100 b.c.).[3] Egypt's national record is a long one, and Israel, not being any such nation, lacks this record. Yet here is an event, allegedly lodged in another nation's historical record, from which the existence of Israel is to be dated—the year of the great hail, in which the flax and barley were destroyed (Exod. 9:31). The anxiety of Israelite belatedness determines that the Passover event—which recognizes and remembers Israel into national and historical existence—also records God's symbolic attack upon Egyptian primogeniture: the historical firstbornness and dynastic continuity of the world's oldest kingdom.

v

The sign of the lamb's blood displaces Pharaoh's violence from the Hebrews to the Egyptians in their place. The sacrificial interpretation of the exodus is repeated in the legislation prescribing the priesthood in Numbers 3:11–13 and again at 8:13–19 (cited above). These texts make "the voice of the latter sign" (Exod. 4:8) specifically point to the Levites:

> And the Lord spake unto Moses, saying,
> And I, behold, I have taken the Levites from among the children of Israel instead of all the firstborn that openeth the matrix among the children of Israel: therefore the Levites shall be mine;
> Because all the firstborn are mine; for on the day that I smote all the firstborn in the land of Egypt I hallowed unto me all the firstborn in Israel, both man and beast: mine shall they be: I am the Lord. (Num. 3:11–13)

The Levite is not driven out of Israel: but neither is he given any land in it.

The logic is that of refinancing a mortgage. In return for a long-standing obligation's having been forgiven, Israel contracts a new one; the contract for the future Levites is accepted in lieu of the older debt's repayment. God gains the right Pharaoh loses, the right of the absolute monarch to the life of his subject, or the subject's firstborn. In taking the tribe of Levi, God takes one of Jacob's younger-born instead. Curiously, of Jacob's first four sons by Leah (Reuben, Simeon, Levi, and Judah), Levi is the only lineage passed over in the threatening of Leahites by Pharaoh's vizier Joseph: *Reuben* offers two of his four sons to Jacob as collateral for *Simeon* and Benjamin after Simeon is taken hostage in Egypt, and *Judah* offers to bear his father's curse forever when he compels Jacob to hazard the only remaining Rachelite (Gen. 42:37, 43:8–9).

The sacrifice of the firstborn is, in a sense, the dreadful content of the Hebrew rite Moses told Pharaoh the Egyptians would find intolerable. Thus it is the sacrifice of *Pharaoh's* firstborn that God exacts in return for the king's not yielding up the Hebrews to go and perform their sacrifice in the wilderness. The conscription of the Levites for service to God in the wilderness implies that God is asking for a sacrifice of Hebrew life itself— even if the Hebrews, treating themselves as shepherds like the patriarchs, might have been sacrificing lambs, not children. "Abel was a keeper of sheep . . . And the Lord had respect unto Abel and to his offering," "the firstlings of his flock" (Gen. 4:2, 4). But the Egyptians hate shepherds (Gen. 46:34), and have been induced to segregate Joseph's clan into Goshen on just this account. Shepherds, like Israelite sacrifices, are an abomination in Egypt (Exod. 8:26, Gen. 46:34). If Egypt had lambs to offer, its sons might be spared—but if it hates shepherds, it may also hate lamb-sacrifice.

With regard to Egyptians eating bread with Hebrews, like objections obtain (Gen. 43:32). When the Hebrews leave Egypt they take with them a custom of eating *unleavened* bread. The shepherd lacks the "culture" of Egypt, and it is precisely in this absence that Mosaic Israel is constituted:

> These are the words of the covenant which the Lord commanded Moses to make with the people of Israel in the land of Moab, besides the covenant which he had made with them in Horeb.
>
> And Moses summoned all Israel and said to them: "You have seen all that the Lord did before your eyes in the land of Egypt, to Pharaoh and to all his servants and to all his land. . . .
>
> I have led you forty years in the wilderness; . . . *you have not eaten bread*, and you have not drunk wine or strong drink; that you may know that I am the Lord your God." (Deut. 29:1–2, 5a, 6, RSV)

Israel is "set apart" from Egypt in regard to a wilderness or lenten diet. In being commanded to put all the leaven out of its houses (Exod. 12:15), the future nation is implicitly told to beware the leaven of the Egyptians. In the pericope of Matthew 16:5–12 and Mark 8:14–21, when Jesus renews this warning in regard to the Pharisees and Sadducees, he may be insisting on a similar distinction between synagogue and church. His apostles cannot yet see it, but Jesus and his teachings are themselves the bread otherwise excluded from their boat, and multiplied for his people; as Paul said, he is the bread of their Passover (1 Cor. 5:7).[4]

vi

It is Moses' mission to make God responsible for the disasters plaguing Egypt, and thus to give the Egyptians cause to expel God's people into the wilderness for their religion. The Passover story contains striking, dramatic reversals upon a scapegoat situation that formerly the Hebrews could not really claim to be theirs. Their expulsion is the logical cultural alternative to the first Pharaoh's program of genocide. We may compare the scapegoat ritual, in Leviticus 16, where one animal is driven into the wilderness to meet a numen and the other animal is sacrificed for sin. The Passover symbolizes—while at the same time it actually averts—both alternatives. The unleavened bread symbolizes an unprepared departure that has nonetheless been prepared for; the blood of the sacrificial lamb provides for the bloodying of the doors that nonetheless signify that these are the places where no (human) blood is to be shed. The Hebrews are not sacrificed, but their firstborn are sanctified; the Egyptian firstborn are not sacrificed either, but their firstborn are killed. And the Hebrews are expelled, but not with sin on their heads. They are sent out to God, not to the demon Azazel. It is their pursuers who are "swallowed up," three days into the wilderness (Exod. 14:3, 15:12).

God's original announcement regarding Pharaoh, in Exodus 4:23, may imply that taking the life of the ruler's son has been a divine object from the start. If so, the son's death might remind us of appeasement sacrifices made in desperate straits, when a royal city is about to fall, or the practice of kings who made their sons "to pass through the fire" (2 Kings 3:27, 16:3, 21:6, 23:10). But Israel in Egypt, like Abraham on Mount Moriah, is forgiven such sacrifices, a gift or redemption that may obscurely anticipate the empty sepulcher in the New Testament. In the Old Testament, however, the celebration of the Passover does not imply the mediation of salvation through the redeeming of an individual victim. The Egyptians are plagued collectively, in the same way that Israel is spared.

"Against any of the people of Israel . . . not a dog shall growl" (Exod. 11:7a, RSV), Moses promises on the eve of the exodus, the suggestion being that what Israel is spared is a pogrom. Hence the atmosphere of a sinister visitation, the vigil behind marked doors, and the angel of destruction ("*evil* angels," in Ps. 78:49). Yet dogs growl against aliens, not locals—the Israelites are naturalized as they depart, at the very moment God claims to be distinguishing between Israel and Egypt (Exod. 11:7b).

As persons who have become strangers in their adopted land, the Hebrews behind their doors in Egypt recall Lot behind his in Sodom. Lot is provided with guardian angels, yet is pressured into offering up his daughters to potentially fatal abuse (to judge by the analogy between

Gen. 19:1–10 and the crime of Gibeah at Judg. 19:16–28). Like the Hebrews instructed by God, Lot is offering a semi-sacred meal at the time of the evil visit, for he is hosting the sacred strangers. The Passover meal is restricted to Israel—that is, in terms of circumcision. Strangers are welcome to it, if they have been circumcised (Exod. 12:43–49): if they have been included in the community of blood that Zipporah included Moses in.

The visitation the angel makes to Egypt must also recall the "Angel of Occupation" that goes with the Israelites in the conquest of Canaan. The sign of blood on the doors corresponds to the red thread on the window of Rahab's exempt house: it told the Israelites that Rahab was to be included in the community that included the Zerahite branch of Judah, whose ancestor's birthright had originally been secured by the same red thread (Josh. 2:18–19, 6:22–25; Gen. 38:28).

Both the sign in the flesh of Exodus 4:24–26 and the sign on the door in Exodus 12:22–23 prevent God from taking life. Thus the Hebrew cult is twinborn with the consecration of the Israelite firstborn as inviolable, with the redirecting of the divine violence toward the Egyptian firstborn. Although it is unmarked houses that are unprotected, it could have been the reverse: the marked houses could have been the proscribed ones—or quarantined ones. The first Pharaoh's purge of the Hebrews, had it been truly thoroughgoing, might have taken this form. Thus the Hebrews arrive at ceremonial religion at the same time they arrive at an identity sufficient for the purposes of sanctioning genocidal violence against them.

Just as the first Pharaoh in his shrewdness creates the Hebrew leadership even while enterprisingly purging it from the womb, so God creates the religious and historical consciousness of Israel even while exposing Egypt to the terrible scrutiny of the angel of destruction. The pogrom that God visits upon the Egyptian majority is something of a preemptive strike on his part, since the logic of scapegoatism typically makes the stranger in society's midst guilty of the disasters engulfing the community as a whole. Moses himself has said that if the Hebrews were to sacrifice in Egypt, they would likely be stoned as foreigners (Exod. 8:26). And indeed, they are expelled that way: God says that they are going to be *driven out*—made into *gērim*, or strangers: "And the Lord said unto Moses, Yet will I bring one plague more upon Pharaoh, and upon Egypt; afterwards he will let you go hence: when he shall let you go, he shall surely *thrust* you *out* hence altogether" (Exod. 11:1). The narrative has already anticipated this result in the account of the critical eighth plague, when Pharaoh finally accepts the request of his servants that he "let the men go, that they may serve the Lord their God" (Exod. 10:7). Reacting to Moses' plan to remove with all his people—men, women, and children—and their possessions, Pharaoh replies: "Not so: go now ye that are men [male], and serve the Lord; for that ye did desire. And they [Moses and Aaron] were *driven out* from Pharaoh's presence" (Exod. 10:11).

The Egyptian year of the great hail was also the year in which the land of Goshen was spared this same sign (Exod. 9:26). Goshen was quite literally passed over. Israel is thus instituted in the form of a tax exemption, like the wheat and rye which were not smitten (Exod. 9:32); the Passover is a national exemption. Narrowly understood, the cultural role of Moses was to found this holiday. As an infant his mother gets Moses exempted from a death sentence on males, and as an adult Moses gets God to spare Israel from the wrath against it in the wilderness. At the center of this story is the institution of the Passover, which the Institutor precipitates into the narrative quite suddenly, before the completion of the deliverance it commemorates. For deliverance must include not only the passing-over itself, but the dismissal of Israel from Egypt. The prescribing of the rite so much overshadows the narrative's ushering in of the actual event that the text has the Lord taking pains to instruct Moses to eat the solemn meal with "your loins girded, your shoes on your feet, and your staff in your hand" (Exod. 12:11)—hardly a condition in which to be observing ceremonial correctness, not to mention to be presiding over a *seder*. The seder cannot be eaten "in haste," because it incorporates the rehearsal and elaboration of so much of this very narrative! Moses receives instructions about excluding leaven from houses and eating unleavened bread for the feast's *seven days*. We can only find these seven days in the narrative itself, if we include the plague of darkness and the journey up to the Reed Sea. The dietary prescription is a recollection of a haste that has scarcely yet been made.

These apparent outrages upon narrative "followability"[5] make a kind of symbolical sense, but only if we agree to let history commemorate the rite, rather than the other way around. For it is the boldest stroke of redactional art to choose the moment of impending deliverance to arrest the story with consecrating and ritualizing of the action—apparently even haste and flight can be made subject to ceremony. The institution of the Passover is hardly less momentous for its being revealed, as it were, upon the eve of the Passover. The ambiguity still haunts the celebration of the Passover in the New Testament, where the Institutor of the Eucharist seems to have understood the basic import of the Mosaic timing very well. The text's observation of the rite, in advance of the occasion it celebrates, transforms the moment of deliverance into an eternal recurrence, and tends to make the moment of deliverance into its own anniversary, eternally recoverable: that is, available for a contemplation that the Hebrews are instructed to share with posterity, even before the moment itself has been properly constituted.

The two kinds of text, rite-prescription and exodus storytelling, come upon the same formulations at the dénouement at Exodus 13:14–17:

> And it shall be when thy son asketh thee in time to come, saying, What is this? that thou shalt say unto him, By strength of hand the Lord brought us out from Egypt, from the house of bondage:
> *And it came to pass, when Pharaoh would hardly let us go,* that the Lord slew all the firstborn in the land of Egypt, both the firstborn of man, and the firstborn of beast: therefore I sacrifice to the Lord all that openeth the matrix, being males; but all the firstborn of my children I redeem.
> And it shall be for a token upon thine hand, and for frontlets between thine eyes: for by strength of hand the Lord brought us forth out of Egypt.
> *And it came to pass, when Pharaoh had let the people go . . .*

The Lord is prescribing this reversion to the events of the past while they have hardly had the opportunity to eventuate as the present.

The sharing with posterity of a communal event is clearly comparable to that solidarity with a kinsman enjoined upon audiences of the patriarchal marriage-saga. But in the exodus the catechizing of the historical moment is the opposite of nostalgic, which is why it is anachronistic. We may think of this as a motion to "make present," rather than to deepen the past, as the various removes within the patriarchal narrative might tend to do. The prescription aligns the moment not only with the New Year, but with the epochal appointment of a new time for the New Year. There are many motions to return to Egypt in the narrative as a whole, but the Passover text itself provides the Hebrews with little space for any reversion to an earlier social settlement. It excludes the temptation of retrospectivity preemptively, by having Moses pre-enact the future of the exodus as a part of the cult, and by drawing Israel toward a day when it will have the Passover in possession, rather than in prospect.

Moses could not come to the Hebrews armed merely with a recital out of a pre-Egyptian past. God's patriarchal pedigree, while it might be sufficient to gain Moses an audience, will not get him a congregation. Yet the present situation requires nothing less. Israel cannot be delivered if it cannot be expelled or excommunicated, and this cannot happen unless it has acquired an identity sufficiently "different" to cause it to be scapegoated. If Israel is not quite a nation dividing from another nation, it may yet be a sect dividing from another sect. But Egypt, while it is a great nation, is too cosmopolitan to be a sect, apart from the cult of Pharaoh himself. Israel, on the other hand, is suddenly a strong sect, but not yet much of a nation. Yet each identity might be regarded as a stand-in for the other.

There may be compelling external reasons why half of a dividing cult and half of a dividing kingdom have been recombined to create the national fable of identity as it is now found in the exodus. Here, however, we are confining our attention to the textual representation of Israel's twofold, historico-religious identity as it is internal to the text of Exodus itself. The history the Hebrews do not quite yet have is partly provided by the rite, while the rite partly commemorates events that have not yet happened.

The watch-night narratives of Exodus 11:1–10 and 12:29–51 are framed by the Passover legislation on both its sides, at Exodus 12:1–28 and 13:1–16. The rite that will confer on Israel the prerequisite of an excommunicable identity commemorates a deliverance that only a prior excommunication would make possible. The two texts prescribing the Passover (Exod. 12:1–28 and 13:1–16) are separated from each other by the first narrative of the actual exodus or departure (at Exod. 12:29–51), so the departure-narrative interrupts the rite as much as the rite based on the departure (the feast celebrating the hasty meal at the departure's imminence) interrupts the narrative. Does the Passover legislation interrupt the watch-night and departure narratives, or do the latter interrupt the rite? Each is interpolated into the other. The narrative is twice interrupted by the supervention of the rite, because the prescriptions for the rite are twice interrupted by the narrative. Neither narrative nor rite, moreover, can be advanced without that interruption—that is, without the explanatory desiderata—each provides the other. *Narrative:* "They were expelling us because we were Hebrews." *Rite:* "We will be Hebrews for their having expelled us."

The text leaves visible both equations. In one, the narrative historicizes the rite, by making the rite occur in the midst of the exodus. In the other, the rite consecrates the narrative, by making the exodus occur in the midst of the Passover. This duplex form reconceives the shepherd's meal of seasonal departure (or his provision for migration) as an epochal departure out of an old nation; and it memorializes and ritualizes that departure by the present pause to observe, apotropaically and preventatively, the shepherd's annual meal. The alternations between narrative and prescription tell us that the interrupted history of Egypt is convertible into the Israelites' national ceremony, while the interrupted meal in Egypt is convertible into the Israelites' national history. Compounding the description of the Passover and the exodus in this way—with each description interrupting the other—the discourse proceeds on two different but coordinated fronts. It is divided to convey the implicit transformation of both ceremonial and historicizing aspects, each by the other. Each half is *in* the keeping of the other, because it implies the keeping *of* the other. The rite will ensure historical survival, and the survivors will conserve the historicized rite.

One thinks of a suggestive episode in a modern Italian novel, Giorgio Bassani's *The Garden of the Finzi-Continis*, as it appeared in the movie version. A Jewish family, celebrating an unhappy Passover in an increasingly hostile and Fascist Italy, has its service twice interrupted by the ringing of the telephone. When the call is first answered, the calling party has hung up. Clearly this call represents an anonymous threat of violent interruption. It is a threat, because it is in the character of ceremonies that they not be interrupted. And yet all sacrifice consecrates the interruption of a life. The tragedy of Jewish identity has been that historically it is a Passover interrupted by a pogrom. The triumph of Israel's identity is that it is formed around an occasion that contains the polar terms in a symbiotic whole. Passover consecrates an interruption in the life of the celebrating community, and incorporates that interruption into its celebrations, surrounding it with a set-apart time and making it holy. Whether the angel at the door is the angel of death, or the angel Elijah, Passover is instituted upon—and is the constituting of—an interruption.

·IV·

ALLEGORIES OF SCRIPTURE

He hath revealed unto thee the Scripture with truth, confirming that which was before it, even as He revealed the Torah and the Gospel. . . . He it is who hath revealed unto thee the Scripture wherein are clear revelations—They are the substance of the Book—and others allegorical. But those in whose hearts is doubt pursue, forsooth, that which is allegorical, seeking dissension by seeking to explain it.

> (after M. M. Pickthall, *The Glorious Koran*, Surah III, 3, 7)

And Reuben said unto them, Shed no blood, but cast him into this pit that is in the wilderness, and lay no hand upon him; that he might rid him out of their hands, to deliver him to his father again. . . .

And Judah said, What profit is it if we slay our brother, and conceal his blood?

Come, and let us sell him . . .

And they drew and lifted up Joseph out of the pit, and sold Joseph . . . and they brought Joseph into Egypt.

> (Gen. 37:22, 26–28, AR)

·15·

"LIKE UNTO MOSES":
THE TEXT OF HISTORY

> And Moses said, "Today you have ordained yourselves for the service of the Lord, each one at the cost of his son and of his brother. . . ." (Exod. 32:29, RSV)

The dual story of the birth of a nation and the birth of a sect, as retailed by the Book of Exodus, takes half its major elements from the story of a dividing nation and half from the story of a dividing sect. In the various considerations that follow, we will supply the two missing shadow-halves: of the other nation, and of the other sect. This means reading Moses and the exodus somewhat "allegorically." The dividing nation and the dividing sect, each being half represented in the narrative, are now going to be understood as internal to Israel itself. Evidence of the representation of an intranational schism is surely already present in the exodus narrative we now have. The ministering Moses is doubled with the priestly Aaron. And the sovereign who forgot Joseph and enslaved the Hebrews and killed their infants is doubled with the one who was brought to treat with Moses as something of an equal and rival: like a party in opposition.—Or a party in exile from power, "in the wilderness."

My purpose here is to show how the landless exodus-Israel that might not quite exist could nonetheless be re-created out of the reserves of historical memory pertaining to the landed state-Israel that did exist: the relation between the extraterritorial Israel and the territorial one is constituted as a double helix, each half of which has been instrumental in generating the literary or ideological depiction of the other. Each Israel conceals a version of itself revealed in the (hi)story of its alternative. At the same time, this structure exposes an abiding difference between the sect and the state, as if they were always at odds. The state always seems eager to say: "I am the people." The authors of Exodus 1 and 1 Samuel 8 seem to reply, with the priest-hero of Nietzsche's *Thus Spake Zarathustra:* "It is a lie! Where there is still a people, there the state is not understood, but hated as the evil eye, and as sin against laws and customs. Many too many are born: for the superfluous ones was the state devised!"

A rapid conjugation of relations indicates that representatives of Yahweh's cult and Israel's land divide the story and its sites in half:

	South	North
Yahweh cult:	Aaron	Moses
	Zadokites	Levites
cult centers:	Temple at Jerusalem	Northern sanctuaries at Bethel and Dan
patriarchal sites:	Abraham's tomb in Hebron	Jacob's pillow in Bethel
	Isaac's well in Beersheba	Rachel's tomb in Bethlehem
tribal sites:	Judah in land of Judah	Joseph's bones in Ephraim
	The spy Caleb in Hebron and the Negeb	Joshua's meeting in Shechem, and his burial in Ephraim
royal capitals:	David made king in Hebron	Saul made king in Shiloh
	Absalom made king in Hebron	Jeroboam found in Shechem

The critics of the Northern kingdom, following the prophet Ahijah of Shiloh, and the apologists for the Southern kingdom, following King Abijah the son of Rehoboam, would each have had their versions of the national history. Each kingdom also may have had its own text of the Mosaic law and its own version of the origin and history of the state. In each kingdom's version of the story, a law of obligation would be revealed at the same time that the leadership of the other state would be convicted of breaking it—and of destroying the nation. The state of Judah had enslaved the tribe of Joseph, which was destined to be free and "Israel"; the people of Joseph had revolted from Judah, which was destined to be sovereign and "Zion." In the Southern version, the latter-day state (the Judah of King Josiah) deuteronomistically sponsors a Mosaic polity, as the Yahwist's God once sponsored Moses the invader by means of the "Southern" Caleb and the Levitical ancestor of the Zadokite and Jerusalemnic priesthood, Aaron. But the Southern version of the Mosaic state seems to be a latter-day discovery, one that follows upon the ministry of the writing prophets. In the Northern version, the Mosaic polity dissents from the Southern state, while Solomon and Rehoboam act the part of the two Pharaohs of Exodus. As Moses the separatist once championed God in Egypt, so God the partisan sponsored Moses in Israel, by means of the "Northern" invader Joshua. In the Southern version, Jacob is buried with Abraham, in the Calebite city of Hebron, the site purchased by Abraham and the first city in which David was king (2 Sam. 2:11, 5:5); furthermore, "to the sons of Aaron" the Israelites "gave the cities of refuge: Hebron" (1 Chron. 6:57, RSV). In the Northern version, Joseph and Joshua are buried at Shechem, got not by the fraud of Jacob's sons but by Jacob's own purchase (so Josh. 24:32 and Gen. 33:19, and cf. Gen. 50:5).

Scholarship has tended to deduce from such evidence the coexistence of two different Israelite traditions, or inheritances: one originally Northern, and Mosaic; and one Southern, and originally Davidic. Each one makes the other somewhat problematic, which is to say, less than wholly heritable, insofar as each inheritance might not belong to the heirs of the other. The Bible as a whole is there to bring them together, yet perhaps only in the late utterance of the so-called deutero-Isaiah do the two traditions really merge within a single ideology. Solomon has been made to speak of Moses; but only rarely do texts such as Psalm 78 stand back from the history to present Moses' exodus from Egypt and David's conquest of Jerusalem as members of a single divine plan.[1] The different strands of Ephraimite and Judahite hopes seem deliberately and programmatically braided and spliced in the prophecy to Jacob's seed and Judah's seed in Jeremiah 33:24–26; nonetheless, even there the Lord's elect are called "two families" (vs. 24). These "two families" seem to have occurred a little before, in the following promises from the same chapter:

> For thus saith the Lord; David shall never want a man to sit upon the throne of the house of Israel;
> Neither shall the priests the Levites want a man before me to offer burnt offerings, . . . and to do sacrifice continually. (Jer. 33:17–18)

The hopes of the nation seem to divide the armorial shield of Israel neatly between two families that have become two parties.

The Israelite could only view the estate into which his tribes and rulers had come, as Moses saw it in Deuteronomy, from a vantage point beyond it. He could see where he had walked up and down the land, with sojourning Abraham and returning Jacob, and yet he was no longer a sojourner. He was now as much a farmer like Cain as a shepherd like Abel; less a migrant like Jacob in Canaan than a subject like Joseph in Egypt. For where Abraham had purchased burial rights in the future Aaronid city of

Hebron at the end of his sojourning, David had purchased the temple site in Jerusalem of the Jebusites at the end of a military conscription. Abraham was buying land in which to settle his people, David a fort from which to rule a kingdom. Thus the Israelite could survey his part of the Lord's original creation and, like the Lord, pronounce it good; but the ownership of the land was passing from clan and family to the state bureaucracy. This was like the fate of the land's ownership during Joseph's royal ministry in Egypt, even while Joseph was naming his sons after their future holdings in Ephraim and Manasseh, and securing a reserve for their families in Goshen.

With the Solomon of 1 Kings, the Israelite of the early kingship could begin to cast his heritage in written and literary form, and approve of it as a divine *fait accompli;* such a people had truly been called out of Egypt and planted in Zion, as if from of old. Yet the Israelite was recasting this heritage in something like its present literary form, as found in the Pentateuch and the Former Prophets, throughout the period from the writing of Deuteronomy to the compiling of Chronicles, which is to say, from the time of the imminent and actual demise of the kingship.[2] Within this body of writings, we find pieces like the "poor laws" of Leviticus 25: laws that appeal almost nostalgically to the divine sponsorship of the exodus at the same time that they try to provide the legal mechanisms for Israel to get itself *back,* when its people have been forced by circumstance to sell their patrimony and alienate their very self-right in order to subsist.

The totality of the Israelite literary inheritance must have been as often alienated from this people as its land and judgments were, insofar as the traditions about Israel belonged to the other half of a divided kingship, or as its texts were the property of a rival priesthood or authorial school, or as the nation itself was going to be lost in Assyria at the fall of the North, or in Babylon at "the captivity of the land." The Septuagint translates the word for the people's assembly or congregation, the Hebrew *qahal,* as the Greek *ecclesia:* both words imply "a people called," that is, "called *together,"* into an assembly.[3] The gathering and compiling of the Scriptures is itself eloquent evidence, albeit literary, of this people's having been so constituted, in the latter day. But insofar as it was *not* together, Israel was still being called out of Egypt, and gathered in Moab. For whether he was under the rule of a Jeroboam in the North or a Josiah in the South, whether he was with Ezekiel under the king of Babylon in the East or with Ezra under the empire of the Persians in the West, the Israelite might well experience his inheritance as divided, and thus as a summons calling him out of any house he might attempt to refather or endow, and beyond any estate he himself could actually hope to inherit. Such a call, issuing from that horizon which his own earthly lot was never to reach, might also have made him—like another Moses—almost infinitely answerable.

Part A. Mosaic History

In his commentary on Paul's use of the word "allegory" in the passage in Galatians 4:24 describing Sarah and Hagar as types for Church and Synagogue, John Chrysostom explains:

> By a misuse of language he called the type allegory. What he means is this: the history itself not only has the apparent meaning but also proclaims other matters; therefore it is called allegory. But what did it proclaim? Nothing other than everything that now is.[4]

But this spirit of contemporization is deeply writ into texts like Deuteronomy itself. "It happened that those predictions took effect after three hundred and sixty-one years," Josephus in his *Antiquities of the Jews* calculates upon the occasion of Josiah's fulfilling the prophecy of 1 Kings 13:1–2 (*Ant.*, X.iv.4; cf. VIII.viii.5). According to 2 Kings 23:16–21, the nameless ninth-century prophet out of Judah who prophesied the Josianic reform of the sixth century impressed the king himself: Josiah refrains from violating the tomb of the ancient prophet from the south (which is also that of an equally impressed professional colleague from the north), and so adorns the national register of historic landmarks with a monument to the righteous. As the New Testament echoes suggest, Jesus almost seems to allude to the same train of events, when he speaks as if there were a kind of Hebraic *kismet*, obliging the hypocritical scribes and Pharisees to "fill up the measure of [their] fathers" in building the tombs of the prophets and adorning the monuments of the righteous (Matt. 23:29, 32).

Nor are such "allegories of Scripture," whereby the experiences of one Israel have been written up as allusions to another, unique to the deuteronomic point of view. Such a contemporizing shift is fundamental to both the instructive repetitions of biblical typology and the diachronic aspect of the parallelisms found in biblical poetic rhetoric: "The Lord sent a word into Jacob, and it hath lighted upon Israel" (Isa. 9:8); prophecy has aimed a message against the Jacob of the past, yet it is intended to land on the Israel of the present. The message can be updated, or the story can be back-dated. We shall be arguing that this diachronic structure can be found embedded in the text of Exodus itself, which purports to apply to the original occasion, and yet contains the possibility of the same temporal shift forward: e.g., Exodus 32:35, "And the Lord plagued the people, because they made the calf, *which Aaron made*."[5] The people are plagued *now*, because they have made that same calf which Aaron made *then*. The sins of the fathers are visited on the heads of the sons: because a sinful present has been revisited by a sinful past. Following the lead of the Aaron who misled them originally, the people are still filling up the measure of their fathers.

Herbert Marks has pointed out to me that here we are arguing that "Moses" and the origins of Israel are related somewhat as "Homer" and his mythic Achaeans are: but while the shift from Homer to his protagonists results in a text that can be described by a classical scholar as "an idealized retrojection based on the poetic tradition's sense of its own glory,"[6] the shift from the Moses of the exodus to the latter-day Mosaic hero of Deuteronomy suggests a historic people's more prosaic expression of its distress and contingency. The result is a text that can be described as a criticizing retrojection based on a received tradition's anxious sense of its own recurrent imperilment.

Pascal seems to get this right, when he describes the kind of book that has created the Jewish nation:

> *Sincerity of the Jews.*—They preserve lovingly and carefully the book in which Moses declares they have been all their life ungrateful to God, and that he knows they will be still more so after his death; but that he calls heaven and earth to witness against them, and that he has [*taught*] them enough.
>
> He declares that God, being angry with them, shall at last scatter them among all the nations of the earth [Deut. 28:64]; that as they have offended Him by worshipping gods who were not their God, so He will provoke them by calling a people who are not His people [Deut. 32:21]; that He desires that all His words be preserved for ever [Deut. 31:21], and that His book be placed in the Ark of the Covenant to serve for ever as a witness against them [Deut. 31:26].[7]

In Isaiah 30, Pascal also notes, Israel's rebellion has caused it to rely on Egypt, and the prophet is told to preserve this folly in written form—"go, write it before them in a table, and note it in a book, that it may be for the time to come for ever and ever" (Isa. 30:8).

In describing this retrojection of the literary tradition of the prophets into Israel's legendary history as based on the Israelite's acknowledgment of his actual history's failings, guilt, shame, self-doubt, and self-forgetfulness—not to mention the humiliating depths of the nation's culpability and disgracefulness before God—we may recur to the story in Exodus and Deuteronomy of the broken tables of the Mosaic law. Such a story can represent to us the great hazard in which the acceptability of the tradition as a whole was repeatedly understood to stand—or to have stood, before its canonization. From our point of view, the restoration of the inscribed law-text is virtually an allegory for the recovery of Israel through the renewal of the law and the covenant: or for the saving of the nation by the conservation of its Mosaic traditions.

The distance between "Hellas" and Israel in this matter speaks volumes for a contrast between Homer and the Bible advanced by Erich Auerbach, a contrast which was already somewhat traditional—for it is found at the place in Pascal we have quoted from—when he presented his telling modern version of it. Auerbach sees the biblical stories as almost morosely indoctrinated by a tyrannical and exclusive claim to veracity that has paradoxically driven a constantly changing, long-term interpretative enterprise of revaluing the texts, on the part of successive covenanted readerships. The biblical characters themselves are no less subject to this kind of pressure in their own lives, during which their status and value as persons is anything but fixed:

> how much wider is the pendulum swing of their lives than that of the Homeric heroes! For they are bearers of the divine will, and yet they are fallible, subject to misfortune and humiliation—and in the midst of misfortune and in their humiliation their acts and words reveal the transcendent majesty of God. There is hardly one of them who does not, like Adam, undergo the deepest humiliation—and hardly one is not deemed worthy of God's personal intervention and personal inspiration. Humiliation and elevation go far deeper and far higher than in Homer, and they belong basically together. . . . Homer remains within the legendary with all his material, whereas the material of the Old Testament comes closer and closer to history as the narrative proceeds.[8]

Let us take an example from the "Deuteronomic History." One version of the name of the Davidic ruler whose entire court was finally deported to Babylon is Jeconiah (2 Kings 24:12–16, NJB, with 1 Chron. 3:16). The record of the kingship in Israel is prefaced by the account of the ark in Canaan, where it was the sons of a much earlier Jeconiah who had failed to respect God's portable throne. As a result, this clan was apparently obliterated to the last man (1 Sam. 6:19, NJB). Might not the same fate be in store for Israel itself, whose kings could not respect the covenant? "Who is able to stand before this holy Lord God?" Auerbach's reader could well ask at the outset, borrowing the words of the early witnesses of the ark (1 Sam. 6:20). But we must then go on to view, in much the same spirit, the whole kingship's dubious ability to stand before history. What follows is my attempt to recognize this pressure toward history, which the Bible puts on the legendary material and received narrations of Moses and the exodus themselves.

The anxious link between "Moses" and Israel, when we consider it in this critical way, suggests a repeated faltering in and recovery of Israel's ideal self. The biblical exodus represents such an interruption in self-consciousness by means of an extended story, in which the nation's identity is "seen through" its jeopardy in the world. The narrative likewise sees Israel through its jeopardized *delivery* into the world, which is then read back into Moses' own infancy story of a borrowed royal sponsorship. The place of Moses in Israel's self-realization is not necessarily a given, but one's identity as a monotheistical Yahwist can hardly be realized except as consciousness arrests itself to contemplate and create a corporate entity distinct from the polytheistic world which it is otherwise immersed in and identified with. Such an arrest in consciousness, according to Deuteronomy, is what was actually to be found in the Sinaitic epiphenomenon: Israel "saw no similitude, only a voice" (Deut. 4:12, AR).

Deuteronomy occupies a critical place in the history of the canon's convergence upon its own project, because this book can be situated in two ways. Either it is the conclusion of the *landless* history of Israel, or it is the introduction to the *landed* history of Israel. It is the *conclusion* of the history that goes back from the wilderness Israel of Moses to the Egyptian Israel of Joseph, to the sojourning pre-Israel of the patriarchs, to the genetic pre-Israel in the seed of Noah's son Shem and Adam's son Seth. Just as the received stories of Near Eastern legend—humankind's loss of the chance of immortality, the divine attempt against the race in the flood, and the building of a Babylonian and cosmic world-empire—had been prefixed to the story of Israel's forebears as that story's prologue, so Deuteronomy was eventually annexed to it as the epilogue. But Deuteronomy itself has cast Moses in the role of the reciter and summarizer of the preceding exodus history. He has to recapitulate this history for the sake of succeeding generations. It is therefore logical to suppose that Deuteronomy originally served such a function as an introduction to a *succeeding* history, namely the history of the landed Israel: apparently Deuteronomy was originally conceived as the prologue to the subsequent history of the judges and kings. Therefore the law text found during the repairs to Josiah's temple—if this law was indeed a document like the Deuteronomy with which it is apparently so much in agreement—would in fact have been the opening discourse for a national history culminating in the reign of the Josiah to whom the book in question was being presented or dedicated. Deuteronomy, in that case, was propaganda for Josiah's own program, if that program was being advanced as the fulfillment of intentions that went back to "Moses."

The deuteronomic history condemns Israel's kings for their sponsorship of idolatry, a sponsorship Josiah was resolved to end forever. But the same history does not fault the kings for ritual uncleanness, or for failure to sacrifice, as we might expect if it had incorporated the norms of the Priestly legislation in Leviticus. And the Priestly legislation, esconced as it now is in one of the first four books of the Pentateuch—along with those four books' Priestly accounts of the Creation, the Flood, Abraham, the priestly offices, and the Mosaic law—does not anticipate Deuteronomy, with its preaching of the purification of motive and circumcision of the heart, and the appointment of a religious capital. Yet it was by means of a code like that in Deuteronomy, and not some other "torah," that Josiah's reign represented itself as recovering the intentions that were God's in the first place, as revealed in his covenanting with Israel in the wilderness. Thus a critical occurrence in the formation of the canon turns on the fixing of the status of Deuteronomy. On the one hand, there is the annexation of Deuteronomy to the "law of Moses" as an epilogue, which creates the five "Books of Moses" that constitute the narrower canon of the Torah, or Book of the Law, but also completes the landless history of Israel; on the other hand, there is the creation of Deuteronomy as the prologue to the history of the landed Israel. The Deuteronomy of the Pentateuch brought with it four books: Genesis, Exodus, Leviticus, and Numbers. These books trace the descent of Moses' wilderness Israel back to Adam and embed the Priestly torah. The Deuteronomy of the subsequent landed history also brought with it four books: Joshua, Judges, Samuel, and Kings. The books trace the career of the Israelite and Mosaic polity forward to the last Judaic kings and embed the deuteronomic historiography. The dual membership of Deuteronomy in the two histories tends to make it the nexus of "the Law and the Prophets," that is, the Torah and the Former Prophets. It ends one pentateuch, or begins another.

An equally important occurrence in the formation of the canon is the fixing of the Priestly narrative within the landless history, which it tends to periodize. Some notable overlapping elements and family resemblances making up the Priestly strand in the first four books of the pentateuchal narrative and law are as follows: Adamic and Noachic man are created in the image of God (Gen. 1:26, 9:6); Noah and the Aaronid priests sacrifice to produce a sweet savour in God's nostrils (Gen. 8:21, Exod. 29:18, Lev. 1:9, 13, Num. 28:2); Noachic man and Israel are forbidden to eat blood (Gen. 9:4, Lev. 19:26), with Israel being given the addition of the use for the blood in sacrifice (Lev. 4:18, 7:2, etc.); Noah, Abraham, and Israel are successively promised by God that he will *establish* his covenant with them (Hebr. *qum* ['confirm,' 'maintain'] in Gen. 9:9, 11; 17:7, 21; Exod. 6:4, Lev. 26:9); and where Noah is promised the perpetual return of seedtime and harvest, Israel is promised that God—in return for obedience to the law—"will give you [Israel] rain in due season, and the land shall yield her increase" (Gen. 8:22, Lev. 26:4). Circumcision is enjoined on Abraham at the time the covenant is promised to him, and yet Ishmael, not Isaac, is the son originally covenanted by this practice. Thus the Priestly strand tends to recognize dispensations as frames within which the covenant relation to God is set out, but also allows for the frames' successive replacement, without any abridgment of the original relation.

It follows that the Priestly legislation, while it emphasizes the adornment of the tabernacle and a service of God that is specifically sacerdotal, does not make Moses legislate the unification of sacrifice at Jerusalem, as we might expect it to if its prescriptions were subsequent to the Josianic revolution memorialized by Deuteronomy.[9] In a Priestly version of the fourth of the Ten Commandments, placed just after a verse proscribing idolatry, God does tell Israel "Ye shall keep my sabbaths, and reverence my sanctuary" (Lev. 26:2; also 19:30): but he does not specify the sanctuary's location, nor point to its specificity, even while the levitical legislation is constantly addressed to the purification of the Israelite camp and the set-apartness of the tent of the meeting. Thus the Priestly author and the deuteronomic author do not communicate or converge on a critical point: each either ignores or is ignorant of the other, in the matter of specifying the sacrality of Jerusalem.

Here we might postulate two different reactions to the Babylonian exile. The deuteronomic historians understood Israel's separation from Jerusalem as the divine punishment for the nation's sin. But a Priestly author, committed to the preservation of "a kingdom of priests, and an holy nation" (Exod. 19:6), dedicated to God throughout the exile, might understand the absence from Jerusalem and the exclusion from the promised land differently; for if the sacrality and possession of Jerusalem had been essential to a Priestly definition of Israel, then Israel's holiness would itself have been violated and profaned by the exilic epoch. Such a blemish would have kept Israel from serving as God's priest forever, and it would have denied the nation its participation in exilic and postexilic epochs comparable to those of Adam, Noah, Abraham, and Moses. For each of these characters bridges between epochs.

The pentateuchal Priestly strand, or compilation—if indeed that is what we must recognize it as—had laid out its own historical torah of Israelite institutions, through its scheme for the successive periods of the revelation from God. But the scope of these institutions tends to be universalist, insofar as such a torah tended to argue for their possession by Israel *apart* from Israel's occupation of the land of Israel, even while the priestly election is uncompromisingly ethnic. The God of the Priestly strand gave Adam dominion over the earth, along with the divine image; he gave Noah a covenant for the everlasting perpetuation of the natural order, and a positive reaction to sacrifice; he gave Abraham the covenant of circumcision even while he included Ishmael—son of an Egyptian mother—in it, and while he established his covenant with Isaac; and he gave Moses and Aaron sacral orders and heritable priestly offices in conjunction with a tabernacle that was portable. Above all, in fact, he gave Moses Aaron: and his descendants. That is how he reconstituted the interruption constituted by the uniqueness of Moses.

Where the Priestly torah breaks off, with the assignment of the tribal portions in Numbers, Deuteronomy has offered to rebegin—with the history that would lead not only to Josiah's Jerusalem, but also to Jeconiah's captivity and asylum in Babylon.

The patron of both the Priestly and the deuteronomic strands in the canon is said to be Moses. A restoration of the religion of Moses characterizes regimes as diverse as those of Jeroboam, Jehoash and Jehoiada, Hezekiah, the Manasseh of 2 Chronicles 33:11–16, Josiah, and Ezra. It obviously helps to know which leader's "Moses" one is talking about. Yet if the reader agrees that one "origin" of the story of Moses' refuge in the Midian is the priestly law about the treatment of the manslayer, he or she would not be able to accept any simple assertion that the story comes from an "early" tradition like "J" (at Exod. 4:19), since the legislation about the parallel duration of asylum comes from a "late" compilation like "P" (Num. 35:28). The resulting etiology would not only be "preposterous," it would also put law and narrative into a new relation of source and resource. The documentarian would have to stop thinking of the laws in Numbers as a priestly supplementation of earlier narrative traditions, if they are also a deduction from an early tradition of Mosaic sanctuary; at the least, he would have to think of an "old" story as an illustration of a putative tradent otherwise only attested in the later Priestly legal corpora.

The literary critic, initially, is also likely to be somewhat disoriented by the suggested correspondence between the legal text and the biographical one. He or she now has to say that the story about Moses appears to be much more a fable about the law in Israel (mixed with a priest-hide-thyself irony) than a character-based story about Israel off collecting itself from the non-being of Egypt and Moses off collecting himself in the limbo of Midian. Not only do we have to integrate two categories of text (or else tradent) that we might well have formerly divided on generic and formalist grounds, we also have to recognize the claims of an art of composition that has had the deep discretion to omit to do this integrating *for* us: we have to do it for ourselves.

The texts we have cited are from two different books in the Pentateuch, two different authors in the old Documentary Hypothesis, and two different genres of composition in the canon: yet they call out to each other in a way that makes them seem "separated at birth." This is one of the old arguments of the source theorists, of course, while "combined at birth" is often the other. Which may only show us that there are almost too many different ways of imagining a source. The matter will hardly be less complicated should we find, for example, that the story of Moses' rustication has another separated twin altogether, in the latter-day political history of the landed Israel. And indeed we do find this, in the story of the career of Jeroboam, the first king of the Northern part of the divided kingdom.

Having read about Mosaic law texts for a priestly Israel and a Mosaic history for a landless pre-Israel, we now come upon a Mosaic kingship for a landed, latter-day Israel. As before, the figure of an incriminated subject is to be separated into the sanctuary of an alternative jurisdiction.

Part B. The Mosaic Revolution and the Northern Kingship

If the whole narrative about the Egyptian Moses coheres—as it were, stereoscopically—with the narrative about the Sinaitic Moses, the stories about Moses the rebel and Moses the reformer must nonetheless come together from two different directions: from an ideal of self-determination and national set-apartness, on the one hand, and from an ideal of constitutional conservation and retrenchment, on the other. Each party, appealing to the Moses of its own tradition, might sponsor a revolution and/or a reform in the name of a Moses whose name had been taken in vain by the other. Each party might institute itself by deinstituting its rival and calling his party's establishment idolatrous. We must attempt to divide the doubled Moses between rival establishments.

In discussing Moses' spokesmanship in relation to Pharaoh, we had occasion to compare the role of the prophets who came before Israel's kings (see chapter 10). When the people ask Aaron to make them gods to replace Moses as the leader who brought them up out of Egypt, they resemble the elders in 1 Samuel who asked Samuel to make them a king to replace the priesthood and to judge them like the nations. An apostate people has again lost confidence in its Yahwist leadership:

> And when the people saw that Moses delayed to come down out of the mount, the people gathered themselves together unto Aaron, and said unto him, Up, *make us gods, which shall go before us;* for as for this Moses, the man that brought us up out of the land of Egypt, we wot not what is become of him. (Exodus. 32:1)

> Then all the elders of Israel gathered themselves together, and came to Samuel unto Ramah,
> And said unto him, Behold, thou art old, and thy sons walk not in thy ways: now *make us a king* to judge us like all the nations. . . .
> That we also may be like all the nations; and *that our king may* judge us, and *go out before us,* and fight our battles. (1 Sam. 8:4–5, 20)

And Samuel says, "I . . . have made a king over you. And, now, behold, the king walketh before you" (1 Sam. 12:1–2).

A parallelism in Hosea 8 brings the histories of king and cult together:

> They have set up kings, but not by me: they have made princes, and I
> knew it not: of their silver and their gold have they made them idols,
> that they may be cut off;
> Thy calf, O Samaria, hath cast thee off; . . . (Hos. 8:4–5)

God's report of Israel's apostasy at Sinai compares with his report in the
kingship initiative. The people worship the calf, and then

> . . . the Lord said unto Moses, Go, get thee down; for thy people,
> which thou broughtest out of the land of Egypt, have corrupted them-
> selves:
> They have turned aside quickly out of the way which I commanded
> them: they have made them a molten calf, and have worshipped it, and
> have sacrificed thereunto, and said, These be thy gods, O Israel, which
> have brought thee up out of the land of Egypt. (Exod. 32:7–8)

Varying from Aaron in verse 4, who credits the deified bull-idol with the
people's deliverance, God in verse 7 credits *Moses,* as if arguing he should
take the people's slight personally and dismiss them as a lost cause. As
Israel put other gods before God and Moses, so it also put the kingship
before God and Samuel. God implies Samuel is another rejected Moses:

> According to all the works which they have done since the day that I
> brought them up out of Egypt even unto this day, wherewith they have
> forsaken me, and served other gods, so do they also unto thee.
> (1 Sam. 8:8)

But God has also just stated that the people have not rejected *Samuel,* only
the God of the exodus himself (1 Sam. 8:7). Either way, Samuel is a
prophet like Moses, because his people remain like Moses' people,
rejecting God or the deliverer who has gone before them, yet seeking to
put the sign or person of a deliverer—the calf, the kingship—in God's
place. Each narrative reports Israel's rebellion against God's *leadership.*

But what about the rival leadership? What is its identity? The anti-
royalist Samuel stands for Moses, but who opposes him? The iconoclastic
Moses opposes Aaron, as the prophetic Moses opposed Pharaoh, but who
did Moses stand for? What did Pharaoh forsake, as Samuel's Israel forsook
the God of the exodus? In the present section, we will consider how an
establishment that is brought to acknowledge "Moses" might have stood
for one that had forgotten "Joseph." It is to the history of the kingship
that we must revert to underwrite the role of Moses as a rebellious subject
of a semi-divine king, while at the same time serving as another divine
being's supreme spokesman. Here it seems significant that Moses is

reported to have murdered an Egyptian overseer. We assume he is an overseer, because Moses meets up with him while he is viewing his people's
burdens (Exod. 2:11): the term resonates throughout the narrative of the
Hebrews' affliction (Exod. 1:11, 5:4–5, 6:6–7). But Moses may be an overseer himself: the oppressive Hebrew in Exodus 2:14 pointedly asks Moses if
he means to kill him, as if Moses might have the authority as well as the
power. Though it is not *said* that the self-divided Moses was an overseer,
that is nonetheless just how his fellow Hebrews originally seem to have
reacted to him. Moses, moreover, is accused of putting himself in place of
Joseph: not so much the Joseph originally accused of presumption by his
brothers, as the Joseph who became the Egyptian vizier who judged his
brothers in place of the ruler, collected taxes for this ruler, created the
state monopoly on land-owning, and segregated the Israelites into
Goshen. Perhaps we can understand the story even better if we suppose
that the oppressive Hebrew stands, himself, in place of one of Pharaoh's
overseers: for Pharaoh seems to treat Moses as an overseer who has
betrayed his terms of office by becoming party to the aspirations of those
in his charge. Moses and Aaron get the lower, Hebrew officers in trouble,
and yet the officers themselves are accused of asking for leave—or a holiday—to go and sacrifice (Exod. 5:17). Like Moses and Aaron, they come
and go, as emissaries between Pharaoh and the people. Pharaoh's taskmasters had set "officers of the children of Israel" over the Israelites
(Exod. 5:14), Hebrews over Hebrews. Solomon, in 1 Kings 12, has done
the same thing in Israel. Moses, then, would only be objecting to himself.

The overall story of Hebrew defiance in Egypt has two halves:

the murder of	the killing of
an actual overseer	the Egyptian officer
by a potential overseer-emissary;	by the young Moses;
the defiance of (rebellion against)	the campaign against
a successor sovereign or dynast	the new Pharaoh
by a presently subject people.	by Moses and Aaron.

Solomon also had an overseer, such as Pharaoh once had in Joseph and
presumably in Joseph's successors; he was Jeroboam, son of Nebat. The
two halves reappear in recombinant form, as renarrativized in 1 Kings 12:

the defiance of (rebellion against)	the rebellion from
an actual sovereign or dynast	Solomon son of David
by an actual overseer;	by Jeroboam his minister;

the murder of	the stoning of
a potential overseer-emissary	Adoram from Judah,
by a former subject-people.	by Jeroboam's Israel.

Like many revolutions, the Mosaic one may be understood on the analogy of a "taxpayers' rebellion," since the escalation of Pharaoh's exactions from the Hebrews figures as a contributing factor in the events leading to the exodus. Jeroboam was in charge of the state's forced labor, which was specifically levied from the house of Joseph (1 Kings 11:28). And yet Jeroboam the labor minister went on to oppose Solomon's son Rehoboam, after having become alienated and a fugitive from Solomon himself; his subsequently rebellious people went on to murder the overseer-emissary of Solomon's successor Rehoboam, after Rehoboam indicated to them that he planned to increase their burden. The rebellious Northerners stone the chief of Rehoboam's labor levy to death when he is sent to them to negotiate for Rehoboam (1 Kings 12:18, "Adoram, who was over the tribute"—in 2 Sam. 20:24 perhaps the same Adoram "was over the tribute" of David).

Thus Moses' leadership, if it is like Jeroboam's, also represents a challenge to the Southern kingship, that is, a judgment on Rehoboam's failure to relieve the burdens—more particularly the *mas* or *missîm*, or levy of forced labor—laid upon the Northern tribes by Solomon (see 1 Kings 4:6, "Adoniram . . . was over the tribute," and 5:13–14, "Solomon raised a levy out of all Israel . . . thirty thousand men . . . And Adoniram was over the levy"). Solomon and his son Rehoboam, like the house of Pharaoh in the story of Moses, "knew not Joseph" (Exod. 1:8). For in the historical period, forced labor was especially Solomon's policy (1 Kings 9:15–24, 11:26–28), a policy that visited on Israel itself the previous fate of the Canaanites who were "put to tribute" in Judges 1:28–35.[10]

Pharaoh's portrait in Exodus, one may suppose, is a deeply veiled critique of Solomon's kingdom as a slave state. For Pharaoh's taskmasters are first called "officers of the *missîm*": "Therefore they did set over them taskmasters [Hebr. *sārê missîm* = chief of the burden or levy] to afflict them with their burdens. And they built for Pharaoh treasure cities Pithom and Raamses" (Exod. 1:11). According to Deuteronomy 17:16–19, a proper deuteronomic king—studious in the levitical law and sponsoring its promulgation by means of written copies of it—would be in sin should he multiply horses, wives, treasures—and public works. Such sin would be a return to the conditions of Egypt: for the king "shall not multiply horses to himself, nor cause the people to return to Egypt, to the end that he should multiply horses: forasmuch as the Lord hath said unto you, Ye shall henceforth return no more that way." More loosely stated, this passage means that the king shall not enslave his people to build the stables, garrisons, and fortified cities that go with building up an ancient Near Eastern military machine. Thus the confounding of Pharaoh finally takes the parabolic form of drowning the chariots and horsemen (Exod. 14:17–18, 28) with which kings like Solomon built up their armies.

In 1 Kings 9:21–22 the text says the Canaanites' children, "that were left after them in the land, whom the children of Israel also were not able utterly to destroy, upon those did Solomon levy a tribute of bondservice unto this day"—"But of the children of Israel did Solomon make no bondmen: but they were men of war." But if these "men of war"—especially if they are "chosen men"—were also *draftees*, then the text's distinction between the army and the labor force begins to erode. As indeed it might: for upon the death of Solomon, only two chapters later, the congregation petitions Rehoboam for relief, "saying, Thy father made our yoke grievous: now therefore make thou the grievous service of thy father, and his heavy yoke which he put upon us, lighter, and we will serve thee" (1 Kings 12:3–4). This "grievous service," in the Hebrew ('sharp or painful servitude'), is almost a technical term in Exodus, as the "cruel bondage" with which Pharaoh had embittered the lives of the Israelites in Egypt and broken their spirit (Exod. 1:14, 6:9, and Deut. 26:6): they were unable to hearken to a deliverer even when he arose and spoke for them.

Pharaoh also failed to hearken to him; so Rehoboam would fail to listen to the reasonable counsels of the elders of his court. Instead, Rehoboam provoked the Northerners, and they rebelled: "So Israel rebelled against the house of David unto this day" (1 Kings 12:19). The people's choice (in 1 Kings 12:4) of the term "grievous service" for Solomon's impositions has thus proven to be an exact one: it warns one of the impending separation of Northern Israel from the rule of Judah, on the analogy of Moses' separation from Egypt: it is the "hard bondage" with which the Egyptians embitter the life of the Israelites from Exodus 1:14.

It is particularly a Pharaoh who "knew not Joseph" who stands accused of the crimes at the opening of Exodus. Not knowing Joseph would mean, in Israel, not knowing—i.e., disenfranchising—Joseph's house: and that is just what Solomon is accused of having done. The conscription of the house of Joseph for Israel's labor force, in the monarchic narrative, is an ironic version of the saving history in the pentateuchal narrative, where the house of Levi is conscripted for Israel's priesthood, in place of the firstborn. But if the former "Israel in Egypt" is the latter-day "house of Joseph in Israel," then who has the part of Israel's deliverer? Who is the latter-day Moses? Who brings the Israel that is Joseph out of the imperial state and into the wilderness to found its cult? The answer is Solomon's overseer, Jeroboam the son of Nebat.

The cause of Jeroboam's first lifting up his hand against his king, in this case Solomon, is stated baldly: "Solomon built Millo"—and refortified Jerusalem (1 Kings 11:26–27). Jeroboam is appointed chief of the labor-levy from Joseph. Then he is called by Ahijah, and thereafter goes into exile in Egypt. When Rehoboam comes to the throne, Jeroboam returns from Egypt. When the house of Joseph seeks relief, Rehoboam promises Jeroboam that he will make the burdens laid upon the house of Joseph yet worse than they had been under the kingship of his father: so Pharaoh makes the Israelites' hard labor worse upon the application of Moses. Jeroboam had fled to sanctuary because Solomon had sought to kill him—because of the prophet Ahijah's prophecy that the successful overseer would lead the secession of the Northern kingdom (1 Kings 11:36–40). In the legendary but extrabiblical material that will feed into Jesus' nativity story in the Gospel of Matthew, this is the same kind of warning that Pharaoh will be given about Moses, as a motivation for his massacre of the Hebrew innocents.

We cannot know, from the record in 1 Kings, all of the details that would fill out a full account of how Jeroboam the overseer came to be Jeroboam the champion of the oppressed and the new spokesman of the North: we lack the stories that constitute the equivalent "preministry of Moses" at the opening of Exodus. But we do not doubt the interest of such an account, for we are told that Jeroboam "lifted up his hand" against Solomon. Our interest is represented in the stories about Moses first going out to his people in Egypt and then waiting out his exile in the land of Midian, as Jeroboam waited out his in the land of Egypt itself. We also cannot know how Moses came to be accepted as the political spokesman for the Hebrew labor force of Pharaoh, apart from the story of his having stood up to the Egyptian overseer who was abusing the Hebrew, but we can repossess ourselves of such an account in the actions of the people in their calling of Jeroboam. Neither can we prove, from the record in Exodus 1, that the Pharaoh who knew not Joseph also sought to thwart the dreaded future embodied in Moses, in the way Solomon attempted to kill the future embodied in the son of Nebat, or in the way that Matthew's Herod attempted to scotch the future at the time that Joseph the carpenter betook himself and his family into Egypt. But again we cannot doubt the interest in such a possibility, and the representation of it, in Solomon's reaction to the prophecy of Ahijah of Shiloh—which is like Herod's reactions to the interpreters of the Scriptures about Bethlehem.

The parallels from Matthew 2 suggest that the stories of Moses and Jeroboam each contain the missing half of the other. Moses killed the first Pharaoh's overseer, and thereafter became the leader of the Hebrew dissent that ended in the exodus from the state of that Pharaoh's successor.

Jeroboam lifted his hand against Solomon, even while becoming his overseer; he colluded with the prophetic party opposed to Solomon, and the people who killed his successor, Rehoboam's overseer Adoram, made Jeroboam the leader of the rebellion that ended in the secession from his state. The story of Moses' preministry begins with his reaction to oppression, leads to his exile, and ends in his return to leadership:

> And it came to pass in those days, when Moses was grown, that he went out unto his brethren, and looked on their burdens: and he spied an Egyptian smiting an Hebrew, one of his brethren. And he looked this way and that way, and when he saw that there was no man, he slew the Egyptian, and hid him in the sand. . . .
> Now when Pharaoh heard this thing, he sought to slay Moses. But Moses fled from the face of Pharaoh, and dwelt in the land of Midian: . . .
> And the Lord said unto Moses in Midian, Go, return to Egypt: for all the men are dead which sought thy life. . . .
> And Moses and Aaron went and gathered together all the elders of the children of Israel: (Exod. 2:11–12, 15; 4:19, 29).

The main line of Jeroboam's early career develops from *both* an original prominence *and* a rebellion, which lead to his exile and return:

> And Jeroboam the son of Nebat, an Ephrathite, . . . Solomon's servant, . . . lifted up his hand against the king.
> And this was the cause that he lifted up his hand against the king: Solomon built Millo. . . .
> And the man Jeroboam was a mighty man of valour: and Solomon seeing the young man that he was industrious, he made him ruler over all the charge of the house of Joseph.
> And it came to pass at the time when Jeroboam went out of Jerusalem, the prophet Ahijah the Shilonite found him in the way; and he had clad himself with a new garment; and they two were alone in the field:
> And Ahijah caught the new garment that was on him, and rent it in twelve pieces: . . .
> Solomon sought therefore to kill Jeroboam. And Jeroboam arose, and fled into Egypt, unto Shishak king of Egypt, and was in Egypt until the death of Solomon. . . .
> And it came to pass, when all Israel heard that Jeroboam was come again, that they sent and called him unto the congregation, . . . (1 Kings 11:26–30, 40; 12:20)

Further, Jeroboam was in Egypt at the coronation of Rehoboam, "for he was fled from the presence of king Solomon, and Jeroboam dwelt in Egypt" (1 Kings 12:2). "To flee from the presence of " means to flee from the reach or jurisdiction of the court: hence the phraseology was also used for the flight of Moses at Exodus 2:15: "Moses fled from the face of Pharaoh, and dwelt in the land of Midian." And like Moses, Jeroboam originally enjoyed the patronage of the ruling house, both before his exile from that house, and before his return from exile to confront it.

Moses is called at Sinai during his exile in Midian, but only after being provoked into becoming the object of Pharaoh's enmity by Israel's suffering itself. Jeroboam is called from his exile in Egypt, but only after being tainted by the prophetic party's enmity to the idolatries of the Davidic regime in Judah. Moses' call at Sinai is framed by the two reports of the death of the Pharaoh: "And it came to pass in process of time, that the king of Egypt died" . . . "the Lord said unto Moses in Midian, Go, return into Egypt: for all the men are dead which sought thy life" (Exod. 2:23a, 4:19). In the Gospel of Matthew the angel in Joseph's third dream partly quotes God from this text: "for they are dead which sought the young child's life" (2:20). But for part of his story Matthew has in fact followed the account of Jeroboam, who "arose, and fled into Egypt . . . and was in Egypt until the death of Solomon" (1 Kings 11:40). For Joseph's second dream had told him he was to "flee into Egypt": "When he arose, he . . . departed into Egypt: And was there until the death of Herod" (Matt. 2:13–15a). Yet Matthew then applies Hosea's reference to the exodus to Joseph's Jeroboam-like departure: "that it might be fulfilled which was spoken of the Lord by the prophet, saying, Out of Egypt have I called my son" (2:15b). From the New Testament parallels and citations we might conclude that Jeroboam returns from exile to fulfill the same sign, or honor the same Mosaic precedent: *the call* out of *bondage Judah sold Joseph* into (Gen. 37:26–28).

Jeroboam is called by the prophet Ahijah, during the reign of Solomon; provoked by Ahijah's prediction, the king tries to kill the man he has formerly patronized. Jeroboam's call becomes a motif, since it happens twice more. Early blanks in Jeroboam's story have been partly filled by the Chronicler, for the "fill" (in 2 Chron. 10:2–3) has then been reproduced in 1 Kings 12:2–3a (MT, missing from the Septuagint, and thus added to our Hebrew text very late): "And it came to pass, when Jeroboam the son of Nebat, who was yet in Egypt, heard of it [i.e., Rehoboam's accession to his father Solomon's throne], (for he was fled from the presence of king Solomon, and Jeroboam dwelt in Egypt:) That they sent and called him." But this call is repeated, resumptively, after the people's rebellion, and so frames it: "And it came to pass, when all Israel heard that Jeroboam was come again, that they sent and called him unto the congregation and made him king over all Israel" (1 Kings 12:20, missing from 2 Chron. 10). As the text now stands, Jeroboam's double call by Israel—along with Israel's rebellion and their election of him—is itself framed by the accession of Rehoboam at Shechem and the fortification of Shechem by Jeroboam (1 Kings 12:1, "And Rehoboam went to Shechem: for all Israel were come to Shechem to make him king"; and 1 Kings 12:25a, "Then Jeroboam built Shechem in mount Ephraim, and dwelt therein"). The call frame is itself framed, by the larger frame of the visitation of Shechem by the two rival kings.

The call of Jeroboam and the visitation of Shechem thus form a double frame around the rebellion of Israel—the intervening narration reporting Jeroboam's advocacy of the Northern cause nonetheless credits Jeroboam himself with instigating the rebellion. Somewhat similarly, Moses is credited with two call stories, one placed in Exodus 3–4, before his first interviews with Pharaoh in Exodus 5, and one placed after, in Exodus 6:1–8. The interwovenness of the texts raises the same questions of temporal order about a "preministry": Was Moses rejected after his call, or was he called after being rejected? Was Jeroboam called by the people and drawn into the rebellion by the opportunity they presented, or was he responsible for drawing the people into rebellion, after he had been singled out by Ahijah's prophecy of his future part in sponsoring it, as Moses had been singled out as a leader by his murder of the overseer?

Parallels and divergences between sequences can be tabulated:

1. Moses kills an overseer who is abusing a Hebrew; he intervenes with a Hebrew abusing his fellow.

1. Jeroboam lifts up his hand against Solomon because of his building projects; he is made overseer of the Josephic labor levy; he is called by Ahijah because of the throne's idolatry.

Conclusions: the Egyptian abuse of the Hebrew in Exodus 2 constitutes a virtual calling of Moses; the throne's abuse of religion in 1 Kings constitutes an offense equivalent to Egypt's offenses against the Hebrews, *but so does its use of the house of Joseph's labor.*

2. The Hebrews reject Moses; Moses guesses he is in danger since his crime is known.

2. Solomon seeks Jeroboam's life; the reader infers that Ahijah's prophecy had become public knowledge.

Conclusions: Moses' murder of the Egyptian functions like a prophecy of the danger he poses to the sovereign or the sovereignty of the state; Jeroboam's collusion with the prophetic party poses a threat to the sovereignty of the state, and functions as an attempt on the sovereign's life.

3. Moses flies to Midian, beyond Pharaoh's jurisdiction.

3. Jeroboam flies to Egypt, beyond Rehoboam's jurisdiction.

4. Moses is called by God; Aaron arrives to support him and his call, and Pharaoh dies.

4. Solomon dies; Rehoboam succeeds him; Jeroboam hears of it and is called by the people.

Conclusions: Moses' being called by God in exile is exchangeable with Jeroboam's being called by the people from exile; the death of an oppressive incumbent functions as the call of new leaders to office.

5. Leaving a father-in-law in Midian, Moses returns to his people.

5. Leaving a host in Egypt, Jeroboam returns to his home.

6. Pharaoh and his court reject Moses' embassy and Pharaoh increases the Hebrews' burdens; their officers complain to Moses (Moses has asked to be able to go a three days' journey to sacrifice).

6. Rehoboam and his young counselors reject Jeroboam's embassy, where the elders advise lenience; Rehoboam vows to increase the burden (after asking for a three-day period to consider the people's petition).

7. Moses complains to God that he has not delivered his people; God promises that Pharaoh will drive the people out of Egypt altogether.

7. God hardens Rehoboam's heart to accomplish Ahijah's word; the people ask what portion they have in David, and secede from Judah.

8. Moses is called by God again as emissary to Pharaoh and Israel, but Israel cannot hearken to him.

8. The people stone the overseer whom Rehoboam sends to them.

Conclusion: again, as at (1), God's call to Moses is equivalent to the polarization of the parties to the conflict. But Moses here changes place with the rejected agent of the oppressor. The people will indeed want to stone Moses, at Exodus 17:4, but Moses also expects his people to be stoned by the Egyptians, for their religion, at Exodus 8:26. Each sequence reverses the cause and the consequence found in the other, but also doubles itself in so doing. Moses is rejected by the Hebrews after he kills the overseer, flies to Midian, and is called by God; he then parts from his father-in-law and returns to his people after the death of Pharaoh and is rejected by the new Pharaoh, and is called (again) by God. Jeroboam is called by Ahijah, is "rejected" by Solomon, and flies to Egypt; after the death of Solomon he is called (again) by the people and parts from his host Shishak and returns to his people, and is rejected by Rehoboam and is called by the people again after the people kill the overseer Adoram.

9. Moses at God's command goes to Pharaoh and does signs and wonders; Pharaoh's heedful advisors remonstrate with him.

9. The people call Jeroboam and make him king.

Conclusion: God's call to Moses equals the popular mandate in Kings (cf. 4–5). Egypt's and Rehoboam's courts both exhibit divided counsels (cf. 6).

10. Moses is permitted by Pharaoh to lead the people's exodus out of Egypt, but Pharaoh finally reneges, and sends his troops after the departed Israelites.

10. Jeroboam leads the secession of the ten tribes out of Judah and is made king of Israel by the people; Rehoboam mounts a force "to bring the kingdom again to Rehoboam" (1 Kings 12:21).

11. God intervenes to make the separation of the people from their former state final.

11. God intervenes to make the separation of the people from their former kingdom final.

12. In the absence of Moses Aaron makes the golden calf.

12. In the absence of Jerusalem Jeroboam puts golden calves at Bethel and Dan.

13. During the instituting of sacrifice Aaron's sons Abihu and Nadab die for offering "strange fire," and Israel mourns them while their father is prevented from doing so.

13. Upon the king's building the high places, Ahijah condemns Jeroboam's house; his son Abijah dies, Israel mourns him, and Nadab later dies for his father's sins, after his father's death.

This narrative double helix shows that the call of Moses, understood very broadly as all the forces impelling him to undertake the leadership of the exodus, has a hidden source in the tradition of the call of a successful schismatic leader. But unlike Jeroboam, Moses is not called by a prophet, but *as* one. We recognize in the call of Moses the call of a prophet, for prophets, like Moses, are called directly by God—only in the case of Elisha is a prophet called by another prophet. The tangle of prophets around the vocation of Jeroboam is typical of a certain kind of call to kingship. Moses is not called as a king; nonetheless, he shares his call with Jeroboam's kind of king. Not all kinds, however: for insofar as his throne belongs to his dynasty, the king is called from the womb, by a prophetic word spoken to his house. But insofar as one house is called to replace another, the word is spoken to one of the king's well-placed and potentially traitorous subjects, who thereafter comes to power through a coup, or through the death of his predecessor. After the establishment of the house of David in Judah, this pattern in Israel is Northern, rather than Southern. A typical example is the anointing of Jehu by a prophetic agent of Elisha in 2 Kings 9:1–3. Jehu is appointed to overthrow the house of Ahab in the reactivated words of Elijah against Ahab: "I will cut off from Ahab him that pisseth against the wall . . . And I will make the house of Ahab like the house of Jeroboam the son of Nebat" (2 Kings 9:8–9). These are words like those originally directed against Jeroboam himself (1 Kings 14:10–11), and they empowered the succession of the house of Baasha.

The missing element on Moses' side of the equation is the call of a potential dynast by a Mosaic prophet like Samuel or Elijah. The missing element on Jeroboam's side of the equation is the divine cowing or defeat of the prophetically condemned house by signs and wonders. But it is only after Moses' murder of the overseer that he is called and empowered by God to deal with Pharaoh with a prophetlike agency that finally leads to him presiding over the destruction of Pharaoh's chariots at the Reed Sea. Similarly, it is only upon the murder of his overseer Adoram that Rehoboam flies in his chariot back to Jerusalem; then a prophet named Shemaiah intervenes with a word of God to prevent Rehoboam's further attempt to bring the North back under the kingship in Judah by military means (1 Kings 12:18, 22–25). Rehoboam mounts a large force to recapture the prize, "to bring the kingdom again to Rehoboam the son of Solomon" (vs. 21), only to have it disbanded. In other words, Shemaiah intervenes in the narrative of the schism where God and Moses intervene—at the Reed Sea—in the narrative of Exodus.

Once he has been made king by the people, Jeroboam goes on to fabricate the golden calves in the North—as Aaron did, once Israel was out of Egypt and in the wilderness. In the absence of the temple, Jeroboam says the calves are the gods which brought his people out of Egypt. In the absence of Moses, Aaron says the calf is the "gods" which brought the people out of Egypt. Moses was on Sinai receiving instructions for building the tabernacle; so also the separated people of the North lack the temple their labor built for Solomon. Aaron's "gods" are thus in place of the Mosaic tabernacle, as Jeroboam's two calves are in place of the Jerusalem temple:

> And Jeroboam said in his heart, Now shall the kingdom return to the house of David:
> If this people go up to do sacrifice in the house of the Lord at Jerusalem, then shall the heart of this people turn again unto their lord, even unto Rehoboam king of Judah, and they shall kill me, and go again to Rehoboam king of Judah. (1 Kings 12:26–27)

This is a scenario also met in the motion of the original Israelites to go back to Egypt, and in their readiness to stone Moses (Exod. 17:4)—as Israel had stoned "Adoram, who was over the tribute" (1 Kings 12:18). Upon the death of Solomon Jeroboam revolted from the new representative of the ascendant dynasty, and took "Israel" out of the Jerusalem-based state to worship in secessionist shrines in the North—to worship, with Israel and Aaron of old, the golden calf, apart from the capital built with Israel's labor. Two of Aaron's four sons, who die at the altar in a repetition of the story of the worship of the golden calf, bear names analogous to those of Jeroboam's sons. With Aaron and Moses and the seventy elders, Nadab and Abihu have dined with God (Exod. 24:1, 11), yet they are numbered among the transgressors who die for sin (Num. 3:4, 26:61). Jeroboam's sons Abijah and Nadab are marked for death by the prophecy of Ahijah against the house of Jeroboam (1 Kings 15:29–30), and they die for the religious missteps of their father's house.[11]

Exodus 32 shows Moses rejecting the golden calf made by Aaron, and Numbers 12 shows God rebuking Aaron's and Miriam's challenge of Moses in the wilderness—God makes Miriam leprous. Moses, at Aaron's entreaty, intercedes to restore Miriam's health and bodily integrity. The question is, if Jeroboam stands in place of Aaron with his calves, as a latter-day Aaron who challenges Moses' pretensions and exalts himself in his place, then who is the Moses that rebukes him? The answer is, the Judaean man whom God sends to come before Jeroboam and deliver his word against the altar at Bethel, in 1 Kings 13. But this instance of a latter-day Yahwist against a latter-day idolator also recalls Moses originally speaking against Pharaoh. For Jeroboam strikes out against the prophetic messenger against Bethel and his arm is frozen in the midst of his evil gesture (vs. 4). Then at Jeroboam's plea, the prophet entreats God, and the king's affliction is relieved (vs. 6). This action is mixed in with the sign God makes of Jeroboam's stricken altar. If the shriveling and unshriveling of the king's arm is also a sign, it is surely the closest one in the Bible to the sign Moses was told to show before Pharaoh, the sign of the prophet's own stricken and cured hand. But Moses never shows this sign, even though it is the one that God says will surely compel Pharaoh's belief. We could argue that only when the man of God came before Jeroboam was the Mosaic sign of the withered hand finally shown in public. As if to confirm that the Exodus text is fulfilled by the action in the 1 Kings text, the first speaks, somewhat reduplicatively, of "the voice [*qôl*] of the latter sign" (Exod. 4:8), while the second text has the Judaean man of god saying, rather heavily, "On that same day he gave the sign, saying, this is the sign that Yahweh spoke" (1 Kings 13:3, AT).

The extended correspondence between the exodus from Egypt and the Israelite schism provides more than a secessionist typology for the Mosaic revolution; it also offers us something like a decisive suggestion for "the genesis of the exodus" itself. Furthermore, the typology points to one reason for the deep investment of the narrative in an ethos both revolutionary and separatist: the story of Jeroboam discovers a basis for this ethos in an intranational experience of fission. This basis is at least as historical as any we might reasonably find in the exodus story proper.

Landed immigrants within a foreign country, such as the Israelites are represented as being in Egypt, cannot themselves constitute a client-state, even if they may in time become an "internal colony." The Israel that revolts from Pharaoh is a state in name only, and it acquires its national holiday, celebrating membership in Israel, anachronistically and prematurely, before it can wholly know itself as a state. Yet the acquisition of the Passover in Egypt is constitutive. There is a similar festal institution for the disaffected Israel of the North. Jeroboam, according to the text of 1 Kings 12:32–33, "ordained a feast in the eighth month, on the fifteenth day of the month, like unto the feast that is in Judah": "So he offered upon the altar which he had made in Beth-el, the fifteenth day of the eighth month, even in the month which he had devised of his own heart." Associated at Leviticus 23:43 with booths which recognized the exodus, this feast serves as a memorial at the seat of the deity Jeroboam declared had delivered Israel from Egypt.

The feast of Jeroboam is historicized on the model of the Passover of Moses. The text of 1 Kings says Jeroboam designated the celebration in the middle of "the month which he had devised in his own heart," making his action very like that of God fixing the date of Passover: "This month shall be unto you the beginning of months . . . In the tenth day of this month . . ." (Exod. 12:2–3). Jeroboam might as well have said, in the words of God instituting the Passover, "This day shall be unto you for a memorial" (Exod. 12:14). Insofar as the Passover refers to the annual departure of the shepherd for new pastures, it refers to a tribal past that precedes the nation. But if it refers to the fission of one nation into two—a fission that is political—it dissimulates Israel's own internal history. Both God and Jeroboam align the feast with the seasonal cycle, God choosing a dividing point for shepherds, Jeroboam for farmers—his is a harvest feast.[12]

Here we may recur momentarily to the laws—the observance of the Sabbath and the prescription of the cult apparatus—that were allegedly being made at the time that the relics of Israel's itinerancy, like the brazen serpent and the ark, were themselves being made. The organization of time into the workweek implies life on the land, more than survival in the wilderness; and it likewise implies regular work within a schedule, more than wandering in the wilderness. Even the manna (in place of the Israelite kitchen) observes this workweek, by doubling its provision the day before the Sabbath (Exod. 16:5). The schedule could apply to life and work on any land, Egypt as well as Canaan.

Similarly, the organization of the cultic apparatus implies life within sacred precincts. And yet, insofar as the apparatus is described as portable, these precincts could be appointed or reappointed and transferred from one place to another, from the wilderness to Shiloh, where the ark was kept, and from Shiloh to Jerusalem, to which the ark was moved, and from Jerusalem to Beth-el, where Aaron's golden bullocks were established in place of the cherubim on the ark. The equipage of an itinerant people's priesthood stands in place of the adornment of a settled people's temples. God's sedan-chair is important to a people mobilized for war, since it allows sacral apparatus to be introduced as a palladium onto the battlefield.

Thus the most important Mosaic legislation, as attested by Exodus, corresponds to the two central facts of the departure from Egypt itself: (1) the dislodgment of a workforce seeking to schedule or reschedule its sacrifices or its holy days, and (2) the appointment of the apparatus for a priesthood seeking to settle or resettle its cult, or else seeking to avoid assimilating a more nomadic existence and a constant military campaign to local practice. The facts of this ancient legislation might apply better to Jeroboam's revolution than to Rehoboam's establishment.

Rehoboam, like Pharaoh in the time of Moses, vows to make the lives of the subject people harder, in reply to the intervention and appeal of their spokesman. Furthermore—again like Pharaoh, after he had used the subject people, or "Joseph," to build the royal cities—Rehoboam was divinely prevented from bringing Israel back within the fold by means of a pursuing army. "The word of God came unto Shemaiah the man of God, saying, Speak unto Rehoboam, the son of Solomon, king of Judah, and unto all the house of Judah and Benjamin, and to the remnant of the people, saying, Thus saith the Lord, Ye shall not go up, nor fight against your brethren the children of Israel: return every man to his house; for this thing is from me" (1 Kings 12:22–24). God rolls back Rehoboam's pursuit of Israel by means of the words of Shemaiah, which stand in place of Moses at the Reed Sea, intervening between opposed parties like the protective pillar of cloud (Exod. 14:19–20). As the waters hearkened to God's rebuke at the sea, so did Rehoboam's army, "an hundred and four-score thousand chosen men," when it "hearkened . . . to the word of the Lord, and returned to depart, according to the word of the Lord" (1 Kings 12:21, 24). To the dispersing army one may compare the disappearance of the dry land upon the completion of Israel's departure from Egypt: "and the sea returned to his strength . . . And the waters returned, and covered the chariots, and the horsemen, and all the host of Pharaoh that came into the sea after them" (Exod. 14:27–28).

The Egyptian troops at the Reed Sea are a double for the stricken firstborn, taken in revenge for the victims of genocide and slavery. The founder of the house of David is not reprehended for instituting the comparable labor levy, but he sins in his numbering of Israel, "eight hundred thousand valiant men that drew the sword": such able-bodied men must have been counted in anticipation of a draft (2 Sam. 24:9–10), even over the objection of David's own general Joab. Therefore the verse in 1 Kings 12 reporting the mustering of Rehoboam's very large force (vs. 21) is critical to our account, because military conscription is a labor levy in another form, even while it is also the means to enforce it. As the Israelites and particularly the Levites were redeemed from the death of the firstborn, so the people who have enlisted with Jeroboam are redeemed from Rehoboam's army. Its disbanding may have this relief in mind.

There is one final congruity between narratives of Israelite migration before the occupation of Canaan and the withdrawal of the North into its own kingdom there. Jeroboam, after the departure of his Israel from their "Egypt"—Judah—built Shechem and Penuel, appointed Bethel and Dan, and established religious houses on the high places (1 Kings 12:25, 28–29, 31–32). This building program completes the "Mosaic" revolution of the North, insofar as its four main sites—Shechem, Penuel, Bethel, and Dan—are all linked to activity that is specifically Yahwist and Josephic.

Three of the places built or appointed by Jeroboam are otherwise established in three so-called "E" stories of Jacob. Jacob purchased Shechem, in the North, from the Hamorites (Gen. 33:19), as the Abraham of the Priestly author purchased Hebron, in the South, from the Hittites, and as the David of a Judahite author purchased the temple site, in Jerusalem, from the Jebusites. At Shechem Jacob "erected an altar and called it El, the El of Israel" (Gen. 33:20, AT). Shechem is not only an El-site, but also a Yahwist one, for it is the first place, after Sinai itself, used for a national assembly in Yahweh's name, as convened by Joshua in Joshua 24. Penuel is similarly identified as both an El-site and a Yahwist one, it being the place where Jacob-Israel first asked the question that God would answer on Sinai, when Moses and Israel learned God's personal name "officially." As for Bethel, it is the place Jacob recognized as the house of God: this he later confirmed—after burying his people's foreign gods near Shechem—with an altar to the El who answered him in the day of his distress and who had been with him wherever he had gone (Gen. 35:1–4). Furthermore, Bethel is the place reconnoitered by spies from the tribe of Joseph at the onset of the occupation depicted in Judges 1:22–26. The Luzzite who is forced to cooperate with the spies, and is thereafter displaced from there to found his own Luz elsewhere, seems to belong to a theme of itinerancy otherwise attaching to Jacob himself; Jacob in effect reconnoiters the same site, upon his departure for the East.

In other words, insofar as Jacob traveled in the path created by the Northern circuit of Jeroboam's Yahwist and El sanctuaries, his itinerary (as found in the texts mainly assigned by traditional scholars to "E") is presented as proto-Mosaic. For each of the named places established by Jeroboam (after the North's departure from the "Egypt" of the South) is said to have been established, in one or another of the preceding biblical narratives in Genesis and Joshua and Judges, as a rallying point for a Yahwist assembly or revelation. We only seem to lack a "Northern genesis" for the sanctuary in Dan. Yet such a missing, pre-Jeroboamic original is found in the report of Judges 18:29–30, where a priest named Jonathan maintains a Yahwist image-worship in that place, formerly called Laish. This priest was descended directly from Moses. The image of Yahweh he maintained there remained in Dan "all the time that the house of God was in Shiloh" (Judg. 18:31). The alignment between Jonathan and Shiloh suggests that the Shilonite priesthood claimed Mosaic descent.

Shechem was purchased by Jacob before his descent into Egypt and used by Joshua after the return to Canaan (Gen. 33:19, Josh. 24:1). Bethel was visited by Jacob before his flight from Esau, and was consecrated after his return (Gen. 28:11–19, 35:1–15). Penuel was visited by Jacob before his reconciliation with Esau and built by Jeroboam after his rebellion from Rehoboam (Gen. 32:30–31, 1 Kings 12:25). Dan was appointed by Jonathan and the Danites before there was a kingship in Israel and again by Jeroboam after he had become king in the North (Judg. 18:14–30, 1 Kings 12:30). Like these other sites, Mount Sinai was also visited twice: first by Moses alone, before he had gone into Pharaoh, then by Moses with Joshua and Israel, after they had come out from Egypt. But if Jacob's journey is made in the footsteps of Northern Israel's, and Moses' journey is made in the footsteps of the Northern Jacob's, then Moses' own journey is made in the footsteps of Jeroboam's withdrawal from the South. It stands to reason that the various scenes of the appointments and revelations at Dan, Shechem, Penuel, and Bethel, inform—even while they are informed by—the greater scene of Moses at Sinai. Our vague feeling that Sinai cannot quite be fixed geographically, as if the mount were following Moses around, may owe something to the itinerancy of the Levites, especially in the North, but it also may owe a good deal to the journeys of Moses' own, latter-day prototypes.

Part C. The Mosaic Revolution and the Kingship in Judah

Jeroboam's altar at Bethel was first condemned by a prophet sent from God "out of Judah." The thing became a sign:

> And when the king heard the saying of the man of God, which he cried against the altar at Bethel, Jeroboam stretched out his hand from the

altar, saying, "Lay hold of him." And his hand, which he stretched out against him, dried up, so that he could not draw it back to himself. The altar also was torn down, and the ashes poured out from the altar, according to the sign which the man of God had given by the word of the Lord. (1 Kings 13:4–5, RSV)

The false prophet who had fatally interfered with the mission of this man of God died knowing better:

". . . For the saying which he cried by the word of the Lord against the altar in Bethel, and against all the houses of the high places which are in the cities of Samaria, shall surely come to pass." After this thing Jeroboam did not turn from his evil way, but made priests for the high places again from among all the people; any who would, he consecrated to be priests of the high places. And this thing became sin to the house of Jeroboam, so as to cut it off and to destroy it from the face of the earth. (1 Kings 13:32–34, RSV)

God, according to the prophecy of Jeroboam's subsequent nemesis Ahijah, "will cut off from Jeroboam him that pisseth against the wall, and him that is shut up and left in Israel, and will take away the remnant of the house of Jeroboam as a man taketh away dung, till it be all gone. Him that dieth of Jeroboam in the city shall the dogs eat; and him that dieth in the field shall the fowls of the air eat" (1 Kings 14:10–11). This colorful denunciation may recall words another man of Judah, David, uttered against another Northerner, Nabal of Carmel (1 Sam. 25:22). For all practical purposes a curse, it becomes proverbial; and God one day sends Elijah to direct most of it against Ahab: "In the place where the dogs licked the blood of Naboth shall dogs lick thy blood, even thine . . . Behold, I . . . will cut off from Ahab him that pisseth against the wall . . . , And will make thine house like the house of Jeroboam the son of Nebat . . . Him that dieth of Ahab in the city the dogs shall eat; and him that dieth in the field shall the fowls of the air eat" (1 Kings 21:19, 21–22, 24). Elijah's protégé Elisha will redirect this prophecy against Ahab's son Joram (2 Kings 9:8–10). Throughout Kings, the prophecies against the North on account of Jeroboam's sin are in counterpoint to the dispensation God makes to Jerusalem and David's house on account of David's election: Jeroboam was a curse, David a blessing.[13] All of the Northern disaster derives from Jeroboam's original apostasy.

This curse seems to be written into the conclusion that the narrative draws at the end of the golden calf episode in Exodus 32 itself: "And the Lord plagued the people, because they made the calf, which Aaron made" (vs. 35). Why describe Israel's apostasy in this double way, unless the text is leaving us the interpretive space we need to postulate an interval between the calf fabricated at Sinai and the ones that furnished Bethel and Dan? The Lord sent disaster upon the North, because Jeroboam had made the calf that Aaron made. The verdict reads like a kind of *prediction.* Another way of saying the same thing is, Jeroboam's revolution has been negatively theologized in the history descending from Jeroboam, even if it has by and large been positively theologized in the traditions attaching to Moses. Jeroboam, in fact, has been made to fear the rallying of the cult to Jerusalem. But the decisive centralization of the cult dates from a much later time, the time of Josiah. Therefore Jeroboam's fear is an *anticipation.* We could even argue that it was *Jeroboam,* not Josiah, who first proposed to centralize the cult, that is, to create—or rather endorse— a pair of *royal* sanctuaries in Bethel and Dan. Yet Jeroboam appears to have moved his own capital three times, from Shechem, to Penuel, to Tirzah; one guesses his program to centralize Northern power needed several tries. Why is anybody's guess: since the moves have not been theologically interpreted, neither have they been assigned a motive.

David's choice of Jerusalem, on the other hand, has been heavily theologized, even in what seems like very old material: at the instigation of the prophet Gad, at the end of a plague, David purchased a building site there, with the worship of God there in mind (2 Sam. 24:18–25). But David did not, in fact, build a temple in the royal city, and when Solomon did, it seems to have rapidly become a kind of polytheistic shrine, with floor space available for any god who could pay the going rate: or who had one of the royal consorts to lobby in his or her behalf.

At the same time that the succession of prophecies against Jeroboam, or against alleged Jeroboamic practice, was turning that king into a byword for Northern apostasy, another, somewhat parallel set of prophecies favoring the throne of David was turning Jerusalem into a guarantee that David's establishment of that city reflected a divine choice in its favor, corresponding to David's choice to put the ark there.[14] For whenever God is found asserting that the throne of David will not want for an heir, it is natural to assume that in God's grace toward David, David's city is (so to speak) thrown into the bargain. And by Hezekiah's time, Isaiah considers Jerusalem to be the main object of God's faithfulness, rather than the king.

The chain of prophecies penalizing "Jeroboam," and the analogous chain endowing "David," converge upon a latter-day fulfillment in the Josianic revolution depicted in 2 Kings 23–24. But the text makes these two chains derive from an original set of prophecies made against Bethel and Jeroboam in 1 Kings 13–14. The Southern prophet who comes to Bethel predicts that the Northern altar will be visited by a latter-day king, "Josiah by name." On that same altar, the man warns, "shall he offer the priests of the high places that burn incense upon thee" (1 Kings 13:2).

Thus the various prophetic words directed toward Jeroboam cast a long shadow across the text of the history of the kingship. His personal destiny is written into the regime of the idolatrous Solomon, his sinful house's fate into that of the murderous Ahab's house, and his polluted altars' desecration into the reform of the avenging Josiah. The effect is to contract the history from the tenth to the sixth centuries into God's prophetic word against the kingship's idolatrous religion. And yet this history only makes the point that the second Ahijah's words against Jeroboam, in 1 Kings 14, do not much differ from the first Ahijah's words against Solomon in 1 Kings 11, for they also invoke the regime's failure to honor the Davidic standard. It was King Solomon, not Jeroboam, who had originally departed from Mosaic obedience: Solomon did not keep God's "statutes and judgments, as did David his father" (1 Kings 11:33; also vs. 38); so Jeroboam, God says, "hast not been as my servant David, who kept my commandments" (1 Kings 14:8) As the culminating summary of the crimes of Manasseh in 2 Kings 21 makes clear, God had promised to secure the safety of an Israel that subscribed "to do according to all that [God had] commanded them, and according to all the law that [his] servant Moses commanded them" (vs. 8). As Solomon departed from his father David, so Manasseh departed from his father Hezekiah, who had destroyed the high places. And as Ahab had sinned and made a grove (1 Kings 16:33; 2 Kings 21:3), so also had Manasseh—but it was Jeroboam who had been the first to do this (1 Kings 14:15), in defiance of the commandment for Canaan's occupation at Exodus 34:13, "ye shall . . . cut down their groves," or Deuteronomy 16:21, "Thou shalt not plant thee a grove." But the children of Israel "forgat the Lord their God, and served Baalim and the groves" (Judges 3:7).

It falls to Josiah to clean up the long-standing mess of the failure to purify religion in Canaan. —Which brings us to the paradoxical point that the prophet Ahijah, in first prompting and virtually appointing Jeroboam to rebel against Solomon, is also ultimately appointing Josiah to undo the policies of Manasseh. For "there remained the grove also in Samaria" (2 Kings 13:6) and as Hezekiah "brake the images, and cut down the groves" in Judah (2 Kings 18:4), so also would Josiah "brake . . . the images, and cut down the groves" (2 Kings 23:14). Josiah also destroyed the idolatrous altars of former kings, including "the altars which Manasseh had made in the two courts of the house of the Lord": he "cast the dust of them in the brook Kidron," as Moses had strewn the powder of the golden calf upon the water at Sinai (2 Kings 23:12, Exod. 32:20).

The nameless emissary to the North from Judah was specific about the identity of the future desecrator of the altar at Bethel, and in the text he is enabled to speak in the yet-to-be invented Isaianic idiom for the advent of a Judaean deliverer-prince, three hundred years in advance of the day to come: "Behold," he tells Jeroboam's altar, "a child shall be born unto the house of David, Josiah by name; and upon thee shall he offer the priests of the high places that burn incense upon thee" (1 Kings 13:2). So we read in Isaiah 7:13–14: "Hear ye now, O house of David . . . Behold, a virgin shall conceive, and bear a son," and 9:6, "and the government shall be upon his shoulder: and his name shall be called Wonderful . . ." The fifth king from the first king Saul—Jeroboam—consecrates the Northern altar, and the fifth king from the last king Zedekiah—Josiah—desecrates it.

As the mixed fate of the prophet out of Judah might suggest, such a dialectic also controls the main narrative of the exodus: Moses is made anathema in one state (Egypt) at the same time he is invested with divine office in another (Israel). The question is, what happens when we map that "Northern" dialectic upon the other, "Southern" one, whereby Aaron is made Yahweh's priest in Israel at the same time that he is ministering to Israel's apostasy from Yahweh in the wilderness? For Aaron's first act of priestly ministration to the congregation (after many such acts toward Egypt) offers itself as a replacement for the departed Moses, as if it stood for a reconsolidation of the priestly service in Jerusalem, upon the departure of a prophetic element (the "Josephic" Moses) out of it. How is Moses brought back into the fold, and the narrative? How does the narrative represent the reappointing of Jerusalem with a Mosaic charge?

As we have elsewhere seen, the most immediate and attested of the commandments—of the Mosaic law, statutes, and inscribed stone tables—concern two obligatory observances: first, the prohibition of the fabrication of religious or cult objects insofar as they pertain to other gods and the corresponding fabrication of religious or cult objects insofar as they belong to the worship of Yahweh; and, second, the observance of the Sabbath as a holy day. So far as these two observances are concerned, the inscribing of laws on stone tables might seem to be somewhat beside the point: the calendar is already fixed in nature by the lunar cycle (though Isaiah's God hates Israel's new moon feasts, in Isaiah 1:14), and the stone tables could be a particularly inconvenient or inappropriate cult object for a migratory people. The rules for the priestly hardware and the ark found in the Pentateuch seem to replace the appointment of the kind of sacred sites where the law tables could be kept. In Deuteronomy, where such a site is in fact appointed, the specifications for the hardware and the tabernacle drop out. The keeping of the tables seems to replace *them.*

The fixing of the texts on stone seems to belong to a "national heritage" and "national confession" mentality that it is probably anachronistic for an early Israel to be credited with. Yet the tablets themselves anticipate their being kept in a sanctuary and a capital, or as a landmark. Weights and measures are kept at the Bureau of Standards, and clock-time is kept at Greenwich: so the stone tables will be deposited in "the ark of the covenant," according to Deuteronomy, and it will be honored in Jerusalem, according to the narrative of the dedication of Solomon's temple. The appointment of Jerusalem with the institutions of the law is surely one of the intentions of the ark narrative, as interpreted *à la* Deuteronomy. David's insistence that "the ark of the covenant of God" (2 Sam. 15:24) remain in Jerusalem, at the time of the court's own flight from the city, may be an early joining of David's choice of Jerusalem with God's choice of the same place in Deuteronomy. The deuteronomic text itself conserves a "standardized" account of the Sinai events, much like the one that everyone must rely on in any attempt to paraphrase the unparaphraseable whole. Moses' instructions to the people at Deuteronomy 27 also prophesy Israel's reaching such a point:

> And it shall be on the day when ye shall pass over Jordan unto the land which the Lord thy God giveth thee, that thou shalt set thee up great stones, and plaster them with plaster:
> And thou shalt write upon them all the words of this law, when thou art passed over, that thou mayest go in unto the land which the Lord thy God giveth thee, . . .
> Therefore it shall be when ye be gone over Jordan, that ye shall set up these stones, which I command you this day, in mount Ebal, and thou shalt plaster them with plaster.
> And there shalt thou build an altar unto the Lord thy God, an altar of stones: . . .
> And thou shalt write upon the stones all the words of this law very plainly. (Deut. 27:2–5, 8)

Presumably such a "lawgiver's Mount Rushmore" would exhibit the code which begins from Deuteronomy's twelfth chapter. This code begins by legislating the confinement of the cult's sacrifices to an elect central place.

This agenda might well strike one as directly contrary to the original spirit of the exodus, which begins from the motion to take Israel's cult out into the wilderness. It obviously makes some sense to explain the stone tables as existing on file, as the record of an agreement or contract, analogous to a deed of title to property, or a written agreement to an engagement for services, or a document of bequeathal, or a certificate of adoption. But the Mosaic tables, in keeping with the spirit of the exodus, are not in fact originally kept in a Sinaitic cairn on the site where they were given—the site where God engaged to make Israel his people, or to hearken unto their initiate's cry for divine adoption. The archival conservation of the tablets in the portable ark is a rather ingenious version of that kind of Near Eastern treaty-keeping in which the contracting parties made their deposition in a fixed repository that was also a landmark (cf. the cairn put between Jacob and Laban in Genesis 31:51–54).

In conjunction with prescriptions for what was to become the temple apparatus, the depositing of the ark in Jerusalem suggests that the narrative of Sinai has been folded over with the story of Zion. And this in turn suggests that not only are we to read Jerusalem for Sinai but, conversely, that we are also to read, in the substitution of Sinai for Jerusalem, the dislodgement of Israel from Jerusalem to some "mount of the congregation" other than Zion (cf. Isa. 14:13). Sinai may not seem so portable as the ark, but if it is less locatable as a place than as a presence, it too belongs to a psychology that seems more Northern and theophanic than Southern and ceremonial. As for the ark itself, one is inclined to describe it as originally a Northern and Mosaic institution that was eventually coopted by David and the capital: for the unification of Israel around Jerusalem. The setting up of the golden calves in the North might then appear as a countermove, an attempt to reclaim an exodus tradition of the South, God's *enthronement* amongst his people, for the renewing of the sanctuaries of the North.

In the incident in Leviticus 10 two of the four sons of Aaron, Abihu and Nadab, die, burnt to death by the divine wrath at the very altar they serve; comparably, the prophet Ahijah accuses Jeroboam of idolatry, and predicts the death of the king's sons Abijah and Nadab. Leviticus 10 is thus an excellent early example of Auerbach's principle that the material of the Old Testament comes closer to history as the narrative proceeds. For while the events of this chapter seem to go back to the story of the Levites whom Moses condemned and executed for following Aaron in the worship of the golden calf in Exodus 32, they also seem to go forward to the death of the sons of Jeroboam whom Ahijah dooms at the division of the kingdom and the appointment of a new Northern priesthood in 1 Kings 12–14. In Leviticus 10 Aaron learns how to deal with a dead body within the sacred precincts without impairing the continuity of his functions as a priest; at the same time he must assent to the loss of half his corporation, while being condemned for not completing a ritual that perhaps cannot be completed for its having been interrupted by the punishment of those who did not complete it! Such a story seems to be made up of two stories, one about the instituting of an Aaronid priesthood, and the other about *de*-instituting it. For in the same measure that the interruption of the priestly or national history has become a part of the original priestly ceremonies, the interruption of the original priestly ceremonies has become a part of the priestly or national history. Thus we can take the report of the death of Aaron's sons Nadab and Abihu to allude not only to the fate of the Northern kingship, but also to the fate of a would-be Aaronid priesthood within it.

The prophet who originally accosted Jeroboam with his destiny as a revolutionary leader bore the name Ahijah (1 Kings 11:29), and so did the prophet who denounced Jeroboam for having departed from Davidic obedience to God and for having made himself other gods and molten images (1 Kings 14:4, 18–19): the two Shilonic prophets seem to be the same man. One must also reckon with the Judaic king Abijah or Abijam: in 2 Chronicles 13:4–9 it is the *king* of this name who accuses Jeroboam of rebellion, idolatry, simony, and ritual fault. And this Abijah especially accuses Jeroboam of having sold away the offices rightly possessed by an Aaronid or Levitical priesthood. The deuteronomistic narrator-editor in 1 Kings 13:32–34 agrees. Jeroboam "made priests for the high places again from among all the people; any who would, he consecrated to be priests of the high places"—*this* was the thing that "became sin unto the house of Jeroboam, even to cut it off, and to destroy it from off the face of the earth" (1 Kings 13:33 [RSV]–34[AV]). In 1 Kings 13:1–10 it is a nameless "man of god" out of Judah who makes the analogous accusations; he comes to Bethel to predict that, in the latter day, the Davidic king Josiah will burn the bones of the evil priesthood at Bethel on its altar: could he have been the voice of an embassy coming directly from King Abijah in Judah? The *altar's* offense, however, is not named by this man of God, except in this: "the priests of the high places that burn incense upon thee" (1 Kings 13:2). Is there a reminiscence here of Aaron's two sinful sons Nadab and Abihu who, in Leviticus 10:1, "took either of them his censer, and put fire therein, and put incense thereon, and offered strange fire before the Lord"?

As a sign of the divine wrath that the altar of Jeroboam is kindling in the presence of the man out of Judah, the altar suddenly smokes in anticipation of the fulfilling of the prophecy of the future burning of men's bones upon it. Jeroboam is paralyzed when he attempts to interfere with the Yahwist prophet, as Moses' sister Miriam was struck with leprosy when she and Aaron objected to Moses' Egyptian wife. But the Southern leadership was no less chargeable, for it was the earlier Ahijah, the prophet of Shiloh, who had accused Solomon of having committed idolatry, and who originally appointed Jeroboam the future king over the ten Northern tribes (1 Kings 11:30–39). A particular occasion of this idolatry was Solomon's Egyptian marriage, which would have sealed his kingship's covenants with Pharaoh.

Three hundred and more years after the Ahijah who commissioned Jeroboam, and the man of God who poured his smoke-generating contumely on the king's practice at the altar, the Judaic king Josiah did indeed burn a Northern shrine, conforming to the ancient denunciation and prophetic sign. At 2 Kings, Josiah's reform (ca. 620 B.C.) is credited with a widely publicized strike against the former sanctuary at Bethel. For Josiah actually goes on to honor and preserve his bygone and anonymous predecessor's memory—the "man of god" who came out of Judah in 1 Kings 13:1. At 2 Kings 23:15–16 Josiah has to come to Bethel to desecrate the graves of those who have served the Northern altars, whereupon he asks the question that serves to align the whole narrative with its beginnings in 1 Kings 13:

> Then he said, What title [or 'monument'] is that that I see? And the men of the city told him, It is the sepulchre of the man of God, which came from Judah, and proclaimed these things that thou hast done against the altar of Beth-el.
> And he said, Let him alone; let no man move his bones. So they let his bones alone, with the bones of the prophet that came out of Samaria. (2 Kings 23:17–18)

Thus "the prophet that came out of Samaria" is *also* Josiah's ancient precursor: Josiah's proscription on desecrating the Judaean prophet's grave seconds the original reverential motions of the old, rival prophet dwelling at Bethel at the time of Ahijah's denunciation of its altar.

The Samaritan rival was a kind of "lying prophet"; he attempted to deflect the man of god out of Judah from his commission, and his partial success in doing this cost the true prophet his life. But then the rival asked to be buried with the Southerner; for the man of Judah's violent death—punishment of his disobedience to one of the original divine conditions set for his prophetic mission—had proved him to be the true prophet. The second prophet prophesies the vindication of the first, and, like Josiah, joins in honoring a vindicated and deceased colleague.

As we have previously noted, the narrative frames the whole royal history by means of the sinful fifth king from the first king Saul, namely Jeroboam, and the sinless fifth king from the last king Zedekiah, namely Josiah. Analogous circular structures seem to be imposed on the story at both ends. Jeroboam, at the instance of the prophet Ahijah, takes Israel out of the Judah that contained Solomon's idolatrous temple only to commit it to the religious sins denounced by—the prophet Ahijah. Josiah finds, in the Book of the Law, what he must have already known—namely, the Mosaic law of devotion to Yahweh—in order to have found the writing in the course of repairing the temple. Likewise, the same king comes to Samaria to learn that the Northern altar was someday to be destroyed by somebody like himself: what he must have already known, again, if that was his purpose in going to Bethel from the outset. Jeroboam speaks as a second Aaron, and provides a model for the religiously compromised first one of Exodus 32. Josiah acts as a second Moses, and provides a model for the devoted latter-day Moses of Deuteronomy—and Exodus 32.

Josiah's strike against the rival sanctuary revives a history of conflict between Southern and Northern cults somewhat atavistically—for the North, as a viable political entity, had fallen to Assyria a century before. Josiah's contemporary Jeremiah prophesies that Jerusalem will become the new ark of the Mosaic covenant with God (Jer. 3:16–17), and Deuteronomy (12:5–6, 10–11, 13–14, 21, 26) legislates the migration of God's name to this single place. The campaign against the high places, regularly associated by the deuteronomic historian with following the example of David, is thus seen as finally leading to Josiah's desacralizing of all worship sites except Jerusalem. But why would the wilderness Moses have been a plausible ideological ally against the shrines in the countryside and the North?

The questions may be, why was worship at the high places so attractive, and what might have dissociated Yahweh's religion from its obvious ritual concomitant, animal sacrifice? The stories of meat-eating in the wilderness seem to offer us a clue. For the deuteronomic Moses disjoins sacrifice to God from meat-eating within the worshiper's home territory: "If the place which the Lord thy God hath chosen to put his name there *be too far from thee,* then thou shalt kill of thy herd and of thy flock, which the Lord hath given thee, as I have commanded thee, and thou shalt eat in thy gates whatsoever thy soul lusteth after" (Deut. 12:21). Deuteronomy decriminalized the eating of meat apart from Jerusalem—now it could be legitimately consumed outside of religious auspices. As Moses separated Israel from the pagan fleshpots of Egypt (Exod. 16:3), so Deuteronomy separated the worshiper from the priestly fleshhooks of local sanctuaries (cf. 1 Sam. 2:13–14, Exod. 27:3, 38:3, Num. 4:14). The deuteronomist divests Jerusalem of exclusive rights over meat sacrifice, even while investing this city with exclusive rights over the divine name and the three major festivals. His law, we may note, sounds much like Jeroboam's speech at 1 Kings 12:28: "*It is too much for you* to go up to Jerusalem." Thus Jeroboam may have originally sanctioned meat-eating in the Northern shrines as an incentive—like Moses giving Israel the quails apart from Egypt—in order to take away from the sway of Jerusalem. The quails carpeted the camp with their flesh for a space it would take a day to travel across (Num. 11:31). Bethel is a day's journey from Jerusalem.

Josiah may not have been the first king to insist on placing God's altar exclusively in the city of David. According to one way of reading 2 Kings 18:22, this may also have been the policy of Hezekiah. Around 690 B.C. he destroyed the brazen serpent kept in the temple, which also housed the ark and the tabernacle (cf. 2 Chron. 5:5). The serpent was portable, and perhaps it was a Northern relic—Hezekiah came to the throne in Judah within a few years of the North's fall. With the prophet Isaiah, he staked his faith on Jerusalem's not being moved. Perhaps this faith required a breach with the exodus past formerly enshrined in the North. For just as it is the deuteronomic word of God that nourishes, and not the literal manna, so it is the word of God that heals, and not the actual serpent (Wisd. of Sol. 16:6–7, 11–12). "The brasen serpent that Moses had made" thus stands opposite "the calf, which Aaron made" (2 Kings 18:4, Exod. 32:35). Deuteronomy only refers to Aaron as someone Israel had to bury (Deut. 10:6, 32:50), but Hezekiah apparently distinguished between Zadokite and other Aaronid and Levitical priests, Levitical priests and other kinds, and other priests and nonpriestly users of the sacrificial auspices (2 Chron. 31:10, 31:2, 29:34, 30:2–4 and 15–18). If this implies an elevation of the status of the sons of Aaron over the other rank and file, it may also imply less status for any Mushite priesthood arriving in Jerusalem from the fallen North.

In the case of either Hezekiah or Josiah, we meet a loss of faith in the saving separatism of the exodus and Sinai in favor of the centrality of Jerusalem and Zion. But the deuteronomic history, following the prophecies of chapter 28 of Deuteronomy itself, ends, like Jeremiah in Egypt, with the captivity. And yet the pentateuchal Moses anticipates the Restoration, by anticipating the occupation of the land, like Ezekiel closing his canon by re-allotting Canaan to the tribes of Israel (cf. Num. 26:53–56 with Ezk. 47:21–23). Joshua likewise divides and apportions the land (Josh. 18:10, 13:7, 23:4) as Ezra rebuilt the temple, the visionary Moses standing in relation to the judge as the visionary Ezekiel stood in relation to the priest. Ezra ends with the Israelites forswearing marriages to "the Canaanites, the Hittites, the Perizzites, the Jebusites, the Ammonites, the Moabites, the Egyptians, and the Amorites" (9:1, 10:3, 5). The discovery and putting away of strange wives at the end of Nehemiah will be the overall history's last version of Israel's repenting of the sins that began in the wilderness. "Pardon, I beseech thee," Moses prays in Numbers 14:19—as if he were referring to the God of Exodus 34:6–7 from a very great remove in historical time—"the iniquity of this people, according unto the greatness of thy mercy, and as thou hast forgiven this people, from Egypt *even until now.*"

·16·

LIKE UNTO AARON: THE GOLDEN CALF AND THE HISTORY OF THE PRIESTLY REVELATION TO ISRAEL

> And the Lord plagued the people, because they made the calf, which Aaron made. (Exod. 32:35)

> How can I curse whom God has not cursed?
>   How can I denounce whom the Lord has not denounced? . . .
> God brings them out of Egypt;
>   they have as it were the horns of the wild ox. . . .
> God brings him out of Egypt;
>   he has as it were the horns of the wild ox. . . .
>   (Balaam's oracles, Num. 23:8, 22; 24:8, RSV)

We can hardly tell if there was a real Moses, as opposed to there being a need to invent him: that is, the need of various latter-day parties, contesting for the endorsement of various national policies, to appeal to the manufactured precedent of an authoritative founder-figure and an authoritative series of founding events. The Davidic party would invent a Moses who served Zion and the Creator and the Lord of hosts (hosts in the narrower, military sense), and who appointed Caleb his land (Judges 1:20) and "the sons of Aaron" their duties in the tabernacle that was to become the temple of Solomon. The Northern party would invent a Moses who appointed the Ephraimite Joshua, remembered Ephraim's father Joseph, challenged an illegal society in which Joseph had become unknown, and removed his people from it. The High Priestly party would invent a Moses who needed Aaron's professional help more than Hur's, in reaction to their own, priestly authority needing support—support to be derived from a relation to "Moses," or from a role in the dissemination of Mosaic rulings and teachings. Yet the priesthood, either the disaffected and dispossessed party of Abiathar in the North or the rival Zadokite party in the

South, would invent a Moses who purged, respectively, the Jeroboamic interlopers and half the Levites, when they were found in the idolatrous service of golden calves, or a Moses who dismissed the deaths—at the altar—of half the sons of Aaron when they introduced "strange fire" into the priesthood's original sacrifices. Later Yahwist moralists (especially the author of Deuteronomy) would invent an aging Moses who appealed, with deliberate anachronism, to Israel's long-standing yet short-lived covenant with God.

Thus all parties might agree upon at least one thing: the appropriation of Moses for various versions of an authoritative narration embodying the national purpose and agenda. Moses' mission became associated with the exodus traditions he taught, or which were taught by persons speaking in his name, and so he became the acknowledged and settled place for each party to recover its roots and traditions, even if, in an act of faith, these roots and traditions had to be transplanted back to a legendary past, in order for the party to make this claim on them. For all of the parties had invested themselves in the Moses of the exodus: yet this is only to say, in a Moses belatedly established by texts like those we now have about him. Moses the Levite and priest, the pilgrim to Kadesh, the dweller in the wilderness, the sojourner in Midian, the planner of an Israelite occupation of Canaan, the teacher of a set of laws or divine judgments, the assayer and proclaimer of the will of the Israelite god, the initiate into the god's ways: none of these biographical elements absolutely requires the association of Moses with an emergence of Israel out of Egypt as a people, or a constituting of that people at Sinai or in Moab as God's nation. It may not only be modesty that keeps Moses out of his account, in Deuteronomy 26:3–9, of the Israelite's confession of the founding history.

Part A. Idolatry and Duality

The tracts of text in Exodus 25–31 and 35–40 concerned with the ("Priestly") blueprint for the tabernacle, like the corresponding texts in Ezekiel 40–48 (those containing a blueprint for the second temple), make the best sense if they are seen as implying a double motion: in Ezekiel's case, a motion to take a cult into exile is also a motion to bring it out from there. In Exodus, as in the golden calf speech of Jeroboam (1 Kings 12:28), the motion to remove from the established rulership is also a motion to relocate the cult. In Moses' case, the reason to go into the wilderness is to provide for auspices apart from the jurisdiction of Pharaoh and Egypt, but this reason has its intra-Israelite counterpart in Aaron's motion to provide for a worship apart from Moses on the theophanically consecrated mountain Sinai. In Jeroboam's case, the comparable reason— or countermotion—is to provide for the cult apart from "David" and the theophanically consecrated Jerusalem temple or "Mount Zion." Given that in the tabernacle texts the cherubs have wings, this initiative has everything to do with the character of the Israelite god as he appears in the theophanies of Ezekiel: you can take Ezekiel's god out of the temple, but you cannot take the temple out of Ezekiel's god.

One of the four faces of the hybrid vehicle for Ezekiel's god is indeed bovine. Yet Ezekiel's conception, with its templar attributes, does not divide the oneness or unity of God. In contrast, Aaron only produces one calf, and yet he refers to it in the plural, as "gods" (Exod. 32:1, 4, 8; Moses also, in vs. 31, refers to "gods of gold"). This detail keeps characterizing Aaron's worship as idolatrous. Here we may pause for theological reflection on the Israelite ban on images. Why do so very many of the normative Mosaic narratives we have visited (and others that we might have looked at, such as that of Gideon and the ephod he makes in Judges 8:24–27) turn so often upon the forbidden recourse to images? Why is this such a *central* narrative "interruption"? What conflict insists on being narrated or reenacted as divisive here? Of course it is the essence of the Yahwist to turn to Yahweh in the same motion that he turns against the images of strange gods. Yet even when the Yahwist turns *to* such an image, as Gideon does, there is a feeling that the worshiper has not wholly abandoned Yahweh, despite a considerable technical mistake about access or service to him. The image-breaking narratives obviously declare that God should not be fetishized in image worship, and that God is an invisible spirit only truly known through the heart. But these truisms need not be peculiar to Israel.[1] God is known in his word in the Bible, but a deity directing his utterance toward a worshiper can hardly be unique to Israel. God is not known by the images of pagan cult, yet the appearance of a deity to a devotee at a shrine or altar or sacrifice or chosen site is hardly unheard of in Israel, and neither, given the ark and the tabernacle, are votive objects. Yet "the idols have spoken vanity" (Zech. 10:2), which means that the true prophet characterizes even vain oracles as idolatrous. Similarly, the fiery theophanies of Yahweh cannot help suggesting that other, artificial images are vain, partly because they are combustible.

The phenomenology of religion in general is not the target of the biblical diatribe. It needs no Moses to tell us that God wants heart service, not eye service. Yet image worship is taboo on several other grounds: whether the image is the bureaucratized remains of animism, or a tool employed in place of a familiar, it cannot copy the truth about Yahweh, or serve the purpose of his worship. Yahweh is not *like* the images. They are many, and he is one; they are dumb, and he is outspoken; they are impassive or indifferent, and he makes his spirits a flaming fire; they nod, he fulminates; they are on the high places, he is everywhere; they are made, yet it is the Maker who dwells in glory. They are mediating likenesses, and he is no likeness—not of anything in heaven or earth.[2] Though he is likened to a great many things, man in particular, there are nonetheless none *like* him. He is solely as he is, and statuary cannot copy his essence without also irremediably denying it. The statues miss God's life, holiness, solity, jealousy, moral character, truthfulness, substantiality, comprehensiveness, and glory. There is no conceding of these attributes to the idols (cf. Isa. 42:8).

In the narratives of Exodus 32–34, it follows, God is revealing himself to Israel *by means of* the destruction of the calf. For the iconoclastic act reveals God precisely at the point where other means for representing him are exhausted. The iconoclastic act is thus itself a form of his worship and service. So the logic whereby the two great tabernacle texts, Exodus 25–31 and 35–40, frame the destruction of the calf and the esoteric revelation of the glory to Moses. This revelation is the logical sequel of the iconoclastic act. In spite of its gold, the idol is not glorious; its *destruction* is glorious, that is, this alone glorifies the living God who is like no other, and whose tabernacle only his *name* can truly exalt.

Because Israel commits idolatry while it is covenanting, treaties with Egypt and Mot, like trust in the military hardware of other states, can also be understood as a defection to idols, and consequently as a failure to glorify the power of God. The rationale for the destruction of the "gods" or idol of Aaron in the midst of the giving of the law now reemerges. God is worshiped in truth by means of the destruction of the images or appearances of false gods, which destroys the *covenant* with them.

The idols were made while the tables were made: the tables forbade idolatry, or convenanting with foreign gods, at the same time the associated legislation was prescribing cherubs for the ark. The tables were broken, and the idols were also broken. Then the tables were renewed, and the cherubs were manufactured out of the same kind of stuff as the idols. The data are peculiarly coordinated, or paralleled in their members, as if they were two different accounts of the same thing, while claiming to be the same account of two different things. For the tables were to come to rest in the Jerusalem-based ark of the deuteronomist, but the Yahwist or Mosaic ark was decorated by cherubs. The covenant is no less a votive object than the bullocks; the cherubs are an acceptable icon, if it is God's holiness and the sacred covenant with him that they guard and represent.

In Aaron's account, moreover, the bullock itself is described with an unforgettable trace of a true theophany:

> And Aaron said, Let not the anger of my lord wax hot: thou knowest thy people, that they are set on mischief.
> For they said unto me, Make us gods, which shall go before us: for as for this Moses, the man that brought us up out of the land of Egypt, we wot not what is become of him.

And I said unto them. Whosoever hath any gold, let them break it off. So they gave it me: then I cast it into the fire, *and there came out this calf.* (Exod. 32:22–24)

Aaron's speech varies from the narrator's own report, by making the emergence of the calf a spontaneous action for which Aaron is not himself responsible. This is virtually Aaron's version of the story of the burning bush, and moreover his version of Balaam's oracles at Numbers 23:22 and 24:8a: Israel came out of Egypt *like a wild ox.* Here then is the Northern miracle missing from the 1 Kings account of Jeroboam's establishment of the rival sanctuaries, where the bullocks must be "gods"—plural—one for the "southern" Bethel, and one for the "northern" Dan:

> Whereupon the king took counsel, and made two calves of gold, and said unto them, It is too much for you to go up to Jerusalem: behold thy gods, O Israel, which brought thee up out of the land of Egypt.
> And he set the one in Beth-el, and the other put he in Dan. (1 Kings 12:28–29)

For why would the text's Moses have called Aaron's bullock "gods," in the plural, at Exodus 32:31, unless Aaron, the ancestor of the Jerusalem priesthood, was being accused preemptively (by a North-favoring author), the very charges against the Jerusalem priesthood being lodged against him that were lodged against the schismatic Northern sanctuaries, its "molten gods," "gods of gold"? Is this what happens when one of Israel's two kingdoms redirects the biblical diatribe against idolatry and non-Yahwist covenants, against Yahwist worship and covenants as found in the other state, in order to make its rival guilty of an indignity to the oneness of God?

The Bible's depiction of Jeroboam accommodating the northern and southern reaches of Northern Israel, by means of two separate divine thrones, each with its own idol, seems to call into question the unity of the deity from the outset, thus invalidating any claim that the idols were originally representations of God's presence. In contrast, the two cherubs that form one (ultimately Jerusalemnic) footstool seem to affirm God's unity, while denying that the cherubs are his image—since God is singular, and the cherubim plural. But Ezekiel's quadrate god was likewise one, and his oneness is successfully taken out of the temple, when the temple falls. Ezekiel's visionary strategy failed in the schism, however, three and a half centuries before. God can seemingly migrate out of the country to Babylon, but he could not migrate out of the city of David, except in the received script of the defection of Aaron.

In the earlier of his two reports to Moses, God attributes the actions of Aaron (at Exodus 32:1–4) to an apostate people; it was they who made the calf and said "These be thy gods, O Israel, which have brought thee up out of the land of Egypt" (Exod. 32:8). The dedication of Solomon's temple is joined to both Sinaitic epiphenomena and Mosaic institutions:

> And the priests brought in the ark of the covenant of the Lord unto his place, . . . under the wings of the cherubims.
> For the cherubims spread forth their two wings over the place of the ark, and the cherubims covered the ark and the staves thereof above.
> And they drew out the staves, . . . and there they are unto this day.
> There was nothing in the ark save the two tables of stone, which Moses put there at Horeb, when the Lord made a covenant with the children of Israel, when they came out of the land of Egypt.
> And it came to pass, when the priests were come out of the holy place, that the cloud filled the house of the Lord,
> So that the priests could not stand to minister because of the cloud: for the glory of the Lord had filled the house of the Lord.
> Then spake Solomon, The Lord said that he would dwell in the thick darkness.
> I have surely built thee an house to dwell in, a settled place for thee to abide in for ever. . . .
> And he said, Blessed be the Lord God of Israel, which spake with his mouth unto David my father, and hath with his hand fulfilled it, saying,
> Since the day that I brought forth my people Israel out of Egypt, . . .
> (1 Kings 8:6–13, 15–16)

Aaron, Jeroboam, and Solomon all dedicate their different shrines with the exodus formula of a deity who brings forth out of Egypt.

In 1 Kings 8:10–11 God's glory prevents Solomon's priests from re-occupying the temple; the Mosaic precedents conclude Exodus:

> And [Moses] took and put the testimony into the ark, and set the staves on the ark, . . .
> And he brought the ark into the tabernacle, and set up the veil of the covering, and covered the ark of the testimony; . . .
> Then a cloud covered the tent of the congregation, and the glory of the Lord filled the tabernacle.
> And Moses was not able to enter into the tent of the congregation, because the cloud abode thereon, and the glory of the Lord filled the tabernacle. (Exod. 40:20–21, 34–35)

The portability of the ark would always be present in the temple, to emphasize before the priests that the sacred relic was the possession of the people descended from the one who had been called out of Moses' Egypt. But, one asks, did this mean they were also called out of Aaron's idolatry?

Parallel to the golden bullocks in the North, the cherubim in the South became part of the Southern (Judaean) definition of God, the God who could hear king Hezekiah's prayer in the time of Sennacherib's siege of Jerusalem. Hezekiah prays not to the deliverer but to the Creator, to the "Lord God of Israel, which dwellest between the cherubims" who "hast made heaven and earth" (2 Kings 19:15 [= Isa. 37:16]). Psalm 80 begins by citing a caring leader, a Northern flock, the house of Joseph, and a theophany: "Give ear, O Shepherd of Israel, thou that leadest Joseph like a flock; thou that dwellest between the cherubims, shine forth"—the tradition of the ark in the wilderness seems close to the text. In Psalm 99 the same description of God's place of presence introduces the celebration of Zion (vs. 1) and the worshiper is exhorted to worship at God's footstool (vs. 5). Thus the cherub texts could be used either in connection with God's transportability—his cloud and chariot—or God's resting place: his temple and throne. Yet Exodus 32 has Moses renounce the Aaronid version of God's vehicle and footstool, the golden calf.

Part B. Exodus and Terminus in Israel's Pre-Exilic Cultic Leadership

Where Solomon's priests and Moses put the law and the golden cherubim, there also did Jeroboam and Moses' brother Aaron put the golden bullocks. The texts that distance Moses from Aaron must also divorce Moses from his own spokesmanship: which may mean, from a High Priestly establishment that Solomon confirmed in Jerusalem: i.e., the priesthood of David's appointee Zadok. For Zadok is preferred over David's other appointee Abiathar, who is found in the defeated party of Solomon's rival Adonijah, at the opening of 1 Kings (1:42, 2:22, 26–27, 35): "So Solomon thrust out Abiathar from being priest unto the Lord; that he might fulfill the word of the Lord, which he spake concerning the house of Eli in Shiloh . . . and Zadok the priest did the king put in the room of Abiathar" (1 Kings 2:27, 35b). Abiathar had been the sole survivor of Saul's slaughter of the priests of Nob (1 Sam. 22:19–20), he had carried the ark of the Lord in the presence of David and shared the king's hardships (1 Kings 2:26), and yet the text identifies his fate with the fulfillment of the prophecy of the "man of God" against the house of Eli in 1 Samuel 2:30–34: Eli would die in his office, but his family would die by the sword. Thus Abiathar is fissioned off from priestly office as the two sons of Eli, Hophni and Phinehas, formerly were, when they died by the sword with the capture of the ark in the time of Samuel. These sons in turn remind us of Aaron's two sons who died at the altar: "Nadab and Abihu died before the Lord, when they offered strange fire before the Lord, in the wilderness of Sinai, *and they had no children:* and Eleazar and Ithamar ministered in the priest's office in the sight of Aaron their father" (Num. 3:4; cf. also Deut. 10:6 and 1 Chron. 24:2). While God rejects an "Aaronid" Eli in favor of a "Mosaic" Samuel, Solomon rejects a "Mosaic" Abiathar in favor of an "Aaronid" Zadok. "I will raise me up a faithful priest," God says (1 Sam. 2:35), in accents of Moses' promise of a deuteronomic successor: "The Lord thy God will raise up unto thee a Prophet from the midst of thee" (Deut. 18:15). Moses declined God's offer to make a great nation of him (Exod. 32:10, Deut. 9:14). But what Moses refused with one hand Aaron got back with the other: "a kingdom of priests" (Exod. 19:6).

Beyond the confirmation of Aaron himself, Moses grants an eternal priesthood to his grand-nephew, Aaron's grandson Phinehas. In Numbers 25 Phinehas acts on behalf of the Aaronid priesthood's sole right to use the sanctuary, by killing a sinful Israelite within it. Aaron's wife was lineally descended from Judah, while Moses' wife Zipporah is Midianite; the sinner whom Phinehas kills was violating it with a woman whom the text identifies as "a Midianitish woman" (Num. 25:6). Aaron and Miriam also object to Moses' having married a Cushite (Num. 12:1). Moses' confirmation of the purist Phinehas anticipates the program of Hezekiah in 2 Chronicles 30–31; the king assigned the Levitical priesthood explicit control over temple sacrifices and monies (cf. Num. 3:32 and 1 Chron. 9:20, 26), after what appears to be a democratic interval permitting the temple's use by everyone answering the royal summons to avail himself of this one-time opportunity.

The priestly genealogies, overall, tell a typical biblical story of the ongoing winnowing of a more elect stock from a less elect one, by (1) splitting off the evil sons Nadab and Abihu from the untainted sons Eleazar and Ithamar, (2) splitting off Eleazar's son Eli—with his remiss sons Phinehas and Hophni—from Eleazar's zealous son Phinehas, and their descendants Ahitub, and Ahitub's son Zadok, and (3) splitting off Zadok from his disgraced nephew Abiathar, who is the son of Ahitub's other son Ahimelech (see 1 Sam. 22:9, 1 Chron. 6:8; but cf. 2 Sam. 8:17 and 1 Chron. 24:6, where Abiathar and Ahimelech have exchanged places as father and son). A second Ahitub is listed as the father of a second Zadok, seven generations later (at 1 Chron. 6:11–12). The genealogies thus suggest that a more Northern, Mushite, and Shilonic priesthood was handicapped and ultimately disqualified, owing to its lack of the patronage of the kingship in Judah—originally David and Solomon's patronage of "Zadok."

The texts seem to recognize two different versions of brokerage with God, that is, of the mediatorial office. In the deuteronomistic version, this office derives from Moses the prophet. But in the Priestly version, it derives from the high or Jerusalem priesthood. In the deuteronomistic version, Moses the prophet confronts the state with the judgments of God on the sins of the rulership. But in the Priestly version, as found in the legislation of Leviticus and Numbers, the priesthood headed by Aaron is appointed by the leadership to atone with God for the sins of the people.

In Moses' name and on Moses' behalf, *the high priest himself* is to function as the prophet among the people—for it is the Priestly version of Moses' commissioning by God (in Exodus 6:1-7:1) that makes Aaron Moses' prophet conclusively, as the two prepare to face Pharaoh the second time.

In 2 Chronicles the Levitical priesthood of the time of Hezekiah is given control over the sacrifices, which are thereupon centralized at Jerusalem; thus Hezekiah also made Jerusalem the place where the Passover is to be celebrated: which is to say, he makes the Passover require a pilgrimage to the City of David in the name of the Lord—so the use of the festal motif of Psalm 118:26 for the Passover in Matthew 21:9. And thus those texts which commission Aaron as Moses' prophet reach out to claim, for officers like Hezekiah's high priest Azariah (2 Chron. 31:10), the spokesmanship for "Moses" that Deuteronomy would presumably relocate in the raising up of a prophet more like Jeremiah than Aaron.

—For if there is one thing that the compound text of Exodus attests to, it is that the law went out of Sinai more than once, and in more than one form. There were two sets of tables, and one of these sets was destroyed by Moses in his anger against a people who had subscribed to the schismatic high priesthood of his own brother Levite. The story of a second set of tables that kept what the first one lost obscurely suggests that the rulers in Zion have kept what the rulers in the North lost, just as they have kept the ark—the ark that latterly the North (Shiloh) lost to the Philistines and that eventually came under the protectorship of the South (David's Jerusalem). The double tradition of calling the "mountain of God" alternately Horeb and Sinai may make the same suggestion of differing Northern and Southern auspices. If it is an alternative to Zion, Sinai also might speak for an alternative to the priesthood of Solomon's temple.

Alternative but parallel cult centers would conserve comparable cult objects: inscriptions, books, and hardware. But insofar as an account of either cult center would be written at the expense of the other, the destruction of the "idols" of the rival center would tend to be written into any representation of the giving of the sacralities of its own. The difference between prohibiting the manufacture of "molten gods" of the "Jahwist" Decalogue of Exodus 34:17 and prohibiting the making of the "gods of silver" and "gods of gold" of the "Elohist" laws of Exodus 20:23 may or may not be the difference between the specifically "molten" temple hardware of Jeroboam and that of foreign idolatry generally; or between Northern bullocks and Southern cherubs. Thus there seems to have been a lot of throwing of stones by people who themselves lived in glass houses. The cherubs were smelted from a collection the Levites made of Hebrew jewelry; the golden bullocks came from the same kind of collection.

The jewelry, in the case of either the cherubs or the bullocks, must in part have been Egyptian, since some of it would have been the jewelry with which the Egyptians gifted the Israelites at the time of their exodus. Analogously, Jeroboam's golden bullocks might have been paid for with dues otherwise levied by the rejected Jerusalem temple. In the time of Josiah, the Book of the Law that Hilkiah finds in the temple is also found in conjunction with such dues. Whatever the circumstances may have been, the text of 2 Kings 22 associates the recovery of the book with the financing of the restoration of the temple. Thus, for "Book of the Law" one may reread, in the light of Exodus, "Mosaic tablets"; and, for "silver . . . gathered of the people," read "precious metals devoted to the priesthood for the (re-)fabrication of cult objects." Thus:

> . . . Josiah . . . sent Shaphan . . . to the house of the Lord, saying,
> Go up to Hilkiah the high priest, that he may sum the silver which is brought into the house of the Lord, which the keepers of the door have gathered of the people:
> And let them deliver into the hand of the doers of the work . . . to repair the breaches of the house, ...
> And Hilkiah the high priest said unto Shaphan the scribe, I have found the book of the law in the house of the Lord. . . .
> And Shaphan the scribe came to the king, and brought the king word again, and said, Thy servants have gathered the money that was found in the house, and have delivered it into the hand of them that do the work, that have the oversight of the house of the Lord.
> And Shaphan the scribe shewed the king, saying, Hilkiah the priest hath delivered me a book. And Shaphan read it before the king.
> (2 Kings 22:3-5, 8-10)

The silver for the renewal of the cult apparatus—in this case the temple itself—is recruited in the same motion that the text of the law or covenant is recovered. Both are "found," both "delivered." Yet Josiah's reform omits any refurbishment of the ark and its cherubs; the emphasis is all the other way, on iconoclastic or iconocaustic purification of the holy place.

Given the parallels for his activity in the Exodus narratives, Josiah proceeds from the discovery of the law to the burning of the golden bullocks, the destruction of the idols that originally parallels Moses' breaking of the tables and commissioning of the cherubs. For the law forbidding idolatry compelled the destruction of Aaron's calf. Thus, on the basis of the new law book,

> . . . the king commanded Hilkiah the high priest . . . to bring forth out of the temple of the Lord all the vessels that were made for Baal, and for the grove, and for all the host of heaven: and he burned them without Jerusalem in the fields of Kidron, and carried the ashes of them unto Beth-el.

. . . And he brought out the grove from the house of the Lord, without Jerusalem, unto the brook Kidron, and stamped it small to powder, and cast the powder thereof upon the graves of the children of the people. . . .

Moreover the altar that was at Beth-el, and the high place which Jeroboam the son of Nebat, who made Israel to sin, had made, both that altar and the high place he brake down, and burned the high place, and stamped it small to powder, and burned the grove. . . .

And the king commanded all the people, saying, Keep the passover unto the Lord your God, as it is written in the book of this covenant.

Surely there was not holden such a passover from the days of the judges that judged Israel, nor in all the days of the kings of Israel, nor of the kings of Judah. . . .

And like unto him was there no king before him, that turned to the Lord with all his heart, and with all his soul, and with all his might, according to all the laws of Moses; neither after him arose there any like him. (2 Kings 23:4, 6, 15, 21–22, 25)

But on the basis of what we have often cited from Deuteronomy, it is not another king who was like Josiah, so much as it was the prophetic, deuteronomic Moses himself. For the language for Josiah's singularity is also that for the singularity of the Mosaic officeholder, in the text's final verdict on him: "And there arose not a prophet since in Israel like unto Moses, whom the Lord knew face to face" (Deut. 34:10).

In 2 Kings 18:5–7, the same claim of singularity has been made for Hezekiah, who is introduced with what seems to be Josiah's epitaph: "after him was none like him among the kings of Judah, nor any that were before him. For he clave to the Lord, and departed not from following him, but kept his commandments, which the Lord commanded Moses" (vss. 5b–6). Hezekiah "trusted in the Lord God of Israel" and "the Lord was with him" (vss. 5a, 7a). The phrases seem to show the pre-Josianic coalescence of Deuteronomy with "David." Josiah's book appears to renew and codify little more than what Hezekiah had already initiated and promulgated a century before, yet without a text: without, in our sense, a "Moses."

Josiah's priest Hilkiah, who found the lost text of the law in the temple debris, is presumably himself a factor contributing to the Pentateuch's portrait of Moses the stone-carver and Moses the furnisher of the tabernacle. Moses' likeness in Deuteronomy can be regarded not only as a mirror that Hilkiah holds up to his prince, but also as presenting to us the self-portrait of a servant of god like Hilkiah. The reformer-priest represents the Jerusalem leadership of the time of King Josiah as a "Mosaic" leadership—i.e., a leadership that departs from the "Pharaoh" of an evil kingship. But what "Pharaoh" was Josiah "departing" from?

Just inside the frame for the deuteronomistic history of the kingship provided by Jeroboam and Josiah are the kings Nadab and Manasseh. Nadab died for his persistence in the sins of his father, Jeroboam. The sins of Josiah's grandfather Manasseh were, according to the history in Kings, of comparable culpability. The reprobate of 2 Kings is reported as having committed virtually every religious sin known to the monarchy: he raised altars for Baal, made a grove, worshiped foreign gods, put idols in the place where only the Name was to go, "used enchantments, and dealt with familiar spirits and wizards," made his son to pass through fire, and led the people to violate the commandments prescribed "according to all the law that [God's] servant Moses commanded them"—"But they hearkened not" (2 Kings 21:2–9). The result of Manasseh's sin is to bring down on Judah the fate of the house of Ahab, whose fate in turn is modeled on that of the house of Jeroboam: "And the Lord spake by his servants the prophets, saying, Because Manasseh king of Judah hath done these abominations, . . . and hath made Judah also to sin with his idols; Therefore thus saith the Lord God of Israel, Behold, I am bringing such evil upon Jerusalem and Judah, that whosoever heareth of it, both his ears shall tingle. And I will stretch over Jerusalem the line of Samaria, and the plummet of the house of Ahab"—for the prophets said that the nation had provoked God's anger "since the day their fathers came forth out of Egypt, even unto this day" (2 Kings 21:10–16).

In making his son pass through fire, had not Manasseh condemned his son, as Pharaoh condemned his firstborn, in not heeding Moses? In shedding innocent blood (vs. 16), had not Manasseh polluted Jerusalem, as Pharaoh had polluted Egypt in oppressing Israel? So Jeremiah warns the kings of Judah and the inhabitants of Jerusalem that God says:

> . . . Behold, I will bring evil upon this place, the which whosoever heareth, his ears shall tingle.
> Because they have forsaken me, and have estranged this place, and have burned incense in it unto other gods . . . and have filled this place with the blood of innocents;
> They have built also the high places of Baal, to burn their sons with fire for burnt offerings unto Baal . . .
> Therefore, behold, the days come, saith the Lord, . . .
> . . . I will make void the counsel of Judah and Jerusalem in this place;
> . . . and their carcases will I give to be meat for the fowls of the heaven and the beasts of the earth. (Jer. 19:3–7).

Jeremiah echoes Ahijah's original denunciations of the house of Jeroboam: "Him that dieth of Jeroboam in the city shall the dogs eat; and him that dieth in the field shall the fowls of the air eat" (1 Kings 14:11). Such predictions recur in the oracles of Elijah and Elisha (1 Kings 21:19, 21–24, 2 Kings 9:7–10). Thus "the Lord spake by his servants the prophets"

(2 Kings: 21:10)—some of their words may even derive from David's oath against Nabal of Carmel (1 Kings 14:10, 1 Sam. 25:22). But by the time of the notice in 2 Kings 21:10–16 the writer does not need to designate the prophets by name: the voice indicting Manasseh has become one with the witness of the text itself. The great circle, from the Moses who stood before Pharaoh to the deuteronomic editors who stood before the history of the Israelite kingdom, has virtually closed. In his conclusive interview with Pharaoh, before the final plague, Moses had said, "As you say! I will not see your face again" (Exod. 10:29, RSV). But the Pharaoh who expelled Moses' Israel from Egypt has finally reversed into the God who is exiling the kingship from the promised land. God hardens his heart against Judah, because Judah has hardened its heart against him: "I will bring upon this city and upon all her towns all the evil that I have pronounced against it, because they have hardened their necks, that they might not hear my words"; "I will scatter them as with an east wind before the enemy; I will shew them the back, and not the face, in the day of their calamity" (Jer. 19:15b, 18:17). This God will not see the face of Israel's kingship again.

But how is Josiah's departure from Manasseh *literalized?* Josiah is saddled by the deuteronomic historians with undoing the legacy of a king who "built altars in the house of the Lord, of which the Lord had said, In Jerusalem will I put my name" (2 Kings 21:4). Manasseh had put other names there, and thus sanctioned other celebrations than the Mosaically prescribed ones; Deuteronomy insists that the proper fear of "this glorious and fearful name, THE LORD THY GOD," is contingent upon Israel's obeying "all the words of this law that are written in this book" (28:58), cultic observances included, and a feature of both the reforms of Hezekiah and Josiah seems to be the centralizing of *the Passover.* Deuteronomy 16 conjoins the keeping of the Name in Jerusalem with the keeping of the holy days in the same place—the holy days are institutions that are as Mosaic as the Name, but that are also specifically connected to the historical departure from Egypt. Thus: "Thou mayest not sacrifice the passover within any of thy gates, which the Lord thy God giveth thee: But at the place which the Lord thy God shall choose to place his name in, there thou shalt sacrifice the passover at even, at the going down of the sun, at the season that thou camest forth out of Egypt" (Deut. 16:5–6). Similarly: "thou shalt keep the feast of weeks, . . . thou, and thy son . . . , the Levite that is within thy gates, and the stranger, and the fatherless, and the widow, that are among you, in the place which the Lord your God hath chosen to place his name there. And thou shalt remember that thou was a bondman in Egypt" (Deut. 16:10–12a). *Thus Deuteronomy also prescribes the existence of a virtually pilgrim nation, that is, one engaged in a perpetual, migratory round, in imitation of the exodus.* Deuteronomy reconstitutes a Mosaically constituted *religio*—one consisting of three annual feasts—by combining it with worship in Jerusalem and the thrice-annual pilgrimage which that involved.

The departure of Moses and his people from Sinai is treated momentously, yet as if it were always happening. The story features the separation of Moses from his father-in-law, repeating his earlier departure from Midian to Egypt. These separation scenes seem fraught with Moses' own doubleness, and thus with the possibility of an ongoing national departure from Moses himself, mirrored in his father-in-law's return to Midian, as well as in all subsequent ideological departures from Moses, mirrored in the people's desire to return to Egypt and in Aaron's fabrication of the bullock. The Mosaic departure from the mount of God, and the sins of the Aaronid priesthood, have also been doubled. Thus the theme of departure *from* the Moses of Sinai and Moab is as deeply written into the narrative as the theme of departure *with* him—from Egypt.

But is there any solid evidence or claim for the earlier existence of a *Mosaic* worship that was priestly, or a bullock priesthood that was Northern and Mosaic? Is there anything more specific than the portrait of Samuel's covenant-brokering as Mosaic, according to our general thesis that the "Mosaic" precedes the fully developed figure of Moses? One discerns a localized, Northern priestly claim upon a putative Mosaic legacy by means of the priestly pedigree found in Judges 18, which cites Moses' own son Gershom (vs. 30). According to this genealogy, there was a non-Aaronid survivor of Moses' line, Jonathan, the son of Gershom, the son of Moses (by Moses' wife Zipporah). Jonathan was the Northern priest who served at the shrine established for the unnamed priest of a man with the Yahwist name Micah; according to the story in Judges 17–18, the nameless priest was more or less kidnapped for the service of the tribe of Dan as it migrated north through Canaan.

This abducted professional is said to have been a Levite, yet a Judahite; a Bethlehemite, yet a stranger in Bethlehem in Judah (Judg. 17:7). His identity is extraordinarily anomalous: he is a priest, yet he does not live in a priestly city, but as a sojourner in Judah; he is from the tribe of Judah, yet he is a landless priest. This jurisdictionally unclaimable character appears to be a kind of Israelite "hedge priest." The man he serves is, at the outset, called Micayehu, "Who is like Yahweh?" He has stolen money from his mother, which she intended to give to the Lord for a statue to be cast for her son. She rewards his honesty in returning her this money by offering it to him outright, but he refuses it and she in turn acquires the statue. "Micah" now owns a shrine and at first he appoints his own son for its priest—there was no king in Israel, and everyone did what was right in his own eyes (Judg. 17:1–6). But when Micah meets the Judahite-Bethlehemite-Levite sojourner, who tells him he is looking for a place, he hires the professional for his household chapel, in the assurance that he will now have a Levite for his priest. It is from this homely situation that the Danites recruit the priesthood for Dan. The priest first comes into contact with them as an advisor to their spying mission in the North. "In those days there was no king in Israel," and the unsettled Danites had been forced to migrate out of the South, and invade the North: ". . . in those days the tribe of the Danites sought them an inheritance to dwell in; for unto that day all their inheritance had not fallen unto them among the tribes of Israel. And the children of Dan sent of their family five men from their coasts, men of valour . . . to spy out the land, and to search it; and they said unto them, Go, search the land" (Judg. 18:1–2). The priest advises them to pursue their invasion of northern Canaan, and on their return the Danites virtually steal him, bribing him out of his service with Micah by means of the promise of a more important job with them, and preventing his rescue by the threat of force; and they steal Micah's entire religious apparatus to boot (Judg. 18:14–20). Then, in the North, they settle with their new-found priest at Laish: "And they called the name of the city Dan. . . . And the children of Dan set up the graven image: and Jonathan, the son of Gershom, the son of Manasseh [Moses], he and his sons were priests unto the tribe of Dan until the day of the captivity of the land. And they set them up Micah's graven image, which he made, all the time that the house of God was in Shiloh" (Judg. 18:29–31).

We are here reading Moses for Manasseh, since that is who Gershom is properly the son of. And why did the Masoretic editors change "Moses" to "Manasseh"? The authors of Genesis etymologize Manasseh to mean "forget"—what does the text here wish to forget? The story is clearly of more than one mind about the priesthood/s in question. On the minus side, the priesthood was local, "lay," unprofessional, opportunistic, for sale, idolatrous, *arriviste*, displaced, "hard-up," replaceable, disordered if not anarchic, and, in short, forgettable (*menešseh*, 'causing to forget'). And it disappeared at the time the ark was lost at Shiloh, before David brought it into Jerusalem. On the plus side, this same priesthood was Yahwistic, Mosaic, Levitical, ancient, established, Shilonic, and Gershonite. And it lasted until the exile. Gershom was the name of the eldest son of Moses, and of the eldest son of Levi. Non-Aaronid Gershonites of the Levitical lineage were serving in the temple service attributed to the time of David, and they were assigned Levitical towns in Manasseh and three other Northern tribes (1 Chron. 6:1, 16–17, 20–21, 31–32, 48, 62). Perhaps it is more significant here that Gershom's name, "a stranger there," is a double for Manasseh's, in that Joseph and Moses both name their sons after their exile. Joseph the father of Manasseh was an exile from Israel in Egypt, but Moses the father of Gershom was an exile from Egypt in Midian. The copyist putting the "n" over the line to change Moses' name to Manasseh's wanted to forget that Moses had ever been in this text; but the name Gershom will not let us forget that Moses was in Midian. That was the place Moses got both his family and his revelation, before taking them out of the South.

The genealogy of the claims upon Moses may now be diagrammed as follows—Jeremiah's frustrated Mosaic ministry forms the final term, before "the day of the captivity of the land" (Judg. 18:30), for reasons yet to emerge.

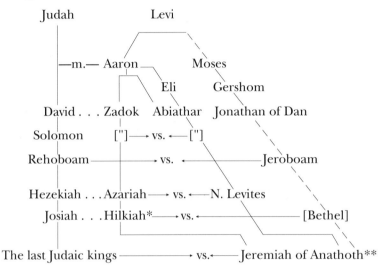

*Jeremiah's father was named Hilkiah
**Abiathar was exiled to Anathoth

Jeremiah may belong in this descent because, according to Jeremiah 1:1, his father bore the same name as Josiah's high priest, Hilkiah. Jeremiah's hometown was the priestly city of Anathoth—to which Solomon exiled David's priest Abiathar (1 Kings 2:26–27) at the time he put Shimei ("the first . . . of all the house of Joseph" [2 Sam. 19:20]) under house arrest in Jerusalem.[3] Jeremiah ben Hilkiah, in other words, may inherit both halves of a long-term antagonism between Aaronid priests in Jerusalem and Mosaic Levites in Ephraim.

The story of the Levite-Mushite priesthood, founded in Dan by Moses' grandson Jonathan, seems to put "Moses" where we might have expected "Aaron." But it is otherwise a good example of the "belated originality" characteristic of stories about Moses himself, as now met in the biblical text. For here we have a report of a kind of latter-day "exodus"—Dan moving out of the South, and thereafter resettling in the North, after the occupation. It constitutes a notable testimony of the confinement of a

Mosaic exodus myth to a more or less purely "Northern" circuit, throughout the historical period, from the judges to the Exile. For the Danites' story is much like that of the occupation itself. The Danites appoint spies; the land they reconnoiter is apparently a good land, and haste is urged in occupying it (Judg. 18:9; cf. Num. 13:30). The spies sent out by Moses reached the brook of Eshcol (Num. 13:23–24); the spies sent out by the Danites returned to Eshtaol (Judg. 18:8). Such a story makes us wonder whether the obscure kidnapped Levite—rather than being replaced by the last-named descendant of Moses—is not himself Moses' original. Yet the story also gives a special plausibility to Jeroboam's latter-day Mosaic pretensions, via his removing of Yahwist worship from Jerusalem to Dan. For the story attests to the Yahwist worship's *already being there,* as it were, "from of old"—from the time of the conquest of the land, the time of the immediate successors of Moses. We meet a certain circularity here: it is as if the Danites were departing from the South to *return* to the North, as the Hebrews from Egypt returned to the land of their forefather Jacob. Those worshiping at Jeroboam's shrines might have thus been assured that they were making the pilgrimage that Moses himself—or the Mushite priesthood in his name—had originally made.

When the Yahwist presented himself before Yahweh, as Mosaic legislation thrice yearly required him to do, he must needs be making a Mosaic pilgrimage to do so. Circularly, once again: the purpose of the pilgrimage was to reconsecrate the shrine, and, at the same time, to set the Yahwist himself apart. Those who rallied to the Lord's name were one with those who assembled at sites that enshrined the memory of Mosaic visitations. We might conclude that the story of the exodus led by Moses once functioned as an etiological myth that supported difficult pilgrimages to Yahwist sanctuaries, both in the North and in the South. But it might have also vindicated the self-exportation of the Danites out of the South and their resettlement in the North, or validated one of the two places where Jeroboam was to resettle Yahwist cult.

We meet the coinherence of the Mosaic origin and destination in the South as well. The proposal Moses makes to Pharaoh, to worship in the wilderness, seems to fit a destination in the oases of Kadesh, where Moses eventually arrives (Num. 13:26, 20:16, 32:8, 33:36, Deut. 1:46, Josh. 14:7). The significance of a journey to Kadesh is hard to see, unless it is already a site consecrated to a pre-Sinaitic worship of Yahweh. Then Yahwist pilgrimages to Kadesh would include Moses' own return there. When the people went the original three days into the wilderness, they found no potable water, apart from miraculous intervention, at Marah (Exod. 15:22–23). This recurs at "the rock in Horeb," where Yahweh plans to meet with Moses—but Moses calls the place Massah and Meribah (Exod. 17:6–7).

The miraculous production of water occurs again at Meribah-Kadesh, at Numbers 20:11. Moses and Aaron fail to sanctify Yahweh here, but the implication of the name is that they were at least at the right place to have done so (cf. *qodeš* with "assert his holiness" at Num. 20:12–13, and also Deut. 32:51).

Deuteronomy begins by locating Moses in the Arabah between Paran and Tophel, eleven days' journey from Horeb, by way of Mount Seir, to Kadesh-Barnea (Deut. 1:1–2). At Horeb God orders the people to depart from it—they have stayed there long enough (Deut. 1:6). The discourse will circle back to the main Sinaitic events, but at the outset it is Kadesh-Barnea that is the place from which Canaan is reconnoitered, where the sentence of detention in the wilderness is carried out, and from which an unsuccessful and rebellious campaign against the Amorites is mounted. God, Moses tells the people, would not listen to their weeping, which is why they have been detained there so long (Deut. 1:45–46). If—as in Deuteronomy 33:2—God's "fiery law" originated from Mount Paran, this agrees with our first notice of Kadesh, which calls it the Fountain of Judgment (Gen. 14:7). Marah is the place in Exodus where the Lord first offers his covenant and cites his commandments: thus Kadesh seems to be the spring and oracle of the law.

Numbers 20:1 reports of Kadesh that Miriam the prophetess "died there, and was buried there." Her brother Aaron dies nearby, on Mount Hor (Num. 20:23–29), where Aaron's son Eleazar was invested with his father's robes of office. Because of the repetitions touched on above, Moses' visits to this neighborhood seem to have him treading in the steps of a Moses who has already been there, as if the "Egyptian" Moses with the refined conscience had been commissioned by God to seek out the desert retreats of the "Hebrew" Moses who worshiped the demon of live volcanoes; or as if the Egyptian Moses had applied to Pharaoh for a visa to visit the tomb-to-be of the Hebrew prophetess who had been instrumental in getting the Israelite pilgrimage-leader born; or, again, as if Moses were going out to meet the historical origins of the Yahweh cult in the wilderness of the Edomite and the Amorite directly south of Judah.

If Kadesh, Hor, and Paran are the originals of the volcanic landscape to which Moses was to return, according to God at Exodus 3:12, then it was Moses' end to find his beginning. Yet Moses also begins at this end, Kadesh having been an original staging-point for the journey that ends where Deuteronomy begins. No man knows the place of Moses' burial, according to the end of Deuteronomy, which thus circles around the points of Mosaic origin and destination in the same way that its hero abides on the threshold of a determinative going out and a determinative coming in.

·17·

SUPPLEMENTARY ORIGINALS

. . . a prophet mighty in deed and word before God and all the
people. (Luke 24:19)

Why did the personage named Moses come to be so important a figure
and subject in the Bible's opening installment, the Pentateuch or the Five
Books? Why did Luke's risen but unrecognized Jesus begin with Moses,
when he modestly undertook to interpret his own presence throughout
the Scriptures to two of his disciples: "And beginning at Moses and all the
prophets, he expounded unto them in all the scriptures the things concerning himself" (Luke 24:27)? What is the basis for this hermeneutic
choice? The answer, that Moses is the founder-figure in the national history that much of the Bible purports to unfold, only does justice to the
coalescence Moses represents if it also recognizes the coalescence of the
whole history. For according to the Moses of Moab, the Sinaitic Moses
stood in *place* of Israel:

> The Lord talked with you face to face in the mount out of the midst of
> the fire,
> (I stood between the Lord and you at that time, to shew you the word
> of the Lord: for ye were afraid by reason of the fire, and went not up
> into the mount;) . . . (Deut. 5:4–5)

The persona speaking in Deuteronomy, in concert with his author, saw in
Moses an Israel-summarizing avatar back onto whom a whole standing
order could be cast. Through Moses Israel could represent itself to God
even in the latter day: and so build on an original Sinatic appointment, "Be
thou for the people to God-ward, that thou mayest bring the causes unto
God" (Exod. 18:19b; RSV, "You shall represent the people before God").

Deuteronomy makes a principle of the truism that the canonization of
Moses must needs reflect the Mosaicization of the canon—the Bible's
instantiation of Moses' particular historical importance may only result
from a belated Levitical and prophetic moralization of the national history. But does the Book of Exodus itself support this view, the view of
Moses as having been created by the texts, as the past's representation to

the future? At Exodus 6:5b, God declares, "I have *remembered* my covenant." This declaration follows on a slightly earlier version, "I have *established* my covenant with them" (6:4)—the ostensible antecedent is the patriarchs. But these seemingly innocent remembrances of the patriarchal "covenant" embed a "structure of recall" if they anticipate Leviticus 26, where God in the wilderness declares that, in spite of the rejection of Israel represented by the fall of Judah and the Babylonian exile, he, the Lord, will again *remember the covenant*—the one he made with those first generations that he brought out of the land of Egypt in the sight of the nations (Lev. 26:45). God's remembering the covenant is like man's remembering the Sabbath—it could never be remembered for the first time.

An essential component in the biblical kerygma of the exodus is this assertion that in delivering Israel from Egypt God "remembered his holy promise, and Abraham his servant" (Ps. 105:42)—the Abraham whom he declared he brought up out of Ur as he declares he brought Israel up out of Egypt (Gen. 15:7, Exod. 20:2). But "Many times did he deliver them . . . he regarded their affliction, when he heard their cry: And he remembered for them his covenant" (Ps. 106:43–45a). At Sinai, in Exodus 32:11–13, Moses asks God to remember his covenant with Abraham: God is not to embarrass himself in front of the Egyptians by having proved an unreliable deliverer to Israel. Despite the appeal to Abraham, Moses is obviously already in a position of having to ask God to remember the exodus! Such a purpose of recoupment, once again, anticipates Deuteronomy.

Who was Moses as he was, and who is merely allegorically like unto him? In which direction should we understand the remove in question: toward the synonymy and interchangeability of the characters called Mosaic, or toward the obliquity of and difference among the characters called Moses? Would these questions arise at all, unless Moses were the name around which Israel gathered the evidence of a crisis of authority, or rather a series of such crises? Insofar as "Moses" was as much a part of the crisis as a part of its resolution, the question was, is Moses available to our contemporaries, or is the appeal to him in fact unavailing?

The Pentateuch, within which the alignment of rememberings and re-rememberings of the exodus is now incorporated, also includes strong references to the return from the exile: the consolidation of the Torah is thus in the nature of a consolation for the great interruptions in national life which took place in Israel from about the beginning of the sixth century B.C. Such a torah must have been a means of renewing the covenant basis of that life, by reinstating it textually. From the fall of Judah in 586 B.C., the Scriptures were a bridge: from an Israel that had gone into exile back to an Israel that existed in history. Ahijah's prophecy against the house of

Jeroboam, made to the queen in 1 Kings 14, promised that God would wipe their house out. But the prophecy reaches far beyond the end of the tenth century: "For the Lord shall smite Israel, as a reed is shaken in the water, and he shall root up Israel out of this good land, which he gave to their fathers, *and shall scatter them beyond the river,* because they have made their groves, provoking the Lord to anger" (1 Kings 14:15). A latter-day, exilic gloss, written hundreds of years after the original events, adds, "This is the day; and what more now?" (JB note).

The pentateuchal references to the hardship of the life of the original emigrants apart from Egypt recall the latter-day experience of those who "went up . . . from Babylon" with Ezra (Ezra 8:1): "For ye know how we have dwelt in the land of Egypt; and how we came through the nations which ye passed by; And ye have seen their abominations, and their idols, wood and stone, silver and gold, which were among them" (Deut. 29:16–17). As in Egypt, the Israelites in Babylon had been "bondmen," yet God had not forsaken them in their bondage (Ezra 9:9). Under Ezra, the emigrants "separated themselves from the people of the lands unto the law of God," and "entered into a curse, and into an oath, to walk in God's law, which was given by Moses the servant of God, and to observe and do all the commandments of the Lord" (Neh. 10:28–29). So the deutero-nomic Moses: "Ye stand this day all of you before the Lord your God . . . That thou shouldst enter into covenant with the Lord thy God, and into his oath, which the Lord thy God maketh with thee this day: That he may establish thee today for a people unto himself . . ." (Deut. 29:10–13; cf. also Exod. 19:8, 24:7). In Nehemiah the people make the analogous com-mitment, after the leaders of the Levites have given an extensive recitation recapitulating the main phases of the nation's history from the election of Abraham to the affliction of the nation "since the time of the kings of Assyria unto this day" (Neh. 9:32). The point of view is that of the editors of the Former Prophets (from Joshua to 2 Kings), a history of the landed Israel that can only have been completed upon the fall of Judah. With the comparable placement of Deuteronomy at the end of the Pentateuch, the history of the landless Israel is likewise completed: upon the death of the Mosaic testator.

The exile's despairing question, "What now?" suggests that the Scrip-tures themselves could provide a "way of escape." Jeremiah wrote telling the exiles to turn their captivity into a virtual land of Goshen—"Build ye houses . . . plant gardens" (Jer. 29:5)—and the letter that went out to Babylon also came into the Bible. All of the Israels that contribute to the portrait of a "nation" that in Egypt became "great, mighty, and popu-lous," a nation called out of foreign bondage to be God's people (Deut. 26:5, 4:20), have also been laid under contribution to make the exile's Israel, now shut up in the wilderness of past history, again present to itself as the people of God's "inheritance"—"as ye are this day," Moses tells his flock (Deut. 4:20). The resonance of an equation between an Israel of the land and one of the text is especially strong if we read such pronouncements over a post-Sinaitic Israel as "performative" utterance that puts the contract with God into effect not only in Moab with Moses, or in Shechem with Joshua, but also in foreign lands with the exiles.

The complete Mosaic testament is ratified and sealed less in Moab than sometime during the exile—in Deuteronomy 28 the exile falls just within the compass of God's promises as made through this text. The old exodus has thus become a call to a new peoplehood, and a means to the catechizing of the present. Israel's doubtful repossession of itself as a landed sovereignty is twinned with its retention of a Mosaic heritage: "The secret things belong unto the Lord our God: but those things which are revealed belong unto us and to our children for ever, that we may do all the words of this law" (Deut. 29:29). For while the voice of this text calls a people back to a putatively Mosaic law, its affirmation of the covenant also seems to resonate with an alignment between an original constituting of the nation as God's people and the "secret" of its future, post-exilic repossession of its homeland: "this day thou art become the people of the Lord thy God"; "Neither with you only do I make this covenant and this oath; But with him that standeth here with us this day before the Lord our God, and also with him that is *not* here with us this day" (Deut. 27:9; 29:14–15).

Jesus began from Moses, but Moses appears to have begun from Hosea. Writing *circa* 750 b.c., less than three decades before Assyria's subjugation of the Northern kingship, this prophet offers us the most important evidence of a date for the first literary coalescence of the ideology of the Mosaic institutions and the story of an exodus from Egypt. Hosea knows much of the essence of the law as it is found in the Decalogue itself: "the Lord hath a controversy with the inhabitants of the land, because there is no truth, nor mercy, nor knowledge of God in the land. By swearing, and lying, and killing, and stealing, and committing adultery, they break out, and blood toucheth blood" (Hos. 4:1–2). He likewise knows about the exodus: "When Israel was a child," his Yahweh says, "then I loved him, and called my son out of Egypt" (11:1). Hosea projects Israel's backsliding upon its original departure from Moses: "at Adam they transgressed the covenant" (6:7, AT, with conjectural "at" for Hebr. "like": at Josh. 3:16 Adam is the place where the waters were held up when the people crossed the Jordan). Thus by the time of Hosea the memory of an ancient migration from Egypt—probably originally that of "Joseph," as the tribe of him "that was separate from his brethren" (Gen. 49:26), or Levi, as the tribe that had no allotment in the land God had provided the Israelite tribes— coexisted with the legal fiction of a contracting with Yahweh to honor a

Mosaic morality. The result is the myth of an ideological leadership that leads to the Sinaitic promulgation: though Hosea mentions neither Moses by name, nor the giving of a law on a mountain.

Indeed, Hosea 12:13 does not, itself, assert that the exodus-leading prophet also participated in (or mediated) a *covenant* between Israel and Yahweh. Yet Hosea's naming of God's instrument in Egypt as a *prophet,* and thus as the type of the writer's own prophetic vocation, surely also implies for the original leader-spokesperson an intercessory function of some kind. But must a prophet's role in delivering Israel from Egypt also imply the role of "Moses" in ministering a covenant to a people at its Sinai? The answer, based on notions of the prophet's function as found in the story of Elijah in 1 Kings 18–19 is roughly yes. This text brings Elijah to Mount Horeb after forty days of flight from Jezebel, and thereupon scripts for God's lonely partisan a decidedly Sinaitic scenario. Similarities between Moses' Sinai and Elijah's Horeb include: (1) the voicing of the complaint that the people have broken their covenant with God or forsaken Yahweh (1 Kings 19:10, 14); (2) the private conference of Yahweh and the prophet at a critical juncture in the landscape (Elijah's lodging in the cave at 1 Kings 19:9 corresponding to Moses' being placed in the cleft in the rock at Exodus 33:22); (3) the divine recommissioning of the alienated prophet on a previously hallowed mountain site; and (4), the extending of the Yahwist mission, among the people, to a loyalist cadre (Moses' purging of the Levites at Exod. 32:25–29, Elijah's appointment to appoint Elisha and the mention of the 7,000 who have not bent the knee to Baal, at 1 Kings 19:15–18, after the purge of Baalists at 1 Kings 18:40). Given our anachronic reading of the claim in 1 Kings 19—that Elijah was virtually a second Moses—the Sinai pericope conversely implies that Moses in the wilderness had suffered the situation of the prophet in Northern Israel. His people had forsaken the covenant: to serve idols (Hos. 4:17, 8:5, 10:5).

For us here, the chief evidence for a prophetic provenance for the moralized exodus narrative is the emergence of Hosea's reference to Egypt out of his declaration of a national or institutional crisis to which prophecy answers. At the opening of his eighth chapter, Hosea has us overhear the divine imperative, and the reason for it: "Set a trumpet to your lips, as a vulture is over the house of the Lord, because they have broken my covenant, and transgressed my law" (Hos. 8:1, RSV [AR]). These words lead to the prediction that—because the Israelites have not known God, have set up the kingship, made the calf of Samaria along with many altars, and written many laws, yet not heeded them—"they shall return to Egypt": from which, once, their God came (Hos. 8:13, 13:4).

Thus the nation's covenant with Yahweh is first invoked, in the dateable literature, *upon the covenant's being broken;* the nation's childhood is defined in terms of the deliverance from Egypt (in Hos. 11:1) *only when the nation has proven to be a wayward adult.* Moreover, Ephraim "shall return to the land of Egypt, and Assyria shall be their king, because they have refused to return"—refused to return, apparently, to Yahweh (Hos. 11:5, RSV). Like Pharaoh's troops at the Reed Sea, or Korah, Dathan, and Abiram in the wilderness (Exod. 15:12, Num. 16:30, 32), Israel "is swallowed up": "among the Gentiles." "For they have gone up to Assyria, a wild ass wandering alone . . . ; Ephraim hath hired lovers" (Hos. 8:8–9). "[He] has spurned your calf, O Samaria," Hosea declares, "A workman made it; it is not God. The calf of Samaria shall be broken to pieces" (Hos. 8:5–6, RSV, after Hebr.). The gods that brought Israel out of Egypt are invoked in proportion to the gathering strength of those forces and idolatries that will bring it back into captivity. Hosea 8 thus provides an early, basic scenario for an apostasy finally enshrined as the idolatry at Sinai. Hosea knows about the apostasy at Baal-Peor (Hos. 9:10b), but invokes such apostasies to pillory "the calf of Beth-aven"—it will become Assyrian booty (Hos. 10:5–6). Covenant, exodus, and wilderness sojourn become visible in Hosea through the default of a *contemporary* Israel.

While the founding history of the covenant always seems doubled with a history of its latter-day imperilment, the covenant also only reaches forward in the same motion that it reaches back. Jeremiah, typically, insists that the return from the captivity will be based on the eternality of God's formerly covenanting with David and the Levites; these covenants, in turn, had been appointed in terms of the divine ordinances governing day and night, heaven and earth (Jer. 33:20–21, 25–26), somewhat like the original covenant with Noah. In Leviticus 26 and Deuteronomy 28 the plagues of the exodus—belonging to traditions of both Egypt and the wilderness— are reread as threats to the future, covenant-breaching nation. Wasted by the enemy, the land of a people who has not observed the Lord's Sabbath will one day enjoy a Sabbath without them (Lev. 26:43). At the same time, Leviticus agrees with the covenant-preaching Jeremiah that the exile will not last forever. Like the man infected with leprosy, who must live beyond the camp only as long as his disease lasts (Lev. 13:45–46), Israel will return; God promises that during the Exile *he will remember the land, and the covenant of their ancestors* (Lev. 26:42, 45–46). This is the language in which God told Moses in Egypt that he had remembered his covenant with the patriarchs, to give their seed possession of Canaan (Exod. 6:3–5).

At the time of Deuteronomy the remembering of the Mosaic past and its *magnalia dei* had itself become the Yahwist "cause" to be rallied to: Israel was not being urged not to forget the Amalekites (Exod. 17:14), but Deuteronomy. There must always be some such custodian of tradition, to warn a nation less against forgetting its Alamo or its Maine than its historical origins and their significance. The Pentateuch puts this spokesman at the end of the trek across the wilderness, in place of the leader who began

it: the forty years' sojourn, between the Moses of Exodus and the one of
Deuteronomy, stands in place of more than four hundred years of God's
covenant with Judah's kings, from David to Josiah. Deuteronomy official-
izes Moses' sponsorship of a tradition he was chosen to conserve as much
as found, even if this role implies the very thing the "original" Moses
would categorically abhor, the routinization of memory.

The deuteronomist might well agree with the psalmist: Isarel's forefathers did not *understand* God's wonders in Egypt (Ps. 106:7). The charge
that Israel has misunderstood God's signs and wonders is slightly different
from the charge of forgetfulness, with its purpose of inculcating a new
mindfulness. But apart from remembering with Deuteronomy and law-
keeping with Leviticus, how *was* the exodus to be understood, or, rather,
re-understood, in the latter day? Texts like Jeremiah 23:7–8 and the second
and third Isaiahs (40–55; 56–66) can tell us that the recoupment in question might take a form very different from Deuteronomy: less a solemn
sanctification of the Mosaic past on behalf of God's continuing interest in
his being properly thanked, than a bold claim upon his direct re-interven-
tion in the present and the immediate future. Jeremiah, in fact, has the
people forget the *deuteronomic* exodus: in subsequent restorations, he says,
"they shall no more say, The Lord liveth, which brought up the children
of Israel out of the land of Egypt" (Jer. 23:7). This prophet often reacts to
the national legacy by dismantling it: the ark at Shiloh where God first set
his name and the name's being at Jerusalem are also things of which Israel
shall no longer speak (3:16, 7:12, 26:6, 9). God institutes some new thing.
Deutero-Isaiah concludes similarly: "it shall be to the Lord for a name, for
an everlasting sign that shall not be cut off" (Isa. 55:13b). Israel's deliverer
will have acted again, without recourse to intermediaries, as he might have
done in the beginning, for Trito-Isaiah says, "It was *neither messenger nor
angel* but his Presence that saved them . . . he redeemed them himself,
. . . throughout the days of old" (Isa. 63:9, JB, after Gr. and Lat. at italics;
contra JPS and AV, "and the angel of his presence saved them").

The words of this last Isaiah, "Then he remembered the days of old,
Moses, and his people" (63:11), implicitly connect God's mindfulness with
the prophet's own activity: it is not only the Lord, but "Isaiah" who recalls
the days of the exodus, reclaiming the saving events while advancing his
prophecy's special role in the people's illumination.[1] Such texts do rather
more than remember that God remembered Israel in Egypt; their
"Moses" is not merely a name for a Mosaic bequeathal ideally governing
Israel's extended historical life as a polity appointed, circularly, to hallow
the exodus with the landless Levites. For what kind of "Moses" would a
prophet, suddenly set down in the midst of the Judah of the Persian
Empire, be recurring to? Answers lie in the prophet's own questions:
"Where is he, the one bringing up from the sea the shepherds of his

flock? Where is he, setting in the midst of them his holy spirit, . . . dividing the waters before them . . . , . . . leading them through the deeps like the horse in the wide-open spaces?" (Isa. 63:11–13, AT). It is the *Holy Spirit*—the wind at the Reed Sea that re-created the aboriginal deep—that now re-creates the prophet. Even if his party's voice has not always been honored—for God's people "rebelled, and vexed his Holy Spirit" (Isa. 63:10a), as they did at Marah, "Because they believed not in God, and trusted not in his salvation," or "believed not for his wondrous works," or "provoked" Moses' own spirit "so that he spake unadvisedly" (Ps. 78:22, 32; 106:33)—it is nonetheless the Holy Spirit that speaks through this latest version of the exodus deliverance. When the Moses of grateful memory rebecomes the Moses of expectant prophecy we are back in the company of the unnamed intermediary of Hosea 12:13: God's spokesman in a crisis-ridden hour, identified with the nation's charismatic beginnings.

In the present book I have tried to suggest the extent to which latter-day crises and covenant breaches—being catalytic for the formation not only of a Mosaic canon but also of a Mosaic mythos—might determine the form and content of the exodus narrative itself. I have grouped much of my earlier discussion of the narrative around the birth of Moses, the revelation of the Name to him, the plaguing of Egypt at his instance or with his appointment, and the instituting of a national feast memoralizing the nation's departure or separation from another nation. We have already touched on the priesthood that is forced into Dan, as an example of a latter-day exodus migration that doubles for the original one. My further discussions of the text of history—really appendices—revisit the narrative under these same heads, as its elements appear in three further "proximate texts" not obviously about the exodus at all, except by way of analogy.[2] Such apparently incidental comparisons show again that the narrative of a veiled origin is almost necessarily fashioned out of sources later than the origin itself claims to be.

Part A. The House of Imram:
The Preservation of a Monotheistic Leadership

The Book of Exodus begins before the birth of Moses, and the exodus the book describes, if we follow the remarks of Solomon in 1 Kings 8, is not fully realized until long after Moses has died, and indeed until Solomon has taken the throne. Yet that is just where the exodus ministry of Jeroboam the son of Nebat began: upon the completion of the Solomonic house-building. The Moses who published God was ideally one with the Solomon who published Moses. "And Samuel said unto the people, It is the Lord that advanced Moses and Aaron, and that brought your fathers up out of the land of Egypt. . . . When Jacob was come into Egypt, and your fathers cried unto the Lord, then the Lord sent Moses and Aaron" (1 Sam. 12:6, 8a). "For thou," says Solomon, taking up Samuel's theme of the Lord's work, "didst separate them from among all the people of the earth, to be thine inheritance, as thou spakest by the hand of Moses thy servant, when thou broughtest our fathers out of Egypt," and "there hath not failed one word of all [God's] good promise, which he promised by the hand of Moses his servant" (1 Kings 8:53, 56b). Yet the Mosaic project that Solomon was completing, according to the lights of Solomon's oration, was the project Jeroboam was only just initiating, according to his own.

In Solomon's oration, the "Northern" champion Moses seems to have been reappropriated for the dignification of the Solomonic Southern kingship and its Aaronid priesthood. And indeed, two of the most significant exodus traditions have given "Moses" a "Southern" provenance: for the Southern oasis of Kadesh is a possible destination for the religious pilgrimage that Moses originally proposes to Pharaoh, and the early assignment of lands in Israel to "Southern" Caleb is credited directly to Moses. Thus the Pentateuch's overall understanding of the exodus event is "through Moses," though other places in the Bible merely understand the event to have taken place "through God" (e.g., Amos 2:10, 3:1).

The prophetic activity that surrounds the nativity of Jesus in Luke's gospel is equivalent to the effects of the Spirit surrounding the birth of Christianity at Luke's Pentecost in Acts 2. Similarly, the adoption of the child Moses by Pharaoh's daughter may claim the exodus for the sponsorship of a royal house. The etymology for the biblical name of Moses' mother, Jochebed (Exod. 6:20, Num. 26:59), makes her name one that *glorifies Yahweh*—she is a virtual embodiment of the first commandment, and her son is one who will see Yahweh's glory. Her nephew Amram (son of her brother Kohath) takes her to wife and becomes the father of Moses and Aaron. Amram has a cousin named Mushi and a paternal uncle named Gershon. Mushi is also the cousin of Moses. Moses has the same Gershon for a maternal uncle, and a Gershom for a son. Gershon (son of Levi) and the Gershonites are threaded throughout the Levitical genealogy, from Genesis 46:11 onwards. Amram is also the father of Miriam, in the genealogy of 1 Chronicles 6:3, but here Amram's aunt-wife Jochebed has dropped out, perhaps because Moses' and Aaron's sister Miriam would also be their aunt-cousin and so confuse an easily discerned patrilinearity, as opposed to concentrating consanguinity: Amram's marriage inverts the genders of the patriarchal case, which gives Abraham's brother Nahor a wife, Milcah, who is also the brothers' niece (Gen. 11:26–29).

Such a tangle within a critical genealogy is not unique to the Bible. The third sura of the Koran, called "The Family [or House] of Imram," identifies the daughter of Moses' mother, by his father Imram, with Mary the mother of Jesus (vss. 35–36). Conformable to this, in the nineteenth sura, called "Mary," Mary is addressed as the sister of Aaron (vss. 16–28). Muslims therefore assume that the name of Jesus' grandfather was Imram, the biblical Amram: the name of Moses' father. The role of Moses' sister, assisting the redeemer's or prophet's mother in delivering her son from the threat of death, makes this typology a perfectly plausible one. If Miriam is in a position to be Moses' aunt, is she not an alternative for the deliverer's mother? The overlaps would result from the genealogy of Moses having been superimposed on the typology of a confessing Yahwist priesthood from Levi, Amram's grandfather.

The successful mothering and nurturing of the Mosaic protagonist within the hostile reign with which that protagonist will take issue—the royal house that has "forgotten Joseph"—might also suggest a latter-day reading of this protagonist's birth story as the rebirth of a Yahwist leadership within either an already established ruling house or a newly ascendant dispensation. Speaking in the Yahwist party voice, Moses spoke as a prophet. But galvanizing a violent action, a Yahwist spokesman acts as a prince or priest or strongman. In that case he belongs in the company of the strongman Jehu in the North, a king who speaks like a prophet at 2 Kings 9:25, and Jehoiada in the South, a priest who promulgates a Mosaic reform at 2 Kings 11:17–18. Jehu was an in-house strongman like Jeroboam, who likewise revolted against his master; Jehoiada is a more quizzical case.

The only bona fide royal infancy story from the royal period when the story of Moses' birth may have been written is in 2 Kings 11. It concerns the priest Jehoiada's removal of the child Jehoash, son of Ahaziah, from among the princes who were to be murdered by Jehoash's grandmother, Jezebel's daughter Athaliah (2 Kings 9:14–27, 11:1–16). Athaliah was the mother of Ahaziah—her son died in Naboth's vineyard during the vengeance of Jehu upon the house of Ahab and Ahab's son King Joram, with which house Ahaziah was allied through his grandmother Jezebel and from which he was partly descended through Ahab's father Omri. Ahaziah's mother Athaliah was the granddaughter of this mighty father in the North, but the point about the fatally wounded Ahaziah is that he dies as a Davidic dynast, smitten in his chariot, dying in Megiddo, and buried "in his sepulchre with his fathers in the city of David" (2 Kings 9:27–28). According to 2 Chronicles 35:20–24, the battle was actually fought at Megiddo, the building of which was part of the original "reason of the levy which king Solomon raised" (1 Kings 9:15). Megiddo is also the place at which Josiah is to die, according to accounts closely parallel to the account for Ahaziah (2 Kings 23:29–30; 2 Chron. 35:22–24).

It is at such critical junctures that we have located both the creation of the textual tradition, and the resort to it: the narrative of the death of

Josiah in 2 Kings is directly preceded by the Lord's resolve to cast off Jerusalem and the house of which he said, after Deuteronomy, "My name shall be there" (2 Kings 23:27; Deut. 12:11, etc.). Similarly, Josiah's death in 2 Chronicles is directly followed by the report that "Jeremiah lamented for Josiah: and all the singing men and the singing women spake of Josiah in their lamentations to this day, and made them an ordinance in Israel: and, behold, they are written in the lamentations" (2 Chron. 35:25).

When it reports the involvement of Ahaziah's father Jehoram, king of Judah, with the sinful house of Ahab and Ahab's son King Joram, the text of 2 Kings anxiously reissues the earlier promises made to David and his heirs that Yahweh would leave them a lamp in God's presence forever (2 Kings 8:19); in 1 Chronicles 28:6–7a, David tells Israel that the Lord made him the same kind of promise, regarding Solomon: "he shall build my house and my courts: for I have chosen him to be my son, and I will be his father. Moreover, I will establish his kingdom for ever." Thanks to Jehoaida's intervention against Athaliah, the promises are kept: he prevents her destroying "all the seed royal" left by her dead son (2 Kings 11:1).

The priest does not act the maternal part alone. Jehoash is originally saved by his aunt Jehosheba, the daughter of King Joram and sister of Ahaziah: she it was who "stole him from among the king's sons which were slain; and they hid him, even him and his nurse, in the bedchamber from Athaliah, so that he was not slain" (2 Kings 11:2). Aunt Jehosheba and the nurse share their roles with Moses' mother Jochebed who hid Moses three months (Exod. 2:2)—not to mention the ministrations of Moses' sister, the scrupulous midwives before her, and the Egyptian princess who in turn will hire the Hebrew nurse who is actually the child's mother. Moses, like Jehoash, is saved by a conspiracy of women.

Moses grew up with his mother, and then she brought him back to Pharaoh's daughter: "and he became her son" (Exod. 2:10). "And it came to pass in those days, when Moses was grown, that he went out unto his brethren, and looked on their burdens" (Exod. 2:11). For six years the son of Ahaziah was kept hidden from Athaliah, harbored with his nurse in the sleeping quarters in the temple of Yahweh and Yahweh's priest. In the seventh year he was crowned, given a copy of the covenant, and presented to the people, in a palace revolution against the Northern queen mother's rule in the South. This revolution, then, was engineered by the priesthood and the royal guard loyal to "David," from which Athaliah had usurped.

Through his father Ahaziah, Jehoash is both Northern and Southern. Moses' nativity story could thus have a "site-in-life" in the various accounts of revolutions harbored within an Israelite house that inadvertently parented its own internecine division. While the God of Exodus means to divide between the House of Pharaoh and the House of Israel, Moses' own life is curiously entangled with both. And while one may wonder how anyone could have been a member of the Egyptian royal household at the same time he was a member of a family of slaves, it is clear from the politics of the two Israelite kingdoms how, through marriage and descent, a member of the royal family in the later half of the ninth century could be party to both Northern and Southern dynasties: King Jehoram of Judah married Athaliah, daughter of King Ahab of Israel, and her son King Ahaziah of Judah was killed on the orders of the Jehu who overthrew King Jehoram of Israel; Athaliah then usurped her dead son's throne rather than see it go to her son's progeny. The restoration of the Davidic king is accompanied by motions that have become very familiar to us from other contexts:

> And Jehoiada made a covenant between the Lord and the king and the people, that they should be the Lord's people; between the king also and the people.
> And all the people of the land went into the house of Baal, and brake it down; his altars and his images brake they in pieces thoroughly, and slew Mattan the priest of Baal before the altars. (2 Kings 11:17–18a)

The iconoclastic outburst that marks the charismatic and kerygmatic phase of the Mosaic religion has again occurred.

A similar reform is attributed to the self-reforming Manasseh of 2 Chronicles 33, who, after he returned from his own Babylonian captivity, "took away the strange gods, and the idol out of the house of the Lord, and all the altars that he had built in the mount of the house of the Lord, and in Jerusalem, and cast them out of the city" (vs. 15). Why is Jehoiada's intervention (2 Kings 11) the one place the deuteronomic history dignifies with this very recognizable sequence of events before the reforms of Hezekiah and Josiah?—Because this is the only place in the history of the Southern kingdom that the divine promises to David's house—always partly conditional upon a reform of the practices begun under Solomon—were actually not kept: during the reign of Athaliah, no heir of David in fact sat upon the throne. The ironic result of Jehu's reform in the North had been the interruption of the continuously Davidic regime in the South. As this regime got back on its feet, it claimed its version of the Mosaic heritage, a covenant between the people and God that also includes a contract between the people and the house of David. If the text of 2 Kings 11:17–18 describes anything like a real event, it must be an important one: the point where the Yahwist leadership in the Jerusalem sanctuary began to work together with "David" to make the institution of the Davidic kingship a permanent part of Israel's *religious* heritage. No parallel development in the national constitution took place in the North.

Every interruption there—nine different dynasties—made its prophets look more and more like the disruptive "Moses," and made its kings less and less like the self-recovering "David." The North could not ultimately survive the curse on Jeroboam. No dynasty was understood as God's gift to the Northern nation, and the Northern ruler least offensive to God, after Jehu, was the one for whom the curse was fulfilled. "They will return to Egypt," Hosea had said, and under Hoshea, thirty years later, their kingdom fell to Assyria.

If the story of Moses' birth is "Northern," then its sequel might well be a vita like that of the Jeroboam, who, in our sense, "remembered Joseph." The Mosaic infancy, through the figure of a child's claim upon life, might also make a regime's claim on the tradition of "Israel," like the nascent Northern kingdom's claim on Yahwist sanctuaries in Bethel and Dan. But the infancy might equally imply the promise of a renewed leadership for the Yahwist cause, as it does in this case from the South. The restoration of Moses to his mother would then stand for a leadership's being recovered for the cause of Mosaic tradition. When Zion says, "The Lord has forsaken me, my Lord has forgotten me," God replies, " 'Can a women forget her suckling child, that she should have no compassion on the son of her womb?' Even these may forget, yet I will not forget you" (Isa. 49:14–15, RSV).

At the same time that Moses' birth story might insinuate the claim of an "Israel" on its own "house" or tradition, the temporary but marked characterization of Moses as a foundling also points to a more radical beginning, of the kind referred to when Israel speaks of itself as having been found as an infant by God in the wilderness: in Ezekiel 16, or Deuteronomy 32:10, where God found Israel "in a desert land, and in the waste howling wilderness; he led him about, he instructed him, he kept him as the apple of his eye," or in Hosea 9:10, where God found Israel "like grapes in the wilderness." The story of the finding of the exposed Moses also calls into question the search for any more historically contingent understandings of the "originality" of Moses' particular mission. Yet the story may fill in a historical *tabula rasa* from the historical record itself, by means of reports of the latter-day survival of Mosaic leaderships.

The identification of Moses' story as anything more than allegorical of his own beginnings, or the beginnings of a particular Yahwist regime, in effect denies Moses' actual function, which is to stand, representatively, in the place of the obscure story of his nation's origins, his own included. This function of Moses as the maker of a beginning in history dictates the *non*-royal aspect of Moses' particular birth story in the first place, since Israel remembered a time when it had no kingship—for it came to royalist politics "late," long after the nations surrounding it had become king-

ships and satrapies.[3] Thus what keeps Moses from being purely a foundling, namely the circumstantiality of history—and hence from being a
child of pure myth, like Romulus and Remus—also keeps him from having
any very secure history of his own: one not transferred from other histories or stories. "The family of Imram" proves a somewhat figurative or
hypothetical one.

Part B. *Keeping the Name upon a Priestly Site in Israel*

> Lord, remember David, and all his afflictions:
> How he sware unto the Lord, and vowed unto the mighty God of
> Jacob;
> Surely I will not come into the tabernacle of my house, nor go up into
> my bed;
> I will not give sleep to mine eyes, or slumber to mine eyelids,
> Until I find out a place for the Lord, an habitation for the mighty God
> of Jacob.
> Lo, we heard of it at Ephratah: we found it in the fields of the wood.
> We will go into his tabernacles: we will worship at his footstool.
> Arise, O Lord, into thy rest; thou, and the ark of thy strength. . . .
> For the Lord hath chosen Zion; he hath desired it for his habitation.
> This is my rest forever: here will I dwell; for I have desired it. (Psalm
> 132:1–8, 13–14)

The Moses of Deuteronomy 12 prophesies the keeping of God's name
upon an exclusive, sacrosanct, and divinely appointed site in Israel, but he
never names the site, of which Deuteronomy keeps its immediate, internal
audience ignorant. The text thus suggests the transfer of such a Yahwist
appointment to a future site, from a past one: on the analogy of the translation of the Name and the ark, from the Sinai of the exodus to the Israel
of Deuteronomy. The place Yahweh will appoint is Jerusalem, but the
ambiguity of Deuteronomy may implicitly acknowledge that this site had
not always been the place where the Name was kept. If some "forebear"
other than Moses himself is wanted, the site in Canaan originally
appointed for the keeping of the Name is in fact the Beth-el of Genesis 28.

At Jeremiah 7:11 it is not Bethel but Shiloh which is the place called by
God's name, but in any case the concept of a place where God causes his
name to dwell would be predeuteronomic. But in Deuteronomy the termi-
nology can apply to one and only one place, the temple in a Jerusalem like
Josiah's. The story of Bethel implies that the patriarch who was named
Israel committed his future namesake to maintaining the priesthood at
Bethel by means of the tithe, in return for a relation to Yahweh. A
Northern author, if he were a Levite, would adopt the story of Bethel

insofar as it could be made to support the provisions of such a maintenance contract. The conservation of the story might well protest or deny the disestablishment of the Levites at Bethel by Jeroboam, even while supporting the establishment or reestablishment of Bethel itself. For while the present story of Genesis 28 (traditionally identified as "JE") ignores Jeroboam's specific innovations—the Aaronid calf and the removal of the Levites from office—it neither disallows the sanctification of Bethel nor resists the "anachronistic," pre-Sinaitic introduction of the name Yahweh (along with the priests who kept that name) into the promises of the patriarchal contract itself.

And what are we to make of the invocation of this contract at Bethel? The so-called Elohist narrative of Exodus 3 suggests that God was called "El" at first, and that only thereafter did he reveal his personal name Yahweh—to the Moses who was commanded to dislodge with Israel from Egypt. The name was vouchsafed to Moses when he was in exile in Midian, when Israel was in bondage in Egypt. Might not this story resonate with overtones of the history of Jeroboam? Jeroboam resolved, presumably during his Egyptian exile from the South, to assert the rights of the North in the face of its Southern bondage under Solomon and his successor. If Jeroboam removed from Judah under the protection of the divine name, as formerly revealed to his Israel and kept in Jerusalem by the sons of Moses' spokesman, Aaron, Jeroboam presumably would have also relocated the Name's service to the sanctuary in Bethel. Moses and his people had exchanged the service of Pharoah in Egypt for the service of Yahweh in the wilderness. Jeroboam and the house of Joseph would now exchange the service of Rehoboam in Jerusalem for the service of the El in Bethel: but now they would call him Yahweh, the God of a new exodus.

The divine name is what Jacob will indeed ask for, not here, but in the subsequent story of Penuel, where the request is evaded. Here it would give Jacob a means of offering a deal to God, or of converting to the prior covenant relation, especially if the parties were to swear an oath for which the Name itself could have been used. It is here that the alleged presumptions of the "Jahwist" ("J") and the "Elohist" ("E") would seem least separable. This is hardly a fatal objection to the Documentary Hypothesis, but it suggests that Northern, Levitical authors had in the Bethel pericope a story somewhat equivalent to the Sinai one, and that it showed that as Moses removed to Sinai, so Israel-Jacob removed to Bethel: to meet and contract with the God who delivers from trouble. But could this predisclosure of the Name to the North alone explain a redactor's joining Yahweh and El stories here, at the place where Jacob's vision coincided with Jeroboam's shrine? Why is Bethel one of the places where the divine name "begins," as it starts to attach to a priestly establishment?

We may revert to the beginning being made by the giving of the Name at Sinai, and ask: What party or establishment at Sinai claims the honor of giving to Israel the name of God? Moses himself is the original administrator of the Name. But the party otherwise most closely related to the giving of the Name at Sinai is the Levites: Moses is a Levite, the Levites rally to the Name at Sinai in the wake of Aaron's apostasy, and use of the Name is a subject of legislation found in both the book of the covenant in Exodus and in the Holiness Code in Leviticus. Thus, the Levites, through Moses and especially in the strand found in the Bethel material, claim priority in the use of the personal name of God. They, through Moses, have revealed the Name to Israel, as Moses once revealed it to Pharaoh: through Moses of old, the Levites possessed the Name in Egypt, even before they were Levites. It was their office to remember the Name. Like Moses they inherited no land, but they took possession of the Name in the land's place. The tax-supported priesthood and the Name's administration and commemoration were allotted to the Levites for their own peculiar inheritance. The text, through the story in Exodus 3, gives Moses the Name in anticipation of the needs of the Levitical corporation.

By giving the Levites their offices, however, the pentateuchal Moses also gives them the Name *back*. In Numbers 1:50 the Levites are assigned to carry the tabernacle and its furniture; in Deuteronomy 31:25 they are said to have regularly carried the ark. Deuteronomy 10 finds Moses issuing a series of laws (perhaps a vestigial decalogue [Deut. 10:12–11:1]), which includes the injunction to swear by the Name (10:20). In the same chapter Moses reports that after he had made the ark and acquired the second set of tables, Aaron died, and Aaron's son, Eleazar, ministered in his father's place (Deut. 10:1–6). But after two removes from Aaron's burial site, Moses says, "*At that time* the Lord separated the tribe of Levi, to bear the ark of the covenant of the Lord, to stand before the Lord to minister unto him, and to bless in his name *unto this day*" (Deut. 10:8). Here Aaron is almost *replaced* by the Levites, in a critical priestly office. The Moses of the text is seconded by the David of 1 Chronicles 15.[4] For when the ark is brought into Jerusalem, David declares that only the Levites are equal to the job; they were absent from the first attempt, and the result was a debacle. Only the Levites can *sanctify themselves* for such a role (1 Chron. 15:2, 12–15); to do this they surely needed the Name.

But why does the office of the Levites regarding the Name need to be reconfirmed? Why do the texts just cited seem to be giving the Levites their *functions* back? The answers may turn on different senses of the way in which the Name was to be kept: by the Levites, or by Jerusalem.

"Jacob vowed a vow" at Bethel (Gen. 28:20), where Jacob spells out what he will do for God (adopt him as his god, and pay a tithe of his gains to him) in return for what he would oblige God to do for him: provide Jacob with food, clothes, protection, and a safe return home. This is a protection which Israel otherwise offered to the priesthood. The chapter concludes with Jacob saying to God, "And this stone, which I have set for a pillar, shall be God's house: and of all that thou shalt give me I will surely give the tenth unto thee" (vs. 22). We conclude that it was the Levites who considered themselves custodians of the Name in which Israel, through the Levites' offices, sacrificed throughout the land, from the time of Canaan's occupation by "the sons of Jacob." For the elements that are in solution in Genesis 28—the predisclosure of the Name and the holiness of God, the treading of the communicant on sacred ground, the pre-rendering of the tithe (which "Israel" promises to God, but which would ordinarily go to the Levites), and the provision for the communicant's welfare (which Jacob secures for himself, but in terms that would ordinarily apply to the Levites)—all support the argument that Jacob figures at Bethel as the patriarchal precursor of a *Levitical* order presiding there.

It follows that the project attributed to Solomon by a deuteronomic historian—the attempt to build in Jerusalem a suitable house for the divine name—implies a "new Bethel": that is, a royal project of reinvesting the Levitical-Mosaic office of the Name's custodianship in a temple priesthood thereupon being made exclusive to Jerusalem. The "house" invested by Solomon with the keeping of the Name in Jerusalem would be an exclusive house of Aaron, which seems to be the house of that priest— Zadok—who supported Solomon's succession to David's throne over Adonijah's. But the project itself (that of making the Jerusalem temple-staff the sole and exclusive keepers of the name of Yahweh) was perhaps more properly Josiah's. For we can see Josiah's activity in Jerusalem in the mirror of this same king's deeds at the "house" at Bethel. Jeremiah had proclaimed the disestablishment of a non-Jerusalemnic name-site in terms reminiscent of Shiloh: "they shall say no more, The ark of the covenant of the Lord: . . . neither shall they remember it; neither shall they visit it; . . . they shall call Jerusalem the throne of the Lord; and all the nations shall be gathered unto it, to the name of the Lord, to Jerusalem" (Jer. 3:16–17). When Josiah returned to Bethel, three hundred and more years after its establishment by Jeroboam, to deconsecrate the altar there, he in effect pronounced that the words attributed to Jacob in the story in Genesis 28—"Surely the Lord is in this place. . . . This is none other but the house of God" (vss. 16–17)—were indeed "the voice of Jacob": the deceptive voice of the local Levites who had tried to claim Jerusalem's election for this shrine. Their claim for Bethel's priority in the use of the Name was thereinafter null and void: as remote from the Jerusalem temple as Mount Sinai in Arabia.

Part C. The Localization of the Burden of Egypt in the Canaan and Israel of
1 Samuel: A Heterodox Exodus Narrative

> After the doings of the land of Egypt, wherein ye dwelt, shall ye not
> do: and after the doings of the land of Canaan, whither I bring you, shall
> ye not do: neither shall ye walk in their ordinances.
> Ye shall do my judgments, and keep mine ordinances, to walk therein:
> . . . (Lev. 18:3–4)

Earlier we broached the possibility of Pharaoh being punished in the form
in which Canaanite-Israelite culture sinned. Curiously enough, the consecration of the Levites and their portage of the ark may help avoid that sin.
There is more than a trace, early in 1 Samuel, of a story that fused the
plaguing of Egypt and the wilderness Israel in a quite distinctive way. This
story first occurs in the prophecy of the man of god against the house of
Eli. The spokesman refers Eli's lineage back to the original ordination of
the Israelite priesthood: "Thus saith the Lord, Did I plainly appear unto
the house of thy father, when they were in Egypt in Pharaoh's house? And
did I choose him out of all the tribes of Israel to be my priest, . . . to burn
incense, to wear an ephod before me? And did I give unto the house of
thy father all the offerings made by fire of the children of Israel?"
(1 Sam. 2:27–28). Here is a priesthood that is appointed before the
exodus, and is assigned the sacrifice for sin during the time of the plagues.
Such a priesthood would surely have been empowered to intervene on
behalf of the sinful Egypt, rather than the sinless Israel. Egypt would thus
be an alternative or "allegorical" Israel.

The possibility is extended by subsequent references in the ark narrative, where, conversely, the corresponding alternative or allegorical Egypt
is the Canaan of the Canaanites. Among our examples of the Egypt-like
plaguing of Canaanite sovereignties we have already touched briefly on
the victorious Philistines of 1 Samuel 5. They capture the ark in battle and
bring it into the enclaves of Philistia, only to be penalized for their success:
by the maiming of the idol of Dagon in Ashod, by panic and tumors in
Gath, and by deathly panic and tumors in Ekron. The deathly panic turns
out to be a plague of mice that ravages the land (1 Sam. 5:9, 11; 6:4–5),
sparing none of the five Philistine cities—i.e., the Philistines' five "lords."
Ekron, in particular, suffers like Egypt: "The hand of God was very heavy
there . . . and the cry of the city went up to heaven" (1 Sam. 5:11–12).

As various scholars have observed, the "exodus pattern" is extraordinarily marked in this part of the narrative, for the Philistines themselves
refer to it explicitly, not once, but twice.[5] When the ark is first introduced
among them, at the battle of Aphek in 1 Samuel 4, Israel's embattled
adversaries refer to a version of the exodus that is decidedly their own:
"these," they say—most likely meaning the cherubim on the ark—"are

the Gods that smote the Egyptians with all the plagues in the wilderness" (1 Sam. 4:8). The editors of the Pentateuch would surely want to emend this, to say that Israel's is the God who, in the wilderness, plagued his own people. After the ark has done the same thing to the Philistines, they consult their priests and diviners. These argue for a course of action that makes their spokesmanship explicitly Mosaic: "Wherefore then do ye harden your hearts," they ask their countrymen, "as the Egyptians and Pharaoh hardened their hearts? when he [God] had wrought wonderfully among them, did they not let the people go, and they departed?" (1 Sam. 6:6; RSV, "made sport of them"). The speaker is recommending, by analogy, that the Philistines let the ark go back to the Canaan of Israel, from whom they have taken it captive into the Canaan of Philistia. According to the analogy, the ark is in the place of the Israelites in Egypt, the Philistines are in place of Pharaoh, the release of the ark from Philistia is in place of the release of the Israelites from Egypt, and the ark's return to Israel is in place of the Hebrews' return to Canaan.

The analogy extends to the Israelite occupation, because the ark is allowed to migrate on its own—in a cart pulled by two milch cows that assent to their being separated from their young—back to the Israelites of Beth-Shemesh. It stops at a landmark in the field of one "Joshua," where the men of Beth-Shemesh sacrifice the cows on a fire of the timbers of the cart. The five lords of the Philistines—who have followed the ark out of Philistia—seeing the finalizing of the sign that it is indeed the ark that has moved the cows, rather than the cows the ark, return home. The princes are not only in the place of the Egyptians who followed the Israelites out of Egypt to be drowned in the Reed Sea, but also in place of the generation that crossed the Reed Sea and died in the wilderness: for that is where the Philistine version has the Egyptians being divinely plagued.

To complete the analogy of the ark's exodus from Philistia to the Israelites' exodus from Egypt, the ark comes back to the Israelites enriched with foreign gold, like the Israelites leaving Egypt. Moreover, the Israelites were carrying the bones of Joseph back to their place—the bones had been put in an ark (*'aron*, 'box,' 'chest'). The Egyptian gold eventually contributed to the adornment of the tabernacle and/or the making of the golden calf. The ark returning from the Philistines was enhanced with an offering of golden mice. The Philistines may have associated the ark with a health-god like Apollo Smintheus ('mousey'), for they are Ionians and thus would have fetishized the deity in the shape in which they sinned as idolaters, which is also the shape in which they have been plagued and punished as sinners. The story of Ahaziah told in 2 Kings 1 strongly suggests that the Baal of the Philistine city of Ekron was a health-god, for the king that sends to him is sick; a little like the Philistine idol of Dagon in the present story, Ahaziah is unable to recuperate from a bad fall.

Thus the ark of 1 Samuel, re-arriving at "Beth-Shemesh" and "Joshua," seems only to have come back to cause death in Israel. The two names compare with those of the last and first judges in the Book of Judges, Samson and Joshua, as if the ark were rolling through history backwards, to re-arrive at an Israel that was in Egypt. For the ark, in the place of Joshua's Israel, back in its home territories, now afflicts its local, Israelite keepers as once the armies of Joshua's Israel, entering the promised land and accompanied by the same ark as their palladium, visited themselves upon the original Canaanites—or as Moses and Aaron once visited God's signs and wonders upon the Egyptians. The logic of the comparison offers to equate the present Israelites with the original Canaanites:[6] because, as Joshua himself told Israel at Shechem, "Ye cannot serve the Lord: for he is an holy God" (Josh. 24:19). The Israelites at the end of the Book of Joshua were no better off than their enemies. Joshua's reasoning at Shechem offers a close enough parallel to the Israelites' reaction in the lethal presence of the repatriated ark at Beth-Shemesh: "Who is able to stand before this holy Lord God?" (1 Sam. 6:20).

The bearing of the ark out of those cities and places that could not serve it in 1 Samuel 4–7—whether the places were Philistine or Israelite—presents us, on the one hand, with an allegory of the exodus, but, on the other, with a latter-day narrative from which some of the narrative of the "original" exodus could derive its contour and meaning. The burden that Israel had become to Philistia in Canaan might well have been a source for the imagery used to reconstruct the burden Israel was alleged to have been to the Egyptians in Egypt. Yet this was also the burden that Israel became to Moses in the wilderness, and would become to God in Israel. Moreover, the burden God was to Israel—whether in the wilderness or in Canaan—was also the burden Israel would become to itself. From a deuteronomistic point of view, it became this burden through idolatry. From a figurative point of view, the burden on Canaan would be Joshua: the story points to precisely this future, with the ark's arrival in "the field of Joshua." But who, allegorically speaking, are the two milch cows separated from Philistia to draw the ark, separated from their family and serving and bearing the ark in that family's place, and immolated at the end of the ark's journey back to its homeland? The cows stand in place of the priestly leaders—Moses and Aaron—who die on the threshold of the occupation.

* * * * *

And what does it mean, for the larger process of the history recorded by the Bible, that Moses did not himself enter the promised land? Surely it means that Mosaic Israel had never quite been realized in history proper, or else that the supersession of such an Israel was something of a foregone conclusion. Mosaic Israel was "somewhere else": in the wilderness with Moses' grave; in the future with a military savior, or a royal patron; in the North, with a schismatic sanctuary; in the South, with a disinherited priesthood; and in the past, with the Judges, before the coming of the national state. Although the various territories—symbolically bequeathed to Israel upon the death of Moses as the testator—were an estate that the tribes "inherited by lot," the legacy was hardly secured without further divine and human intervention: only with the coming of the state, in the time of David, did Israel expand from within to occupy the borders that the storied Moses had reached and defined from without. It was presumably from the vantage point provided by the monarchy (as in Solomon's deuteronomistic dedication of the temple in 1 Kings 8–9) that Israel was able to review and summarize its traditional history as a series of backdrops lifting on the present actualization of Israel, and so visualize Moses foreseeing Israel's inheritance from a peak outside of it. When God makes his covenant with Abraham, he says it was he (and therefore not Terah) who brought his servant out of "Ur of the Chaldees" (Gen. 15:7, *contra* 11:28, 31), and he promises to give Israel the land from Sea to River (Gen. 15:18). But the kingship that won this possession, according to 1 Samuel 8, established itself at the same time that Israel gave up the Mosaic "kingship of God."

The grand chronology of the story of Israel, from the Creation to the Exile, thus embeds a double strand, one piece prophesying an Israel of God, and the other lamenting it. In the one tradition Moses comes to announce the exodus, and the accession of Yahweh to the divine throne of Israel's consciousness; but in the other, Moses makes Israel's history a recall to its lost faith in this original revelation. When Moses of one pentateuchal tradition reports that God has visited the people, the people understand, and even (according to the Septuagint) rejoice: Moses' and Aaron's signs and words are that convincing (Exod. 4:31). But in a second tradition, the people refuse to hear approximately the same report, so broken is their spirit (Exod. 6:9). If we reject the optimistic report that Moses was well received, we must then accept the pessimistic report that he was rejected. We stand upon the threshold of a people's faith in Moses, but we face both ways.

At Sinai God tells Moses that he will allow the Israelites to overhear God speaking to his servant in the cloud, so "that the people may hear . . . and believe thee for ever" (Exod. 19:9). But as late as John 5:46, Jesus is accusing the Jews of having failed to believe this Moses: the Moses in whom they claim to put their hope is actually the one who accuses them— of their perpetual unbelief. When the people despair of making a prompt invasion of Canaan, Yahweh asks Moses, "How long will it be ere they believe me?" (Num. 14:11). Hebrews 3:18 might well conclude that the generation that was saved from Egypt at the first could not be saved thereafter, because it did not believe. On the other hand, the great homily on faith subsequently found in Hebrews 11 takes heart from an ideal investment like the one depicted in and through a Moses—the Moses of, say, Numbers 12:7, "faithful in all [the Lord's] house." The text says that it was this faith, "the evidence of things not seen," that caused Moses to forsake the treasures of Egypt, behold him who is invisible, and keep his eye on the reward.

The passage from Hebrews 11 frames Moses' faith in the unseen with others' faith in him, for it starts from the faith of his parents in their son's existence (vs. 23), and ends with the faith of his people who were able to cross the Red Sea as if on dry land (vs. 29). There is scarcely any need for the homilist to mention the miraculous intervention of God, if Israel's deliverance from the Sea was accomplished by the miracle of the people's faith in Moses. The Egyptians tried to walk on the water, but they could not: because, the context implies, they lacked the necessary faith. Yet almost the opposite is the case in the actual Book of Exodus, where it is the children of Israel themselves who do not believe until the miracle at the Sea has been divinely performed for them: presumably to help their unbelief, their lack of faith in their savior (cf. Ps. 78:22, 32, with Exod. 14:31).

As for Moses himself, at the end of his own pilgrimage he stands on a national border he will not cross, giving endorsement to tribal boundaries he will not see, and prescribing the landless Levitical inheritance and the priestly cities of refuge from the standpoint of his own, deeper disqualification from inheriting in Israel. Such a figure may not lack faith, but by the same token he may need it. For the "symbolic" of this life is to be found in the boundaries it mediates. Putting Egypt behind him as a resource, and keeping Israel ahead of him as a reward, Moses is an honored but twice-alienated Hebrew whom God buries outside the promised land beyond Jordan, and an honorary but twice-excommunicated Egyptian who perishes in the wilderness beyond the Reed Sea. He is presented in this way not in despite of his appointment to be the great raiser of consciousness in Israel, but because of it: only such a subject, coming from outside Israel, could make Israel his proper object—and his people the servant of God, rather than the slave of the state. Through such a Moses passes the identification of Israel with its own historical limits, and thus with itself, rather than with Moses. For Moses found Israel in Egypt, but put it up for adoption in the desert. Whether in Midian, Sinai, or Moab, Moses' own existence typically occupies a perilous threshold between two territories or jurisdictions, and so, perforce, defines him for either side as one coming from abroad or beyond. His was a generation that perished in the desert, yet lived in a numinous interval between worldly dispensations. He suffered a speech impediment, yet voiced the name of God. Moses' whole life—like the Passover, and the Tetragrammaton itself—is the constituting of an interruption.

NOTES

Preface

1. See my early position paper, "On literature and the Bible," *Centrum* (University of Minnesota), II:2 (Fall 1974): pp. 5–6, 14, 15, 21, 28–29, from which I have adapted most of this and the next paragraph.

2. "Under What Lyre" (1946), in *Collected Poems,* ed. Edward Mendelson (New York: Random House, 1976), pp. 259–60: the sixth commandment of the "Hermetic Decalogue," which ends by telling its audience to "trust in God; and take short views."

3. See the famous essay of Claude Lévi-Strauss, "The Structural Study of Myth," *Journal of American Folklore* 57 (1955): 428–44, at sec. 4.11.2: "our method eliminates a problem which has been so far one of the main obstacles to the progress of mythological studies, namely, the quest for the *true* version, or the *earlier* one. On the contrary, we define the myth as consisting of all its versions. . . ." For the analogous univocal rule (from Maimonides) governing traditional Torah interpretation, see Jon D. Levenson, "The Eighth Principle of Judaism and the Literary Simultaneity of Scripture," in *Journal of Religion* 68 (1988): 205–25: three different biblical laws regarding the manumission of the slave necessarily issue in a fourth law when the texts are synchronized in the Talmud. For the relevance of these laws to the subject of this book, see the use made of them in chapter 4, and reference there (in note 20) to J. Weingreen, "The Deuteronomic Legislator—A Proto-Rabbinic Type," in *Proclamation and Presence: Old Testament Essays in Honour of Gwynne Henton Davies,* ed. John I. Durham and J. R. Porter [1970] (Macon, Ga.: Mercer University Press, 1983).

4. "Master of the tale . . .": see Meir Sternberg, *The Poetics of Biblical Narrative: Ideological Literature and the Drama of Reading* (Bloomington and Indianapolis: Indiana University Press, 1985), p. 75. To generalize from the master of individual tales and cycles to the master of the whole narrative corpus and chronicle is sometimes to go too far, of course, despite the remarkable homogeneity, overall, of biblical storytelling techniques and concerns. The lack of so-called doublets in the so-called Davidic court history, for example, deprives the teller of what is elsewhere to be regarded as a resource.

5. For this notice of *Studien zur Komposition des Pentateuch* (Berlin and New York: de Gruyter: 1990), I am wholly dependent on the reviews of Joseph Blenkinsopp, *Catholic Biblical Quarterly* 54 (1992): 312–13, and John Van Seters, *Journal of Biblical Literature* 111 (1992): 122ff. Van Seters's own theory, of a late, unified composition of the major narrative, is found in his *In Search of History: Historiography in the Ancient World and the Origins of Biblical History* (New Haven: Yale University Press, 1983). The typical view is that of Klaus Koch, in *The Growth of Biblical Tradition,* 2d ed., trans. S. M. Cupit (New York: Charles Scribner's Sons, 1969): that early oral

traditions only began to be written up late in the day, i.e., toward the end of the period encompassed by the major narrative. My own opinion, for what it is worth, is that narratives concerning the patriarchs and David's family are early, and narratives concerning Moses and the Former Prophets are later, and that the evidence is to be found in the congruities between the subject matters in question.

Acknowledgments

1. Cf. the headnote to "The Hittite Laws" in James B. Pritchard, *Ancient Near Eastern Texts Relating to the Old Testament,* 3d ed. with Supplement (Princeton: Princeton University Press, 1957), p. 188: "The laws, as they have come down to us, represent two tables. . . . A label which is accidentally preserved . . . proves that— possibly in a different arrangement—there existed a third tablet." Cf. also Confucius, *The Analects,* III.15: "When the Master went inside the Grand Temple, he asked questions about everything. Someone remarked, 'Who said that the son of the man from Tsou understood the rites? When he went inside the Grand Temple, he asked questions about everything.' The Master, on hearing of this, said, 'The asking of questions is in itself the correct rite.' " (Trans. D. C. Lau [Harmondsworth, U.K.: Penguin Books, 1979], p. 69.)

2. *Moses and the Deuteronomist, A Literary Study of the Deuteronomic History, Part One: Deuteronomy, Joshua, Judges* (New York: The Seabury Press, 1980), esp. chap. 2, pp. 25–72. (Reissued at Bloomington: Indiana University Press, 1993.)

Chapter 1: The Face of Moses

1. Cf. Robert M. Torrance, *The Comic Hero* (Cambridge, Mass.: Harvard University Press, 1978), pp. 12–59, for Odysseus and the Aristophanic protagonist.

2. For the strict limitations that critical study of the texts themselves might impose on Moses' historicity, see Geo Widengren, "What do we know about Moses?" in *Proclamation and Presence: Old Testament Essays in Honour of Gwynne Henton Davies,* ed. John I. Durham and J. R. Porter [1970] (Macon, Ga.: Mercer University Press, 1983), pp. 21–47. Widengren's study is, among other things, an extremely valuable guide to biblical references to Moses in 'pre-deuteronomic' strata of the texts mentioning or alluding to him.

3. The glow on Moses' face may be the shine of massive scar tissue or hardened skin from a burn, according to William H. Propp. "The Skin of Moses' Face— Transfigured or Disfigured?" *Catholic Bible Quarterly* 49 (1987): 375–86. There is no decisive evidence in the story of the veil at Exodus 34:29–35, nor in the preceding exposure of Moses to God's glory at Exodus 33. But the glow or stigmata in the second story would answer to the question put in the first, "how shall it be known that [Moses has] found favor in [God's] sight?" (Exod. 33:16, RSV), or that he has seen God's glory? The suggestion about the burn is originally that of B. D. Eerdmans, *The Covenant at Mount Sinai Viewed in the Light of Antique Thought* (Leiden: Burgersdijk and Niermans, 1939), pp. 20–22, with reference to the alleged effects of Moses' working in a Midianite smithy. Propp explains the tradition of Moses' horns as thus being half-correct, 'hornified' (calloused to the hardness of horn) being as plausible a translation of *qaran* as 'shone.' He concludes that we should read Exodus 34:29–30, 35, as reporting "the skin of his face was burnt to the hardness of horn," and as an early notice of *keratosis.*

"The sight of the glory of the Lord was like devouring fire on the top of the mount in the eyes of the children of Israel," we read at Exod. 24:17; Moses is in this mount forty days (vs. 18) before he views that glory (Exod. 34:5–6) and the need for the veil is introduced. (The intervening passages contain the first long set of prescriptions for the cult and its furniture, *including the veil,* and the episode of the golden calf.) Moses' shielding of Israel from God's fiery presence at Sinai is referred to in Deuteronomy 5:3–4 and 18:16. Moses must be shielded (by God's hand) in Exodus 33:22, at the sight of the glory. He thus stands on a mount of disfiguration.

The legendary material about Moses is likewise strongly in favor of the idea of the burn, and much of it takes us back to the origins of Moses' call at the burning bush. The legends say: (1) Moses was so important that his face is engraved forever on the sun; (2) Pharaoh tried to kill the infant Moses, but Pharaoh's officer Haman, finding the child at home in an oven where he seemed to be burning in a great fire, assumed the parents' compliance with his master's will; he did not perceive that it was the child's glorious face that flamed so brightly; (3) the princess who rescued Moses did so because when she touched his basket she was cured of abiding sores on her face, her new beauty astonishing her maidservants. And finally (4), Moses as a young child was tested for his covetousness toward Pharaoh's sacrosanct crown: a platter with the crown on it and a platter of live coals were put before him. He reached for the crown, and a guardian angel deflected his hand to the coals—Moses took one and put his hand to his mouth in pain. The resulting burning of his tongue made him lisp the rest of his life. These ideas are all taken from the summaries of rabbinic material in Joseph Gaer, *The Lore of the Old Testament* (New York: Grossett and Dunlap, 1966), pp. 137, 141–44; they associate Moses with burns, disfiguration, and a countenance that cannot be beheld directly or without aversion. We can combine this evidence with the report that upon confronting the burning bush Moses *hid his face:* i.e., he anticipated his need for the veil, in shunning the heat. The story of the burning bush ("E") is not attributed to the author of the veil notice ("P"), but if we are looking at a unified tradition, then its different ramifications may be found in different sources, without the loss of a common coherence (cf. the quotation from Lévi-Strauss in Preface note 3, *supra*).

4. By the same token, the Egyptian courtiers touched by the plague of boils were unable to present themselves in court before their god-king. Herodotus gives an account of the particular cleanliness of the Egyptians (*Histories*, 2.35ff.), who are continually washing their linens; their priests shaved every other day to guard against the presence of lice while attending to their religious duties. No wonder the Egyptian magicians were unable to bring forth lice in competition with Moses. That, the magicians say, "is the finger of God" (Exod. 8:19). Exodus twice directs attention to the magicians' plight, as if God were bent upon incapacitating a Levitical priesthood, making its stigmatized representatives unpresentable before their Lord. The same motive of stigmatization may hide within the veil: this may also be the finger of God.

5. See Moses Hadas, *Introduction to Classical Drama* (New York: Bantam Books, 1977), chap. 3, "Sophocles," esp. pp. 42–49.

6. The dissolving of "Moses" into exodus motifs and covenant motifs tends to support Eduard Meyer's claim that Moses is not a historical figure (*Die Israeliten und ihre Hachbarstämme* [Halle: Martin Niemeyer, 1906], p. 451). Meyer's work is cited as a major source by Freud in *Moses and Monotheism,* trans. Katherine Jones (New York: Knopf, 1939), p. 16 (or in *The Complete Psychological Works of Sigmund Freud,* ed. and trans. James Strachey [London: Hogarth Press, 1964], vol. 23, p. 13), where the quest for the historical Moses leads this investigator away from the dou-bleness of the biblical Moses and the texts about him into the postulation of two

different historical characters who correspond to the service of two somewhat
gnostically opposed deities—the Egyptian Aton and the levitical Jahve (see esp.
pp. 48, 54, 55–56, in the Jones trans. of Freud's book [all further citations are from
this trans.]). According to Freud, the original, gentile Moses was an Egyptian who
converted the Hebrews in Egypt to the worship of the universal sun-god Aton, but
who also led his new people out of post-Akhenaton Egypt. A subsequent generation rebelled against their teacher and betrayed him in the wilderness. The blood
of this "suffering servant" and "lost leader" then watered, even as it transformed,
the consciences and Yahwist religion of his Jewish persecutors and successors. On
the Freudian view, a deuteronomic Moses might be presumed to say to the Levites,
echoing the midrash in *Sifre,* "if you are my ministers, I am Moses, and if you are
not my ministers, I am, as it were, not Moses" (cf. Piska 346: "When I proclaim His
Name, He is great, but when I do not, (He is not great,) if one may say such a
thing—*Therefore ye are My witness, saith the Lord, and I am God* (Isa. 43:12)—when
you are My witnesses, I am God, but when you are not My witnesses, I am not God,
if one may say such a thing": *Sifre: A Tannaitic Commentary on the Book of Deuteronomy,* tr. Reuven Hammer (New Haven and London: Yale University Press, 1986),
p. 359). At Deuteronomy 33:9b–10a, Moses says of the Levites: "they have observed
thy word, and kept thy covenant. They shall teach Jacob thy judgments, and Israel
thy law." Freud's last will and testament seems to be conceived in about the same
spirit, the traitorous and loyalist Levites corresponding to Freud's own disciples
and legatees in the psychoanalytic movement.

The best antidote to Freud, in this respect, is Martin Buber. For Buber it is
Israel's will to existence that seeks and finds fulfillment in and through the narrative—a narrative involving a constitution, a genealogy, a tradition, a record, and a
culture. Even though Buber's emphasis is not at all "deuteronomic" in our sense,
he has been the great guide to the theological dimension of this narrative, especially in *Moses: The Revelation and the Covenant* [1946] (New York: Harper & Row,
1958). In both Buber's book and the present one, Moses is above all the human
protagonist of the Book of Exodus (all of the likenesses implied by my title depend
upon our postulating such a Moses to start with). Yet this putative protagonist has
here become the point of departure for the depiction of a composite being whose
existence depends largely on figures and movements that reach far beyond the
bounds of Exodus itself.

7. José Ortega y Gasset, *The Revolt of the Masses* [1929; English, 1932] (New
York: W.W. Norton, 1957), p. 154.

8. Ortega y Gasset, *Revolt of the Masses,* p. 154.

9. See above all Gerhard von Rad, *Old Testament Theology,* Vol. 1: *The Theology of
Israel's Historical Traditions,* tr. D. M. G. Stalker (New York: Harper & Row, 1962),
"The Conception of Moses and his Office," pp. 289–96.

10. "Hymn of Victory of Mer-ne-Ptah (The 'Israel Stela')," in James H.
Pritchard, ed., *Ancient Near Eastern Texts,* 3d ed. (Princeton: Princeton University
Press, 1957), p. 378 n. 18: Israel, in the line *Israel is laid waste, his seed is not,* "is
written with the determinative of people rather than land." For commentary on
the subject here, see Herbert N. Schneidau, *Sacred Discontent: The Bible and Western
Tradition* (Berkeley/Los Angeles/London: University of California Press, 1976).
p. 134, in "The Hebrews Against the High Cultures: Pastoral Motifs," pp. 104–73.

Chapter 2: "The Voice of the Words": The Moses of Deuteronomy

1. Maurice Blanchot, *The Writing of the Disaster,* trans. Ann Smock (Lincoln: University of Nebraska Press, 1986), p. 63.

2. After "On literature and the Bible," *Centrum* II:2 (Fall 1974): 25. "Exhort one another every day," a similarly contemporizing text in Hebrews says, "as long as it is called 'today,' " and it quotes "Today when you hear his voice do not harden your hearts as in the rebellion" (Heb. 3:12–15, RSV; Ps. 95:7). The passage in the *Centrum* article goes on to compare "In the day that thou eat thereof thou shalt die" with "this day thou shalt be with me in paradise" (*ibid*, pp. 25–26). Almost everything said there, in connection with the actualization of Israel in the deuteronomic present, has been thought out by means of von Rad, *Old Testament Theology*, Vol. 1, *Theology of Israel's Traditions*, "Deuteronomy," pp. 219–31.

3. The likeness between the Moses of Deuteronomy and Jeremiah emerges in other ways. Jeremiah composed a kind of personal testament, and expressed his faith in a future in the promised land. As the martyr of the servant songs of Isaiah 40–55, he may have become a literary subject, as has the deuteronomist's Moses. He was forbidden the temple precincts, and was sent into hiding (Jer. 36:5, 19); so Moses was hidden from the people while he was fasting in Sinai. Jeremiah communicated to the king through his secretary, Baruch; so Moses communicated to Israel through his mouthpiece, Aaron.

4. The phrase "packaged prophetism" for Deuteronomy is aptly used by B. Davie Napier as a summary rubric in his section on this book in *Song of the Vineyard: A Theological Introduction to the Old Testament* (New York/Evanston/London: Harper & Row, 1962), pp. 230ff. See also his article in *The Interpreter's Dictionary of the Bible*, 5 vols. (Nashville: Abingdon, 1962–76), *sub* prophecy. Napier, *Song*, p. 231, quotes Eric Voegelin for this point of view on the effect of Deuteronomy (Voegelin assuming from the complaints of Jeremiah that the Josianic reform had failed): "Far from resulting in a new response of the people to the living word of Yahweh . . . the prophetic effort (Deuteronomy) derailed into a constitution for the Kingdom of Judah which pretended to emanate from the 'historical' Moses. The past that was meant to be revitalized in a continuous present now became really a dead past; and the living word to which the heart was supposed to respond became the body of the law to which the conduct could conform." (Voegelin, *Israel and Revelation* [Baton Rouge: University of Louisiana Press, 1956], p. 377).

5. For this second point of view on Deuteronomy, which I propose be *combined* with the first, see esp. Robert R. Wilson, *Prophecy and Society in Ancient Israel* (Philadelphia: Fortress Press, 1980), pp. 156–66.

6. Franz Kafka, *The Diaries: 1914–1923*, ed. Max Brod (New York: Schocken, 1949), pp. 195–96, for the full passage. Compare Reinhold Niebuhr's moralization, in *The Nature and Destiny of Man: A Christian Interpretation*, Vol. II, *Human Destiny* (New York: Chas. Scribner's Sons, 1964), p. 308: "Each individual has a direct relation to eternity; for he seeks for the completion of his life beyond the fragmentary realizations of meaning which can be discerned at any point in the process where an individual may happen to live and die. The end of an individual life is, for him, the end of history; and every individual is a Moses who perishes outside the promised land." See IV [II] Esdras 7:119–20 (alt. 49–50), in a passage about the human inability to take possession of a paradise: "How does it profit us that an eternal age is promised us, whereas we have done works that bring death? And there is foretold us an imperishable hope whereas we are so miserably brought to futility?" (tr. G. H. Box, in R. H. Charles, ed., *Apocrypha and Pseudepigrapha of the Old Testament* [Oxford: Clarendon Press, 1913], Vol. 2, p. 591). In contrast, Deuteronomy insists on the fullness of Moses' life (after Gen. 6:3, where God declares that a man's "days shall be an hundred and twenty years"), without any proto-apocalyptic motif

of Moses' entry on the land; yet it treats his life as the culmination of Israelite history up until this point.

Chapter 3: The Broken Law-Book

1. The death penalty is specified for violations of the ten commandments of the law as given at Exodus 20, in the following legal texts beyond it:

  I. worship of other gods, Exod. 22:20, Deut. 17:2–5; cf. also the penalty for breaking the ban, Lev. 27:29;

  II. idol-worship where it is Molech-worship (child sacrifice to an idol), Lev. 20:2; cf. also the same penalty for conjuring the dead, Lev. 20:27;

  III. taking the Name in vain, Lev. 24:16; cf. also Deut. 18:20;

  IV. sabbath-breaking, Exod. 31:15;

  V. parent abuse and parent-cursing, Exod. 21:15, 17;

  VI. murder, Exod. 21:12, 14;

  VII. adultery, Lev. 20:10, Deut. 22:22; (incest: Lev. 20:11ff. passim; bestiality: Exod. 22:19, Lev. 20:15–16); cf. also the ordeal of jealousy in Num. 5:12–31 with the information that the original Near Eastern penalty for the guilty wife was drowning (failure to pass the water test);

  VIII. theft of persons, Exod. 21:16; Deut. 24:7 particularly indicates theft of persons *for sale;* see also Exod. 22:2, which allows the cattle-thief caught in the act to be killed with impunity;

  IX. false witness: cf. Exod. 23:7, against preferring a murder charge against the innocent: "I will not justify the wicked," when combined with the death penalty at Lev. 24:16 for taking the Name in vain, seems to make such perjury, or lying under oath to prosecute a false charge, a capital crime.

  [X. covetousness: cf. the Sermon on the Mount, Matt. 5:22: "the judgment" (the death penalty for murder), which Jesus imposes on anger, might be generalized to apply to all intentional sin.]

Cf. Albrecht Alt, *Essays on Old Testament History and Religion,* (Garden City, N.Y.: Doubleday & Co., Anchor Books, 1968), *sub* "The Origins of Israelite Law," esp. pp. 156–57. See chapter 5, *infra,* for the attempt to situate these mortal offenses in biblical narrative.

Chapter 4: The Book of the Covenant

1. Michael Fishbane, *Biblical Interpretation in Ancient Israel* (Oxford: Clarendon Press, 1985), pp. 384–85, makes this point by similar means. Cf. John Milton, *Paradise Lost,* VIII.633ff.: "Be strong . . . and keep / His great command."

2. For further on the Josianic reform or "revolution," see chapter 15, Part C; chapter 16, Part B; and chapter 17, Part B, *infra.*

3. For a précis of my ideas in this matter, emphasizing allegorical relations between narratives on either side of the Mosaic massif but within the Law and the Former Prophets, see "Allegories of Scripture," in *Shofar: An Interdisciplinary Journal of Jewish Studies* 11:2 (Winter 1993), Bible Issue, ed. Stanley Goldman: 127–66. Almost all of the comparisons in this article are observed, considered, researched, and annotated by Edward L. Greenstein in his masterful article "The Formation of the Biblical Narrative Corpus," in *American Jewish Studies Review* (Cambridge, Mass.) 15 (1990): 151–78. Greenstein proposes not so much to appreciate the distribution and effect of the phenomenon, as to set out the various means of assessing its genetics or formation.

4. George E. Mendenhall, "Covenant Forms in Israelite Tradition," in *The Biblical Archaeologist Reader 3*, ed. Edward F. Campbell, Jr., and David Noel Freedman (Garden City, N.Y.: Doubleday & Co., Anchor Books, 1970), pp. 25–53; (= *Law and Covenant in the Ancient Near East*, Biblical Colloquium: Pittsburgh, 1955); *Interpreter's Dictionary of the Bible*, sub "Covenant"; *The Tenth Generation* (Baltimore and London: Johns Hopkins University Press, 1973), pp. 174–97 and p. 200 n. 5; and Dennis J. McCarthy, S. J., *Treaty and Covenant* (Rome: Biblical Institute Press, 1978), *passim*. See as well Delbert R. Hillers, *Covenant: The History of a Biblical Idea* (Baltimore and London: Johns Hopkins University Press, 1969), esp. pp. 25–97.

5. James B. Pritchard, ed., *Ancient Near Eastern Texts Relating to the Old Testament*, Third Edition with Supplement (Princeton: Princeton University Press, 1969), p. 203, "Treaty between Mursilis and Dupp-Tessub of Amurru" [Historical Introduction]: "Aziras was the grandfather of you, Duppi-Tessub. He rebelled against my father, but submitted again to my father. When the kings of Nuhasse land and the kings of Kinza rebelled against my father, Aziras did not rebel. As he was bound by treaty, he remained bound by treaty . . . ," etc. This work hereafter cited as *ANET*.

6. Pritchard, *ANET*, p. 529, "Hittite Treaty": 'Treaty of Suppiluliumas and Aziras of Amurru': [*Preamble:*] "These are the words of the Sun Suppiluliumas, the great king, the king of the Hatti land, the valiant, the favorite of the Storm-god. [*Military Clauses:*] . . . He who [lives in peace] with the Sun [the Hittite monarch] shall live in peace also with you. But he who is an enemy of the Sun, shall also be an enemy [with you]."

7. Pritchard, *ANET*, p. 531, in the Akkadian "Treaty between Niqmepa of Alalakh and Ir- ᵈIM of Tunip": "4. If any booty coming from my land is sold in your land, you must seize it, together with the one who sells it, and hand it over to me. 5. If a fugitive slave, male or female, of my land flees to your land, you must seize and return him to me, (or), if someone else seizes him and takes him to you, [you must keep him] in your prison whenever his owner comes forward, you must hand him over to [him]." Note also extradition of fugitives in treaties between Egypt and the Hittites, in *ANET*, pp. 200, 203, 204–05.

8. Pritchard, *ANET*, pp. 534ff., "The Vassal-Treaties of Esarhaddon," an Akkadian treaty from Assyria, virtually an airtight loyalty oath to the crown prince Ashurbanipal, including commitments not to conspire with his court to bump him off, esp. pp. 535–37. Cf. *ANET*, pp. 531–32, "Treaty between Niqmepa of Alalakh and Ir-ᵈIM of Tunip": "2. [If in your land] there is [a plot against me, and] they plot [to . . . , and you hear of it], you will search for them . . . 3. If someone from my land [*plots against me*], you must [. . .] and you must not conceal it from me, and if he lives in your land, you must extradite him."

9. Pritchard, *ANET*, "The Lipit-Ishtar Lawcode," p. 159. The following quotation is from *ANET*, p. 161.

10. After Pritchard, *ANET*, p. 192 (Hittite Laws, no. 63). For the following point about material scarcity, cf. Joseph Isenbergh, "Why Law?" *The University of Chicago Law Review* 54 (1987): 1117–23 (review of R. M. Unger, *The Critical Legal Studies Movement*, Harvard University Press, 1986).

11. For further on Jeroboam and the Northern revolution from the South, see chapter 15, part B, *infra*.

12. Sir Leonard Wooley, in *History of Mankind, vol. 1:* Jacquetta Hawkes and Sir Leonard Wooley, *Prehistory and the Beginnings of Civilization* (New York and Evanston: Harper & Row: 1963), p. 491. Cf. "The Code of Hammurabi," no. 6, in Pritchard, *ANET*, p. 166, "If a seignior stole the property of church or state [lit., 'of

god or palace'], that seignior shall be put to death," and also no. 8, in the same place, and in the same vein.

13. Cf. "The Hittite Laws," no. 173, in Pritchard, *ANET,* p. 195: "If anyone rejects the judgment of the king, his house shall be made a *shambles.* If anyone rejects the judgment of a dignitary, they shall cut off his head. If a slave rises against his master, he shall go into the *pit."* And "The Code of Hammurabi," in *ANET,* p. 167, no. 15, "If a seignior has helped either a male slave . . . or a female slave escape . . . he shall be put to death," and no. 19, "If [a seignior] has kept that [fugitive] slave [from no. 17] in his house (and later the slave has been found in his possession), that seignior shall be put to death." Harboring a runaway slave is fined in terms of wages in "The Hittite Laws," no. 24 (*ANET,* p. 190).

14. "Code," no. 1, Pritchard, *ANET,* p. 166, "If a seignior accused another seignior and brought a charge of murder against him, but has not proved it, his accuser shall be put to death." And no. 14, on kidnapping among seigniors. Ibid., p. 167, no. 22: "If a seignior committed robbery and has been caught, that seignior shall be put to death." The death penalty, however, is comparatively rare in the Code of Hammurabi. It is meted out to a seignior's wife who connives in his murder because of another man (no. 153), and to the false accuser of a seignior of sorcery (no. 2), as well as murder. In general, the Code seems designed to regulate the justice pertinent only to the seigniors—and moreover to keep them alive—as if they alone merited the benefit of law.

15. "Code," no. 14, theft of a son, and no. 15, escape of a slave, in Pritchard, *ANET,* pp. 166–67.

16. The present considerations have been very much influenced by Edward L. Greenstein, "Biblical Law," chap. 2 in *Back to the Sources: Reading the Classic Jewish Texts,* ed. Barry W. Holtz (New York: Summit Books, 1984), esp. pp. 96–98. Cf. also J. Weingreen, "The Deuteronomic Legislator—A Proto-Rabbinic Type," in *Proclamation and Presence: Old Testament Essays in Honour of Gwynne Henton Davies,* ed. John I. Durham and J. R. Porter [1970] (Macon, Ga.: Mercer University Press, 1983), pp. 76–89.

17. "The Hittite Laws," no. 7, in Pritchard, *ANET,* p. 189.

18. "Code of Hammurabi," nos. 201, 200, in Pritchard, *ANET,* p. 175.

19. "On the Jewish Question, II" (review of Bruno Bauer, *The Capacity of Present-Day Jews and Christians to Become Free*): text from *Karl Marx: Selected Writings,* ed. David McLellan (New York: Oxford University Press, 1977), p. 60.

20. On the term *habiru* in relation to the legislation on the Hebrew slave and its revision, I am following J. Weingreen, "The Deuteronomic Legislator—A Proto-Rabbinic Type," in *Proclamation and Presence,* ed. Durham and Porter, pp. 76–89.

21. *The Targum Onqelos to Exodus [The Aramaic Bible, Vol. 7],* tr. Bernard Grossfeld (Wilmington, Del.: Michael Glazier, 1988), p. 52. I owe the idea of using the Targum of Onkelos here to Meir Sternberg, following his citation in a joint presentation at Indiana University, "On Eagles' Wings," chaired by Herbert Marks for the Indiana University Institute for Advanced Study, Oct. 17, 1992. Sternberg has inspired most of the present passage.

For the thought here, cf. the conclusion of C. S. Lewis's account of his conversion to God in the Trinity Term of 1929: "The words *compelle intrare,* compel them to come in, have been so abused by wicked men that we shudder at them; but, properly understood, they plumb the depth of the Divine mercy. The hardness of God is kinder than the softness of men, and His compulsion is our liberation." The author writes of himself—"alone in that room in Magdalen, night after night, feeling . . . the steady, unrelenting approach of Him whom I so earnestly desired not to meet"—as unable to escape the deity who was "Reason itself," but who would not prove comfortably reasonable: "the reality with which no treaty can be made was upon me." ("Checkmate," in *Surprised by Joy: The Shape of My Early Life* [New York: Harcourt, Brace and Co., 1956], pp. 228–29.)

22. "Liminal community": see chapter 6, at notes 16 and 21, *infra*, citing Victor Turner, *Structure and Anti-Structure* (Chicago: University of Chicago Press, 1969), esp. chaps. 4–6.

23. Perry Miller, *The New England Mind: The Seventeenth Century* [1939] (Boston: Beacon Press, 1961), pp. 398–99.

24. This discussion is indebted throughout to Delbert R. Hillers, *Covenant: The History of a Biblical Idea*, pp. 98–119, esp. pp. 100–106, and Richard Elliott Friedman, "Torah and Covenant," in *The Oxford Study Bible, Revised English Bible*, ed. M. Jack Suggs, Katharine Doob Sakenfeld, and James R. Mueller (New York: Oxford University Press, 1992), pp. 154–63. On the general theme here, the relation of the Abrahamic to the Mosaic covenant, see David Noel Freedman, "Divine Commitment and Human Obligation," in *Interpretation* 18 (1964): 419–31. A barebones Middle Assyrian deed of royal gift (within the reign of Ashuruballit, 1363–28 B.C.) is found in Pritchard, *ANET*, p. 220. Hillers quotes another such from Ugarit: "From this day forward Niqmaddu son of Ammistamru king of Ugarit has taken the house of Pebeya [. . .] which is in Ullami, and given it to Nuriyana and to his descendants forever. Let no one take it from the hand of Nuriyana or his descendants forever. Seal of the king." (Hillers, *Covenant*, p. 105.)

25. A. Leo Oppenheim, *Ancient Mesopotamia: Portrait of a Dead Civilization* [1964] (Chicago: The University of Chicago Press, Phoenix Books, 1968), pp. 286–87.

26. A special case of the land-grant form occurs in the documentation of the royal gift from a king to a god. See "A Royal Decree of Temple Privilege" (Pharaoh's decree), in Pritchard, *ANET*, p. 212, which provides that "prophets [in the temple's service] . . . are exempt [from the corvée] for the length of eternity by the decrees of the King of Upper and Lower Egypt." And *ANET*, p. 32, from a narrative, "I [the king] made this decree . . . 'An offering which the King gives to [the god] Khnum, the Lord of the Cataract Region, Who Presides over Nubia, in recompense for these things which thou wilt do for me: I offer to thee thy west [lands] in Manu . . . ,' " etc. Yahweh's donation of land to his human subject obviously reverses the form of a human subject's donation to his patron deity. But Jacob's vow at Bethel is an example of the dedication of a repayment-gift.

27. Cf. Edward Chiera, *They Wrote on Clay* [1937] (Chicago: University of Chicago, Phoenix Books, 1957), pp. 180ff. In the case at Nuzi, the would-be buyer paid the landowning peasants to adopt him as a dependent and to bequeath him their land, in return for the new possessor's taking care of the legator in his old age by means of a subsidy. In this way poor peasants exchanged their land for some other consideration—money, care—and thus evaded a statute against their selling their land and removing themselves from the local tax-roll of landowners. See Pritchard, *ANET*, p. 219 (H.1–2), for Nuzi "Sale-Adoption" texts; cf. further, chapter 6, note 2, *infra*. For the ownership of the land of Israel, cf. chapter 5, note 10, *infra*.

Chapter 5: The Two Tables, and the Morality That Legislates

1. The interpretation of uncleanness as disorder, or as *violations* of order, has been advanced in Mary Douglas, *Purity and Danger: An Analysis of Concepts of Pollution and Taboo* [1966] (Harmondsworth, U.K.: Penguin Books, Pelican Books, 1970), chap. 3, "The Abominations of Leviticus," pp. 54–72; Philip Soler, "The

Dietary Prohibitions of the Hebrews," *New York Review of Books* 26:10 (June 14, 1979): 24ff. Robert Alter offers strictures on some unsound or fanciful semiology, on the part of Soler, in the matter of "cutting" and dividing in words as opposed to actual sacrificial practice, in "A New Theory of Kashrut," *Commentary,* Aug. 1979, pp. 46–52; Alter nonetheless reacts positively to the basic reasoning.

The general premises of this chapter closely resemble those of Frye, "Crime and Sin in the Bible," in *Northrop Frye: Selected Essays 1974–1988,* ed. Robert D. Denham (Charlottesville: University Press of Virginia, 1990), pp. 255–69.

2. Cf. Calum M. Carmichael, *Law and Narrative in the Bible: The Evidence of the Deuteronomic Laws and the Decalogue* (Ithaca and London: Cornell University Press, 1985), in general for this chapter, and pp. 142–50 on the present topic of Reuben and Esau. Note Carmichael's p. 150: "To repeat: Esau is not as described in the law. He is not a stubborn and rebellious son, who is also a glutton and a drunkard." *However:* Esau's Hittite marriages constitute a defiance of various Mosaic and deuteronomic pronouncements, and Genesis makes clear that Esau married "out" *before* he was disinherited (Gen. 26:34), even though it is part of the art of the narrative that the parental objections to his marriages should only be lodged *afterwards* (Gen. 27:46, 28:1). To my mind, this frame for the story is what links the law and the narrative: Esau *is* as described in the law.

3. See the listing of the major texts indicating the death penalty for transgressions against the Exodus 20 Decalogue at chapter 3, note 1, *supra.*

4. I am referring here to David Weiss Halivni, *Midrash, Mishna and Gemara: The Jewish Predilection for Justified Law* (Cambridge, Mass.: Harvard University Press, 1986), esp. pp. 14–16.

5. Finding the Decalogue in the Psalms depends on: (1) reading the exodus-God of Ps. 81:9–10 ("no strange god be in thee") as counting for Commandment I (Exod. 20:1–3); cf. also Ps. 44:20, "If we have forgotten the name of our God, or stretched out our hands to a strange god," for Commandments III and I; (2) reading Ps. 24:3–4, with its ascent into *the hill of the Lord* by the person who has not sworn deceitfully, as referring to III and IX; and (3) reading Ps. 50:16–20, with its reference to toleration for thieves, adulterers, and the loan of the mouth to deceit and slander, as referring to a torso of VIII, VII, and IX, as per the order of transgressions in Jer. 7:9 (where the people *steal,* murder, *commit adultery,* and *swear falsely:* murder has been left out of the Psalmist's list); cf. Hos. 4:2 (where the people swear, lie, *kill, steal,* and *commit adultery* [= VI, VIII, VII]).

6. For these two points, see von Rad, *Old Testament Theology,* Vol. I, *Theology of Israel's Traditions,* pp. 276–77. The disposal of the dead in the Bible is of course no real cult, but something like the opposite, the means to separate the dead from the living, "out of . . . sight" (Gen. 23:4). The influence of the dead over the living only seems to turn up with regard to narrow ethical issues: i.e., the sacrifice of the red heifer in Numbers 19 is for a killing that has not been solved, and that would pollute the ground, at Deut. 21:1–9. Exceptions such as Saul and Samuel's ghost help prove the rule.

7. So Nohrnberg, "Princely Characters," sec. vi, in Jason P. Rosenblatt and Joseph C. Sitterson, Jr., eds., *"Not in Heaven": Coherence and Complexity in Biblical Narrative* (Bloomington: Indiana University Press, 1991), pp. 74–75.

8. Von Rad, *Old Testament Theology,* Vol. I, *Theology of Israel's Traditions,* pp. 26, 209.

9. Rape (plus pillage) is discussed as programmatic for the biblical history-telling, in my "Allegories," in *Shofar* 11:2 (Winter 1993): 127–66, esp. 135–48. Some aspects of the program can be re-discovered in recent and current feminist

studies of gendered violence in the Bible, e.g., Mieke Bal, *Lethal Love: Feminist Literary Readings of Biblical Love Stories* (Bloomington and Indianapolis: Indiana University Press, 1987). The sexual politics of the Bible, it must be emphasized, turns as much on racial relations—on genetics and genealogy—as on love-hate and need-fear relations between the sexes. See Sternberg's reading of the rape of Dinah as an ideological test-case, in *Poetics*, 445–75, the reaction of Danna Nolan Fewell and David M. Gunn, "Sternberg's Reader and the Rape of Dinah," in *Journal of Biblical Literature* 110:2 (Summer 1991): 193–211, and Sternberg's reply, "Biblical Poetics and Sexual Politics: From Reading to Counterreading," *JBL* 111:3 (Fall 1992): 463–88.

10. Israel is God's "inheritance," thanks to Moses' prayer for the people's reacceptance by God at Exod. 34:9: "I pray thee, go among us . . . and take us for thine inheritance" ("I will take you to me for a people," God says at Exod. 6:7). The *land* is said to be the possession of God at Lev. 25:23 and Josh. 22:19, and Jer. 16:18. David's chagrin, in 1 Sam. 26:19, at his being prevented "from abiding in the inheritance of [Yahweh]" cuts two ways: i.e., it is a scandal that his position with Saul should exclude him either from the land-residence he inherits and is owed as a tribal Yahwist or from the Yahwism he inherits and subscribes to as a tribal land-resident. The *people* are God's inheritance at Ps. 28:9. The *tribes* are this, at Isa. 63:17 and 47:6, and the Jerusalem temple is this at Ps. 79:1. The *land* is the inheritance of Yahweh at 1 Sam. 10:1, 26:19, and 2 Sam. 20:19 and 21:3. It is to be Israel's legacy at Deut. 4:38 and 4:21, "that good land, which the Lord thy God giveth thee for an inheritance." The Pentateuch says very often that the Levites own no land, i.e., do *not* inherit in this way. See Jacques Guillet, *Themes of the Bible* (Notre Dame, Ind.: Fides, A Fides Spire Book, 1964), pp. 171–223, esp. 206–10 and p. 222 n. 218, and Roland de Vaux, *Ancient Israel, Volume 1: Social Institutions* (New York, Toronto: McGraw-Hill, 1967), chap. 11, "Economic Life," pp. 164–77.

For the land as a theological theme, see the the admirable, brief remark of Yehezkel Kaufmann, *The Religion of Israel*, trans. and ed. Moshe Greenberg (Chicago: University of Chicago Press, 1960), p. 241: "Possession of the land is the earliest eschatological motif of Israelite religion." See also von Rad, *Old Testament Theology*, Vol. I, *Theology of Israel's Traditions*, pp. 296–305, "The Granting of the Land of Canaan" (esp. pp. 299f., on the reversals on "the theological basis of all legislation concerning land tenure in ancient Israel" [p. 300]). And see Buber, *Moses: The Revelation and the Covenant* [1946] (New York: Harper & Row, Harper Torchbooks, 1958), "The Land," pp. 172–81, esp. p. 174, on the propriety of regarding the land as the concrete content of the revelation to *Moses:* but for various reasons I cannot agree with this without qualification. The land, I have argued in chapter 5, sec. v, is in fact the concrete content of the revelation to *Abraham* (or "the forefathers"); furthermore, the words "the land that I will show you" allude—however obliquely—to the survey or specification or map attaching to a deed provided to Israel apart from and prior to the Mosaic legislation (though also included in it).

11. "Is not every Vice possible to Man described in the Bible openly?"—so the Laocoön Group engraving (*Poetry and Prose of William Blake*, ed. Geoffrey Keynes, Nonesuch Library edn., p. 582).

12. "The river" (as indicated by the word's determinative) was regarded as the river's *god*, one capable of making a judgment. Examples of the river or the water as the divine judge of various adulteries and sexual procurements (and their denials) are "Code of Hammurabi," nos. 132 and 133a, in Pritchard, *ANET*, p. 171;

"The Middle Assyrian Laws," nos. 17, 22, and 24, in *ANET,* pp. 181, 182. For the mutual execution of the man and the woman, in "Code," no. 129, see note 15 *infra.*

13. Prof. David Noel Freedman explained his idea to me and others at his seventieth birthday luncheon in May 1989, at a Bible conference at University of California, Riverside. The scheme fits into his understanding of "The Earliest Bible," in *Backgrounds for the Bible,* ed. Michael P. O'Connor and D. N. Freedman (Winona Lake, Ind.: Eisenbrauns, 1987), pp. 29–37.

14. The defectiveness of the human heart is a leitmotif in Jer. 3:17, 7:24, 11:8, 16:12, 23:17, 23:26; God takes up this burden at Gen. 6:5, 8:21.

15. "Hittite Laws," nos. 197–198, in Pritchard, *ANET,* p. 196; "The Middle Assyrian laws," nos. 15 and 23, in *ANET,* pp. 182, 183. Ravishing another man's daughter is punished by a kind of *talio* in the Assyrian laws, no. 55: the father of a ravished virgin may take the ravisher's wife (in marriage), and give the daughter to the ravisher in marriage, in *ANET,* p. 185. See also "Code of Hammurabi," no. 129, in *ANET,* p. 171 ("If the wife of a seignior has been caught while lying with another man, they shall bind them and throw them into the water. If the husband of the woman wishes to spare his wife, then the king in turn may spare his subject"—no such provision for interfering with the law regarding this capital crime is found in Deut. 22:22); in Code, no. 130, the forcing of another's *betrothed* is a capital crime (*ANET,* p. 171), it being a kind of robbery of the other males involved.

16. See Pritchard, *ANET,* p. 196, for "Hittite Laws": no. 197 for the places where adulterers get caught (it is rape in the mountains and adultery in the house), and no. 198 for the husband's right to spare the transgressing wife's life ("If a man seizes a woman in the mountains, it is the man's crime and he will be killed. But if he seizes her in (her) house, it is the woman's crime, and the woman shall be killed. If the husband finds them, he may kill them then, there shall be no punishment for him."). But the husband may also spare both the wife's life and that of her fellow adulterer. The king may also order them killed—or spare them—one guesses without consulting the husband if he does not see fit to do so. If the lady invites the man, according to "Middle Assyrian Laws," no. 16 (*ANET,* p. 181), there is no crime (i.e., the husband is out of luck). This cannot explain why Potiphar's wife is so ready to concoct the story of Joseph's aggression, perhaps before Joseph the tale-teller can report her to his master as faithless; she minimizes the risk of an unfavorable disclosure to her husband without ever having been in much danger before the law.

17. Cf. Michel Foucault, *Discipline and Punish: The Birth of the Prison,* tr. Alan Sheridan (New York: Random House, Vintage Books, 1979), 3.3, "Panopticism," esp. pp. 195–200, citing the military archives of Vincennes near the end of the seventeenth century, for the regulations and system for the "lock up" of a town stricken by the plague. Measures involved the confinement—virtually the incarceration—of all persons within their houses, as well as the town within itself: "Every day, too, the syndic goes into the street for which he is responsible; stops before each house; gets all the inhabitants to appear at windows (those who live overlooking the courtyard will be allocated a window looking onto the street at which no one but they may show themselves)"; when people failed to appear at their windows, the monitors knew that the sick or dead were being concealed. This purpose of surveillance of the house, as visited by the "intendents" or legalized informants, made the window into a confessional.

Chapter 6: The Birth of the Life of Moses

1. "Some commentators have wondered whether this is a form of irony directed toward the Egyptians, but in the light of the favorable portrayal of the Egyptian princess, this is hardly likely": so Brevard S. Childs in *The Book of Exodus: A Critical, Theological Commentary* (Philadelphia: The Westminster Press, The Old Testament Library, 1974), pp. 18–19. I do not agree. The princess belongs to the house of Pharaoh, and Pharaoh's house is to be despoiled. The prediction of the enriching of Israel is made in the vicinity of the story of the wages (Exod. 2:7–9, Exod. 3:21–22), and in the prediction that "each woman shall ask of her neighbor" clothing to be put on the Hebrew's sons and daughters. The irony lies in the prediction's already being partly fulfilled, i.e., in the appropriation of Pharaoh's house for the nurturing of a despoiler whom God is yet to commission.

2. For adoption procedures, cf. Pritchard, *ANET,* p. 175, "Code of Hammurabi," no. 192, which implies "You are my son" is an adoption formula, with *ANET,* p. 173, nos. 170–171, "my children!" (= the offspring of the speaker's slave-concubine, adopted by the free father). Again, cf. the Neo-Babylonian certificate of record in *ANET,* p. 547, item no. 19, in which a brother adopts his prostitute-sister's 17-day-old son: he "came to . . . his sister, stating as follows: 'Give me your . . . son . . . , that I will rear him, and he will be my son.' " The famous testamentary disqualification of the treacherous would-be successor of the ill Hattusilis and the installation of another "son" (Mursilis) in his place is certainly based on adoption procedures: "I, the king [Labarnas Sr., i.e., Hattusilis], called him [Labarnas Jr.] my son, embraced him, exalted him, and cared for him continually. But he showed himself a youth not fit to be seen . . . Enough! He is my son no more! . . . Behold, Mursilis is now my son . . . In place of the lion the god will [set up another] lion." (Quoted from O. R. Gurney, *The Hittites,* 2d ed. 1954 [Harmondsworth, U.K.: Penguin, Pelican Original, 1966], p. 171.) With this compare God's adoptive motions toward David's son in 2 Sam. 7:14 ("I will be his father, and he shall be my son"); toward the king who is speaking in Ps. 2:7 ("I will declare the decree: the Lord hath said unto me, Thou art my Son; this day have I begotten thee"); and toward "Ephraim" in Jer. 31:9 ("I am a father . . . and Ephraim is my firstborn"). See also *ANET,* p. 174, "Code of Hammurabi," nos. 185–186, for "taken" in the passage quoted in the text; and also the citation of *ANET* in the next note. Cf. also Jer. 33:26: "Then will I cast away the seed of Jacob, and David my servant, so that I will not *take* any of his seed to be rulers over the seed of Abraham, Isaac, and Jacob." For the Nuzi archives, see Edward Chiera, *They Wrote on Clay* [1937] (Chicago: University of Chicago, Phoenix Books, 1957), pp. 180ff., and Pritchard, *ANET,* p. 219 (H. 1–2), for Nuzi "Sale-Adoption" texts (as cited in chapter 5, note 28, *supra*). For a large collection of examples, i.e., of documents providing orphans with parents and childless persons with heirs, see Elizabeth C. Stone and David I. Owen, *Adoption in Old Babylonian Nippur and the Archive of Mannum-Mešu lissur* (Winona Lake, Ind.: Eisenbrauns, 1991).

3. "Code of Hammurabi," no. 185, from Pritchard, *ANET,* p. 174. See also "The Laws of Eshnunna," no. 33, in *ANET,* p. 162: "If a slave-girl by subterfuge gives her child to a(nother) man's daughter, (if) its lord sees it when it has become older, he may seize it and take it back." This law seems to name the parties to the transaction whereby Jochebed's son Moses is recovered for Yahweh.

4. See Pritchard, *ANET,* p. 547 (no. 19) as cited in note 2, just above; and *ibid.,* p. 543 (no. 13), for an Old Babylonian formulaic declaration for rescinding this same kind of adoption and thereby disinheriting the adoptee, "You are not my son." The "No People Mine" of Hos. 1:9 (AT) is not only a disinheriting formula,

but also a divorce formula of the "You are not my spouse" kind: thus Hos. 2:2, "she is not my wife, neither am I her husband."

5. Sir James Frazer, in *Folk-Lore in the Old Testament: Studies in Comparative Religion, Legend and Law*, abrdgd. edn. (New York: Tudor Publishing Co., 1923), p. 266. See also Martin P. Nilsson, *The Mycenean Origin of Greek Mythology* [1932] (New York: W. W. Norton & Co., Norton Library, 1963), pp. 124ff., on Amphion and Zetes founding Thebes (so *Odyssey* XI.262ff.) and building the walls of the city: "The well-known version of the myth occurs, however, first in the Antiope [fragments] of Euripides. . . . It has a feature which is found in true foundation myths. The twins were exposed to die but were saved by shepherds, just as were Romulus and Remus or Cyrus."

6. See Pritchard, *ANET,* "The Legend of Sargon," p. 119: "My mother was a high priestess, my father I knew not / . . . / My mother, the high priestess, conceived me, in secret she bore me. / She set me in a basket of rushes, with bitumen she sealed my lid. / She cast me into the river which rose not (over) me. / The river bore me up and carried me to Akki, the drawer of water. / Akki, the drawer of water lifted me out as he dipped his e[w]er. / Akki . . . [took me] as his son (and) reared me."

7. George E. Mendenhall, *The Tenth Generation: The Origins of the Biblical Tradition* (Baltimore and London: Johns Hopkins University Press, 1973), p. 14.

8. Frye, *The Secular Scripture: A Study of the Structure of Romance* (Cambridge, Mass. and London: Harvard University Press, 1976), p. 102.

9. Thucydides, *The Peloponnesian War,* I.1 (1, 3), Crawley trans.

10. Livy, *History of Rome*, I, 3–4, trans Aubrey de Sélincourt (Penguin Books). Cf. Frazer's irony, *Folk-Lore in the Old Testament*, abrdgd. edn. cit., p. 265: "She [Rhea Silva] fathered them on the god Mars, but her hard-hearted uncle [Numitor's brother Aumulius] refused to admit the plea, and ordered the two babes to be thrown into the river."

11. Herodotus, *Histories,* I.105, as cited by Otto Rank, *The Myth of the Birth of the Hero and Other Writings,* ed. Philip Freund (New York: Random House, Vintage Books, 1957), p. 27.

12. Rank, "The Myth of the Birth of the Hero," in *op. cit.*, p. 37–39.

13. I am echoing Childs, *The Book of Exodus*, pp. 8–19 (esp. the "rags to riches" story and its description, pp. 8 and 10, and remarks on threatening a labor supply, p. 11). Much of what follows is otherwise a version of Freud, *Moses and Monotheism,* trans. Katherine Jones (New York: Knopf, 1939), pp. 7–16, and Otto Rank, "The Myth of the Birth of the Hero," in vol. cit. at note 11, *supra.* I am also close to Lord Raglan, *The Hero: A Study in Tradition, Myth, and Drama* (1949) (New York: Vintage Books, 1956), pp. 173–85: out of twenty heroes and twenty-two criteria for the heroic life-cycle, Raglan's Oedipus gets full marks; Theseus and Moses tie for second at twenty each (but Moses gets "several of them twice, or, if we include Josephus' account, even three times" [p. 181]). See also the citations from Wisdom 10:13–14 and 11:14 in the next note.

Childs follows H. Gressmann, *Die Anfänge Israels* (Schriften des AT I.2²: Göttingen, 1922), in arguing that the "pogrom" was originally directed at Moses' own nativity and has only latterly been directed at the population explosion. Most of the extra-biblical material cited in note 18 *infra* supports such a conclusion. But the narrative of Exodus 1–2 has chosen to make the "pogrom" the antecedent of the birth, not the other way around. Annunciation materials are mainly suppressed from the birth story, because it is not Moses and Israel but God that is being announced to Egypt, and not Moses to the Hebrews or Egyptians. Temporally speaking, Moses is "caused" by the genocidal plan, to show that although nothingness is impossible with the Creator, he likes working in a resistant medium.

14. Cf. Richmond Lattimore, *The Poetry of Greek Tragedy* (Baltimore: Johns Hopkins University Press, 1958), "Oedipus Tyrannus"; reprinted in *Literature in Critical Perspectives: An Anthology*, ed. Walter K. Gordon (New York: Appleton-Century-Crofts, 1968), pp. 204–14. Cf., also, Lattimore, *Story Patterns in Greek Tragedy* (Ann Arbor: University of Michigan Press, Ann Arbor Paperbacks, 1969), pp. 8–9: "the foundling, or we might call him the exposeling." For Moses as a vindicated exposeling, note Wisdom of Solomon 11:14 (NJB), "for the man whom long before [the Israelites] had exposed and later mockingly rebuffed, they felt only admiration when all was done," and compare Wisdom's providential care over Joseph: "She did not forsake the upright man when he was sold . . . she accompanied him down into the pit, nor did she abandon him in his chains until she had brought him the sceptre of a kingdom and authority over his despotic masters, thus exposing as liars those who had traduced him" (Wisd. 10:13–14, NJB). The two passages show how the hero-motifs of exposure and vindication typically work together as a pair.

15. The premier example is "The Hymn of the Pearl" from The Gospel of Thomas; for a version, see Bentley Layton, tr., *The Gnostic Scriptures* (Garden City, N.Y.: Doubleday & Co., 1989), pp. 370ff. The pearl descends into the Egypt of the material world, and is subsequently redeemed from there. The pearl is understood as a figure for the soul: the soul of the microcosm might well be in the shape of the soul of the macrocosm, since the pearl has the spherical shape of the cosmic World-Body, as shaped to and by the World-Soul in Plato's *Timaeus*. Andrew Marvell's poem "The Pearl" has much the same Neoplatonic implication.

16. Cf. Arnold van Gennep, *Rites of Passage*, tr. M. B. Vizedom and G. L. Caffee [1960] (Chicago: University of Chicago Press, Phoenix Books, 1969), esp. pp. 10–11, "rites of separation," "transition," and "incorporation," and pp. 65–115 with the use of the term "novitiate"; Victor Turner, *Structure and Anti-Structure* (Chicago: University of Chicago Press, 1969), esp. chaps. 4–6; and the present chapter, note 21 *infra*, with text.

17. *Moses and Monotheism*, Jones trans., p. 13, " 'National motives,' in Rank's terminology, had tranformed the myth into the form now known by us." So Rank, in *The Myth of the Birth of the Hero*, ed. Freund, p. 83, note. Rank points out here that the biblical account demythologizes ("re-converts") the myth, i.e., tells us what the story would be if there were no "family romance" and one's parents were indeed humble folk.

18. In the midrash on Exodus (slightly miscited by Rank, *op. cit.*, p. 17n) astrologers advise Pharaoh that a woman is currently pregnant with Israel's redeemer; so Shemot Rabba 1:18 with 1:24 (*Midrash Rabba, Exodus*, tr. S. H. Lehrman [London: Socino, 1939], pp. 25, 31), on the appropriateness of water as the form of death (because of Num. 20:12–13 and the Song at the Sea). Cf. Josephus, *Antiquities*, I.ix.2: the astrologers are "sacred scribes" who tell Pharaoh that about this time (of the oppression of the Hebrews with the building of the pyramids) there will be a child born to the Israelites who, if brought up, would reduce the Egyptians' power and raise the Israelites', and attain for himself an immemorial glory; the Targum of Jonathan names the prophets as Jannes and Jambres, otherwise of 2 Timothy 3:8 ("Now as Jannes and Jambres withstood Moses, so do these also resist the truth: men of corrupt minds, reprobate concerning the faith").

At *Antiq.*, I.ix.3, God comes as a messenger to Amram to tell him in a dream that the child with whom his wife is pregnant is the one that the Egyptians are presently intent upon destroying, and that the child will be secreted from the vigilance of the destroyers: after being brought up in a surprising way, he will deliver the Hebrew people and become famous beyond Israel; and his brother will be given an eternal priesthood. At *Antiq.,* I.ix.7, Moses is presented by his foster mother at court; he rejects the embrace of the king, and treads down his diadem when the king puts it on his head (other versions have him reach for the diadem himself—see *supra,* chapter 1, note 3). One of the original Egyptian prophets now steps forward to identify Moses as the child of the soothsayers' prediction. (Moses, however, continues to be sponsored by the royal house, and, in *Antiq.,* I.x, is made Pharaoh's general for a successful expedition against the Ethiopians. At *Antiq.,* I.xi.1, Moses flees Egypt, owing to intriguers' jealous plots against his life—no murder of an overseer is mentioned.)

In another story, Pharaoh dreams that a tender kid outweighs the entire Egyptian court, when tried in a balance by an old man. Interpreting this dream, Pharaoh's counselor Balaam advises that a son will be born to Israel, who will destroy Egypt; his counselor Jethro/Reuel lectures Pharaoh on the Hebrew God's patronage of the Israelite's forefathers, and he is banned to Midian; and his counselor Job tells him to use his own judgment; Balaam then advises genocide, the plan to which Pharaoh hearkens. To forestall the effects, all the Hebrew husbands, following the example of Amram, their chief priest, divorce their wives. Amram is persuaded to rescind this program, however, on the basis that they are denying life to unborn girl-children. Miriam, who makes this argument, also has a prophetic dream of Moses, in which the messenger tells her to tell her parents the message that their unborn son will be cast into the waters and that through him the waters will become dry. So, variously, Ginzberg, *The Legends of the Jews* (Philadelphia: Jewish Publication Society of America, 1909–38), Vol. II, pp. 296ff., and *The Jewish Encyclopedia,* Vol. 9 (New York: Funk and Wagnalls, 1905), p. 47, citing several rabbinic sources (Exodus Rabba 1.24, etc.). Joseph Gaer, *Lore of the Old Testament* (New York: Grossett and Dunlap, 1966), pp. 141–42, also tells the story of Pharaoh's threatening dream (in Arab folklore, that of a young man mounted on a lion who throws Pharaoh into the sea), and the idol-breaking earthquake that lead his stargazers to tell him that on this night a child that will destroy Egypt has been born to Amram the Levite (cf. *Otzar Midrashim* [1915], ed. J. D. Eisenstein, cited by Gaer). Miriam is the prophet of the birth at Exodus Rabbah 1.22 (*Midrash Rabba, Exodus,* tr. S. H. Lehrman, p. 28). Matthew knows of the parents' divorce; prophetic dreams; consultations with diviners, soothsayers, scribes, and stargazers; infant massacre by a hostile tyrant; and—perhaps—Gabriel's alleged interference in some of this.

19. George E. Mendenhall, *The Tenth Generation,* p. 200. Cf. Freud's version of James H. Breasted's ideas, in *Moses and Monotheism,* Jones trans., p. 101: "In Egypt monotheism had grown—as far as we understand its growth—as an ancillary effect of imperialism; God was the reflection of a Pharaoh autocratically governing a great world Empire."

20. So Martin Buber, *Moses: The Revelation and the Covenant* [1946] (New York: Harper & Row, Harper Torchbooks, 1958), p. 44: "When Moses came to the Midianites, he entered the range of life of the Fathers." What Moses "saw" in the burning bush, Buber deduces, was a theophany of that deity who was especially the Fathers' god.

21. This description echoes Victor Turner, *Structure and Anti-Structure: The Ritual Process,* chaps. 4–6. See also the same author, "Betwixt and Between: The Liminal Period in *Rites de Passage,* " in J. Helm, ed., *Proceedings of the American Ethnological Society for 1964* (Seattle, 1964), pp. 4–20, and "Process, System, and Symbol: A New

Anthropological Synthesis," in *Daedalus: Journal of the American Academy of Arts and Sciences*, Summer 1977, pp. 61ff., esp. pp. 66–73, where Turner sketches various kinds of role-reversal and their ludic and dramaturgical content in relation to the liminal phase of rites of passage (p. 69: "I see liminality, in tribal societies, even when they have inhabited a single ecological environment for a long time by any measure, as the provision of a cultural means of generating variability, as well as of ensuring the continuity of proved values and norms"). The several ways in which the wilderness existence of the Israelites (plagues, demoralization, destruction of sinners) mirrors and revisits the people's former existence in Egypt fits Turner's model. Forty years is not, of course, the duration of the passage for the individual, but for a society: every forty years a society becomes, biologically speaking, a new society, as the children of its former infants succeed them by passing into *their* "majority," i.e., by becoming the new majority. The "ludic" element, however, seems lacking in the Bible, apart from the quail-feast, the calf orgy, and the one feature that gets picked up in Shakespeare's *Tempest:* the preservation or continual restoration of the freshness of the Israelites' clothing during the critical *passage* through the trial period (Deut. 8:4, 29:5, Neh. 9:21).

22. Michael Fishbane, *Biblical Interpretation in Ancient Israel*, (Oxford: Clarendon Press, 1985), pp. 358–60, discusses the typological mechanisms pertaining to Joshua, as a "retrojective redescription" of Moses, in satisfying textual-exegetical detail.

23. So William Foxwell Albright, *Yahweh and the Gods of Canaan* (Garden City, N.Y.: Doubleday, Anchor Books, 1969), p. 37.

24. I am following L. Rost, "Weidewechsel und altisraelitischen Festkalendar," in *Zeitschrift für Alttestamentliche Wissenschaft* (Giessen, Berlin), 52 (1934): 161–75, after Childs, *The Book of Exodus*, p. 189.

Chapter 7: Sojourner in Midian

1. Pritchard, *ANET,* "The Legend of Sargon," p. 119, as quoted above, chapter 6, note 6.

2. I hardly need to say here that my "solution" to the problem of the names Reuel, Jethro, and Hobab is only a "reading," deliberately incognizant of attempts to explain the names on the basis of (1) posttextual misunderstanding, (2) textual misunderstanding and omissions, and (3) pretextual omissions and origins, as they might pertain to tribal name-practice, kinship relations, and genealogy: as in, e.g., Albright, *Yahweh and the Gods of Canaan* (Garden City, N.Y.: Doubleday, Anchor Books, 1969), pp. 38–42. (The difficulty with such "archaeological" explanations is that often they tell us a good deal about the biblical and extrabiblical context *of* the narrative but nothing much about the context *within* the narrative, which, in this case, is Moses' need for sanctuary—comparable to Sisera's—and not the relations among Kenites, Midianites, Hebrews, and Israelites apart from this need.)

3. Cf. Robert Alter, *The Art of Biblical Narrative* (New York: Basic Books, 1981), pp. 47–62, esp. 49, 52–58.

4. Alter, *Art of Biblical Narrative*, pp. 53–54, on Gen. 24; and p. 56 on Gen. 29:14–15: Laban's "affirmation of kinship" with Jacob is followed by "an overture to a bargaining session" that "reveals incidentally that Laban has already been extracting labor from his kinsman-guest for a month."

5. The Hagarenes are deduced from two notices: Ps. 83:6, in the parallelism, Edom / Ishmaelites :: Moab / Hagarenes (i.e., a kingdom / a nomadic group, twice), and the defeated Hagarites of 1 Chron. 5:18–20 with 5:10 ("[Israel] dwelt in their tents [= the Hagarites' tents] throughout all the east land of Gilead").

6. "Social puberty," after van Gennep, *Rites of Passage*, tr. M. B. Vizedom and G. L. Caffee [1960] (Chicago: University of Chicago Press, Phoenix Books, 1969), p. 65.

7. Herodotus, *The Histories*, II.37: "They practice circumcision, while men of other nations—except those who have learnt from Egypt—leave their private parts as nature made them. . . . They are religious to excess, beyond any other nation in the world, and here are some of the customs which illustrate the fact. . . . They circumcise themselves for cleanliness' sake, preferring to be clean rather than comely." (Trans. Aubrey de Sélincourt, Penguin Books.)

8. As noted, e.g., by Gerhard von Rad on Gen. 18, *Genesis* (Philadelphia: Westminster, 1961), p. 200. Von Rad quotes *The Odyssey* XVII.485–87, about the gods visiting men in various shapes and disguises and investigating human wickedness, apropos the three men who visit Abraham and receive his hospitality. See also *Odyssey* IX.265–70, Odysseus to Polyphemus, on respect for Zeus the Hospitalier (Xenios). Cf. also Hermann Gunkel, *The Legends of Genesis: The Biblical Saga and History*, trans. W. H. Carruth [1901] (New York: Schocken Books, 1966), p. 93: "the story of the three men who visit Abraham is told among the Greeks by Hyrieus at Tanagra (Ovid, *Fasti*, V., 495 ff.)." Another analogue is Ovid, *Metam.*, VIII.629ff.; Baucis and Philemon receive Jupiter and Mercury in mortal guise, after a thousand homes have barred their doors against them. At *Metam.*, I.220ff., Lycaon attempts to disgrace Jupiter, here too in human guise, with a meal of human flesh; Deucalion and Pyrrha survive the universal flood that Jupiter thereupon sends to punish the race; they only do this by chance, but it is their piety that thereafter earns them a means to re-people the world once it has drained. Abraham becomes many peoples' father at Sodom's destruction and Lot's wife's sterilization.

Chapter 8: Delivering Justice: The Prehistory of Mosaic Intervention

1. John Wain, "A Song About Major Eatherly," ll. 21–28; from *Weep Before God* (London: Macmillan & Co., St. Martin's Press, and Toronto: Macmillan Co. of Canada, 1961). (Major Eatherly was the pilot for the plane that dropped the atom bomb on Nagasaki. The epigraph to the poem cites reports of his having suffered mental disorders after the war. Wain's poem does not imply the pilot was less sinned against than sinning, and remembers that he refused a pension for his services.)

Chapter 9: "Thus I Am to Be Remembered": Sinai and the Name

1. "The God of several Psalms": e.g., Ps. 18:2, 31, 46; 28:1, 31:3, 42:9, 71:3, 89:26, 94:22. For "the Mighty One of Jacob . . . the stone of Israel" in Gen. 49:24, cf. Isa. 49:26, 41:16; Ps. 132:2, 5. God comes *from* Sinai in Moses' Song (Deut. 33:2), and in Deborah's (Judg. 5:5). He comes *upon* Sinai at Exod. 19:20, 24:16, and Neh. 9:13; so also Galatians 4:24.

2. Hans-Georg Gadamer, *Truth and Method* (New York: The Seabury Press, A Continuum Book, 1975), "The model of the Platonic dialectic," pp. 325–33, and esp. p. 330, which I echo. A conversation ideally "converts" its parties' activity of "talking at cross-purposes" into an exchange between partners, as if each were in possession of the missing half of the other's discourse.

3. Childs, *The Book of Exodus*, p. 50, on vs. 14 ('I am He who is' versus—and as—'I am who am'), and pp. 60–71. For the topic of this chapter generally, I am also indebted to Th. C. Vriezen, *An Outline of Old Testament Theology* (Engl. edn., 1958) (Newton, Mass.: Ch. T. Branford Co., 1961), "The Names of God,"

pp. 194–98, "The Revelation of God," pp. 233–69, esp. 235–38, and von Rad, *Old Testament Theology,* Vol. I, *Theology of Israel's Traditions,* pp. 179–221, esp. pp. 203ff.

4. Childs, *The Book of Exodus,* pp. 62–63, 596. "I will be merciful to whom I will be merciful" is of course only partly an equivalent for "I will be that I will be," precisely because it is so much fuller: "I will do what I will do *in the particular way that I will do it*"—it specifies *how.*

5. *Odyssey* IX.366, 408: *ou tis.* Cf. Vriezen, *Outline of Old Testament Theology,* p. 236: "*Yahweh does not mention His name;* but at the same time he does more than this."

6. Gerhard von Rad, *Old Testament Theology,* Vol. I, *Theology of Israel's Traditions,* p. 182, and pp. 179–89 generally.

7. Cf. John Calvin, *Institutes of the Christian Religion,* tr. Henry Beveridge (Grand Rapids: Wm. B. Eerdmans, 1964), vol. 1., pp. 59–60: "This far, indeed, we differ from each other, in that every one appropriates to himself some peculiar error; but we are all alike in this, that we substitute monstrous fictions for the one living and true God—a disease not confined to obtuse and vulgar minds, but affecting the noblest, and those who, in other respects, are singularly acute. . . . Hence that immense flood of error with which the whole world is overflowed . . . there is scarcely an individual to be found without some idol or phantom as a substitute for the Deity. Like water gushing forth from a large and copious spring, immense crowds of gods have issued from the human mind, every man giving himself full license and devising some peculiar form of divinity, to meet his own views. It is unnecessary here to attempt a catalogue of the superstitions with which the world was overspread. The thing were endless; and the corruptions themselves, though not a word should be said, furnish abundant evidence of the blindness of the human mind" (I.v.11, 12). Paul's reading of this instinct toward idolatry, at Romans 1:23, 25, which converts the glory of God into a lying image made in the likeness of the creature, refers to the golden calf, since it echoes the same idea at Ps. 106:19–20: "They made a calf in Horeb, and worshipped the molten image. Thus they changed their glory into the similitude of an ox that eateth grass" (cf. also Jer. 2:11).

8. For *I am he,* see, above all, Isa. 52:5–6: "And all day long my name is being blasphemed; therefore my people will know my name; in that day, therefore, [they will know] that I [am] he, the one foretelling: yes, I" (AT). We have quoted Hos. 1:9 in the text ("And he said, call its name 'Not-My-People,' for you['re] not my people and I['m] not 'I-Am' to you" [AT]). Compare also Deut. 32:39a: "See now, that I—myself—am he, and there is no god(s) besides me" [AT].

God's "I-am-ness" and his reflexive self-identification can be derived from the statement "Yahweh is God" (1 Kings 18:39), when it is put into the first person, "I am I"; and from several biblical passages that then translate across the first to the third person: i.e., "I am Yahweh," "I am [he]," and "I am the one (who . . .)." For *I am Yahweh,* cf. Isa. 58:9, "And you will call, and Yahweh will answer; you will cry, and he will say, 'here—I!' " (AT); and Isa. 42:8, "I am Yahweh, that is my name and my glory I'll not give to another, or my praise to the idols" (AT). (The formula "I am he" is presumed by the arrest of Jesus in John 18:4ff: "Then Jesus . . . said to them, 'Whom do you seek?' They answered, 'Jesus of Nazareth.' Jesus said to them, 'I am he.' Judas, who betrayed him, was standing with them. When he said to them, 'I am he,' they drew back and fell to the ground. Again he asked them, 'Whom do you seek?' And they said, 'Jesus of Nazareth.' Jesus answered, 'I told you that I am he . . . ' " [RSV]. Using the double-nuanced language of John, Jesus might well stun his audience by saying, "I am the new content of the old scriptural formula, 'I am he.' ")

Note that half the formula used by the Pharaoh, in the text of this chapter's epigraph, finds parallels in the writing prophets, where "as I live" is a frequent oath of God's commitment to his will: cf. esp. Jer. 46:18, "*As I live*, saith the King, whose name is the Lord [YHWH] of hosts, Surely as Tabor is among the mountains, and as Carmel by the sea, so shall he come," and Ezk. 20:3, 31. (See also Jer. 5:2 with 22:5, 22:24, 38:16; Ezk. 5:11, 14:16–20, 16:48, 17:16–19, 18:3, 33:11; 34:8, 35:6–11; Isa. 49:18.)

9. Said to be an inscription on an Egyptian temple to Neith, at Sais (700 BC?); see Plutarch, *De Iside* 9 (*Moralia* 354), where the goddess is the Egyptian Athena, or Isis (veil = Gk. *peplon*, robe). Cf. also Vulgate Wisdom of Solomon 7:27 (Wisdom comprehends "the beginning, and consummation, and the middle of times"), and Revelation 1:8 ("I am Alpha and Omega, the beginning and the ending, saith the Lord, which is, and which was, and which is to come, the Almighty"; cf. Isaiah 48:12, "I am He, I am the first, / and I am the last" [RSV]).

10. The varieties of self-ownership, self-definition, self-disposal, and self-loss in Shakespeare are endless. One instance may speak for them all: the Bastard (Falconbridge) in *King John*, I.i.175, "I am I, howe'er I was begot."

11. So Paul Ricoeur, "Towards a Hermeneutic of the Idea of Revelation," in his *Essays on Biblical Interpretation*, ed. and intro. Lewis S. Mudge (Philadelphia: Fortress Press, 1980), p. 96.

12. The classic study is Albrecht Alt's, "The God of the Fathers," in his *Essays on Old Testament History and Religion*, Anchor Books edn., pp.1–100.

Chapter 10: Prophet unto Pharaoh

1. Pritchard, *ANET*, p. 66 (Tablet IV, ll. 4–26). See Alexander Heidel, *The Babylonian Genesis* (Chicago: University of Chicago Press, 1963), p. 37, for the "images" in this passage as a *garment* that Marduk's word of command makes disappear and reappear, in a demonstration perhaps even closer to that of Moses turning a rod into a snake and back into a rod again.

2. If we just stick to finding Leviticus's twenty-sixth chapter in Ezekiel, without an appeal to all kinds of comparable holiness-legislation in the two texts, we still come up with a rich catch. See esp. the covenant-avenging "sword" of Lev. 26:25, with Ezek. 21, *passim*. See also the catalogue of Jerusalem's crimes at Ezek. 22, and the price paid for them at Ezek. 17:12–21. For echoes of this price in Lev. 26, compare Ezek. 4:16–17 and Lev. 26:26, 39; Ezek. 5:10 and Lev. 26:29; Ezek. 12:14–16, 22:15 and Lev. 26:33; Ezek. 5:15 and Lev. 26:32; Ezek, 6:4 and Lev. 26:30–31; Ezk. 6:8–9 and Lev. 26:39–41. Ezekiel can also illuminate specifics of the pentateuchal narrative; e.g., the demotion of the Levites in Ezek. 44:10–14 is arguably a source of the story-line found in Num. 18:1–8, 19:20.

3. If we follow the implications of the Documentary Hypothesis as they have sometimes been expounded, the prestige of the first account of the history ("J," united monarchy period) was countered by a second ("E," northern monarchy period); the prestige of the second necessitated the assimilation of the first to it (J +E, fall of the Northern monarchy). The combination (JE) set the pattern for the third ("P," survival of the Southern priesthood). (The Priestly author— "voice," text, tradition—well attested by Priestly and non-Priestly doublets, was in possession of his own sequence of narratives describing the Creation, the Flood, the Abrahamic covenant and the Abrahamic site Hebron, and the Mosaic vocation.) Finally, the example of the Priestly torah—Leviticus, chiefly—going beyond the "Book of the Covenant" (traditionally placed by scholars in the exodus texts of E), could have inspired, or been inspired by, the supplementations and editorial-

izing of a fourth author ("D," writing during the times of the latter-day Southern monarchy and its fall—different parts of D either suppose or do not suppose the magnification of Josiah and the fatality of Mannaseh, or the disestablishment of the Jerusalem monarchy and the "return to Egypt" of the refugees). Thus no one portion of the text is immune from being quoted against another, "the word against the word."

4. Richard Elliott Friedman, *Who Wrote the Bible?* (New York: Simon and Schuster, Summit Books, 1987; Harper and Row, Perennial Library 1989), chaps. 11–12. But *contra* Friedman's case, on a pre-deuteronomic date for P's ideas, an exile could have composed P, and left out the Josianic-deuteronomic legislating of Jerusalem as the only cult center, precisely because he could not know—must necessarily have doubted—that Jerusalem would ever be this center again. Traditional links between both the holiness and ritual legislation of P and the ethnic purism and the temple rules of the exilic prophet Ezekiel also remain valid. Friedman's notable idea that a Jerusalem temple was sized in order to incorporate a given relic—the tabernacle—conforms to what we know about temples and museums generally: parts of them may be built around the housing of a principal decoration or donation. But a 1:2 relation between tabernacle specifications and the temple's inner-sanctum measurement may equate different texts, without really settling their dates.

5. Using the phrase of David at 1 Sam. 25:22, the prophets extend vengeance to the last man in the condemned person's party, all who "pisseth against the wall," or every male (1 Kings 14:10, Ahijah's prophecy against Jeroboam, for not following David; 1 Kings 21:21–22, Elijah's prophecy vs. Ahab, using Ahijah's prophecy vs. Jeroboam; 2 Kings 9:8, Elisha's prophecy and commissioning vs. Ahab's family for following Jeroboam). Cf. also 1 Kings 16:1–7, the Lord's word to the prophet Jehu ben Hanani, vs. Baasha for following Jeroboam; the phrase is lacking, but the prophecy is fulfilled according to the type (1 Kings 16:11). The first of the prophets against Jeroboam was the anonymous man out of Judah (1 Kings 13:1). The prophecy–and–fulfillment pattern from 1–2 Kings includes the following:

> 1 K 15:29, the narrator notes the fulfillment of prophecies against Jeroboam, after Baasha's murder of Nadab.
>
> 1 K 16:11, the narrator notes the prophecy against Baasha has been fulfilled, after Baasha's murder by Zimri.
>
> [1 K 21:29, God announces to Elijah that he will defer Ahab's punishment to the king's son and house: i.e., the prophecy will not be fulfilled except belatedly.]
>
> 1 K 22:38, the narrator notes the prophecy against Ahab as fulfilled, after his bleeding to death in Samaria from a battle wound.
>
> 2 K 9:25–26, Jehu notes the fulfillment of the prophecy of Elijah (at 1 K 21:19) against Ahab and family, after he has killed Ahab's son Jehoram.

We are to compare and contrast the interlocking pattern of the promises to "David" at 1 Kings 2:33; 11:12–13, 11:32–38 (esp. vs. 32), 15:4–5; 2 Kings 8:19; 19:34. The texts dis-electing Jeroboam and (re)electing David are readily understood as two halves of one zipper. See further, chapter 15, notes 13 and 14, *infra*.

6. For God's word in the Bible generally, cf. Gerhard von Rad, *Old Testament Theology*, Vol. 2., *The Theology of Israel's Prophetic Traditions*, tr. Stalker (Evanston and New York: Harper & Row, 1965), pp. 80–98, "The Prophet's Conception of the Word of God," and esp. pp. 152–55, on Isaiah.

7. As found in Martin Buber, *Moses*, Torchbook edn., pp. 62–64.

8. E.g., Elijah and drought, 1 Kings 17:1; Elisha and rain, 2 Kings 3:16–17, 20; Elisha, famine and rain, 2 Kings 6:25 with 7:2; Elisha and famine, 2 Kings 8:1, and, *a fortiori*, the "famine" of the word of God in Amos 8:11. In Ps. 147:17–18 the word goes forth in the way that frost, ice, and the wind go forth; in Ps. 148:8 the violence of the weather and the elements fulfills his word; and in Isa. 55:10–11 the word descends from heaven like rain and fertilizes the earth, before returning to God—in this case, God says (at vs. 11) his word does not return to him without accomplishing the purpose for which God sent it. Cf. also Joel 2, threatening the "day of the Lord" (vss. 1, 11, 31) in terms of darkness (vss. 2, 10), earthquake and eclipses (vss. 10, 31), and armies that may also be locusts (vss. 2–9, with vs. 25 ["the locust . . . my great army which I sent among you"]).

9. Childs, *The Book of Exodus*, pp. 132–51, esp. 147–49.

Chapter 11: The Burden of Egypt

1. Nohrnberg, "On literature and the Bible," *Centrum* II:2 (Fall 1974): 29.

2. *The Jewish Encyclopedia*, Vol. 10 (New York: Funk and Wagnalls, 1907), *sub* "Plagues," at p. 70, col. A: "R. Jose the Galilean says: 'The Egyptians in the Red Sea suffered fifty plagues. In Egypt the "finger of God" was recognized by the ten plagues; but at the Red Sea God's powerful "hand" was visible [Ex. xiv. 31, Hebr.], which being multiplied by five fingers makes fifty plagues.' "

3. The biblical succession of whole and presentable persons includes Enoch (Gen. 5:22, 24), Noah (Gen. 6:9), Abraham (Gen. 17:1, 24:40), the sons of Aaron (Lev. 21:17–21), David, if he is the Psalmist (Ps. 15:2, 18:32, 56:13, 101:6, 119:1–3, etc.), Naaman (2 Kings 5:14, with Exod. 4:7 and Lev. 14:11, etc.), Hezekiah (2 Kings 20:3, Isa. 38:3), and Isaiah (6:5–7). We may compare God's presentation of himself to Moses, when he makes all his goodness go before him (Exod. 33:14, 19, with the vision of God at 24:10; cf. also Lev. 26:21 with 23–24 [". . . if ye walk contrary unto me, . . . I will bring seven times more plagues upon you . . . Then will I also walk contrary unto you]"). Moses' veil, we have guessed, also makes him *un*whole.

4. Martin Buber on Gen. 2:4: *Kingship of God* (New York: Harper & Row, Harper Torchbooks, 1973), p. 113.

5. The members of forecast, enactment, and report are posited, explained, theorized, and applied by Meir Sternberg, *The Poetics of Biblical Narrative: Ideological Literature and the Drama of Reading* (Bloomington and Indianapolis: Indiana University Press, 1985), chap. 11, "The Structure of Repetition: Strategies of Informational Redundancy," esp. pp. 375–93. Sternberg, pp. 106ff., implies that this structure is found in the biblical rhetoric of performative utterance.

6. Here we are noting, with Meir Sternberg, *Poetics*, pp. 104–109, that the preliminaries and realizations found in prophecy-and-fulfillment models for the rhetoric of the biblical ideology, and for the divine or prophetic predictive activity generally (the "if . . . then" or the "conditions . . . fulfillment" structure of, say, 1 Kings 6:12, 8:20, 12:15) appear at the outset in God's speech-act of "Let there be light: and there was light" (Gen. 1:3); hence the Psalmist's reasoning, "for [the Lord] commanded, and they were created" (Ps. 148:5). Cf. Isaiah 9:7, "The zeal of the Lord of hosts will perform this"; Psalm 119:106, "I [= the confessing psalmist] have sworn, and I will perform it"; Jeremiah 1:12 "I [= God] will hasten my word to perform it"; Job 23:14, "he [= God] performeth the thing that is appointed"; Ezekiel 37:14, "then shall ye know that I the Lord have spoken it, and performed it"; Job 42:2, "I know that thou [Job's God] canst do all things, / and that no purpose of thine can be thwarted" (RSV); Isaiah 46:10–11, where God is "Declaring the end from the beginning, and from ancient times the things that

are not yet done, saying, My counsel shall stand, and I will do all my pleasure: . . . I have purposed it, I will also do it"; Isaiah 48:3, "I have declared the former things from the beginning; and they went forth out of my mouth, and I shewed them; I did them suddenly, and they came to pass." Contrast Isaiah 43:19, "Behold, I will do a new thing; now it shall spring forth," taken with 65:17, "behold, I create new heavens and a new earth: and the former shall not be remembered, nor come into mind." Of course all such tributes to the absolute efficacy of the deity have much in common either with the flattery of Near Eastern potentates or else with the actual enhancement of royal prerogatives.

7. For parallel discussions of texts in these terms, see Robert Alter, *The World of Biblical Literature* (New York: Harper-Collins, Basic Books, 1992), pp. 74–75, and Burke O. Long, "Framing Repetitions in Biblical Historiography," *Journal of Biblical Literature* 106 (1987): 385–99.

Chapter 12: The Genesis of the Exodus

1. "Manumission of a female slave and her daughter, June 12, 427 B.C.," after Pritchard, *ANET,* p. 548. In Exod. 11:5, "from the firstborn of Pharaoh that sitteth on his throne, even unto the firstborn of the maidservant that is behind the mill," the slave-girl is parallel to the prisoner in Exod. 12:29, "from the firstborn of Pharaoh that sat on his throne unto the firstborn of the captive that was in the dungeon." Cf. Isa. 42:6–7, 16, for the release from darkness and captivity.

2. For the creator in Isaiah, cf. 40:12, 22, 26; 42:5, 16b ("I will make darkness light"), 45:6–7 ("there is none beside me . . . there is none else. I form the light, and create darkness"), 45:18, 51:10; 54:9 ("For this is as the waters [days?] of Noah unto me"); 65:17 ("For, behold, I create new heavens and a new earth"), etc.

3. "Hymn to the Aton," in Pritchard, *ANET,* p. 370.

4. So the Babylonian Creation Epic, in Pritchard, *ANET,* p. 61 (Table I, ll. 5, 22), pp. 66–67 (Table IV, ll. 48, 96–100, 137–140).

5. "Hymn to the Aton," in Pritchard, *ANET,* p. 370.

6. The creator-god's conquest of the Old Testament chaos-monster and the Near Eastern combat myth are variously presented in Frank Moore Cross, *Canaanite Myth and Hebrew Epic: Essays in the History of the Religion of Israel* (Cambridge, Mass.: Harvard University Press, 1973); Theodore H. Gaster, *Thespis: Ritual, Myth, and Drama in the Ancient Near East,* 2d rev. ed. (Garden City, N.Y.: Doubleday, Anchor Books, 1961); Martin Buber, *Moses,* Torchbook edn., p. 79; and Jon D. Levenson, *Creation and the Persistence of Evil: The Jewish Drama of Divine Omnipotence* (San Francisco: Harper & Row, 1988), esp. pp. 14–46, 53–99. For the Classical equivalents, see Joseph Fontenrose, *Python* (Berkeley and Los Angeles: University of California Press, 1959), *passim.* The connection between the Song at the Sea and cosmogonic conquest is treated at length in Cross, *Canaanite Myth,* chap. 6, pp. 112–44.

7. For this scruple as an essential part of the poetics of the main line of biblical storytelling, see Sternberg, "Ideology of Narration," in *Poetics,* esp. pp. 126–28 ("All the narrative battles against pagan tradition take place underground, by way of allusion and parody detectable by the initiate alone" [p. 128]). I am arguing that this scruple is *not* so apparent in the poetry, and that, moreover, one example, the Song at the Sea, intends to be the rhetorical climax of events and prose that lead up to and issue in it.

8. Pritchard, *ANET,* p. 369 (600th stanza of "Amon as the Sole God")

9. Fontenrose, *Python,* p. 425. Cf. Pritchard, *ANET,* pp. 333–34, the purification formula for the "Temple Program for the New Year Festival in Babylon": "They

purify the Temple, / The god Marduk from Eridu, who dwells in the temple Eudul, The god Kusug . . . , / The deity Ningirim who listens to prayers, / The God Marduk purifies the temple, / The God Kusug draws the plans, / The deity Ningirim casts the spell. / Go forth, evil demon that happens to be in this temple! / May the god Bel kill you, evil demon! / Wherever you are, be suppressed." However elusive, the demon in question has clearly earned a kind of place in both the cult and its shrines. The Hebrew Satan may be his Yahwist majesty's loyal opposition and devil's advocate, but he has earned no comparable cult, for in the Old Testament there are no prayers or apotropaic spells to protect against him—though the Book of Job may suggest that there *ought* to be!

10. Pritchard, *ANET,* p. 368 (100th stanza of "Amon as the Sole God").

11. This reading of the Epic is Thorkild Jacobson's, in Henri Frankfort et al., *Before Philosophy* [= *The Intellectual Adventure of Ancient Man,* 1946] (Harmondsworth, U.K.: Penguin, Pelican Books, 1954), pp. 183–99.

12. Tiamat's proposal, *pace* God's at Gen. 1:26 " 'Let us make man in our image,' " is quoted from Pritchard, *ANET,* p. 62 (Tablet I, l. 125): "monsters" is supplied by the translator, E. A. Speiser, at a defect in the text (we can guess that the editor of the Anchor Bible *Genesis* has this right).

13. The Babylonian creation/enslavement of humankind: in Pritchard, *ANET,* p. 68 (Tablet VI, ll. 1–36): ". . . I will establish a savage, 'man' shall be his name. . . . He shall be charged the serving of the gods / That they might be at ease!" And: "Out of his [Kingu's] blood they fashioned mankind. / He [Ea] imposed the service and left free the gods." And: "Ea . . . had created mankind, / Had imposed upon it the service of the gods."

14. Pritchard, *ANET,* p. 66 (Tablet IV, ll. 4–26). See above, chapter 10 note 1 and text, for this status-winning wonder as a sign, and chapter 11 note 6, for the promise-performance trope for the Creator's activity. (Here we are emphasizing God's power to do what he wills with the same freedom he has to speak; in chapter 10 we are emphasizing God's power to earn assent by a demonstration of his powers—to *command* assent.)

15. If the word is essentially God's, then a prophet's failure to invoke it, use it, or fully comply with it is a Marduk-like arrogation of God's power. See Sternberg, *Poetics,* pp. 106–107, for virtually the same points.

16. Isa. 63:7–19 is cited by Buber, *Moses,* Torchbook edn., p. 36, where he translates this text (vs. 11, AV, "Then he remembered the days of old, Moses, *and* his people, saying, Where is he that brought them up out of the sea with the shepherd of his flock? . . .") as "He remembered the days of old, the drawer-forth [= Moses] of his people. . . ." These "days of old" (as also in Isa. 51:9, "the generations of old") seem to recall the Flood and the Creation, though they can also be the heyday of God's conquest of Canaan, as in Ps. 44:1–3, for example.

17. Otto Rank, *The Trauma of Birth,* and, in Freund, ed., *The Myth of the Birth of the Hero,* "Life Fear and Death Fear," pp. 263–79. Cf. Rank in Freund, p. 265: "As I have already pointed out in *The Trauma of Birth,* it seems to me essential for the understanding of the neurotic to go at the human problem from the side of fear, not from the side of instinct; that is, to consider the individual not therapeutically as an instinctive animal but psychologically as a suffering being"; and p. 268, "In this case [of birth trauma], . . . fear is a reaction to the trauma of separation. . . . The fear in birth, which we have designated as fear of life, seems to me actually the fear of having to live as an isolated individual, and not the reverse, the fear of the loss of individuality (death fear). That would mean, however, that primary fear corresponds to a fear of separation. . . ."

Chapter 13: The Creation of Israel (I): The Exodus and the Numbering of Israel

1. Cf. the following analysis in the text, and "Atrahasis," in Pritchard, *ANET,* pp. 104–106, "Old Babylonian Version," where the god's measures in fact begin with an *anti*-Flood: "The land became wide, the people became numerous, / The land bellowed like wild oxen. / The god was disturbed by their uproar. / Enlil heard their clamor And said to the great gods: / 'Oppressive has become the clamor of mankind. / By their uproar they prevent sleep. / Let the flour be cut off for the people, / In their bellies let the greens be too few. / Above let Adad make scarce his rain, / Below let not flow the flood, let it not rise from the source.' " (Trans. E. A. Speiser, *ANET,* p. 104, i.1–13, *sans* textual marks.) The Flood stories are in Pritchard, *ANET:* Sumerian, "The Deluge" (= Ziusudra), p. 42–44; Babylonian, "Gilgamesh," Tablet XI, pp. 93–96; Babylonian (and Neo-Assyrian) "Atrahasis," pp. 104–106; and Alexander Heidel, *The Gilgamesh Epic and Old Testament Parallels* (Chicago: University of Chicago Press, 1963), pp. 80–92, 102–19.

2. *Causa,* in the "epic" and functioning in the inceptive sense I am referring to, is found at several places in the Western narrative tradition, where, in general, the etiology of disaster has been assimilated to a *casus belli* ('occasion for war'), or other occasion for wrath, and then shrunk to occupy the epic *propositio.* Examples of such propositions concerning cause and blame are found at the openings of Homer's *Iliad* and *Odyssey,* Virgil's *Aeneid* (the inceptions of Bks. I *and* VII), Lucan's *Pharsalia,* Statius's *Thebiad,* Petrarch's *Africa,* and Milton's *Paradise Lost* (the cause of God's making the world, however, was his desire to impart his good [*Par. Lost,* VII.190]). The cause of the Trojan War was perhaps the gods' desire to thin out the human population, before it was the strife between the gods over the golden apple (Scholiast on *Iliad* 1.5, *contra* Apollodorus, *Epit.* 3.1–2), *contra* the source of so many dead at Troy being the wrath of Achilles, or the falling out between Achilles and Agamemnon (*Iliad* 1.1ff.; cf. the prose paraphrase in Alexander Pope's first note to his translation: "Sing, O Goddess, that Wrath of *Achilles,* which prov'd so pernicious to the *Greeks:* We only know the Effects of it, that it sent innumerable brave Men to the Shades, and that it was *Jove's* Will it should be so. But tell me, O Muse, what was the Source of this destructive Anger?").

3. Robert Alter, *The Art of Biblical Narrative* (New York: Basic Books, 1981), p. 165, reads the murder and/or sale of Joseph into slavery this way.

4. See sources cited in chapter 6, note 18, for the warnings about Moses which Pharaoh receives in extra-biblical legend.

5. So Marx, in essence, on the "everyday Jew," in "On the Jewish Question," in *Selected Writings,* ed. McLellan, pp. 60–61.

6. Cf. Jon D. Levenson, *Sinai and Zion: An Entry into the Jewish Bible* (Minneapolis: Winston Press, 1985), *passim.*

Chapter 14: The Creation of Israel (II): The Exodus and the "Visiting" of Israel

1. Arnold van Gennep's term, *Rites of Passage,* Phoenix Books edn., p. 65.

2. Freud's observation that circumcision is originally an Egyptian institution implies that the Bible does not know this, or else does not want to. Why then assign its instituting to the covenant with Ishmael, whose mother was an *Egyptian?* Circumcision is "pre-Egyptianized" from the time of Genesis 17: God insists Ishmael be circumcised because he knows Ishmael's offspring will be practicers of circumcision—Ishmael, after all, will marry an Egyptian (Gen. 21:21). But having Abraham

himself adopt such a practice (as if from Egypt) to express ethnic solidarity with the Hagarene leaves God free to impose it on Moses to express Moses' ethnic solidarity not with Egypt but with Midian, i.e., with a patriarchal past and with the tribal practice of scarification for coming-of-age. Cf. *Moses and Monotheism,* Jones trans., pp. 37–38, 49, 66 ("Here [with Abraham] the opportunity was taken to deal a decisive blow at the Egyptian origin of the custom of circumcision. Jahve was said to have already demanded it from Abraham, to have instituted it as a sign of the bond between him and Abraham's descendants. This, however, was a particularly clumsy invention. . . . An Israelite, finding himself in Egypt, would have had to recognize all Egyptians as brothers, bound by the same bond. . . ."). At the last citation Freud indirectly brings in Josh. 5:5, to prove that the Bible also "knows" the practice to be Egyptian: yet the prior case of the half-Egyptian Ishmael is entirely omitted from his discussion.

3. Henri Frankfort, *Ancient Egyptian Religion: An Interpretation* [1948] (New York: Harper & Row, Harper Torchbooks, 1961), p. 41.

4. For intratextual and numerological backgrounds relating the New Testament bread to the Old Testament shewbread, making this reading of "the leaven of the Pharisees" clearer than it may be here, see John Drury, "Understanding the Bread: Disruption and Aggregation, Secrecy and Revelation in Mark's Gospel," in Jason P. Rosenblatt and Joseph C. Sitterson, Jr., eds., *"Not in Heaven": Coherence and Complexity in Biblical Narrative* (Bloomington: Indiana University Press, 1991), pp. 98–119, 239.

5. "Followability" is the term of Martin Price, in "The Fictional Contract," in *Literary Theory and Structure: Essays in Honor of William K. Wimsatt,* ed. Frank Brady, John Palmer, and Martin Price (New Haven: Yale University Press, 1973), pp. 174–84.

Chapter 15: "Like unto Moses": The Text of History

1. Cf. James A. Sanders, *Torah and Canon* (Philadelphia: Fortress Press, 1972), p. 20. The very early witness of a pair of verses on the occupation, at Judges 1:20–21, makes Moses assign Hebron to Caleb, while at the same time pairing this with Benjamin's failure to drive the Jebusites from Jerusalem—"the Jebusites dwell with the children of Benjamin in Jerusalem unto this day." The latter report sounds pre-Davidic (*contra* the Hebron and Jerusalem of 2 Sam. 5:1–13), and the distich as a whole offers to make Moses older than Jebus (i.e., antedates Judaic claims to Southern territory with a state of affairs that is pre-Davidic, and therefore suggests that the tradition of Moses is at least as old as that of peaceful coexistence with the Jebusites). David's alleged use of Psalm 18, with its apparent allusion to Moses' name (at 2 Sam. 22:17, comparable to the allusion to the princess at Exod. 2:10), also suggests the antiquity of a tradition of Moses.

2. Cf. Sanders, *Torah and Canon,* esp. pp. 91–96.

3. Cf. Paul Hanson, *The People Called: The Growth of Community in the Bible* (San Francisco: Harper & Row, 1986).

4. *In Epist. ad Gal. comm.,* J. P. Migne, *Patrologia Graeca,* vol. 61, p. 662, as cited in Robert M. Grant, *A Short History of the Interpretation of the Bible* (1963 edn.) (New York: Macmillan, 1966), p. 96.

5. Childs, *The Book of Exodus,* p. 557, explains that although there is a problem in the line, it "is not one of textual corruption," and then asserts that "the last three words appear to be a clumsy, secondary addition": hence he parenthesizes them. But if we take the alleged addition to be an originary supplement that reverses the priority of the calf the people made into the effect of the one that

Aaron made, we can guess the reason—to tar Aaron *and* his latter-day followers—for an addition that converts the line into an example of the "poesis of an origin" (cf. Gk. *poiein,* 'to make').

6. Gregory Nagy, *The Best of the Achaeans: Concepts of the Hero in Archaic Greek Poetry* (Baltimore and London: Johns Hopkins University Press, 1979), p. 8; Herbert Marks, letter of Sept. 12, 1992 to the author.

7. *Pascal's Pensées* (New York: E. P. Dutton, Dutton Everyman, 1958), p. 177, no. 630. (No. 325 in the H. F. Stewart trans. [New York: Random House, Modern Library College Editions, n.d.], p. 181.)

8. Erich Auerbach, *Mimesis: The Representation of Reality in Western Literature,* tr. Willard Trask (Garden City, N.Y.: Doubleday and Co., Anchor Books, 1957), p. 15. See pp. 5–19.

9. Arguments for a relatively early date for "P" have been recently presented by Richard Elliott Friedman, *Who Wrote the Bible,* chaps. 11–12, pp. 188–216, on P and the court of Hezekiah (*regnat* 716–687 B.C.). See chapter 10 note 4 *supra.*

10. The Solomon of 2 Chronicles 2:18 conscripts the foreigners in the land to be "hewers [of timber] in the mountain" and "bearers of burdens." Deut. 29:11 recognizes such workers—"thy stranger that is in thy camp"—as a class subject to covenanting, along with wives and children. But 1 Kings 5:13, 15 makes them "a levy out of all Israel," Solomon thus submitting his own people to the fate of the subject (but covenanted) Gibionites, "hewers of wood and drawers of water," at Josh. 9:21–27.

11. For this observation see David Damrosch, "Leviticus," in Frank Kermode and Robert Alter, eds., *The Literary Guide to the Bible* (Cambridge, Mass.: Harvard University Press, 1987), pp. 69–72, and *The Narrative Covenant: Transformations of Genre in the Growth of Biblical Literature* (San Francisco: Harper & Row, 1987), pp. 266–78; with Edward L. Greenstein, "The Formation of the Biblical Narrative Corpus," *AJS Rev.* 15 (1990): 171. Greenstein notes that Eli's sons Hophni and Phinehas yield their place to a newly sanctified Eleazar, son of one Abinadab (1 Sam. 7:1); he is appointed to keep the ark returned from the Philistines. The name of this Eleazar's father suggests the replacing of one set of Aaronids—Abihu and Nadab—by another set, Eleazar and Ithamar: Abinadab = *abi[hu]* + *nadab.*

12. The week of the original creation when conflated with the aftermath of the Flood ("God made a wind blow over the earth, and the waters subsided" . . . "in the first month, the first day of the month, the waters were dried from off the earth" [Gen. 8:1, 13, RSV]), the week of Passover, and the week of the Feast of Booths all have in common a putative or actual date at the ending or rebeginning of the year (Gen. 8:13, Exod. 12:2, 23:16, 34:22); and they also have in common taboos on various "sabbatical" periods of work (Gen. 2:2–3, Exod. 12:15–17, 20:10–11, Lev. 23:35, Num. 29:12). Given the Near Eastern association of the New Year's festival with the reinstallation of the king, we may say that the biblical or Mosaic festival tends to make *God* the reinstalled "king." (For a much more complete development of the analogies between the Priestly creation narrative as liturgy, and the priestly festive institutions as the creation, see Jon D. Levenson, *Creation and the Persistence of Evil: The Jewish Drama of Divine Omnipotence* [San Francisco: Harper & Row, 1988], pp. 66–99.) The human head of the Israelite state *also* gets himself installed in this way, in the particular cases of Solomon and, more importantly, of his and his son's Northern rival, Jeroboam. But the tradition has been Mosaicized.

Let us retrace the route to this conclusion, which comes from attempting to read a feast of national set-apartness as one more "supplementary original" for the idea of the exodus. But in the present case the latter-day historical prototype is to be found in an institution by the kingship itself, rather than in, say, Hosea's festal motions, which are back toward a dwelling of Israel in a wilderness apart from any kingship.

The feast of Ingathering or annual Thanksgiving came to be known commemoratively as the Feast of Booths ("Tabernacles"). Leviticus 23:42–43 asserts that the booths which the celebrants are to occupy have a Mosaic provenance: "all that are Israelites born shall dwell in booths: That your generations may know that I made the children of Israel to dwell in booths, when I brought them out of . . . Egypt: I am the Lord your God." The first place the Israelites camped, upon leaving Egypt, was outside of a point of departure and arrival named Succoth (Exod. 13:20, with 12:37 and Num. 33:5); "Booths" is thus the southernmost station of the exodus proper. The name of the feast in both Deuteronomy 16:13 and Leviticus 23:34 also presumes booths, in contrast to Numbers 29:12–38, which specifies the exact contents for the eight days of sacrifice otherwise prescribed by Leviticus for this feast.

The booths could well derive from the temporary shelters built and occupied by migrant workers in the fields at harvest time, but how did they come to be associated with the Mosaic exodus? Who politicized them as a national, historical memorial? Even though the name Succoth ("booths") has been gotten into both the Exodus narrative (at 12:37, 13:20) traditionally assigned to "E," and into the head position in the list of the stations in Numbers (33:5), these cases are without any hint of an association with a seasonal festival: the Passover already occupies such a place in Exodus, and the itinerary in Numbers is more or less its own calendar. Exodus wedges the "Egyptian" Succoth into the Passover texts between the death of the firstborn and the second set of ritual injunctions.

The law of Moses concerning the three major Israelite festivals, as it is found in Deuteronomy 16:16, and as it is invoked in Ezra 3 and Nehemiah 8, relocates the feasts, with the thrice annual presentation of males before Yahweh, to Jerusalem. If this practice is to be linked with the original sacrifice of the firstborn in Egypt, then the action of King Jeroboam in 1 Kings 12:32 may also suggest the adapting of an exodus tradition to a city-based cultus: "And Jeroboam appointed a feast on the fifteenth day of the eighth month *like the feast that was in Judah*" (RSV). The subsequent description (vs. 33, ". . . the month which he had devised of his own heart . . ." [RSV]) calls our attention a second time to any given feast's being subject to the various political reinstitutions of its observance. The Feast of Booths is used in this opportunistic way by Solomon at the dedication of the temple (1 Kings 8:2), and again by Ezra and Nehemiah (Ezra 3:1–6, Neh. 8:14–18). Thus Jeroboam appears to have re-scheduled a traditional feast—Booths—exactly one month later, Booths being regularly placed in the middle of the seventh month (Lev. 23:34, Num. 29:12–38, Ezek. 45:25). In 1 Kings 8 "the feast" in Judah has not yet got its other name, but it seems to be a version of Booths all the same. By putting it a month later, Jeroboam moved an observance celebrated at the end of the year (if we adopt indications at Exodus 23:16, 34:22) to the beginning: that is, to an inaugural date like the one occupied by the Passover.

Where Josiah had celebrated a major Passover at the refounding of Israel's covenant relation to God, Ezra—in the rededication of the temple after the return of Israel from the Babylonian exile—will celebrate a major Feast of Booths (Neh. 8:14–18). The name Succoth was also attached to the place of encampment and house-building at which Jacob arrived upon his return to the promised land (after departing from Esau, Gen. 33:16–17)—Jacob could thus be a forerunner of

Ezra. When Solomon dedicates the temple he holds his feast "before the Lord our God, seven days and seven days, even fourteen days" (1 Kings 8:65), which is explained as seven days of dedication and seven of feast (2 Chron. 7:8–9). But who put such a feast (which again appears to be Booths) into a relation with the commemoration of the exodus, as found in Leviticus 23:24?

The feast is called "Booths" in both Leviticus and Deuteronomy. Should we be asking: Who named Ingathering after a place named in the text of Exodus? Is the answer Jeroboam, armed with a Mosaic interpretation of the festival? If so, then the distance Moses put between Rameses and Succoth at the Passover (Exod. 12:37) can be equated with the psycho-political space that Jeroboam put between Jerusalem and Bethel at the Feast. The meaning would be, "You must keep the Feast, Ingathering, because it was on that day that Jeroboam brought Israel out of Judah as Moses once brought Israel out of Egypt." Ingathering would have thus been politicized to stand for Israel's latter-day immigration into the Northern kingship. Thus would Jeroboam's feast be remembered.

13. Comments in the narrative, whether those of the narrator or the internal characters, in regard to the Northern kingship and the Southern throne, are regularly "theologized": for Jeroboam this means "rejected by the God of a latter-day priesthood in Judah"; for David, his throne, and his city, it means "revered (likely enough retrojectively) by the God of Judah." The initial case of the latter is God's promise to David—as Nathan reports it—that, even though his son sins, nonetheless God's "mercy shall not depart away from him" (2 Sam. 7:15). See chapter 10 note 5 *supra* for some of the internal commentary in question. An excellent exposition of the elemental unity of the text of the royal history from Solomon to Jeconiah in 1–2 Kings is that of E. Theodore Mullen, Jr., "The Sins of Jeroboam: A Redactional Assessment," in *The Catholic Biblical Quarterly* 49:2 (1987): 212–32.

14. The choice of Jerusalem for David's sake is first found in God's promise to Solomon, at 1 Kings 11:12–13, 32–38, and in Ahijah's commission to Jeroboam to rebel, at 1 Kings 11:31–32. This election is reaffirmed by the narrator at 1 Kings 15:4–5 and 2 Kings 8:19, and by the prophet Isaiah at 2 Kings 19:34.

Chapter 16: Like unto Aaron: The Golden Calf and the History of the Priestly Revelation to Israel

1. To some extent I am repeating here von Rad, *Old Testament Theology*, Vol. I, *Theology of Israelite Traditions*, pp. 212–19. What the Moses of Deuteronomy "sees" in the burning bush is less an image of God than an audition of him; the fire on Sinai, comparably, is not really God's image, but his *word:* "And the Lord spake unto you out of the midst of the fire: ye heard the voice of the words, but saw no similitude; only ye heard a voice" (Deut. 4:12). *Contra* images, see, successively, Hos. 8:4–6, 13:1–3; Jer. 10:1–16; Isa. 44:9–20; and Wisdom of Solomon 12:27–16:12.

2. Cf. St. Thomas Aquinas, *De Veritate*, q. 17, art. 4, resp. 3: "A false opinion about [God] is the contrary of a true opinion. In this sense idols are called 'falsehoods,' opposite to the divine truth, because false opinion concerning idols is the contrary of true opinion concerning the unity of God." (Trans. Robert Mulligan, S.J., *Truth*, vol. 1 [Chicago, 1952], p. 113). See also Moses Maimonides, *The Guide for the Perplexed*, tr. M. Friedlander (Dover Publications: n.p., 1956), Pt. 3, chap. 44, p. 356: "If there had only been one figure of a cherub [at Exod. 25:18], the people would have been misled and would have mistaken it for God's image which was to be worshipped, in the fashion of the heathen; or they might have assumed that the angel [represented by the figure] was also a deity, and would have thus adopted a

Dualism. By making two cherubim and distinctly declaring 'the Lord our God, the Lord is One,' Moses clearly proclaimed the theory of the existence of a number of angels; he left no room for the error of considering those figures as deities, since [he declared that] God is one, and that He is the Creator of the angels, who are more than one."

3. Richard Elliott Friedman, *Who Wrote the Bible*, pp. 125–26, 146. Distinctions between Aaronid and Mushite (Mosaic) priesthoods are obviously basic to some of my readings, and they may well extend beyond the exile. See further, Richard Elliott Friedman, *The Exile and Biblical Narrative: The Formation of the Deuteronomistic and Priestly Works* (Chico, Calif.: Scholars Press, 1981). Not less interesting is the pioneering proto-sociological analysis of Paul D. Hanson, *The Dawn of Apocalyptic* (Philadelphia: Fortress Press, 1975), *passim*, which categorizes different branches of post-exilic prophecy by opposing visionary and charismatic Mushite sects to pragmatic and bureaucratic Zadokite sects (both being found within the restored Israel). For the differing political identities and roles of Nehemiah and Ezra in post-exilic Israel, I am content to go with the summary account of Bo Reicke, *The New Testament Era: The World of the Bible from 500 B.C. to A.D. 100*, tr. David E. Green (Philadelphia: Fortress Press, 1968), pp. 13–23. Reicke's brief account, based on deductions from the dangerous revolt of Syria from Persia and indications in the books bearing the Israelite leaders' names, suggests that the scribe Ezra may have been much closer to prophetic and revolutionary circles than the Persia-supporting administrator Nehemiah. In my argument I do not, however, really take or have any strong positions on the recurrent biblical question of who's whose; I confine myself merely to noting within the major narratives the evidence of the pressure to be *somebody's*.

Chapter 17: Supplementary Originals

1. The arguments, along with the paraphrase of Isaiah 63:11, are partly after Paul D. Hanson, *The Dawn of Apocalyptic* (Philadelphia: Fortress Press, 1975), p. 89. See chapter 16 note 3 *supra*.

2. "An analogy," Luther explains, "is an assimilation . . . in virtue of which one thing agrees with another in its peculiar characteristics and becomes like it" (*Lectures on Romans*, tr. William Pauck [Philadelphia: The Westminster Press, 1961], p. 334: on the "proportion of faith" in Rom. 12:6, where "analogy" means, roughly, *criterion*).

3. See Martin Noth, *The History of Israel*, 2d ed., tr. P. R. Ackroyd (New York: Harper & Row, 1960), pp. 164–224, and Albrecht Alt, *Essays on Old Testament History and Religion*, Anchor Books edn., *sub* "The Formation of the Israelite State," esp. pp. 226–38, contrasting with Israel the Canaanite tendency represented in the federation of the Philistine city-states.

4. For the intratextual links in this paragraph, see Paul D. Hanson, "1 Chronicles 15–16 and the Chronicler's Views on the Levites," in *"Sha'arei Talmon": Studies in the Bible, Qumran, and the Ancient Near East Presented to Shemaryahu Talmon*, ed. Michael Fishbane and Emanuel Tov (Winona Lake, Ind.: Eisenbrauns, 1992), pp. 69–77.

5. James S. Ackerman, "Who Can Stand before YHWH, This Holy God? A Reading of 1 Samuel 1–15," in *Prooftexts* 11 (1991): 1–24, citing especially David Daube, *The Exodus Pattern in the Bible* (London, 1963), pp. 73–88, and Lyle M. Eslinger, *Kingship of God in Crisis: A Close Reading of 1 Samuel 1–12* (Decatur, Georgia, 1985), p. 196–201, 204, 209f., 221; cf. also David Damrosch, *Narrative Covenant*, pp. 188–91.

6. Ackerman's refined point, "Who Can Stand before YHWH," *loc. cit.*, p. 8.

GENERAL INDEX

Thanks to T. Buckman, S. Fahringer, Sarah Wright, Stephanie N.

SCRIPTURAL INDEX

JAMES NOHRNBERG has taught Bible and literature classes at Harvard and Yale, and at the University of Virginia, where he has been Professor of English since 1975. He is the author of *The Analogy of* The Faerie Queene.